Political Theories of International Relations

Political Theories of International Relations

From Thucydides to the Present

DAVID BOUCHER

Oxford University Press

1998

OXFORD
UNIVERSITY PRESS

Great Clarendon Street, Oxford OX2 6DP

Oxford University Press is a department of the University of Oxford.
It furthers the University's objective of excellence in research, scholarship,
and education by publishing worldwide in

Oxford New York
Auckland Cape Town Dar es Salaam Hong Kong Karachi Kuala Lumpur
Madrid Melbourne Mexico City Nairobi New Delhi Taipei Toronto
Shanghai

With offices in
Argentina Austria Brazil Chile Czech Republic France Greece
Guatemala Hungary Italy Japan South Korea Poland Portugal
Singapore Switzerland Thailand Turkey Ukraine Vietnam

Oxford is a registered trade mark of Oxford University Press
in the UK and in certain other countries

Published in the United States
by Oxford University Press Inc., New York

British Library Cataloguing in Publication Data
Data available

Library of Congress Cataloging in Publication Data
Data available
ISBN-13: 978-0-19-878054-0
ISBN-10: 0-19-878054-0

Typeset by Hope Services (Abingdon) Ltd.
Printed in Great Britain by
Biddles Ltd
King's Lynn

ACKNOWLEDGEMENTS

This book was first conceived in 1986 when I was lecturing in the philosophy of international relations at La Trobe University in Melbourne. It was there that I wrote an article on Hobbes for the four-hundredth anniversary of his birth, organized by Conal Condren of the University of New South Wales, Sydney. I would like to thank Conal for his strong support and encouragement in Australia, and subsequently since my return to Britain. The paper was published as 'Inter-Community and International Relations in the Political Philosophy of Hobbes', *Polity*, 23 (1990), 207–32. I am grateful to the editor for allowing me to use this article as the basis of Chapter 6 of this book. I first wrote the overall scheme while a research fellow at the History of Ideas Unit, Australian National University, under the title 'The Character of the Philosophy of International Relations and the Case of Edmund Burke', which was published in the *Review of International Studies*, 17 (1991), 128–48. I subsequently taught the philosophy of international relations in the Department of Political Science in the Faculty of Arts, Australian National University, and at the University of Wales, Swansea. I would like to thank all those students who contributed to the refinement of my ideas and who forced me to aim for clarity and intelligibility, not something easily achieved by some-one brought up in the school of philosophical idealism.

I am grateful to Henry Hardy of Oxford University Press, who saw my initial proposal through the review process and who gave me encouragement to pro-ceed, and Tim Barton, who has kept a keen eye on the project since. I am also indebted to Fiona Little for the careful copy-editing of the typescript. Helen Simpson was a rigorous proof reader and saved me from a number of infelicities, while Ruth Marshall was patient and encouraging. I am grateful to a large number of friends and colleagues for their support over the years, but I would particularly like to thank Terry Nardin for reading the whole of the typescript and for giving me the benefit of his penetrating and perceptive criticisms. I have tried as best I can to address them and follow his advice. I take full responsibility, how-ever, for the inadequacies that remain. I am also indebted to my friends Lawrence Wilde and Andrew Vincent for the benefit of their specialist advice on the chap-ters on Hegel and Marx respectively. W. H. Greenleaf has been a formative influ-ence on my work, and it was he who first introduced me to conceiving the history of political thought in triadic terms, which I have developed and adapted to the field of the political theory of international relations in this book.

Once again I have to express my deep gratitude to my wife Clare and my daugh-ters Lucy and Emma for their forbearance and toleration.

D.B.

Swansea
March 1988

CONTENTS

viii   *Contents*

DETAILED CONTENTS

Introduction

1

THE CHARACTER OF THE POLITICAL THEORY OF INTERNATIONAL RELATIONS

There has been a proliferation in the number of courses offered in, and an upsurge in student demand for, international relations theory under the auspices of political science and international relations departments. Many of these courses, and the literature related to them, refer to the classical political thinkers and their views on international relations, yet no text is available for students to familiarize themselves in detail with such theories. F. Parkinson's *The Philosophy of International Relations: A Study in the History of Thought*[1] is too far-ranging, and consequently terribly superficial, for this purpose, although interesting in its own right as a catalogue of who said what, at any level of discourse, where, and when about the significant issues in the discipline. A more recent study focuses more narrowly upon the principal philosophers in political theory, suggesting that international theory cannot be distinguished from and is a continuation of political theory. It deals chiefly with the classic texts in the traditional canon of political theorists, whether or not they had anything significant or explicit to say about international relations theory.[2] The traditional canon of texts is not always the best place to look for what the great theorists had to say about the subject. Plato's *Laws* and Hobbes's *De cive*, for example, add significantly to what they have to say about international relations in *The Republic* and *Leviathan*. The traditional canon also filters out philosophers whose principal contribution has been to tackle and advance our understanding of international relations issues. These writers include Vitoria, Grotius, Vattel, and Pufendorf, but also Thucydides, who is not strictly speaking a philosopher, but who nevertheless has a philosophy permeated by the non-Platonic element in Greek philosophy. In this respect Thucydides ranks alongside Machiavelli and Burke, whose practical concerns were thoroughly impregnated by philosophical principles of interpretation.

International Relations Theory and the Political Theory of International Relations

The theories of international relations that, in both their behaviouralist and anti-behaviouralist forms, dominated the sub-discipline for sixty years or so, self-consciously rejected political theory in an attempt to establish their own intellectual credentials. Despite being subject to similar pressures, international theory rejected the option taken by political theory of defining itself in terms of its illustrious past and missed the opportunity of firmly anchoring itself on sound philosophical foundations. Paradoxically the 'English school' represented by Wight and Bull, far from strengthening the intellectual heritage, undermined it by failing to employ discriminating criteria to differentiate genuinely philosophical contributions from the merely polemical. The emphasis upon taxonomy averted the gaze from the quality of argument, and the terms 'Hobbesian', 'Grotian', and 'Kantian' became simply emblematic of certain positions rather than philosophical arguments.

The sub-disciplines of political theory and international relations theory within the discipline of politics in the twentieth century have tended to go their separate ways. To a large extent international relations, along with its theoretically oriented practitioners, pronounced a unilateral declaration of independence in order to establish its credentials as a worthwhile and practically relevant academic activity. Political theory, traditionally conceived, and international relations theory were deemed to inhabit two distinct universes of discourse.[3] Three examples from the post-1945 period will serve to illustrate three tendencies in the process of differentiation. On the one hand David Easton's assault upon traditional political theory and his redefinition of the term to refer to the formulation of hypotheses for empirical testing was also carried forward in international relations. Kenneth N. Waltz, more sympathetic than most to classical political theory, has quite rightly pointed out that the term 'theory' is used very loosely among specialists in international relations, often referring to any work that rises above mere description and includes some analysis. Rarely does it 'refer only to work that meets philosophy-of-science-standards'.[4] The criterion of what constitutes good theory betrays a prevalent belief among theorists of international relations that explanation must aim to approximate the achievements of natural science. This does not mean that Waltz subscribes to the 'covering-law' model of explanation, which seeks to establish invariant or probable associations in repeated occurrences. Theories, in Waltz's view, aim to explain why the associations or laws obtain. It is a conception of theory more in keeping with the social sciences, and specifically economics, than with 'much of traditional political theory, which is concerned more with philosophic interpretation than with theoretical explanation'.[5]

The fostering of a dichotomy between political theory and international relations theory was particularly pronounced in the work of Martin Wight, the doyen of the English school, who was, unlike Waltz, vehemently anti-behaviouralist.

Political theory, he argued, is mainly preoccupied with speculation about the state, whereas international theory concerns itself with the international community of nations. Political theory, he contentiously thought, was progressivist in that it concerned itself with the good life, and had developed a vocabulary singularly suited to the business of dealing with the control of social life. He equally contentiously described international theory as non-progressivist because its subject-matter was concerned with state survival in a context of repetition and recurrence. When international relations theory is understood in these terms, there is no body of theory in international relations comparable with the classic texts in political theory.[6] By using such a narrowly stipulative definition of political theory, Wight cut international theory off from a rich source of stimulus. He bemoaned the fact that what international theory there was had to be extracted from a scattered diversity of sources. 'International Theory', Wight told us, could 'be discerned existing dimly, obscured and moreover partitioned, partly on the fringe or margin of ordinary political philosophy and partly in the province of international law.'[7] Despite protesting that international theory approximates not to natural science, but to philosophy, Wight engaged in an activity that looks more like pre-Darwinian biology than philosophy. Having stipulatively defined the rare genus international theory, he set about classifying its species and subspecies. Wight described his adventures in theory as 'an experiment in classification, in typology, and . . . an exploration of continuity and recurrence, a study in the uniformity of political thought: and its leading premise is that political ideas do not change much, and the range of ideas is limited.'[8]

A second form of anti-behaviouralist theory in international relations brought the sub-discipline no closer to a reconciliation with political theory. From among a wide range of fashionable short-lived attempts theoretically to reorient the discipline emerged the activity of constructing models, or perspectives, to act as tools of analysis in explaining international relations. The perspectives of Realism, with its emphasis upon power and security, pluralism, with its focus upon interdependence and transnational relations, and structuralism, with its central themes of dominance and dependence, offered ready-made theoretical frameworks which could be refined and applied for value-free post-behavioural social scientific explanation.[9] Mervyn Frost argues that all of the dominant approaches, including the so-called classical approach of Wight, Bull, Vincent, and others, give epistemological priority to the facts. This is what he has called the bias towards 'objective explanation' in the sub-discipline, and is the main reason why normative political theory has been largely neglected.[10] The result, in Chris Brown's words, is 'an undertheorised and limited conception of international relations'.[11] His view is that international relations theory has to be seen embedded in the broader project of social and political theory. The growing acknowledgement that there is a need for reconciliation is evident. Scott Burchill, for example, denies the need for an autonomous international relations theory because the discipline is not analytically distinct from social and political theory, and Howard Williams has gone so far as to suggest that in many ways 'the study of political theory is the study of international relations'.[12]

There were opportunities when one could have expected a political theory of international relations to emerge. Late-nineteenth-century imperialism, the Boer War, the two world wars, and the Vietnam War provided points at which the sub-disciplines converged, but never so closely that they were ever in danger of breaking down the contrived distinction between domestic and international political theory. The philosophers T. H. Green, Bernard Bosanquet, Bertrand Russell, John Dewey, George Santayana, and R. G. Collingwood, the sociologist L. T. Hobhouse, the economist J. A. Hobson, the historian of political thought Ernest Barker, and the classicist Gilbert Murray were all passionately interested in the political theory of international relations. They made significant contributions to and generated heated debates about it. While political theorists never ceased to be alarmed at the changing world in which they lived and were acutely aware of the issues to which a system or community of sovereign states gave rise, they never succeeded in making any significant impact on shaping the sub-discipline of international relations. International relations theorists developed their own vocabulary and concepts, indifferent to the overtures from some of the most significant political philosophers of the twentieth century.

What were the fundamental circumstances which made international relations as a sub-discipline unreceptive to political theory playing a greater role in its development? Both sub-disciplines were subject to many of the same pressures in their initial formations. They emerged under the auspices of both law and history, while at the same time wishing to differentiate themselves from both as integral aspects of the nascent discipline of politics. Political theory and international relations theory justified themselves in terms of their practical relevance, in keeping with the intensely practical nature of the subject-matter of politics. In order to avoid the charge often levelled against the discipline of politics in general, especially by such writers as Seeley, that politics historically conceived could be nothing more than mere empiricism, an intellectually unedifying gathering of facts, both political theory and international relations theory sought to establish their philosophical credent..ls. Political theory as it emerged at the turn of the century defined itself in terms of its past, reflecting to some extent its disciplinary origins, but also the dominance of philosophical Idealism, which contended that philosophy was indistinguishable from the history of philosophy. Political theory constructed a canon of texts which served as its legitimizing pedigree. The post-Second World War dominance of positivism within the discipline of politics, privileging inductive and deductive knowledge—empirical observation and analytic statements—over the opinion of values, and the emphasis upon the analysis and explanation of ordinary language made popular by Wittgenstein and Austin in philosophy, led to the near-death of normative political theory in the 1950s. While the patient had not quite stopped breathing, Laslett's pronouncement of the death of political theory in 1956 and Strauss's claim that the body was in a state of putrefaction in 1959 were symptomatic of political theory's near-demise.[13] The myth of the tradition, as it is sometimes called, has persisted and has proved to be remarkably adaptive to criticism. While logical positivism exacted its toll on normative political philosophy it did not succeed in displacing the great texts in the history of political thought from their central place in the discipline of politics.[14] Despite the charge made by David Easton and his followers that the reliance of political theory upon the classics was now redundant, except for the formulation of hypotheses that could be empirically tested, Leo Strauss, Sheldon Wolin, Hanna Arendt, Eric Vögelin, Isaiah Berlin, and John Plamenatz drew heavily upon past thinkers in order to make contemporary political points.

This is not the place to show how the canon of great texts in political theory was constructed in Great Britain and America in the decades at the turn of the century in response to an expanding student population and the need to educate future leaders in civic and political matters. Unlike political theory, international relations theory allied itself closely with law, and particularly with international law. The First World War generated a considerable impetus for understanding the conditions of world peace and for exploring the means of establishing and sustaining them. The improvement of the condition of mankind by means of 'scientific study' (meaning scholarly and systematic study) and the application of scientific methods to social problems were the primary goals of the sub-discipline. The euphoria that accompanied the establishment of the League of Nations and the consensus that surrounded the idea of liberal internationalism during the 1920s generated a widespread belief that reason and rationality, given the appropriate conditions, would lead to the shared values of liberal democracies becoming manifest in international agreements for the fostering of a shared harmony of interests and the establishment of permanent peace and security. Such a strong belief in the power and efficacy of reason was necessarily premised on the belief that education in international affairs would lead to progress in world understanding and co-operation. Along with the chairs founded at Aberystwyth by David Davies in 1919 and at London by the Cassel Trustees in 1923 came the conscious attempt to establish a canon of classic texts relating to the origin and development of the Law of Nations. In the most ambitious and significant publishing vent..re in the history of thought in international relations, the Carnegie Institution of Washington undertook to republish a large number of texts in Latin and vernacular languages, with English translations, in order to make the knowledge they contained more easily accessible to scholars and more widely available to the interested public in all countries of the world. Under the auspices of the Carnegie Endowment for International Peace the works of Ayala, Belli, Bynershoek, Gentili, Grotius, Legnano, Pufendorf, Rachel, Suárez, Textor, Vattel, Vitoria, Wheaton, Wolff, and Zouche were published.

It is curious that this putative tradition never attained central importance for international relations theorists. The Wall Street Crash of 1929, the Japanese invasion of Manchuria in 1931, Hitler's rise to power in Germany in 1933, the withdrawal of Japan and Germany from the League in 1935, and the Italian invasion of Abyssinia in 1935 confirmed the view of sceptics that faith in human reason for the deliverance of world peace was misplaced. Such disillusionment injected a new realism into perceptions of international relations.[15] It is ironic that the Woodrow Wilson Professor of International Politics at the University College of

Wales, Aberystwyth, was responsible for producing the most renowned and scathing attack on Wilson's liberal internationalism, or Utopianism as E. H. Carr called it. Carr argued that the Utopian search for a standard of ethics outside of politics and to which politics must conform was 'doomed to frustration'. It was a mistake, he argued, to identify a universal harmony of interests with the interests of each state. *Laissez-faire* in both the internal market and international relations was a paradise for the strong, but not for the economically weak: 'State control, whether in the form of protective legislation or of protective tariffs, is the weapon of self-defence invoked by the economically weak. The clash of interests is real and inevitable.'[16]

During the post-1945 period most writers interested in the political theory of international relations have been happy to concur with Martin Wight's observation that with the exception of Thucydides' *History of the Peloponnesian War*, which is not a work of philosophy at all, there are no classic texts in the philosophy of international relations. Even Andrew Linklater, who has done a great deal to revive interest in some of the classic thinkers, drives a wedge between the political theory of international relations and political theory proper by suggesting that the former considers issues that the latter does not. International political theory questions the legitimacy of the division of humanity into states, and the assumed primacy of obligations to the state over those to humanity. This, however, is a stipulative definition, as stipulative as Wight's definition that political theory is speculation about internal matters of state and international theory is speculation about relations among states.

This is not to say that political theorists of international relations believe that there is no heritage in the history of thought in international relations. In fact, they believe that there is a considerable heritage scattered throughout a vast variety of literature. The reluctance to acknowledge or to establish a canon has had a regrettable consequence. This consequence I call intellectual egalitarianism. Because international relations theory is first defined as an exceedingly rare and rather shy creature, ar., one of any degree of fame in whatever area of achievement who happens to have said something on the subject has a right to be heard. The quality of theorizing is secondary to the fact of theorizing. The obvious need to expand the traditional classic political theory canon to incorporate international theorists has resulted in a failure to apply appropriate qualitative criteria in discriminating who should and who should not be included.

Invoked alongside the great political philosophers such as Hobbes, Rousseau, and Hegel are the international jurists Grotius, Pufendorf, and Vattel, polemicists such as Cobden, Bright, and Hobson, and writers of distinction such as Tolstoy, Wells, and Huxley, along with distinguished statesmen such as Lincoln, Bismarck, Gladstone, and Churchill. Whereas in the realm of practical politics, including issues of international justice, everyone's voice may have a claim to be heard, in the theory of these issues, notwithstanding the postmodernist discomfort with silences, some voices may have nothing of importance to say. It is only those thinkers who were able to see in the transitory events emerging issues, which they articulated and addressed at a level of sophistication that was at once rigorous, intellectually demanding, and visionary, who have a legitimate claim to be counted among the political theorists of international relations. There are many other levels of discourse, some of which are theoretical, upon which talk about international relations may occur, but to pretend that they are all philosophical or have the status of the political theory of international relations is to do a great disservice to the discipline and to condemn it in perpetuity to include in its canon of texts the mediocre and mundane alongside the truly original and important. Even the better surveys and anthologies travel up and down this continuum of levels of discourse, applying what appears to be a principle of intellectual egalitarianism.[17] For example, despite Martin Wight's claim that 'international theory is the political philosophy of international relations', he presents us with a classificatory catalogue of everyone who said anything about international relations in a project that Hedley Bull approvingly describes as an exercise to rediscover, assemble, and categorize everything that has been said on international relations throughout history.[18] The reason for this is the intensely practical nature of the discipline, which is understandable given the enormity and emotiveness of the issues. But if practical considerations are to act as the criteria of why one person's thoughts and not another's are included in a study, we need to be quite clear about what we are doing. The practical impact of the likes of Frederick the Great, Stalin, Hitler, Churchill, and Kissinger was no doubt immense, and what they said gives us a genuine insight into the ways in which they perceived the world and how these perceptions informed their actions. Such a focus is wholly legitimate and intrinsically interesting, and may suggest some practical lessons. Such a focus is best suited to the construction of what have been called 'belief systems' in international relations, which help us to understand foreign policy decisions at a variety of levels of analysis, relating to cognitive psychology, the cultural context, the dominant ideology, or internationally shared assumptions and beliefs. Exponents of the 'belief systems' approach have, however, been far from clear in what a belief system is, how it is related to the individual, and in what relation it stands to action. In a collection of essays justifying t..is approach, John MacLean and Michael Dillon suggest, for example, that belief systems are constitutive of their own reality, while Barbara Allen Robertson and Margot Light maintain that an external reality stands outside the belief system and is only imperfectly represented by it. In other words, we encounter both a denial and an affirmation of the mind/object dichotomy, but no sound reasons are given for why we should accept either.[19]

The study of the theory of international relations, however, stands in a different relation to the events. Instead of the thought illuminating the events, as in the case of Stalin, Churchill, and others, the events illuminate the thought which is intended to transcend them. Thus, for a theory of the human predicament that the English Civil War betrays, we look not to Oliver Cromwell or Charles II but to Thomas Hobbes, and for the general principles of international relations to emerge out of the Thirty Years War and the Napoleonic Wars we look not to the participants and their representatives at the congresses of Münster and Osnabrück, out of which came the Treaties of Westphalia, or the Congress of Vienna, which re-established the *ancien régime*, but instead to Pufendorf, Wolff,

Vattel, and Hegel, whose theories extrapolate from these events the growing importance, autonomy, and integrity of the state as an actor, or even a personality, in international relations, and present in a different way the dilemma of one's loyalty to humanity and one's obligations to one's *patria*. Furthermore, when attempting to discern the theoretical importance of the discovery of the New World we look not to the opinions of Columbus, Cortés, and Pizarro, but instead to the theories of property of Vitoria, Grotius, Pufendorf, and Locke which legitimated or denied the basis of the European conquest of America. It is the events, then, which give rise to the problems which the philosophers address, and from which they imaginatively attempt to formulate principles which they incorporate into systematic theories directed not so much to the resolution of the particular problems out of which they arose, but primarily to the place of those problems generally in the human predicament. Of contemporary political theorists of international relations Terry Nardin is highly sensitive to the danger of conflating unalike activities under the guise of theory. To theorize about something, he argues, is to invoke concerns different from those of the moralist, citizen, statesman, or philosopher.[20]

Up until a decade ago there was very little interest in, or recognition of, the place of ethical and political theory in international relations, neither in the contribution which the history of thought nor contemporary normative theory might have to make to understanding and responding to the ethical and political dilemmas of the modern world. The four decades following 1950 have aptly been christened the 'forty years' detour', in which for the most part values might permissibly be allowed a role in the choice of issue to be investigated but not in its analysis.[21] The publication of John Rawls's *A Theory of Justice* in 1970 served to stimulate a return to grand theory, the repercussions of which were taken up in the political theory of international relations by Charles Beitz, Michael Walzer, Terry Nardin, and Mervyn Frost. While the works of these writers often draw upon the classic theorists, the tendency is much more pronounced in John Vincent, Michael Donelan, Andrew Linklater, Justin Rosenberg, Janna Thompson, and Chris Brown.

The mistake that theorists of international relations made was to cut themselves adrift from the mainstream of political theory in order to develop their own theories and concepts. The consequence was to deprive themselves of the powerful background theories in which to embed their own thought. The acknowledgement that many of the pressing world issues of today are at once political and ethical, and that the answers to them need to be firmly anchored in a systematic and comprehensive political theory, has led a number of theorists to explore the viability of various 'background' theories. Thompson and Brown, for instance, investigate the value of 'cosmopolitanism' and 'communitarianism' in their various guises and their capacities to generate and sustain answers to international issues of justice and rights.[22] Frost follows Ronald Dworkin's method of drawing up a list of settled norms in international relations. He then asks whether they can be sustained by the background theories of utilitarianism, contractarianism, and rights-based justifications. Frost's own theory is a version of communitarianism, or what he calls a constitutive theory, derived from Hegel. Brown also subscribes to this constitutive theory, which refuses to privilege individuals over communities.[23] Nardin's approach, while not normative in the sense of justifying or recommending states' conduct, looks at the nature of the association that gives rise to the law and morality of the international community.[24] Adapting Oakeshott's distinction between civil association and enterprise association, with their respective non-instrumental and instrumental rules, Nardin suggests that the international community is best understood as a form of civil association which he calls practical, and in which the rules are constraints upon the actions of states with different values, cultures, interests, and beliefs. The rules are not instrumental in achieving substantive goals and purposes, but instead provide the framework in the context of which the various goals adopted by independent states can be pursued.[25]

Increasingly, political theorists, such as John Rawls, David Miller, Onora O'Neill, and Brian Barry, have come to acknowledge that the concerns of international relations are a continuation of, and indistinguishable from, the traditional issues of political obligation, sovereignty, citizenship, and distributive justice. Critical theorists such as Habermas, Cox, and Linklater, anti-foundationalist postmodernist international relations theorists, such as James Der Derian, R. B. J. Walker, and Jim George, and postmodernist political theorists, such as William Connelly, Richard Rorty, and François Lyotard, have explored the implications of postmodernism for the dominant approaches to international relations, particularly Realism, and for the issue of human rights.

The Classic Texts in the Political Theory of International Relations

In this book my intention is to retrieve the intellectual heritage of the political theory of international relations on the assumption that its severance from international theory in the twentieth century has been contingent and accidental rather than logical or necessary. Furthermore, it is my view that if we are to understand the full import of the classic political theories of international relations we cannot assume that no disservice is done to the theory by detaching it from the rest of what a theorist is trying to argue. When we look, for example, at theories which justify or condemn the colonization of the Americas with reference to what is permitted under the Law of Nations, they are hardly intelligible unless we identify the theory of property which informs the discussion. The important distinction which informs politics at that time is that between the landed and landless. To be a landholder defined one's political persona. Questions of what might disqualify one from holding land, and of the violations of the Natural Law or Law of Nations by which a title may justifiably be transferred, were issues that adventurers, monarchs, and the Church were anxious to have settled in their favour. In this respect the theories of property of such notable thinkers as Grotius, Pufendorf, and Locke take on new significance in so far as they had a considerable bearing upon questions of legitimating claims to American land. To take another instance, omission of a discussion of Hegel's theory of the importance of the master–slave relationship in the process of recognition and the development of individuality obliterates the whole basis of his remarks on the relations among states.

Events have a place in this book in so far as they set the problems which the philosophers address. The first part of this book bears the burden of carrying the detail of the changes in the international system through the Athenian Empire, the Macedonian Empire, the Roman Republic and Empire, and the Holy Roman Empire and on to the change of balance in medieval Church–empire relations, the emergence of a system of city-state relations in Italy, and the rise of the establishment of the nation-state system in Europe whose formalization was greatly assisted by the Peace of Westphalia and the Peace of Utrecht. It is, however, the aspiration to seek in the transitory something which reveals in a systematic and coherent manner the more fundamental springs of action that will be my main concern. Thucydides, for example, directed his work not at the passing tastes of a contemporary audience, but to posterity in the hope that his observations would be of enduring significance, given that in his view human nature is in perpetuity more or less the same, and that events are repeated in some fashion or other.[26] The emphasis of discussion is upon the philosophically interesting and rigorous theorists. This is not to suggest that the mediocre may not provide a fitting context for our understanding of the classic thinkers, as Quentin Skinner's work in the history of ideas demonstrates, and where appropriate I invoke thinkers whose philosophical credentials are not exactly bona fide.

It is my intention to present the political theory of international relations not chronologically, but thematically in relation to the criteria which inform the actions of states. This entails a conceptualization of the whole of the history of the political theory of international relations in the West. The purpose of this book is to offer such a characterization and to illustrate it with reference to the philosophers who have contributed most to our understanding of international relations. It is argued that three distinct ways of thinking about criteria of conduct in international relations are discernible in the classical literature. These traditions, or ways of thinking, are not classificatory categories within which to place particular thinkers, but, on the contrary, are tools of analysis which enable us to explore the theories of these philosophers and relate them to each other in a thematic framework. It is argued that within any one philosopher's work elements from all three traditions are to be discerned, but that in all cases one of these has a tendency to dominate the other two. Consequently, the book is organized into three parts, each one of which focuses upon the predominance in particular philosophers of one of the tendencies.[27] In the next chapter I give a brief overview of the three traditions which provide the frame of reference for the whole book. In other words, it is a fundamental premise of this book that all philosophers of international relations attempt to accommodate three competing claims on their attention: the need to relate conduct to interests, that is, the recognition that there is an internal spring to action; the need to constrain that conduct with ethical standards which rise above the merely contingent, that is, the recognition of external constraints to the internal springs to action; and the need to allow these springs to be responsive to changing historical pressures, that is, the recognition that ethical standards which are absolute may stand in too abstract a relation to those contingencies to which they are meant to apply. Philosophers have balanced these claims differently, with varying degrees of success, designating greater or lesser degrees of importance to one or another of them.

Modern Characterizations

The purpose of this section is to criticize, in general terms, the predominant types of characterization of the history of the political theory of international relations, before offering in Chapter 2 an alternative which will serve as the conceptual framework in terms of which the thinkers discussed in the rest of the book can fruitfully be explored. For as long as there have been communities of people, there have been relations among them, and as far as we know such relations provoked people to think about them. There have been many ways of thinking about international relations, giving rise to various schools of thought. The formation, disintegration, and regrouping of schools appear to have been particularly volatile in the last two or three decades,[28] but prior to the First World War there was a certain degree of stability in what may be called patterns of philosophical thinking about international relations. It is to these philosophies, which Michael Banks rightly claims 'have no equal in contemporary scholarship',[29] that this analysis is devoted, but it is nevertheless my intention to trace these philosophical trends through the international relations theories of the twentieth century. There has been no shortage of suggestions about how we should study the classic theories of international relations, but the predominant way of characterizing the literature has been in terms of two polarized categories. The traditions of Realism and Idealism[30] are identified and placed in opposition to each other as exemplifications of radically different conceptions of international relations. Hans Morganthau, for example, characterizes the history of modern political thought as a Manichaean competition between the two categories.[31] Each category has allied to it different theories which coexist in mutual antagonism with those of the other.

John H. Herz has given a thorough account of the assumptions of both traditions in his *Political Realism and Political Idealism: A Study in Theories and Realities*.[32] Political Realism contends that experience unequivocally shows that conflict is inherent in relations among individuals, and among societies. It is therefore prudent and imperative that we make preparations for dealing with such conflicts. It is necessity, rather than choice, which impels us to be prepared. Power and security are the principal concerns of the Realist. Without power there can be no security in international relations. To pursue the ideals of peace and a universal world community in which there is a harmony of interests is to leave the state vulnerable to the ambitions of unscrupulous external powers. The reality of relations between states is that each will try to gain advantage over the other.

The international state system, to put it in Hedley Bull's terms, is an 'anarchical society',[33] but this does not mean that there is no order, only that there is no ultimate authority to enforce order. There is an order which is more or less the result of a delicate balance of power, in which each state, or alliance of states, attempts to counteract the power of others. Such order as does exist is fragile and precarious, always subject to being shattered by the interests and ambitions of those states which feel that the current order is too restrictive of their actions.

Political theorists who typically fall into this tradition are Thucydides, Machiavelli, Hobbes, and Spinoza. In order to accommodate other thinkers who share certain of the Realist assumptions, a modification of the tradition has to be made. Herz calls this the 'new Realism'.[34] In this respect, Burke's emphases upon tradition, established institutions, and social pressures in shaping ideas and attitudes, and in consequence influencing the behaviour of states, are seen as important extensions of Realism. Similarly, Marx's contention that economic power was concentrated in the hands of an élite, animated by the profit motive and compelled to exploit other nations, falls within this extension of Realism. Both Burke and Marx, however, are acknowledged to fit uneasily into this Realist tradition.

Within the Idealist, or Utopian, tradition the fact that conflict exists and is manifest in the relations between states is readily conceded. The tendency is, however, not to accept conflict as an unavoidable and inevitable consequence of the human condition. Rather than accept conflict as the norm, it is seen as a perversion of the natural harmony of interests. It therefore behoves the philosopher to search for the just and ideal condition of harmonious relations between states. Ethics and not interests should be the guide to international relations. Philosophers within t...s tradition are uneasy with, and shy away from, the ideas of national interest and brute force overriding moral considerations. There is a tendency towards internationalism, or a stress upon the rights and obligations of sovereign states. These rights and obligations are reciprocal, and usually based upon some notion of a higher transcendental or Natural Law, but not invariably. There is, then, an ideal which transitory interests must not be allowed to overrule.

Political theorists who are typically associated with the Idealist, or Utopian, tendency in international relations are Plato, Aquinas, Grotius, Locke, and Kant. Other thinkers like Burke and Marx, who sit uneasily in the Realist tradition, can also be claimed as exponents of, or adherents to, the second. Burke, for instance, was vehemently opposed to the idea of Reason of State and did not subscribe to the view that national interests override moral laws.[35] Marx can also be associated with this tradition because of the Utopian element in his thought. After capitalism had run its course, he believed, there would be an international stateless society.

The Realist tradition is closely allied with empiricism in politics. The empiricist approach takes each event on its merits, allowing expedience and prudence to be its guide. The Utopian, or Idealist, tradition is closely associated with rationalism, that is, each event is judged in terms of general abstract principles, to which, of course, Burke was strongly averse.[36]

The classification of the whole of the history of the theory of international relations into two antithetical categories did, as I have briefly intimated, fail to accommodate comfortably some thinkers whose inclusion tended to undermine the efficacy of the category to which they were assigned. The response to such procrustean tactics has been varied.[37]

Martin Wight, most famously and most influentially, developed a threefold categorization at the centre of which stands a fundamental question: what is the nature and character of international society? It is the answers given to this question which purportedly differentiate thinkers into his three traditions of Realists or Machiavellians, Rationalists or Grotians, and Revolutionists or Kantians.

The Realist tradition emphasizes international anarchy, power politics, and warfare, and is distinguished from the others by its reliance on the inductive method. It concentrates on the facts of the case rather than upon what ought to be. Wight contends that the Realist tradition rests upon three 'scientific' presuppositions. First there is the mechanistic view of international politics which views relations among states in terms of balance and equilibrium, the so-called balance of power. Secondly, there is the biological theory associated with Darwin and the infamous struggle for survival. The third theory upon which Realism rests is a psychological one, particularly evident in Hobbes's egoism, but Wight argues that almost all psychological theories lead to Realism because they tend towards determinism and undermine the place of ethics in human behaviour. Rationalists believe that international society consists of states constrained by custom, law, and obligations which arise from many different types of co-operation and interaction amongst themselves. This tradition is associated with Natural Law, a belief in an ordered cosmos regulated by immutable laws appropriate to all creatures, including humans. Revolutionists have a passionate belief in the unity of humankind and they see international society transcending its parts. They are cosmopolitans rather than internationalists.

Hedley Bull, for example, reformulates the existing categories and adds a third. The Realist tradition he calls Hobbesian, and for him it is epitomized by the view that international politics is analogous to a state of nature. The Idealist, or Utopian, tradition he calls Grotian, and it is characterized by the view that politics between nations takes place within the framework of an international society governed by law. The additional category, which he grafts onto the first two, he names the Kantian tradition, in which interstate relations are superseded by a transnational community of humanity. Here the coincidence of the interests of all human beings projects a universalist perspective.[38] Martin Wight, from whom Bull borrows and develops the traditions, says of the third that its emphasis upon the universality of humanity does not in itself distinguish it from the Grotian tradition, because in Grotius himself we find conceptions of both a society of humanity and a society of states. The distinguishing features of the tradition are a dissatisfaction with the existing system of states and a belief in the rational progress of human affairs towards a more desirable condition.[39]

Wight sometimes called exponents, or exemplars, of the various traditions Machiavellians, Grotians, and Kantians, or alternatively Realists, Rationalists, and Revolutionists.[40] On Wight's characterization Burke is deemed a Grotian because of the presupposition of an international society based upon a more fundamental natural or providential, order, in which war, while constrained by convention and the 'Law of Nations', must, in the absence of authority, be reverted to for upholding justice in international relations. But, as R. J. Vincent has rightly pointed out, while Burke and Grotius have certain affinities, it would be perverse to identify the Englishman with the Rationalists, Wight's alternative name for the tradition, because Burke's most famous work, the *Reflections,* is vehemently anti-rationalist.[41] Burke, Vincent contends, exhibits elements from all three traditions, and if he is to be classified at all it is best to revert to the old right–centre–left continuum, that is, the categories of Conservatism, Liberalism and Revolutionism. Vincent argues that 'Burke was a conservative, but a conservative with the range of vision to marshal rationalism as well as realism on behalf of the cause'.[42] Vincent's suggestion, however, is naïve. Such political categories are notoriously amorphous, and even anachronistic when related to Burke. Indeed, the attribution of such political appellations to Burke depends very much upon the perspective from which his pronouncements are considered. In India, for example, the introduction to a new edition of Burke's speeches on the impeachment of Warren Hastings describes him as a 'liberal political philosopher'.[43]

The purpose of formulating a third tradition was, of course, to accommodate those philosophers of international relations who sat uneasily in the conventional Realist and Idealist categories. To make the characterization less procrustean than it was by identifying a third tradition was in itself an advance. But is the resolution satisfactory? In reformulating the traditions of Realism and Idealism and adding to them a third, the focus becomes the end product, or conclusion of the theories, that is, whether they postulate anarchy, international society, or universalist values. The ways in which thinkers reach their conclusions differ significantly, and a resemblance in conclusion may serve to disguise more fundamental and philosophically important divergences in arguments and assumptions. For example, to identify Hobbes and Filmer as exponents of absolute monarchy is inconsequential in comparison to their significant differences over, to take just one instance, the source of the authority of the sovereign and the constraints upon the arbitrary exercise of power.

There is a common difficulty that all these different conceptions share. They see each of their traditions as mutually exclusive and autonomous categories, without adequately explaining the relations between them, or between the traditions and the thinkers who are said to exemplify them. The traditions are little more than classificatory categories into which thinkers are forced irrespective of the embarrassing elements which appear to be ill at ease in their putative homes. If the focus of the activity is upon accommodating a thinker to a tradition, then at least one of four strategies appears to be adopted to maintain the integrity of the characterization, but each of them serves to undermine the whole enterprise. First, there is what we may call the Wight strategy of constantly changing the traditions, and their central focuses, in response to each thinker who formally deviates from his patterns. Wight saw his exploration of the history of ideas in international relations primarily as 'an experiment in classification, in typology . . .'.[44] This explains his curious propensity continuously to add subcategories to the traditions like species to a genus, and borders dangerously upon defeating the whole point of classification by inventing a new category for each thinker.

Wight's immensely influential approach is based upon a principle of historical method which in the subject of political theory, with which he wished to bring about a *rapprochement*, came under considerable attack in the 1960s. Like Arthur O. Lovejoy's infamous unit ideas, the currency in which Wight deals is ideas that recur with very little variation in different contexts, like coins that change hands, and whose value is little affected by inflation. The voices are ones with which we can engage because they speak the same language and address the same perennial problems. Such assumptions have long been undermined by historians of ideas such as Skinner, Pocock, and Dunn, drawing on the philosophies of Collingwood, Wittgenstein, and Austin, who in their different ways attempt to demonstrate that meanings change in different contexts, even though the words are ostensibly the same.[45]

The recent reaction against dominant discourses in the theory of international relations from both critical theorists and postmodernists, irrespective of their different substantive purposes, is to adopt the strategy of exposing historically constructed myths. Theories, it is suggested, are practices, the result of human artifice, which give rise to, or construct, relationships of power. Power relationships are dispersed throughout a multiplicity of practices, exerting varying degrees of authority but standing in no necessary relation to each other, nor together exhibiting a rational or teleological development towards some desired end. The uncovering of layer upon layer of social practices, and the demonstration of how power relat.⌄ns have been socially constituted, is itself an historical endeavour, more fashionably known as 'archaeology' or 'genealogy', which in international relations theory has taken the form, for example, of undermining the dominant discourse of 'Realism' by showing that its reified historical exemplars and sanctified texts when read in the context of their contemporaneous social practices may appropriately be interpreted or read as anti-Realist. From the perspective of historical materialism, Justin Rosenberg, for example, takes the city-state system of ancient Greece and the state system of Renaissance Italy, which are central to orthodox Realist balance of power international political theory, and pronounces that his aim is 'partly to call the Realist's bluff by taking a closer look at these pre-modern geopolitical systems: can we trust the historical references, or are they hiding something?' 'Well, it turns out that when Thucydides, for instance, is "restored" to his original context and his statement that the real reason for the Peloponnesian War was the growth in Athenian power, he could not mean "geopolitical power" on the modern realist definition . . .'.[46] Postmodernists such as R. B. J. Walker and Jim George explicitly aim to 'disrupt

Realist textual certainty' by exposing Realist interpretations of canonical thinkers such as Thucydides and Machiavelli as parodies and caricatures.[47] As opposed to the use of history in establishing the orthodoxy in international relations theory, we have the use of history as a weapon in the fight against orthodoxy in the theory of international relations.

An alternative to Wight's way of coping with the pitfalls of classification is the Bull strategy of maintaining the traditions, acknowledging those aspects of a theory that do not fit, and then cursorily dismissing them. It has been suggested that Bull's main contribution to the theory of international relations is his ability to make sharp distinctions and careful definitions.[48] This, R. B. J. Walker contends, 'takes us into the realm of classification and typology'[49]—a realm, of course, that he inhabits with his mentor Martin Wight.

The third strategy is to retain the labels of Realist and Idealist and to redescribe their content, enabling the theorist of international relations to reallocate thinkers into more comfortable homes despite their self-perceptions. This is the route that Martin Griffiths takes when he contends that, rather than the meaningless category of Realism as traditionally conceived in international relations, we should adopt Robert Berki's quite different formulation, which transforms the self-styled Realists Hans Morganthau and Kenneth Waltz into Idealists, and the self-styled Grotian Hedley Bull into a 'Realist'.[50] While this may be intellectually self-edifying, such re-description adds little to our understanding.

The fourth and most radical strategy is to employ entirely different categories, as Chris Brown and Janna Thompson do in using the concepts of communitarianism and cosmopolitanism.[51] Linklater's distinction between men and citizens also alludes to this perspective. The two categories are to some extent related to the debate in mainstream political theory between liberal individualism and communitarianism. The liberal individualist, while emphasizing universal characteristics of human nature, such as the psychological motivation of pleasure and pain, nevertheless recognizes the subjective self-determining features of human action. The liberal pr_es highly the individual setting his or her own goals and being able to step back from them and subject them to criticism if desired. While we are motivated by the same things, as Hobbes argued, we are at liberty to put different values on them. Another version of this subjectivism is that of Mill, who argued that each person has a unique personality and has a conception of what is good for him or her which is different from everyone else's. The experiences of other people, on this view, do not provide grounds for overriding my view of what is good for me. Mill was concerned, of course, about the tyranny of the majority as a possible consequence of democracy. In opposition to this Will Kymlicka identifies perfectionism in politics. He uses the example of Marxian perfectionism. Perfectionist politics of any kind, including such ideologies as Nazism or Fascism, sets a clear idea of what is good and devotes the resources of society almost exclusively to achieving it. This is what Michael Oakeshott has famously identified as rationalism in politics. It is the politics of certainty because it believes that by the exercise of reason and the rejection of tradition answers to problems can be arrived at with certainty. Rationalism is also the politics of perfection because the answer arrived at with certainty is taken to be the best answer.[52]

Communitarianism is a philosophical point of view that steers a course between individualism and universalism. On the other hand, Marxist perfectionism claims that a person's good is the same as everyone else's; it is our capacity to produce free of being alienated from ourselves and from the product of our work. Communitarianism contends that our conception of the good is neither unique nor one which we share with everyone else. What we regard as good for ourselves is related to the cultural traditions and ways of life in which we participate. Liberalism believes in the principles of self-determination, that is, the making of choices on the basis of the beliefs that we hold and the values we have, and also in the freedom to question those beliefs. It believes in a neutral state which in some way sets the framework within which competing conceptions of the good can be pursued. Communitarianism is much less individualist and much less universalist than either of these positions. It believes in the idea of the common good, or what Rousseau called the General Will. Kymlicka argues, for example, that in liberal societies there is a notion of the common good, but it is adjusted to the preferences and the conceptions of the good of the people who live in them. A communitarian society, on the other hand, formulates substantive conceptions of the good which defines a society's way of life and acts as a criterion against which individual preferences can be judged. He argues that a community's 'way of life forms the basis for a public ranking of conceptions of the good, and the weight given to an individual's preferences depends on how much she conforms or contributes to this common good'.[53] The state is not then committed to neutrality but takes precedence over the differing individual conceptions of the good and their claims to the resources and freedom needed to pursue them. A communitarian state, he argues, should encourage individuals to conform to the common good and discourage them from pursuing their own conceptions. Kymlicka maintains that communitarianism is a form of the perfectionist state. It differs, however, from Marxist perfection..m. Marxism ranks conceptions of the good in terms of a transhistorical criterion. Communitarianism ranks conceptions of the good in relation to the current practices pursued in a society.

Liberals see the self-determining self as prior to the social roles he or she participates in. Typically many liberals talk of Natural Rights which we hold independently of society. Communitarians, on the other hand, believe this to be a wholly fallacious view of the self. Our lives and personalities are shaped by the social circumstances in which we find ourselves, and we simply cannot step back from them and be neutral in our judgements. The self is said to be embedded or situated in existing and ongoing social practices. This is not a denial of self-determination, but instead a recognition that self-determination operates in the context of social roles. The state conceives its role as enabling us to become more deeply embedded in those roles in order to understand them better and to promote self-fulfilment. It does not see itself as protecting rights against society and enabling us to stand back from those roles in order to criticize them. MacIntyre maintains that our communal values set the horizons of the goals that we set for ourselves. Our situatedness contributes to the sort of person we are, and therefore puts limits on the sorts of goals we think it legitimate to pursue. Sandel argues that the self cannot be conceived as prior to the ends it pursues. The self is in fact constituted by those ends, and not separated from them. By being embedded in some shared social context, many of the ends that constitute us are not chosen, but given.[54] The state is therefore seen as an enabling state in that it creates the conditions for us to come to identify our shared constitutive ends, and removes the obstacles for us to pursue them in conformity with the common good. What we have is a recognition of sharing a good in conformity with others, and it has value in knowing that my good is also the good of my fellow citizens. There is no such thing as the unencumbered self independent of his or her socially constituted ends.

The communitarian also denies that individualism can give a firm basis to state legitimacy. Charles Taylor argues that a state which purports to be neutral fails to give credence to the idea of a shared common good which justifies the sacrifices people are asked to make in order to sustain the welfare of the state. The demands of the state will only be accepted as legitimate if citizens feel part of a common life which is valued as an all-important good, not just as an aggregate of individual wills, whose continuance and enhancement are seen as of intrinsic importance, not instrumentally as the means of promoting their own individually conceived ends.[55]

Cosmopolitans are those theorists who posit a world community consisting of individuals, or individuals represented through states and subject to a common moral law. The communitarians, on the other hand, posit the individual and his or her morality firmly grounded in the community. The formation of the individual, and his rights and duties, is generated by historically based moral communities, the morality by which they are regulated having been internally precipitated, rather than externally received. This conceptualization of the last two centuries of the history of the theory of international relations focuses upon the source of values rather than the causes of conflict.

A focus upon the conclusion or the desired end result, that is, a cosmopolitan or communitarian community,[56] leads to the perverse outcome of associating thinkers whose questions and reasons for reaching their conclusions are very different. Brown subsumes Kant, the Utilitarians, and Marx under the cosmopolitan category. The desirability of the end result, however, obviously hinges on the arguments used to reach the conclusion; in other words we are talking about different world communities.

Brown does suggest that we should avoid two common misconceptions about cosmopolitanism: first, that it has no necessary connection with the desire for a world government, and secondly, that it is universalist, but that not all universalist doctrines are cosmopolitan. Subscription to some kind of moral order whose source is not community-based seems to be all that constitutes the differentia of this category. This would lead to the apparently perverse conclusion that Plato and Aristotle were cosmopolitans, even though they thought that the *polis* was the natural community which shaped and moulded the citizen. If it is the idea of uni-

versal moral standards which is doing all the work, then the idea of cosmopolitanism needs to be more specifically defined as one element associated with it,
but not invariably so. As we will see, Plato and Aristotle could not conceive of a
higher association than the *polis*, and both believed in qualitative differences
between human beings within and without the community, yet both subscribed
to universal moral laws above those formulated by each people for itself. If
restricted to the two categories allowed us by Brown and Thompson, we would
have to say that Plato and Aristotle were at once communitarian and cosmopolitan. The personified Laws in the *Crito* tell Socrates how they have taken him and
shaped him into what he is, and that he owes a greater loyalty to them than to his
natural parents, yet the source of justice is transcendental and not conventional.
The point is this: universal or cosmopolitan rights can have their source in agreement, or be declaratory, meaning that their source is independent of human
design. Either way communitarianism and cosmopolitanism do not turn out to
be mutually exclusive, or even opposed categories.

On the other hand Thompson and Brown contend that the communitarian is
unlikely to acknowledge the possibility or desirability of a world community.[57]
Brown suggests that communitarians of the Hegelian and neo-Hegelian persuasion would not see a world community as a necessary step beyond the state,
'because it could not provide any resource for the creation of individuality and
personality on top of those already to hand in the modern state'.[58] Hegel's views,
and indeed Rousseau's, are faithful representations of the communitarian attitude
to cosmopolitanism, and as we will see in Chapter 14 Hegel's view constitutes the
exception rather than the rule.[59] In this respect Brown fails to make the crucial
distinction that the Hegelian communitarians always made, and that is between
international relations as they currently stand and as they might yet become.

The categories of cosmopolitanism and communitarianism do in fact generate
a good deal of confusion when applied to the details of particular thinkers' arguments. We have a cosmopolitanism that cannot envisage the disintegration of the
state system, but instead sees its transformation into an ethically conceived confederation of states bound by three types of right, constitutional, interstate, and
cosmopolitan (Kant), and a communitarianism that conceives the disintegration
of the state system and the extension of the ethical community to encompass the
world (Green and Bosanquet).[60] Furthermore, in Marx we have an appeal to a
cosmopolitanism whose attainment is frustrated by alienation, exploitation, and
estrangement, coupled with a strong communitarian belief that human nature in
addition to having a general form is in its substance historically constituted.

Onora O'Neill's distinction between universalist and particularist accounts of
reasoning about action is a variation of the cosmopolitan and communitarian
division, and captures in essence much of what I have covered in detail in this
book. The ancient universalists, she argues, supported their arguments for the
universal form, scope, and content of ethical principles with demanding metaphysical and epistemological ideals. Justice was inextricably linked to conceptions
of the good life and of virtuous character. In other words, justice and virtue were
part and parcel of their universalism. The idea of the good was fundamental to

ethical thinking about inclusive universal principles and the way in which they were to be realized for the person and the polity. Particularism for her is a very broad-ranging category often associated with historicized versions of Aristotelianism. It limits virtue in its scope to the contingencies of local norms and practices. What is virtuous is dictated by the circumstances and position of the person, and therefore cannot be universal in scope. Modern universalists, she argues, in their attempts to jettison the baggage of the metaphysics of the person, maintain that justice should be neutral between different conceptions of the good and have next to nothing to say about virtue. The two most notable examples in this respect would be John Rawls and Brian Barry, who associate justice with the terms of reasonable agreement. This is what Barry calls justice as impartiality. Barry maintains that, given that we have irresolvable differences over what constitutes the good life, 'justice as impartiality offers a fair basis of agreement for people with divergent conceptions of the good'.[61] Barry does not, however, want to exclude particularist considerations as being ethically relevant in the discharge of universal obligations.

Modern-day particularists, O'Neill argues, not only reject universalism, but also seem disinclined to say anything about justice. Instead they concern themselves with anchoring 'the claims of virtue in judgements about the shared particularities of tradition, practice and community'.[62] Here she has in mind communitarians such as Sandel and Taylor and particularist feminists such as Carol McMillan and Carol Gilligan. There are nevertheless distinguished particularists who try to reconcile their ideas with universalism and concepts of international justice. David Miller, for example, contends that for ethical particularism personal attachments, relationships, and membership are ethically significant because they give rise to obligations that we may not have to others who stand in different or in no relation to us. Does this view of ethics exclude obligations that we might have to humanity, and if not in what relation do they stand to particularistic obligations? Miller maintains that our relationship to other members of humanity is not merely as individuals, but that we are also related as members of groups or nations. He argues that ethical particularism is not incompatible with a doctrine of basic human rights. Both the universalist and the particularist can agree that certain conditions—call them basic rights—are essential for living a recognizably human life. These may include basic levels of bodily integrity, individual freedom, and material resources. The main area of contention, however, is over *who* has the obligation to ensure that these basic rights are enjoyed. For the particularist it is one's co-nationals who are responsible for protecting basic rights, such as the relief of hunger. In relation to outsiders, however, we may have an obligation to protect their basic rights, perhaps through redistributive justice, when they are unable to protect them for themselves. This is not an unqualified obligation. The failure of a community to protect the basic human rights of its members may be the consequence of bad policies, or of a reluctance by the privileged to concede their vested interests. An outside community that decides that its own welfare requirements take precedence over those of the needy in another country does not directly violate their rights. That community may be charged with doing nothing to prevent their rights being violated, but under the circumstances the inaction may be justified. Miller concludes that the type of ethical particularism he wants to defend is not therefore incompatible with ethical universalism in the form of acknowledged basic human rights. The obligations corresponding to these rights, however, are primarily the responsibility of co-nationals. Justice does not therefore require us to intervene in all cases to protect the human rights of foreigners, 'though humanitarian considerations may lead us to do so'.[63]

The characterization that I present of the traditions of Empirical Realism, Universal Moral Order, and Historical Reason is dialectical. I do not want to suggest that self-consciousness is the criterion of these traditions, although it may often be the case that a thinker is conscious of occupying a place in a particular tradition, nor do I wish to claim that they are anything more than abstractions. They are characterizations of styles of thinking about the criteria of conduct in international relations which have surfaced and been intimated from time to time in the history of European philosophy. The focus is not upon the substantive ends, such as a specific type of order, or upon a cosmopolitan or communitarian view of the world, but instead upon the criteria invoked to guide, justify, or recommend state conduct. No one thinker fits perfectly into any one tradition, nor are the styles of thinking meant to act as classifying categories into which to force particular philosophers. The traditions stand in a dialectical relation to each other, and there are constant tensions between them. Within the work of any one writer we see attempts to resolve the tensions by employing one of the categories to subordinate the other two. Below I sketch the bare outlines of the traditions with the intention of providing an overview, which as the details transpire in the various chapters will necessarily be qualified and extended.

The argument of this chapter has simply been this: a philosophical focus, the focus of the political theory of international relations, largely excludes many of the polemical and ideological thinkers illegitimately invoked in response to the legitimate need to expand the political theory canon in order to include writers with a more specific focus upon international relations. Attempts to characterize the history of the political theory of international relations have in their different ways been inadequate. All of them fail to relate the traditions to each other, and to individual thinkers in a meaningful way. Furthermore, their traditions are classificatory categories, used, it seems, for the purposes of labelling.

Notes

1. F. Parkinson, *The Philosophy of International Relations: A Study in the History of Thought* (Beverly Hills, Sage, Calif., and London, 1977).
2. Howard Williams, *International Relations in Political Theory* (Buckingham, Open University, 1992).
3. Raymond Aron complained that 'theory' has become a much over-used and abused

word, particularly in the field of international relations where the most banal observations are dressed up under the guise of theory. See 'What is a Theory of International Relations?', *Journal of International Affairs*, 21 (1967).

4. Kenneth N. Waltz, *Theory of International Politics* (New York, McGraw-Hill, 1979), 1.

5. Waltz, *Theory of International Politics*, 6. Twenty years earlier Waltz had developed his famous analysis of war in terms of three images, the internal psychology of man, the internal structure of the state, and the structure of the world state system, by drawing upon the insights of classical political theorists, tempered nevertheless by the assumptions of contemporary social science. See Kenneth N. Waltz, *Man, the State and War: A Theoretical Analysis* (New York, Columbia University Press, 1959).

6. Martin Wight, 'Why is There No International Theory?', in H. Butterfield and M. Wight (eds.), *Diplomatic Investigations: Essays in the Theory of International Politics* (London, Allen and Unwin, 1966), 18.

7. Martin Wight, *International Theory: The Three Traditions*, ed. Gabriele Wight and Brian Porter (London and Leicester, University of Leicester Press, 1991), 1. Michael Donelan also subscribes to this view in his *Elements of International Political Theory* (Oxford, Oxford University Press, 1990), 1.

8. Wight, *International Theory*, 5.

9. This characterization became widely accepted and still acts as a useful heuristic device for teaching international relations to students. The most influential perpetrators of what has been called the inter-paradigm debate are Richard Little and Michael Smith with their immensely popular reader, *Perspectives on World Politics*, 2nd edn. (London, Routledge, 1991). The list of what passes as theory in the field of international relations could be extended considerably, but it would not add anything to the point that international theory has on the whole developed independently of political philosophy, to the detriment of the former and, I may add, of the latter. For surveys of the various 'theories' of international relations see K. J. Holsti, *The Dividing Discipline: Hegemony and Diversity in International Theory* (London, Allen and Unwin, 1987); Ken Booth and Steve Smith (eds.), *International Relations Theory Today* (Cambridge, Polity, 1995); and A. J. R. Groom and Margot Light (eds.), *Contemporary International Relations: A Guide to Theory* (London, Pinter, 1994).

10. Mervyn Frost, *Ethics in International Relations: A Constitutive Theory* (Cambridge, Cambridge University Press, 1996), 12, 18–19.

11. Chris Brown, *International Relations Theory: New Normative Approaches* (London, Harvester Wheatsheaf, 1992), 83.

12. Scott Burchill, 'Introduction', in Scott Burchill, Andrew Linklater, Richard Devetak, Matthew Paterson, and Jacqui True, *Theories of International Relations* (Basingstoke, Macmillan, 1996), 7–8; and Williams, *International Relations in Political Theory*.

13. In criticizing contemporary political philosophers, A. H. Hanson argued that they have abandoned the claim to offer any practical guidance and 'remain content with the intellectually exciting but politically sterile task of teasing out linguistic puzzles'. See 'Political Philosophy or Political Science', an inaugural lecture (Cambridge, Leeds University Press, 1956), 7.

14. Chris Brown largely attributes the parting of the ways to the demise of normative moral philosophy following the First World War. This does not explain why international theorists did not take the route of political theorists and define themselves in terms of their pedigree. See Brown, *International Relations Theory*, 84–9.

15. William C. Olsen and A. J. R. Groom, *International Relations Then and Now: Origins and Trends in Interpretation* (London, Routledge, 1991), chaps. 4 and 5.

16. E. H. Carr, *The Twenty Years' Crisis 1919–1939* (London, Macmillan, 1939; 2nd edn. 1946), 60.
17. See Martin Wight, *International Theory*; Torbjörn L. Knutsen, *A History of International Relations Theory* (Manchester, Manchester University Press, 1992). For anthologies see Howard P. Kainz (ed.), *Philosophical Perspectives on Peace* (London, Macmillan, 1987); John A. Vasquez (ed.), *Classics of International Relations*, 2nd edn. (Englewood Cliffs, NJ, Prentice Hall, 1990); Evan Luard (ed.), *Basic Texts in International Relations* (London, Macmillan, 1992).
18. Hedley Bull, 'Martin Wight and the Theory of International Relations', in Wight, *International Theory*, p. xi. The quotation from Wight appears on p. 1.
19. Richard Little and Steve Smith (eds.), *Belief Systems and International Relations* (Oxford, Basil Blackwell, 1988).
20. Terry Nardin, *Law, Morality and the Relations of States* (Princeton, Princeton University Press, 1983), p. xi.
21. Steve Smith, 'The Forty Years' Detour: The Resurgence of Normative Theory in International Relations', *Millennium*, 21 (1992).
22. Janna Thompson, *Justice and World Order: A Philosophical Inquiry* (London, Routledge, 1992); Brown, *International Relations Theory*.
23. Frost, *Ethics in International Relations*, and Chris Brown, 'The Ethics of Political Restructuring in Europe—The Perspective of Constitutive Theory', in Chris Brown (ed.), *Political Restructuring in Europe: Ethical Perspectives* (London, Routledge, 1994), 167.
24. Following Oakeshott, Nardin takes the task of philosophy to be the identification and examination of the postulates that sustain and constitute given human practices. See Michael Oakeshott, *Experience and its Modes* (Cambridge, Cambridge University Press, 1933) and *On Human Conduct* (Oxford, Clarendon Press, 1975).
25. Nardin, *Law, Morality and the Relations of States*.
26. Thucydides, *History of the Peloponnesian War*, trans. Rex Warner, rev. edn. (Harmondsworth, Penguin, 1972), 1. 22.
27. This is not the place to rehearse the well-worn arguments for and against various approaches in the history of ideas. I have addressed and criticized the major positions in my *Texts in Context: Revisionist Methods for Studying the History of Ideas* (Dordrecht, Martinus Nijhoff, 1985).
28. See Michael Banks, 'The Evolution of International Relations Theory', in Michael Banks (ed.), *Conflict in World Society* (London, Wheatsheaf, 1984), 3–21.
29. Banks, 'The Evolution of International Relations Theory', 5.
30. Banks names these traditions Realism and Liberalism (ibid. 5–7), whereas E. H. Carr refers to them as Realism and Utopianism. See Carr, *Twenty Years' Crisis*, 22–89.
31. H. J. Morganthau, *Politics among Nations*, 5th edn. (New York, Knopf, 1978), 3.
32. Chicago and London, The University of Chicago Press, 1951.
33. See Hedley Bull, *The Anarchical Society: A Study of Order in World Politics* (London, Macmillan, 1984).
34. Herz, *Political Realism and Political Idealism*, 25.
35. The aspects of Burke's thought that can be related to different traditions will be explicated in more detail in due course.
36. Carr, *Twenty Years' Crisis*, 28.
37. Kenneth W. Thompson suggests that 'We may be awaiting a new synthesis, an outlook that strives with more determination to combine the ideal and the real'. See K. W. Thompson, 'Idealism and Realism: Beyond the Great Debate', *British Journal of International Studies*, 3 (1977), 209.

38. Bull, *The Anarchical Society*, 25. Also see Hedley Bull, 'Society and Anarchy in International Relations' and 'The Grotian Conception of International Society', in Herbert Butterfield and Martin Wight (eds.) *Diplomatic Investigations: Essays in the Theory of International Politics*, (London, Allen and Unwin, 1966); and Hedley Bull, 'Hobbes and the International Anarchy', *Social Research*, 48 (1981). Graham Evans offers a variant of the three traditions which has the same source of inspiration as my own, namely W. H. Greenleaf. G. Evans 'Some Problems with a History of Thought in International Relations', *International Relations*, 4 (1974).

39. Martin Wight, 'An Anatomy of International Thought', *Review of International Studies*, 13 (1987), 224. Also see Hedley Bull, 'Martin Wight and the Theory of International Relations', *British Journal of International Studies*, 2 (1976), 101–16; and Brian Porter, 'Patterns of Thought and Practice: Martin Wight's International Theory', in Michael Donelan (ed.), *The Reason of States* (London, Allen and Unwin, 1978), 64–74.

40. Bull, 'Martin Wight and the Theory of International Relations', 104. Banks names the third tradition 'radical' (Banks, 'The Evolution of International Relations Theory', 7). Thinkers usually placed in this tradition are Kant, Marx, and Mazzini. Also see G. L. Goodwin, *World Institutions and World Order* (London, Bell and Sons, 1964), 12.

41. R. J. Vincent, 'Edmund Burke and the Theory of International Relations', *Review of International Studies*, 10 (1984), 206, 216, and 217–18, n. 6.

42. Vincent, 'Edmund Burke and the Theory of International Relations', 216. Andrew Linklater is also influenced by Wight in his characterization of the history of the philosophy of international relations. See Andrew Linklater, *Men and Citizens in the Theory of International Relations*, 2nd edn. (London, Macmillan, 1990).

43. V. K. Saxena, 'Introduction', in Edmund Burke, *Speeches on the Impeachment of Warren Hastings* (Delhi, Discovery Publishing House, 1987) 2 vols., i, p. x. This accords with the liberal utilitarian view of Burke dominant at the end of the 19th century, and the beginning of the 20th century.

44. Wight, *International Theory*, 5.

45. For critiques and assessments of these ideas see my *Texts in Context*.

46. Justin Rosenberg, *The Empire of Civil Society: A Critique of the Realist Theory of International Relations* (London, Verso, 1994), 62 and 82–3.

47. Jim George, *Discourses of Global Politics: A Critical (Re)Introduction to International Relations* (Boulder, Colo., Rienner, 1994), 194–5; R. B. J. Walker, *Inside/Outside: International Relations as Political Theory* (Cambridge, Cambridge University Press, 1993), 30–48 and 65–6.

48. R. J. Vincent, 'Hedley Bull and Order in International Politics', *Millennium*, 17 (1988), 195–213.

49. Walker, *Inside/Outside*, 69.

50. Martin Griffiths, *Realism, Idealism and International Politics* (London, Routledge, 1992).

51. Brown, *International Relations Theory*; Janna Thompson, *Justice and World Order*.

52. Michael Oakeshott, *Rationalism in Politics and Other Essays*, new and expanded edn., ed. T. Fuller (Indianapolis, Liberty, 1991), 5–42.

53. Will Kymlicka, *Contemporary Political Philosophy: An Introduction* (Oxford, Oxford University Press, 1990), 206.

54. Michael Sandel, *Liberalism and the Limits of Justice* (Cambridge, Cambridge University Press, 1982), 55–9 and 152–4.

55. Kymlicka, *Contemporary Political Philosophy*, 225.

56. Brown, *International Relations Theory*, 44.
57. Thompson, *Justice and World Order*, 120. Chris Brown, 'International Political Theory and the Idea of World Community', in Ken Booth and Steve Smith (eds.), *International Relations Theory Today* (Cambridge, Polity Press, 1995), 91.
58. Brown, 'Idea of World Community', 103–4.
59. Thompson includes a useful chapter on nationalism as a form of communitarianism.
60. More will be said on this issue in Chapter 16 of this book.
61. Brian Barry, *Justice as Impartiality* (Oxford, Clarendon Press, 1995), 119.
62. Onora O'Neill, *Towards Justice and Virtue: A Constructive Account of Practical Reasoning* (Cambridge, Cambridge University Press, 1996), 17.
63. David Miller, *On Nationality* (Oxford, Clarendon Press, 1995), 80.

2

EMPIRICAL REALISM, UNIVERSAL MORAL ORDER, AND HISTORICAL REASON

Having looked at the general position of the political theory of international relations and explored the alternatives available for characterizing its history, I want in this chapter to offer the organizing framework that provides the structure of this book. Without going into the complexities of methodological debate I want simply to state some of the principles that have informed my approach.[1] One of the important insights of Gestalt psychology is the realization that the brain is constantly working to group series of electrical impulses generated by retinal stimulation into simple objects based on a whole series of factors, including previous experience. Quite simply, in severe cases we feel uncomfortable and disoriented when the stimuli are confusing and render us incapable of clear imagery. The concept of a Gestalt switch and the illusions of perception are familiar to us all. In the realm of philosophy Hegel offered comparable insights. The mind must rest dissatisfied with a confusing mass of detail which exhibits no intelligible pattern. Thought thinking about thought seeks to render it intelligible or rational. In other words, we try to make sense out of masses of detail over long time frames by discerning in it some intelligible pattterns, if only to see it as the continuation of an argument or a shared way of thinking. For those who look at the world rationally, the world looks rational in return. This is not to say that irrationality, contingency, and randomness are ignored, but all these factors somehow have to be explained or understood not merely as disconnected incidents, but in their relations with the broader stream of thought. Every concrete affirmation of a position is at the same time a denial of something else, and to relate it to this something else is to add a dimension of intelligibility that the author may not himself or herself have provided. Despite the endless disputes over the period and geography covered by the historical concept of the Renaissance, only some literary and artistic figures perceived themselves as living through and making a contribution to it. The lack of self-perception of the Renaissance does not render those other souls who lived through it (wherever and whenever it may have been) non-participants. Methodological discussions largely revolve around the question of what appropriate constraints ought to regulate and even constitute the intelligibility sought in historical studies.

In what follows I lay out three ways of thinking discernible in discussions of philosophical and ethical issues in the political theory of international relations. They are what Oakeshott calls 'ideal characterizations' because they are never found in their pure form articulated by any one thinker or having an independent and autonomous existence at any particular time or place. Each tradition is related dialectically to the others as thesis the first, antithesis the second, and synthesis the third. Elements of each may be found in particular thinkers, and genuine attempts may be discerned to resolve the opposed tendencies, or to accommodate them as coexisting. What follows is not a formula to be applied to the various thinkers to produce a contrived and stylized comparative study. Instead the framework acts as a reference point which sometimes comes to the fore, but which is never meant to dominate the discussions.

Empirical Realism

The first tradition may be termed Empirical Realism. Those philosophers who fall within its compass view human beings as discrete, autonomous, sensing individuals. These individuals have their own needs, desires, interests, and aspirations. The springs of action are radically subjective. The criterion of goodness is pleasure, and that of badness, aversion. In so far as we desire the same things our interests come into conflict. Right conduct is dictated by our desires and interests. Hobbes, of course, has given the most sophisticated rendition of this view, in which he argues that Natural Rights are dictated by right reason, and their justification for use is merely the fact that we have them. They are, in fact, rules of prudence, and not moral imperatives. Whereas Machiavelli had uneasily divorced political expediency from morality, in Hobbes expediency becomes equivalent to morality. There is no ultimate moral law which guides our will, nor any ultimate moral end to which our actions must be directed. The satisfaction of desires is temporary, and we are condemned never to experience fulfilment, because the attainment of one satisfaction leads to the desire for another. Machiavelli puts this view admirably when he says: 'human appetites are insatiable, for by nature we are so constituted that there is nothing we cannot long for'.[2] At its most pessimistic points, exponents of the ideas associated with this tradition contend that men are more naturally inclined to do evil than they are to do good. Diodotus, as reported by Thucydides, suggests that 'Cities and individuals alike, all are by nature disposed to do wrong, and there is no law that will prevent it'.[3] Everything and everyone is a means to an end, and has to be justified in terms of its, or his, usefulness.

The implications of this view of human nature, as self-interested and unconstrained by any universal higher moral laws, are profound for civil society. Thucydides, Machiavelli, and Hobbes, the archetypal exemplars of this tradition in the history of the political theory of international relations, all assume a permanent human nature which can be modified and constrained by human laws and conventions. Without a strong authority capable of enforcing a code of rules which minimize the conflict inherent in human relations, no commodious living would be possible. Strong government is necessary to modify human nature, but such modifications are fragile, and civil society is perpetually threatened by the probability, even inevitability, that human interests, driven by ambition or impelled by crisis, will triumph over convention and revert to a situation where self-interest and chaos reign. This, of course, is the condition which Hobbes is both warning against and constructing a set of political arrangements to prevent, but it is most forcefully portrayed by Thucydides in his description of the plague in Athens, during which time there was a complete breakdown of civil society.[4] Furthermore, all three see chance, or fortune, as an important factor in human affairs, although they all differ in their beliefs about the degree to which it can be tamed. Thucydides is totally pessimistic in this respect; Machiavelli believes that those who possess *virtù* have some chance of harnessing fortune, but his optimism fades as the malice of fortune makes his own circumstances irredeemable; Hobbes is the most optimistic of the three in believing that this element of chance, so destructive when unconstrained, can almost be completely eliminated from politics by the great Leviathan.

In international relations, where no ultimate authority possesses the requisite power to enforce compliance with rules of conduct, states pursue their own interests in a sphere devoid of justice. Friedrich Meinecke articulates this element in the tradition when he argues that in domestic politics it is both possible and desirable that morality, justice, and power to be in harmony with each other, but in international relations such a harmony is unachievable in the absence of an ultimate power capable of upholding justice.[5] Fear and distrust of other states provide the motive for increasing one's power by prosecuting wars to subdue those who when the scales change will seek to subdue you. The paradox is, however, that having gained power, the fear of losing it impels the state to acquire more. For Hobbes, states, like individuals, are constantly seeking power, not simply because of the del.ght one gets from exercising it, but because power cannot be maintained 'without the acquisition of more'.[6] This echoes Alcibiades' justification of Athens's Sicilian expedition, in which he warns: 'The fact is that we have reached a stage where we are forced to plan new conquests and forced to hold on to what we have got, because there is a danger that we ourselves may fall under the power of others unless others are in our power.'[7] States must always be in a condition of readiness for war, being, as Hobbes suggested, both forewarned and forearmed, by which he meant that they must maintain an extensive intelligence network in addition to a well-armed militia.[8]

In this tradition national interest is paramount. Disagreements between states are viewed as conflicts of interest.[9] Alliances are entered into in order to further national interests in enhancing one's security against potentially hostile powers. Underlying this view is the notion that states in the international sphere are predatory, and that each has to look out for itself or suffer the humility of being dominated by others. International relations take place in a competitive and hostile environment in which there are winners and losers. Necessity, the desire for security, and the fear of being dominated force states to act in ways which attempt to maximize their interests, but which do not necessarily accord with conventional morality. The doctrine of *raison d'état* is central to this tradition and dictates the course a state must take, often in defiance of considerations of ethics or justice, to preserve its vitality and strength. In Meinecke's view the essence of those acts motivated by *raison d'état* is 'a high degree of causal necessity, which the agent himself is accustomed to conceive as absolute and inescapable'.[10]

Talk of the Laws of Nature and Natural Rights is not absent from this tradition, but these are conceived naturalistically, rather than ethically. It is a Law of Nature, for example, that the strong dominate the weak, and that we have a Natural Right to acquire everything that it is in our power to do. These are not ethical imperatives in that no one is obliged to let themselves be dominated, or to allow another unlimited acquisition at the expense of others without a moral justification.

This tradition does not exclusively sustain a commitment to either communitarianism or cosmopolitanism. Hobbes, for example, maintains that there is no justice or injustice independent of the sovereign. The will of the sovereign is equated with law and justice. Each society has its moral code recognized and sustained by its sovereign power. The principles of human nature are universal, but the moral code by which subjects are constrained is particularistic. There is no justice or injustice in the international sphere in the absence of a sovereign power to establish and enforce a code of ethics. Whereas individuals are the ultimate unit of value, he posits neither a universal community of humanity, nor an institutional cosmopolitanism through which universal notions of justice can be promoted. On the other hand, utilitarianism, which puts a similar emphasis to Hobbes upon pleasure and pain as the subjective springs of action, is cosmopolitan. In ethics it posits a form of consequentialism in which right and wrong are determined by consequences, the criterion of good and bad consequences being the utility principle of the greatest happiness of the greatest number. For Bentham, values are not generated by a sovereign and do not emanate from a political community; in..ead they have their basis in the principles of pleasure and pain. In Bentham's view each person has a duty to promote the happiness of humanity, and this is usually most efficiently attained through institutions such as the family and states which have no intrinsic value as such, but have a claim on us in so far as they promote the general happiness. The principle of the greatest happiness for Bentham is at once universal and cosmopolitan. He was not, however, a proponent of world government, but had the consequences of such a form of government contributed more to the general happiness it is something he would have had to advocate. On the principle of the greatest happiness of the 'citizens of the world' Bentham opposed both war and colonization because of their 'inutility'.[11]

Universal Moral Order

The second tradition, sometimes referred to as Idealist, Utopian, or Rationalist, is perhaps better described as that of a Universal Moral Order, to avoid confusion with the distinctive philosophical concepts associated with the other terms. The basic idea at the heart of this tradition is perhaps best summed up in the words of a contemporary political theorist of international relations. The universalism to which this tradition refers is of the 'covering-law' type which 'holds that there is one God, so there is one law, one justice, one correct understanding of the good life or the good society or the good regime, one salvation, one messiah, one millennium for all humanity'.[12] It is a tradition which, in Onora O'Neill's words, allied justice with virtue. It was universal in form in that it posited that there are certain ethical principles which are applicable to all and not merely some cases. It is also theoretically universal in scope in that certain fundamental principles were deemed to be cosmopolitan, but often in reality it fell far below being universal in scope in disregarding women, slaves, barbarians, and heathens.[13]

This tradition of a Universal Moral Order is able to encompass cosmopolitan and communitarian theories which posit fundamental moral laws, and thus Plato, Aristotle, and the Stoics are accommodated. What it excludes is naturalistic universal ethical theories which argue that human nature, red in tooth and claw, should override conventional morality and our obligations to states, uniting us in a common humanity. Morality was often taken to be a product of convention by Greek sophists, and in many instances it was related more explicitly to self-interest. Sometimes morality is opposed to nature and deemed unnatural, and at others it is viewed as continuous with human nature, facilitating the realization of human potential. Conventional morality in many instances was rejected, and a universal naturalistic ethic replaced by an emphasis upon natural equality and a denial of primary loyalty to the *polis* along with the rejection of familial and social ob..gations. The divisions between social groups within the *polis*, and more generally between Greeks and barbarians, were deemed unnatural. Democritus and Hippias posit something very like this. Antiphon, however, is a perfect exemplar. These views will be looked at more fully in Chapter 3. A universal naturalist ethic belongs in the tradition of Empirical Realism.

There is no necessary connection between universal rights and foundationalist ethics, nor are they necessarily justified deontologically, as Kant suggests. Utilitarians justify universal human rights with consequentialist arguments, but subscribers to the tradition of Universal Moral Order do not wish to equate ethics with expediency or usefulness. That is not to say that they do not revert to consequentialist arguments from time to time to justify moral conduct. There are certainly elements of consequentialism in Grotius, Pufendorf, and Vattel, which have led some interpreters to mistake the part for the whole and see them as veiled utilitarians.

Those whose views contribute to this tradition do not deny that the selfish interests and passions of individuals are strong. They maintain that they should, however, in no way act as a guide to personal conduct. The base animal appetites are to be fought against and renounced. There are ideals, higher laws, or natural and universal ethical rights, which are independent of human artifice, and with which positive laws and conventions must be consistent. This ethical sphere is not the creation of human beings: it is something to be apprehended or discovered by the exercise of pure reason. Alternatively, in the Natural Rights thinkers the tradition was secularized and the rights deduced from innate and self-evident human attributes, such as natural sociality. Having said that, the religious element is rarely absent.

Natural Rights theorists of the sixteenth and seventeenth centuries, while emphasizing the individual, do not lose sight of the community and of the moral constraints upon individual and state actions. Furthermore, the collectivist consciousness implied by the Natural Law and early Natural Rights theorists gives way to a more radical individualism in the later Natural Rights theories.[14] D. M. Mackinnon encapsulates this later shift in emphasis effected by Natural Rights theories when he argues that their exponents are 'no longer concerned with constraints and limitations, but rather with demands and permissions'.[15] Basil Wiley expresses a similar sentiment when he contends that the older conception of Natural Law emphasized its regulative character, whereas Natural Rights theorists extol the liberating character of nature.[16] At the heart of this idea of human rights lies the idea that man has inherent virtues which give rise to reciprocal moral claims. We are inherently moral prior to the emergence of any civil society, and we possess our moral rights not by virtue of being a citizen, but by the very fact of our humanity. Civil society is the creature of man, or of God expressing Himself through man.

Many modern conceptions of human rights that are universalist, such as the European Convention on Human Rights (1953) and the American Convention on Human Rights (1978), clearly have their source in agreement. Hedley Bull's subscription to the idea of human rights is not grounded in an absolutist transcendental ethic, but instead rests upon convention. On a philosophical level Rex Martin's *A System of Rights* argues against the prevalent idea that a right is a valid claim, proposing instead that it is an established way of being treated or of acting, and that whatever valid claim one wishes to present as a putative human right simply dissolves if it is not acknowledged as a civil right by given communities.[17]

In the Realist tradition the view of human nature was pessimistic ('men are always more ready for evil than for good'),[18] but in the tradition of a Universal Moral Order the conception of human nature is much more optimistic. St Thomas Aquinas, for example, contends that 'it is clear that there is in man a natural aptitude to virtuous action',[19] and that we must all help each other to achieve the virtue potential within us. Right action is not action motivated by self-interest, or *raison d'état*, but that which is in conformity with law or innate moral principles. Relations between states are seen to be regulated by moral or transcendental principles, which may find expression in international law. Justice, then, is not dependent upon a secular power for its enforcement; it exists independently of states, and acts as a standard by which their actions may be judged, as well as a moral constraint upon the pursuit of blatant national interest. Whereas Hobbes equates the will of the sovereign with right and wrong, justice and injustice, Pufendorf, for example, contends that it is 'no more possible for a civil sovereignty to create goodness and justice by precept, than it is for it to command that poison lose the power to waste the human body'.[20] Within this tradition political society is continuous with, and not a radical departure from, the state of nature. The pre-civil condition, unlike in the Empirical Realist tradition, is generally viewed as social.

In the Realist tradition the possession of power was justification enough for its use to acquire more. The Laws of Nature, devoid of ethical content in Thucydides, both justify and explain state aggression. Athens, with the power and ability to acquire an empire, was compelled to do so by the Laws of Nature, which dictate that the powerful rule the weak; that one must rule wherever one can; that self-interest overrides considerations of justice; and that others will rule over you if you do not rule over them. Fear and the need for security, and the dictates of self-interest, compel both the acquisition of an empire and the reluctance to let it go. The Athenians justified their imperialism by claiming that they were doing nothing against the Laws of Nature. They were doing no more, the Athenians claimed, than any other state would do in their position. All this is anathema to the Laws of Nature postulated in the second tradition. Cicero is responsible for the quintessential statement of the character of Natural Law in this tradition. In his most famous statement he argues that

there will not be different laws at Rome and at Athens, or different laws now and in the future, but one eternal and unchangeable law will be valid for all nations and for all times, and there will be one master and one ruler, that is, God, over all, for He is the author of this law, its promulgator, and its enforcing judge.[21]

War is not wholeheartedly condemned in Christian ethics. It is regarded as an evil to which we may have to revert to uphold justice in the international sphere. But such wars have to be prosecuted with the purest of motives. Aquinas is quite clear that three stringent conditions have to be met before war can be justified. First, the body which declares war must have vested in it the authority to do so. Secondly, the reason for going to war must be that of a just cause. The state which is subject to attack must deserve such action being taken against it. And, thirdly, those who embark upon war must do so with the proper and right intent. Wars must be entered into only to achieve some good object, or to avoid an evil being done to one's own or someone else's state. If the three conditions are not met, then war is not just. Aquinas argues that 'it can happen that even when war is declared by legitimate authority and there is just cause, it is, nevertheless, made unjust through evil intention'.[22] Even when the basis of such Natural Law becomes secularized there is no question of its moral imperative being weakened. Hugo Grotius, who is frequently invoked as the leading figure in severing the connection between Natural and Divine Law, nevertheless maintained its immutability. The absoluteness and self-evidence of the Natural Law, Grotius claimed, is such that it can not even be altered by God. Just as mathematics deals with figures in abstraction, the Law of Nature can be discovered by reason in abstraction from any particular circumstances.[23] For Grotius the Law of Nations, or *jus gentium voluntarium inter civitates*, arose from the relationships which develop and pertain between states. Through consensus, grounded in experience, the Law of Nations developed. The function of Natural Law in relation to the Law of Nations was to constrain the acts of rulers to ensure that they remained within certain bounds.[24] For Grotius, war can only be legitimate if there is just cause, which requires an injury to be received by one's own state, or a perception of excessive violation of the Laws of Nature and of Nations perpetrated against other states.[25] Even when a state acts with just cause against another, moderation should always be practised.[26] In the theories of Grotius the Law of Nature becomes the assertion of the principle of having respect for one another's rights; that is, having rights implies a certain duty on the part of others to respect them. The Law of Nations is restrained by the rights and duties embodied in the Natural Law. It is a distinctly ethical doctrine, which views moral action in terms of obedience to law.[27] Right action is that which conforms to law, and conflict between nations constitutes a conflict of rights. Natural Rights theories reach their zenith, of course, in Locke and during the American and French revolutions, in which the rationalistic element in the tradition becomes excessive, society becomes subordinate to individual rights, and the doctrines become more radical, or subversive, in opposing any authority which appeared to transgress, or deny, such rights.

A number of qualifications need to be made at this point. Within this tradition reference is made to Natural Law and the Law of Nations, but the relation between the two is by no means constant, nor is it necessarily always apparent. The Law of Nations may sometimes be equated with the Natural Law, and at other times viewed as the result of general consent, or agreement, but nevertheless as consistent with Natural Law. The Natural Law is not always posited as superior, and indeed the Roman Stoics did not view it as a constraint or measure of positive law. It is the Christian adoption of Natural Law that injects a much more actively judgemental element in.ʊ it. We must also remember that to postulate the universality of the Natural Law and the Law of Nations meant in practice the universalization of Christian ethics, which are imposed upon the infidel. For example, Vitoria's arguments relating to the American Indians are based upon universal rights which take priority over those of the communities he discusses, and to be in breach of these constitutes legitimate grounds for intervention. Vitoria was convinced that not only Christians but also the American Indians, by the exercise of right reason, could apprehend for themselves the Natural Law. Given that the Spanish had to act in conformity with the Natural Law, they had every right to expect the American Indians also to do so.

Grotius, Pufendorf, and Vattel, in seeking to put Natural Law and Natural Rights on a scientific foundation, liberated discussions about politics and international relations from theology without severing entirely the religious connection. Kant, however, went even further. It was not knowledge of man's anthropology which yielded moral principles, but the a priori concepts of pure reason. Kant's categorical imperative is the criterion of right action: if something is right for me to do, then it must be right for everyone else to do. Moral categories are imperative directives to act, and are good in themselves and not for their consequences. Ends are not for Kant the basis of morality.

It is clear from what has been said that the two traditions of Empirical Realism and Universal Moral Order in the political theory of international relations are antithetical; they are polar opposites. Realism postulates interest and expediency as criteria of state action, while the tradition of a Universal Moral Order postulates conformity to rule or principle: the former is a finite, empirical, and pragmatic criterion; and the latter universal, generalized, and abstract. Each is one-sided in that it cannot accommodate the insights of the other, yet each has a positive value in over-emphasizing an aspect of what motivates the actions of states. The Realist tradition is of value because it emphasizes how radically subjective action is. Action is self-propelled; the springs of action are internal to the actor. No general law or principle which stands outside the actor is the source of any action. A state never acts for the sake of conforming to a rule or principle, but at least in some sense, however weak, acts to fulfil an interest, or satisfy a desire. Similarly, the tradition of a Universal Moral Order emphasizes something of value: that no action is so capricious that it is entirely subjective, and that desire without a regulative principle of reason is an impossibility.

The Realist tradition is defective, however, in that its criterion of state action can be used to justify any form of expediency which gives one state advantage over another; the advantages to be gained from co-operation are perpetually overshadowed and threatened by the ever-present danger of the conflict inherent in human relations breaking down what is, for the Realist, always nothing more than a fragile peace. Morality in international relations, for the Realist, is expediency. Expediency rooted in experience is a transitory and inconsistent guide to conduct: friends become enemies, enemies become friends, depending upon what relative advantage is to be gained from adopting such a stance. It is a criterion, to paraphrase Hegel, immersed in finite matter, totally one-sided, and inadequate as a guide to conduct.

The tradition of a Universal Moral Order emphasizes the general principles or rightness of state action at the expense of interest. Its general principles are abstract and have to be translated to apply to specific situations. Which principles apply to what situations is often a matter of expedient choice. Abstract principles are also notorious for conflicting with each other when applied to concrete situations, and the choice of what principle to apply depends very much upon what type of self-image a state projects of itself to the world. If, for example, it sees itself as the upholder of the moral principle of freedom, it will initiate, or intervene in, interstate conflicts which it sees as necessary to preserve the value of freedom. If it is the kind of state that views war as inherently evil, then considerations of freedom become secondary concerns in its deliberations about interstate relations.

The fundamental premise of this tradition appears to be this: irrespective of what states do and what leaders of states think, there is a right course of action independent of the individual interests and desire of the state. In relation to the action of individuals, Collingwood has expressed the absurdity of the one-sidedness of the tradition well. He argues that rationalists, or intellectualists, maintain that 'there is a right thing to do, whose rightness is independent both of its being done and of its being thought or imagined. It is not merely the case, on this theory, that right is right though nobody does it: we must add that right is right though nobody thinks it'.[28]

Historical Reason

What was needed, then, in the history of the political theory of international relations, was a criterion of state action which explained more adequately what characterized interstate relations, and which also provided a standard of conduct in terms of which the rationality of the actions of states could be judged. The problem was to overcome the deficiencies of the two antithetical traditions by creating a real unity, or synthesis, in which the positive elements of both became incorporated into a new and more adequate viewpoint. Stated simply, the problem that had to be resolved was this: how could rational state action escape the mere immediacy of self-interest and expediency, and at the same time avoid conforming to abstract principles which appear to stand above, and fail to reflect, national interests and aspirations? The answer was to formulate a criterion that was not immersed in immediate state interests, nor at the same time entirely divorced from them. It was to be found in the historical process itself and in the traditions of states' associations with others: a criterion, to paraphrase Rousseau, which would unite utility and justice. The criterion would have to be general in that it was not rooted in the immediacy of the present and, indeed, was still in the process of formation as history unfolded, but it would not be so general and abstract as to postulate a pre-existing set of principles to which international law must conform. Morality would cease to be seen as mere prudence or expediency or, indeed, as the expres⌣.on of the divine voice in our souls. Morality, as Rorty suggests, must be seen as 'the voice of ourselves as members of a community, speakers of a common language'.[29] Here, instead of conflating morality and prudence, as Hobbes did, a distinction may be maintained between morality, which is equated with community interests, and prudence, which is equated with personal interests and may sometimes conflict with community interests.

Within this third tradition, which may be termed Historical Reason, we find that human nature is not a fixed entity. Human beings have developed their characters and natures over time, and within the context of historical societies. To put it in Hegel's terms, every man is a child of his times,[30] and for Marx also, the individual was what he was because of what he did, and how he did it, and those modes of behaviour were inextricably linked with changing modes of production and the social relations generated by them. Relations between nations were similarly a reflection of the productive process, the former of which change as the modes of production follow their historical course. Hegel and Marx have typically been seen as representatives of opposed views of international relations. Hegel is seen to be a communitarian holding the view that such relations as the family, civil society, and the state are constitutive of our selves. The community generates what Walzer calls the 'thick morality' that gives meaning and guidance in our lives. On the other hand, Marx is seen as a cosmopolitan thinker who posits a universal human essence from which individuals have become alienated through exploitation and to which communities have been prevented from aspiring because of estrangements from each other. It is clear on closer analysis, however, that for both thinkers recognition within the context of social relations is constitutive of our selves as persons. The historical process gives a content to human capacities which can only develop in social relations in a historical process.

Individuals and states alike are what they are because of their relations with others of their kind. The relations themselves give rise to the conventions and perceptions in terms of which the associations are continued and valued. In the case of individuals, Dilthey argues that they stand at the centre of systems of interaction, within each of what he calls the cultural systems, or external organizations of society; 'values, rules and purposes are developed, and made conscious and consolidated by reflection'.[31] Each of the systems possesses 'an inner regularity which conditions its structure and this structure in turn reciprocally determines its development'.[32] Earlier, this idea had been extended from the internal organization of the state to its relations with other states, by, for example, Rousseau, Burke, Hegel, and the British Idealists.

Hegel, of course, has been vilified from all quarters for glorifying war and exalting the state. He has been held responsible for both world wars, for Fascism and Nazism, and for totalitarianism.[33] He has always had his defenders, however, against such a crude Realist interpretation.[34] What can be said unequivocally against his detractors is that he was not purporting to recommend a state of affairs, and always maintained that in the realm of Spirit, as opposed to nature, one could not predict what human ingenuity might bring about.[35] Philosophy, Hegel argues, cannot give instruction because 'it always comes on the scene too late to give it'.[36] *The F..ilosophy of Right* is principally concerned to show the historical process by which a state comes to develop its customs, laws, institutions, and constitution, but it also shows that states in the current world system are autonomous and the arbiters of their own wills. Individuality, Hegel argues, is the awareness of oneself as distinct from other selves,[37] but just as a person can never be an actual person without rapport with others, so the 'state is as little an actual individual without relations to other states'.[38] Whereas contracts between individuals within states are much more extensive, because of mutual interdependence, than those conducted between states, there is nevertheless a sense of identity between the European states which has modified aggressive behaviour.[39] Relations between states, Hegel argues, 'depend principally upon the customs of nations'.[40] Although Hegel's logic precludes the possibility of a universal state and the total elimination of war, it nevertheless implies a movement beyond the condition about which he theorized. Indeed, it is implied that groupings of states may have sufficient traditions in common to live harmoniously with each other. He says, for example, that 'The European peoples form a family in accordance with the universal principle underlying their legal codes, their customs, and their civilization. This principle has modified their international conduct accordingly in a state of affairs [i.e. war] otherwise dominated by the mutual infliction of evils.'[41]

Bernard Bosanquet argued early in this century that patriotism and humanitarianism are compatible. Patriotism has in fact given rise to all that we now consider general principles of humanity. Following T. H. Green's example he believed human progress consisted in consciousness of a common good in which the well being of others is closely tied-up with one's own. My duties to humanity come about by a gradual extension of those I regard as included in the common good. To put it in contemporary terms, the tradition of Historical Reason posits a thick conception of morality deeply embedded in the practices of a living developing society. This thick morality gives rise to a thin universalism rather than vice versa. This universal moral minimalism is crucial for the purposes of transnational criticism and solidarity, but it is no substitute for the values thickly conceived in the context of the practices of a society.[42] The universalism that eminates from this tradition to different degrees is what Walzer calls reiterative. It differs from covering-law universalism in focusing upon the particularistic and pluralizing aspects of morality.[43]

In the work of T. H. Green it is the recognition of a wider and wider range of people we regard as our neighbours and are prepared to include in the moral community that gives rise to our obligations to each other. As Green says, 'It is not the sense of duty to a neighbour, but the practical answer to the question Who is my neighbour? that has varied.'[44] This differs from the Natural Law foundation to the community of humankind in positing a historical identity to the moral obligations incurred, first to the family, then to the tribe, the nation, and the state, and finally to humanity. The broadening of the community within which the common good prevails brings with it an extension of the obligations owed to a larger number of people and eventually to humanity as a whole. From the Natural Law perspective this sentime... to treat everyone as part of a world moral community is there from the outset, and the obligations to humanity, far from having a historical basis, are innate, and whether we recognize and act upon them or not makes no difference to the fact that they exist. And if we come to acknowledge them at a later time it does not alter the fact that they were there from the beginning.[45]

The emphasis upon a historically emerging criterion of conduct immediately opens itself up to the charge of relativism and subjectivism. The code of conduct is strictly speaking relational, rather than relative. Exponents of this third criterion are historicist in that they relate the ethical code to prevailing circumstances, but they are not necessarily relativists in that they do not generally suggest that one code is as good as another. Hegel and Marx both contend that the prevailing code of morality is a function of the times which gave rise to it, but both provide criteria in terms of which one moral code can be said to be better than or preferable to another. Bradley's position best exemplifies the response to the charge of relativism. He argues in good communitarian fashion that the idea that moral rules fell full-fledged from heaven is preposterous. Human nature evolves in the historical process, beginning with a base animal nature and gradually reaching higher degrees of 'specification and systemization' in the context of a community. Every person is a child of the times and must realize himself or herself as such. Morality at any given stage is an established fact passed on to the individual as an objective accomplishment of past and present generations, expressing the power of the law and the truth of my own nature in a higher self above the caprice of my own opinions. He goes on to contend that

> Here (as we have seen) all morality is and must be 'relative', because the essence of realization is evolution through stages, and hence existence in some one stage which is not final; here, on the other hand, all morality is 'absolute', because in every stage the essence of man *is* realized, however imperfectly: and yet again the distinction of right in itself against relative morality is not banished, because from the point of view of the higher stage, we can see that lower stages failed to realize the truth completely enough, and also, mixed and one with their realization, did present features contrary to the true nature of man as we now see it. Yet herein the morality of every stage is justified for that stage; and the demand for a code of right in itself, apart from any stage, is seen to be the asking for an impossibility.[46]

The tradition of Historical Realism continues into the twentieth century through the British Idealists and the contemporary ethical doctrines of Terry Nardin and Mervyn Frost. The Marxist variant has found expression in the structuralism of Gunder Frank and Johan Galtung, the critical theory of Jürgen Habermas, Robert Cox, and Andrew Linklater, and the historical materialism of Justin Rosenberg. Postmodernism has affinities with this tradition in contending the historical conditionality of our social standards but, unlike the school of Historical Reason, asks us to suspend our epistemic and moral judgement.

I have suggested that there are three traditions, dialectically related and offering different criteria for state action. They are related to individual thinkers in that elements from each appear in any one, or body of, work, with one of the traditions dominating the other two. In subsequent chapters the details of these traditions will be explored in relation to specific thinkers.

Notes

1. I have elsewhere given extended consideration to the methodology of studying the history of ideas. After finding serious flaws in the proposals of Greenleaf, Pocock, and Skinner I argued for a methodological pluralism, the main benefit of which, to borrow one of J. S. Mill's insights, is the need constantly for self-justification in the face of competing ideas. Furthermore, different approaches bring to the surface of interpretation different, and not always incompatible, images and insights. See my *Texts in Context: Revisionist Methods for Studying the History of Ideas* (Dordrecht, Martinus Nijhoff, 1985). For reasons of consistency, I have capitalized such terms as Natural Law, Law of Nature and Natural Rights, even though in the texts under discussion this may not always be done.

2. Machiavelli, *The Discourses*, ed. Bernard Crick, trans. Father Leslie Walker (Harmondsworth, Penguin, 1970), 268.

3. Thucydides, *History of the Peloponnesian War*, trans. Rex Warner, rev. edn. (Harmondsworth, Penguin, 1972), 3. 45.

4. Thucydides, *Peloponnesian War*, 2. 53.

5. Friedrich Meinecke, *Machiavellism: The Doctrine of Raison d'État and its Place in Modern History* (London, Routledge, Kegan Paul, 1962; first pub. 1924), 14.

6. Thomas Hobbes, *Leviathan* (Harmondsworth, Penguin, 1981), 161.

7. Thucydides, *Peloponnesian War*, 6. 18. Cf. Machiavelli, *The Prince*, trans. George Bull (Harmondsworth, Penguin, 1974), 135, and *Discourses*, 442.

8. Thomas Hobbes, *Man and Citizen*, ed. Bernard Gert (London, Harvester, 1978), 261. Cf. Machiavelli, [The prince] 'should never take things easy in times of peace, rather use the latter assiduously, in order to be able to reap the profit in times of adversity' (*The Prince*, 90).

9. See Joseph Frankel, *National Interest* (London, Macmillan, 1970).

10. See Meinecke, *Machiavellism*, 6. The conception of the three traditions in relation to the internal affairs of states owes a great deal to W. Dilthey, M. Oakeshott, R. G. Collingwood, W. H. Greenleaf, D. Germino, and David Cameron.

11. See Jeremy Bentham, 'A Plan for an Universal and Perpetual Peace', in Howard P. Kainz (ed.), *Philosophical Perspectives on Peace* (London, Macmillan, 1987), 128–36. For a discussion of Bentham's ideas on international relations see Stephen Conway, 'Bentham on Peace and War', *Utilitas*, 1 (1989), 82–101. Bentham, along with Adam Smith and James Mill, articulated the general liberal opposition to imperialism. They rejected it on the grounds that colonization brought little or no economic benefit to Britain; that the view that colonies provided relief for England's surplus population was fallacious; and that England gained no political advantage from holding colonies. J. S. Mill dissented from these views and justified a British Empire comprising colonies settled by whites, and dependencies populated by non-settlers in Asia and Africa. See Eileen P. Sullivan, 'Liberalism and Imperialism: J. S. Mill's Defence of the British Empire', *Journal of the History of Ideas*, 44 (1983), 599–617.

12. Michael Walzer, 'Nation and Universe', *The Tanner Lectures on Human Values*, 11, ed. G. B. Peterson (Salt Lake City, University of Utah Press, 1990), 510.

13. Onora O'Neill, *Towards Justice and Virtue: A Constructive Account of Practical Reasoning* (Cambridge, Cambridge University Press, 1996), 11.

14. See David Cameron, *The Social Thought of Rousseau and Burke: A Comparative Study* (London, Weidenfeld and Nicolson for London School of Economics, 1973), 41–60; A. P. d'Entrèves, *Natural Law*, rev. edn. (London, Hutchinson, 1972), chap. 4; R. J. Vincent, 'Western Conceptions of a Universal Moral Order', *British Journal of International Studies*, 4 (1978), 20–46; R. J. Vincent, *Human Rights and International Relations* (Cambridge, Cambridge University Press, 1986), 4–37; and F. Parkinson, *The Philosophy of International Relations: A Study in the History of Thought* (Beverly Hills, Calif., and London, Sage, 1977), 9–26.

15. D. M. Mackinnon, 'Natural Law', in H. Butterfield and M. Wight (eds.), *Diplomatic Investigations: Essays in the Theory of International Politics* (London, Allen and Unwin, 1966), 79.

16. Basil Wiley, *The Eighteenth Century Background* (London, Penguin, 1965), 23.

17. Rex Martin, *A System of Rights* (Oxford, Clarendon Press, 1993), 2 and 93.

18. Machiavelli, *The Florentine History*, trans. W. K. Marriot (London, J. M. Dent, 1976), 306.

19. Aquinas, *Selected Political Writings*, ed. A. P. d'Entrèves (Oxford, Blackwell, 1974), 127.
20. Samuel Pufendorf, *On The Law of Nature and Nations: Eight Books* (1672), trans. of the 1688 edn. by C. H. Oldfather and W. A. Oldfather (Oxford, Clarendon Press, 1934), bk. ii. iii. 5. Also see David Boucher, 'Reconciling Ethics and Interests in the Person of the State: The International Dimension', in Paul Keale (ed.), *Ethics and Foreign Policy* (Sydney, Allen and Unwin, 1992), 53.
21. Cited by d'Entrèves, *Natural Law*, 25.
22. Aquinas, *Political Writings*, 161.
23. Hugo Grotius, *On the Law of War and Peace*, in M. G. Forsyth, H. M. A. Keens-Soper, and P. Savigear (eds.), *The Theory of International Relations: Selected Texts from Gentili to Treitschke* (London, George Allen and Unwin, 1970), 66.
24. Cf. Parkinson, *Philosophy of International Relations*, 36.
25. Hugo Grotius, *On the Law of War and Peace*, in M. G. Forsyth, H. M. A. Keens-Soper, and P. Savigear (eds.), *The Theory of International Relations: Selected Texts from Gentili to Treitschke* (london, Allen and Unwin, 1970), 70 and 71.
26. Hedley Bull, 'The Grotian Conception of International Society', in Herbert Butterfield and Martin Wight (eds.), *Diplomatic Investigations: Essays in the Theory of International Politics* (London, Allen and Unwin, 1966), 60. Also see H. Lauterpacht, 'The Grotian Tradition in International Law', *British Yearbook of International Law*, 27 (1946), and Grotius, *Law of War and Peace*, 78.
27. Vincent, *Human Rights and International Relations*, 25. Other philosophers of importance in this tradition would be Pufendorf, Vattel, and Kant.
28. R. G. Collingwood, 'Lectures on Moral Philosophy for M-T 1921', MS, Collingwood Papers, DEP 4, Bodleian Library, Oxford, fo. 16.
29. Richard Rorty, *Contingency, Irony and Solidarity* (Cambridge, Cambridge University Press, 1989), 59.
30. G. W. F. Hegel, *The Philosophy of Right*, trans. T. M. Knox (Chicago, Benton, 1952), preface, 6.
31. W. Dilthey, *Selected Writings*, ed. and trans. H. P. Rickman (Cambridge, Cambridge University Press, 1976), 236.
32. Cited by Michael Ermath, *Wilhelm Dilthey: The Critique of Historical Reason* (Chicago, University of Chicago Press, 1978), 123.
33. See e.g. L. T. Hobhouse, *The Metaphysical Theory of the State* (London, Allen and Unwin, 1951; first pub. 1918), 26–43 and 138–49; D. A. Routh, 'The Philosophy of International Relations: T. H. Green versus Hegel', *Politica*, 3 (1938), 224–5; E. F. Carritt, *Morals and Politics* (Oxford, Oxford University Press, 1935), 107 and 114; E. F. Carritt, 'Hegel and Prussianism', *Journal of Philosophy*, 15 (1940), 315–17; Karl Popper, *The Open Society and its Enemies*, (London, Routledge and Kegan Paul, 1977; first pub. 1945), vol. ii. For an interesting account of the debate regarding Hegel's responsibility for the First World War, see John Morrow, 'British Idealism, "German Philosophy" and the First World War', *Australian Journal of Philosophy and History*, 28 (1982), 380–90.
34. See e.g. Henry Jones, 'Why We are Fighting', *Hibbert Journal*, 13 (1914–15), 61–5; and Henry Jones, *The Principles of Citizenship* (London, Macmillan, 1919), 100–3; T. M. Knox, 'Hegel and Prussianism', *Journal of Philosophy*, 15 (1940), 51–63; and the exchange between Knox and Carritt and Spender in the same volume, pp. 219–20 and 313–17; Shlomo Avineri, 'The Problem of War in Hegel's Thought', *Journal of the History of Ideas*, 22 (1961), 462–74; Shlomo Avineri, *Hegel's Theory of the Modern*

State (Cambridge, Cambridge University Press, 1972), chap. 10; Peter P. Nicholson, 'Philosophical Idealism and International Politics: A Reply to Dr Savigear', *British Journal of International Studies*, 2 (1976), 76–7; Andrew Vincent, 'The Hegelian State and International Politics', *Review of International Studies*, 9 (1983), 191–205; and Steven B. Smith, 'Hegel's Views on War, the State, and International Relations', *American Political Science Review*, 77 (1983), 624–32.

35. G. W. F. Hegel, *Reason in History*, trans. Robert S. Hartman (Indianapolis, Bobbs-Merrill, 1953), 68–70.
36. Hegel, *Philosophy of Right*, preface, 7.
37. Hegel, *Philosophy of Right*, §322.
38. Hegel, *Philosophy of Right*, §331.
39. Hegel, *Philosophy of Right*, §333 and *Zusatz* to §339.
40. Hegel, *Philosophy of Right*, §339.
41. Hegel, *Philosophy of Right*, *Zusatz* to §339.
42. Michael Walzer, *Thick and Thin* (Notre Dame, Ind., University of Notre Dame Press, 1994).
43. Walzer, 'Nation and Universe', 513.
44 . T. H. Green, *Prolegomena to Ethics*, 4th edn. (Oxford, Clarendon Press, 1899), 247.
45. Michael Donelan, *Elements of International Political Theory* (Oxford, Clarendon Press, 1990), 10–11.
46. F. H. Bradley, *Ethical Studies*, 2nd edn. (Oxford, Clarendon Press, 1927), 192.

PART I

Empirical Realism

3

THE PRIMACY OF INTEREST: CLASSICAL GREECE

The tradition of Empirical Realism has its roots deeply embedded in the non-Platonic elements of Greek political thought. It emerges clearly in the work of the sophists, whose ideas were influential in informing the basic assumptions of Thucydides' *History of the Peloponnesian War*. Just as Plato's dialogues encompass different points of view, Thucydides' text also takes the form, although much less systematically, of contests of competing ideas. In order to make sense of Thucydides and the assumptions that he made in characterizing the human condition, it is imperative to discern the identity of the political associations, their relations with each other, and the beliefs that permeated the age and structured the horizons within which he formulated his own ideas. I want in this chapter to sketch in some detail the historical and intellectual landscape of classical Greece in order to demonstrate how deeply Thucydides is embedded in it, and how far removed in thought and practice it was from anything that we are now familiar with.

The Independent *Polis*

Classical Greece consisted of numerous autonomous political and social units known as *poleis*, perhaps as many as 1,500,[1] notoriously independent in outlook, but in practice subject in varying degrees to pressures from the more powerful Greek city-states,[2] or from the ambitions of their non-Greek neighbours, the relatively primitive Scythians and Thracians who threatened the eastern and western settlements, and the sophisticated Lydians and Persians who respectively subjected the Greek settlements of Asia Minor to their suzerainty in the sixth and fifth centuries BC.[3] The Greek city-states varied considerably in size, with many having fewer than 5,000 male citizens, while the great majority had under 10,000.[4] Athens at the time of the Peloponnesian War had a citizen population of about 40,000 men, of whom about 21,000 could afford to purchase the equipment to serve as hoplites,[5] the heavily armed Greek infantry named after the round convex shield, the *hoplon*, that they wore to protect themselves in phalanx warfare.[6] This form of warfare replaced that of the aristocracy, who when the cavalry dominated were the only ones to be able to afford horses. Phalanx warfare depended upon a sense of community between the leaders and the middle class. Hoplites had to face the enemy together, each protecting with his shield the sword arm of the comrade immediately to his left.[7] Those citizens who were of more modest means were eligible to man the warships. With the considerable increase in naval power consequent upon the acquisition of an empire, the poorer citizens became politically stronger. Although Athens was liberal in its citizenship policy, Pericles sought to arrest its expansion by restricting citizenship to males who could prove Athenian parentage on both sides.[8]

Athens relied upon the citizen body and about six thousand alien residents for its fighting force, and may have had cause to regret adopting a restrictive policy with the heavy losses sustained during the Peloponnesian War. Instead of relying upon its manpower, Athens exacted tribute from the empire. The total population of Athens was between 215,000–300,000, while Sparta's was slightly less, at between 190,000–270,000,[9] of whom fewer than 4,000 would have been citizens of military age.[10] Sparta was therefore reliant upon its allies in the Peloponnesian League for military assistance. Sparta was eternally vigilant in relation to its large unarmed helot, or serf, population and declared war on it annually to dispose of dissident elements.

Few *poleis* possessed over four hundred square miles of territory, and many, such as Aegina with thirty-three and Delos with two, considerably less. Sparta and Athens were among the larger *poleis* with 33,000 and 1,000 square miles respectively. The *polis* was not simply a city-state, but also encompassed the countryside and its inhabitants. As many as 80 per cent of citizens were country dwellers, with a considerably smaller percentage at Athens because of its reliance upon the sea.

Over a long period Athens had expanded to unite the whole of Attica, which belonged to its citizens. In order to protect its sea interests Athens built a double-walled defensive corridor from the city to the port of Piraeus, enabling it to displace country dwellers during the Peloponnesian War with relative impunity from the conventional war strategy of the devastation of the countryside by Sparta, which invaded Attica almost every year from 431 BC to 425 BC, destroying the corn and, contrary to the established conventions of warfare, vines and olive trees. One of the main sources of opposition in Athens to the war was the enforced separation of the country dwellers from their land, a theme that surfaces prominently in Aristophanes' *The Acharnians*, written in 425 BC, and *Peace*, written in 421 BC, in which Attic farmers longing to be reunited with the land comprise the chorus. Sparta had effectively ceased its policy of devastation in Attica after 425 BC, but as late as 411 BC Aristophanes has his characters extolling a return to the land as the principal benefit of peace.[11] The plague that struck Athens in the second year of the Peloponnesian War was attributed, according to Plutarch, to Pericles' policy of compelling the 'country people to crowd inside the walls'.[12]

Sparta's relationship with the land was different. Spartan territory was not co-extensive with the land of its citizens. The land of the Spartan citizens was tended by helots, whereas the land beyond was cultivated by the *perioeci*, who were free men responsible for their own affairs and who contributed to the upkeep of the army and were also called upon to serve. In return they enjoyed the protection of the most formidable fighting force in Greece.

The *polis* was an organized way of life which was incapable of extensive territorial expansion without destroying its character. It was believed that a *polis* had natural or optimal limits that should not be exceeded. Writing almost a century after Thucydides, Aristotle argued that 'To the size of states there is a limit, as there is to other things, plants, animals, implements; for none of these retain their natural power when they are too large or too small, but they either wholly lose their nature, or are spoiled'.[13] Athens had expanded to encompass the whole of Attica, but its imperialist aspirations of the fifth century BC were not territorial. The Athenian Empire was tribute-paying and in return enjoyed the protection of Athens's navy. Membership was not, however, voluntary. The Delian League which Athens led after the expulsion of the second Persian invasion of 480 provided security of markets, the sea, and life.[14] Athens refused the right to secede for the fear that the Persian threat might re-emerge. By 454 BC, when Athens transferred the treasury funds from Delos to Athens, no member could doubt that membership was compulsory, that withdrawal was forbidden, and that the Athenians were the undisputed imperial power.[15]

Many Greek *poleis* sent out settlers to colonize territories, but each constituted an independent *polis* administratively free of the mother state, but often enjoying a close but ambiguous relationship with it. The Athenians appear to have reduced tributes to the League when it appropriated land for its colonists.[16] The attachments between *poleis* and their colonies were sentimental and religious, and might predispose them to provide mutual assistance in war. Wars between colonies and the mother countries, while frowned upon as bad form, were not regarded as rebellion. If a *polis* tried politically to impose itself upon its colony it invariably met with a hostile response, as Corinth, a member of the Peloponnesian League, c..d in 433 BC when Corcyra (Corfu) sought the assistance of Athens to repel the mother country, a dispute which Thucydides highlights as one of the ostensible causes of the Peloponnesian War.[17]

The expansion of Greece by colonizing a great deal of the Mediterranean did nothing to create a pan-Hellenic state; it simply multiplied the number of autonomous *poleis*. The independent *polis* was the centre of unity and attachment, but the state was not, as it became in the sixteenth and seventeenth centuries, an abstract entity. It was essentially a corporation of citizens who when they went to war did so not in the name of Athens or Sparta, but as Athenians and Spartans. There was very little sense of working for the common good of Hellas as a whole, and indeed, where interest prescribed, alliances with non-Greek powers were made to gain advantage over rival Greek city-states, as Athens did with Persia against Sparta at the beginning of the fourth century BC after defeat in the Peloponnesian War.

There were, of course, broader focuses of unity than the *polis*. The practice of third-party arbitration, for example, had become widely accepted, indicating that there was an intimation of universal justice beyond the borders of the *polis*.[18] Subscription to a distinction between particular and universal law is well documented in Greek literature and philosophy. Sophocles' Antigone, for example, refers to Laws of Nature that are timeless, and justifies breaking the laws of the state by arguing that they are at variance with the laws of heaven.[19] Socrates, of course, posited an immutable transcendental sphere of forms, in accordance with which our mutable world of existence should be fashioned approximately to conform. In the *Rhetoric* Aristotle distinguishes between universal and particular laws, the former of which are universal principles of morality independent of human agreement.[20] And in the *Nicomachean Ethics* he talks of two types of political justice, natural and conventional: 'It is natural when it has the same validity everywhere and is unaffected by any view we may take about the justice of it. It is conventional when there is no original reason why it should take one form rather than another and the rule it imposes is reached by agreement, after which it holds good'.[21] The sophists, as we will see, took a different view, and it remains to be seen to what extent Thucydides took their views as his exemplar.

Identity and Difference

The Greeks saw themselves as sharing a common inheritance in social customs, religion, and language, while at the same time being conscious of their different ethnic attachments, the major ones of which were the Dorians and Ionians.[22] The Greek *poleis* saw themselves as part of the same civilization, but as having attained different levels in the civilizing process. They were qualitative differences of degree based upon intellectual, cultural, and political achievement. Plato, representing Socrates, who was a contemporary of Thucydides, talks of the Greeks as a common people, among whom armed conflict was to be considered civil strife informed by the int_ation of reaching agreement. War, properly speaking, occurred between Greeks and non-Greeks.[23]

Non-Greeks were 'barbarians', which did not necessarily mean they were enemies. They were, indeed, regarded as inferior, but it is not entirely clear upon what grounds. In Thucydides, for example, the distinction does not appear to be racial.[24] Indeed, for him, war was the great leveller of barbarian and civilized societies.[25] Antiphon the sophist, an Athenian contemporary of Thucydides, questioned any naturalistic grounds for the distinction: 'none of us is marked off as either barbarian or Greek; for we all breathe the air with our mouth and nostrils and [eat with our hands?]'.[26] Hippocrates, who was born about the same time as Thucydides, provides us with the first known attempt to establish a natural distinction between Greeks and barbarians on scientific grounds by positing a relation between climate and racial characteristics.[27] Many of the images of the relationship between Greeks and barbarians equate it with that of the natural superiority of men over women.[28] Aristotle intimates that the relationship is the same as that of master and natural slave, and is based on the distinction that slaves have a capacity for understanding reason, but not for exercising it. Those who refuse to submit to the guidance of their superiors have to be restrained by force, 'for war of such a kind is naturally just'.[29]

In general the differentiation of Greeks and barbarians on racial grounds was much less pronounced in the classical than in the Heroic ages of Greek history, when the distinction came to rest much more upon moral, intellectual and religious superiority.[30] Isocrates, for example, suggests that the pupils of Athens 'had made the name of Hellas distinctive no longer of race but of intellect, and the title of Hellene a badge of education rather than of common descent'.[31] It was the threat of common danger from the barbarian Persians that for the first and last time facilitated a certain degree of unity based on the consciousness of a shared Greek heritage. The Hellenic League was formed in 481 BC when Sparta and Athens acknowledged the division of Greece into two exclusive leagues.[32]

Above all it was religion that both identified and differentiated the Greeks. It provided the common bond in that it was a pan-Hellenic religion conventionally comprising twelve deities. The gods resided on top of Mount Olympus, presided over by Zeus and Hera, his queen. The gods each exercised specifically demarcated powers separately over the aspects of the cosmos, or the elements, or human events like war and peace, or personal qualities.[33] The importance of religion cannot be overestimated. No distinction was made between religious and secular activities. All collective activities had a religious significance, and religion permeated all levels of society. As Andrewes suggests, 'every Greek activity was linked with the cult of some god to an extent which makes our civilisation seem, by comparison, nakedly secular'.[34] The various religious festivals and holy days were observed and celebrated in a variety of ways, some by all Greeks, others by ethnic groups, and still others by individual *poleis*. Truces were sometimes arranged between combatants so that the celebration of games or festivals could proceed.[35] The religious leagues, or *amphictionies*, comprised *poleis*, or ethnic groups, or both, and celebrated one or a number of festivals at a common shrine. Examples of such leagues are the Delphic and that of the Dorian cities.

What made the common identity a diversity was the fact that the *polis* provided the institutional social framework within which religious worship functioned. The *polis* was the instrument through which the individual participated in common or pan-Hellenic religious festivals and shrines. Each *polis* had its own representative, the *theoriai*, to conduct ceremonies at common sanctuaries. The *poleis* were bound to respect each others' shrines and sanctuaries at the risk of incurring the wrath of the gods. To be excluded from the religious practices of the *polis* was effectively to be deprived of citizenship. The elaborate ritual communal practices, such as banquets and games, not only engendered social cohesion, but also defined one's status as a citizen. In Athens during the Peloponnesian War, for example, the festivals continued as a mark of defiance even when the enemy occupied Attica.[36]

Accusations of impiety were serious matters. It was an offence against both the gods and the community. Impiety was, however, not a clearly defined offence.

Because Greek religion was anthropomorphic and the gods lived lives analogous to those of humans, but on a much higher plane, they could be depicted as succumbing to the ordinary vices. Aristophanes, for example, depicts the gods as suffering from deprivation of food and sex, and losing their sovereignty over the universe.[37] The desecration of altars, revelation of secrets of a cult, or blasphemous sayings, all might constitute impiety.[38] Denial of the existence of the gods was a particularly serious offence. Protagoras, for example, who with reference to gods said, 'I have no means of knowing either that they are or that they are not,' was tried in Athens, one of the more liberal *poleis*, for impiety in about 411 BC, and either fled or was banished, losing his life when the ship upon which he departed sank. And it was for denying the existence of the gods and putting others in their place that Socrates was tried in 399 BC. There are numerous instances of famous people being charged with impiety, including Anaxagoras, despite his friendship with Pericles, and Euripides, who was accused by Cleon, Pericles' successor.[39]

Thucydides' attitude to impiety is ambivalent. Piety and success in political life appear, for him, to be closely allied, and even successful tyrants such as the Pisistratids are portrayed as pious. Alcibiades, who was suspected by the demos of having tyrannical aspirations, but for whom Thucydides nevertheless has a qualified regard, could not maintain the link. His private life inflamed the demos, and his enemies engineered his recall from the ill-fated Sicilian expedition on a charge of impiety, at which point he defected to Sparta; he returned to Athens at a later date to resume his political career.

Thucydides appears to hold a utilitarian view of religion. It provides the social cohesion necessary for morality to flourish. Fear of the gods and the love for one's city, enacted through the plethora of religious rituals, practices, and festivals, instil in citizens a piety respectful of laws and institutions. A lack of piety encourages disrespect for the law and undermines the fear of divine punishment for wrongdoing. Impiety dissolves the social conventions conducive to the common good, and engenders an individualistic self-seeking that destroys a social cohesiveness. The spiritedness and daring of the Athenians, which gave them the courage to defy the conventions of siege warfare and abandon Athens when under threat from Persia, was at the same time a corrosive force. When the plague hit Athens in the second year of the war, the constraints of piety were fearlessly and recklessly abandoned and civil society collapsed. Similarly, the erosion of piety was a significant factor in the collapse of civil association consequent upon the civil war in Corcyra. The sanctity of temples was disregarded, and party community rested not upon religious grounds, but upon a partnership of crime (*Peloponnesian War*, 3. 82). Immediately after Pericles' Funeral Oration, in which he calls upon his fellow citizens to sustain their 'daring spirit' (2. 43), Thucydides graphically describes the plague that so relentlessly led citizens to become 'indifferent to every rule of religion or of law' (2. 52), and which precipitated 'a state of unprecedented lawlessness' (2. 53). On the other hand, Thucydides praises the Pisistratids, dictators of Athens from 546 BC to 511 BC, for their devotion to religious institutions, which included making 'all the proper religious sacrifices' (6. 54). Although Thucydides mentions the purification of Delos by Pisistratus, he does not draw out its political implications (3. 104). Herodotus, however, sees it as part of Pisistratus' policy to consolidate his power.[40] It was also an assertion of the primacy of Athens among the Ionians in the region.

Religion was to be judged upon its consequences. It is quite clear that when Thucydides sees no advantage in conforming to the superstitions of religious divinations, he speaks of them contemptuously. In describing the Athenian defeat at Epipolae in 413 BC, for example, when the Athenian 'position, so far from improving, was getting worse every day in every respect', Thucydides disparagingly says of Nicias that he 'was rather over-inclined to divination and such things', following the postponement of withdrawal on the recommendation of the soothsayers who saw the eclipse of the moon as a sign not to set sail (7. 50). Furthermore, Thucydides castigates the Athenians for not accepting responsibility for the Sicilian catastrophe and instead blaming 'the prophets and soothsayers and all who at the time had, by various methods of divination, encouraged them to believe that they would conquer Sicily' (8. 1). In the Melian Dialogue the Athenians warn of the danger of abandoning faith in the ability of men to save themselves and turning instead to the false hope engendered by soothsayers and oracles (5. 103). Finley goes so far as to say that Thucydides 'detested the soothsayers and oracle-mongers who were a plague in wartime Athens'.[41] Thucydides' account of the war, he suggests, is almost wholly secular. Furthermore, Finley contends that there are no grounds 'to think that policy-making was ever determined or deflected by reference to divine will or divine precept'.[42]

It is true that Thucydides betrays a certain hostility towards divination (3. 104; 5. 26; 7. 50), but he was perfectly willing to believe that natural phenomena were signs from the gods. It was more the interpreters that he distrusted. The Peloponnesian War was, for Thucydides, the greatest that had ever occurred (1. 1). A criterion of its greatness was that it gave credibility to past prodigies, by the sheer scale of portents that became manifest:

Wide areas, for instance, were affected by violent earthquakes; there were more frequent eclipses of the sun than had ever been recorded before; in various parts of the country there were extensive droughts followed by famine; and there was the plague which did more harm and destroyed more life than almost any other single factor. All these calamities fell together upon the Hellenes after the outbreak of war. (1. 23)

There is, as Hornblower argues, no suggestion that the Athenian Empire had divine sanction,[43] but the passage just cited indicates that there was divine retribution consequent upon the war occasioned by the empire. In discussing the outbreak of war, Thucydides merely reports upon the extent of prophecies and 'oracular utterances' without comment (2. 8).

It was in the sphere of warfare that divination came into its own. The danger and uncertainty that accompany war made it all the more imperative to determine the disposition of the gods at every stage. A 'besought' consultation, as opposed to a 'self-offering' sign, carried more authority by the fact that it was besought. Oracles were notoriously ambiguous in their advice and had, for the most part, to be interpreted. The oracle was not usually expected to initiate advice, but rather to respond to specific alternatives.[44] It is well attested that divination had a more significant influence on conduct, even to the detriment of the city, than Finley allows. Sparta, it has to be said, was far more scrupulous in its observance than Athens, but was not averse to using religion as a pretext to disguise an underlying motive (1. 126–39). Holladay and Goodman, in opposition to Finley, argue that there are ten cases in a thirty-eight-year period when 'earthquakes and bad omens' led to the abortion of expeditions which damaged the interests of both Sparta and its allies. The authors contend that 'even the hardheaded Thucydides accepted this scrupulousness for a fact and did not attempt to rationalise it by producing more material explanations'.[45]

If divination was important in war, how important was war for the Greeks? It is largely from Herodotus and Thucydides that we get the impression that warfare was the pre-eminent activity around which life revolved. No Greek city was militaristic in the modern sense. War was not regarded as necessary to human development, nor as a good in itself.[46] There is no doubt, however, that military organization and citizen militias were extremely important to the *polis*; only the poorest, who could not afford to serve, escaped military service. Even Socrates served as a hoplite in at least two battles, and Thucydides was himself a soldier. Are we, then, to believe Clinias, the Cretan, in Plato's *Laws* when he tells us that citizens 'are all engaged in a continuous lifelong warfare against all cities whatsoever', or that 'the normal attitude of a city to all other cities is one of undeclared warfare'?[47]

War and *Stasis*

Many commentators tell us that war was simply a fact of life for the Greeks, to which resort was made as a matter of course. Momigliano and Garlan, while endorsing this view, p_.nt to the paradoxical fact that the Greeks gave remarkably little attention to articulating the concept of war, or to trying to discover its causes. They explain this apparent neglect by suggesting that war was so much a part of life, a natural phenomenon about which nothing could be done, that they took it for granted.[48] This is not an altogether convincing explanation. Thucydides himself, of course, analysed the fundamental cause of the Peloponnesian War, and traced the dissolving and pernicious effects that war had upon social cohesion. During the blackest periods of the war in Athens anti-war plays were entered in the competitions, which means that they had to be chosen by the archon in charge of the festival, and the chorus paid for by a wealthy citizen. Euripides' *The Trojan Women* was staged a short time after the massacre of the males and the sale of the women and children of the tiny island of Melos by the Athenians in 416 BC, to which Thucydides devotes a disproportionate amount of space, indicating the depths to which he thought Athens had sunk (5. 84–116). *Lysistrata*, the third of Aristophanes' war plays, was staged in 411 BC, after the humiliating defeat of the Athenian navy on the Sicilian expedition in 413 and the

Spartan occupation of part of Attica. Andrewes tells us that even though a great deal of time was spent engaged in warfare, the Greeks did not much relish the prospect.[49] Even Sparta, whose society and citizenry were most rigorously organized on military lines, had by the fifth century BC pursued a cautious policy towards foreign involvements. Its main concern was to preserve the delicate balance in its domestic affairs that persistently threatened to degenerate into civil strife.[50] For Thucydides, Sparta's strength was not in its military force, but in the organization and stability of its regime, which was the oldest in Greece, having remained unchanged for 400 years.[51]

Relations among Greek *poleis* were not characterized by unrelenting hostility.[52] The nature of Greek warfare, which was strictly limited to campaign seasons, made the concept of total war simply unintelligible.[53] Greek warfare conformed with the predilection for competitions, whether in athletics, drama, or comedy. Even Plato's dialogues are not so much accounts of conversations as records of intellectual competitions, in which the participants often become irritable at being outmanœuvred by Socrates. Protagoras, for example, refers to fighting 'many a contest of words'.[54]

Greek *poleis* put a very high premium upon settling conflicts between them quickly and decisively, perhaps in one or two major confrontations. Phalanx warfare was a close-range, terrifying, bloody clash of armies, confronting each other eight deep, protected by bronze armour and heavy round shields, with spears and swords for combat. The aim was to break through the phalanx, reducing the opposing army to disarray and causing the men to turn and flee, thereby providing the space and opportunity to cut them down from behind. It is estimated that about 15 per cent of the men would die in these clashes, but it was not the common practice to pursue and massacre the hoplites who fled on the breaking of the phalanx.[55]

By the time of the Peloponnesian War such clashes, along with the practice of the devastation of crops, ceased to be as effective. Athens, because of the poor quality of its soil, developed trading links and created for itself a formidable sea presence, protecting its access to the sea by a long double wall to the port of Piraeus. The refusal of Athens to engage in combat with the superior forces of Sparta and its allies was completely alien to conventional practice. During the Peloponnesian War the clash of opposing hoplites became a much less decisive factor in the conflict.[56]

War was not resorted to on any pretext, and peace was indeed a value that the Greeks, as the poets and historians testify, held dear. The ambassadorial system that emerged was designed not only to agree upon the terms of peace, but also to avert war, as Thucydides, for example, copiously illustrates. The history is one not only of warfare, but also of the extensive representations made by envoys from the various *poleis* caught up in the conflict.[57]

Of more importance than external relations to the Greeks was the internal order of the *polis*. The Greeks were preoccupied with *stasis*, which Watson defines as 'the use of armed force inside a city to alter the way it was governed'.[58] The term is in fact much broader in meaning than this. Its referents range from political groupings and factional rivalry, or intrigue, to hostile civil war, and in its pejorative sense it provided the occasion to invite the intervention of outside support. In its pejorative sense, it was characterized by Greek writers as the central threat to civil society.[59] Plato, for example, contends that the lawgiver should give primacy to organizing a city with 'regard to the internal warfare which arises, from time to time, within the city, and is called, as you know, *faction*—a kind of war any man would desire never to see in his own city'.[60] Earlier Herodotus had argued that 'internal strife is worse than united war in the same proportion as war itself is worse than peace'.[61] One of the most graphic and disturbing accounts in Thucydides is not of interstate war, but of the civil war in Corcyra in 427 BC and the successive revolutions in other Greek cities. With reference to the leaders of factions, Thucydides argues that 'In their struggles for ascendancy nothing was barred; terrible indeed were the actions to which they committed themselves, and in taking revenge they went farther still. Here they were deterred neither by the claims of justice nor by the interests of the state' (3. 82).

The New Learning

The openness of Athens to the outside world made it the centre for the exchange of new and exciting ideas in all aspects of learning, some of the ideas of which caused great consternation because of their religious and political implications. These are the ideas which circulated in Thucydides' Athens, but he did not, as we will see, subscribe to the more extreme views.

Pericles, for whom Thucydides shows the greatest admiration, was profoundly curious about the new scientific theories that were circulating. He may have been responsible for inviting Anaxagoras of Clazomenae to Athens, where he was maintained for many years at Pericles' expense. Anaxagoras was a materialist who thought that imperceptible particles of everything exist in all matter, and that each coheres with others of its kind to form the objects with which we are familiar. Bread, for example, contains tiny particles of blood and bone which when consumed join with those already in the body. Nothing can be created that does not in some form already exist. Mind, or reason, separates and arranges the totality of the mass of particles, but nevertheless plays a minimalist role in his theory.

His importance lies in the fact that he denied that the sun was a god, and postulated that it must be a stone, white hot with intense flames, ignited by friction, and probably many times larger than the Peloponnese. The moon, too, was a stone which, being lower than the sun, reflected its heat and light. Furthermore he was able to explain solar eclipses scientifically, which undermined the perception of their occurrence as portents divinely instigated.[62] Pericles, whom Plutarch describes as 'steeped in the so-called higher philosophy and abstract speculation',[63] is said to have calmed the minds of his people by giving them an astronomy lesson on the occasion of an eclipse.[64] Thucydides' reference to an eclipse during the first summer of the war intimates, contrary to the impression he gave when referring to the increased incidence of eclipses as a criterion of the greatness of the war (1. 23), that their occurrence has a scientific, rather than a divine, cause (2. 28).

Similarly, Thucydides' description of the plague at Athens, another criterion of the greatness of the war, betrays a clinical precision dismissive of supernatural explanations. Hippocrates (*c*.460–377 BC), of course, maintained that it was only the lack of understanding that led men to attribute diseases to gods. All diseases have antecedent natural causes.[65] In addition to the causes, the Hippocratic writings lay great emphasis upon diagnosis and prognosis, and in this respect they show affinities with Thucydides. *Stasis*, or civil war, for example, is viewed as a disease, the causes of which are ambition and greed-generating competition, which fail to be fully contained by the law and which escalate beyond political intrigue to armed conflict. The diagnosis varies according to the attendant conditions: 'In the various cities these revolutions were the cause of many calamities—as happens and always will happen while human nature is what it is, though there may be different degrees of savagery, and, as different circumstances arise, the general rules will admit of some variety' (3. 82). The cure is the re-institution of civic values, and the preventative medicine is to ensure that the institutional framework exists to prevent the subversion of those values by self and group interests. Thucydides' description of the plague in Athens interestingly leaves the question of cause to one side, leaving open the possibility of a medical or divine explanation. He says that he is satisfied merely to describe the symptoms so that future generations may recognize it. He does, however, do much more than this. Poole and Holladay argue that Thucydides made an original contribution to the advancement of medical knowledge, which was ignored by contemporary practitioners. He discovered for the first time the principles of contagion and acquired immunity, which he deduced from factual observation. In this respect Thucydides was more empirically minded than the Hippocratics who are said to have influenced him, but who in fact were the victims of their own a priori theories about the tr...1smission of diseases.[66]

It is not so much the natural as the ethical theories in circulation that are of interest here. Professional teachers were in great demand in Athens, a democracy in which it was important to be able to put one's case eloquently and persuasively. The sophists, such as Protagoras, professed to teach wisdom and virtue. The self-importance that many of them exuded, the agility of their minds in making wrong appear right, and the shocking nature of their teaching made them at once the targets of fun and charges of impiety. Aristophanes' *The Clouds*, for example, ridicules the four fundamental elements of sophist teaching: its impiety, its scientific speculation, its new morality, and the art of rhetoric. Socrates, although the views attributed to him bear no relation to his own, is the representative sophist who announces that 'The first thing you'll have to learn is that with us the gods are no longer current'.[67] The person of Wrong in the same play denies that there is such a thing as justice, and boasts, 'I was the one who invented ways of proving anything wrong, laws, prosecutors, anything. Isn't that worth millions—to be able to have a really bad case and yet win?'[68]

The sophists and allied thinkers of fifth-century Athens, many of whom travelled extensively and were not natives of the city, provide the range of political and ethical theories that comprise the context of Thucydides' views. What they have in common is the denial that law has a divine origin. The great lawgivers, such as Lycurgus and Solon, had been deemed to receive their laws from the gods, but observations of variations in moral practices once thought to be natural and universal cast doubt upon their transcendental origin and immutability. The sophists addressed themselves to the question of the relation between *physis* and *nomos*. For them *physis* meant reality, or nature, and *nomos*, convention or law. They all agreed that morality has its origin and basis in convention. Furthermore they exhibited a common scepticism about the possibility of attaining absolute knowledge.[69] They disagreed, however, on the relation in which convention stood to nature. Antiphon and Callicles, for example, contend that conventional morality is opposed and inimical to nature. Nature replaces convention as the criterion of right action. Far from denying absolute standards, they substitute for the transcendental a natural standard of conduct. Antiphon and Callicles differ considerably, however, in the specifics of their arguments. In Antiphon's scientific speculations primacy is given to natural formations over those of artifice,[70] and he confirms what Plato contends in the *Laws*, namely that there is a close connection in the writings of the sophists between physical science and naturalistic theories of ethics.[71] The principal surviving fragments come from his work *Truth*, the title of which is meant to convey the idea that it is an investigation into reality (*physis*) at the expense of appearance.[72] He wants to show that the laws of society are adventitious and their consequences capricious and often detrimental to nature. Nature's consequences are determinate: if its laws are transgressed the punishment quickly follows. The injunctions of nature compel us to pursue the maximum pleasure and to avoid pain, the former being beneficial and the latter harmful.[73] Conventional morality should be complied with only if the harm suffered in breaking it would be greater. There is no suggestion of destroying society, but instead an injunc..on to follow nature's dictates which are consistent with self-interest. Antiphon argues that 'A man, therefore, would practise justice in the way most advantageous to himself if, in the presence of witnesses, he held the laws in high esteem, but, in the absence of witnesses, and when he was by himself, he held in high esteem the rules of nature.'[74] Antiphon's naturalistic emphasis led him to postulate a natural equality which dissolved social distinction and superordinate relations among nations. Greeks and barbarians, on natural criteria, which have primacy over conventional, are naturally equal. There is then a unity of the human race. It is not clear whether he thought divisions into separate states were wholly conventional, nor whether he believed that a natural harmony exists. The fact that he recommends faithfulness to conventional morality when it cannot be deviated from with impunity implies the necessity for such constraints. Elsewhere he extols the virtues of concord based on education, friendship, inner purpose, and the elimination of fear.[75]

Callicles adopts an even more radical position, which most commentators have encapsulated in the dictum 'might is right'. He was not a sophist, but he clearly associated with them, and nothing is known of him apart from the portrayal in Plato's *Gorgias*. He is believed to have been a real person, active in politics during the Peloponnesian War. Callicles wished to subvert and transform conventional morality on the grounds that it is opposed to nature, which is itself the absolute standard of justice. He did not wish to deprive justice of its favourable evaluative connotation, but wished instead to divest it of its conventional content and replace it with a content dictated by nature. For him the strong ought to rule by virtue of their superior strength: 'nature . . . demonstrates that it is right that the better man should prevail over the worse and the stronger over the weaker . . . right consists in the superior ruling over the inferior and having the upper hand'.[76] These principles are just as applicable among animals and states as they are between individuals. They are the principles of natural justice which give the strong the right to take anything they like from the weak. Plato is not, however, referring merely to physical strength. It is those who are powerful in both body and mind who possess the natural right to rule in their own interests.[77]

The idea of equality is conventional subterfuge perpetrated by weaklings to deprive the strong of their natural entitlements. Inequality is in fact the natural condition of animals, humans, and states, and the inequitable distribution of resources its just corollary. Conventional justice on Callicles' logic is unnatural and thus harmful. The weak should submit to the strong in accordance with the natural order. Nature's law, then, is the criterion of right conduct which rejects any obligation to abide by conventional morality, and proposes its replacement by an absolute criterion of Natural Right and justice.[78]

Callicles' position is quite distinct from that of the sophist Thrasymachus, who defines justice as that which is in the interest of the stronger. Collectively, of course, the weak may constitute the stronger element in society, and what they dictate as just in their own interests is just. He is not equating the content of morality with what nature dictates. It is not an argument about Natural Rights and natural justice, but instead, as far as Thrasymachus is concerned, a question of observable empirical evidence. Every government, whatever its composition, is the strongest element in society and enacts laws in its own interest which it enforces against lawbreakers as a matter of justice.[79] It is an affirmation of convention which justifies despotism, but which leaves conventional morality devoid of content.

Thrasymachus' ethical position is more closely allied to those of Protagoras and Democritus, who believed that morality is indeed conventional, but not inconsistent with nature. Conventional morality is necessary for social life, but does not constitute an opponent of human nature. Protagoras and Democritus both visited Athens, the former more conspicuously than the latter. We have already seen that Protagoras' scepticism about the possibility of knowledge of the existence of the gods led to a charge of impiety. Furthermore he replaced the theocentric with an anthropomorphic criterion of truth: 'man is the measure of all things—alike of the being of things that are and of the not-being of things that are not'.[80] By this Protagoras means that what seems true to me is true for me. Individual persons, not humanity as a whole, are the measure. It is not sense perception but judgement that constitutes the measure. In looking at the sun sense experience presents it as about thirty centimetres in diameter, whereas one's judgement may estimate it many times larger than the Peloponnese.[81] There is no criterion independent of our separate judgements by which to ask which is true, but the states of mind that make the judgements are not all equally good.

The sophist is like a physician who makes the unhealthy mind healthy, not by exchanging a false opinion for truth—all opinions are equally true—but by making one opinion appear less good than another. All agree that anarchy is less good than order, and the youth who prefers anarchy has to be persuaded that order is the greater good.[82] Justice and morality do not exist by nature; they are the product of convention consequent upon the bitter experience of incessant and internecine conflict destructive of humanity. The virtues of self-restraint, or conscience, and a sense of justice develop 'to bring order into our cities and create a bond of friendship and union'.[83] Whereas morality is not natural, it is nevertheless necessary and consistent with nature in its capacity for the better preservation of humankind. In this respect it is like a second nature to us, imperative for the maintenance of social life and the preservation of the species.

The laws of society educate the young in the constraints upon behaviour, and the purpose of punishment is education and not revenge. The civic virtues were capable of being taught and acquired, and Protagoras himself professed to teach them.

The criterion of what is better and worse upon which Protagoras' ethical theory rests is, of course, liable to vary with men's opinions. Democritus thought that he could overcome this deficiency in Protagoras. He argued that the assertion that all judgements are true simply cannot be sustained because by definition the proposition that all judgements are untrue must also be true, and hence renders the initial proposition false.[84] For Democritus all that exists in reality is atoms and void. Atoms differ in shape, size, and mass, but they are devoid of qualities like colours, odours, and sounds which exist by convention. Sense perceptions, then, exist only for us, and each is equally valid. We cannot through sense perception know anything as it really is. This type of knowledge is illegitimate because the senses reach a point at which sound, colour, and smell become imperceptible. Legitimate knowledge, is however, attainable by the exercise of reason.[85]

For Democritus nature and convention are not opposed. The possession of intelligence enables humans to create and transform their own environment, which supplements rather than denies nature. The constraints are self-imposed in the sense that men recognize that just behaviour is not an external imposition, but something which man is disposed to impose upon himself.[86] Human nature is capable of being modified by education, and the modification constitutes a reorganization of the atoms of which people are composed. To disrupt the harmony and balance of the atoms in the soul by immoderate acts is inimical to human happiness. Choosing right conduct is aided by the criteria of pleasure and displeasure, with the proviso that not all pleasures are beneficial. Well-being, or freedom from disturbance or wonder, is the consequence of the proper discrimination of pleasures.[87] Personal happiness can be attained only in the context of the city, which sustains the social relations consistent with humans' transformed, or second, natures. The existence of the city requires adherence to justice, and law is designed to promote human happiness. We become aware of the excellence of law through obedience to it. The soul regulated by law develops a sense of shame and conscience, making wrongdoing inconceivable, even in private.[88] Law, even though it is conventional, is of immense benefit to humanity. The role of education in inculcating virtue cannot be overestimated. Fewer people attain virtue by their natural qualities than by training.[89] Education reinforces our own self-control.

Without respect for law, envy generates conflict resulting in civil strife. Democritus, like his contemporaries, is far more concerned with civil war than he is with external conflict. Personal distress is far easier to bear than public distress, which destroys any hope of rescue. Reversion to a state of anarchy, in which animals live, is the consequence of the breakdown of civil society. Divisions between the rich and poor can be averted by beneficence. Democritus argues that 'It is only possible to produce great deeds, even wars among cities, through concord: otherwise it is impossible.'[90]

Democritus, then, identifies personal well-being with the well-being of the state, and self-interest with the common interest. It is in our interest to cultivate the well-ordered soul, to be virtuous, just, and obedient to law. The condition of well-being in Democritus has an internal source, whereas this is not evidently the case with Thucydides.[91]

The moral argument of Thucydides gives emphasis to the propensity of conventions and institutions to modify human nature and improve the human condition. The advent of a stable and settled way of life arising from the development of law and morality diminishes uncertainty and fear, which are the precipitates of aggressive behaviour. It was the strength of the Spartan constitution, which had remained unchanged for four hundred years, that gave Sparta its strength (1. 18). It was a constitution that identified the public and private interest. Athens too was at its strongest when private interest and ambition did not deviate from the interest of the state. The coincidence of private and common interest sustained by good laws, piety, and education engenders a love for the city which comprises its strength (2. 40). Like Democritus and Protagoras, Thucydides warns of the destructive power of *stasis*, but the elimination of uncertainty and fear within the *polis* is not reflected in the external sphere, in which relations remain volatile. It is when self-interest within the state deviates from the common interest, as it did in Athens after Pericles, that internal strife and overextended external ambition lead to the ruination of the city. Pericles himself was not opposed to imperialism; he merely warned the Athenians not to weaken themselves by expanding the empire during the war (2. 65). Thucydides' view that self-interest and greed lost Athens its empire does not mean that he was himself opposed to the institution of empire, only that self-interest and greed are not worthy motives for an imperial policy, though the interest of the state may well be.

Is he like Callicles and Antiphon in postulating nature as the criterion of right action? Contrary to the postmodernist interpretation of Thucydides, human nature for him is a fixed entity capable of providing the basis for prediction. Unmodified by morality, the individual will maximize utility in conformity with perceived interest. The power to do so with impunity leads to a disregard for moral constraints. The Athenians, in pursuing their imperial policy, often appealed to nature as the justification, explanation, and recommendation of their actions. It was, however, the appeal to nature translated into stark realism that impelled Athenians to believe that they were above moral restraints both as citizens and as a state, which had disastrous consequences both internally and externally, culminating in the catastrophic defeat of the Sicilian expedition and the ultimate humiliating surrender to Sparta. The most that the Athenians can be read as saying is that nature prescribes a code of conduct that overrides appeals to morality and justice when there is an imbalance of power (1. 76; 3. 45; 5. 105; 7. 77), not that might prescribes right. There is clearly a scepticism which Thucydides shares about the capacity of convention to control nature.[92] As to its desirability, the fact that war strips away convention and reduces men to pursuing their immediate interests is for him regrettable (3. 82). It is, for Thucydides, an observable fact that human nature subverts conventions when fear and uncertainty prevail, reducing the human condition to savagery and barbarism. What made Athens great, for example, was respect for, and equality before, the law, and the treasured possessions of courage and loyalty. Openness to the world and faithful friendship made Athenians dependable, identifying their own interests with those of the city. The fragility of these virtues which Pericles extolled was exposed by the plague. Unprecedented barbarism followed unequalled virtue.

In Thucydides' view, then, nature is not a criterion of right action, nor is might equivalent to right. Human nature is destructive of civil society and civilized conduct, and threatens to subvert the constraints which modify it. The conventional institutions of the city which modify human behaviour are both necessary and desirable, but nevertheless fragile.

Notes

1. Peter T. Manicas, 'War, Stasis, and Greek Political Thought', *Comparative Studies in Society and History*, 24 (1982), 677.
2. Adam Watson, *The Evolution of International Society* (London, Routledge, 1992), 49.
3. M. I. Finley, *The Ancient Greeks*, rev. edn. (Harmondsworth, Penguin, 1971), 6–61.
4. M. I. Finley, *Politics in the Ancient World* (Cambridge, Cambridge University Press, 1991), 59.
5. Paul Woodruff, 'Introduction', in *Thucydides on Justice, Power and Human Nature* (Indianapolis, Hackett, 1993), p. xiv.
6. John Keegan, *A History of Warfare* (London, Hutchinson, 1993), 248.
7. Michael Gagarin and Paul Woodruff, 'Introduction', in *Early Greek Political Thought from Homer to the Sophists* (Cambridge, Cambridge University Press, 1995), p. xi.
8. A. R. Burn, *Pericles and Athens* (London, English Universities Press, 1956), 91–3.

9. Estimates of the populations of Greek city-states are notoriously difficult to arrive at. The figures used here are those of Victor Ehrenberg, *The Greek State* (Oxford, Blackwell, 1960), 33.

10. It was almost unheard of for Spartan citizenship to be conferred upon a foreigner. Herodotus reports that during his lifetime (*c.*490–425 BC) the Spartans did it only once, when they were desperate to secure the military services of Tisamenus, who accepted on condition that his brother Hagias also be made a citizen. See Herodotus, *The Histories*, trans. Aubrey de Sélincourt, rev. edn. (Harmondsworth, Penguin, 1972), 591 [ix. 35].

11. Aristophanes, *Lysistrata*, in *Lysistrata, The Acharnians, The Clouds*, trans. Alan H. Sommerstein (Harmondsworth, Penguin, 1973), 229:

    NEGOTIATOR: I'm ready to go back to my husbandry now.
    AMBASSADOR: And I'm wanting tae do some manuring.

    Also see Antony Andrewes, *Greek Society* (Harmondsworth, Penguin, 1991), 166.

12. Plutarch, 'Pericles' in *The Rise and Fall of Athens: Nine Greek Lives*, trans. Ian Scott-Kilvert (Harmondsworth, Penguin, 1960), 201.

13. Aristotle, *The Politics*, ed. Stephen Everson (Cambridge, Cambridge University Press, 1988), 1326a, 35–9.

14. T. R. Glover, *The Ancient World* (Harmondsworth, Penguin, 1972), 110.

15. H. D. F. Kitto, *The Greeks*, rev. edn. (Harmondsworth, Penguin, 1971), 67; Finley, *Ancient Greeks*, 122; Finley, *Politics in The Ancient World*, 63.

16. Burn, *Pericles and Athens*, 85.

17. Watson, *Evolution of International Society*, 48; A. R. Burn, *The Penguin History of Greece* (Harmondsworth, Penguin, 1990), 88; and Thucydides, *History of the Peloponnesian War*, trans. Rex Warner, rev. edn. (Harmondsworth, Penguin, 1972), i. 31–55.

18. Ehrenberg, *The Greek State*, 105–6.

19. Sophocles, *Antigone*, in *Antigone, Oedipus the King, Electra*, trans. Robert Fagles (Harmondsworth, Penguin, 1994), 450–61.

20. *Aristotle on Rhetoric: A Theory of Civic Discourse*, trans. George A. Kennedy (Oxford, Oxford University Press, 1991), i. 13.

21. Aristotle, *Nicomachean Ethics*, trans. J. A. K. Thomson (Harmondsworth, Penguin, 1973), 157.

22. Andrewes, *Greek Society*, 84–5.

23. Plato, *The Republic*, trans. Desmond Lee, 2nd edn. (Harmondsworth, Penguin, 1987), 258–9.

24. See Michael Palmer, 'Machiavellian *virtù* and Thucydidean *areté*: Traditional Virtue and Political Wisdom in Thucydides', *Review of Politics*, 51 (1989), 374.

25. W. B. Gallie, *Understanding War* (London, Routledge, 1991), 36.

26. There is a dispute about whether Antiphone the sophist was the same person as Antiphon of Rhamnus, to whom Thucydides refers (8. 68 and 8. 90) and who is reputed to be his teacher. The evidence seems weighted against this. See Mario Untersteiner, *The Sophists*, trans. Kathleen Freeman (Oxford, Blackwell, 1954), 228–32. The quotation is taken from Antiphon's fragment *On Truth*.

27. Cited in W. K. C. Guthrie, *The Sophists* (Cambridge, Cambridge University Press, 1971), 153.

28. See Edith Hall, 'Asia Unmanned: Images of Victory in Classical Athens', in John Rich and Graham Shipley (eds.), *War and Society in the Greek World* (London, Routledge, 1993), 110, 112, and 123.

29. Aristotle, *Politics*, 7–9, 11, and 178.
30. Plutarch, for example, tells us that after the defeat of the Persians at Platea in 479 BC the Greeks consulted the oracle at Delphi to enquire what sacrifice should be made. The answer was to extinguish all fire in the land because it had been contaminated by the barbarians, and to rekindle it from the altar at Delphi before making sacrifice. See Plutarch, 'Aristides', in *The Rise and Fall of Athens*, 132. Herodotus relates how Egyptians would not, on religious grounds, kiss Greeks, use their cooking implements, or eat meat cut with a Greek knife. See Herodotus, *Histories*, 145 [II. 42].
31. Coleman Phillipson, *The International Law and Custom of Ancient Greece and Rome* (London, Macmillan, 1911), 126.
32. P. A. Brunt, 'The Hellenic League against Persia', in *Studies in Greek History and Thought* (Oxford, Clarendon Press, 1993), 47–83.
33. Hayden V. White, *The Greco-Roman Tradition* (New York, Harper and Row, 1973), 22–6.
34. Andrewes, *Greek Society*, 254; and cf. Pauline Schmitt-Pantel, 'Collective Activities and the Political in the Greek City', in Oswyn Murray and Simon Price (eds.), *The Greek City from Homer to Alexander* (Oxford, Clarendon Press, 1990), 200.
35. M. D. Goodman and A. J. Holladay, 'Religious Scruples in Ancient Warfare', *Classical Quarterly*, 36 (1986), 152.
36. Schmitt-Pantel, 'Collective Activities and the Political', and Christine Sourvinou-Inwood, 'What is *Polis* Religion?', in Murray and Price (eds.), *Greek City*, 210, 212, 298–9, and 301; and Kitto, *Greeks*, 137–8.
37. See Alan Sommerstein's introduction to Aristophanes' *Lysistrata, The Acharnians, The Clouds*, trans. (Harmondsworth, Penguin, 1973), 17. The idea occurs in *The Birds*.
38. M. I. Finley, *Aspects of Antiquity: Discoveries and Controversies*, 2nd edn. (Harmondsworth, Penguin, 1977), 65.
39. Gilbert Murray, *Euripides and his Age* (London, Oxford University Press, 1965), 25–7; and Untersteiner, *Sophists*, 5.
40. Herodotus, *Histories*, 64 [I. 64].
41. Finley, *Aspects of Antiquity*, 52–3.
42. Finley, *Politics in the Ancient World*, 26–7.
43. Simon Hornblower. *Thucydides* (London, Duckworth, 1987), 183.
44. Robert Parker, 'Greek States and Greek Oracles', *History of Political Thought*, 6 (1985), 297, 299, 301–2, and 307.
45. Goodman and Holladay, 'Religious Scruples in Ancient Warfare', 155.
46. Graham Shipley, 'Introduction: The Limits of War', in Rich and Shipley (eds.), *War and Society in the Greek World*, 19.
47. Plato, *The Laws*, trans. A. E. Taylor (London, Dent, 1934), 2.
48. Arnaldo Momigliano, 'Some Observations on Causes of War in Ancient Historiography', *Studies in Historiography* (London, Weidenfeld and Nicolson, 1966), 120; and Yvon Garlan, *War in the Ancient World* (New York, Norton, 1975), 17–18. Finley, for example, contends that 'War was a normal part of life' (*Politics in the Ancient World*, 67; cf. Finley, *Ancient Greeks*, 63).
49. Andrewes, *Greek Society*, 161.
50. Manicas, 'War, Stasis, and Greek Political Thought', 682.
51. Leo Strauss, *The City and Man* (Chicago, University of Chicago Press, 1978), 146.
52. Watson, *Evolution of International Society*, 50.
53. Manicas, 'War, Stasis, and Greek Political Thought', 677.
54. Plato, *Protagoras*, trans. W. K. C. Guthrie (Harmondsworth, Penguin, 1987), 33.5a.

55. Keegan, *History of Warfare*, 244–54.
56. Andrewes, *Greek Society*, 166.
57. Adam Watson, *Diplomacy* (London, Routledge, 1982), 85–6; and Phillipson, *International Law and Custom*, 302–46.
58. Watson, *Evolution of International Society*, 52.
59. Manicas, 'War, Stasis, and Greek Political Thought', 680; Finley, *Politics in the Ancient World*, 61 and 111; Finley, *Ancient Greeks*, 59–60. W. G. Runciman argues that *stasis* was not a significant factor in the decline of the *polis*. Other societies experienced exceptionally high levels of violence, but were nevertheless able to perpetuate their institutions in a reasonably stable way. See Runciman, 'Doomed to Extinction: The *Polis* as an Evolutionary Dead-End', in Murray and Price (eds.), *Greek City*, 349–50.
60. Plato, *Laws*, 5.
61. Herodotus, *Histories*, 525 [viii. 3].
62. Murray, *Euripedes*, 23–4; Burn, *Pericles and Athens*, 23; Burn, *Penguin History of Greece*, 47–8; John Mansley Robinson, *An Introduction to Early Greek Philosophy* (Boston, Houghton Mifflin, 1968), 182–3. Also see G. B. Kerford, 'Anaxagoras of Clazomenae', in Paul Edwards (ed.), *The Encyclopedia of Philosophy* (New York, Collier Macmillan, 1967), i. 115–17.
63. Plutarch, 'Pericles', 169.
64. Simon Hornblower, *A Commentary on Thucydides* (Oxford, Clarendon Press, 1991), 284.
65. Burn, *Penguin History of Greece*, 271–2.
66. J. C. F. Poole and A. J. Holladay, 'Thucydides and the Plague of Athens', *Classical Quarterly*, n.s. 29 (1979), 296–300. Also see Hornblower, *Thucydides*, 131–2.
67. Aristophanes, *The Clouds*, in *Lysistrata, The Archarnians, The Clouds*, 122.
68. Aristophanes, *Clouds*, 154.
69. See W. K. C. Guthrie, *The Greek Philosophers from Thales to Aristotle* (London, Routledge, 1991), 66.
70. Untersteiner, *Sophists*, 240.
71. Ernest Barker, *Greek Political Theory* (London, Methuen, 1977), 75 and 77; and Plato, *Laws*, 889–97.
72. Kathleen Freeman, *The Pre-Socratic Philosophers* (Oxford, Blackwell, 1946), 394.
73. Robinson, *Introduction to Early Greek Philosophy*, 250–3; and Guthrie, *Sophists*, 290–1.
74. Antiphon, 'On Human Nature', repr. in Barker, *Greek Political Theory*.
75. Freeman, *Pre-Socratic Philosophers*, 402–3.
76. Plato, *Gorgias*, trans. Walter Hamilton (Harmondsworth, Penguin, 1971), 78 [483].
77. Callicles says: 'My belief is that natural right consists in the better and wiser man ruling over his inferiors and having the lion's share' (*Gorgias*, 87 [490]).
78. See e.g. Guthrie, *Greek Philosophers*, 102; Robinson, *Introduction to Early Greek Philosophy*, 255; Barker, *Greek Political Theory*, 81; and Understeiner, *Sophists*, 328.
79. Plato, *Republic*, 78 [338e–339].
80. This is the opening sentence to his book *Truth*, cited by Plato in *Theaetetus*, trans. F. M. Cornford (Indianapolis, Bobbs-Merrill, 1957), 31 [152].
81. For an excellent discussion of the meaning of Protagoras' dictum see Jonathan Barnes, *The Presocratic Philosophers* (London, Routledge, 1992), 541–4.
82. Robinson, *Introduction to Early Greek Philosophy*, 248.
83. Plato, *Protagoras*, 55 [322c]. Protagoras explains the origin of morality with the aid of a myth in which the virtues are bestowed upon man by Zeus, who feared the

destruction of humanity. The mythological character of the story is reinforced by its opening line: ' Once upon a time'. See *Protagoras*, 52 [320d].

84. Sextus Empiricus, *Selections from the Major Writings on Scepticism, Man and God*, trans. Sanford G. Etheridge and (ed.) Philip P. Hallie (Indianapolis, Hackett, 1985), 157.
85. Barnes, *Presocratic Philosophers*, 559–61; and Robinson, *Introduction to Early Greek Philosophy*, 201–4.
86. Cynthia Farrar, *The Origins of Democratic Thinking: The Invention of Politics in Classical Athens* (Cambridge, Cambridge University Press, 1988), 239.
87. Freeman, *Pre-Socratic Philosophers*, 316.
88. Guthrie, *Sophists*, 69.
89. Jacqueline de Romilly, *The Great Sophists in Periclean Athens* (Oxford, Clarendon Press, 1992), 52 and 172. Law in itself is not sufficient to make men good. Wisdom and knowledge resulting from good education are likely to make people act for the right motives. See Jonathan Barnes, *Early Greek Philosophy* (Harmondsworth, Penguin, 1987), 267.
90. Cited in Robinson, *Introduction to Early Greek Philosophy*, 232.
91. Because of the fragmentary nature of the evidence for Democritus' thinking, a much more individualistic, as opposed to collectivist, interpretation can be constructed. See Farrar, *The Origins of Democratic Thinking*, 193.
92. Peter R. Pouncey, *The Necessities of War: A Study of Thucydides' Pessimism* (New York, Columbia University Press, 1980), 86.

4

THUCYDIDES' *PELOPONNESIAN WAR*

The *History of the Peloponnesian War* has been described as the only acknowledged classic text in international relations, and its author has been applauded for his scientific analysis of interstate politics.[1] It is ostensibly an account of the war between Sparta and its allies and Athens and its allies that took place 431–404 BC, punctuated by the precarious peace of Nicias (421–414 BC). It is because the book is much more than a chronicle of events, and because a theoretical position can be extrapolated from it, that it has become an exemplar for critics and sympathizers alike of the philosophy of Realism in international relations. For some, it is the archetypal statement of power politics, equating might with right,[2] or the epitome of alliance politics and the delicate balance of power.[3] For others the *Peloponnesian War* is the quintessential expression of the security dilemma which is occasioned by the ambiguity of intention, offensive or defensive, consequent upon the build-up of another country's military capacity.[4] Furthermore, Thucydides has been identified as the prototype structural Realist and an implied third-image theorist who sees the major causes of war not within the psychology of man, or the internal structure of the state, but primarily within the state system itself.[5]

Thucydides is not for every theorist of international relations an unremitting Realist. Many have detected, in varying degrees of mitigation, a moralism that tempers or even bemoans the cold-hearted and clinical ruthlessness of some of the historical characters he portrays. Michael Smith suggests that Thucydides' Realism is tempered by 'a sense of brooding tragedy, a profound regret that this is the way of the world'.[6] An extension of this view portrays Thucydides as a moralist intimating the inappropriateness of the depraved and shrewd Athenian Realism, in such passages as the Melian Dialogue, to such a noble people as the Athenians. On this reading the *Peloponnesian War* is a morality play in the spirit of classical Greek tragedy.[7]

Because of the centrality of Thucydides' text to the traditions of Realism and neo-Realism, postmodernist international relations thinkers have complained of the selective privileging of aspects of the history by the proponents of the dominant paradigms. Jim George argues, for example: 'illustrating that the "great texts" of International Relations can be read in ways entirely contrary to their ritualized disciplinary treatment is, consequently, to open up space for other ways of reading *global life*, effectively and powerfully blocked off under a foundationalist textual regime.'[8] They object to the appropriation of Thucydides exclusively in terms of his scientific rationalism and universal laws of behaviour, which are grounded in self-interest and power politics. Thucydides presented as a clinical detached observer not only displays an epistemological naïvety in believing that the Athenians generally told things as they really were (the correspondence theory of truth), but ignores the extent to which he became passionately involved with the subject-matter. In writings of the 1960s a new emphasis emerges on the personality of Thucydides, the art as opposed to the science of the writer, and his role as a moralist.[9] The aim is to demythologize Thucydides. The primacy of the sovereign state and the construction of the insider/outsider dualism in modern international relations theory generate an anachronistic reading of the *polis* and its perception of external threat, which appears not to have been a fundamental preoccupation of the Greeks.[10] A more sensitive reading of Thucydides reveals not a timeless body of laws with mathematical certainty, but the articulation of a range of practical moral options appropriate to a context, and embedded in political argument, from which various courses of action can be chosen.[11] It has to be said, however, that even though a range of options is presented, and in some cases the options refer to different ways in which the state interest may be served, not a moral option versus *raison d'état*, the argument resting on the grounds of justice and morality wins out only once (*Peloponnesian War*, 1. 86–7). In this respect, however, the most that can be said is that Thucydides as a matter of empirical observation concludes that might has a tendency to subvert right, not that he equates might with right, nor that he approves of the subordinate role of morality.

Thucydides' *History of the Peloponnesian War* is the most famous account of a single war that we have had handed down to us. It is not a history in the sense that we would understand the term today. Thucydides himself composed the speeches that the principal characters speak, keeping as closely as possible, he says, to the general sense of the words that were used. The speeches, in his view, reflect what 'was called for by each situation' (1. 22). The judge of what was 'called for' was, of course, Thucydides himself. The purpose of the history is not to provide a mere narrative account of the war. Although the focus of his history is on the war itself, his purpose is not to understand the events for their own sake, but to establish and illustrate universal traits of human behaviour. His history is essentially a study of human nature and the effects of the war upon action. He has a pessimistic view of human nature and clearly finds repugnant the way Athens disregards moral considerations in its imperial conduct. The book's purpose is didactic: it is meant to teach the reader certain lessons about the behaviour of individuals and of states. He is concerned with the psychological effects of war. Furthermore, he is concerned to demonstrate the tension between the injunctions of justice on the one hand and the demands of empire on the other. The Athenian spokesmen he cites often claim that an imperial power cannot afford to sacrifice self-interest for considerations of justice. This interest of which they speak, however, is at first the interest of the community and the empire, but evidently pronouncements of collective interest gradually become pretexts for self-interested gain.

Thucydides' assumption is that the events of the past, given what human nature is, 'will, at some time or other and in much the same ways, be repeated in the future' (1. 22). His history, then, was meant to have lasting significance, not as an account of a war, but as a source of generalizations about human behaviour, in the context of changing political and security challenges. I can find little grounds for Cynthia Farrar's claim that the *Peloponnesian War* is a 'possession for all time' not because history repeats itself, but because it accentuates the reader's ability to assess and respond to ongoing experience.[12] The two propositions are not mutually exclusive, but, on the contrary, mutually inclusive. The capacity for human nature to degenerate to a predictable basic condition when faced with extreme adversity is the basis of what one learns from experience, and from which one can enhance one's own capacity to respond.

Human history, then, is the dimension in which human nature unfolds, but that nature is not made by history; it is modified by great leaders who can strike an identity between the individual and common good, and by religious institutions, but when they cease to function as constraints there is a reversion to a human nature which is fixed and whose manifestations depend upon the context in which it is called upon to act. In this respect Thucydides does not predominantly belong in the company of those who profess Historical Reason as the criterion of ethical conduct. He does not deny that there are universal laws of humanity which give hope of salvation to all those who are distressed (3. 84). Neither Thucydides nor any of his speakers suggests that justice is a vacuous convention, nor that nature provides a better basis for law. Even when Athenian imperialism is justified on grounds of human nature, it is recognized by Thucydides and Pericles that the desire to rule where one can must be constrained by common prudence. Some justifications of action are, however, more devoid of moral considerations than others. The Athenians at Sparta before the outbreak of the war justified the empire as a normal precipitate of human nature, but did not, as the Athenians did in the Melian Dialogue, deny the relevance of any considerations of right and wrong.[13] Interest, both common and individual, does tend to predominate over justice in the motives of the actors and provides the justificatory, explanatory, and recommendatory nexus around which all else revolves in Thucydides.

The *History of the Peloponnesian War* is not a work of political philosophy, nor is it a sustained theoretical account of war and its relation to the actions of individuals and states. Intermittently, in the speeches and in Thucydides' own comments on the events which take place, we are able to glimpse at the theory which is intimated, but nowhere fully formulated and made explicit. It is we who have to construct the theory for ourselves. Furthermore, apart from a celebration of the strength of Sparta, and the portrayal of a brief glorious moment in the history of Athens at the peak of its power under Pericles and presiding over the empire, it is a history of failure and degeneration perpetrated by the actions of men unable to practise moderation in their personal ambitions. It is a deeply pessimistic account in that Thucydides offers no remedies or precautions for avoiding the consequences of war.[14]

Athens and Sparta on the Eve of the War

The *polis* is for Thucydides the fundamental unit in international relations, and he at no point intimates a pan-Hellenic solution to conflict among the city-states. In fact he neglects to inform us of Pericles' attempt at a pan-Hellenic initiative following the Persian War.[15] The bipolar balance of the Spartan and Athenian alliances was the outcome of an historical process, in which the natural inclination to dominate resulted in the domination of each alliance by a formidable power. The two principal states in the conflict, Athens and Sparta, were entirely different in character. Athens had newly emerged as a democracy after suffering a century of political instability. Pericles was its effective leader. The principle of freedom of speech and the importance of the assembly in Athenian politics gave every citizen the opportunity to rise to prominence without having to achieve elective office. Pericles' successor, Cleon, who advocated the death penalty for the Mytilenians, rose to power as an effective demagogue.

The buildings were grand, and partly paid for out of the proceeds of the empire. Learning was fostered and the arts were encouraged. Few of the great cultural figures in Greece between 500 BC and 300 BC failed to visit Athens. As Pericles says in the Funeral Oration, Athens was 'open to the world' (2. 39). Its government and way of life were in the view of many Greeks models to be emulated.

Because of the infertility of its soil Athens was not self-sufficient and had to foster trading links with its neighbours and with countries as far away as Asia Minor. Athens was the centre of commerce and culture in Greece. Its role in expelling the Persians and leading the Delian League, out of which the empire grew, made Athens the most formidable sea power in Greece, able to control the Aegean and the eastern Mediterranean. Pericles' refusal to enter into traditional warfare with Sparta reflects the extent to which it dominated the sea and saw its military strength in the navy.

Sparta was a complete contrast with all the other city-states in Greece. Its geographical isolation, different Greek dialect and ethnic origin (Dorian as opposed to Ionian), fertile soil, and self-sufficiency turned Sparta's attention not to the sea, but to the development of its military organization, tactics, and weapons. All those things that Athens valued, the development of philosophical criticism, promotion of the arts, and extensive contact with foreigners, Sparta forbade.[16] Sparta did not send out colonies with the exception of one; did not encourage the visits of foreigners; did nothing to promote art and literature; had no fine buildings; and did not encourage commerce. Spartan society was very heavily regulated. Strict discipline, including public whipping contests, prepared young boys for military service. Spartan citizens constituted a professional army which developed as a consequence of subjecting peoples who outnumbered them, that is, the helots, upon whom they relied as agricultural workers. Sparta had a constitution four hundred years old, which was the envy of conservative Greek states for its stability and combined elements of aristocracy, monarchy, and democracy.

In characterizing Athens and Sparta, Thucydides warns us not to be deceived by appearances. If Sparta became deserted, Thucydides argues, it would be difficult for future generations to imagine the extent of its power. Its lack of magnificent temples and monuments deludes us into thinking that it was not as powerful as it actually was. In the case of Athens, the grandeur of its buildings would lead us to think that it was twice as strong as it actually was. Thucydides concludes that 'We have no right, therefore, to judge cities by their appearances rather than by their actual power' (1. 10). From the end of the Persian Wars to the beginning of the Peloponnesian War, Thucydides argues, although there were periods of relative calm and peace, on the whole both Athens and Sparta were either engaged in quelling revolts among their allies or fighting with each other. Both states, then, 'were consequently in a high state of military preparedness and had gained their military experience in the hard school of danger' (1. 18). It should also be added that both before and after the Persian Wars Sparta had made a number of unwelcome interventions in Athens's affairs, including the attempt to prevent the rebuilding of her city walls (1. 90–3).[17]

Immediately prior to the outbreak of the Peloponnesian War, Greece had become polarized, and most of the Hellenic world was allied to one of the major powers. Those city-states that were not committed viewed the situation carefully in order to decide in which direction to turn (1. 1). Neutrality was a precarious policy to adopt, and those states which adopted such a stance had cause to regret it. The Corcyreans, for example, bemoaned their short-sightedness when they maintained that 'We used to think that our neutrality was a wise thing, since it prevented us being dragged into danger by other people's policies; now we see it clearly as a lack of foresight and as a source of weakness' (1. 32). The Corcyreans showed themselves to be acutely aware of the bipolar structure of the Greek world in appealing to the Athenians to pay due heed to the consequences of the Corcyrean fleet falling into the hands of Corinth and its Spartan allies. Such a situation would significantly strengthen the Peloponnesian alliance, and if war came Athens would have to face the combined fleets of Corcyra (Corfu) and the Peloponnese (1. 36).

It was the dispute between Corcyra and Corinth that constituted the immediate cause of the war in that it implicated both Sparta and Athens. Athens, believing that war with Sparta was inevitable, and not wishing to see the Corcyrean fleet fall into the hands of the Peloponnesians, decided to enter into a limited conditional defensive alliance with Corcyra. This alliance committed Athens to action only if any of its allies were attacked from outside. Such a treaty did not contravene the existing agreement that held between Athens and Sparta. Corinth sailed against Corcyra and was prevented from gaining complete victory by the intervention of Athens. In the view of Corinth, this constituted a breach of the peace treaty between the Peloponnesian and Athenian alliances.

Following closely upon this dispute, another conflict arose between Athens and the Peloponnese. Potidaea, a colony of Corinth, was actually allied to Athens, paying tribute to the Athenian alliance. Athens, fearing that Corinth might attempt to turn Potidaea against it, made certain stringent demands of its ally. Potidaea was to dismantle its fortifications, send hostages as security to Athens, and expel

Corinthian magistrates. Potidaea revolted, and Corinth came to its aid against the Athenians, who sought to suppress the rebellion against the alliance. Athens got the better of the Corinthian and Potidaean forces and blockaded Potidaea. Corinth decided to petition Sparta to declare war against the Athenians. The Spartans agreed and called together their allies to vote on the decision. A majority decided in favour of war, but urged restraint until the allied forces could prepare themselves for prolonged military action. Delaying tactics were employed by sending delegations to Athens. Finally, Sparta gave Athens an ultimatum which made no reference to the previous hostilities which had constituted a breach of the treaty, but instead stated that 'Sparta wants peace. Peace is still possible if you will give the Hellenes their freedom' (1. 139). In other words, Sparta called upon Athens to renounce its empire and liberate its subject city-states. Athens declined the invitation.

Fear: The Real Reason for War

It is generally acknowledged that Thucydides made a significant contribution to our understanding of war in distinguishing between its ostensible, immediate, and official justification on the one hand and its unstated, long-term, deep causes on the other.[18] This is a continuation of his fascination with appearance and reality. The deep-rooted cause of the Peloponnesian War that Thucydides discerned was a universal spring, or cause, of human action, *fear*.[19] Fear of its allies defecting to Sparta made Athens resist attempted acts of secession from the empire. Fear, however, is rarely sufficient in itself to motivate large-scale actions.

In relation to the Persian Wars, prior to the acquisition of the empire, the Athenian delegation at Sparta declares that the motives for action in expanding its influence were *fear* of Persian expansion, the desire for honour, and the pursuit of self-interest (1. .'5). Fear, however, occasioned by uncertainty, resulting in anticipation, and generating both beneficial and detrimental consequences, is the foundation of Thucydides' understanding of the dynamics of the Peloponnesian War.[20] Fear, then, is a powerful motive for action: and this, Thucydides claims, was the 'real reason' for the war: 'What made war inevitable was the growth of Athenian power and the fear which this caused in Sparta' (1. 23). What Thucydides is suggesting, then, is that Sparta was compelled to enter into war by Athens.[21] There was really no alternative.

Sparta's fear of Athens is confirmed by Thucydides in numerous places. A few examples will suffice. In explaining why Athens had become powerful he suggests that the 'real fears' of Sparta were of 'the sudden growth of Athenian sea-power and by the daring which the Athenians had shown in the war against the Persians' (1. 90). In the 'Dispute over Corcyra' (1. 31–55) the Corcyreans who address the Athenians in the hope of Corcyra being allowed to join the alliance also recognize Sparta's fear of Athens: 'Sparta is frightened of you and wants war' (1. 33). The Athenians also appear to acknowledge this fact in conceding that 'whatever happened, war with the Peloponnese was bound to come' (1. 44). A further example is afforded in the section entitled 'The Debate at Sparta and Declaration of War' (1. 66–88), in which the Corinthians attempt to gain Spartan support in their dispute with Athens over Corcyra; Thucydides says that

> The Spartans voted that the treaty had been broken and that war should be declared not so much because they were influenced by the speeches of their allies as because they were afraid of the further growth of Athenian power, seeing, as they did, that already the greater part of Hellas was under the control of Athens.   (1. 88)

Thucydides does not, however, record Pericles' attempt to allay the fears occasioned by the growth of Athenian power. Aware of the mounting concern felt by Sparta, Pericles invited delegates from all over Greece to discuss the security of shipping, the restitution of sanctuaries destroyed by the Persians, and the common sacrifices owed as a result of the wars. Plutarch says that he mentions this 'as an illustration of Pericles' lofty spirit and of the grandeur of his conceptions'.[22] One could equally impute the motive of fear of Sparta's reaction to the build-up of power, given that Pericles' predilection was to avoid the uncertainty and danger of battle.

The emotion of fear also figures prominently in the revolt of Mytilene (428–427 BC). In trying to gain the support of Sparta, the Mytilenians justify their revolt against Athens by suggesting that faith has been broken on the Athenian side. Athens no longer wishes to treat Mytilene as an independent equal, but to subject it, like other states, to Athenian power. Fear here works at two levels. First, mutual fear, or an equality of fear, would prevent breaches of faith. The proposition is, then, that a balance of fear engenders mutual respect. It is because there is no longer an equality of fear that Athens thinks that it can act in such a way as to subject Mytilene. Second, it is the Mytilenian fear of the growth of Athenian power that impels it to revolt, even though it realizes that it is premature and a high-risk strategy. Sparta was, of course, the focus of aspirations for the liberation of Greece from the grip of Athens, and the Mytilenians appealed to both this and their own fear in calling upon Sparta to assist them: 'Be the men, therefore, that the Hellenes think you and that our fears require you to be' (3. 14). Another dimension of fear appears in Pericles' Funeral Oration. It is the Athenian fear of recrimination that impels it to hold on to the empire whether it wants to or not.

Fear, as we saw, is one of the fundamental causes of action. Fear, the desire for glory, and the pursuit of self-interest are, for Thucydides, universal characteristics of human nature. Fear of being dominated if one does not dominate is the principal motive behind both the acquiring of an empire and, having acquired it, the refusal to give it up. This is illustrated by Euphemus. He argues that it is only by subjugating the Ionians and the islanders that Athens can preserve its freedom against Sparta. He states quite categorically that 'it is because of fear that we hold our empire in Hellas' (6. 83).

Fear, then, has a central explanatory role throughout Thucydides' *Peloponnesian War*. Fear drove Athens to build up its empire, and it was Spartan fear of this empire that caused the Peloponnesian War. Furthermore, it was Athens's fear of recriminations that impelled it to hold on to and expand the empire. There is no suggestion that fear is equated with rational decisions. Often the decisions precipitated by fear turn out to be to the detriment of the city. Ambition and self-interest are factors which complicate the causes of war and extend beyond fear, leading to overextension and ill-conceived hopes of gain.

Imperialism and Human Nature

What is remarkable about Thucydides' account is the brutal honesty of the characters. No attempt is made to disguise their motives, except in the case of Nicias and the Sicilian expedition (which backfires upon him), or to offer a legitimate pretext for Athenian imperialism.[23] On the whole Thucydides gives little emphasis to the economic factors that would justify Athenian imperialism; instead he emphasizes the psychological. Imperialism is justified on the grounds of expediency, security, ambition, the desire for glory, and the natural desire to want more and to dominate, but never on moral grounds. The empire is justified by its supporters for the good of Athens, not for the common good of the members of empire (3. 37). Holding on to it is a protection against recriminations. When the Mytilenians revolt against the empire, however, they wish to equate self-interest with the common interest (3. 14). Whereas Cleon, Pericles' successor, sees the revolt not simply as an attempt to increase power, which would be justifiable, but as an attempt by appealing to Athens's enemies to destroy her, which makes such action by an ally reprehensible. Cleon censures Mytilene for putting 'might first and right second' (3. 39).

Thucydides assumes that human nature is more or less the same wherever you find it (1. 84), and that human nature both explains and justifies human action. In relation to imperial...m, speakers in various debates invoke human nature both as an explanation and as a justification of Athenian imperialism. In the Mytilenian Debate (3. 36–50), Diodotus invokes human nature to explain why Mytilene rebelled against Athens, and why such nature should be a mitigating factor in discerning the appropriate punishment. The assumption that Thucydides employs throughout the *Peloponnesian War* is that individuals are utility maximizers making rational choices in accordance with their interests. The complicating factors are introduced by what may be called, following David Gauthier, straight maximization, in which individuals are prepared to sacrifice the long-term common good for individual short-term gain, and constrained maximization, in which each citizen benefits from constrained self-interested behaviour—one may call it enlightened self-interest (see Thucydides' assessment of Pericles, 2. 65, and the Civil War in Corcyra, 3. 82). It is apparent from Thucydides' account of human nature in relation to the progressive development of Greek political life and organization in the archaeology that he believes that constrained maximization is the rational option for human beings.[24]

In the international sphere, the characteristics of individuals are attributed to states. There is no natural order or harmony in the relations among states. The order that exists is created and sustained by the powerful and by force of nature the powerful will always impose their power within their sphere of influence, and 'it has always been a rule that the weak should be subject to the strong' (1. 76). States, like individuals, are motivated by fear and self-interest, and appeal to justice only when that interest is served (1. 76 and 5. 105). Appeals to interest are consistent with security, 'whereas the path of justice and honour involves one in danger' (5. 107). In the view of Athens, gaining an empire is quite in accordance with the Laws of Nature. It is a Law of Nature that the weak become subject to the strong, and when the opportunity of aggrandisement is offered by superior strength (1. 76) considerations of right and wrong are sacrificed to self-interest. Euphemus, the Athenian, confirms this in his contribution to the Debate at Camarina. He says: 'When a man or a city exercises absolute power the logical course is the course of self-interest' (6. 85).

The Natural Right of the stronger to rule over the weaker is rather a simplistic explanation and justification of imperialism. It might be a successful strategy if applied circumspectly in hegemonic conditions, but becomes positively dangerous when pursued in a bipolar context, as Thucydides himself shows. Athenian action seemed to lack perspective during the war. The reaction against Melos was disproportionate to its size and strategic value, and bordered on the obsessive, making an example of the Melians to other cities which refused to join the empire, in order to eliminate neutrality and opposition. The Sicilian expedition was an obvious overextension of power, motivated by the desire to conquer Sicily and the Greeks in Italy, and to make inroads into the Carthaginian Empire, with the ultimate goal of returning with the new troops acquired to attack the Peloponnese (6. 90). The Sicilian expedition was also an underestimation of the resolve of Sparta, because of its lack of enthusiasm for aiding Melos, successfully to intervene when its interests were threatened (7. 18).

The Natural Right of which Thucydides speaks is a universal characteristic of human beings and states and therefore not restricted to Athenian imperialism. The exercise of this right is contextual in that there are circumstantial limits beyond which it becomes counter-productive. Sparta had reached that limit and could not, given its subject helot population, expand further without jeopardizing its security, and this was a limitation its leaders acknowledged. Pericles believed that in the circumstances Athens had reached the optimum size of empire and should not expand further. Alcibiades, on the other hand, failed to see the contextual constraints upon the Natural Right of the strong to rule over the weak, and overextended Athens to the point of ruin.[25]

Questions of morality in international politics are subordinate to the idea of *raison d'état*. This is not to say that justice and compassion are entirely out of place. The Athenians believed that given the power that they held they should be praised for being far more just than anyone had a right to expect (1. 76). Athenians, although capable of acts of gross barbarity, for example against the people of Melos, were also capable of acting with restraint against the enemies they defeated.[26] The fact that the Athenians decided to take a second vote on the fate of Mytilene was precipitated by pangs of conscience, or remorse, at the cruelty of the initial sentence.[27] Self-interest, not justice, was nevertheless still the criterion appealed to in deciding and changing the fate of the Mytilenians.

The order that is created is precarious and perpetually subject to threat from those, who, when they see an opportunity to further their interests, do not hesitate to take it. As Diodotus says: 'Cities and individuals alike, all are by nature disposed to do wrong, and there is no law that will prevent it' (3. 45). In the Melian Dialogue, for instance, the Athenians argue that in the absence of international law states have to be constrained by force. The notions of justice and injustice are therefore inapplicable to the interstate sphere. Each state has an obligation to look after its own state interest in deciding its course of action. It is in the interests of each state, if it has the power, to rule where it can: 'it is a general and necessary Law of Nature to rule wherever one can' (5. 105).[28] The Athenians throughout the *Peloponnesian War* justify their imperialism not in terms of justice and injustice, but with reference to the claim that they are doing nothing that any other state would not do in similar circumstances and with the same degree of power. Such a view reflects Thrasymachus' claim in the *Republic* that justice is what is in the interests of the stronger.

The Burden of Empire

The exercise of power imposes certain necessities upon the imperial state, acting as constraints to which a non-imperial power may not be subject. Considerations of justice should give way to the primacy of interest in matters concerning empire. Nothing should jeopardize the existence and success of the empire. In the Mytilenian Debate we hear strong arguments against letting one's judgement be swayed by compassio.. and considerations of decency. Such things 'are entirely against the interests of an imperial power' (3. 40). Cleon argues that to destroy the whole population of Mytilene would be to act in the interests of the empire. To spare them would be an act of folly. Such acts of compassion are a luxury that can be engaged in only if the empire is relinquished. The interests of the empire demand that the Mytilenians be punished. It is no more than the Mytilenians would have done to Athens had they been successful in their revolt. Indeed, it was they who perpetrated the wrong and who will not be satisfied until Athens is destroyed, because an enemy who has been injured and escapes is more dangerous than one who has done an injury and also suffered one. And, as if all these considerations were not enough, the ultimate appeal is to the Laws of Nature: 'for it is a general rule of human nature that people despise those who treat them well and look up to those who make no concessions' (3. 39). The Athenians do not accept Cleon's argument and are instead swayed by that of Diodotus. It is interesting, however, that the argument of Diodotus is predominantly concerned with the interests of Athens. The debate, then, is not about what would be just, but about which course of action—to destroy the population of Mytilene or to exercise leniency—would be in the best interests of Athens.

The degree of activity required to create and sustain an empire forecloses the possibility of retreat with impunity. Pericles emphasizes the imperative need for continuous activity, and for resisting any inclination towards rest. Having once procured an empire there is no turning back. The hatred incurred in administering an empire makes it positively dangerous to contemplate giving it up. There is no alternative but to maintain the empire. He says quite explicitly: 'Your empire is now like a tyranny: it may have been wrong to take it; it is certainly dangerous to let it go' (2. 63). Only certain people are of value when a state embarks upon an imperialistic course of action. Pericles speaks contemptuously of those citizens who are apathetic or inactive. He contends disdainfully that they are fit only to be ruled over as slaves by a foreign power. It is men of action who make it possible for the inactive to exist at all. Athens, Pericles boasts, is the greatest city in the world because its love of the life of activity has impelled it to spend 'more life and labour in warfare than any other state, thus winning the greatest power that has ever existed in history, such a power that will be remembered for ever by posterity' (2. 64).

The argument of Alcibiades in persuading Athens to launch the Sicilian expedition further illustrates how the burden of empire locks the state into a certain course of action. He argues that it is impossible to know what the optimum size of the empire should be. Athens, however, has reached a stage where new conquests have to be pursued and past gains consolidated. The justification for this is that 'we ourselves may fall under the power of others unless others are in our power' (6. 18). But more importantly, Alcibiades argues, a city which is used to action will quickly be ruined if it turns to inaction. In other words, for the sake of survival Athens must continue with its policy of imperialism. Gaining new experiences in conflict keeps the city in a state of high preparedness for any external threat. Activity or continuous action in extending and maintaining the empire is to be highly valued.

In summary, imperialism and human nature are integrally related. A state that has the ability to acquire an empire is compelled to do so by the Laws of Nature, which dictate that the powerful rule the weak; that one must rule whatever one can; that self-interest overrides considerations of justice; that others will rule over you if you do not rule over them. Fear and the need for security, dictates of self-interest, compel both the acquisition of an empire and the reluctance to let it go. In essence, the Athenian claim is that they are doing nothing against the Laws of Nature and nothing that others would not do in similar circumstances. Appeals to the Laws of Nature in explanation and justification of Athenian imperialism do not in fact explain why it was Athens in particular, and not another Greek city-state, that became so powerful and dominated Hellas in the fifth century BC.

The Athenian Character

Human nature is not something that can be allowed to be exercised without restraint. Laws and conventions within states serve to constrain and modify human nature. Peter H. Judd argues that in the mind of Thucydides the purpose of governmental institutions is to bring about a transformation in human nature and thus modify behaviour in such a way that the continued existence of society is assured.[29] Governments, although not immune from the desires and aspirations of self-interested individuals, have a greater capacity than the individual for promoting the common good. The strain of war, and the great sufferings inflicted as a consequence, can lead to the erosion of traditional conventions and the liberation of human nature.

It was the Persian Wars which liberated Athens from some of its traditional constraints and enabled one of its distinguishing characteristics to come into being and develop. This was Athenian 'daring'. Throughout the history Athenian daring is highlighted as one of the distinguishing characteristics of that city-state, and it is what enabled Athens to build up her power and acquire an empire. The Corinthians in the Debate at Sparta and Declaration of War recognized this trait in the Athenian character. In comparing Sparta with Athens, the Corinthians claim that the Spartans are too conservative and cautious, whereas the Athenians are adventurous and innovative: 'they prefer hardship and activity to peace and quiet' (1. 70). Athenian daring allows them to take risks, whereas the Spartans' lack of confidence in their own judgements always makes them stop short of what they are capable of doing. The anonymous Athenian contributors to the debate similarly emphasize Athens's daring as one of the marks of its greatness. Against the Persians, the Athenians claim, 'the courage, the daring that we showed were without parallel' (1. 74). This daring was manifest in the decision to abandon the city, take to the ships, and face up to the danger. Such a course of action required courage as well as dar...g. In the Funeral Oration of Pericles we find him praising the courage and daring of Athens. This daring was well directed by the intelligence or resolution (*gnome*) of Athenian leaders, which complemented the daring or zeal of the people. *Gnome*, when understood as intelligence in Thucydides, is contrasted with passion and anger, and when understood as rational action or planning is contrasted with chance or uncertainty (*tyché*).[30] Sparta certainly suffered from ill fortune or chance, but also succeeded by resolve or intelligence (5. 75; cf. 2. 87). It is the combination of intelligence and daring that makes Athens special.

Pericles urges his contemporary Athenians to 'resolve to keep the same daring spirit against the foe' as their ancestors had done (2. 43). It was this quality which led to the acquisition of power, and not power which generated this quality.[31] It was this very same daring, however, which caused other Greek cities to fear Athens's rebuilding programme after the war (1. 90), and which liberated individuals to disregard the conventional constraints of the city, and also to embark upon hopeless adventures in disregard of the intelligence that had once directed

Athenian daring towards the honour and glory of the city. Pericles was able to harness the positive side of Athenian daring, but, as Plutarch tells us, he resisted their 'more reckless impulses'.[32]

In abandoning the city, under the extreme pressure of war, Athens was forced to break with its traditional practices and customs, thus liberating itself, to a certain extent, from the constraints that operated in other cities. One such constraint, as we have already seen, was that of piety. Steven Forde points out that traditional piety would have imposed constraints on the use and abuse of power, on its accumulation, and on the ends towards which it could be directed. Such constraints operated in the name of, and appealed to, justice.[33] Daring overcame the conventional constraints of justice and eliminated ethics from the sphere of international relations.

In addition to Athenian intelligence and daring, the peculiarly emotional attachment to the city that the citizens of Athens had, and were encouraged to cultivate, distinguished them from the citizens of other Greek cities. When Pericles entreats his fellow citizens to look upon Athens as a lover, he is pressing for a strong erotic attachment. In the Funeral Oration Pericles says that the Athenians should gaze upon the greatness of Athens every day and 'become her lovers' (2. 43).[34] Hornblower suggests that Thucydides appears here to be using a phrase that was already part of the political currency of Athens.[35] This erotic attachment to the city inspires devotion in a way that the traditional values of piety and community no longer could. Love provides the social cohesion that the liberation of human nature by the Persian Wars and the encouragement of individual freedom would not provide.[36]

In summary, a combination of daring directed by intelligence to the interest of the state, a love of action rather than tranquillity, and a strong emotional love of the city distinguished Athens from other Greek city-states. It was these qualities that made it strong. In relation to the Persian Empire or, later, the Roman Empire Athens was quite distinct. It was not territorially ambitious, and remained a provincially defined *polis*. It was an empire of the sea, or thassalocracy.[37]

The Paradoxical Effects of War

Paradoxically these same qualities, when individual self-interest entrusted to chance replaced the guiding role of intelligence, destroyed Athens. Lowell Edmunds argues that the opposition of intelligence and chance, the former principally associated with Pericles, provides the central theme in Thucydides. He suggests that intelligence gradually gives way to chance as the *History* progresses.[38] The Spartans, however, demonstrate quite late in the *Peloponnesian War* their ability to overcome chance by the use of their intelligence or resolution (5. 75).[39]

Various Athenians warn of the dangers of overconfidence. Diodotus, in the Mytilenian Debate, tries to change the Athenians' attitude to slaughtering the whole population of the city by claiming that any people in their position would have done the same. The idea that fortune is on one's side, he claims, is a significant factor in engendering a mood of overconfidence in a people: 'for sometimes she does come unexpectedly to one's aid, and so she tempts men to run risks for which they are inadequately prepared' (3. 45). It is especially the case that where city-states are concerned fortune leads them into believing that they are more powerful than they actually are. Nicias does try, in the Launching of the Sicilian Expedition, to warn the Athenians against allowing their successes to give them a false sense of their invincibility. Spartan misfortune and not Athenian design accounts for their recent successes. It is no time for risking everything on new adventures. Nicias warns his fellow citizens not to 'indulge in hopeless passions for what is not there' and that success is gained not by wishful thinking, but by foresight (6. 11–14). It is Alcibiades, however, whose personal ambitions Nicias warns against, and who persuades the Athenians to launch the Sicilian expedition. While the degeneration is not as unrelenting as Lowell implies, it is nevertheless undeniable that Thucydides saw success precariously balanced against the vicissitudes of chance.

War puts into jeopardy everything that has been gained and established in the progress of civilization and empire. It leads to a lowering of moral standards within the city and results in a progressive degeneration of human behaviour, which is reflected in the transformation of action informed by the ideal of the common good to the unrelenting pursuance of individual self-interest. Thucydides states this quite clearly when he says:

In times of peace and prosperity cities and individuals alike follow higher standards, because they are not forced into a situation where they have to do what they do not want to do. But war is a stern teacher; in depriving them of the power of easily satisfying their daily wants, it brings most people's minds down to the level of their actual circumstances. (3. 82)

War is always a prec..rious and dangerous mode of action to embark upon because its course and consequences are unpredictable. At one time luck can appear to favour a state, but suddenly fortune can change.

The Corinthians at the allied conference in Sparta, meeting to ratify the decision to go to war, show themselves acutely aware of the unpredictability of the turns of fortune during the course of war. They inject a note of caution into the proceedings in arguing that to go to war is to be blind to the fact that the confidence which spurs them on is illusory. Ill-conceived plans may often succeed as a matter of chance because the enemy is even more inept. Moreover, what at first appears to be an excellent plan may turn out to be a disastrous failure. This is indeed a premonition of the catastrophic Athenian expedition to Sicily. The Corinthians warn us that practice often falls far short of theory. To execute plans with the same degree of confidence as they are conceived is almost impossible because the presence of fear always makes us fall short of the ideal (1. 120). With this circumspect and astute knowledge of the precariousness of war the Corinthians advocate a distinctly limited objective. Having been the victims of aggression, they claim, it is appropriate to go to war, but once security against the Athenians has been established, that will be the 'proper time' to return to peace (1. 121).

The Spartans, too, attempted to impress upon the Athenians the folly of rushing into things on the basis of having had a taste of good fortune. After the Athenian success at Pylos in 425 BC the Spartan representatives who went to Athens warned the Athenians about being overconfident. They argued that Athens was now in a position to consolidate its good fortune by holding what it had gained as well as achieving for itself honour and reputation. They urged the Athenians not to make the mistake of those who, having gained an unexpected and extraordinary success, press on in the hope of more. It is those who have experienced changes, both good and bad, who are reluctant to trust in the hope that their luck will continue (4. 17). Athens, having experienced good and bad fortune, decided to ignore the Spartan advice and press for further victories.

Because of its daring Athens was much more inclined to trust in fortune than was Sparta. Thucydides comments on this aspect of Athenian character after telling how the Athenians had responded to the return of two of the generals, Pythodorus and Sophocles, from Sicily, by banishing them because they had accepted peace when it was within their grasp to take over the island. This was the effect on Athenians, Thucydides claims, of the present run of good fortune. They believed that everything was attainable and that nothing could go wrong: 'It was their surprising success in most directions which caused this state of mind and suggested to them that their strength was equal with their hopes' (4. 65). This false perception of the capacity of Athens for success in foreign adventures is manifest in the Sicilian expedition, which was 'undertaken with hopes for the future which, when compared with the present position, were of the most far-reaching kind' (6. 31).

What has been said so far can be summarized in four pertinent paradoxes which explain the degeneration and defeat of Athens. First, fear is the cause of both seeking, establishing, and maintaining security on the one hand, and generating fears in others who at once threaten that security on the other. Fear drove Athens to create its empire, and fear of the power of that empire drove Sparta to declare war on it. There is no state of equilibrium, then; everything is constantly in flux. Secondly, human nature impels cities to exercise power over others. It is a Law of Nature to rule where one can. But this propensity towards imperialism in external affairs leads to the very thing that erodes the constraints on human nature in internal affairs. War, as Thucydides says, is a 'stern teacher' (3. 82). It throws the conventions of civilized life into turmoil and confusion. When this happens human nature shows its true colours. It proves unable to keep passion in check, disregards justice, and opposes anything superior to itself. Envy leads men to exalt vengeance 'above innocence and profit above justice' (3. 84). The breakdown of laws and conventions in internal affairs leads to a disregard for the 'general laws of humanity which are there to give a hope of salvation to all who are in distress' (3. 84). Human nature, because of a lack of an ultimate authority in the external sphere, can be a positive driving force in bringing glory and honour to the city. When the internal constraints of law and convention have become eroded, human nature undermines authority in internal affairs, and leads to irrational excursions into the external sphere in order to satisfy private ambitions rather than to further common interest. Thirdly, the justification and explanation of the empire in terms of the natural right of states to look to their own interests, and to seek more at the expense of other states, paradoxically justify the individual self-interest which leads to the destruction of Athens. The fourth paradox is similarly destructive of order and security. Daring, the very thing that distinguished the Athenian character from that of other Greek cities, and enabled Athens to become an imperial power, was also the very thing that caused its decline. When the harsh teaching of war begins to break down the internal conventions and authority internal to the city, daring has that propensity to accelerate the process.

In addition to these paradoxes, the language in which Athens conducts its deliberations among citizens and between itself and other cities becomes increasingly couched in terms that are destructive of the community of speech upon which the discourse depends. The independence of the *polis* was paramount, but the language of the Athenians, and increasingly their actions, denied the putative equality of Greek city-states, asserted the primacy of self-interest, and rejected justice as a criterion of right conduct. Through the debates at Corcyra, Mytilene, Melos, and Camarina we saw successive and more blatant appeals to interest. In the last of these speeches, for example, Athens sought to renew its alliance with Camarina against Syracuse. The Syracusan envoy, Hermocrates, made the obvious accusation against Athens, accusing it of destroying the liberty of Greek city-states and pursuing its interests in disregard of those of others. Alliances, being based on a community of trust, lacked credibility when backed by a language of self-interest. Camarina did not feel able to ally itself with either side.[40]

I now want to turn to look at how these factors were involved in the gradual decline of Athens and its institutions.

The Decline of Athens

In his reply to the Spartan ultimatum Pericles claimed that the ancestors of Athens had made their city great not because of good fortune, but because of their wisdom. They had defeated the Persians not by means of material resources, but because of their daring. Very soon after Pericles made this speech, ill fortune struck in the second year of the war, and this ill fortune was exacerbated and compounded by the very thing that had made Athens great, its daring. Thucydides does not tell us that Pericles himself was blamed for the plague that hit Athens. His policy of herding people in from the countryside and forcing them to live in close quarters was believed to be the cause of the plague.[41]

When the plague came to Athens, so severe were its symptoms and so ill-equipped were the Athenians to deal with it that the failure of prayers in the temples and the ineffectiveness of oracles led to their contemptuous rejection. In the face of this natural disaster the conventional restraints of piety upon human nature immediately began to break down. The plague ushered in a period of 'unprecedented lawlessness' (2. 53). Observing how quickly people's fortunes changed, individuals became excessively self-indulgent. The prospect of death from the plague impelled them to seek the pleasure of the moment. They disregarded the law and exercised no self-restraint: 'No fear of god or law of man had a restraining influence' (2. 53).

This, then, was the beginning of the decline, which was compounded by the death of Pericles two and a half years after the outbreak of the war. Pericles himself and his policies had acted as restraining influences on the unbridled self-interest of Athenians. His death, in the view of Thucydides, was the crucial turning-point in the actions of Athens. From this point on the shift in balance from the good of the city to self-interested adventurism signifies the progressive degradation of the city. Pericles had held the view that an Athenian victory would be assured if Athens exercised a degree of patience and caution; saw to it that the navy was well maintained; and avoided the temptation to add new territories to the empire while the war was still in progress. Those who succeeded him, however, disregarded this policy and embarked upon ventures fuelled by personal and private ambition which appeared to have little to do with the conduct of war, but which had serious consequences for both the Athenians and their allies. When such policies succeeded they brought profit and credit to individuals, and when they failed they impaired the capacity of the state to wage war. Pouncey sums up Thucydides' view nicely when he says: 'Athens lost the war, in Thucydides' opinion, because her leaders pursued personal ambitions (*idias philotimias*) and personal profit (2. 65. 7), and ultimately undid their city by becoming involved in personal feuds (*diaphoras*—2. 65. 12).'[42]

Just as human nature and Natural Right were invoked to explain and justify imperialism, they were also invoked to account for the self-interestedness of individuals. In the Mytilenian Debate of 427 BC Diodotus the Athenian puts forward a fatalistic, and implicit, despondent, view of the capacity of human laws and conventions to keep human nature in check. He argues that as long as ambitions are fed by pride and insolence, and for as long as poverty impels men to act boldly and their lives are dominated by ceaseless passions, the impulses of men will always lead them to act dangerously. It is simply impossible, Diodotus argues, for the force of law or any other means of restraint to prevent human nature pursuing a course of action once it has decided upon it (3. 45).

Of considerable significance in the degenerative trend was the civil war in Corcyra in 427 BC. It was here that the world seemed to be turned upside-down and that an example, or precedent, was set for others to follow. What made this civil war, or *stasis*, distinctive was the considerable involvement of Athens and Sparta in the internal politics of this single Greek *polis*.[43] During the civil war people were, because of personal hatred or because debtors did not wish to repay the money they owed, acting recklessly, and all on the pretext of protecting the democracy. Thucydides comments: 'as usually happens in such situations, people went to every extreme and beyond it. There were fathers who killed their sons;

men were dragged from the temples or butchered on the very altars; some were actually walled up in the temple of Dionysus and died there' (3. 81).

Following the Corcyrean civil war nearly all of the Hellenic world became embroiled in intrigues and disputes. Competing parties within states appealed to outside forces for help. Democratic parties called upon Athens, and oligarchic parties appealed to Sparta. In peacetime such activities would have been unthinkable, but during war each party could look to an alliance to damage its opponents.

Each revolution seemed to reach new heights of savagery in the methods used to seize power and in the atrocities committed in seeking revenge. In what is perhaps one of the most famous passages in the book (3. 82), Thucydides describes how these unprecedented acts of human excess precipitated a revolution in language. All fixed points of moral and common decency had disintegrated, and now even language underwent transformation. To keep pace with the changing nature of events, words changed their meanings: acts which were once described as thoughtless aggression were now considered courageous and befitting a party member. Delay and caution became known as cowardice. To see a problem from all points of view was frowned upon. Such a person would be unfit for action. A real man was distinguished by his fanaticism, and it was regarded as a legitimate act of self-defence to plot against your enemies behind their backs. A man with violent opinions could be trusted, whereas someone who voiced objections to them could not. Party membership became a stronger tie than that of the family because party members could be relied upon to do anything for whatever reason. Party members had confidence in each other, not because of a common religious bond, but because they were fellow criminals. The parties themselves were formed with a view to ousting the incumbent government, rather than out of a desire to enjoy and promote the laws. To vanquish your opponent through an act of treachery led to you being credited with superior intelligence.

It was not so much that the words lost their meaning—a contentious translation of what Thucydides says[44]—but that their evaluative and descriptive contents became unstabl.. Loyalty, for example, retained its favourable evaluative connotation, but what were regarded as acts of loyalty changed. The changes were mainly in the referents of words, but not wholly. Kinship, for example, remained kinship, but the esteem in which it was held diminished.[45] What usually takes generations to transpire came about overnight. The point that Thucydides is trying to make, and which is well put by Terence Ball, is that 'Conceptual confusion and political chaos are one and the same', and hence there is a correlation between communicative disarray and the breakdown of community.[46]

In Thucydides' view, it was 'Love of power, operating through greed and through personal ambition' (3. 82) which brought about the evils he describes. Once the struggles broke out a violent fanaticism came into play. Leaders of parties duped the people into thinking they were promoting political equality for all, whereas really they were consolidating aristocracy. Neither justice nor considerations of the interests of the state deterred the extremes that men went to. Their criterion of action was pleasure. There was no room for conscience in a city which valued those who could put forward a clever argument to justify disgraceful acts.

Citizens who held moderate views were held in suspicion and eliminated for not taking sides. The less intelligent triumphed over the more intelligent by launching themselves straight into action and thus gaining the advantage over those who deliberated before acting. The civil war in Corcyra, then, heralded the general breakdown of law and order in the Hellenic world, and allowed human nature to show its true colours.

In what turned out to be a prophetic piece of insight, the Corinthians announced in the Debate at Sparta prior to the declaration of war that 'Athenian daring will outrun its own resources' (1. 70). A peace treaty was made between Sparta and Athens after ten years of war. The treaty was in force for six years and ten months but was never fully honoured by either side.

Athens, during this period, continued its expansionist aims, ignoring the warning that Pericles had given about extending the empire. The Athenians voted to send sixty ships to Sicily. One of the commanders, Nicias, believed that it was a mistake and that the ostensible reason for going, to help an ally, was in fact a shallow pretext to conquer the whole of Sicily. He argued that 'this is no time for running risks or for grasping at a new empire before we have secured the one we have already' (6. 10). He warned that Alcibiades, who was young and had recently been chosen as one of the commanders of the fleet, was motivated by self-interest and was out only for personal gain. Alcibiades appealed to the Athenians to remain faithful to the character and institutions which they had. One aspect of that character was, of course, daring, and the Athenians remained true to it by embarking upon the expedition to Sicily. Nicias, in a further attempt to halt the folly, changed his tactics by exaggerating the amount of resources that would be needed to win the engagement. Far from his assessment deterring the Athenians, they became impassioned with a new enthusiasm. Such was their daring that the prospect of new conquests and gains inspired them to vote the full amount that Nicias claimed would be needed.

We should not exaggerate the extent to which Thucydides blamed leading individuals such as Nicias and Alcibiades for the disaster. Both men, although different in character, lacked the *gnome*, or reason, of Pericles. It is true that Thucydides saw the competition among politicians for the approval of the demos as responsible for the fall of Athens (2. 65), but although Nicias and Alcibiades were both motivated by personal gain, Thucydides thinks that the demos was largely to blame. Piety and success in political life, as we have already seen, for Thucydides, are important allies. Even successful tyrants, such as the Pisistratids, are portrayed as pious and possessing virtue (6. 54), which puts them on a par with the richly admired Spartan leader Brasidas, who is described in similar terms (4. 81). Alcibiades, who was suspected by the demos of having tyrannical aspirations, but for whom Thucydides nevertheless had a qualified regard, failed to sustain the link between piety and political success. His personal life was characterized by licence and excess, giving rise to suspicions about his political ambition. It was this, Thucydides tells us, that had much to do with the subsequent downfall of the city (6. 15). It is not Alcibiades' conduct *per se* that he is indicting, but the response of the demos to it. His private life inflamed the demos, and his enemies engineered his recall from the ill-fated Sicilian expedition on a charge of impiety, at which point he defected to Sparta and played a leading role (which Thucydides exaggerates) in its counter-offensive against the Athenians before returning to Athens to resume his political career. Thucydides is suggesting that it was the recall of Alcibiades by the demos, depriving the expedition of his excellent qualities in war (6. 15), that resulted in such catastrophe.[47]

Although Nicias is portrayed as cautious and superstitious, and really not up to the job of leading the Athenian expedition, he saw, in the spirit of Pericles, the futility of trying to expand the empire when the time was not propitious. He was unable to restrain his fellow Athenians from reacting with passion to the frustration of their ambitions instead of with reasoned calm.[48] His demise at the hands of Sparta and her allies was, Thucydides thinks, least deserved among men of his time. Nicias had practised a law-bred virtue, in his obsession to preserve his reputation and to be a successful general, that was consistent with the traditions and expectations of his countrymen in a competitive and ambitious culture (7. 86).[49]

The Sicilian expedition was the longest undertaken from Athens and became famous because of the brilliant spectacle it made and for 'its astonishing daring' (6. 31). It ended, however, in total victory for the Syracusans and their allies. It was, Thucydides says, 'the greatest action that we know of in Hellenic history— to the victors the most brilliant of successes, to the vanquished the most calamitous of defeats; for they were utterly and entirely defeated; their sufferings were on an enormous scale; their losses were, as they say, total; army, navy, everything was destroyed . . .' (7. 87).

This news had a devastating effect upon Athens and inspired the whole of Hellas to turn against her. In the eighth book of the *Peloponnesian War* considerations of national interest left the centre of the stage and personal intrigues and power struggles of self-seeking individuals predominated. Self-interest became the glaring and obvious factor motivating every individual both inside and outside Athens. War had destroyed even the last vestiges of community spirit, and had brought democracy to an end in Athens with the oligarchic coup of 411 BC. The war continued with Athens suffering further defeats. It lost twenty-two ships to the Peloponnesians, who then encouraged Euboea to revolt.

It was this new defeat, Thucydides claims, which caused an even greater panic than the Sicilian disaster. There were now no ships and no more crews. Civil disturbances broke out at the prospect of the Peloponnesians following up their victory by marching on Athens. However, the Peloponnesians lacked the daring of the Athenians and did not follow through. The Athenians deposed the Four Hundred who comprised the oligarchy and voted to give power to the Five Thousand. Some minor military successes followed, but Sparta was the victor in 404 BC and demanded the dissolution of the empire.

The war ruined Athens and severely weakened Sparta. Throughout Thucydides we see human nature being assigned an increasingly insidious role in the degeneration of Greece. Human nature impels individuals and states to aggression, resulting ultimately in their complete degradation. The primacy of interest in Thucydides is not, however, an individual interest, which more often than not is divisive and destructive of the community. The collective interest of the *polis*, directed by the *areté* of noble leaders, is the primary value to which he subscribes. He does not deny the notion of universal justice; he simply acknowledges that for better or worse it has no constraining force in a system composed of states unequal in power.

Notes

1. Thucydides, *History of the Peloponnesian War*, trans. Rex Warner rev. edn. (Harmondsworth, Penguin, 1972). See Martin Wight in H. Butterfield and M. Wight (eds.), *Diplomatic Investigations: Essays in the Theory of International Politics* (London, Allen and Unwin, 1966), 33; and R. G. Gilpin, 'The Richness of the Tradition of Political Realism', *International Organisation*, 38 (1984), 291.
2. Martin Wight, *Power Politics*, ed. Hedley Bull and Carsten Holbraad, 2nd edn. (Harmondsworth, Penguin, 1986), 24. Wight suggests that it is 'One of the supreme books on power politics'. Also see Michael Joseph Smith, *Realist Thought from Weber to Kissinger* (Baton Rouge, La., Louisiana State University Press, 1986), 4. Also see Clifford Orwin, 'The Just and the Advantageous in Thucydides: The Case of the Mytilenian Debate', *American Political Science Review*, 78 (1984), 485.
3. Torbjörn L. Knutsen, *A History of International Relations Theory* (Manchester, Manchester University Press, 1992), 32.
4. Nicholas J. Wheeler and Ken Booth, 'The Security Dilemma', in John Baylis and N. J. Rengger (eds.), *Dilemmas of World Politics* (Oxford, Clarendon Press, 1992), 35.
5. R. O. Keohane, 'Theory of World Politics: Structural Realism and Beyond', in A. Finifter (ed.), *Political Science: The State of the Discipline* (Washington, DC, American Political Science Association, 1983), 507–8; and Kenneth N. Waltz, *Man, the State and War: A Theoretical Analysis* (New York, Columbia University Press, 1959), 12, 159, and 211.
6. Smith, *Realist Thought*, 10.
7. F. M. Cornford, *Thucydides Mythistoricus* (London, Arnold, 1907), chap. 13.
8. Jim George, *Discourses of Global Politics: A Critical (Re)Introduction to International Relations* (Boulder, Colo., Rienner, 1994), 196.
9. For an excellent discussion of these tendencies see W. R. Connor, 'A Post Modernist Thucydides?', *Classical Journal*, 72 (1977), 289–98.
10. R. B. J. Walker, *Inside/Outside: International Relations as Political Theory* (Cambridge, Cambridge University Press, 1993), 65–6.
11. Hayward R. Alker, Jr., 'The Dialectical Logic of Thucydides' Melian Dialogue', *American Political Science Review*, 82 (1988), 805–20; also see Daniel Garst, 'Thucydides and Neorealism', *International Studies Quarterly*, 33 (1989), 3–28.
12. Cynthia Farrar, *The Origins of Democratic Thinking: The Invention of Politics in Classical Athens* (Cambridge, Cambridge University Press, 1988), 129.
13. See Denis Proctor, *The Experience of Thucydides* (Warminster, Aris and Phillips, 1980).
14. Jacqueline de Romilly, *Thucydides and Athenian Imperialism* (Oxford, Blackwell, 1963), 357.
15. See Plutarch, 'Pericles' [17], in *The Rise and Fall of Athens: Nine Greek Lives*, trans. Ian Scott-Kilvert (Harmondsworth, Penguin, 1960), 184–5.

16. T. R. Glover, *The Ancient World* (Harmondsworth, Penguin, 1972), 131.
17. Graham Shipley, 'Introduction: The Limits of War', in John Rich and Graham Shipley (eds.), *War and Society in the Greek World* (London, Routledge, 1993), 11.
18. See Shipley, 'Introduction', *War and Society in the Greek World*, 11; and M. I. Finley, *The Ancient Greeks*, rev. edn. (Harmondsworth, Penguin, 1971), 63.
19. It is a matter of contention whether Thucydides formulated this deeper cause in the original conception of the *Peloponnesian War*, or whether he inserted it at a later date. See Proctor, *The Experience of Thucydides*, 177–91.
20. For an important comparison of the crucial role fear plays in the theories of Thucydides and Hobbes see G. Slomp, 'Hobbes, Thucydides and the Three Greatest Things', *History of Political Thought*, 9 (1990).
21. Leo Strauss, *The City and Man* (Chicago, University of Chicago Press, 1978), 174.
22. Plutarch, 'Pericles' [17], 185.
23. See e.g. Christopher Bruel, 'Thucydides' View of Athenian Imperialism', *American Political Science Review*, 68 (1974), 14.
24. Also see Farrar, *The Origins of Democratic Thinking*, 143.
25. Also see Strauss, *City and Man*, 191.
26. See Steven Forde, 'Classical Realism', in T. Nardin and D. Mapel (eds.), *Traditions of International Ethics* (Cambridge, Cambridge University Press, 1992), 73.
27. Proctor, *The Experience of Thucydides*, 91.
28. This was not an unusual view among the Greeks. Democritus, for example, argued that 'by Nature ruling belongs to the stronger'. See Michael Gagarin and Paul Woodruff (eds.), *Early Greek Political Thought from Homer to the Sophists* (Cambridge, Cambridge University Press, 1995), 157.
29. Peter H. Judd, 'Thucydides and the Study of War', *Columbia Essays in International Affairs*, 11 (1966), 187.
30. See Connor, 'A Post Modernist Thucydides?', 55 n. 9.
31. Also see Strauss, *City and Man*, 171.
32. Plutarch, 'Pericles' [20], 187.
33. Steven Forde, 'Thucydides on the Causes of Athenian Imperialism', *American Political Science Review*, 80 (1986), 437.
34. Rex Warner's translation does not bring out this strange erotic element of the love of Athens. He translates the phrase thus: 'What I would prefer is that you should fix your eyes every day on the greatness of Athens as she really is, and should fall in love with her' (2. 43). The translation used in the text is that of Hornblower. See fn. 35.
35. Simon Hornblower, *A Commentary on Thucydides* (Oxford, Clarendon Press, 1991), 311.
36. Forde, 'Thucydides on the Causes of Athenian Imperialism', 439.
37. Peter T. Manicas, 'War, Stasis, and Greek Political Thought', *Comparative Studies in Society and History*, 24 (1982), 684.
38. Lowell Edmunds, *Chance and Intelligence in Thucydides* (Cambridge, Mass., Harvard University Press, 1975).
39. Simon Hornblower, *Commentary on Thucydides*, 226; and Hornblower, *Thucydides* (London, Duckworth, 1987) 69–70.
40. For an interesting discussion of these aspects of Thucydides see James Boyd White, *When Words Lose their Meanings* (Chicago, University of Chicago Press, 1984), chap. 3.
41. Plutarch, 'Pericles' [34] , 201.
42. Peter R. Pouncey, *The Necessities of War: A Study of Thucydides' Pessimism* (New York, Columbia University Press, 1980), 39.

43. Marc Cogan, 'Mytilene, Plataea, and Corcyra: Ideology and Policy in Thucydides, Book Three', *Phoenix*, 35 (1981), 1.
44. John Wilson, ' "The Customary Meanings of Words were Changed"—Or were they? A Note on Thucydides 3,82.4', *Classical Quarterly*, 32 (1982), 18–20.
45. Clifford Orwin, '*Stasis* and Plague: Thucydides on the Dissolution of Society', *Journal of Politics*, 50 (1988), 834–5; and Strauss, *City and Man*, 147 n. 8.
46. Terence Ball, 'Hobbes' Linguistic Turn', *Polity*, 17 (1985), 746.
47. For interesting discussions of Thucydides' attitude towards and relationship with Alcibiades see P. A. Brunt, 'Thucydides and Alcibiades', in *Studies in Greek History and Thought* (Oxford, Clarendon Press, 1993), 17–46; H. D. Westlake, 'The Influence of Alcibiades on Thucydides, Book 8', in *Studies in Thucydides and Greek History* (Bristol, Bristol Classical Press, 1989), 154–63; and Michael Palmer, 'Alcibiades and the Question of Tyranny in Thucydides', *Canadian Journal of Political Science*, 15 (1982), 103–24.
48. Farrar, *The Origins of Democratic Thinking*, 174.
49. What Thucydides could have meant by attributing *areté* to Nicias is a matter of contention. See e.g. A. W. H. Adkins, 'The *Areté* of Nicias: Thucydides 7.86', *Greek, Roman and Byzantine Studies*, 16 (1975), 379–92; and Michael Palmer, 'Machiavellian *virtù* and Thucydidean *areté*: Traditional Virtue and Political Wisdom in Thucydides', *Review of Politics*, 51 (1989), 365–85.

5

MACHIAVELLI, HUMAN NATURE, AND
THE EXEMPLAR OF ROME

There is a great deal of truth in the view that Machiavelli 'is a chameleon: he takes on the coloration of his critics'.[1] He is at once a satanic teacher of evil and an elevated moral soul; a friend to tyrants and a teacher of republicans; a patriot and a calculating opportunist; an impartial, detached political scientist and a partisan political satirist.[2] It is quite remarkable how diverse the interpretations have been, yet among theorists of international relations it is equally remarkable how this spectrum of interpretation is reduced to a monochrome, with differing shades of grey. Wight sees Machiavelli as the inaugurator of the Realist tradition, being the first since the Greeks to analyse 'politics without ethical presuppositions', identifying the wickedness of men as the origin of the state whose main purpose is to restrain them.[3] For M. J. Smith, Machiavelli is the exponent of an instrumental morality positing the state as the boundary of the common good, a sentiment echoed by Prezzolini in attributing to Machiavelli the view that 'the state is the ultimate end and that there is nothing better in which man can participate'.[4] If one accepts this, then Stawell's view, that 'of all writers he [Machiavelli] perhaps has done most to harm the cause of internationalism',[5] becomes plausible. It was not that Machiavelli was opposed to internationalism, but it was, in his view, unlikely to come about by consent. It could, however, be achieved by conquest. For Steven Forde, Machiavelli is the purest of Realists, absolving states of all moral responsibilities, endorsing 'imperialism, the unprovoked subjugation of weaker nations, without reservation and without limit'.[6] Utility, then, becomes the guiding principle, and a wholly secular view of politics predominates.[7] For Fukuyama it is the desire for glory that constitutes the fundamental spring of action in princes and republics and provides the key to understanding Machiavelli.[8] The adoption of such a pagan principle is explicable if one follows Meinecke's view that Machiavelli was 'a heathen . . . to whom the fear of hell was unknown'. For Meinecke, Machiavelli was 'the first person to discover the real nature of *raison d'état*.[9]

Critical international relations theorists have stigmatized such views as stereotypical and unreflective. They emanate from the uncritical reification of a supposed tradition of thinkers in international relations. Effectively the injunction to which we are being asked to subscribe is to be less anachronistic and more historical in our treatment of Machiavelli, that is, to put the tradition to the question and generate the opportunity for critical reflection on the false images of the age. R. B. J. Walker argues that above all Machiavelli was concerned with citizenship and civic *virtù* and its relation to military affairs. Closely related to this is Machiavelli's emphasis upon courses of action being recommended, judged, and understood circumstantially. Walker concludes that 'we have, in a specifically Renaissance humanist language, in the images and metaphors of Machiavelli the poet rather than Machiavelli the prototypical political scientist or Realist, an account of political life as occurring in time'.[10]

The purpose of this chapter and the next is to show that Machiavelli was indeed a much more complex thinker than Realist interpretations generally allow. At the same time I want to suggest that his own experience of practical politics, associated with his passion for ancient and recent history, disposed him to allow Realist principles to dominate his conclusions. Having diagnosed the problems of internal and external relations as a Florentine Second Chancellor discharging his duties as secretary to the government departments of the Ten of War from July 1498, and then the Nine of the Militia from 1507 until the fall of the republic and the return of the Medici in 1512, he used his time in exile to refine his diagnosis, dwell upon the prognosis, and distil a remedy from the lessons of ancient and recent history.

Machiavelli's Method

The method he adopts is not, however, inductive. He does not present us with general laws based upon observation. Nor is his method hypothetico-deductive. We are presented not with hypotheses subject to falsification by evidence, but with maxims rhetorical./ illustrated by example. He is not the dispassionate observer and value-neutral analyst that the positivistic scientist demands,[11] but instead a committed partisan whose studies are through and through normative and thoroughly impregnated with value judgements.[12] His aim to achieve a greater degree of certainty in the attainment of political knowledge should be seen as a plea not for political science but for political education. It is based upon the deeds of the great rulers and commanders of the past and the success of the Roman Republic, the lessons of which may be modified according to circumstances or invented anew should none be appropriate.[13] In *The Discourses* Machiavelli quite clearly tells us that 'one never finds any issue that is clear cut and not open to question' (*Discourses*, 1. 6, p. 121). Certainty, or even a high degree of probability, is vitiated by the presence or absence of the variables *fortuna* and *virtù* (to which I will return) in all Machiavelli's political scenarios, and this renders the attribution of scientific intent highly dubious.

If there is a genuine scientific comparison to be made it is with medicine. Medicine is, for Machiavelli, nothing 'but a record of experiments, performed by doctors of old, upon which the doctors of our own day base their prescriptions' (*Discourses*, I. preface, p. 98). Like the writings of many of his contemporaries, Machiavelli's work is replete with medical analogies and metaphors. The comparison of the human body with the body politic was commonplace, and the identification of common ailments in the latter demanded common cures. Statesmen are likened to physicians called upon to cure political disorders. Machiavelli suggests, for example, that 'in every large city there inevitably occur unfortunate incidents which call for the physician, and the more important the incidents the wiser should be the physician one looks for' (*Discourses*, III. 49, p. 526). Furthermore the physician must purge the state of malignities to restore 'health to the body' (*Discourses*, II. 5, p. 290). And again in *The Prince* Machiavelli contends:

When trouble is sensed well in advance it can easily be remedied; if you wait for it to show itself any medicine will be too late because the disease will have become incurable. As the doctors say of a wasting disease, to start with it is easy to cure but difficult to diagnose; after a time, unless it has been diagnosed and treated at the outset, it becomes easy to diagnose but difficult to cure. So it is in politics.   (*The Prince*, 39)[14]

It must be emphasized that the physician embodies a good deal of doubt and chance in diagnosing and speculating upon the seriousness of an illness and in prescribing a remedy. The remedy may be simple and effective, or so complicated that the patient's life may be put at risk. The methods used during the Renaissance to heal the sick were, of course, very different from ours. They were frequently brutal and excruciatingly painful. If the ailment did not improve after a period of indulgence, the pains of the patient 'should be coerced with severity'.[15] This is certainly consistent with what Sheldon Wolin calls Machiavelli's economy of violence.[16] A political ailment should be caught in its early stages and dealt with severely and effectively before it becomes untreatable or requires such drastic measures that the life of the state is put in danger.[17]

Where does one get the experience to be a physician of the state? The answer is in history. This is what many commentators refer to as Machiavelli's historical method,[18] but it is neither historical nor a method.[19] Machiavelli's own political experience, associating with and observing some of the most notable political actors of his day—Cesare Borgia, Pope Julius II, the Emperor Maximilian, King Louis XII of France—impressed upon him conclusions which he sought to confirm by the authority of historical examples, ideally from Rome, another instance from antiquity, and one from more recent times. In his discussion of the importance of religion to instil fear and respect, and to strengthen social cohesion, for instance, Machiavelli cites the examples of the Romans, the Samnites, and Savonarola (*Discourses*, I. 11–15, pp. 139–52). History, for Machiavelli, is not so much a sequence of events happening in time as a series of transhistorical exemplars, a vast storehouse of examples, which he was not averse to 'interpreting' or altering to substantiate his political points.

As a humanist Machiavelli fully subscribed to the cult of antiquity, and saw Republican Rome as the great city-state to be emulated. Like Petrarch, he idealized the Roman Republic. Petrarch invoked Roman antiquity as an ideal that the prince should restore in order to abate the decay of medieval society.[20] Machiavelli purported to shun the Utopias of philosophers in favour of the harsh realities behind appearances, but what he did instead was to present an idealized picture of Rome—a golden age—to act as the touchstone of political success (*The Prince*, 90–1).

What grounds did he have for believing that we could learn lessons from the distant past? Human nature for Machiavelli, as for Thucydides, is not historically constituted, although it is nevertheless institutionally modified and capable of exhibiting peculiarly national characteristics (*Discourses*, III. 43, pp. 517–19). Because of an underlying constancy in human nature, 'everything that happens in the world at any time has a genuine resemblance to what happened in ancient times. This is due to the fact that the agents who bring such things about are men, and that men have, and always have had, the same passions, whence it necessarily comes about that the same effects are produced' (*Discourses*, III. 43, p. 517).[21] This is what Chabod calls 'the immutability of human passions', [22] and we should not therefore abjure imitation, 'as if the heaven, the sun, the elements and man had in their motion, their order, and their potency, become different from what they used to be' (*Discourses*, I, preface, pp. 98–9).[23] This constancy of human nature does not, however, preclude variety in disposition and imagination. It is this variation which in similar circumstances brings one man success and another grief.[24]

Human Nature and Politics

To say that the passions are constant tells us nothing about their content. Machiavelli's view of human nature is extremely pessimistic, and entirely consistent with that of Thucydides. Like Hobbes after him, Machiavelli maintains that most men are envious o. others and more inclined to belittle achievements than to admire them (*Discourses*, I. preface, p. 97). Of human beings Machiavelli contends that 'Envy, Sloth and Hatred are their companions, and with them go Cruelty, Pride and Deceit'.[25] The desires of men know no bounds, yet their capacity to attain them falls far short, and having achieved what is good they become bored and complain. In Machiavelli's view, 'we are so constituted that there is nothing we cannot long for' (*Discourses*, II. preface, p. 268), and men are driven by their natures from one ambition to another. The desire to acquire more is common among men (*The Prince*, 42). Furthermore, 'men are inclined to think that they cannot hold securely what they possess unless they get more at others' expense' (*Discourses*, I. 5, p. 118). Not only are men straight utility maximizers resentful of constraints, they are also untrustworthy and 'will always do badly by you unless they are forced to be virtuous' (*The Prince*, 127).[26] Men are easily corrupted and not bound even by the bond of love, which they break when it is in their interests to do so. It is fear rather than love 'strengthened by a dread of punishment which is always effective' in constraining their natures (*The Prince*, 97).

This does not mean that everyone to an equal degree shares and acts upon these perennial traits without compunction or compassion. Indeed, they are more evident in some groups than in others. On the whole, although the populace is fickle, it is less ambitious than the nobility. The nobility wants to dominate, while the populace wants only not to be dominated (*Discourses*, I. 5, p. 116). The enmities that persist between the people and the nobles are as a consequence both 'serious and natural'.[27] It is in the power of those who govern to make men good and virtuous by subjecting them to good laws and institutions, but they should always assume the worse-case scenario when making these provisions:

All writers on politics have pointed out, and throughout history there are plenty of examples which indicate, that in constituting and legislating for a commonwealth it must needs be taken for granted that all men are wicked and that they will always give vent to the malignity that is in their minds when opportunity offers. (*Discourses*, I. 3, pp. 111–12)

For Machiavelli morality is subordinate to politics. Political activity creates and sustains the conditions within which morality can flourish. There is in Machiavelli no sense in which the law of the prince or republic has to mirror or conform to a higher pre-existing and universal moral code. Morality comes into being as a consequence of the emergence of political communities.

Machiavelli argues that the first communities banded together for the purpose of security. In order to achieve this aim they designated a strong and courageous man to lead them. Threats to the safety of this man, and hence to security, gave rise to distinctions between goodness and honesty on the one hand, and wickedness and dishonesty on the other. Those who constituted a threat were blamed, and those who were overtly grateful to the leader were praised and respected. It was with the enactment of laws to prevent evil that the idea of justice came into existence (*Discourses*, I. 2, pp. 106–7). Such views were not uncommon in antiquity, of which Machiavelli was a student. Polybius, for example, attributes goodness and justice, as well as honour and disgrace, to social relations and protection by the brave against imminent dangers. Initially, however, 'the condition of life among men was this,—herding together like animals, and following the strongest and bravest as leaders'.[28]

There cannot, in Machiavelli's view, be a universal common good. Political activity is designed to promote the common good within the community, and prudent foreign adventures should be undertaken to enhance it at the expense of the foreigner. When Machiavelli talks of the common good it is always from the perspective of one state; the courses of action recommended to improve it are generally to the detriment of another. Morality among nations is not a consideration in the Machiavellian calculus, because morality is sustained within the state by strong, stable government.

States are, Machiavelli tells us, driven by ambition to dominate each other, and this gives rise to mutual jealousy and hatred. Machiavelli thinks it perfectly permissible, given such circumstances, to engage in deceit and fraud in relation to other states in order to improve the common good of one's own. A circumspect general, for example, should promise the defenders of a town under siege amnesty and assure them that the common good is not under threat, and that it is only a few ambitious citizens who are to suffer. The populace, anxious for a swift settlement, 'shuts its eyes to any trap which may underlie generous promises. Innumerable cities have by this means been reduced to servile states' (*Discourses*, III. 12, p. 442).

The implication of Machiavelli's view of human nature is that everything is in flux and motion (*Discourses*, I. 6, p. 121). The natural propensities inherent in man make every form of government, to differing degrees, unstable and subject to transformation. The Polybian cycle of government in which the pure forms of monarchy, aristocracy, and democracy give rise sequentially to tyranny, oligarchy, and anarchy is subscribed to by many Renaissance humanists, including Machiavelli. The cycle is one, Machiavelli claims, through which all common-wealths go. Very rarely would a state return to a form of government that it had just overthrown, and very few states have the strength and vitality to be able to complete the cycle more than a few times before ceasing to exist (*Discourses*, I. 2, pp. 106–9). The cycle is, however, an ideal characterization of the life of a single state, and it can theoretically repeat the full cycle until it becomes exhausted. What prevents this is the existence of other states. While some cities, or states, are feeling the benefits of their pure forms of government, others are experiencing the ills of the degenerate forms. What often happens is that the cycle is broken by the subjugation of the weaker state by the stronger and better-organized state. Thus the cyclical view of government has little predictive power.

Cecil H. Clough has argued that Machiavelli, in fact, believes in human progress: 'This, in the simplest terms, meant that primitive society consisted of groups of savages, each group under a king, and that there was gradual develop-ment to the zenith of civilization exemplified by the Italian cities, and Florence above all.'[29] The cyclical theory, Clough maintains, fits within the broader theory of evolutionary progress. I fail to see how such a theory of progress can be sus-tained. In every area of human activity that Machiavelli considered significant, his contemporary Italy con.pared unfavourably with republican Rome. Its mixed constitution was superior; its pagan religion was better used in the service of the state and fostered more manly virtues than Christianity; its military was better organized and constituted; and its imperial policy was the model to be emulated.[30]

Experience of the Ancients: Macedonia

I have suggested that Machiavelli's view of human nature and the subordination of morality to politics postulates a dynamic view of the relations among nations, each of which has its own common good which it is prepared to enhance at the expense of others. There are, of course, constraints, but they are prudential rather than moral and relate to the wisdom, capacity, and credibility of foreign adventures, rather than to their justness. The main problem with the states of contemporary Italy was not that they were motivated by greed and ambition, but that they lacked the wisdom, capacity, and credibility for success, and were instead dominated by foreign powers, reliant upon mercenary militia rather than a citizen army, and brought to their knees by a religion with its gaze fixed firmly in the stars. As a consequence the condition of Italians, Machiavelli contends, 'is more enslaved than the Hebrews, more servile than the Persians, more dispersed than the Athenians, without a head, without order, beaten, despoiled, torn, pillaged, and having endured ruin of every sort'.[31] Having been at the heart of the great Roman Empire, how could the condition of Italy have plummeted to such a deplorable low, and what could be done to retrieve the situation? It was to his beloved ancients that Machiavelli turned for the answer. In their company he felt fully at home, relaxed, forgot his considerable cares, and drank of their wisdom. Through his reading in the evenings, Machiavelli maintains, 'I enter the ancient courts of ancient men, where, received by them lovingly, I feed on the food that alone is mine and that I was born for. There I am not ashamed to speak with them and to ask them the reason for their actions; and they in their humanity reply to me'.[32]

At the end of the Peloponnesian War, Greece was still bedevilled by wars which resulted in the erosion of city-state autonomy, and by a significant Persian presence and influence in Greek affairs. Persia's preoccupations away from its western borders did not make it feasible to conquer European Greece, but it nevertheless wished to prevent Athens, Sparta, or Corinth from dominating the peninsula. The King's Peace orchestrated by Persia gave rise to various manœuvres and alliances involving Thebes, Corinth, Sparta, and Athens and designed to prevent a preponderance of power in the hands of one city-state. The European Greek city-states comprised for a short time a system based on rules and agreements, supported by money and diplomatic initiatives from Persia.[33]

In the eastern part of the Greek world dynasties emerged as a consequence of the constraints imposed by the King's Peace in the European Greek peninsula and because of a weakening of Persian control over the coastal and adjacent regions of Asia Minor, but by the middle of the fourth century BC Macedonia began to expand and dominate. During the 340s Philip II dominated Greek politics, and by 338 he controlled the mainland. He acceded to the throne in 360 or 359 at 24 years of age, and consolidated his position by murder and bribery. He was, in Demosthenes' view, an 'unscrupulous and clever opportunist'.[34]

He was able to combine the role of king with that of mercenary commander, distributing the territorial spoils of his conquests to his troops. In 337, capitalizing on the anti-Persian pan-Hellenic sentiment he sensed, Philip convened a council of Greek city-states, which he called upon to join him on an expedition to Asia Minor to defeat the Persians.[35] Isocrates had already called upon Philip to unite the Greeks against the Persians, but apart from the glory of conquest the Macedonian king needed a vast Asian empire to maintain his expensive forces.[36] Isocrates had hoped that the union would be voluntary, but Philip's well-disciplined, well-paid, and formidable force, with a wanton disregard for campaign seasons, brought it about by force.

Philip was assassinated in July 336, an event which delayed rather than aborted the Persian campaign. His son Alexander, who was not above suspicion in the incident, seized his inheritance with a fervour that was to transform the known world. Philip's death occasioned the opportunity for dissidence, and Alexander's first task was to impress himself upon Macedonia's enemies in the north, Thrace and Illyria. He then brutally destroyed a recalcitrant Thebes before embarking upon a twelve-year campaign in Asia.

The army of 37,000 was modest in size, and included 5,000 cavalry. Alexander combined light-armed infantry, javelin-men, and archers with cavalry charges, backed by a 9,000 strong infantry phalanx.[37] By 332 Alexander had gained Syria and Palestine and was advancing in Egypt, and two years later declared himself the legitimate heir to the Persian Empire. He was by example an inspiring figure, at once generous and ruthless. He was also daring to the point of recklessness. He risked his own life with scant regard for his succession, and populated the far-flung corners of his empire with sparsely garrisoned Alexandrias. The Greek mercenaries he stationed in these remote areas quickly became disaffected.

Alexander's empire was not institutionally united, but instead the sum of various titles united in his person. He was King of Macedonia; President of the League of Corinth, the members of which remained relatively autonomous; reputed Pharaoh of Egypt; and the great King of Persia, although most of the Persian Empire evaded his control.[38] Following Alexander's death from fever in 323 at the age of 33, the next fifty years were characterized by bitter internecine struggle between his generals and their heirs for the spoils of an empire fragmenting into kingdoms: the kingdom of Macedon, the empires of the Seleucids incorporating Syria and much of Asia Minor, and Egypt, which was controlled by the Ptolemies.

Some writers have taken Plutarch's life of Alexander the Great to demonstrate a genuine cosmopolitan principle at work, in which the distinction between barbarian and Greek was to give way to mutual equality, and citizenship of the *polis* to membership of the universal empire, governed by one law and one system of justice.[39] There is certai..ly evidence that Alexander wished to unite the higher races of Macedonia, Greece, and Persia, but this was not his policy towards others. Alexander appointed Persians to senior military positions and encouraged his generals to marry Persian women, and he himself wore Persian dress. The policy was not one that greatly pleased the Greeks, and after his death many abandoned their Persian wives.

For Machiavelli, both Philip II and Alexander the Great were men of *virtù* and were invoked as exemplifications of good political practice, but not without some reservations. Philip is praised for the organization of his Macedonian army, which made him less subject to fortune's malice (*The Prince*, 87), and for seizing the opportunity to dominate Greece while other states languished or absorbed themselves in comedies (*Art of War*, 725).[40] He was not afraid to transform the institutions and personnel in the provinces he conquered, moving 'men from province to province as shepherds move their sheep' (*Discourses*, I. 26, pp. 177). Like all those who from low origins or low fortune become great, he practised fraud well (*Discourses*, II. 13, pp. 310–2). While in charge of the Theban army he led it to victory and then deprived the Thebans of their liberty (*The Prince*, 79). Philip's greatest mistake was not to avenge a wrong done to one in his court, and instead to reward the wrongdoer, so enraging the victim that he assassinated the King of Macedonia (*Discourses*, II. 28, pp. 367–9).

Alexander, like Caesar, was lavish with other people's money, which only served to increase the reputations of the two men at home (*The Prince*, 94). Both were wise enough to aspire to imitate great leaders—Alexander emulated Achilles, and Caesar, Alexander (*The Prince*, 90)—and neither was afraid to face danger in the front rank of his troops (*Art of War*, 725). Both were audacious in the face of fortune, but even they were thwarted by her might.[41]

Alexander is praised for the power of his oratory in inspiring his troops (*Art of War*, 661), and for having achieved greatness by arming his own people.[42] Along with his father, Philip, Alexander is admired for having conquered the world (*Art of War*, 725). It was the ambition of their successors that lost the empire (*The Prince*, 44). But it is not the Macedonian example that the modern prince or republic is urged to imitate, but the example of the state that crushed it. In this respect, as Butterfield tells us, Machiavelli entered 'with an almost medieval rigidity into the Renaissance cult and imitation of ancient Rome'.[43]

Experience of the Ancients: Rome

It was Rome which at the end of the sixth century BC freed itself from its Etruscan kings and became an aristocratic republic with two consuls. It first consolidated its position in Italy and the Greek southern Italian colonies, and then conquered the entire Mediterranean area, including north Africa and the Hellenistic east, eventually incorporating large parts of western Europe into its diverse empire. The Roman Republic lasted from 509 BC until the defeat of Mark Antony by Gaius Octavius in 31 BC. *Imperium populi Romani* emphasized the dominance and pride of the people who constituted a great nation, whereas the Augustan *imperium Romanum* retained the favourable evaluative connotations of pride, duty, and national self-respect; the idea of the dominance of the people was replaced by the idea of a higher personality to whom the citizen owed respect.[44] Although Augustus was ostensibly first among equals (*princeps*), he effectively became a monarch, a willing recipient of the homage and loyalty traditionally afforded to the *imperium populi Romani*. He was in some works of art depicted as a pharaoh and by implication associated with the gods. Egypt was an immense source of wealth and not formally a province, but instead the property of the *princeps*. Augustus saw his own prestige and honour resting not upon the formal powers assigned to him but upon the authority (*auctoritas*) he exuded, consolidated by his immense wealth and the power to dominate by patronage.[45] His imperial successors gradually adorned a majestic aura leading to deification. From AD 282 emperors were no longer required to be ratified by the Senate, and by the end of the empire citizens were compelled to prostrate themselves before the emperor, with only the most important of his entourage allowed the honour of kissing the hem of his splendidly adorned garments.[16]

The end of the Roman Empire is conventionally dated 476 with the deposition of the last emperor in the West, Romulus Augustulus, as a consequence of the invasion of the western provinces by the barbarian Huns, Vandals, Visigoths, and Ostrogoths.[47] The empire was, however, weak and in disarray long before, and had transferred its centre to Byzantium in the East under the Emperor Constantine, who in 313 AD proclaimed Christianity as the preferred religion of the empire. Christianity, while fulfilling the need to promote social cohesiveness, turned men's eyes away from earthly glory and secular honour and towards salvation and the rewards of heaven.[48] The eastern part of the empire was to endure for a thousand years after its western counterpart. Its demise came with the conquest of Constantinople by the Turks in 1453.

It was the Roman Republic that Machiavelli admired: its form of government; its method of expansion; and its use of religion, particularly in relation to military affairs.

Let us first take its form of government. After 510 the Etruscan kings of Rome were replaced by two consuls, who were chosen by an assembly of adult male citizens. In addition the consuls were advised by the Senate, composed of former magistrates. These three elements characterized the whole of the republican period, which was effectively aristocratic rule, constrained with varying degrees of intensity by the popular assembly.[49] Unlike in Athens, the tenure of offices was restricted to one year, a principle that was not blatantly disregarded until the closing century of republicanism in Rome. The Senate was composed of a more or less permanent membership.[50] The people were originally divided into what were effectively castes, the patricians purportedly descended from the ancient tribal aristocracy, and the plebeians or common class, the former of which initially dominated the offices of government. The first two centuries of the republic saw the manifestation of competition and rivalry between the patricians and plebeians, known as the st..uggle of the orders; and the plebeians gradually forced concessions, including their own assembly, *concilium plebis* (471 BC). In 342 BC the plebeians were admitted to the consulate, and as a consequence a mixed nobility emerged.[51] In 286 BC the decisions of the *concilium plebis*, plebiscites, became binding not only for plebeians, but also for patricians.[52] Divisions from then on were largely based on wealth and not caste.

Polybius likened this form of government to Lycurgus' Spartan constitution. The Roman constitution was, Polybius thought, the best existing in his time, because it combined elements of monarchy in the consuls, of aristocracy in the Senate, and of democracy in the power wielded by the people, and this constituted the foundation of its stability.[53] The source of stability, however, is more likely to have been the dominance of the Senate. It had no legal or constitutional authority for dominating the government, but did so nevertheless because of its own standing and prestige, that is, *auctoritas senatus*.[54]

Machiavelli admires Rome because it had judiciously incorporated elements of monarchy, aristocracy, and democracy, and far from seeing harmony as necessary to the well-being of a city, contends that the clashes between the dispositions of the populace and the upper class brought about the blend of estates that constitutes the 'perfect commonwealth'. It is this clash, Machiavelli argues, that brings about all legislation conducive to liberty (*Discourses*, I. 1–6, pp. 100–18), and what contributed in no small part to the greatness of Rome was the capacity to indict publicly those citizens who constituted a danger to the freedom of the state (*Discourses*, I. 7, p. 124). In the case of Manlius Capitolinus, for example, we have an exemplary citizen, perverted by envy and an overwhelming desire to rule, embarking upon a rebellion against the Senate and the laws of Rome. Although the populace took delight in that which disadvantaged the nobility, the Tribunes of the plebeians nevertheless indicted Capitolinus and sentenced him to death (*Discourses*, III. 8, pp. 426–7). Capitolinus was a man out of tune with his times, because had Rome had a corrupt populace he would have succeeded in becoming a tyrant. This confirms, for Machiavelli, 'that a bad citizen cannot do much harm in a republic that is not corrupt' (*Discourses*, III. 8, p. 426).

It was this lack of corruption that rendered safe for Rome the provision for a temporary dictator with limitations upon his powers. In conditions of extreme peril, whether occasioned by internal or external factors, a republic is unable to act swiftly and decisively and would come to grief without recourse to an emergency dictatorship. It is only when corruption has set in that a dictatorship can prove harmful to a republic. It was not this provision, Machiavelli argues, that made it possible for Caesar to become a tyrant, but the power he attained as a seasoned military commander which precipitated his self-proclamation. Dictators proclaimed according to the law ensured the preservation of the Republic in times of danger. (*Discourses*, I. 33–4, pp. 190–6).

It was, Machiavelli believed, the patriotism and loyalty of Rome's citizens, and their lack of corruption, that made it possible to retain freedom and liberty throughout the tumultuous clashes of patricians and plebeians. The Roman populace exhibited a basic goodness, piety, and loyalty which ensured, in the absence of corruption, that the governance of Rome was better facilitated. In contemporary times the German people still exhibited such goodness and piety. In contrast, modern Italy was corrupt and nothing good could be expected of its citizens (*Discourses*, I. 55, pp. 243–4).

The second element of Republican Rome that Machiavelli admired was its method of expansion. It did not attempt to enslave its neighbours, and indeed entered into different types of relation with its allies according to circumstances, extending citizenship when appropriate, or when forced by the social wars, and sharing the spoils of war with her Italian allies in foreign campaigns around the Mediterranean and Greece. The underlying conception of Roman *imperium* was not territorial, although it did enter into landed relations, but instead one of command by an *imperator* and obedience to those commands. As Andrew Lintott suggests, in all the relations into which the Romans entered with other peoples, even those they called friends and allies, they 'expected their commands to be obeyed, even when they allowed a great deal of *de facto* autonomy and frequently exercised power by indirect means'.[55] Rome endeavoured, where possible, to place the landed gentry in control of its provinces, making it clear from the outset on whose pleasure their survival depended.[56] Up until the mid-third century BC Roman influence was largely confined to Italy. Campaigns against Carthage and in Greece, as well as against the kingdoms of Asia Minor, formerly part of the Macedonian Empire, resulted in a considerable increase in territory and exposed the weaknesses in a system of government so heavily reliant for its functioning upon tradition and authority.[57]

Rome was always at pains to emphasize the justness of its wars, which were motivated not only by greed, but by a concern for the safety of its allies.[58] Like other dominant powers, however, it did not allow considerations of justice to interfere with its self-interest.[59]

For Machiavelli imperialism is merely the extension of the natural impulse to want more, and to get it if one has the capacity to do so. Living upon one's own resources is not a virtue to which the human condition inclines us (*Discourses*, I. 1, p. 102). Not every commonwealth is constituted to follow this impulse, but because human affairs are always in motion a commonwealth instituted to preserve its *status quo* may be forced upon a contrary course of action for which it is ill-equipped in the intensely competitive environment of international relations. As a matter of prudence, then, a commonwealth should be designed for expansion because

it is impossible for a state to remain for ever in the peaceful enjoyment of its liberties and its narrow confines; for, though it may not molest other states, it will be molested by them, and, when thus molested, there will arise in it the desire, and the need, for conquest. It will find, too, that, when it has no external foe, there will be one at home, for this seems necessarily to happen in all large cities. (*Discourses*, II. 19, pp. 335–6)

If a commonwealth is designed for expansion, in the event that it should by circumstances be forced to do so, those additional lands and subjects acquired (on the proviso that the Roman methods are followed) can be held with greater ease (*Discourses*, I. 6, pp. 121 4). Machiavelli's fundamental assumption in all this is that power promotes security (*Discourses*, I. 1, p. 102), and without security the liberties of a republic are in jeopardy. As Skinner quite rightly suggests, 'the pursuit of dominion abroad is thus held to be a precondition of liberty at home'.[60]

In order to convert a city into a great empire it is necessary to ensure that a large male population is acquired. There are two ways of ensuring this: either by attracting foreigners by making access to the city and residence in it relatively easy, or by forcing people to inhabit it by destroying the towns that lay around it and thus compelling their populations to move into the city. Rome took the latter course and by the time of the reign of its sixth king had 80,000 bearers of arms living in the city. The principle, Machiavelli argues, is analogous to good farming. The first branches of a plant are cut off in order that the roots may strengthen and produce more productive and fruit-bearing branches (*Discourses*, II. 3, p. 282). Rome also allowed relatively free access to foreigners, and was thus, in conjunction with the first method of gaining a large male population, able to raise 280,000 men and arm them. Athens and Sparta, Machiavelli argues, never reached the grandeur of Rome because they did not use the same methods of enlarging their male populations, and were consequently never able to raise more than 20,000 men under arms each.

Continuing the analogy with nature, Machiavelli argues that a slender trunk cannot support heavy branches. If a small republic attempts to extend itself and subject larger republics, it will experience a great deal of difficulty in supporting them. The branches become too heavy for the trunk and the least wind weakens the tree. This is what happened to Sparta. Having a slender trunk, discouraging foreigners from entering its city, it took over most of Greece, but as soon as Thebes rebelled and the others followed suit, the trunk was stripped of its branches. Rome, however, had such a strong and powerful trunk that it could easily support the largest of branches. It was the procedure of strengthening the trunk and then expanding its territories that made 'Rome great and exceedingly powerful' (*Discourses*, II. 3, p. 283).

If a city wishes to expand, it may study three methods which republics have used in the past and which serve as lessons for future action. First, there is the method of forming leagues of several republics in which 'no one of them had preference, authority or rank above the others' (*Discourses*, II. 4, p. 283). There are distinct disadvantages to this method, which outweigh its advantages. Its advantages are that it does not necessarily involve war, and that it is relatively easy to hold the new areas incorporated into it. The disadvantages are that such a league of republics finds it difficult to expand because each member is distinct and has its own resources. This makes consultation difficult and decision-making a slow process. Further, such leagues are not as enthusiastic about acquiring new dominions because they all share in the expansion and do not appreciate acquisitions as much as would one republic which enjoys the benefit of the whole.

Such leagues, Machiavelli contests, seem to have fixed limits beyond which they will not go. Twelve to fourteen communities appear to be the optimum size. When this size is reached they believe that they can easily defend themselves against all comers. Necessity does not require them to expand their dominions, and because all share in further expansion they may not feel that there is any advantage in acquiring more territories. Gaining more allies in the confederation would enhance the possibility of confusion and inaction by making the decision-making process more cumbersome. Further, to subject territories to the rule of the confederacy would, they believe, have no particular advantage.

When such leagues reach their optimum size and they feel they have provided well for their security, they tend to engage in two activities. In the first place, they offer security and protection to others who are willing to pay for it, and secondly, they are prepared to hire out armies of mercenaries to princes who need arms to execute their enterprises. Cesare Borgia was one such prince who used mercenaries, and Florence also hired French and Swiss arms. Such confederacies are not effective in increasing the number of subjects, and quickly fall into ruin if they exceed their optimum size.

A second method of expansion, of which Machiavelli disapproves, is to make 'states subjects instead of allies' (*Discourses*, II. 4, p. 284). Sparta and Athens followed this method and were unable to hold on to the dominions they had conquered. It is a difficult and tiresome task to take over the government of a subject city, especially if that city has been used to self-rule. In order to do this you need strong armed forces. If such a means of expansion is undertaken, Machiavelli argues, it is essential to gain help from allies and to expand the population of your own city. Sparta and Athens had recourse to neither of these and thus were eventually ruined (*Discourses*, ıı. 4, p. 285).

The third method of expansion, which the Romans undertook and which Machiavelli recommends be followed, is that of 'forming alliances in which you reserve to yourself the headship, the seat in which the central authority resides, and the right of initiative' (*Discourses*, ıı. 4, p. 284). The Romans made many alliances with states in Italy and reserved the right of issuing orders in the empire. Rome's allies soon fell under the influence of that city and shed blood on its behalf. The great armies of allies which went out of Italy to transform kingdoms into provinces of the empire subjected to the rule of the empire people who were already accustomed to being ruled by kings. The territories were administered by Roman governors and had been conquered by armies carrying the Roman insignia. They therefore recognized Rome as their superior and bowed to its authority. Rome's allies in Italy soon found themselves encircled by subjects of Rome, and found that they were being overshadowed by the sheer enormity of the city, which was extremely well armed and protected. Fearing their position in relation to Rome, the allies formed a league to reduce Rome's power. Against its might and strength the Italian allies soon crumbled, and ended up themselves not allies but subjects of Rome.

By increasing its population through a policy of destroying the towns outside its walls, and by allowing relatively free access to the city, Rome laid such firm foundations that it was able to build an empire with the help of its Italian allies, and then to subject those very allies to its rule. No other empire before or after that of Rome has adopted these methods. It is because such methods have not been imitated, and indeed have been considered to be of no consequence or relevance, that Italy has 'become the prey of anybody who has wanted to overrun this land' (*Discourses*, ıı. 5, p. 288)

The third feature of the Roman Republic that Machiavelli thought ought to be imitated was the pagan religious practices that contributed to the social cohesiveness of its citizens. Religion in Rome was an effective means of social control whose offices were in the hands of the aristocracy.[61] The Roman calendar was divided into days when public business could be entered into, and those when for religious reasons it could not. Because the priests sat in the Senate, combining religious and political power and authority, meetings of the Senate were exempt. The taking of auspices was a matter of course in sanctioning or discouraging public acts, and unfavourable signs could be used to prohibit public business on days for which it was previously scheduled. The declaration and conduct of war was integrally related to religious rituals and practices. Mars the war-god was the object of constant cult worship, and the soldier's oath of loyalty sworn to an officer, and his successors, on each period of military service was the solemn *sacramentum*.

The Roman religion was civic in that the greater good of the state was at the heart of the religious cults that worshipped such gods as Jupiter, Juno, and Mars. The Roman people attributed their extraordinary success to their piety. For such religious devotion the gods had rewarded them. Where piety was such an important publicly defining mode of practice, the favour of the priests was eagerly sought, and their advice readily accepted, to ensure the continuing good grace of the gods. Such reverence provided politicians with a considerable degree of manipulative control. Accusations of impiety were extremely serious and were used to discourage acts of disloyalty to the state. Religion was a means by which fear could be focused and organized for the benefit of the state.

Polybius viewed this 'scrupulous fear of the gods' as the most important distinguishing feature giving strength to the Roman Republic. Its importance for him was not as an exhibition of genuine and sincere piety on the part of the nobles, but as an effective means of social control. He maintains that 'to my mind, the ancients were not acting without purpose or at random, when they brought in among the vulgar those opinions about the gods, and the belief in the punishments in Hades: much rather do I think that men nowadays are acting rashly and foolishly in rejecting them.'[62] This is the view of Roman religion that Machiavelli echoes.

Of those people to be praised, Machiavelli says, founders of religions deserve to be put on the top of the list, because it is they who give the strongest foundations to the state. This is not to say that Machiavelli was devoutly religious, although, making the fideistic distinction between faith and reason, he subscribed to the conventional commonplaces of Christianity.[63] Christianity, for him, was the true religion, which had been corrupted with catastrophic consequences by its self-seeking guardians. Its interpreters had emphasized Christianity's other-worldliness and humility instead of its vigour and sanctioning of the love and honour of one's *patria*.[64] Machiavelli's political, rather than theological, judgement of religions is in terms of their practical secular effects. He praises the religion instituted in Rome by Numa because it was used 'as the instrument necessary above all others for the maintenance of a civilized state' (*Discourses*, I. 11, p. 139). In this respect, Christianity's emphasis upon humility had proved a hindrance to such an objective, 'especially when used in dealing with arrogant men who, either out of envy or for some other cause, have come to hate you' (*Discourses*, II. 14, p. 312). In other words, he has a purely instrumental view of religion, when viewed politically. It is an invaluably useful tool to be used by governments in keeping order in the state. The fear of God is the most effective means of instilling into the populace discipline, obedience, and order. Without the fear of God a state either falls into ruin or needs to be subjected to the fear of a prince.

The existence of a religion in itself is not sufficient to keep a state in order. In Machiavelli's view, religion has to be 'properly used' (*Discourses*, I. 13, pp. 146–7), and by this he means that due respect should be shown to its ceremonies and institutions, that is, its rituals and practices should be maintained without corruption. The reason is, again, instrumental. If rulers do not show due reverence and respect for religion and appear to be contemptuous of it, then people will be less strong in their faith and question either the authority of the leader or the desirability of the religion.

The fact that Christianity had not been used well in Italy, and that its ceremonies had not been maintained uncorrupted was, in Machiavelli's view, the reason why his contemporary Italy was in such a sorry plight. He contends that 'The first debt which we, Italians, owe to the Church and to priests, therefore, is that we have become irreligious and perverse' (*Discourses*, i. 12, p. 144). Machiavelli bemoans the fact that the Roman Catholic Church did not possess the temporal strength and authority to subordinate to itself the whole of Italy, and to provide leadership in spiritual and secular matters. Worse still, its weakness was compounded, since because of its recourse to foreign allies to protect its own territories, it prevented other Italian states from taking the lead.

Religion not only reduces a people to obedience in the internal affairs of a state, it also inspires them in their foreign enterprises. Machiavelli says quite explicitly that 'It was religion that facilitated whatever enterprise the senate and the great men of Rome designed to undertake' (*Discourses*, i. 11, p. 139).

In military affairs the use of religion is one of the best methods available for inspiring loyalty and promoting a courageous spirit in preparation for battle. In *The Art of War* Machiavelli states:

Also very powerful in keeping the ancient soldiers well disposed were religion and the oath sworn when they were taken into service, because in all their transgressions they were threatened not alone with the ills they could fear from men but with those they could expect from God. This condition, mingled with other religious customs, many times made every sort of undertaking easy for the ancient generals, and always will make them so, where religion is feared and observed. (*Art of War*, 661)

Machiavelli contends that the use of soothsayers, diviners, and oracles should be judicious. The Romans made extensive use of auguries 'in entering upon military enterprises, in leading forth their armies, on engaging in battles, and in all their important enterprises, whether civic or military' (*Discourses*, i. 14, p. 148). In their armies they had officials called poultrymen who were responsible for taking auspices. Before a military encounter the poultry would be brought out, and if they pecked at the corn it was considered a good omen from the gods. If they did not peck it was a bad omen.

The Roman leaders were, in Machiavelli's view, so astute that if they considered a time right for attack they would ignore auspices that suggested the contrary. They would do so, however, in a way that did not appear irreverent. In an important engagement against the Samnites the poultry failed to peck, but the head poultryman judged that the time was nevertheless right to attack. His deceit came to light and was conveyed to the consul Papirius, who warned his nephew the messenger to mind his own business well, because as far as his army was concerned the poultry had pecked. Careful not to have his own irreverence exposed, Papirius placed the head poultryman at the front of the army, where he was accidentally killed by a Roman javelin. The consul announced that the gods favoured them in the death of the poultryman who had lied, and thus they were absolved of blame. This, for Machiavelli, was a fine example of a consul 'knowing how to accommodate nicely his plans to the auspices' (*Discourses*, i. 14, p. 150). The practice of consulting auspices when well used almost always inspired 'troops to go confidently into battle, the which confidence almost always leads to victory' (*Discourses*, i. 14, p. 150).

In summary, then, irrespective of its effect on the soul, or upon prospects of salvation, Machiavelli is concerned only with the temporal effects of religion. Christianity had led men into effeminate ways, teaching them to spend too much time on their knees looking up to their heavenly reward, instead of standing up courageously and looking to their affairs on earth. He looked to the pagan religions because they valued courage, honour, and glory, qualities that promoted civic virtue. The new generation of Italians needed such inspiration if it was to rise to the challenge that it faced.

The fourth feature of the Roman Republic that Machiavelli admired was its citizens' militia, with its strict disciplinary code, and its brutal system of punishment, which instilled in soldiers a greater fear of the consequences of failure than of the enemy. Polybius tells us, for example, that

it sometimes happens that men confront certain death at their stations, because, from their fear of the punishment awaiting them at home, they refuse to quit their post: while others, who have lost shield or spear or any other arm on the field, throw themselves upon the foe, in hopes of recovering what they have lost, or of escaping by death from certain disgrace and the insults of their relations.[65]

Military command and power were not clearly distinguished from civilian positions of authority. The command of armies fell to consuls and praetors, who when the empire expanded became governors over the conquered territories. Military command offered considerable opportunities for the acquisition of wealth, the dispensation of patronage, and support in elections to republican offices. Towards the end of the republic and during the first two hundred years of the Principate the mi..tary sometimes held the decisive hand. The struggle for political power often depended upon the loyalty of the contestants' armies.[66] Sulla, for example, achieved a position of power by military might after a civil war, and his attempt to prevent a repetition by a programme of legislation dating from 82 BC, which was intended to regulate magisterial offices and curb the power of the tribunes, was rapidly dismantled or ignored.[67]

Rome during the early period of the republic did not have a standing army. Landowners were called upon as part of their citizen duty—as central to their public persona as the right to vote in the assembly—to enter military service, at their own expense. When campaigns were limited to Italy and confined to seasons, the property-owners were less likely to face financial ruin. As campaigns became more distant and sustained, many small farmers left the land and therefore ceased to be liable for military service. In response to the growing crisis in recruitment, but also for reasons of power and influence among the aristocratic groupings, the property qualification, long thought to be the basis of a soldier's loyalty, was abolished at the end of the second century BC. Armies now became extremely reliant upon their commanders for a share in the spoils of booty, and their happiness and discipline depended upon the commander fulfilling this need. In turn, the gratitude of the military could be used by the commander to bolster his political ambitions.

The growth of the empire necessitated admitting troops of non-Italian origin into the military, recruited from all parts of the empire and united, at least in part, by a common duty to Rome.[68] By the second half of the first century BC, during the Flavian dynasty, with the exception of the praetorian guard, less than 50 per cent of soldiers attached to the legions were born in Italy. The auxiliaries in Britain, for example, were usually levied from newly conquered areas, and included Germans, Gauls, Spaniards, and soldiers from the Orient.[69]

The Art of War

Of his major writings, *The Art of War* was the only one to be published in Machiavelli's lifetime, and it became an extremely popular treatise, but it did not succeed in displacing the standard tracts on warfare, which continued to appear in new editions and which, like Machiavelli's, harked back to the Ancients.[70] In it he extols the virtues of a citizen army, motivated to train diligently on public holidays in preference to the pursuit of more trivial pleasures. His ideal was a combination of the Greek and Macedonian phalanx with the Roman legionary composition and chain of command. He placed a great deal of emphasis upon infantry and greatly undervalued the importance of cavalry in both Roman and modern Italian warfare. Although he follows Polybius in many of his details of Roman warfare, Machiavelli's contemporary experience of mercenary troops, who relied heavily upon cavalry, disposed him to ignore the historian's strictures. The defeat of the Roman army by Hannibal in 216 BC Polybius attributes to the superior cavalry forces c. the Carthaginians: 'a lesson to posterity that in actual war it is better to have half the number of infantry, and the superiority in cavalry, than to engage your enemy with an equality in both'.[71] The Romans did, in fact, reorganize their cavalry and, aided by a strong constitution and determined consuls, went on to regain Italy and incorporate most of the known world into their empire. Machiavelli contends, however, that peoples who value cavalry more than infantry, as modern Italy herself did, are exposed to dangers of all kinds. The ruination of Italy by constant foreign interventions is attributed to 'no other sin than that she has given little attention to soldiers on foot and put all her soldiers on horseback' (*Art of War*, 602). Cavalry serve useful associated functions in war, such as scouting and pursuing a routed enemy, but are next to useless in the field, which is the principal arena of battle.

While he was not a slave to the method of example, he could not reconcile himself to the view that modern military inventions may have the advantage over the ancients. The German use of the pike, for example, while useful in repelling a cavalry attack, was positively dangerous should the cavalry dismount and cut into the unarmoured pike-men with swords. The Romans were again superior in that their armour and swords equipped them well for both defensive and offensive engagements. A combination of German pikes and muskets, with the Roman shield and sword, was the ideal equipment for the infantry (*Art of War*, 598–601). While he was prepared to concede a role for artillery, mainly to augment the function of the javelin and bow, he did not envisage its importance or potential for the transformation of warfare (*Art of War*, 635–8; cf. *Discourses*, II. 17, pp. 321–8). Firearms, in particular the harquebus (the forerunner of the musket), in Machiavelli's view, were of little use in battle except for frightening peasants and cavalry with the noise (*Art of War*, 625 and 654).

Machiavelli's apparent *naïveté* in practical military organization, although such matters were entrusted to him among his formal duties as secretary to the Ten of War,[72] has led many commentators to pronounce this aspect of his writings the least 'modern'. Federico Chabod suggests 'that he who in his political thought was a man of the Renaissance became a man of the thirteenth century when he turned his attention to military matters'.[73] Anglo attests this view when he contends that *The Art of War* 'would be more properly regarded as perhaps the greatest—though certainly not the last—medieval compilation'.[74] Furthermore, Azar Gat suggests that Machiavelli's belief in the efficacy of history as a storehouse of examples for his political theories was found most wanting in military matters. Gat argues, 'it was in the military sphere—rapidly and decisively influenced by technological change—that this outlook on history and theory faced an almost immediate breakdown'.[75]

It is also well recognized that Machiavelli's military ideas go far beyond these practical prescriptions. The aim of establishing a conscripted citizen militia is to take the responsibility for security and the prosecution of war out of the hands of a privileged self-interested élite. Military training in a responsible citizens' militia is designed to revive civic virtues, and values of honour, courage, loyalty, and national pride associated with the ancients and lost to Machiavelli's contemporary Italy. In Machiav_.li's view, the importance of having good arms is imperative. He goes so far as to say that 'The art of war is all that is expected of a ruler' (*The Prince*, 87). Neglect of such an art is one sure way of losing your state. Machiavelli's advice to a prince is that he should indulge himself more systematically in military exercises in peacetime than in war, in order to reap the benefit if circumstances change for the worse (*The Prince*, 87–90).

The arms a republic or a prince should possess are not those of mercenaries or auxiliaries. Machiavelli's diplomatic experience had taught him that neither is to be trusted. The experience of Florence in using Paolo Vitelli in its conflict with Pisa, and his betrayal of his employer when victory was in sight, were enough to turn Machiavelli permanently off the use of mercenary troops.[76] Mercenaries are little better than useless, having no reason to fight other than the small amount of pay offered. This is not sufficient to make them loyal or lay down their lives (*Discourses*, I. 43, p. 218). In *The Prince* Machiavelli issues an even sterner warning: 'Mercenaries and auxiliaries are useless and dangerous. If a prince bases the defence of his state on mercenaries he will never achieve stability or security' (*The*

Prince, 77). They are simply not to be trusted. They lack the fear of God, which makes them ill-disciplined, disloyal, cowardly, and afraid. They are thirsty for power, but also faithless, and in war they either desert you or disperse. These sentiments are echoed once again in *The Florentine History*, when he refers to the use of mercenaries as an 'irrational and perverted method of carrying on war'.[77] Mercenary leaders are ambitious, but their ambitions in external affairs are self-interested and detrimental to the common good.[78] The condition of Italy was, in Machiavelli's view, a consequence of the ambitions of mercenary leaders.

Of all soldiers, auxiliaries are the most dangerous to use in military campaigns. They are paid for by your ally and remain loyal to his command. Machiavelli argues that a prince or a republic should adopt any course of action other than to allow auxiliary forces into the state to defend it. Experience shows us, he argues, that an 'ambitious' prince or republic has no better chance of gaining a city or province than to be invited in to protect it. He who is so ambitious as to invite the aid of auxiliaries is attempting to gain what he has little chance of keeping. Ambition can often blind a man into striving to satisfy a present desire without giving due heed to the evils that may befall him as a consequence (*Discourses*, II. 20, p. 341). After the Vitelli affair Machiavelli did in fact spend much of his time organizing, recruiting, and inspecting a Florentine militia force, which was to reduce her reliance upon auxiliary and mercenary troops.

To rescue Italy from the barbarians required a well-trained, civically motivated citizens' militia, led in the first instance by a prince strong enough to impose his will upon a corrupt people. Money would not guarantee him success in military affairs. The 'sinews of war lay not in money, but in good soldiers' (*Discourses*, II. 10, p. 301). Gold, of course, is necessary, but good soldiers are capable of getting it for themselves. It is, therefore, important to arm your own subjects, because in arming them, you arm yourself. However, in annexing new territories to your own, you should ensure that you disarm the people you have conquered.

The four elements identified, government, method of expansion, religion, and military organization, cannot be taken in isolation from Machiavelli's knowledge of more recent history and his own diplomatic experience. These together are interwoven with his exposition of the doctrine of *raison d'état*, and the complex interrelationship between *virtù*, *fortuna*, and *necessità*. These interrelations, the appropriate form of government, and the course of action to be pursued are circumstantially contingent. What is ideal in one set of circumstances may be unwise in another. The condition of contemporary Italy, Machiavelli believed, required a strong prince to fulfil the role of delivering the Italian people from the barbarians.

Notes

1. J. H. Geerken, 'Machiavelli: Magus, Theologian or Trickster?' *Machiavelli Studies*, 3 (1990), 95.
2. Some representative examples will suffice. Numerous interpreters have viewed his

teaching as evil. The seminal modern example is Leo Strauss, *Thoughts on Machiavelli* (Seattle and London, University of Washington Press, 1969). He is viewed as an elevated moral soul by B. Croce, *Politics and Morals* (London, Allen and Unwin, 1945), and Sebastian de Grazia, *Machiavelli in Hell* (Princeton, Princeton University Press, 1989). Frederick the Great condemned him as a friend to tyrants before adopting the methods himself. Rousseau, of course, saw *The Prince* as an advice book to republicans exposing the actions of monarchical rulers. For a view firmly placing Machiavelli in the civic republican humanist tradition see J. G. A. Pocock, *The Machiavellian Moment* (Princeton, Princeton University Press, 1975). With the rise of Italian nationalism Pasquale Villari claimed Machiavelli as an illustrious forerunner in *The Life and Times of Niccolò Machiavelli*, trans. Linda Villari (London, Benn, 1929). It is more generally accepted, however, that Machiavelli was a Florentine patriot. See e.g. Hanna Fenichel Pitkin, *Fortune is a Woman* (Berkeley, University of California Press, 1984). The classic view of Machiavelli as a political scientist is in Leonardo Olshki, *Machiavelli the Scientist* (Berkeley, Gillick, 1945), Herbert Butterfield, *The Statecraft of Machiavelli* (New York, Collier-Macmillan, 1967), James Burnham, *The Machiavellians: Defenders of Freedom* (London, Putman, 1943), and Ernst Cassirer, *The Myth of the State* (New Haven, Yale University Press, 1946). Garrett Mattingly counters this view by arguing that *The Prince* is a political satire. See Mattingly, 'Machiavelli's *Prince*: Political Science or Political Satire?', *American Scholar*, 27 (1958). An interesting development of Rousseau's and Mattingly's positions is to be found in Mary C. Dietz, 'Trapping the Prince: Machiavelli and the Politics of Deception', *American Political Science Review*, 80 (1986). She argued that Machiavelli attempted to dupe Lorenzo de' Medici into following the advice of *The Prince* in order to effect his downfall. A further development of this line portrays Machiavelli's vision of the world as one populated by confidence tricksters, engaged in different ways in the subtle art of public relations. See Wayne A. Rebhorn, *Foxes and Lions: Machiavelli's Confidence Men* (Ithaca, NY, Cornell University Press, 1988).

3. Martin Wight, *International Theory: The Three Traditions*, ed. Gabriele Wight and Brian Porter (London and Leicester, University of Leicester Press, 1991), 16 and 161. For Parkinson and Carr he is the first important pioneer of Realism. See F. Parkinson, *The Philosophy of International Relations: A Study in the History of Thought* (Beverly Hills, Calif., and London, Sage, 1977), 31, and E. H. Carr, *The 20 Years' Crisis 1919–1939* (London, Macmillan, 1939; 2nd edn. 1946), 63.

4. Michael Joseph Smith, *Realist Thought from Weber to Kissinger* (Baton Rouge, La., Louisiana State University Press, 1986), 10; and Giuseppe Prezzolini, *Machiavelli* (London, Hale, 1968), 51.

5. F. Melian Stawell, *The Growth of International Thought* (London, Thornton Butterworth, 1929), 79.

6. Steven Forde, 'Classical Realism', in T. Nardin and D. Mapel (eds.), *Traditions of International Ethics* (Cambridge, Cambridge University Press, 1992), 64.

7. Richard W. Sterling, *Ethics in a World of Power* (London, Oxford University Press, 1958), 237; and Torbjörn L. Knutsen, *A History of International Relations Theory* (Manchester, Manchester University Press, 1992).

8. Francis Fukuyama, *The End of History and the Last Man* (Harmondsworth, Penguin, 1992), 184.

9. Friedrich Meinecke, *Machiavellism: The Doctrine of Raison d'État and its Place in Modern History* (London, Routledge and Kegan Paul, 1962; first pub. 1924), 29 and 41.

10. R. B. J. Walker, *Inside/Outside: International Relations as Political Theory* (Cambridge, Cambridge University Press, 1993), 39. Also see Jim George, *Discourses of Global Politics: A Critical (Re)Introduction to International Relations* (Boulder, Colo., Rienner, 1994), 194–7.

11. Burnham, *The Machiavellians*, 29–35.

12. Strauss, *Thoughts on Machiavelli*, 11. Cf. the not uncommon view represented by Parel: 'He brought to the field of political enquiry the scientific spirit of detachment, which like a steel frame holds together his doctrines and gives them durability.' See Anthony Parel, 'Introduction: Machiavelli's Method and His Interpreters', in Anthony Parel (ed.), *The Political Calculus* (Toronto, University of Toronto Press, 1972), 3. Parel admits, however, that Machiavelli is not wholly detached, but that the elements of ideology and injunction that remain 'are kept within the bounds of scientific spirit' (p. 5).

13. Niccolò Machiavelli, *The Discourses*, ed. Bernard Crick, trans. Leslie J. Walker, rev. Brian Richardson (Harmondsworth, Penguin, 1970), I. 39, p. 207.

14. Niccolò Machiavelli, *The Prince*, trans. George Bull (Harmondsworth, Penguin, 1961).

15. Beroaldus, cited by A. H. Gilbert, *Machiavelli's Prince and its Forerunners* (Durham, NC, Duke University Press, 1938), 27.

16. Sheldon Wolin, *Politics and Vision* (Boston, Little Brown, 1960), 195–238.

17. See e.g. *The Prince*, 39–40: 'Political disorders can be quickly healed if they are seen well in advance (and only a prudent ruler has such foresight); when, for lack of a diagnosis, they are allowed to grow in such a way that everyone can recognize, remedies are too late.'

18. Butterfield, *The Statecraft of Machiavelli*, 23–33: and Sydney Anglo, *Machiavelli* (London, Paladin, 1971), 243.

19. Machiavelli did, of course, write history, and sometimes paused to impart the moral to the reader. After describing the banishment of Cosimo de' Medici from Florence in 1433, Machiavelli says of those who banished him that 'It would have been better for them to have died than to have allowed Cosimo to get off with his life, or to have allowed friends of his to be left behind in Florence. Great men should not be struck at, or, if they are, it should be to utterly destroy them' (*The Florentine History*, trans. W. K. Marriot (London, Dent, 1976), 177).

20. István Bejczy, 'The State as a Work of Art: Petrarch and his *Speculum principis* (xiv, 1)', *History of Political Thought*, 15 (1994), 314.

21. Cf. 'If the present be compared with the remote past, it is easily seen that in all cities and in all peoples there are the same desires and the same passions as there always were. So that, if one examines with diligence the past, it is easy to foresee the future of any commonwealth, and to apply those remedies which were used of old; or, if one does not find that remedies were used, to devise new ones owing to the similarity between events' (*Discourses*, I. 39, pp. 207–8).

22. F. Chabod, *Machiavelli and the Renaissance* (New York, Harper Torchbooks, 1958), 132.

23. Cf. 'men are born and live and die in an order which remains ever the same' (*Discourses*, I. 11, p. 142).

24. Letter No. 116 in *Machiavelli: The Chief Works and Others*, ed. Allan Gilbert, (Durham, NC, Duke University Press, 1989), 895–6. Even though characters vary, we are obstinate in the character we have.

25. 'Tercets on Ambition', in *Chief Works*, 736.

26. Elsewhere in *The Prince* Machiavelli says, 'men are wretched creatures who would not keep their word to you' (p. 100).

27. *History of Florence* in *Chief Works*, 1140.
28. *The Histories of Polybius*, trans. Evelyn S. Shackburgh (Bloomington, Ind., Indiana University Press, 1962), vi. 5–6.
29. Cecil H. Clough, *Machiavelli Researches* (Pubblicazioni della Sezione romanza dell' Istituto Universitario orientale, Napoli Studi, V. 3, 1967), 83.
30. These elements will be discussed in Part III.
31. For this quotation I use *The Prince*, trans. Harvey C. Mansfield Jr. (Chicago, Chicago University Press, 1985), 102.
32. Letter to Francesco Vettori, 10 Dec. 1513, in *The Prince*, trans. Mansfield, 109–10.
33. Adam Watson, *The Evolution of International Society* (London, Routledge, 1992), 62–8.
34. Cited in J. K. Davies, *Democracy and Classical Greece*, 2nd edn. (London, Fontana, 1993), 249.
35. John Keegan, *A History of Warfare* (London, Hutchinson, 1993), 258. The alliance was named the League of Corinth.
36. A. R. Burn, *The Penguin History of Greece* (Harmondsworth, Penguin, 1990), 332.
37. F. W. Walbank, *The Hellenistic World* (London, Fontana, 1992), 31.
38. Ernest Barker (ed. and trans.), *From Alexander to Constantine* (Oxford, Clarendon Press, 1956), 17.
39. See e.g. Derek Heater, *Citizenship* (London, Longman, 1990), 9–10. For the relevant extract from Plutarch see Barker (ed.), *Alexander to Constantine*, 6–8.
40. Machiavelli, *The Art of War*, in *Chief Works*.
41. Machiavelli, 'Tercets on Fortune', in *Chief Works*, 748–9.
42. Letter dated 26 Aug. 1513, in *Chief Works*, 925.
43. Butterfield, *The Statecraft of Machiavelli*, 46.
44. Richard Koebner, *Empire* (Cambridge, Cambridge University Press, 1961), 11.
45. David Shotter, *Augustus Caesar* (London, Routledge, 1991), 32–3. Machiavelli blamed Augustus for providing the conditions for corruption in disarming the Roman people. See Larry I. Peterman, 'Machiavelli's Dante and the Sources of Machiavellianism', *Polity*, 28 (1987).
46. Olga Tellegen-Couperus, *A Short History of Roman Law* (London, Routledge, 1993), 116–17.
47. Averil Cameron, *The Later Roman Empire AD 284–430* (London, Fontana, 1993), 187–8.
48. Hayden V. White, *The Greco-Roman Tradition* (New York, Harper and Row, 1973), 120. The Roman Empire will be examined more closely in relation to the tradition of a Universal Moral Order.
49. Michael Crawford, *The Roman Republic* (London, Fontana, 1992), 22–3.
50. M. I. Finley, *Politics in the Ancient World* (Cambridge, Cambridge University Press, 1991), 58.
51. White, *Greco-Roman Tradition*, 89; and Crawford, *Roman Republic*, 24–5.
52. Tellegen-Couperus, *Short History of Roman Law*, 7–8.
53. Polybius, *Histories*, vi. 3–11. Polybius says: 'For it is plain that we must regard as the *best* constitution that which partakes of all these three elements'; and 'every form of government that was unmixed, and rested on one species of power, was unstable' (vi. 3 and 10).
54. Shotter, *Augustus Caesar*, 8.
55. Andrew Lintott, *Imperium Romanum* (London, Routledge, 1993), 41–2.
56. Crawford, *Roman Republic*, 137.

57. Shotter, *Augustus Caesar*, 9.
58. Crawford, *Roman Republic*, 68.
59. Lintott, *Imperium Romanum*, 34.
60. Quentin Skinner, *Machiavelli* (Oxford, Oxford University Press, 1981), 73.
61. H. D. Jocelyn suggests that 'what distinguished Roman politicians from their foreign contemporaries was the fact that they supervised the whole apparatus of their community's official cult themselves, instead of leaving it in the hands of separate priesthoods recruited from elsewhere in their own or from another social class' ('The Roman Nobility and the Religion of the Republican State', *Journal of Religious History*, 4 (1966–7), 92).
62. Polybius, *Histories*, VI. 56.
63. Dante Germino, 'Second Thoughts on Leo Strauss's Machiavelli', *Journal of Politics*, 28 (1966).
64. de Grazia, *Machiavelli in Hell*, 89.
65. Polybius, *Histories*, VI. 37.
66. Tellegen-Couperus, *Short History of Roman Law*, 82.
67. J. F. Gardner, 'Introduction', *Caesar: The Conquest of Gaul* (Harmondsworth, Penguin, 1982), 8.
68. Keegan, *A History of Warfare*, 270.
69. R. G. Collingwood, *Roman Britain* (London, Oxford University Press, 1924), 20–1.
70. Anglo, *Machiavelli*, 139–41.
71. Polybius, *Histories*, III. 117. In *Discourses*, II. 18, pp. 328–33, Machiavelli discounts this evidence.
72. See J. R. Hale, *Machiavelli and Renaissance Italy* (Harmondsworth, Penguin, 1961). Also see Marvin Lunenfeld, 'The Art of War in Renaissance Florence: Leonardo, Machiavelli and Soderini', *Machiavelli Studies*, 3 (1990), 43–78.
73. Chabod, *Machiavelli and the Renaissance*, 103 n.
74. Anglo, *Machiavelli*, 142. Also see Michael Mallet, 'The Theory and Practice of Warfare in Machiavelli's Republic', in Gisela Bock, Quentin Skinner, and Maurizio Viroli (eds.), *Machiavelli and Republicanism* (Cambridge, Cambridge University Press, 1990), 173–80. For a slightly more sympathetic view see Felix Gilbert, 'Machiavelli: The Renaissance of the Art of War', in Peter Paret (ed.), *Makers of Modern Strategy from Machiavelli to the Nuclear Age* (Princeton, Princeton University Press, 1984), 11–31.
75. Azar Gat, 'Machiavelli and the Decline of the Classical Notion of the Lessons of History in the Study of War', *Military Affairs*, 52 (1988), 203.
76. Hale, *Machiavelli and Renaissance Italy*, 27–33.
77. Machiavelli, *History of Florence*, in *Chief Works*, 1285.
78. Russell Price, '*Ambizione* in Machiavelli's Thought', *History of Political Thought*, 3 (1982), 392.

6

THE PRIORITY OF THE SECULAR: THE MEDIEVAL INHERITANCE AND MACHIAVELLI'S SUBORDINATION OF ETHICS TO POLITCS

The idea of the unity of the Roman Empire and of a universal society was strongly perpetrated by Roman theorists and by Christian thinkers when the empire and Christendom became synonymous with the vision of a spiritual community. The rule of Caesar marks the point at which the empire began to be conceived as more than conquered territories to be exploited, and instead as a broader community to which Rome had responsibilities. We should not lose sight of the fact, however, that although the relation between Rome and subject kingdoms was vague and imprecise, obedience to the commands of the emperor was an expectation. The extension of citizenship was not merely a magnanimous gesture, and within Italy it was a forced concession, but a means by which to exercise greater control over the élite in client states. Citizenship was a privilege, not a right, and socially differentiated a class owing allegiance to Rome. It was not until AD 212 that Caracalla extended citizenship tu most free men in the empire. Citizenship itself was a form of social cohesion designed to bolster allegiance to Rome, with its emphasis upon valour, loyalty, duty, and love of the empire.

With the adoption of Christianity as the official religion of the empire and the transference of the seat of the emperor to Constantinople, the ideal of the unity of the empire disintegrated in the face of barbarian invasion. This compounded a process that was already in motion during the fourth century, when fewer Roman soldiers were evident in the western territories, and subdivisions of the empire were made for administrative convenience. From the fifth century the empire in the West became a patchwork of small states in which political power depended upon land and fortifications, and allegiance was secured by kinship ties and vendettas. This political disintegration and fragmentation precipitated ideas of attachment to a broader focus of unity, Christendom. It was, Denys Hay tells us, 'the largest unit to which men in the Latin west felt allegiance in the middle ages'.[1] The various orders of monks and friars were truly international and in many areas, and not always without resentment, enjoyed dispensations from the secu-

lar obligations of ordinary subjects. Although the Pope was the universal symbol
of unity, in practical terms local loyalties to the clergy prevailed, many of whom
were dominated by a powerful nobility.[2] The unity of Christendom was never a
political reality, and referred instead to a spiritual unity to which secular rulers
were nevertheless deemed to be subordinate, the authority of both being divinely
ordained.

The Empire, the Church, and State

It is often suggested that the papal claim to universal allegiance was severely
damaged by the re-emergence of the empire as a political force. Charlemagne's
coronation in 800 is seen to be a significant turning-point, but as Geoffrey
Barraclough suggests, this should not be exaggerated. The new emperors had no
pretensions to a universal empire, and their ambitions were largely territorially
confined, excluding England, the countries of northern Europe, and Spain. After
the collapse of the Carolingian state and the transfer of the seat of the Holy
Roman Empire to Germany, France itself renounced the ideal of imperial
suzerainty.[3] The medieval empire was one of the many political actors to emerge
from feudal Europe and had no rights higher than states that had consolidated
internal political power and could make their presence felt. Expression to such an
idea was given by the thirteenth-century legist Azo when he contended, 'today
every king seems to have the same power as the emperor; therefore, he can do as
he pleases'.[4] After the mid-1350s the emperor was little more than the king of
Germany. Feudalism in Europe was at once a principle of stability and disorder.
The fortresses, fortified towns, and farmhouses, as well as the medieval castle,
were places of safety and security. Social relations were elaborately conceived in
terms of contractual obligations regulating all aspects of life, and even the duty
owed to one's king was taken to be enshrined in a contract between the ruler and
his vassals. The idea of arbitrary rule was anathema to the political subject of the
Middle Ages.[5] Such feudal relations permeated society, resulting in an ambiguous
array of duties and obligations associated with individuals (or corporations) who
could be both lords and vassals in the complex hierarchy of feudalism. The destabilizing factor which provided ample opportunity for private warfare was the
medieval principle of liberty, which could be invoked to protest that a lord had
broken his bond, and to renounce the homage and fealty due to a superior
power.[6] The prince or king lacked the centralized power characteristic of later
periods, and had insufficient revenue and authority to employ universal con-
scription in the prosecution of his wars.

The role of the nobility was to rule and bear arms. The king, or prince, considered himself to be a nobleman, indeed the 'first noble', who should distance
himself from this class as its ruler, while at the same time having a determined
place in its etiquette as a member.[7] Governmental authority and military strength
remained elusive for medieval rulers to monopolize, and warfare became

enmeshed in a code of chivalry and manners that was often tangential to the practice it ostensibly regulated. The laws of chivalry related to all forms of conduct engaged in by the feudal class which were not directly specified in feudal obligations. The illusion was perpetrated that chivalry, with its elaborate code of honour, regulated the conduct of nobles in the castle and princely court. The life of a knight was deemed both virtuous and pious, and was thought to be an imitation of the ancients. The numerous orders of chivalry founded in the fourteenth and fifteenth centuries espoused the highest ethical and political ideals. Challenges were frequently issued by princes to settle political disputes by duel, in order to spare the blood of many, but the duels seldom actually took place. Heralds were the keepers of the code of chivalry, and they acted as bearers of warnings and ultimatums in times of war, and occasionally negotiated peace treaties on behalf of their masters. Ambassadors were the principal diplomatic representatives in the employ of the greater European states, and nuncios and procurators conducted the lesser business of great princes and nobles and of corporations which were afforded diplomatic rights. In addition, heralds were part of a developing hierarchical system of diplomacy.[8]

Huizinga tells us that chivalry both contributed to serious political mistakes and served to disguise calculated interest as generosity of spirit. He argues that 'The chivalrous prejudice often caused resolutions to be retarded or precipitated, opportunities to be lost, and profit to be neglected, for the sake of a point of honour; it exposed commanders to unnecessary dangers. Strategic interests were frequently sacrificed in order to keep up the appearance of the heroic life'.[9] It was to the chivalrous sentiments which the genre of advice books to princes appealed, and that Machiavelli's own *The Prince* ridiculed.

During the later medieval period, as political and military power became consolidated and centralized within states, the policies of rulers were characterized more by *raison d'état* than by chivalrous ideals.[10] The state was, of course, much less centralized than it later became; less clearly differentiated from the person of the ruler; less independent of ecclesiastical influence; but its authority was nevertheless acknowledged as distinctly political, and frequently the legitimacy of the ruler was deemed to derive from the people, who were seen in some way to be the expression of God's will. On criteria which define the state as an abstract entity, having a legitimate monopoly of force, possessing internal and external sovereignty, that is, having an authority greater than that of any lord or nobleman in the land, and independent of an external authority such as the emperor or Pope, it could be suggested that the state begins to appear in the sixteenth century, particularly in Renaissance Italy.[11] If one is prepared to accept that such criteria are a matter of degree, then recognizable signs of the emergence of states can be discerned from the twelfth to the fourteenth centuries.[12] It was in Renaissance Italy, however, from the beginning of the fourteenth to the middle of the fifteenth century, that the modern manner of permanent diplomacy arose as a response to the emerging autonomous state and to the greater reliance of princes upon mercenaries, who were not wholly trustworthy and needed to be supplemented by authoritative representatives. By 1460 permanent embassies were commonplace throughout Italy, reflecting the preponderance of city-states or communes claiming independence.

In Machiavelli's view the expansion of the Roman Empire had serious deleterious consequences for the west. First it destroyed nearly all of the princedoms and republics in Europe, Africa, and Asia. Secondly, this led to a considerable reduction in opportunities for competent men to arise outside Rome (*Art of War*, 623).[13] Furthermore, in abandoning the traditional seat of the empire, the western part fell prey to corrupt officials and hordes of barbarians (*History of Florence*, 1034).[14] The consequent fragmentation of the empire did not regenerate the opportunities for competent men to arise because old ways and customs, once destroyed, are not easily regained, a condition exacerbated by the erosion of ancient values by the adoption of Christianity (*Art of War*, 623). Machiavelli catalogues a liturgy of vicissitudes that befell Italy and the role of Christianity in provoking and prolonging dissensions. He argues that the papacy of the later Middle Ages was not strong enough to hold the country, but at the same time would not allow any other power to do so (*History of Florence*, 1061). At the end of the thirteenth century the Emperor Rudolph, having no interest in retaining Italy, allowed many cities to buy their liberty and change their forms of government (*History of Florence*, 1063).

Burckhardt says of Renaissance Italy that 'Intrigues, armaments, leagues, corruption and treason make up the outward history of Italy at this period'.[15] Hale paints a similar picture when he says, 'International relations were dominated by rulers, monarchs, and popes, whose word held just so long as their interests were maintained'.[16] It was a period which Meinecke sees as dominated by utilitarian calculations about the usefulness of political alliances and obligations with scant regard for religious or moral constraints, within a context of determinate rules regulating the rights, duties, and privileges of the widely established system of permanent embassies.[17] In the Italian context the struggle between the empire and papacy, along with the French preoccupation with the Hundred Years War, produced a power vacuum that was quickly filled by the emerging more or less autonomous city-states, which absorbed into themselves many of the smaller city communes delegated their freedom by the emperor or Pope. The power vacuum emerged following the eradication of the influence of the emperor in Italy, who shortly after the beginning of the fourteenth century acknowledged that it was a place where he could do little more than sell privileges and titles, the election of a French Pope, Clement V, who removed his *Curia* to Avignon in 1309, and the subsequent return to Rome in 1377 of Gregory XI, when the Great Schism reduced papal influence further, giving rise to two rival popes and for a short period three.[18] Disputes which increasingly arose between the papacy and the empire over the source, scope, and exercise of coercive authority were generally applicable to city-states, kingdoms, and principalities as well as to the dominion of the emperor.

It was in the course of these debates that a secular view of politics was forged, and the theoretical foundation was laid for its complete expression in the writings of Machiavelli. During the later Middle Ages the question of the relation between the Church and State became the focus of political writings, testifying to the emergence of a developing political consciousness among secular rulers. The Church wished to impress upon such rulers its supremacy in all matters temporal and spiritual. One of the most forceful assertions of papal supremacy was made by John of Salisbury (*c*.1115?–80). He argued that the sword of the prince, by which he meant the temporal power of jurisdiction, was conferred by the Church, and that the prince was in effect an instrument of the Church discharging a sacred, but nevertheless inferior, function. Because the sword was stained with blood it was unworthy to be wielded by the priesthood, whose hands were preserved for the spiritual sword.[19] By the middle of the twelfth century his view was widely accepted by the clergy, and it was officially adopted by the papacy in the opening decades of the thirteenth.[20]

The doctrine of papal supremacy was widely questioned, and the primacy of the secular asserted in temporal government. Augustine had, of course, paved the way for thinking about the secular and divine in terms of the principles of the city of God and the city of man. This distinction found institutional expression in the thinkers of the later medieval period, such as John of Paris, Marsilius of Padua, and Dante, assisted in their secularism by the popularity of the Arab philosopher Averroës (1126–98), who synthesized the long tradition of Aristotelian interpretation to which he belonged. Averroëistic Aristotelianism presented a number of serious implied criticisms of accepted theological views. He argued that nothing can be born out of nothing, hence the universe must always have existed, thus implicitly denying Creation. He also denied personal immortality by contending that the soul is not individual, but universal. Humanity is eternal in the common reason of mankind. Individuals have a finite existence. Furthermore, he distinguished between the conclusions of philosophical reasoning and the revealed truths of the Qur'ān, arguing that in a conflict between the two the latter should prevail. His contention was sufficiently ambiguous to give rise to the suspicion that he condoned the view that something that is theologically false might be philosophically true.[2]

John of Paris contributed to the political debate of the later Middle Ages in response to a dispute between King Philip IV of France (*c*.1250–1306) and Pope Boniface VIII over the king's assertion of a right to tax the Church and its minions in his territories. John of Paris wished to distinguish more clearly between the two jurisdictions of the Pope and the king, without pronouncing on who was to decide the boundary. The secular and spiritual spheres were separate and independent. Secular authority is established first in time, but priestly authority is higher in dignity because of its ministry to the higher end of our being. The former is not, however, derived from the latter, and is in fact superior in some matters, namely the secular. Both derive their legitimacy from God.[22] The clergy, he believed, did not have a legitimate coercive authority, but a spiritual authority, with a moral sanction, deriving from a universally acknowledged right to preach, from which derives the jurisdiction to pronounce certain activities sinful, such as usury, but others, he contended, such as disputes over property, are properly to be judged by the secular power.[23] Neither the Pope nor the ruler has lordship over the goods of the laity, which are acquired 'by the personal art, labour or industry of individual people'.[24] Only in cases of extreme public or spiritual necessity can the respective powers justify the appropriation of the property of the laity.

Marsilius of Padua and William of Ockham

The question of the jurisdiction of the papacy and of the emperor was one of the crucial issues affecting perceptions of international relations in the later medieval period. The distinction between, and independence of, the secular and spiritual authorities was further refined by Marsilius of Padua. Marsilius supported Ludwig of Bavaria against Pope John XXII, who excommunicated Ludwig in 1324 for failing to submit himself for papal approval after the disputed imperial election of 1314. The dispute continued throughout the pontificate of Clement VI and was not resolved until after Ludwig's death in 1347, when the independence of the electors was acknowledged. Marsilius had a practical influence upon politics during Ludwig's invasion of Italy (1327–30), his coronation in Rome, the deposition of John XXII, and the election of his successor.[25] Ludwig entered Rome in 1328 and appointed Marsilius to rule on his behalf. J. W. Allen suggests that in his hounding of clerics Marsilius 'acquired, it seems, quite a reputation for cruelty: a thing, perhaps, not easy to do in fourteenth-century Italy'.[26]

Marsilius's scientific and medical training predisposed him to approach answering such questions as 'what is the source of political authority?' and 'what are the proper relations between Church and state?' by means of observation and induction, rather than by the deductive methods typical of medieval theologians. There are many respects in which Marsilius's thought draws upon Averroëistic Aristotelianism. First he makes the distinction between faith and reason, being careful not to deny the ..uth of revelation. Knowledge held on faith is not self-evident, nor have philosophers been able 'to prove by demonstration its nature' (*Defensor pacis*, I. v. 10).[27] Matters of faith we hold 'by simple belief apart from reason' (*Defensor pacis*, I. ix. 2). About governments established by God we can say very little, but we can enquire into the origins, that is, the first causes and principles, of governments instituted by human artifice (*Defensor pacis*, I. xii. 1). Outside society individuals are subject to all kinds of dangers, including those from our perverse natures and from other people. Society arises from a recognition of common needs which can only be satisfied by a large association of individuals. Morality does not exist prior to society. It emerges from the need to regulate antisocial conduct. Quarrels and disputes have to be arbitrated with reference to a standard of justice. Marsilius suggests that as society slowly developed, a guardian became necessary to make this code of justice and to establish institutions to restrain excessive wrongdoing; to repel external attacks; to make provisions for common services and maintenance; and also to administer to the spiritual needs of individuals.

Marsilius's theory of morality is a direct denial of medieval orthodoxy, and leans towards the Averroëistic secularism which was so at variance with Christianity. Justice and our sense of right and wrong arise from the acknowledgement of human perversity and the recognition of the need to co-operate. There is no suggestion of a pre-existing order of justice which is independent of society and which men must come to know. Indeed, such things are outside the bounds of human demonstration and therefore logically excluded from his discussion. Laws and rules regarding human action are derived from observations about what is consistent with human association. Reason acting on experience demonstrates that certain actions are inimical to human association. Rules must therefore be formulated with reference to our desire to co-operate. Those things which are consistent with this desire are pronounced 'right' and those things inconsistent with it 'wrong'. This is a prudential or utilitarian view of ethics which emphasizes the usefulness or expediency of having a code of ethics, and as J. W. Allen tells us, 'It gets rid at once of the transcendental element in ethics'.

In the *Defensor minor* this radical doctrine is considerably modified and accords much more closely with the conventional theological teaching. Marsilius reiterates the distinction he had made between Divine Law instituted by God (only God and his son Jesus could act as judges), and the human law instituted by the human legislator and juridically administered by those authorized to do so. The implication is that Marsilius is denying the jurisdiction of the ecclesiastical courts. In chapters 8 and 13 of *Defensor minor* Marsilius makes it clear that human laws must be in accordance with Divine Laws. He maintains that 'Divine Law commands obedience to human rulers and laws which are not contrary to Divine Law' (*Defensor minor*, 23).[28] Divine Law takes precedence over human law when the two come into conflict. When such laws deviate from Divine Law the Christian is absolved of the obligation to obey the secular ruler. The judge of such discrepancies is not to be the clergy, but the individual. Here Marsilius is affirming the right to resist t, rants. At the end of the *Defensor minor*, despite its aparent endorsement of the sovereignty of the emperor, he suggests that the people can revoke the authority that they have conferred upon him. We see in Marsilius elements from the traditions of both Empirical Reason and a Universal Moral Order. It is clear, however, that in the more substantive treatise, *Defensor pacis*, the transcendental element of universalism is largely dismissed.

The relationship between the *Defensor pacis* and the *Defensor minor* has led to considerable disagreement among scholars. What they agree upon is that the *Defensor minor* is an imperial tract expressing a firm commitment to the role of the emperor and the legitimacy of the empire. On the one hand there are those who see aspects of the latter representing a profound change of doctrine from that expressed in the earlier treatise. On this reading it is denied that the *Defensor pacis* represents a justification for absolutist imperial rule. Instead it is seen as a thoroughly republican tract. The *Defensor minor*, on the other hand, is seen as a reflection of his changed circumstances, and a strong endorsement of imperial rule.[29] However, some interpreters have seen the two treatises as consistent. Here it is argued that Marsilius was an imperial absolutist from the start and that the *Defensor minor* merely makes more explicit his long-standing views. The *Defensor pacis* has been widely read as a republican tract because of its emphasis upon the consent of the people, or 'the weightier part thereof', in the legitimation of political power. The populist interpretation of Marsilius is put forward by both Quentin Skinner and Alan Gerwith.

There is much evidence in the *Defensor pacis* to support the republican interpretation. In chapter xii of Discourse I, for example, Marsilius attempts to 'demonstrate' the source of the power to make laws and the power to punish their transgression. The legitimate maker of law, or the legislator, he argues, is the whole body of the people. The reason why people join together in communities is to avoid the uncertainties of living in a lawless and precarious condition, and to enjoy the benefits of a peaceful existence. He maintains that 'Those matters, therefore, which can affect the benefit and harm of all ought to be known and heard by all' (*Defensor pacis*, I. xii. 7).

It is clear, however, that he does not intend a purely democratic assembly in which majority rule prevails. He maintains that the views of some elements of the population should rightly carry more weight than others. A community of free citizens, he argues, will obey the law that it has self-imposed, whereas if law is imposed upon the people without their authority by despots, however good that law, it 'would be endured only with reluctance' (*Defensor pacis*, I. xii. 6). The authority to make law, then, resides in the people, or the weightier part thereof, but this does not mean that the people personally have to legislate. Legislative authority can be conferred upon a person or persons by the people. Those who exercise legislative authority on behalf of the people do not exercise it unconditionally. The people, which is the primary legislator, determines the conditions. If authority is delegated in this way, then the laws enacted and the institutions established must have the approval of the primary legislator.

It may, however, be misleading to read the *Defensor pacis* as solely a republican tract, and the danger is ...at we read our present conception of sovereignty back into Marsilius's tract. It is difficult to understand what Marsilius was trying to get at if we do not have a clear picture of the historical context. Italy comprised numerous city-states. The Italian peninsula was divided into two areas: the lands of the empire and the lands of the Church, that is, the north and the south papal states. Marsilius's theory is based upon the experience of Padua under the empire. In this context there was deemed to be a hierarchy of sovereignty with the emperor at the pinnacle. The emperor was theoretically sovereign, but often in practice the city-states were relatively autonomous and exercised *de facto* sovereignty. There was, then, a discontinuity between theory and practice. Overall in the later works there is a slight change of emphasis. Here he accepts the universal empire as the context of political life. There is an overall consistency in his thought between the models set out in *Defensor pacis* and the *Defensor minor*. In the latter he introduces a hierarchy of sovereignty. Given the contemporary background, there was no contradiction between talking of republicanism and the emperor's authority over the city-states.[30]

The pro-imperial view of Marsilius links the legislator with the emperor. The book is dedicated to Ludwig of Bavaria, and the *Defensor pacis* and *Defensor minor* together are taken to sustain the imperial view. Marsilius also wrote a short work entitled *On the Transfer of the Empire* (*De translatione imperii*) in order to cast doubt upon the legitimacy of the papal claim that the Pope could appoint and depose emperors by transferring the imperial seat. At the time of writing this tract Marsilius sought the protection of Ludwig of Bavaria, who was at odds with the papacy over his royal imperial jurisdiction over Germany and northern Italy.

Marsilius takes the Roman Empire to signify a universal monarchy encompassing the jurisdiction of Rome over its many territories, the seat of which was transferred to Constantinople in the reign of the Emperor Constantine. The papacy claimed the right to transfer the seat of the empire on the basis of a document known as the 'Donation of Constantine'. The document was believed to date from the fourth century and granted dominion over the lands of the empire to the Pope on the authority of the Emperor Constantine I. It was not until the Renaissance that the document was revealed as a forgery, but its authenticity was widely questioned even during the Middle Ages. Marsilius of Padua questioned the interpretation put upon the document, and not the authenticity of the document itself.

In the *Defensor pacis* Marsilius argues that all authority over individuals derives from the community. In Discourse II he derives the power of the emperor from the Roman people. In this respect the human legislature appoints the emperor, but ultimately it is the work of God acting through human actions. It should be remembered that the Pope was in Avignon at this time, and did not control Rome. In Discourse II, Chapter xii. 1 he talks of the origin of the empire. It was a corporation of provinces in which the Roman people had the authority to make laws for the whole world. The legislator who was the delegate or representative of the community granted ecclesiastic jurisdiction. He argues that it was on Constantine's authority that the Church of Rome was granted 'leadership' over other churches and bishops (*Defensor pacis*, II. xxii. 9).

Constantine decreed that maintenance of the faith was to be regulated by the Bishop of Rome, but not determined by his personal whim. Obedience to the Church of Rome was given by the other Churches voluntarily and was grounded upon reverence for its example and the calibre of its leaders. The habit of custom, Marsilius argues, amounted to election. Neither Christ nor any of the Apostles decreed priority upon Rome. Peter, from whom popes claim descent, had no special authority over the other Apostles, and if he had, it would have had to have been with their consent (*Defensor pacis*, II. xxii. 13). Marsilius argues that after the death of Constantine and when the imperial seat was vacant popes illegitimately tried to claim that their priority derived not from the emperor or the consent of the other Churches, but from Divine Law (*Defensor pacis*, II. xxii. 20). Furthermore, he complains that more recent popes, such as Boniface and Clement V, have extended these preposterous claims into the political realm and maintained that no ruler can exercise the temporal sword without their authority.

Marsilius extends his critique of papal pretensions in *On the Transfer of the Empire*. Its purpose is to show that the current holder of the title of Roman Emperor occupied his position wholly in accordance with the established selection procedures. Furthermore, to whatever extent the papacy had a role in effecting the transference of the imperial crown to the Franks and eventually to Germany, its involvement was not necessary, but merely honorary. The ceremonial custom of the papal crowning of new emperors did not alter the fact that imperial authority was derived from a source independent of papal control.[31] He contended, for example, that in modern times the Pope merely confirmed the selection of the seven German electors. The emperor 'is crowned by the Bishop of Rome for the sake of ceremony rather than on account of some necessity' (*Transfer of the Empire*, 81).

In contrast to the two positions taken on the relationship between the *Defensor pacis* and the *Defensor minor*, Cary J. Nederman maintains that both treatises argue something similar, but that that similarity, unlike in the imperial interpretation, does not consist in a consistent absolutism. Instead, he maintains that in both treatises Marsilius trades in ambiguity. In other words, Marsilius hedges his bets. In both treatises he argues that empire may be a legitimate form of rule, depending upon the circumstances, but that its legitimacy ultimately rests upon the more fundamental principle of the consent of the people.[32] Nederman argues that the *Defensor minor* is meant to be logically consistent with its predecessor, and constitutes an application of its main precepts to a particular question.[33] He argues that the *Defensor pacis* talks of political communities in general and gives no special status to any particular constitutional or geographical political arrangement. The *Defensor minor*, however, applies the general principles to the example of the imperial government rather than to national or city-state regimes. Like any other polity it has its origins in the consent of its 'corporate community' or human legislator, and the papacy has no greater right to interfere in its affairs than it does in the affairs of any other temporal political authority.[4] Nederman argues that in neither the *Defensor minor* nor the *Defensor pacis* does Marsilius give his unequivocal endorsement to universal government under the empire. He concedes that there are circumstances when it might be appropriate. He maintains that on practical grounds an empire would unite members of the same faith more effectively than a religious universal leader. This amounts to a criticism of papal power, rather than a recommendation for empire. His main concern is to rein in papal authority, and in doing so he is prepared to enlist the empire.

Marsilius also wants to maintain that law depends upon sanctions for its enforcement, and that strictly speaking only human law could be demonstrated to have this character. The will of the legislator is the source of law. As d'Entrèves says: 'will and not reason is the constituent element of law'.[35] It is only the state which has 'the authority to give commands to the subject multitude collectively' (*Defensor pacis*, iii. iii, pp. 431–2). Divine Law is exclusively concerned with religious values in relation to salvation and therefore has no coercive character. The clergy have no legitimate coercive powers, and their function should be merely pastoral. Although religious persecution would be taken out of the hands of the clergy, he does not wish to embrace toleration. Because of the temporal usefulness of religion the state itself would provide the function of persecution.

The human legislator, whether he is a prince or an emperor, in Marsilius's theory must constitute a government of unity and peace. The purpose of government, although the result of the recognition of common needs and the necessity to repress perverse natures, is to create and sustain the conditions which bring *tranquillitas* or peace to the community. Peace and tranquillity are not ends in themselves, but the condition which promotes human development and progress in the arts and sciences. He is largely talking about the attainment of peace within the nation, and intimates that language is a natural criterion for the division of the world into states. He even suggests that nature provides wisely in envisaging wars between them. Discord, which is opposed to tranquillity, has a destructive effect. He takes the case of Italy to 'demonstrate' or prove his point. When Italy enjoyed peaceful relations among its inhabitants it experienced all the fruits of progress, and incorporated most of the habitable world into its empire. When discord arose in Italy it became weak and vulnerable to foreign invasion and domination; and this once proud people is now treated with contempt.

The theme of the separation of Church and State and the question of the relation of the Church to the empire were extensively addressed after 1328 by William of Ockham (*c.*1285–*c.*1347), one of the most eminent theologians of the fourteenth century. After fleeing from Avignon when suspected of heresy, he joined the court of Ludwig at Pisa and then at Munich. He spent the rest of his life defending apostolic poverty, denying the claims of papal absolutism in secular and ecclesiastical matters, and asserting the independence of the authority of the emperor and other secular rulers from the authority of the Church. Like Marsilius, Ockham believed that the claim of the papacy to absolute power in temporal and ecclesiastical matters had led to untold violations of rights, generated endless conflicts, and undermined the legitimacy of secular rulers. Furthermore, the clai..i was contrary to scripture and therefore dangerous and heretical. If such a claim were true, 'then Christ's law would involve a most horrendous servitude' to the Pope, who could 'therefore by right deprive the king of France and every other king of his kingdom without fault or reason. . . . This is absurd.'[36] Human government, Ockham argued, is a consequence of the Fall, after which God conferred two powers in order to prevent endless destruction: the powers to institute rulers and to acquire private property. Irrespective of their faith, these are powers which all human beings possess, and are not derived from, nor dependent upon, the papacy. The authority of the Roman Empire, then, prior to Constantine's conversion, was wholly legitimate and not granted to him by the Church.[37] Furthermore, Ockham casts doubt upon the authenticity and interpretation of the Donation of Constantine supposedly granting the Pope authority over the empire.

For Ockham legitimate political power derives from and rests upon the consent of the people.[38] This, of course, poses him a problem relating to the foundation of the Roman Empire. He is certain that by the time of Christ and the Apostles it did possess 'true jurisdiction', which is attested to by the fact that they did not question the authority of the empire, but instead criticized abuses of its power. Ockham confesses his ignorance as to when the empire might have acquired legitimacy and speculates about the way in which it might have done so. First, it may have extended its authority by the willing consent of subject peoples in some regions, and or by usurping rule in others, which later became translated into willing consent. Secondly, a true empire may have been established by just war. The conditions of a just war for Ockham relate specifically to injuries received, and not, as with Machiavelli, necessities perceived. Direct attack, or the refusal by a defeated enemy to make reparations after taking property, and other crimes and injustices legitimately inviting punishment, constitute grounds for just war. The perpetrators of such injustices can be rightfully subdued to one's power. Ockham suggests that a combination of both methods probably transformed Rome from a tyrannical to a legitimate empire, but a third ground appears to be wholly absent, that is, 'special divine ordinance revealed by a special miracle, as Moses' rule over the children of Israel was established'.[39]

Political Experience of Machiavelli

The period between the late fourteenth century and the end of the fifteenth century saw Italy relatively isolated from the ambitions of the rest of Europe. It was nevertheless under threat from the Ottoman Empire, and was not without the occasional intrusion of foreign allies called in by one state or another to assist in its struggle against the others. By the fifteenth century Naples, Venice, Florence, Milan, and the papal states were the main political actors, but none of them on its own could dominate the other four, nor any two together gain significant advantage over any other two. This period was beset by petty rivalries and struggles for influence seemingly unconstrained by moral and religious considerations. Mattingly goes so far as to say that 'in Italy, power was temporal in the strictest sense of the term. It was naked and free, without even the most tenuous connection with eternity'.[40] Power and force became supreme political values and played a considerable part in securing the allegiance of supporters and maintaining one's state. Much of Machiavelli's advice is directed towards these matters. In pursuit of this value war became endemic to the Italian states system. The Italian city-states up to 1494 co-existed in a precarious equilibrium. In the first half of the fifteenth century Milan under the Sforzas looked as if it might become the dominant Italian state, and in order to prevent this Florence allied with Venice. When Venice became more powerful in the latter part of the century Florence changed its allegiance at different times to Milan or Naples.

Machiavelli thought that none of the Italian states were well equipped for war. He contended that the lesser princes took up arms for gain, led by mercenary generals with 'dastardly armies' in a country full of 'slothful rulers' (*History of*

Florence, 1079). The weak cities of Italy 'defended themselves by uniting with whoever conquered' from among the stronger emerging states of Europe.

The weakness of Italian city-states in 1494 invited the outside intervention of France and Spain, each eager to ensure that the other did not become dominant to the detriment of the other. Such outside intervention led to a decline in the independence of Naples, Milan, and Florence. Machiavelli's contemporary Francesco Guicciardini (1483–1540), writing in the late 1530s, suggested that the Florentine policy of switching allegiances was a deliberate attempt by Lorenzo de' Medici, the Magnificent, to maintain the Italian situation in 'a state of balance'.[41] The idea of maintaining an equilibrium as a method of defence was, of course, to become much more widely acknowledged and accepted when the European family of states became more fully developed after 1494 and particularly in the eighteenth century.

Robert R. Sullivan has suggested that Machiavelli has elements of a theory of balance of power which have not been sufficiently well noticed. He suggests that Machiavelli first adumbrates a static theory and supplements it with a dynamic theory. The static theory postulates a state that is powerful enough to deter other states from attack because of the formidable task of overcoming her, yet not so formidable as to make neighbouring states so insecure that they are compelled to attack out of fear. This is an ideal type which it would be imprudent to emulate simply because of Machiavelli's fundamental assumption that things are constantly in flux. This leads to what Sullivan calls the dynamic theory, in which the state is viewed not as a mechanism, but as a developing organism which is either rising or declining. He argues that states, like individuals, are prone to be lazy, arrogant, and careless with the power that they have endeavoured to acquire. Having reached optimum security, states recklessly pursue empire, causing their decline and decay, or alternatively they relax and corruption sets in, allowing other states to makes gains in the power stakes. Sullivan portrays Machiavelli's conception of the state as a self-rectifying organism in which declines are the catalysts for compens...ory stimuli to rise.[42] His interpretation asks us to stretch the imagination beyond credulity.

Machiavelli's theory is not one of balance of power, but one of attainment and preservation of power. The attainment of power must be commensurate with one's ambitions, that is, the pursuit of a policy of expansion must appear both credible and feasible. All states decline, even Rome, and what one can best hope for is to retard that process, but no one has succeeded in doing it indefinitely. To retard the process, periodic and often brutal renovations of the principal institutions of state have to be undertaken in order to prevent corruption from setting in. This entails reinvesting the fear and awe that accompanied the establishment of these institutions so that individuals fear the consequences of neglecting their ceremonies and customs. Most important, of course, religious institutions should be periodically renovated (see *Discourses*, I. 12, pp. 142–6, and III. 1, pp. 385–90), but good laws which are the foundations of good arms and the state should also be duly returned to their pristine condition. Cleomenes, the successor of Lycurgus, had all the euphors killed to prevent them from obstructing his renewal of the laws, a policy that would have been successful had not the Macedonians attacked and defeated Sparta when her forces were inferior (*Discourses*, I. 9, p. 134).

The motivating factor among great leaders for expansion is ambition for glory, and what Machiavelli advises is not judicious balance of power, but judicious expansion disguised by appearances that mask the reality: 'men in general are as much affected by what a thing appears to be as by what it is, indeed they are frequently influenced more by appearances than by the reality' (*Discourses*, I. 25, p. 175). That is the course that Rome pursued in relation to the other Italian states before becoming strong enough to subject them to herself.

The Italian situation of the fifteenth and sixteenth centuries has frequently been identified as the birthplace of the modern states system.[43] Machiavelli saw at close quarters the actions of princes in the name of their states. Florence, Burckhardt tells us (with some exaggeration), was the first modern state.[44] It was one of the most wealthy and culturally exciting cities in Europe. Political thought, commerce, and the arts all flourished. By the time Machiavelli was in the employ of the government, Florence was going through a period of what Hale calls 'crumbling imperialism'.[45] It was trying to maintain its authority over territories which appealed to foreign powers to aid them in their quest for liberation. One such conflict was that with Pisa, which began in 1496 and was the main burden upon Florence until 1509. The war was costly and was fought against a people vehemently opposed to living under Florentine rule. The Florentine reliance upon Italian and Swiss mercenaries, as well as French auxiliaries, proved disastrous. It was to repair relations between Florence and France that Machiavelli was called upon to conduct his first major mission in 1500. It was at this time that he realized most forcefully the need to act swiftly and boldly rather than to appear weak and indecisive because of delays. He was unable to give King Louis XII the assurances he required about payment because of the indecision and procrastination of his Florentine superiors. Machiavelli was humiliated by the taunts that the French made about the ...significance of Florence, and about how her ludicrous self-importance far outweighed her military and financial capacities.[46]

Machiavelli was to make four missions to Louis XII's court in France, in 1500, 1503, 1510, and 1511. Louis XII lacked political imagination and vision beyond 'present convenience'.[47] Machiavelli also travelled to Germany in 1507 on a mission to the Emperor Maximilian's court. He found him far too generous, and although Machiavelli admired his army, which consisted of a citizens' militia, he wondered how long the emperor could continue to pay for it with such a generous nature. Machiavelli says of Maximilian: 'being extremely liberal, he adds difficulty to difficulty; and although generosity is a virtue in princes, yet it is not enough to satisfy one thousand when there are twenty thousand more who are in need.'[48]

It was the missions to Cesare Borgia (the Duke Valentino) and Pope Julius II, however, which made the most profound impression upon Machiavelli. He was able to make a careful study of Cesare Borgia during three missions: to Urbino in 1502, to Imola in 1502–3, and later to Rome. Borgia was Machiavelli's exemplar of the man with *virtù*. In Rome Machiavelli was able to observe Pope Julius II, who was responsible, along with fortune, for Cesare Borgia's downfall, and for ruining Italy. At Urbino the menacing character of Borgia, and his lack of compunction in perpetrating the most brutal and heinous acts out of political necessity, fascinated Machiavelli. Machiavelli thought him to be a courageous and magnificent leader whose appetite for new territory and glory was insatiable. At Imola Borgia seems to have taken him into his confidence on many occasions. For a period of over three months Machiavelli reported back to Florence about Borgia's plans and about his impressions of this awe-inspiring leader, whose reputation for lust and cruelty was notorious. Borgia was anxious to impress upon Machiavelli the mutual benefits that would accrue if Florence were to give him support. This was the message that Machiavelli conveyed in his dispatches to the Ten of War. He was impressed by the secrecy with which the duke conducted his affairs: 'things to be kept silent are never mentioned to us, and are carried on with wonderful secrecy' (*Legations*, 11. 19, p. 127).[49] He revealed his plans to no one until he ordered them to be carried out (*Legations*, 11. 82, p. 142). Even the reason for the execution of Remirro (or Rimirro) di Orco, whom Machiavelli describes as the 'chief man of this Lord' (*Legations*, 11. 81, p. 141), was left to speculation.

In reporting that Remirro had been found cut into two pieces in the public square in Cesana, Machiavelli says that no one is quite sure about why he died, 'except that so it has pleased the Prince, who shows that he can make and unmake men as he likes, according to their deserts' (*Legations*, 11. 82, p. 142). In *The Prince* he suggests that the methods by which the Duke Valentino acquired and pacified the Romagna are worthy of imitation. Remirro had a reputation for excessive brutality which served to keep the nobles of the Romagna in check. In order to deflect their hatred, Machiavelli contends, Cesare Borgia had Remirro decapitated: 'The brutality of this spectacle kept the people of the Romagna for a time appeased and stupefied' (*The Prince*, 58). Remirro was in fact a well-known enemy of Paolo Orsini, one of the confederates who rebelled against Cesare Borgia and seized Urbino in 1502. Choosing not to rely upon the arms of the French, the duke turned to deceit to rid himself of the conspirators. Remirro may have been killed to demonstrate to Paolo Orsini the sincerity of Cesare Borgia's overtures for reconciliation. Having regained the confidence of the conspirators, and during a celebration of their united success in capturing Senigallia, Cesare Borgia left the room, and his men captured and executed the conspirators (see *The Prince*, chapter vii).[50] In the *First Decennale* covering the history of Florence from 1494 to 1504, Machiavelli gives credit to Cesare Borgia for the amazing feats he and his men accomplished: the duke 'with his soldiers did wonders, storming Faenza in short order and turning Romagna upside down', and in capturing the ex-confederate traitors Fermo, Vitelli, and Orsini, so 'sweetly this basilisk whistled' (*First Decennale*, 1454, ll. 394–5).[51] The basilisk, or cockatrice, is reputed to have been hatched by a serpent out of the egg of a cock. It could kill by a glance. Borgia's ability to lure his prey demonstrated how adept he was at appearing something that he was not.

Machiavelli did have some reservations about Cesare Borgia during his mission to Imola. He thought that the duke's government was founded on good fortune, and that perhaps such unheard-of fortune led him to be overconfident about what he could attain (*Legations*, II. 82, p. 142). These observations are reinforced in the *First Decennale*. Machiavelli implies that the duke's success rested largely upon having the support of his father, Pope Alexander VI. When the Pope died the states of the duke crumbled. The duke is scorned for being easily tricked by Cardinal della Rovere, who had been exiled by Alexander VI. In return for the duke's support for election to pontiff, della Rovere promised him the position of captain-general of the papal militia. Machiavelli comments that 'the Duke lets himself be carried away by that rash confidence of his, and believes that the words of another man are going to be surer than his own have been' (*Legations*, 13. 18, p. 143). So cunning was Julius II that Duke Valentino 'believed he would find in another such pity as never he knew himself' (*First Decennale*, 1455, ll. 473–4). Rovere, who became Julius II, reneged on his promise as soon as he was confident that Duke Valentino could not retaliate, ordered him to surrender the castle at Forlì and other strongholds in the Romagna, and had him arrested when he refused: 'So we see that this Pope is already paying his debts very honourably, and that he cancels them with the cotton of the ink stand' (*Legations*, 13. 61, p. 157).

When Julius II had established himself firmly in the papacy he went on the offensive to regain the papal territories that had been lost. In August 1506 he took Perugia in a campaign which showed him to be audacious and daring in the face of overwhelming odds. This demonstrated to Machiavelli that there was nothing that could not be achieved if a ruler was prepared to act in conformity with his fortune. Shortly afterwards Julius II moved on to Cesana and declared to a delegation from Bologna that he did not feel bound by the agreements of his predecessors, nor by those that he himself had made when forced to do so because necessity dictated the circumstances. He succeeded in taking Bologna with the aid of French soldiers.

By 1510 Julius II was deeply concerned about the influence of French and German powers in Lombardy. After defeating Bologna he went on to Venice, with which he concluded a peace treaty, to mount a campaign against the foreigners. Florence was now in a difficult position because both France and the papacy had been her traditional allies. Soderini, the gonfalonier of Florence, sent Machiavelli to France to attempt a reconciliation, which proved unsuccessful. With due caution, wary of Julius II's extraordinary good luck, Machiavelli recommended that Florence support France in the conflict. Florence in fact took a neutral stance, but not without arousing the suspicion in Julius that Soderini was sympathetic to France. In an attempt to gain the support of Florence, Julius became determined to restore the Medici. Soderini succumbed to external and internal pressure, allowing Giuliano de' Medici to return to Florence in September 1512. Machiavelli was imprisoned and later released under a general amnesty upon the election of Cardinal Giovanni de' Medici as Pope Leo X in 1513. He was the first Florentine Pope, and his election strengthened support for the government and the Medici family. In a letter to Francesco Vettori, Machiavelli lays the blame for the condition of Italy firmly at the feet of Julius II: 'I am now ready to weep with you over our ruin and servitude, which, if it does not come today or tomorrow, will come in our time. And Italy will owe that to Pope Julius . . .'[52]

In discussing the bearing that fortune has on the affairs of state later in *The Prince*, Machiavelli describes Pope Julius II as being impetuous in his actions. His impetuosity was so well suited to the times that his manner of proceeding with his affairs was always successful. Impetuousness in these circumstances achieved more than any other pontiff could have done even by the use of the utmost prudence. However, Machiavelli strikes a note of caution. The pontiff's life was so short that he did not live long enough to experience a turn in the tide of fortune: 'If there had come a time when it was necessary for him to act with circumspection he would have come to grief: he would never have acted other than in character' (*The Prince*, 133). In a letter to Vettori, Machiavelli describes Julius II as 'unstable, hasty, rash and stingy'.[53] To act consistently in character was a common trait of Cesare Borgia, who was far too self-confident; the Emperor Maximilian, who was over-cautious and hesitant; and Julius II, who was invariably impetuous. All could have achieved much more had they been able to adapt to circumstances and changes of fortune. This lesson of the need to be flexible Machiavelli learnt from Cardinal Volterra on the day Julius II was elected, and again two years later from the tyrant of Siena, Pandolfo Petrucci, whom Cesare Borgia thought a great master of treacherousness. Petrucci told Machiavelli 'that to avoid falling into error we must shape our course according to events from day to day, and must judge of things from one hour to another, for time and circumstances are more powerful than human intelligence'.[54] Machiavelli was indeed sceptical about the ability of rulers to be flexible: 'because . . . since men in the first place are short-sighted and in the second place cannot command their natures, it follows that fortune varies and commands men and holds them under her yoke'.[55]

It is not, then, open to any ruler to deliver his country from danger, or to perpetuate the conditions for good and loyal citizenship free of corruption. Only men or women with a heightened sense of the appropriate and necessary thing to do in given circumsta...ces, and possessing the requisite *virtù* to act accordingly and the ambition conducive to the common rather than the private good, will attain glory and prolong success.

In *The Prince* Machiavelli is concerned almost exclusively with the difficulties that princes encounter in acquiring their principalities, and the complex balance that prevails between the internal and external affairs of state. *The Prince* is a distillation of Machiavelli's experience primarily designed to provide new princes with the technical rules of statecraft to expedite their smooth passage through turbulent times. Machiavelli also offers his own practical experience in order to supplement his treatise.

The Prince was first dedicated to Giuliano de' Medici, who in 1513 looked the most likely to succeed to the new composite principality that Cesare Borgia had created. He did not in fact inherit these territories, but received others, which upon his death in 1516 were added to those of Lorenzo de' Medici, a new prince faced with the problem of reconciling the new territories to his established Florentine principality. *The Prince* was then dedicated to Lorenzo, who personally appeared a most unlikely candidate to act in the manner that Machiavelli prescribed. This gives rise to the question of Machiavelli's sincerity. Was *The Prince* merely a confidence trick to gain employment, or even a clever ploy to dupe Lorenzo into acting so despicably that he would bring about the downfall of his own government? I have argued elsewhere that, given Machiavelli's desperate desire to work in government and how precarious his position was, having been imprisoned and suspected of plotting against the Medici, and how unlikely it was that he could extricate himself from being implicated in Lorenzo's activities and gain the favour of the new government, let alone receive the credit for the return of republicanism, it is most improbable that he would have taken the risk. In order to ingratiate himself with Lorenzo de' Medici it is likely that Machiavelli indulged in insincere flattery, and he may have harboured severe doubts about Lorenzo's capacity to take on the task of liberating Italy from the barbarians. On the other hand there is no reason to believe that Machiavelli was not sincere in the methods he thought necessary to accomplish the task.[56] In the *Discourses* upon the first ten books of Livy, which appears to have been written shortly after *The Prince*, Machiavelli dwells predominantly upon the problems of creating and maintaining political stability in both republics and princedoms, especially in the former, because he thought a mixed form of republican government more likely to achieve long-term stability.

Machiavelli has a great deal to say about the maintenance of internal affairs, but such advice for the most part falls outside the scope of this book. What is important to note, however, is that internal affairs are to a large extent dependent upon external affairs. In *The Prince*, chapter xix, Machiavelli argues that providing that external affairs are under control, and providing that no conspiracy has already hatched, domestic affairs too will remain under the ruler's control.

The Conditions for a Successful State

What, then, does a state need in order to keep external affairs under control, and in order to expand its territory successfully, given that expansion is the only prudent course of action for the strong and capable state? Machiavelli begins to answer this question in chapter xii of *The Prince*. The soundest foundations of any state are 'good laws and good arms' (*The Prince*, 77), and good laws depend upon good arms. For purposes of defence against foreign aggression, Machiavelli adds an additional condition. You must have good allies, and you will always have good allies if you have good arms (*The Prince*, 103). Both good laws and good allies, then, are dependent upon having good arms. Having good arms, however, is not quite enough to ensure success. Religion, as we have seen, not only reduces a people to obedience in the internal affairs of a state, it also inspires them in their foreign enterprises. Machiavelli says quite emphatically that 'It was religion that facilitated whatever enterprise the senate and the great men of Rome designed to undertake' (*Discourses*, I. 11, p. 139). Religion in Rome was used 'as the instrument necessary above all others for the maintenance of a civilised state' (*Discourses*, I. 11, p. 139).

In addition to the prudent use of religion, Machiavelli believed that a further ingredient had to be present in order to inspire states and their armies to achieve great things. He calls this element 'necessity'. Given his view of human nature, Machiavelli believes that 'men never do good unless necessity drives them to it' (*Discourses*, I. 3, p. 112). Necessity, whether natural or manufactured, is a factor in human affairs which compels people and rulers to do things which for the most part they would not otherwise do. In other words, it acts as the volitional force particularly in activating latent or nascent *virtù*. Without it, Machiavelli contends, the achievements of human beings would not have been so great (*Discourses*, III. 12, p. 440). Necessity focuses the mind and restricts choices to essentials. Necessity does not automatically lead to inspired action, but provides the motivation for it: 'God does not want to do everything Himself, and take away from us our free choice and our share of the glory which belongs to us' (*The Prince*, 135). Without it, where choice and freedom are too much in supply; 'confusion and disorder become everywhere rampant' (*Discourses*, I. 3, p. 112; I. 1, pp. 100–4).

Necessity can be circumstantially generated, or the product of deliberate contrivance. Circumstantially, necessity is not of one's choosing. It can be a natural phenomenon such as over-population, drought, famine, disease, or geographical constraints. Where natural necessity does not exist to prevent men from becoming complacent, slothful, lazy, and effeminate, laws should be substituted to regulate conduct likely to precipitate such decline. On the other hand, necessity can result from the strength of one's neighbours, the corruptness of one's people, or an understanding of human nature. Such adversity to the prudent man is the opportunity for inspired action (*Discourses*, I. 51, pp. 234–5). Necessity drives people to perform 'glorious deeds'. It is, following Livy, 'the last and best of all weapons' (*Discourses*, III. 12, p. 443).

Rulers and army commanders have long utilized necessity for inspiring their troops to fight courageously. Machiavelli substantiates his claim with an example from Livy. Vettius Messius, faced with the prospect of losing his life with no avenue of escape, inspired his troops by saying: 'Follow me. There is neither wall nor rampart in the way, but just armed forces to oppose armed forces. In valour we are equal, but in necessity which is the last weapon and the best of all, you have the advantage' (*Discourses*, III. 12, p. 443).

Rulers and commanders have even manufactured necessity where it was lacking. This is what I have called contrived, or engineered, necessity. Here the ruler exercises his political imagination by contriving necessity to shape circumstances to his own advantage.[57] Rulers and commanders have therefore gone to great lengths to engineer the constraints of necessity to bring to bear upon their own troops. Machiavelli contends that 'Some have forced their men to fight through necessity, taking from them every hope of saving themselves except by winning' (*Art of War*, 662). Of the many necessities with which we are faced, the 'strongest is that which forces you to conquer or to die' (*Art of War*, 662). Here religion can judiciously be combined with necessity. The fear of eternal damnation is far greater than the mere fear of death . The necessity of saving one's soul was 'very powerful in keeping the ancient soldiers well disposed' (*Art of War*, 661).

Contrived necessity can be counter-productive if steps are not taken to remove or alleviate the necessity under which the enemy labours. Thus if the route is left open for the enemy to retreat, or to perceive an advantage, as opposed to annihilation in defeat, he will not feel the pressure of necessity to stand and fight at all costs. In the case of the Roman general Camillus, when he captured the city of Veii it was conveyed to the populace that 'to deprive the enemy of a last necessity to defend it' (*Discourses*, III. 12, p. 443), those citizens found without arms would not be harmed. The removal of such necessity need only be apparent because the ordinary people, eager for a peaceful conclusion to hostilities, 'shuts its eyes to any trap which may underlie generous promises' (*Discourses*, III. 12, p. 442).

Machiavelli's conception of just war hinges upon the idea of necessity. A war is just if necessity compels you to enter into it. Quoting Livy (9. 1. 10), Machiavelli suggests that 'War is justified, if necessity forces one to it, and to arm is a duty, if in arms lies one's hope' (*Discourses*, III. 12, p. 442). Fear of the enemy and the desire for security constitute such necessity (*The Prince*, 135, and *Discourses*, III. 12, p. 442). The justness of a war is judged not by absolute moral criteria, but by subjective standards of perceived safety, security, and advantage. The common good of the state, even if it is achieved at the expense of other states, is the only justification that need be given.

To sum up so far: good arms, good laws, and good allies, although indispensable in making a state great, need to be supplemented by religion and necessity to ensure that citizens and armies perform to their optimum. But this is not all that contributes to the greatness of a state.

Fortune, or *fortuna*, plays a significant part in all human affairs, and however strong a state may be, or however well its plans are laid, fortune can intervene and dash all hopes of success. Human beings are endowed with freedom of will, but often this will is broken ⌐y what Machiavelli calls the malice of fortune. In chapter xxv of *The Prince* Machiavelli actually quantifies what part fortune plays in human affairs. In his view fortune governs about half of our actions, leaving the rest in our own control. Fortune tends to strike hardest against those who are ill prepared for its force. Even Cesare Borgia, who had risen to power because of good fortune and who had then built firm foundations to maintain his gains, found that fortune was, when it struck, simply irresistible.

In *The Prince* and *The Discourses* Machiavelli emphasizes that the actions of leaders have to be suited to the times. When fortune changes you must be capable of adapting your actions to accommodate it. The problem is that few people are capable of changing their ways to suit the times. This is because we find it impossible to go against our natures. If we are successfully pursuing one course of action, when fortune changes we find it hard to believe that it is no longer prudent to pursue the same policies that have served us so well in the past. In his 'Tercets on Fortune', Machiavelli is extremely pessimistic about our ability to do other than what fortune wills. In talking about fortune's palace, in which the wheels turn one way, and then another, turning against each other and then suddenly changing direction, he contends that

while you are whirled about by the rim of a wheel that for the moment is lucky and good, she is wont to reverse its course in mid circle. And since you cannot change your character nor give up the disposition that Heaven endows you with, in the midst of your journey she abandons you.[58]

While individuals find that their characters are so fixed that they cannot adapt to changing circumstances, principalities may suffer more than republics from changes in fortune. Republics are more able to court fortune's favour because of the diversity of character that the citizens exhibit. But even in the case of Rome fortune eventually prevailed. In book II, chapter 29 of *The Discourses*, Machiavelli talks of fortune as if it possesses a will. Throughout his works fortune is portrayed as a woman who is fickle and who prefers young men, who are more inclined to be bold and impetuous than older men. Machiavelli suggests that fortune must be treated roughly: the more you beat her, the more power you exert over her. But, all in all, fortune cannot entirely be opposed. You can 'weave its warp, but cannot break it' (*Discourses*, II. 29, p. 372). The roads of fortune cross at the most unlikely points, and one should never despair because hope is never extinguished.

We are not all equally subject to the whims of fortune. Some are more able than others to seize the opportunities she offers and ride the waves to success, and having achieved success, remain more capable of placing it upon firm foundations. Those people who possess *virtù* are those whom fortune most favours. *Virtù* for Machiavelli is not moral virtue. He has in mind ancient pagan *virtù*, literally translated as 'that which befits a man'. It is a combination of valour and courage, but above all it points to balanced judgement and astuteness. In essence, it relates to that quality of adaptability which is necessary to alter your ways to suit changing circumstances. *Virtù* is also the quality which enables you to exercise your political imagination in recognizing and contriving necessities and in acknowledging opportunities when fortune sends them, but more than this, it is the ability to seize those opportunities, whatever they may be, and turn them to one's advantage.

In chapter VI of *The Prince* Machiavelli singles out a number of people who he thinks gained power by means of *virtù*. These were Moses, Cyrus, Romulus, and Theseus. For these men of *virtù* fortune did nothing more than provide them with the opportunities. Without such opportunities their *virtù* would have come to nothing, and without *virtù* fortune's opportunities would have been missed. In *The Discourses* Machiavelli portrays fortune as choosing those it wants to attain great things: 'it chooses a man of high spirits and great virtue who will seize the occasion it offers him' (*Discourses*, II. 29, p. 371).

Virtù is found not only in individuals, but also in armies. In the Roman army, Machiavelli claims, order promoted both *virtù* and ardour. No action was performed unless it was sanctioned by a regulation. In this army 'we find that no one ate or slept or went wenching or performed any other action, military or domestic, without instructions from the consul' (*Discourses*, III. 36, p. 504). Disciplined and instilled *virtù* of this kind enabled ardour to be used in such a way that no circumstances could discourage or demoralize the army.

One may say in summary that necessity impels a prince or republic possessed of *virtù* to act upon the opportunities that fortune provides. But the picture is not complete without integrating the place of ambition in Machiavelli's theory of the state and international relations. Ambition is a human characteristic, Russell Price argues, which Machiavelli generally tends to associate with the *grandi*, or the ruling class, of whom there would be very few in a state. Even in republics those who aspire to public office would be relatively few.[59] It is a characteristic of which Machiavelli disapproves when it is detected in the actions of individuals in internal affairs.

Machiavelli closely associates ambition with corruption. He describes it as an appetite contributory to the ruin of most states. Ambition leads to rule by faction, which is subversive of law. The wicked are drawn to faction because of ambition and avarice, whereas the good are drawn by necessity for protection (*History of Florence*, 1146). To be driven by ambition is to strive for status, power, or office with a view to promoting one's own self-interest, or that of one's relatives or associates. This is what Machiavelli calls 'private ambition' (*Discourses*, III. 22, p. 469), which is accentuated self-interest, desirous of personal glory rather than the glory of the state. Private ambition is, like Rousseau's particular will, by definition opposed to the common good, and indeed destructive of it. It is to private ambition that Machiavelli attributes the ruin of Italy in general and of Florence in particular ('The [Golden] Ass', 762; 'Tercets on Ambition', 736; and *Discourses*, I. 7, pp. 124–7).[60] A land in which the people are ambitious and cowardly, as in Italy, opens itself to all sorts of harm ('Tercets on Ambition', 737). A new prince of a composite principality has to beware of his enemies calling for outside assistance, which they do either out of 'excessive ambition or because of fear' (*The Prince*, 38). In *The Discourses*, Machiavelli shows how ambition can be dangerous to a republic. In Rome it was common for the populace or the nobility to become arrogant when either side felt that it had the upper hand. There is a tendency for those who seek to rid themselves of injuries to inflict similar injuries on others. It is as if people need to be ill-treated, or to ill-treat others. This passing 'from one ambition to another' is one of the ways by which a republic becomes dissolved (*Discourses*, I. 46, p. 224). Those citizens 'who live ambitiously' first tend to seek not to be ill-treated by securing their safety by means of seemingly honest methods. They offer assistance to others to protect them against the powerful. Their power begins to grow, and neither citizens nor magistrates wish to offend such persons: 'it is not very difficult after that for them to do just what they please and to give offence in their own turn' (*Discourses*, I. 46, p. 224). Once ambitious people have succeeded, 'there is not a thing so unjust, so cruel, so avaricious that they do not dare to do it. Hence they make laws and statutes not for the public benefit but for their own; hence wars, truces, alliances are decided not for the common glory but for the pleasure of a few' (*History of Florence*, 1146).

Ambition in relation to foreign affairs is on the whole a much more laudable motivation, on condition that it is joined with 'a valiant heart' and 'well armed vigour' ('Tercets on Ambition', 737, ll. 91–2). Ambition can be transformed by the man of *virtù* into patriotic vigour.[61] Wars, of course, can be prosecuted out of private ambition and for personal gain to the detriment of the state, but those that are motivated by public ambition and that benefit the common good are to be encouraged. In this respect the methods of Manlius, the Roman consul, are to be emulated. His actions were devoid of personal interest, and directed instead to the benefit of the state and public advantage. He treated everyone harshly and did not therefore attract factions to grow up around him (*Discourses*, iii. 22, p. 469). Expansionist ambitions in the sphere of international relations are perfectly acceptable because among states there is no universal code of ethics to restrain them. Thus 'Ambition uses against foreign peoples that violence which neither the law nor the king permits her to use at home (whereof home-born trouble almost always ceases)' ('Tercets on Ambition', 737, ll. 97–100). The criterion of the wisdom of such activity is whether such expansionist policies redound to the glory of the state and the common good of its citizens. There are two principal reasons why states embark upon war. First, wars arise out of extreme necessities which result in whole peoples seeking new territories elsewhere, invariably displacing another people or destroying them. Such wars are brutal and horrific, but sometimes necessary. Wars are also due to the ambitions of princes and republics who wish to establish an empire. Here a people need not be displaced, providing they pledge their obedience to the new ruler, and laws and customs may often be kept in place (*Discourses*, ii. 8, p. 294).[62] This was the method of Alexander the Great and the Romans. Successful conquests of this kind are to be praised on condition that a state has the capacity to hold the conquered territories. To use troops paid for by others, that is, auxiliaries, in order to further the ambitions of the state is dangerous because in winning a territory the auxiliaries may turn around and attempt to subjugate you. It is quite natural for neighbouring states to have ambitions to dominate each other, but they should only do so if they have the capacity, or are compelled to do so from necessi., or out of the fear of being dominated.

Reason of State

The decline of the papacy and empire as important focuses of universalism gave way to a Realism of naked power politics propelled by an undisguised *raison d'état*.[63] Ideas of state necessity and public utility overriding the rights of individuals for the common benefit were widespread before the Renaissance in Italy. Justifications for Reason of State were couched in familiar religious terms, and related to the law of God and the Natural Law. Lesser acts of immorality or sin, including deceit well used for a good cause, impelled by necessity, were often deemed permissible to avert greater wrongs. In cases of extreme necessity even extraordinary levies on the wealth of the Church were permissible. The medieval ruler was, however, more constrained than the prince whom Machiavelli envisages; Roman, Germanic and feudal customs and laws required him to take counsel on important public issues. He was not completely at liberty to decide what necessity required for the security of the realm.[64] We have already seen the extent to which Machiavelli saw at first hand the unveiling of these constraints. His cynicism was widely shared among his contemporaries. Guicciardini, for example, through the character of Bernardo, suggests that constraints of conscience in relation to war are misplaced: 'Therefore when I talked of murdering or keeping the Pisans imprisoned, I didn't perhaps talk as a Christian: I talked according to the reason and practice of states.'[65]

Machiavelli's theory of the Reason of State, a theory which both Pocock and Skinner considerably underplay in emphasizing his association with humanist rhetoric,[66] needs to be constructed with reference to both *The Prince* and *The Discourses*, along with his other writings. The specific precepts of the doctrine of *raison d'état* are contingent upon the circumstances in which a ruler finds himself. In general, *raison d'état* is operationalized *virtù*, that is, doing what is necessary for the interest of the state. Knowledge is power, and all rulers must equip themselves with it. Meinecke sees necessity as the linchpin of the whole theory of *raison d'état*. It constitutes, for him, a causal necessity dictating national interest and providing the impetus to ignite *virtù* into action and to force the masses into conformity with what the man of *virtù* and circumstances require.[67] Necessity, in other words, restricts choices, and in many instances leaves no choice, and it impels actions that reason may lack the strength to generate and that open up a divide between politics and morality.

The relation between necessity and Reason of State is not, however, causal in a naturalistic sense. Necessity does not provide the necessary and sufficient conditions for acts of *raison d'état*. The imagination and thought of the man of *virtù* always mediate, comprehending the situation and conceiving the possibilities, and even manufacturing necessity when required. The idea of *raison d'état* in Machiavelli is an ennobled concept animated by the high moral ideal of the common good which is depe..dent upon political stability, the only context in which ordinary moral values and the values of citizenship can flourish. It is a product of the recognition, as Meinecke suggests, that power, justice, and morality are capable of working in harmony within the state, but not within the wider context of relations among states: 'Justice can only be upheld, if power exists which is able and ready to uphold it.'[68]

There are certain basic things that political actors need to know in order to gain glory for themselves and their states. Glory, the principal reward of astute political action, is gained by those who are founders of religions, republics, and princedoms, and those who at the head of armies have increased their own territories or those of their country (*Discourses*, I. 10, p. 134). It is imperative that those who are founders and commanders organize the institutions over which they have authority in such a way as to facilitate their future maintenance. Corrupted institutions provide the opportunity for achieving glory by the renovation and renewal of basic principles.[69] Glory is not commensurate with power. Power used well and successfully, that is, for the common good, commits the ruler's name to posterity. Praise is also afforded those who benefit mankind through arts and sciences. Infamy is due to those who subvert all these positive achievements.

First, as has already been suggested, rulers need to be well versed in human nature. Knowing the human character is a fundamental prerequisite of successful political action. History is the best teacher of human nature and of how to act in order to overcome its potentially damaging consequences. The possession of knowledge is a powerful ally in the quest for political stability.[70]

Secondly, any such action has to be informed by an intricate understanding of the complex interrelations between necessity, *virtù*, and fortune, and of how they in turn relate to good laws, good arms, and public-spirited ambition. Necessity will often require courses of action that ordinary morality abjures. The prudent man of *virtù*, ambitious for glory and the betterment of the common good, seizing the opportunities that fortune presents, will do what is necessary for the preservation and promotion of the welfare of the state.

And, thirdly, having acquired the requisite knowledge and having the character to act in accordance with it, the ruler should observe rules of statecraft which, if followed without succumbing to the qualms of conventional morality, will lead to greater stability. Such rules are not a recipe for certain success. Given the complexities of the human condition, nothing can ever be certain: 'no government should ever imagine that it can adopt a safe course of action; rather it should regard all possible courses of action as risky' (*The Prince*, 123).

The condition of a stable state is a successful foreign policy, which invariably includes war as an instrument of policy. The virtues associated with war help promote those qualities of citizenship and patriotism necessary to keep corruption at bay. Both the love of one's country and the hatred of neighbouring princes and republics are in Machiavelli's view natural (*Art of War*, 662; *Discourses*, III. 12, p. 441). War and interstate rivalry had been such a significant aspect of Machiavelli's experience that he states quite emphatically in chapter XIV of *The Prince* that the ruler 'should have no other object or thought, nor acquire skill in anything, except war, ..s organization, and its discipline. The art of war is all that is expected of a ruler . . .' (*The Prince*, 87). By this Machiavelli does not mean merely the art of military tactics and command. The prince must also be well versed in statecraft. The ruler must therefore be eternally vigilant, or, as Hobbes was later to suggest, he must be forewarned and forearmed (*The Prince*, 87, 88, 90). Foreknowledge of the possible shape of events and their likely outcomes is fundamental to successful political activity.[71]

It was the necessity of eternal vigilance in a state system in which war was endemic that diplomacy flourished, not only for just representation, but also to convey news of developments,[72] a service in which Machiavelli himself was employed. To be unprepared is, in Machiavelli's eyes, one of the cardinal political sins. The Romans had such foresight, and when they sensed that there was trouble on the horizon they took immediate steps to check it (*The Prince*, 40, 87, 88, 90). Unpreparedness is a consequence of political illusion: the belief that success breeds success and the consequent refusal to alter one's course of action when circumstances change; a trust in hope rather than in one's own capacities; a belief that it is worth upsetting one's plans in order to avert war, while in fact it is merely postponed to one's own disadvantage (*The Prince*, 43); and the belief that an ally that one has helped become great will not in turn ruin one (*The Prince*, 44).

Fear is an extremely potent weapon in the arsenal of a ruler who has to assume the worst of human nature. It is much better to be feared than to be loved, because love is a fickle emotion, but fear can be effectively instilled 'by a dread of punishment which is always effective' (*The Prince*, 97). Fear keeps people in check. The ruler of *virtù*, always attuned to the 'ambition, licentiousness, lamentation and avarice' of the populace ('The [Golden] Ass', 772, l. 136), has to have the strength of a lion and the cunning of a fox. Here Machiavelli is directly contradicting the genre of advice books to princes, which almost invariably speak of the power of love in maintaining the allegiance of the people. John of Salisbury, for example, contends that the prince 'desires love more than fear. . . . For love is stronger than death; and the military formation that is tied together by the bonds of love will not break easily.'[73]

Machiavelli's advice to princes is contingent upon the type of principality the prince has, and whether, if acquired in war, he has used his own arms and *virtù* or relied upon foreign arms and fortune. Hereditary principalities are relatively easy to maintain because 'it is enough merely not to neglect the institutions founded by one's ancestors' (*The Prince*, 33).

In new principalities the task is much more difficult. Composite principalities consist of new appendages joined to an old state. To secure his hold on these new possessions a prince is compelled to destroy the family of the old prince (*The Prince*, 36), taking care not to exacerbate hostility by changing the laws and taxes. Machiavelli emphasizes this point when he says 'there is nothing to worry about except the ruler's family. When that has been wiped out there is no one left to fear' (*The Prince*, 46). If you destroy the family of the former prince, the people having been used to living in obedience to a monarch will succumb to the power of the new prince (*The Prince*, 49). A prince will not incur the wrath of his new subjects if he refrains from being 'rapacious and aggressive with regard to the property and women of his subjects' (*The Prince*, 102). In particular, it is especially important that the 'prince must abstain from the property of others; because men sooner forget the death of their father than the loss of their patrimony' (*The Prince*, 97). In provinces that differ in language and custom the prince should consider residing, or sending out a small colony. Only a small number of people need be dispossessed, so insignificant a number that they need constitute no threat in their opposition. Rule by force is simply too expensive and dangerous because the billeting of soldiers in large numbers causes considerable resentment. Both princedoms and republics should set themselves up as the protectors of the smaller states that surround them, taking care to deter the intervention of foreign powers and the aggrieved individuals who invite them (*The Prince*, 39).

An acquired state that has been used to freedom and liberty living under its own laws will not take kindly to being deprived of its liberty and will before long destroy the conquering power, justifying its actions by appeal to freedom and the traditional institutions of its city (*The Prince*, 48). The safest way to keep such a territory is to devastate it.

In completely new states, Machiavelli argues, the difficulty in maintaining them depends upon the ability of the ruler. If the new state is acquired through the exercise of one's ability rather than through good luck, the ruler is in a strong position. Moses, who led the Israelites out of Egypt, Cyrus, the founder of the Persian Empire, Romulus, the legendary founder and king of Rome, and Theseus, king of Athens and hero of Attica, are highlighted as individuals who did not have to rely on good fortune for their success. They surmounted untold difficulties in establishing their states, but then maintained them with ease. New principalities that are acquired with the aid of good fortune and with the use of foreign arms stand on very poor foundations indeed. They are acquired with ease, but are extremely difficult to hold on to. Those who buy their way into power, or are granted it by the favours of others, fall into this category. They are suddenly elevated from obscurity, but lack the talents necessary for commanding because they have no troops who are loyal and devoted to them. To demonstrate this point, Machiavelli uses one of his many examples from nature as an analogue: 'governments set up overnight, like everything in nature whose growth is forced, lack strong roots and ramifications. So they are destroyed in the first bad spell' (*The Prince*, 54). Some princes, however, who possess great *virtù* may not so easily come to grief. If they are able to lay foundations after the event, as other princes did before, then they may be able to hold on to what fortune has provided them. Cesare Borgia came to power by employing the arms of others and by means of the favours of Pope Alexander VI. He soon began to build his own army, and laid firm political foundations in the Romagna for attaining further glory. Had he not succumbed to illness at the time of Alexander's death, Cesare Borgia's *virtù* would have won him even greater honours: 'and if what he instituted was of no avail, this was not his fault but arose from the extraordinary and inordinate malice of fortune' (*The Prince*, 55).

Following the example he learned from Cesare Borgia, Machiavelli recommends that one should never declare one's intentions. The ruler should simply act (*Discourses*, I. 44, p. _0). Thus one should not declare one's intention to kill someone, because it may provoke a reaction which is extremely dangerous. It is much better to kill your intended victim outright 'for a dead man cannot contemplate vengeance' (*Discourses*, III. 6, p. 400). When a ruler inflicts harm upon great men it is a mistake to believe that the old injuries are cancelled out by new benefits. Those injured merely await the opportunity to avenge themselves (*Discourses*, III. 4, pp. 394–5, and *The Prince*, 61). Cruelty has to be used well. It has to be employed once and for all to secure one's position and then it should be used sparingly if possible. In this way men's minds will be put at ease and the ruler will win their confidence when benefits are conferred.

In *The Prince*, chapter XVIII, drawing upon his own experience, Machiavelli argues that great successes have been gained in modern times by those who give their word lightly. He contends that the people are so simple that it is easy to trick them with cunning. People are deceived by appearances, and as long as the ruler appears to have the virtues most admired in a prince, while being capable of acting quite to the contrary, he will easily dupe the people. Fraud, while usually considered reprehensible, is 'praiseworthy and glorious' in the conduct of war. To outsmart the enemy by trickery and deceit is a perfectly legitimate tactic in war. The defence of one's country justifies the most extreme courses of conduct:

For when the safety of one's country wholly depends on the decision to be taken, no attention should be paid either to justice or injustice, to kindness or cruelty, or to its being praiseworthy or ignominious. On the contrary, every other consideration being set aside, that alternative should be wholeheartedly adopted which will save the life and preserve the freedom of one's country. (*Discourses*, III. 41, p. 515)

It must be emphasized that Machiavelli continually stresses that the end towards which all these seemingly immoral actions are to be directed is to be a good end. Such actions must be directed to the maintenance of political stability and the promotion of the common good. However, as I have already suggested, he is concerned only with the common good of the ruler's own state, and not with that of those states he conquers and subjects. His doctrine of *raison d'état* presents a policy of state action in its relations with other states in a purely one-sided manner. He does not assume a balance in which equilibrium is the goal. Only out of the most extreme necessities should one rely upon such a precarious path to peace as alliances with others to avert war. The primary goal is security, upon which one should build at every advantage. He works upon the principle that a state should do unto others before anything is done to it. For Machiavelli there is no universal common good. The state is the provider of the stable conditions in which morality and good citizenship can flourish, and the outside environment composed of other states constitutes a constant threat to that stability.

In Machiavelli, then, we have a continuation of the theme of the denial of any universal ethical standards by which states should direct their actions. Morality emerges within the context of societies which are established for protection. The state provides the environment within which morality can flourish, and in which citizens can develop all of the conventional virtues. The realm of politics, while guided in its ultimate end by moral considerations, cannot afford to be constrained by the ethics of the ordinary citizen. There is a tension between politics and morality which cannot be resolved. Morality must be subordinate to politics if statesmen and states are to sustain the necessary flexibility for creating and maintaining a stable political environment both internally and externally.

Notes

1. Denys Hay, *Europe: The Emergence of an Idea* (New York, Harper and Row, 1966), 56.
2. Torbjörn L. Knutsen, *A History of International Relations Theory* (Manchester, Manchester University Press, 1992), 16.
3. Geoffrey Barraclough, *History in a Changing World* (Oxford, Blackwell, 1957), 101.
4. Cited by Gaines Post, '*Ratio Publicae Utilitas, Ratio Status*, and "Reason of State" ', in *Studies in Medieval Legal Thought* (Princeton, Princeton University Press, 1964), 277.

5. David Boucher and Paul Kelly, 'The Social Contract and its Critics', in David Boucher and Paul Kelly (eds.), *The Social Contract from Hobbes to Rawls* (London, Routledge, 1994), 10–11. Also see R. W. and A. J. Carlyle, *A History of Medieval Theory in the West* (Edinburgh, Blackwood, 1970), iii. 150.

6. Cary J. Nederman and Kate Landon Forhan, 'Introduction', in Cary J. Nederman and Kate Landon Forhan (eds.), *Medieval Political Theory—A Reader* (London, Routledge, 1993), 12–13.

7. Norbert Elias, *The Court Society* (Oxford, Blackwell, 1983), 117.

8. Garrett Mattingly, *Renaissance Diplomacy* (London, Cape, 1955), 30–3.

9. J. Huizinga, *The Waning of the Middle Ages* (Harmondsworth, Penguin, 1976), 95.

10. Barraclough, *History in a Changing World*, 103.

11. This view is propounded by Quentin Skinner, *The Foundations of Modern Political Thought* (Cambridge, Cambridge University Press, 1978), vol. ii. 349–58; and Quentin Skinner, 'The State', in T. Ball, J. Farr, and R. L. Hanson (eds.), *Political Innovation and Conceptual Change* (Cambridge, Cambridge University Press, 1989), 90–131.

12. See Post, '*Ratio Publicae Utilitatis*', 241–309; and Antony Black, *Political Thought in Europe 1250–1450* (Cambridge, Cambridge University Press, 1992), 186–191.

13. Niccolò Machiavelli, *The Art of War*, in *The Chief Works and Others*, ed. Allan Gilbert (Durham, NC, Duke University Press, 1989), 3 vols.

14. Niccolò Machiavelli, *The History of Florence*, in *Chief Works*.

15. Jacob Burckhardt, *The Civilisation of the Renaissance* (London, Phaidon, 1944; first pub. 1860), 57.

16. J. R. Hale, *Machiavelli and Renaissance Italy* (Harmondsworth, Penguin, 1961), 15.

17. Friedrich Meinecke, *Machiavellism: The Doctrine of Raison d'État and its Place in Modern History* (London, Routledge and Kegan Paul, 1962; first pub. 1924), 30.

18. Denys Hay, *Europe in the Fourteenth and Fifteenth Centuries* (London, Longman, 1970), 165 and 273–94. For a brief period between 1367 and 1370 Urban V returned to Rome, but he was driven back to Avignon by his enemies.

19. John of Salisbury, *Policraticus*, ed. and trans. Cary J. Nederman (Cambridge, Cambridge University Press, 1990), iv. 3, p. 32.

20. Charles Howard McIlwain, *The Growth of Political Thought in the West* (New York, Macmillan, 1932), 234.

21. G. G. Coulton, *Studies in Medieval Thought* (London, Nelson, 1940), 121–9.

22. John of Paris, *On Royal and Papal Power*, in Cary J. Nederman and Kate Landon Forhan (eds.), *Medieval Political Theory—A Reader* (London, Routledge, 1993), 164–5.

23. Black, *Political Thought in Europe*, 52–4.

24. John of Paris, *On Royal and Papal Power*, 166.

25. Black, *Political Thought in Europe*, 58.

26. J. W. Allen, 'Marsilio of Padua and Medieval Secularism', in F. J. C. Hearnshaw (ed.), *The Social and Political Ideas of Some Great Medieval Thinkers* (New York, Barnes and Noble, 1923).

27. Marsilius of Padua, *Defensor pacis* trans. Alan Gerwith (Toronto, Toronto University Press, 1986).

28. Marsilius of Padua, *Defensor minor and De translatione imperii* trans. Fiona Watson and Cary J. Nederman (Cambridge, Cambridge Univeristy Press, 1993).

29. This is the position of Alan Gerwith in his *Marsilius of Padua and Medieval Political Philosophy* (New York, Columbia University Press, 1951).

30. I owe this point to Joe Canning.
31. See Cary Nederman's introduction to the *Defensor minor and De translatione imperii*.
32. Cary J. Nederman, *Community and Consent: The Secular Political Theory Of Marsiglio of Padua* (Lanham, U.S.A., Rowman and Littlefield, 1994), 22–3.
33. Cary Nederman, 'The Problem of Empire in Marsiglio of Padua', *History of Political Thought*, 16 (1995).
34. Nederman, introduction to *Defensor minor and De translatione imperii*, p. xix.
35. A. P. d'Entrèves, *The Medieval Contribution to Political Thought* (Oxford, Clarendon Press, 1939), 86.
36. William of Ockham, *A Short Discourse on Tyrannical Government*, ed. A. S. McGrade (Cambridge, Cambridge University Press, 1992) II. 3, p. 23.
37. Ockham, *Discourse on Tyrannical Government*, III. 13, p. 97.
38. Black, *Political Thought in Europe*, 70.
39. Ockham, *Discourse on Tyrannical Government*, IV. 10, p. 125.
40. Mattingly, *Renaissance Diplomacy*, 57.
41. Francesco Guicciardini, 'The Balance of Power among the Italian States', in Evan Luard (ed.), *Basic Texts in International Relations* (London, Macmillan, 1992), 382.
42. Robert R. Sullivan, 'Machiavelli's Balance of Power Theory', *Social Science Quarterly*, 54 (1973), 262–4.
43. See e.g. Martin Wight, *Power Politics*, ed. Hedley Bull and Carsten Holbraad, 2nd edn. (Harmondsworth, Penguin, 1986), 30.
44. Burckhardt, *The Civilisation of the Renaissance*, 48.
45. Hale, *Machiavelli and Renaissance Italy*, 25.
46. Quentin Skinner, *Machiavelli* (Oxford, Oxford University Press, 1981), 7.
47. See Peter E. Bondanella, *Machiavelli and the Art of Renaissance History* (Detroit, Wayne State University, 1973), 30.
48. Cited in Bondanella, *Machiavelli*, 31. This point is expanded upon in *The Prince*, chap. XVI.
49. Niccolò Machiavelli, *Legations*, in *Chief Works*, 120–61.
50. See also Niccolò Machiavelli, 'A Description of the Method Used by Duke Valentino in Killing Vitellozzo Vitelli, in *Chief Works*, 163–9.
51. Niccolò Machiavelli, *First Decennale*, in *Chief Works*.
52. Letter no. 134, in *Chief Works*, 926.
53. Letter no. 128, in *Chief Works*, 910.
54. Cited in Sydney Anglo, *Machiavelli* (London, Paladin, 1971), 28; Skinner, *Machiavelli*, 9; and, Hale, *Machiavelli and Renaissance Italy*, 67.
55. Letter no. 116, in *Chief Works*, 897.
56. See David Boucher, 'The Duplicitous Machiavelli', *Machiavelli Studies*, 3 (1990), 163–72.
57. K. R. Minogue, 'Theatricality and Politics: Machiavelli's Concept of Fantasia', in B. Parekh and R. N. Berki (eds.), *The Morality of Politics* (London, Allen and Unwin, 1972), 153.
58. 'Tercets on Fortune', in *Chief Works*, 747, ll. 109–14.
59. Russell Price, '*Ambizione* in Machiavelli's Thought', *History of Political Thought*, 3 (1982), 383–445.
60. 'The [Golden] Ass' and 'Tercets on Ambition', in *Chief Works*, 762 and 736.
61. Anthony Parel, 'Machiavelli Minore', in Anthony Parel (ed.), *The Political Calculus* (Toronto, University of Toronto Press, 1972), 191.
62. Also see Price, '*Ambizione*', 395.

63. Knutsen, *A History of International Relations Theory*, 26–7; and Adam Watson, *The Evolution of International Society* (London, Routledge, 1992), 153–8.
64. Post, '*Ratio Publicae Utilitatis*', 274.
65. Francesco Guicciardini, *Dialogue on the Government of Florence*, ed. Alison Brown (Cambridge, Cambridge University Press, 1994), 159.
66. J. G. A. Pocock, *The Machiavellian Moment* (Princeton, Princeton University Press, 1975); and Skinner, *The Foundations of Modern Political Thought*, vol. i.
67. 'A high degree of causal necessity, which the agent himself is accustomed to conceive as absolute and inescapable, and to feel most profoundly, is therefore part of the very essence of all action prompted by *raison d'état*.' (Meinecke, *Machiavellism*, 2; cf. 6, 37).
68. Meinecke, *Machiavellism*, 14.
69. See Hanna Fenichel Pitkin, *Fortune is a Woman* (Berkeley, University of California Press, 1984), 52–3.
70. On the importance of knowledge see Alkis Knotos, 'Success and Knowledge in Machiavelli', in Anthony Parel (ed.) (Toronto, University of Toronto Press, 1972), *The Political Calculus*, 83–98.
71. Robert Orr, 'The Time Motif in Machiavelli', *Political Studies*, 17 (1969), 193.
72. Mattingly, *Renaissance Diplomacy*, 58–62.
73. John of Salisbury, *Policraticus*, iv. 3, p. 34; also see p. 35.

7

INTER-COMMUNITY AND INTERNATIONAL RELATIONS IN THE POLITICAL PHILOSOPHY OF HOBBES

F. Melian Stawell, in one of the first general histories of thought in international relations, has little to say about Hobbes's contribution to understanding the relations among nations,[1] but more recently Hobbes's impressionistic, suggestive, cursory characterization of the international sphere as the nearest analogue to the state of nature has made his name synonymous with the doctrines of Realism and Reason of State.[2] Hobbes has now become the rival of Machiavelli in lending his name to a distinct tradition of thought in international relations,[3] to which they both belong, along with Thucydides, Bacon, Bodin, Hume, and Treitschke. When writers of the twentieth century are considered, the names of E. H. Carr, Hans Morganthau, and Winston Churchill are usually added to the list.[4]

Hobbes, in a number of places, invites the comparison of international relations with the unmitigated war of everyman against everyman which is characteristic of the mere state of nature in which Hobbes's individualism is at its most rampant. War is the declared disposition to resolve conflicts of will by resorting to force.[5] There never was a time, Hobbes admits, when this disposition was sufficiently prevalent to constitute a condition in which every individual was at war with every other. The nearest thing which approximates such a condition is the relations which pertain between states (*Leviathan*, 266). Since they have no common sovereign to hold them in awe, there is neither justice nor injustice in the international sphere.[6] In consequence, nations 'live in the condition of a perpetuall war, and upon the confines of battel, with their frontiers armed, and canons planted against their neighbours round about' (*Leviathan*, 266). When physical hostilities cease there is no condition of peace, but merely a breathing-space during which time preparations are made for the next encounter.[7] This pessimistic view of international relations is reiterated in *A Dialogue between a Philosopher and a Student of the Common Laws of England*. In answer to the question whether there can be a lasting peace between nations, the lawyer answers that no such condition can be expected 'because there is no Common Power in this World to punish injustice: mutual fear may keep them apart for a time, but upon every visible advantage they will invade one another'.[8] We should not lose sight of the fact, however, that internal conflict, or civil war, constituted for Hobbes a much greater 'inconvenience' than war among nations.[9]

Interpretations of Hobbes

Much has been written about Hobbes's place in the history of political thought, and in particular about his relation to the Baconian revolution and the emergence of modern science with its materialist-mechanistic outlook. Traditionally Hobbes has been portrayed as a materialist inspired by the new science of his age, adapting the laws of bodies in motion to the deductive examination and explanation of the human condition in its civil and ethical dimensions.[10] He has been seen as the forerunner of utilitarianism, deducing political philosophy from egoistic psychology and grounding moral and political obligation in enlightened calculated self-interest.[11]

Against the mechanistic utilitarian Hobbes, other commentators have sought to ally him with the Christian Natural Law tradition. Most notably, A. E. Taylor and Howard Warrender have argued that moral obligation exists in the state of nature and is grounded in divinely ordained Laws of Nature which are independent of the will of the sovereign. In this respect he is seen as the forerunner of a Kantian deontological ethics.[12] Leo Strauss highlighted the defects in both these interpretations, suggesting that Hobbes's political philosophy relied neither upon the moral principles of Christian Natural Law, nor upon a theory like Spinoza's, in which purely naturalistic principles are the ground of morality.[13] Oakeshott has extended this interpretation by agreeing that Hobbes's emphasis upon the fear of violent death as the one passion that lay at the root of morality consititutes a break from the Aristotelian and Scholastic view, while at the same time denying that Hobbes's break w..h the past was complete. The idea that civil society counteracts with all the power at its disposal the passion of pride or vanity is, Oakeshott contends, an echo of the Christian-Stoic tradition. Furthermore, late Scholastic nominalism had begun the process of emancipating the emotions and displacing reason in favour of will and imagination a long time before Hobbes developed these themes.[14] Nominalists contended that the nature of a thing, that which makes it this thing rather than that, was constituted by its individuality. Both in God and in man the will takes precedence over reason. What constitutes the individuality of man is not self-consciousness, but the act of willing.[15]

Interpreters of Hobbes's International Relations Theory

Hobbes's admirers and adversaries in the study of international relations have tended to take the purported correspondence between the individual in the state

of nature and the nation in its relations with other nations at face value,[16] meticu-
lously pursuing the questions of how far the analogy can be empirically substan-
tiated, and in what respects it needs to be modified to accommodate modern
international relations. Hedley Bull, for example, contends that 'we are entitled to
infer that all of what Hobbes says about the life of individual men in the state of
nature may be read as a description of the condition of states in relation to one
another'.[17] Furthermore, Bull contends, 'it is legitimate to ask how far world politics today resembles Hobbes's account of the state of war'.[18] To avoid labouring
the point, this tendency can be illustrated with reference to one aspect of Hobbes's
state of nature. Hobbes argues that in the state of nature we are all more or less
equal in body and mind. Differences which do occur are not significant enough
for you to be able to secure something for yourself so confidently that no one else
will desire it or try to take it away from you. The weakest of persons has the
strength to kill another through deceit or cunning, or by entering into an agreement with others who are similarly threatened by the danger. It is this condition
of natural equality and mutual fear which compels us to exercise power over
others in order to establish security. 'Power', Hobbes argues, 'if it be extraordinary, is good, because it is useful for protection; and protection provides security.
If it be not extraordinary, it is useless; for what all have is equally nothing' (*Man
and Citizen*, 49; cf. *Elements of Law*, 70; *Leviathan*, 183). Even when a relative
advantage has been gained in the acquisition of power, with its consequent implications for security and commodious living, its continued enjoyment can only be
procured by 'the acquisition of more' (*Leviathan*, 161). In summary, it is natural
equality which is partially to blame for the mutual fear which drives men in the
state of nature to the acquisition of power after power (*Man and Citizen*, 113;
Leviathan, 161).

Modern commentators have assumed that if the analogy between individuals
and nations is to hold, or if it is to be compelling, the principle of natural equality must be equally applicable. Beitz, for example, contends that the analogy is
only acceptable if a number of conditions are met, one of which is that 'states have
relatively equal power (the weakest can defeat the strongest)'.[19] This condition of
equality, the commentators suggest, simply cannot be sustained because history
shows us that there have always been vast discrepancies between the powers of
individual nations. The condition of nations is far more tolerable than that of
individuals because of the absence of fundamental equality.[20] States are simply
not as vulnerable as individuals in a state of nature[21] because 'in modern international society there has been a persistent distinction between great powers and
small'.[22] The advent of nuclear weapons, however, has introduced a new element
into the equation. If nuclear proliferation advances at its present rate, Gauthier
argues, 'then an ever increasing number of nations will come to share this dread-
ful equality. And so we may look to Hobbes's account of the natural condition of
mankind, with a view to understanding better our own international situation.'[23]
The equality of which Gauthier speaks is that of equal vulnerability to nuclear
weapons, a point which is contested by both Beitz and Bull. They both contend
that it is simply not the case that states are, or even are potentially, equally

vulnerable: 'states are highly unequal in this sense as well, as a result of their varying levels of retaliatory capabilities (and hence of deterrent strengths) and of
nuclear defences.'[24] Mark A. Heller has extended the argument by contending
that because states are not essentially equal, they do not all feel the state of nature
to be intolerable to the same degree. Furthermore, the incentive to leave the international state of nature is not as strong as that which impels association in the
original state of nature. The rulers of states, weighing their public and
private interests, will, Heller believes, allow the latter to dominate over the former,
and make them averse to relinquishing sovereignty to a world government. The
main thrust of Heller's argument is that the state in almost all respects is very
unlike the individual person, and that therefore it is a mistake to consider the situation of the former to be analogous to the latter in a state of nature,[25] and he
warns us not to follow Hobbes in the 'fallacy of confusing the natural man with
the political state'.[26]

Although many commentators recognize that Hobbes himself did not wish to
push the analogy between the relations of individuals and the relations of states
too far,[27] there is certainly a prevalent tendency to take the analogy too seriously,
and a failure to heed Oakeshott's warning that Hobbes 'could not deny himself the
pleasure of exaggeration'.[28] It is these exaggerations which tend to be seized upon
at the expense of a sensitive understanding of what Hobbes's view really was. He
alerts us himself to the fact that we should not take arguments by analogy, or correspondence, literally when he comments upon Aristotle's comparison of bees
and civil society. Hobbes says: 'When Aristotle calls them political or social creatures, he did not intend it really that they lived a civil life, but according to an
analogy, because they do such things by instinct as truly political creatures do out
of judgement'.[29]

Two articles have appeared in the last decade which present a more considered
view of what Hobbes was trying to convey to us about states in their relations with
each other. Murray Forsyth has argued that Hobbes's state of nature is more complex than is usually perceived. Individuals in a condition of war with each other
represent only the first phase, which becomes modified into a condition of groups
of various kinds in their relations with each other prior to the establishment of a
commonwealth by institution.[30] In addition, Donald W. Hanson has argued that
concentration upon the idea of a state of nature has inhibited our appreciation of
Hobbes as a philosopher of peace. He suggests that if we focus instead on Hobbes's
view of psychology and human nature we achieve a much more adequate understanding of his political theory. Hanson contends that Hobbes's theory of human
psychology is 'perfectly abstract', and not a matter of cataloguing specific character
traits. The mind, for Hobbes, is therefore malleable and susceptible to the educa-
tive processes which have to be instituted by the Leviathan in order to eradicate the
causes of internal dissension and 'to eliminate the sorts of ambitions in domestic
politics that he thinks lead to adventurism and imperialism'.[31]

In this chapter I wish to explore the relations which Hobbes believed to operate between communities in what Forsyth calls the modified state of nature, and
to highlight certain principles and constraints, in particular the role of honour, in

making the human predicament less precarious than it is in the mere state of nature in which individuals are at war with each other. For this purpose I wish to introduce a distinction between the hypothetical, or logical, state of nature and the historical pre-civil condition. The former is constructed by Hobbes through scientific, or philosophical, demonstration, that is, the achievement of conditional knowledge by tracing the 'Consequences of one Affirmation, to another' (*Leviathan*, 148). The historical pre-civil condition is something which we have to construct from Hobbes's various and scattered statements. But why should we want to do this, given that he did not believe that the state of nature ever existed? History, Hobbes tells us, is knowledge of facts and results from sense and memory (*Leviathan*, 147). In *De homine* (On Man), written in 1658, he contends that histories, that is, the registers of fact, are especially useful, for they 'supply in abundance the evidence on which rests the science of causes; in truth natural history for physics and also civil histories for civil and moral science' (*Man and Citizen*, 50). Philosophy for Hobbes, of course, is nothing other than the science of causes and effects.[32] In comparing the logical state of nature with the historical pre-civil condition we will see that Hobbes did actually believe that the modified, as opposed to the mere, state of nature did exist in pre-civil times. In both accounts he believed that relations between warring groups, rather than warring individuals, constituted the norm, and that the hostility was considerably alleviated by the emergence and development of constraints upon the actions of groups in their relations with others.

Furthermore, it is the purpose of this chapter to identify what Hobbes believed the relations among states to be, and in what ways and by what means he thought they could be improved. We will see that, for Hobbes, relations among states are *not* very like relations among individuals in the mere state of nature. Instead relations among states can more fruitfully be seen as analogous to a modified, or non-social community, stage of the hypothetical state of nature, and the historical pre-civil condition. It will also be suggested that Hobbes gave advice on how relations between states could be improved, and believed that not only had there been, but also there could continue to be, progress in this respect. It should be made clear at the outset that the purpose of this essay is not to improve our understanding of the relations among states, but instead to improve our understanding of what Hobbes had to say about such matters.

Hypothetical State of Nature

In articulating his account of man in the hypothetical state of nature, Hobbes, it is well known, relies heavily upon Thucydides.[33] War to the Greeks was a fact of life, and each *polis* had to prepare itself for the eventuality. It was considered to be an instrument of policy which was frequently invoked in disputes between *poleis*. Although the focus of Thucydides' *History of the Peloponnesian War* is the hostilities between Athens and Sparta during the period 431 to 404 BC, the work is essentially a study of human nature, its role in the relations between states, and the effects of war upon the internal relations of the state. Thucydides assumes that the events of the past, given what human nature is, may be profitably studied because there is a tendency for them, 'or at least their like', to be repeated.[34] He believed, therefore, that what he had to say was of lasting significance, not as an account of war, but as a source of generalizations about human behaviour. Hobbes used Thucydides as a source both in his account of the logical, or hypothetical, state of nature, and in the actual, or historical, account of communities in pre-civil times.

Thucydides shows that the Athenian representatives in their justification of imperialism in the Debate at Sparta believed that it was consistent with human nature to want to hold on to their empire for reasons of 'honour, fear and profit'.[35] In *Leviathan* Hobbes identifies three characteristics of human nature which are the cause of conflict: competition, diffidence, and glory (*Leviathan*, 185). On the surface Hobbes's causes of conflict appear to differ from those which cause the Athenians to retain and expand their empire, but when we look at the consequences of Hobbes's three characteristics it is clear that what he had in mind was very similar to Thucydides' causes. Hobbes says that competition makes people 'invade for Gain', and this is the equivalent of 'profit' in Thucydides: diffidence makes people invade 'for Safety', and this is the equivalent of 'fear'. Glory makes men invade 'for Reputation', and this is equivalent to 'honour' (*Leviathan*, 185). It is fear, however, which is for both authors the most powerful driving force in human nature. It is fear which serves to explain and justify a significant amount of human behaviour. Fear in the relations between individuals and between states serves to explain and justify the consequent conflict, while the lack of fear in the internal affairs of a state, that is, the absence of a power to keep men in awe, explains degeneration into civil war.

For Thucydides it was the fear of Persian expansionism which compelled Athens to acquire an empire, and it was the fear that the allies of Athens might defect to Sparta whic.. led it to maintain its empire by resisting all attempts at secession.[36] New conquests were pursued and past gains consolidated on the justification that 'it is as necessary for us to seek to subdue those that are not under our dominion, as to keep so those that are: lest if others be not subject to us, we fall in danger of being subjected unto them'.[37] Indeed, when Pericles addresses the Athenians who were critical of him for implicating Athens in the war with Sparta he reminds them that 'already your government is in the nature of a tyranny, which is both unjust for you to take up and unsafe to lay down'.[38] Paradoxically, it was fear which inspired the quest for security in the creation of an empire, and it was fear which led to its destruction. The real reason for the Peloponnesian War, Thucydides claims, was 'the growth of the Athenian power; which putting the Lacedaemonians into fear necessitated war'.[39]

What is most disturbing and striking about Thucydides' account of fear, and the role of human nature in general, is the extremely pessimistic tone which permeates the work; this deepens as during the course of the war the conventional constraints upon human nature disintegrate and any sense of a community spirit is dissolved and replaced by an unremitting self-interestedness, exhibited in leaders as well as ordinary citizens, that destroys all remnants of civility. There is little sign in Thucydides of the possibility of deliverance out of the chaos consequent upon human nature, but the fact that he wrote for the instruction of posterity would seem to suggest that he had hopes that lessons could be learned and such catastrophic consequences avoided in the future by perspicacious leaders.

Hobbes's reading of Thucydides' would have reinforced in him both the negative and positive consequences of fear, and he tried to explicate them in his logical construction of the state of nature. Hobbes's optimism is brought into sharp relief when juxtaposed with Thucydides's pessimism. For Hobbes mutual fear is the cause of conflict between individuals, but it is also the means of their deliverance from the mere state of nature in which natural equality engenders 'continuall feare, and danger of violent death' (*Leviathan*, 186). In this condition of mutual distrust and intense competition 'we can neither expect from others, nor promise to ourselves the least security' (*Man and Citizen*, 113) Fear, Hobbes contends, is 'The Passion to be reckoned upon' (*Leviathan*, 200). By fear he does not simply mean the immediate fear of another person, or other persons, but also the anticipation or foresight of those evils which may befall one at a future time. To anticipate future evil impels us to make provisions for avoiding it. Hobbes contends that 'It is through fear that men secure themselves by flight indeed, and in corners, if they think they cannot escape otherwise; but for the most part, by arms and defensive weapons; whence it happens, that daring to come forth they know each other's spirits' (*Man and Citizen*, 113 n.).

Anticipation of future consequences, whether bad or good, is based upon our experience of the past and affords us the foresight or prudence required for survival in the state of nature. Conjectures based upon experience are always uncertain and often fallacious because of insufficient knowledge of all of the circumstances. However, the more experience one has, the more prudent one will be in having one's expectations confirmed (*Leviathan*, 97; cf. *Leviathan*, 137). It is clear from what Hobbes says in his various accounts of the human predicament that he did not, even in his logical or hypothetical state of nature, envisage a quantum leap from the war of everyman against everyman to civil society. There is an intermediate stage in which communities form and enter into relations with each other in a modified state of nature.

It is not simply fear which precipitates this condition, but also 'Desire of such things as are necessary to commodious living' and the hope of attaining them (*Leviathan*, 188). Furthermore, it is not merely prudence which delivers us from our condition, but 'Reason', or 'right reason' (*Leviathan*, 188, and *Man and Citizen*, 123),[40] which reveals to us the dictates, or laws, of nature conducive to peace. Unlike prudence, reason is not based upon experience alone (*Leviathan*, 115), but is acquired through the apt imposition of names, and by means of an ordered method of establishing the connections among them. It is reason which 'suggesteth convenient Articles of Peace, upon which men may be drawn to agreement' (*Leviathan*, 188).

The world populated by individual sensing beings gradually develops through the fruits of experience, namely prudence, and the discovery of the dictates of reason, into a dynamic and changing collection of individuals, confederacies, and alliances of convenience, which through expediency, self-interest, and the desire for a better life enter into relations with other people. Among the purposes of such groups are internal security against each other; protection against other groups, or external enemies; taking those things which others have cultivated or built; and voyages of plunder. What we have in the hypothetical state of nature, then, is a complex set of relationships. Those between individuals; those between individuals and groups; and those between groups and other groups. All of these relationships grow from a condition of mutual fear and hostility and develop into tentative trust and temporary harmony. Our morbid fear of death and our vanity impel us to associate, even if that association may often result in conflict. The dictates of reason incline us towards association. Reason tells us that peace is more conducive to the preservation of life than war; that if others are willing to give up certain of their rights in the interests of peace then we should also be similarly inclined; and that having made a covenant, even if it is made through fear, we should be faithful to it (*Leviathan*, 190 and 201; cf. *Elements of Law*, 79).

The relations among individuals in the state of nature very soon lead to a modification of the one-to-one relation between equals. The natural inclination towards accumulating power to provide security acts as a catalyst to those who fear your power, or envy your possessions, to come together for mutual gain (*Leviathan*, 183 and 184). The very first, or fundamental, Law of Nature indicates that we should enter into security agreements, or form security communities by force. Reason tells us that we should endeavour as far as possible to procure peace, but if there remain people who persist in their hostile demeanour towards us we are at liberty to take all steps necessary to '*seek, and use, all helps, and advantages of Warre*' (*Leviathan*, 190).[41] In *The Elements of Law* Hobbes tells us that '*mutual aid is necessary for defence*' (*Elements of Law*, 101), and that we can only attain 'safety and commodity' by the 'mutual aid and help of one another' (*Elements of Law*, 100).[42] Furthermore, in anticipation of the future danger occasioned by natural equality a man should endeavour to 'prevent such equality before the danger cometh, and before there be necessity of battle' (*Elements of Law*, 73). To this end, Hobbes tells us in *The Citizen*, we may 'get some fellows' and 'enquire out for auxiliaries of war', so that if there must be hostility we will not be without help in the conflict (*Man and Citizen*, 118–19). In *Leviathan* we are told that there is no hope of defence against destruction 'without the help of Confederates' and that 'Feare of oppression, disposeth a man to anticipate, or seek ayd by society: for there is no other way by which a man can secure his life and liberty' (*Leviathan*, 204 and 163). If a person sees that he has no more power to overcome than that of a solitary individual, that person 'may probably be expected to come prepared with forces united, to dispossesse, and deprive him, not only of the fruit of his labour, but also of his life, or liberty' (*Leviathan*, 184). In other words, Hobbes is suggesting the impossibility of individuals unattached to groups surviving in the hypothetical state of nature.

In the Athenian justification of imperialism, and the Melian Dialogue, Thucydides articulates the Athenian belief that the international sphere is devoid of the notions of justice and injustice. There is no natural order in the relations between states. The order which exists is created and sustained by the powerful: 'It has always been a rule that the weak should be, subject to the strong.' [43] Each state has an obligation to look after its own self-interest in deciding its course of action, and it is in the interests of each state, if it has the power, to rule where it can. Indeed, the Athenians go so far as to say of men that 'for certain by necessity of nature, they will everywhere reign over such as they be too strong for.'[44]

These precepts of nature which Thucydides applied to interstate relations are translated by Hobbes into the relations between individuals. In the state of nature, where there is no commonly acknowledged authority, we get our auxiliaries of war by either consent or conquest. If we are able to subject people to our will we have a right, grounded upon superior power, to take whatever action we deem appropriate and necessary, for purposes of security, to ensure that those we have in our power continue to remain so 'for the time to come' (*Elements of Law*, 73–4).[45] Hobbes argues that '*a sure and irresistible power confers the right of dominion and ruling over those who cannot resist; insomuch, as the right of all things that can be done, adheres essentially and immediately unto this omnipotence hence arising*' (*Man and Citizen*, 119).

To unite by agreement into a small confederacy, or to exercise one's power over a small number of people, affords little security in the state of nature. Where the numbers are small on each side in a conflict the addition of a few more to either side is bound to secure the enlarged group victory.[46] It is therefore necessary that the number of confederates of auxiliaries of war be of such a large proportion that the addition of a few to the enemy's side 'may not prove to them a matter of moment sufficient to assure the victory' (*Man and Citizen*, 167).

It is clear, however, that such large groupings, because of diversity of opinion, desires and mutual envy, remain highly unstable alliances (*Leviathan*, 225). Even in the face of a common enemy, Hobbes believes, when imminent danger has the benefit of concentrating the mind, the diversity of opinion on how best to deploy their forces will, in the face of a small group united under one head, result in defeat. The transfer of right, in such circumstances, to a single head, if it is only temporary (that is, for the duration of the battle or the war), brings no lasting security. When the immediate danger has subsided, and there is no common enemy to unite them, their diverse opinions and interests surface and the bond that held them together in adversity dissolves when the common fear wanes (*Leviathan*, 225).

Even in this crude condition a code of honour appears to be evident. To enter into a confederacy with others in which everyone expects the same degree of defence is an expedient measure, but to attempt then to deceive your confederates and thus break the covenant is an act of folly which leaves you in a position where your only means of safety and defence is your individual power. If you were to be allowed entry into another confederation, it would only be by the error of the confederates, an error which cannot be relied upon. The most likely scenario is that you will be cast out of the confederation you deceived by breaking your covenant and left to perish as an outcast unable to procure the protection of another confederation because it is publicly known that you give your word lightly (*Leviathan*, 101). To act in such a manner is to act against the dictate of reason which tells us to do nothing that would contribute to our own destruction.

Furthermore, one joins a confederation for purposes of protection, and in doing so one sets a value on the power of the others to fulfil that expectation. In this respect one is honouring those in whose trust one places oneself. It is to those who have a reputation for prudence in matters of war and peace, Hobbes argues, that we are more likely to entrust the exercise of power over us. Having thus honoured a person, or persons, in joining a confederacy, it is an expression of dishonour to leave. The question of justness or unjustness does not arise, 'for Honour consisteth onely in the opinion of Power' (*Leviathan*, 156). A confederacy slighted by a sign of dishonour would, we may assume, in order to redeem and protect its reputation and deter others from similar acts of dishonour, take revenge on those who tried to leave.

Hobbes appears to be contending, then, that non-social communities, that is, confederacies of auxiliaries of war, rather than individuals, are the norm in the hypothetical, or logically constructed, state of nature. Relations between these groups, although not cordial, are nevertheless constrained by the Laws of Nature and honour. In *The Elements of Law* Hobbes contends that the Law of Nature commands us in war not to be carried away by our passions and indulge in gratuitous cruelty with no prospect of future benefit. A mind disposed to cruelty without necessity is at variance with the Law of Nature (*Elements of Law*, 100). Only fear can be used in justification of taking a life, but fear predominantly manifests itself as actions which are dishonourable and which betray one's own weaknesses. Courageous and magnanimous men do not perpetrate cruelty. There is no law in war which makes cruelty an injustice; 'yet there are those laws, the breach whereof is dishonour. In one word, therefore, the only law of action in war is honour; and the right of war providence' (*Elements of Law*, 101). In *A Dialogue between a Philosopher and a Student of the Common Laws of England*, Hobbes, through the medium of the philosopher, goes further and argues that if an injury has been inflicted upon you then a defensive war is justifiable, but if the injury is reparable, and reparation has been offered, it would be iniquitous to invade on that pretext. He contends that 'Necessity and Security are the principal justifications, before God, of beginning of War' (*A Dialogue*, 159).

In view of the fact that the fundamental Law of Nature is an inclination towards peace, even though there is no common authority acknowledged by the various confederations in the state of nature, all those people engaged in mediating for peace must be given security and safe conduct. In other words, if peace is the end, the means of procuring that end must be guaranteed: 'neither can peace be had without mediation, nor mediation without safety' (*Man and Citizen*, 145; cf. *Elements of Law*, 87; *Leviathan*, 213).

In summary, Hobbes's hypothetical, or logically constructed, state of nature begins with individuals in their hostile relations with each other. Soon the original position becomes converted into a condition principally comprising confederacies of auxiliaries of war, the individual outside of which has little prospect of survival, and relations between which are less than cordial, but more conducive to safety and commodious living than life in the mere state of nature.

The Historical State of Nature

I now want to turn, more briefly, to the question of what Hobbes actually thought the pre-civil condition was like. In Hobbes's view, 'there had never been any time, wherein particular men were in a condition of warre one against another' (*Leviathan*, 187), and therefore the natural liberty of which Hobbes speaks is a convenient fiction designed to impress upon the reader the necessity of strong government. It may also be inferred that the natural equality of sexes of which Hobbes speaks had no historical basis. Whereas women figure significantly in the hypothetical state of nature, or at least in its unmodified stage, they disappear altogether from Hobbes's view of what the past was actually like, with the exception of the Amazon women whom he invokes to substantiate his hypothetical account of the natural equality of the sexes in the state of nature. Filmer, for example, was critical of Hobbes's logical account of the state of nature on the grounds that it was both misleading and superfluous.[47] It was misleading because such a condition never existed, and superfluous because in the historical examples which Hobbes gives he appears to subscribe to the idea of the natural, paternal foundation of dominion.

Hobbes admits that the mere state of nature has no historical basis, but this does not, however, apply to the modified state of nature which he did think actually existed. The modified state of nature comes into being, on the logical account, by means of institution and conquest. Hobbes, in the historical account, begins with the equivalent of the modified state of nature, but invokes patriarchal authority as the foundation of the social cohesiveness of the groups, which grow and develop by means of the procreation of their members; by conquests; by individuals joining for protection, or being enticed to join because of their skills; or by the institution of a larger group at the instigation of a number of heads of households in agreement with each other.

All countries, Hobbes admits, originally comprised numerous families over which there were lords or masters (*Leviathan*, 158). Sons, and presumably daughters, are born into the protection of a family, and owe allegiance to the father, or mother, who exercises dominion (*Man and Citizen*, 117). Such allegiance is owed on the ground that he, or she, who is nourished and preserved owes everything to the preserver (*Man and Citizen*, 213). 'Dominion by Generation' (*Leviathan*, 253) was a common foundation of government in pre-civilized communities, and 'originally the Father of every man was also his Soveraign Lord, with power over him of life and death' (*Leviathan*, 382). Such goods and lands as the children hold are at the pleasure of the father, or master (*Man and Citizen*, 184; *A Dialogue*,

163). A family, Hobbes contends, 'is a little city' (*Man and Citizen*, 217), which having grown numerous by the multiplication of children, the conquest of persons who become its servants, and voluntary subscription to its laws by those 'furnished with Arts necessary for Mans life' (*A Dialogue*, 159) in return for protection, cannot be put under the power of another 'without casting the uncertain die of war' (*Man and Citizen*, 217).[48]

The fathers of families, then, which may include acquisitions by conquest and consent, and not each and every individual in the pre-civil condition, enjoy a natural liberty. By right of this natural liberty, and in the absence of a common lord or master, each father who rules over a family is obliged to follow no counsel other than his own, and possesses 'a common right in all things' (*Man and Citizen*, 184; cf. *A Dialogue*, 159). Thus, the institution of a commonwealth by consent is not in the hands of each individual in the pre-civil condition, but is the preserve of fathers of families who are at liberty to renounce their power (*Leviathan*, 382) and join together in great aristocracies. Great monarchies, however, tend to arise as a result of one small family increasing its territory and the wealth of its subjects, by means of engaging in war (*A Dialogue*, 161). In this respect the historical pre-civil condition appears to follow a similar process to that which can be inferred from Hobbes's account of the hypothetical modified state of nature. There leaders of communities, and not individuals, would institute commonwealths by consent, or enlarge themselves by conquest.

Thucydides, in his *History of the Peloponnesian War*, describes how the ancient inhabitants of Hellas lived in small scattered communities, which through fear of invasion cultivated only the bare necessities for their existence. Because of the uncertainties of their lives they tended to be semi-nomadic, preferring to uproot themselves and move on rather than build permanent dwellings which would attract the attention of invaders. Their condition of life was very like that which Hobbes later ascribed to people in the hypothetical state of nature and the historical pre-civil condition. Thucydides says:

For it is evident that that which is now called Hellas, was not of old constantly inhabited; but that at first there were constant removals, every one easily leaving the place of his abode to the violence always of some greater number. For whilst traffic was not, nor mutual intercourse but with fear, neither by sea nor land; and every man so husbanded the ground as but barely to live upon it, without any stocks of riches, and planted nothing (because it was uncertain when another should invade them and carry all away, especially not having the defence of walls); but made account to be masters, in any place, of such necessary sustenance as might serve them from day to day: they made little difficulty to change their habitations.[49]

Communities were constantly subject to the raids of pirates, who plundered booty out of self-interest and in order to maintain the weaker people in their own communities. The activities of pirates were regarded as honourable, and on land a similar system of armed robbery prevailed.

In *The Elements of Law*, *The Citizen*, and *Leviathan*, Thucydides' account of ancient times in Greece provides Hobbes with an illustration of the relations between communities in the pre-civil condition. Hobbes argues that, not only among the Greeks, but in all nations, composed as they were of numerous families, it was considered just and honourable (*Leviathan*, 224) to engage in rapine as 'a trade of life' (*Elements of Law*, 100); to enrich your community by '*booting*' or '*taking prey*' (*Man and Citizen*, 267); and 'to robbe and spoyle one another' (*Leviathan*, 224). Even though there is no Law of Nature governing 'living by rapine' (*Man and Citizen*, 166) in these relations between non-social communities, or families, a code of honour developed. Raiding parties on their expeditions for booty observed the 'Lawes of Honour', in that they desisted from cruelty and spared men their lives 'and instruments of husbandry' (*Leviathan*, 224), 'lest by too much cruelty they might be suspected guilty of fear' (*Man and Citizen*, 166). In other words, whereas there is no historical[50] parallel to the mere state of nature, Hobbes was able to confirm his logical construction of inter-community relations in the modified state of nature with reference to the behaviour of actual communities, in particular those of the Amazon women, Saxon and other German families, the American Indians, and the paternal communities of Ancient Greece. Sovereignty by institution, the logical consequence of the state of nature, is nevertheless an historical rarity, with paternal dominion and dominion by conquest being far more prevalent. This apparent discrepancy between the logical, or hypothetical, institution of a commonwealth and the historical, or actual, evolution of commonwealths nevertheless has the same implication for Hobbes's view of political obligation, because 'In summe the Rights and Consequences of both *Paternall* and *Despoticall* Dominion, are the very same with those of a Soveraign by Institution' (*Leviathan*, 256).

Relations among Commonwealths

It has been shown that both in the hypothetical state of nature and in the historical pre-civil condition certain constraints served to regulate relations among non-social communities. It is now appropriate to consider the relations between civil societies, or commonwealths, which according to Hobbes remain in a state of nature in their relations with each other, and to look at his advice for improving the relations. The liberty which a commonwealth has, Hobbes claims, is the same as that which every person would have in the absence of civil laws or a sovereign power to keep him in awe. A commonwealth has the absolute liberty to do whatever it judges to be most conducive to its benefit. The freedom of a commonwealth is not that of its subjects, but the freedom 'to resist, or invade other people' (*Leviathan*, 266).

A commonwealth is instituted for two particular reasons: first to ensure peace and security at home, and secondly to guarantee mutual aid against external enemies. To this end the sovereign is empowered to '*use the strength and means of them all, as he shall think expedient, for their Peace and Common Defence*' (*Leviathan*, 228). The swords of war and justice are inseparable and are therefore to be invested in the same sovereign power (*Elements of Law*, 111–12; *Man and*

Citizen, 177–9). Since the sovereign has an obligation to uphold peace and security, that body, or person, must be the judge of what is necessary for fulfilling the obligation.[51] To the sovereign falls the power of making war and peace with other nations. He is the judge of whether war would be in the public interest and how large an army would be needed to engage in battle (*Leviathan*, 302, and *A Dialogue*, 59). In addition he must have the power to raise the necessary revenue to pay for foreign engagements (*Leviathan*, 298, and *A Dialogue*, 61). As sovereign he is also the supreme commander of the army, and whoever he appoints as general, the 'Soveraign Power is alwayes Generallissimo' (*Leviathan*, 235; cf. *Leviathan*, 117).

Hobbes tells us that two things are necessary for the defence of the people. First, the sovereign must be forewarned of potential hostility, and this is equivalent to that dimension of fear in the state of nature which facilitates anticipation. It is necessary to the defence of the commonwealth to have spies who discover the deliberations and thoughts of potential adversaries. The gathering of intelligence in order to anticipate the actions of other states is 'no less necessary to the preservation of the state, than the rays of light are to the conservation of man' (*Man and Citizen*, 261). Secondly, the sovereign must ensure that the state is forearmed against the possibility of attack. To this end it is necessary to raise money; to have a well-armed militia; to maintain a navy; and to build forts. It is too late to make these preparations after an attack, or when hostilities are imminent. If a ruler does not use his power to gather adequate intelligence about other nations, and prepare his own for the eventuality of war, he is in breach of his duty to provide security for his subjects.

In order to forestall potential attack it may be necessary, from time to time, to engage in sabotage and other clandestine activities, the purpose of which is to destabilize the governments of foreign powers. A sovereign must, Hobbes suggests, do 'whatsoever shall seem to conduce to the lessening of the power of foreigners whom they suspect' (*Man and Citizen*, 262; cf. *Leviathan*, 364). Such tactics are perfectly legitimate in the absence of a common authority and laws which define what is and is not just. In consequence, 'Force, and Fraud, are in warre the two Cardinall vertues' (*Leviathan*, 188).

Just as equality between individuals is not conducive to peace because of mutual fear, which precipitates insecurity, equality between commonwealths has a similar effect. There can never be peace, Hobbes argues, when the fears of states are equal (*Leviathan*, 684), nor can learning flourish when commonwealths have no 'leasure from procuring the necessities of life, and defending themselves against their neighbors' (*Leviathan*, 683). War is beneficial to progress in that it unites smaller cities into larger and great commonwealths. It is not against the Laws of Nature, or honour, that upon all sorts of pretexts commonwealths invade their neighbours to subdue them by means of force, or attempt to reduce their power by other means when they see an advantage can be gained. In *A Dialogue between a Philosopher and a Student of the Common Laws of England*, the philosopher contends that 'the most visible advantage is then, when the one Nation is obedient to their King, and the other not' (*A Dialogue*, 57). This, of course, is a salutary warning that internal insecurity has profound implications for external security.

It appears from Hobbes's account of international relations that nations inhabit the equivalent of the mere state of nature for only a short time because the fear which is a consequence of natural equality inspires them to bring about an imbalance of power. As in the modified state of nature, auxiliaries may be procured by conquest, or by covenant. Leagues of commonwealths, Hobbes argues, are perfectly legitimate and profitable for such time as they last. Without a common power to keep them in awe, however, when a new fear arises, or when a commonwealth believes a greater profit can be gained by breaking its covenant, the league is dissolved. However, we can assume that the same disincentive which deters individuals in the state of nature from breaking their agreements would also apply to states. A state which is publicly known to enter into treaties and alliances lightly might find that foreign agreements and allies are hard to come by.

Just as Hobbes believed that non-social communities, or families, in the pre-civil condition lived by looting and robbing, he also believed that nations have enriched themselves in similar ways: 'as small Familyes did then: so now do Cities and Kingdomes which are but greater Families' (*Leviathan*, 224). The relations between commonwealths were in Hobbes's view far less hostile than those between individuals in the hypothetical mere state of nature. He says, for example, that 'in the war of nation against nation, a certain mean was wont to be observed' (*Man and Citizen*, 166). Excessive cruelty and unnecessary laying to waste the means of working the land were regarded by some nations, as they had been by families, as dishonourable. In days of old great commonwealths like Rome and Athens engaged in acts of booting and plundering in their relations with other commonwealths. This practice itself was not dishonourable, but Hobbes believed that it was not a very sensible way of going about improving the condition of the people of a commonwealth, and should 'not be brought into rule and fashion' (*A Dialogue*, 267). Although this injunction would serve to moderate international relatioи, Hobbes justifies it on the ground of enhancing internal commonwealth affairs. In his view, an increase in riches through the spoils of war and foreign tribute is a matter of chance: 'For the militia, in order to profit, is like a die; wherewith many lose their estates, but few improve them' (*A Dialogue*, 267). The economy of a commonwealth needs to be put on a firmer foundation than this. The sovereign has a duty to enact laws which promote those things which contribute to a more certain increase in wealth and thus satisfy the desire for commodious living. To this end he should encourage those things which are conducive to the greater productivity of the soil and seas, and foster the development of mechanical skills and navigation.

Hobbes gives a good deal of prudential advice to the sovereign on how to conduct international relations. The defence of a nation, he suggests, consists not only in being adequately prepared for battle, but in the avoidance of 'unnecessary wars'. A monarch who is too impetuous in his prosecution of wars will soon bring ruin to the commonwealth (*Elements of Law*, 184). Furthermore, the monarch should take heed of counsel, and of the experience and intelligence gathered by those who have travelled abroad. It is a grave mistake to rely solely upon one's own capacities and rashly make war, or peace, without entering into consultation. It is imperative that the monarch gains 'Knowledge in some measure of the strength, Advantages and Designs of the Enemy, and the Manner and Degree of the Danger that may from thence arise' (*A Dialogue*, 63). In seeking such counsel it is necessary to beware of those who are ambitious for command in the military. Such men have an inclination to prolong the causes of war because honour in their profession can only be attained by war (*Leviathan*, 162). Ultimately, however, and without consultation if the circumstances necessitate, the monarch is the judge of what, and how much, is necessary for maintaining the security of his subjects. A prudent sovereign, then, would not put the safety of his subjects at risk by engaging in wars inspired by ambition and vainglory.

Even though Hobbes says that commonwealths are in their relations in a condition of war, he nevertheless envisaged considerable commerce between them. This would follow, of course, from his view that one of the two passions which dispose us to seek peace is the hope that by our industry we may satisfy our desires for 'such things as are necessary to commodious living' (*Leviathan*, 188), and these things would include foreign commodities not produced in the domestic market. In *The Elements of Law* he contends that it is a Law of Nature that foreign traffic and trade be allowed to be conducted without discrimination. Indeed, to discriminate against a nation is to demonstrate your hostility towards it. Such discrimination as, for example, the Athenians in their ports and markets practised against the Megarians is a cause of war (*Elements of Law*, 87). One of the inconveniences of the war of all against all is that we are unable to enjoy commodities imported from overseas. No commonwealth, Hobbes suggests, is self-sufficient in the commodities it needs, and each produces more of some things than it can consume. The surplus facilitates the importation of foreign goods (*Leviathan*, 295). It is not the sovereign, however, who is best equipped for the organization of this trade. Hobbes argues that 'In a Bodie Politique, for the well ordering of forraigne Traffique, the 1..ost commodious Representative is an Assembly of all the members; that is to say, such a one, as every one that adventureth his mony, may be present at all the Deliberations, and Resolutions of the Body, if they will themselves' (*Leviathan*, 281). The sovereign does, however, on the grounds of national interest, have the authority to determine the places where trade is to be conducted, and which commodities are to be imported and exported. The purpose of such intervention is to prevent merchants trading in commodities, such as noxious substances, which are pleasurable but harmful (*Leviathan*, 299), and thus detrimental to the nation.

It was Kant who most forcefully recognized the potential of commerce to lead to progress in international relations. The commercial spirit, he believed, was incompatible with war,[52] and the gradual development and proliferation of trade would reduce the possibility of war. It is clear that Hobbes believed that the desire for a more commodious life, which includes the enjoyment of foreign goods, acts as an incentive to desist from unnecessary wars. Foreign traffic is better facilitated between commonwealths which have entered into agreements of mutual interest, whether for profit or mutual security (*Leviathan*, 286). Peaceful relations between nations enrich the internal condition of commonwealths.

Hedley Bull has argued that 'The conception of progress is, of course, entirely absent from Hobbes's account of the international state of nature, which presents the behaviour of states in terms of static and unchanging principles.'[53] My account of how Hobbes perceived the international sphere, and his advice to sovereigns for the better conduct of their relations, coupled with his belief that trade contributes to our desire for commodious living, which war obviously disrupts, indicates that Hobbes believed progress to be both possible and desirable in international affairs, as long as the sovereign was guided by prudence and the laws of honour (*Leviathan*, 188). Progress, of course, does not mean steady and unrelenting improvement. There may be periods during which regression takes place, just as society itself can degenerate into civil war. But such regressions are not irretrievable, and in the long term relations between states have improved, mainly because they are not subject to 'static and unchanging principles'. The obligation of the sovereign is to procure the safety of the people, and 'by safety here, is not meant a bare Preservation, but also all other Contentments of life' (*Leviathan*, 376). Foreign commerce, of course, contributes to these contentments. The human mind, or that which it desires and honours, is extremely malleable. The sovereign in this respect educates the people into the right ways of thinking in order to minimize both external and internal disorder,[54] both of which impair the sovereign's ability to fulfil his obligation to maintain the safety of the people. Among those things which contribute to internal disorder, and should therefore be avoided, Hobbes highlights imperialistic expansionism, which overextends the state, and the conquering of territories which remain ununited and are a burden better lost than retained (*Leviathan*, 375).

If states are in the equivalent of a state of nature, how can their relations progress or improve? The Law of Nations, Hobbes tells us, is nothing other than the Law of Nature (*Leviathan*, 394). Fear and the desire for commodious living, combined with the dictates of reason, would, one assumes, bring out modifications equivalent to those which occur in transforming the hypothetical mere state of nature into its modified form. In other words, the condition of states is not like the war of all against all, but instead analogous to the hypothetical modified state of nature and the historical pre-civil condition.

The question must arise as to whether this implies an extension of the logic of *Leviathan* to entail the likely creation of a world state.[55] This question has been asked on many occasions and answered by suggesting that the logic is not applicable to states because states are not really like men.[56] My point is that states are not like individuals, but they are like the non-social communities in the modified state of nature (and for that matter the historical pre-civil condition) to which Hobbes thought the logic of instituting a commonwealth applicable. In essence, then, the logic ought to apply to states. It appears, however, that Hobbes did not believe that it was possible to create by institution a universal society of nations. The incentive in the state of nature to institute a commonwealth is for internal peace and security against external enemies. Once a commonwealth has achieved a certain size and wields a certain power, both objectives have been achieved, and even though relations between states are potentially hostile, life is far more commodious than the lives of those individuals in a condition of liberty in the state of nature, or as members of a group in pre-civil times. This is because the sovereign provides sufficient internal and external security to allow industry to flourish. A number of states may unite for the purpose of security and give allegiance to a sovereign power, but this will then be a larger commonwealth rather than a peaceful alliance of states. It is conceivable on Hobbes's logic that a super-state could arise, but having arisen it would immediately lack the external threat against which the new Leviathan of states was instituted to protect each member. In the absence of external threat, would relations within the super-state begin to crumble? It is also conceivable, on the basis of conquest, which is as valid a claim to sovereignty as that of institution, that a world state could emerge through imperialist expansionism. Hobbes, in fact, rejected both possibilities on practical grounds.

In so far as a sovereign has an obligation to protect his subjects from one another and from external enemies, the possibility of discharging that obligation successfully becomes less likely as the size of the territory grows. There appears to be an optimum size beyond which the probability of insecurity becomes greater. If, like an individual, a state is forced to acquire more power in order to hold on to that which it has, the possibility of overextending itself is very real. Nevertheless, Hobbes did believe in progress in the relations between states—the move away from plundering and pirating, for example, constituted an improvement—but as in the relations between individuals and between communities, there is always the danger of reverting to a condition of hostility. Without a common power, of course, states are more likely to revert to a condition of war, as experience shows, than a commonwealth which has a sovereign at its head is likely to degenerate to a condition of civil war.

It is clear that agreements and conventions, particularly regulating trade, mitigate the consequences of an international state of nature, but can they, in Hobbes's view, ever be elevated to the status of international law? The answer seems to be in the negative. For Hobbes, punishment is a logical corollary of law, and punishment depends on the sword of the sovereign. Law without punishment is an illusion. Furthermore punishment must be sufficiently severe to deter crime. Security is achieved not so much by the compact to establish or institute a commonwealth, as by the punishments enforced by the sovereign entrusted with authority.[57]

In summary, then, Hobbes does not believe that there is any higher law ordained by a force outside of human will. Justice and injustice are consequences of the institution of a sovereign who determines what is just and enforces it. As we saw, Machiavelli struggled in his own mind with the tension between what is morally right and what is expedient for the ruler to do. In Hobbes this tension is resolved, and morality is equated with expediency. Law is equated with the will of the sovereign, and the question of its justness does not really arise. We do not ask whether a law is just or not, but merely who made it. It is enough that it is authoritatively enacted by the legitimate sovereign, even if that sovereign is simply *de facto*. In the international sphere, in the absence of a sovereign, there is no justice or injustice, but there are principles relating to honourable and dishonourable acts which serve to restrain excessive acts of cruelty or recklessness. Furthermore, a whole range of considerations of a prudential nature serve to make international relations far more civilized than relations among individuals in a state of nature characterized as a war of everyman against everyman.

Notes

I am grateful to the participants in the Hobbes symposium, University of New South Wales, 1988, for their penetrating probing of my argument. Without undervaluing the contribution of others I would like to mention three in particular, C. A. J. Coady, Carole Pateman, and J. G. A. Pocock, who inspired me to make some modifications. I am also indebted to the anonymous readers who made invaluable suggestions for improvement, and to the participants in the History of Ideas Seminar, Australian National University, and the members of the Philosophy Department, Trent University, Canada, who commented upon versions of this chapter.

1. F. Melian Stawell, *The Growth of International Thought* (London, Thorton Butterworth, 1929).
2. See e.g. John H. Herz, *Political Realism and Political Idealism: A Study in Theories and Realities* (Chicago and London, The University of Chicago Press, 1951), 24–5; Graham Evans, 'Some Problems With a History of Thought in International Relations', *British Journal of International Studies*, 4 (1974), 720; Michael Walzer, *Just and Unjust Wars: A Moral Argument with Historical Illustrations* (New York, Basic Books, 1977), 5–12; F. Parkinson, *The Philosophy of International Relations: A Study in the History of Thought* (Beverly Hills, Calif., and London, Sage, 1977), 37–40; Charles R. Beitz, *Political Theory and International Relations* (Princeton, Princeton University Press, 1979), 15–66; Martin Wight, 'An Anatomy of International Thought', *Review of International Studies*, 13 (1987), 222–3. For a discussion of Martin Wight's categorization of international thought into Realists, Rationalists, and Revolutionaries see Hedley Bull, 'Martin Wight and the Theory of International Relations,' *British Journal of International Studies*, 2 (1976), 101–16.
3. Martin Wight refers to the tradition as Machiavellian, contrasting it with the Grotian and Kantian traditions. See Bull, 'Martin Wight and the Theory of International Relations', 104. Bull prefers to use Hobbes as the epitome of the tradition. See Hedley Bull, 'Society and Anarchy in International Relations', in H. Butterfield and M. Wight (eds.), *Diplomatic Investigations: Essays in the Theory of International Politics* (London: Allen and Unwin, 1966), 35–50; and Hedley Bull, *The Anarchical Society: A Study of Order in World Politics* (London, Macmillan, 1984), 24–7 and 46–51. Also see Donald W. Hanson, 'Thomas Hobbes's "Highway to Peace"', *International Organization*, 38 (1984), 331. Hanson says: 'There is, in any case, a recognisable "Hobbesian tradition" in the study of international relations, whether it has been faithful to Hobbes or not . . .'.
4. See e.g. Bull, 'Martin Wight and the Theory of International Relations', 104; and Evans, 'Some Problems with a History of Thought', 720.

5. 'The estate of men in this natural liberty is the estate of war. For WAR is nothing else but that time wherein the will and intention of contending force is either by words or actions sufficiently declared; and the time which is not war is PEACE' (Thomas Hobbes, *The Elements of Law Natural and Politic*, 2nd edn., ed. M. M. Goldsmith (New York, Barnes and Noble, 1969), 73). 'For what is WAR, but that same time in which the will of contesting by force is fully declared, either by words or deeds? The time remaining is termed PEACE' (Thomas Hobbes, *The Citizen*, in *Man and Citizen*, ed. Bernard Gert (London, Harvester, 1978), 118). 'So the nature of War, consisteth not in actual fighting; but in the known disposition thereto, during all the time there is no assurance to the contrary. All other time is PEACE' (Thomas Hobbes, *Leviathan, or The Matter, Forme, & Power of a COMMON-WEALTH, Ecclesiasticall and Civill*, ed. C. B. Macpherson (Harmondsworth, Penguin, 1981), 186).

6. 'before the names of Just, and Unjust can have place, there must be some coercive Power' (*Leviathan*, 202). Cf. 'For before covenants and laws were drawn up, neither justice nor injustice, neither public good nor public evil was natural among men any more than it was among beasts' (Thomas Hobbes, *On Man* [*De homine*], trans. Charles T. Wood, T. S. K. Scott-Craig, and Bernard Gert in *Man and Citizen*, 43.

7. Hobbes, *Man and Citizen*, 260–1.

8. Thomas Hobbes, *A Dialogue between a Philosopher and a Student of the Common Laws of England*, ed. Joseph Cropsey (Chicago and London, The University of Chicago Press, 1971), 57.

9. See Deborah Baumgold, *Hobbes's Political Theory* (Cambridge, Cambridge University Press, 1988), 78.

10. W. H. Greenleaf, 'Hobbes: The Problem of Interpretation', in Maurice Cranston and Richard Peters (eds.), *Hobbes and Rousseau* (New York, Doubleday Anchor, 1972).

11. Quentin Skinner, 'Hobbes's *Leviathan*', *Historical Journal*, 7 (1964), 321.

12. Skinner, 'Hobbes's *Leviathan*', 321.

13. Leo Strauss, *The Political Philosophy of Hobbes: Its Basis and its Genesis* (Oxford, Clarendon Press, 1936).

14. Michael Oakeshott, *Rationalism in Politics and Other Essays*, new and expanded edn., ed. T. Fuller (Indianapolis, Liberty, 1991), 278.

15. Oakeshott, *Rationalism in Politics*, 280.

16. Joseph Frankel has summed up the Realists' relation to Hobbes admirably. He says, 'It does not make much difference whether the adherents of the theory of power politics postulate a basic lust for power, an *animus dominandi*, or regard it as a derivative from the anarchic state of international relations. In both cases they tend to draw an analogy between the international system and Hobbes's state of nature in that the units—the states and the individuals respectively—are threatened in their survival and hence seek security, the only ultimate basis for which is force' (Joseph Frankel, *National Interest* (London, Macmillan, 1970), 49–50).

17. Hedley Bull, 'Hobbes and the International Anarchy', *Social Research*, 48 (1981), 721. Cf. Ibid. 725 and 727; Bull, 'Society and Anarchy in International Relations', 38 and 45; Bull, *The Anarchical Society*, 46 and 49. Also see Howard Warrender, *The Political Philosophy of Hobbes* (Oxford, Clarendon Press, 1966), 118; David P. Gauthier, *The Logic of Leviathan* (Oxford, Clarendon Press, 1969); 207; Stanley Hoffman, *Duties Beyond Borders: On the Limits and Possibilities of Ethical International Politics* (New York, Syracuse University Press, 1981), 36.

18. Bull, 'Hobbes and the International Anarchy', 721.

19. Beitz, *Political Theory and International Relations*, 36. Cf. Bull, 'Hobbes and the

International Anarchy', 733–4; Bull, *The Anarchical Society*, 46; Warrender, *The Political Philosophy of Hobbes*, 119; Gauthier, *The Logic of Leviathan*, 207.

20. Gauthier, *The Logic of Leviathan*, 207.
21. Warrender, *The Political Philosophy of Hobbes*, 119; Bull, *The Anarchical Society*, 46.
22. Bull, *The Anarchical Society*, 50; cf. Beitz, *Political Theory and International Relations*, 40.
23. Gauthier, *The Logic of Leviathan*, 207–8.
24. Beitz, *Political Theory and International Relations*, 41. Cf. Bull, 'Hobbes and the International Anarchy', 733. It may be said, however, in Gauthier's defence, that when he wrote the rate of proliferation which was evident during the 1950s and 1960s showed little sign of abating. It seemed to many that more and more countries would soon acquire the capability of inflicting unacceptable damage on each other by means of a nuclear strike. This is essentially what Robert McNamara termed finite deterrence and was premised on the fact that beyond quite modest levels of weapons the curve plotting potential damage begins to flatten significantly. There were some grounds, then, for Gauthier to infer that with the potential spread of finite deterrence, something resembling an equality of vulnerability might ensue. I am indebted to Michael W. Doyle for this qualification.
25. Mark A. Heller, 'The Use and Abuse of Hobbes: The State of Nature in International Relations', *Polity*, 13 (1980), 27–8 and 31.
26. Heller, 'The Use and Abuse of Hobbes', 32.
27. See e.g. Bull, 'Society and Anarchy in International Relations', 45; Bull, *The Anarchical Society*, 49; Bull, 'Hobbes and the International Anarchy', 727; Gauthier, *The Logic of Leviathan*, 207; and Beitz, *Political Theory and International Relations*, 37. Hobbes tempers the analogy by saying that because sovereign powers uphold 'the Industry of their subjects; there does not follow from it, that misery, which accompanies the Liberty of particular men' (*Leviathan*, 188).
28. Michael Oakeshott, *Hobbes on Civil Association* (Oxford, Blackwell, 1975), 54. The essay from which I quote was originally the introduction to Blackwell's 1946 edition of *Leviathan*.
29. *The English Works of Thomas Hobbes of Malmesbury*, ed. Sir William Molesworth (London, John Bohn, 1841), v. 89. For the prevalence of arguments of correspondence in the 16th and 17th centuries see W. H. Greenleaf, *Order, Empiricism and Politics* (Oxford, Oxford University Press for the University of Hull, 1964).
30. Murray Forsyth, 'Thomas Hobbes and the External Relations of States', *British Journal of International Studies*, 5 (1979), 196–209.
31. Hanson, 'Thomas Hobbes's "Highway to Peace" ', 329–54.
32. Oakeshott, *Hobbes on Civil Association*, 17.
33. See Strauss, *The Political Philosophy of Hobbes*, 64–5, 74–5, 79–80, and 108–10; R. Schlatter, 'Thomas Hobbes and Thucydides', *Journal of the History of Ideas*, 6 (1945); Walzer, *Just and Unjust Wars*, 4–13; Peter R. Pouncey, *The Necessities of War: A Study of Thucydides' Pessimism* (New York, Columbia University Press, 1980), appendix, 'Human Nature in Hobbes', 151–86; G. Klosko and D. Rice, 'Thucydides and Hobbes's State of Nature,' *History of Political Thought*, 6 (1985); Terence Ball, 'Hobbes' Linguistic Turn,' *Polity*, 17 (1985); C. W. Brown, 'Thucydides, Hobbes, and the Derivation of Anarchy', *History of Political Thought*, 8 (1987); and, C. W. Brown, 'Thucydides, Hobbes, and the Linear Causal Perspective', *History of Political Thought*, 10 (1989). Also see Thomas Hobbes, 'Of the Life and History of Thucydides', in *The English Works*, vol. viii, pp. xiii–xxxii. In his verse autobiography Hobbes singles out

Thucydides as the one author who has pleased him most of all because Thucydides had contended that 'Democracy's a Foolish Thing, Than a Republic Wiser is one King' (Thomas Hobbes, 'The Life of Mr Thomas Hobbes of Malmesbury' (Exeter, The Rota, 1979), 4).

34. Thucydides, *History of the Peloponnesian War*, trans. Thomas Hobbes in *The English Works*, vol. viii, 1. 22. I use Hobbes's translation in order to emphasize the relation between the two thinkers.

35. Thucydides, *Peloponnesian War*, 1. 76.

36. Thucydides, *Peloponnesian War*, 1. 75–76.

37. Thucydides, *Peloponnesian War*, 6. 18.

38. Thucydides, *Peloponnesian War*, 2. 63.

39. Thucydides, *Peloponnesian War*, 1. 23.

40. Hobbes says that 'By right reason in the natural state of men, I understand not, as many do, an infallible faculty, but the act of reasoning, that is, the peculiar and true ratiocination of every man concerning those actions of his, which may either redound to the damage or benefit of his neighbours' (*Man and Citizen*, 123).

41. Cf. 'reason therefore dictateth to every man for his own good, to seek after peace, as far forth as there is hope to attain the same; and to strengthen himself with all the help he can produce, for his own defence against those, from whom such peace cannot be obtained; and to do all those things which necessarily conduce there unto' (*Elements of Law*, 74). 'But the first and fundamental Law of Nature is, *that peace is to be sought after, where it may be found; and where not, there to provide ourselves for helps of war*' (*Man and Citizen*, 123).

42. Cf. 'For this matter nothing else can be imagined, but that each man provide himself of such meet helps, as the invasion of one on the other may be rendered so dangerous, as either of them may think it better to refrain than to meddle' (*Man and Citizen*, 167).

43. Thucydides, *Peloponnesian War*, 1. 76. This is not to suggest that Thucydides necessarily agreed with the views he was reporting.

44. Thucydides, *Peloponnesian War*, 5. 105. Cf. 'of man we know for certain, that by a natural necessity wherever they are the stronger, there they will reign' (*Thucydides, Peloponnesian War*, 5. 104 n. 1).

45. Cf. 'But the conqueror may by right compel the conquered, or the strongest the weaker (as a man in health may one that is sick, or he that is of riper years a child), unless he will choose to die, to give caution of his future obedience' (*Man and Citizen*, 119).

46. 'for the odds on the other side, of a man or two, giveth sufficient encouragement to an assault' Hobbes, *Elements of Law*, 101.

47. Sir Robert Filmer, *Observations Concerning the Originall of Government, Upon Mr. Hobs Leviathan*, repr. in *Patriarcha and other Political Works of Sir Robert Filmer*, ed. Peter Laslett (Oxford, Basil Blackwell, 1949), 239.

48. Cf. 'By this it appears, that a great Family if it be not part of some Common-wealth, is of it self, as to the Rights of Soveraignty, a little Monarchy; whether that Family consist of a man and his children; or of a man and his servants; or of a man, and his children, and servants together: wherein the Father or Master is the Soveraign. But yet a Family is not properly a Common-wealth; unlesse it be of that power by its own number, or by other opportunities, as not to be subdued without the hazard of war' (*Leviathan*, 257).

49. Thucydides, *Peloponnesian War*, 1. 2.

50. By the term 'historical' I merely wish to suggest the recorded past as known by Hobbes himself.

51. 'that himself is Judge of Necessity' (Hobbes, A Dialogue, 64; cf. Leviathan, 234–5 and 360).

52. See Howard Williams, Kant's Political Philosophy (Oxford, Basil Blackwell, 1983), 15–16; Wight, 'An Anatomy of International Thought', 224; Immanuel Kant, in M. G. Forsyth, H. M. A. Keens-Soper, and P. Savigear (eds.), The Theory of International Relations: Selected Texts from Gentili to Treitschke (London, George, Allen and Unwin, 1970), 181, 188, and 220. Kant says: 'In connection with the life of the agriculturalist, salt and iron were discovered which were perhaps the first articles that were sought far and near, and which entered into the commercial intercourse of different peoples. Thereby they would be first brought into a peaceful relation to one another; and thus the most distant of them would come to mutual understanding; sociability and pacific intercourse' (Ibid. 220). This is not to suggest that Kant thought commercial relations to be a necessary and sufficient cause of international peace. See Michael W. Doyle's illuminating article 'Liberalism and World Politics', American Political Science Review, 80 (1986), 1151–69. It should also be emphasized that both Hume and Adam Smith recognized the importance of commerce in this respect.

53. Bull, 'Hobbes and the International Anarchy', 730.

54. Cf. Hanson, 'Thomas Hobbes's "Highway to Peace" ', 347–52. Hobbes contends that the minds of the common people 'are like clean paper, fit to receive whatsoever by Publique Authority shall be imprinted in them' (Leviathan, 379). Hobbes is quite explicit about the possibility of progress in internal affairs. He says: 'So, long time after men have begun to constitute Common-wealths, imperfect, and apt to relapse into disorder, there may, Principles of Reason be found out, by industrious medita-tion, to make their constitution (excepting by externall violence) everlasting' (Leviathan, 378). It is true that he did not exhibit the same degree of optimism about progress in international relations, but it is clear from what he says that sovereigns will learn to act in ways which contribute to significant improvements in international relations. Even Kant believed that periods of regression occur, but that in the long run progress is made.

55. This question is addressed by various contributors to Timo Airaksinen and Martin A. Bertman (eds.), Hobbes: War among Nations (Aldershot, Avebury, 1989).

56. See Heller, 'The Use and Abuse of Hobbes', 21–32.

57. For a good discussion of Hobbes's thoughts on law see Baumgold, Hobbes's Political Theory, 108–13.

PART II

Universal Moral Order

8

THE PRIORITY OF LAW AND MORALITY:
THE GREEKS AND STOICS

The categories of communitarianism and cosmopolitanism proposed by Chris Brown, and discussed in Chapter 1, when applied to ancient history imply a discontinuity between the Greeks with their emphasis upon the city-state, and the fulfilment of one's life as a citizen, and the Stoic and Roman conception of the cosmos of humanity to which we belong as citizens of the world. My category of a Universal Moral Order better captures the continuity that is to be discerned between the Greek and Roman periods. There were many Greeks who saw no incompatibility between living one's life as a citizen within a *polis* that was naturally limited in size, and at the same time being subject to a Universal Moral Law. What is important in the order of questions that this category predicates is not whether a person is a citizen of a *polis* or state, but from what source the moral law is derived. In this respect law that is declaratory, rather than made, discovered rather than enacted, betrays the idea of a pre-existing moral order that is not dependent upon the state, nor subject to change in its fundamentals by the arbitrary will of humans.

In distinguishing between nature and convention many Greek thinkers viewed morality as a product of the latter. The putative social contract theories of Antiphon, Hippias, Callicles, Democritus, Protagoras, Thrasymachus, and Glaucon postulate a morality that is the product of self-interest. In some instances morality is regarded as opposed to nature, and therefore unnatural, while in others it is viewed as consistent with nature facilitating human potential and constraining the destructive tendencies of the straight utility maximizer. What they have in common is that morality is a human invention which contingently arose to serve the interests of individuals threatened by the unconstrained behaviour of others. Morality in this respect is intra-societal and does not extend beyond the borders of the state, unless such an extension serves an interest. Such a morality is particularistic, but could be extended over the whole world by a policy of imperialism, or extended by example or agreement founded on rational self-interest. Alternatively, conventional morality can be rejected in favour of a universal naturalistic ethic, which overrides particularistic ethical codes.

The naturalistic tendencies of many of the moral conventionalists led them to question any primary loyalties to the *polis*, and to posit a natural equality which dissolved conventional social hierarchies within and between states. Social distinctions and the division of the world into Greeks and barbarians was simply unnatural. There are signs of this naturalistic universalism in Democritus and Hippias,[1] but they are much more pronounced in Antiphon. Antiphon believed, as we saw in Chapter 3, that mankind is united in nature, naturally equal, and subject to nature's laws. The Laws of Nature, however, posit quite a different ethic from conventional morality and dictate courses of action which are purely self-interested, even to the extreme detriment of the interests of others, and license, from the position of natural equality, inequalities based on the natural relations of dominance and compliance.

This is the sort of thing the Athenians complain of in Plato's *Laws* when they suggest that the teachers of such views 'actually declare that the really and naturally laudable is one thing and the conventionally laudable quite another . . . and hence the factions created by those who seek, on such grounds, to attract men to the "really and naturally right" life, that is, the life of real domination over others, not by conventional service to them'.[2]

The idea of state citizenship, or of fulfilling one's life in the *polis*, does not depend upon a particularistic morality, nor is it incompatible with the idea of a Universal Moral Order to which all citizens in all *poleis* are subject. Both Plato and Aristotle could not conceive of a higher association beyond the *polis*, yet both were committed to the idea of a universal morality. Similarly, many of the Stoics saw no incompatibility between loving one's fatherland and at the same time acknowledging our common humanity and membership of one world-wide moral community. Cosmopolitanism does not necessarily imply an institutional cosmopolitanism nor need communitarianism restrict a shared morality to the boundaries of a nation state

The Greeks

We have already seen how intensely religious Greek life was, and how religion could not clearly be distinguished from citizenship and its duties and obligations. Laws were similarly inextricably imbued with religious content, and were often thought to be little more than the application of religion to civic and social life. They are often referred to as the sacred or unwritten laws. To disobey the law was consequently an affront to the gods, who when angered in some way had to be appeased because it was from them that the laws derived. The gods were the source of law. The Spartans, for example, believed that Lycurgus in his constitution merely declared the will of the real lawgiver, Apollo.[3] There are, of course, notable parallels in other cultures. Moses and Numa delivered the word of God and the goddess Egeria, respectively, to their people.

The sentiments expressed in Greek literature and the philosophies of Plato and Aristotle combat the claim of the Sophists that morality is a convenient fiction, nothing more than a pragmatic response to the practical inconveniences of mutual co-operation. The Chorus in Sophocles' *Oedipus the King* sing of a law independent of human will:

> For there are laws enthroned above;
> Heaven created them,
> Olympus was their father,
> And mortal men had no part in their birth.[4]

In another of Sophocles' plays, Antigone, in defiance of a decree of Cleon, buries her brother on the grounds that she is obeying the dictates of a higher law which overrides human law.[5] Plato wants to demonstrate that there is a sphere which stands outside the transitory world of experience. The changing and unstable world of Becoming is contrasted with the world of Being, a realm of absolutes in which there are immutable eternal forms conforming to the rational law of the cosmos. Law or Justice is discovered rather than made. The apprehension of this rational law would enable us to overcome the variability and uncertainty of the world of Becoming. Aristotle in the *Rhetoric* invokes Sophocles to illustrate his own distinction between *specific* and *common* laws: '*specific* being what has been defined by each people in reference to themselves, and *common* that which is based on nature; for there is in nature a *common* principle of the just and unjust that all people are in some way divine, even if they have no association or commerce with each other . . .'[6]

The idea of a Universal Moral Law in the thought of Plato and Aristotle was not incompatible with their view that the *polis* was the natural association in which human potentials can flourish. Whereas the thinkers that we have dealt with in the Empirical Realist tradition viewed society as little more than a collection of individuals, Plato and Aristotle viewed the state, or *polis*, as an organism. The state for Plato was the individual amplified to a larger scale. Justice in the individual was for him the same as justice in the state. This was because both were manifestations of the transcendental and immutable form of justice.

The good of the social organism for Plato takes priority over that of the individuals who comprise it. He therefore believes that it is imperative that guardians be chosen who are 'most likely to devote their lives to doing what they judge to be in the interest of the community, and who are never prepared to act against it'.[7] Although Aristotle is critical of Plato's state, complaining that the unity is in fact a perversity of nature, he nevertheless develops the organic view further. He argues that because human beings are not self-sufficient they are naturally compelled to associate in order to sustain life. The state, which is the highest form of association, exists to promote the good life. The state is the fulfilment of the individual, and logically prior to its parts. The individual is inexplicable in isolation from the whole (*Politics*, 4).[8] The citizen in relation to a state, not any particular state, is like an arm or a leg in relation to the body. The good of each part is dependent upon and inseparable from the good of the whole (*Politics*, 185).[9] Like Plato, Aristotle believes that the same virtues which individuals possess can be found in exactly the same form, and have the same nature, in the state (*Politics*, 157).

Although the state, or *polis*, is natural—the organic unity of, and superior to, its parts—it is subject to a moral law that is independent of the will of the sovereign. In this respect the law is not created, but discovered by reason. Aristotle argues that 'he who bids the law rule may be deemed to bid God and Reason alone rule, but he who bids man rule adds an element of the beast; for desire is a wild beast, and passion perverts the minds of rulers, even when they are the best of men' (*Politics*, 78; also see 80).

Both Plato and Aristotle believe that there is an optimum size for the social organism, and that expansion beyond it is detrimental to its nature. Aristotle, for example, argues that both experience and reason tell us that well-governed states have strictly limited populations. Good order in the state requires good laws, and a large multitude, he suggests, simply cannot be orderly (*Politics*, 162–3). The very idea of a universal social organism is, for both Plato and Aristotle, unnatural.

Within Greece itself Plato and Aristotle believed that there were qualitative differences to be discerned among poleis in the degree of civilization which each had attained. The differences in degree depended upon the extent to which reason promoted the common good of the citizens of each *polis*. Because the Greeks shared a common civilization and religion, their relations, in Plato's view, were naturally friendly. Disputes between the Greek city-states which resulted in armed conflict were 'internal and domestic', and indicative of a sickness affecting the social organism. Such conflicts were to be viewed as civil strife and could only be honourably entered into if the intention was to restore peace. This could be the only just and civilized course of action among friends. Employing established, and inventing new, forms of defence will in fact deter other states from attacking the well-prepared *polis* (*Politics*, 172). Aristotle argues that the military state, unaccustomed to peace because its citizens have never been taught by their legislator to value it, is in fact far more unstable that the peace-loving state: 'For most of these military states are safe only while they are at war, but fall when they have acquired their empire; like unused iron they lose their edge in time of peace' (*Politics*, 178).

Relations between Greeks and non-Greeks, or barbarians, were, however, naturally hostile. And whe.. conflict of this sort arose it could rightly be called war; the constraints of friendship were not a consideration, and 'enslavement and destruction' were perfectly acceptable and permissible.[10]

Why was war between Greeks and barbarians natural? Aristotle provides the answer. He makes a distinction between natural free men and natural slaves. Natural slaves are the living property or instruments of naturally free men. Those people who are compelled to live by the work of their bodies, and who can understand reason but do not possess it, are natural slaves and require to be ruled in order to prevent passion ruling their lives (*Politics*, 6–7). He says, for example: 'it is better for them as for all inferiors that they should be under the rule of a master' (*Politics*, 7). Furthermore, Aristotle suggests that nature is purposive in that it has made animals for the use of human beings, who in acquiring them naturally practise the art of war. War includes hunting, 'an art which we ought to practise against wild beasts, and against men, who though intended by nature to be governed, will not submit; for war of such a kind is naturally just' (*Politics*, 11). The study of war, Aristotle says, should be with a view to establishing sufficient military strength to prevent enslavement of the citizens of one's own state. Beyond this, war should be directed towards those who deserve to be enslaved (*Politics,* 178). The barbarians, who understand reason but who do not possess it in the same degree as the Greeks, deserve to be enslaved. But he does not sanction imperialistic adventurism, or self-interest, as the motive for ruling over other peoples. If an empire is to be acquired, he insists, it should be 'for the good of the governed, and not for the sake of exercising a general despotism' (*Politics,* 178).

In Aristotle's mind there appears to have been no inconsistency or incompatibility between, on the one hand, the views that the *polis* is organically self-sustaining and constrained and that peoples are divided into Greeks and barbarians and, on the other hand, the view that all peoples are subject to universal rational moral laws. The Christian fathers similarly had no difficulty in postulating a universal Natural Law while at the same time believing that Europeans, Jews, and Africans comprised a clear hierarchy of races. Natural equality need not be a presupposition of such a law. Aristotle, of course, was the teacher of Alexander, who ignored his teachings on the *polis* and who attempted to overcome the divisions between Greeks and Persians in the idea of a universal concord and fellowship. In Alexander there is a sense of natural equality, at least between the Greeks and Persians, based upon a religious conviction which led him to believe that God had charged him with the mission of harmonizing and reconciling the world. Plutarch writes of Alexander that he

did not overrun Asia in the spirit of a brigand, or as if it were a booty and the spoils of war. . . . He wished to show that all things on earth were subject to one principle (*logos*) and included in one polity (*politeia*), and that all men were one people; and he demeaned himself accordingly.[11]

There was no institutional unity to the empire of Alexander, nor does he seem to have had aspirations of creating a world state. Instead he united in himself the titles of King of Macedonia, King of Persia, Pharaoh of Egypt, and President of the League of Corinth, the members of which retained a considerable degree of autonomy.[12]

With the emergence of the Macedonian Empire the city-state ceased to be the centre of moral life. The ethical theories of a self-sustaining moral and political unit had to be transformed in order to accommodate the idea of a universal empire. The shift of focus had already begun when such Sophists as Antiphon found a fundamental unity of humanity in our common nature. In other quarters Hellenism was beginning to be seen not as a natural attribute, but as a cultural attainment, shared with those whose intellectual, rather than racial, characteristics had been shaped by a similar education. Isocrates saw in the rise of Macedonia the possibility of the realization of a greater unity. The division between Greek and barbarian, then, was not natural, and what is more, it was permeable. Conversion was a matter of individual intellectual effort.[13] The Cynics had abandoned the ideals of Plato and Aristotle in denying that the man of virtue and wisdom was subject to the law of any particular state. Wise men were related to each other in sharing a universal wisdom, and the law to which they were subject was that of virtue. Community ties were customary and conventional, and the institutional constraints associated with them were to be abandoned by the man of wisdom, who transcended such encumbrances. The vast majority of humanity was, however, foolish and ignorant. Cynicism was a negative doctrine in its rejection of the constraints of the city-state and its conventional values, and was not as such a celebration of cosmopolitanism.

The Epicureans provided a further example of a turning-away from the city-state. They placed the individual in a cosmic context, but did not succeed in providing a firm moral foundation. Following the atomism of Democritus they posit a cosmic physical determinism in which morality is a resident alien. They believed that the gods were indifferent to the circumstances of ordinary mortals, and did not therefore provide moral guidance.[14] Pleasure was the goal of Epicureanism, but this did not entail a crude hedonism. Pleasure was derived from an absence of pain and a lack of turmoil in the soul, and not from overindulgence in sensual desires. It is the pleasure of the mind at rest above that of desire satisfied: 'For we do everything for the sake of being neither in pain nor in terror.'[15] The Epicurean should avoid situations which arouse emotions and cause perturbations: 'The purest security is that which comes from a quiet life and withdrawal from the many.'[16] This includes retreat from political life, except in extreme circumstances, in preference to a life spent in friendship with a small number of associates. Justice for Epicurus is that which is useful in human associations to prevent mutual harm. It is agreed proscriptions among individuals or nations. This is not to say that anything that is agreed must be just. Some agreements are naturally entailed in the development of society, and only those are just which benefit all of the members of a society that makes them.[17] Injustice is not intrinsically bad, but is to be avoided because of the unsettling effects of the fear of detection on committing a crime. No one can be confident of escaping detection.[18] The inevitable anxiety resulting from committing crimes outweighs their appeal, and therefore acts as a deterrent.

The Greek and Roman Stoics

Epicureanism, as MacIntyre suggests, provides the rationale for withdrawal from public life, whereas Stoicism offers better reasons for participation in it.[19] For the Stoics a necessary part of their doctrine of appropriation is a natural concern for other human beings. It is in the writings of the Stoics that we encounter the firmer foundations upon which the tradition of a Universal Moral Order was built. From roughly 300 BC, when Zeno (*c.*336–264 BC), a native of Cyprus, ventured into Athens, to about AD 200, Stoic philosophy played an important part in the intellectual life of the ancients. The fragmentary nature of the early surviving writings has given rise to allegations of inconsistency between an apparent materialism and an intellectual, or rationalist, spiritualism. Zeno believed that philosophical theory has three elements, which concern nature (*physis*), character (ethics), and rational discourse (logic), and none of which is separate from the others.[20] The

Stoics maintained that only bodies exist, and that in relation to these there are two principles in the universe, activity and passivity: 'The passive, then, is unqualified substance, i.e., matter, while the active is the rational principle [*logos*] in it., i.e., god. For he being eternal and [penetrating] all of matter, is the craftsman of all things.'[21] Bodies, then, are not merely material, but a unity of *physis*, or nature, and *logos*, or a rational principle. This does not mean that everything in nature is rational. Nature is law governed and rationally ordered, and therefore is intelligible, and this is its rational principle or *logos*. Plants and animals, although distinctive in nature and intelligible because they conform to the rational coherence and order of the universe, do not possess rationality as their guiding principle.[22] Men, are, however, guided by this principle of rationality. Such a principle entails a free will which appears to be at odds with what some commentators suggest is a Stoic determinism, or fate, implying that as a result of a string of causes everything is as it should be in this law-governed rational universe.[23] Chrysippus the Stoic does, however, attempt to retain the notion of moral responsibility while subscribing to the idea of inexorable Laws of Nature. He distinguished between basic and proximate causes. The former relate to those qualities that make a thing what it is. It is fated that men have the bodily parts they have, and which constitute them as men, and that they will one day die. The physical world is determined, and so are human beings in so far as they are part of it. Proximate causes are things that are possible, but may not happen. A person may die tomorrow as the result of a car crash, but it may not happen if he chooses to travel by train. That which is fated is for Chrysippus not that which is necessary in any deterministic sense of the word. Certain things are in our power to change, and thus we are morally responsible. A single physical action can be performed for different reasons. Walking away from a fight may be cowardly if it is to save one's own skin, or courageous if at the risk of losing one's reputation one backs down in order to avoid inflicting harm on another.[24] If fate was deterministic then all causes would have to be basic, and there would be no proximate causes. He argued that all true things in the past are necessary because they have already happened and are no longer subject to change, and the same may be said about things that have happened in the present. In relation to the future it is fate that what happens does happen, that what will be will be. But he did not mean by this that it must be.[25]

The Stoics' most forceful injunction was to live according to nature. This nature was not a primary impulse to pursue pleasure. The primary impulse that men share with animals is that of self-preservation. Like Plato and Aristotle the Stoics did not interpret nature merely in terms of brute instincts, but instead saw it as correlative with reason. In man the endowment of reason supervenes on the impulse to self-preservation, and as rational creatures we are forbidden by right reason to do anything that is inconsistent with nature. Actions constrained by right reason are what Zeno called appropriate.[26] To live according to nature was to be guided by one's reason.

This for the Stoics translated into a personal ethic, not (as it did for Plato and Aristotle) into an ethics of citizenship.[27] Reason as a guide to conduct was for the Stoics universal, and because reason and nature, including human nature, are synonymous this meant that there were universal Laws of Nature to which we are all subject. To live according to reason is to live both socially and morally. Only beings possessed of reason are capable of living morally, and living morally entails living socially. On the question of whether justice and morality are natural or conventional, then, the Stoics maintained that they are natural because they follow from man's rationality.[28] In other words, the cultivation of reason, which alone belongs to man, inevitably gives rise to a social life governed by morality and justice. The universe is law-governed and exhibits reason, which implies a rational lawgiver, namely God.[29] The principles of Natural Law were ideal in that they could only become manifest if men attained perfect rationality. One such principle was that of equality. Zeno taught, for example, that as rational creatures we are naturally equal. The distinction between Greeks and barbarians, as it was for the Cynics, was merely conventional. The woman was equal to the man, the slave to the master. There was no such thing as a natural slave, only enslaved individuals finding themselves in that condition through folly and wickedness.

In practical terms, the weakness that exposed Stoicism to the criticism of the Sceptics was the distinction between the wise man and the fool. In this respect the early Stoics resemble the Cynics. The world state is composed of wise men, and only fools live in actual states. Diogenes Laertius reports that Zeno denigrated general culture and believed that 'all those who are not virtuous are hostile and enemies and slaves and alien to each other, parents to children and brothers to brothers [and] relatives to relatives'.[30] Chrysippus thought that the wise share a common citizenship of the city of the world.[31] In fact the idealism of early Stoicism, with its tendency to become divorced from the world as it was, positing a law to be emulated, but of no man's making, exposed it to the critical gaze of the Sceptics. Carneades, who was later to be the Realist whom Grotius singled out for a sustained attack, made it his vocation to expose its weaknesses, so much so that he could say: 'If there were no Chrysippus, I would not be.'[32] Carneades argues that there is no certain criterion of truth,[33] on the basis of which he subjects the major doctrines of Stoicism to dissolving scrutiny. He argues that there is no such thing as Natural Law, and that the laws of states are conventional expressions of self-interest. Justice, or attending to the interests of others, is nothing but folly. All kingdoms and empires are acquired by war, and necessarily entail inflicting injury on others and their gods. It was not by justice that the Romans acquired their empire and riches, and they would be obliged to revert to dwelling in huts if they returned all that did not justly belong to them.[34]

Reason and nature, for the Stoics, dispose us to practise the fundamental virtues of justice, courage, prudence, and temperance. Virtue is indivisible, and it is therefore not possible to possess one to the exclusion of the others. One is either virtuous or not; there are no half measures. Virtue is intrinsically good and is pursued for its own sake, 'not because of some fear or hope or some extrinsic consideration'.[35]

Although the Law of Nature is a guide to personal conduct, we are unambiguously social creatures living in particular states and subject to their laws. In this respect an appropriate action, that is, one according to reason, is to love one's father-

land, and among the goods external to oneself is a 'virtuous fatherland'.[36] But ultimately we are united as rational creatures in a single cosmopolis, or city of God. All
men, then, should consider themselves to be fellow citizens subject to a common
order.[37] This vision of the world-state is not, however, fundamentally political. It is
primarily religious in emphasizing our common place in a rationally ordered cosmos, regulated by a supreme lawgiver, and ethical because of its emphasis upon reason as the universal bond of mankind. It was these elements, rather than a
conception of the state, or world-state, that gave the Stoics lasting significance.

In the second century BC Panaetius of Rhodes, the then head of the Stoic school,
taught a modified form of Stoicism in response to the dissolving criticisms of the
Sceptics, which gave hope to those who had not yet attained virtue, but were striving towards it.[38] He was concerned with the man on probation making progress
towards attaining wisdom, not by the exercise of perfect virtue, but by means of
services or duties regularly rendered. He rejected the traditional Stoic psychology
which traced all the faculties back to reason, and instead suggested that the
psyche had both rational and irrational parts which had to be accommodated.
Unlike the earlier Stoics, he posited that external things such as property and
health are goods to be valued and pursued, not merely because they give content
to virtue and a domain for its exercise, but also because they are valuable in themselves as long as they do not come into conflict with virtue.[39] The life of perfect
apathy, for Panaetius, was not a possibility. Unlike his predecessors, who emphasized wisdom above all among the virtues, Panaetius emphasized temperance, or
soberness. To act with decorum was of much greater practical import. In his
political philosophy, like many Greek philosophers before him, he favoured a
mixed constitution incorporating elements of monarchy, aristocracy, and democracy. He had many discussions with the historian Polybius, and like him admired
the Roman constitution. For Panaetius the Natural Law was not an ideal regulating the community of wise men, but a principle, embodied in varying degrees in
actual states, by which their actions could be appraised. The exercise of political
power could only be distinguished from force, and justified as legitimate, with
reference to the justness of its exercise and the rightness of its aims. Panaetius'
form of Stoicism, accepting elements of Platonism, Aristotelianism, and the criticisms of Carneades, was acceptable to his Roman friends, among whom were to
be counted Scipio Africanus Minor (185–129 BC), the principal interlocutor in
Cicero's *Commonwealth*.[40]

McIlwain suggests that some of the Stoic doctrines, such as universal citizenship and the brotherhood of man, made it well suited to a state that was gradually incorporating the peoples of the known world under its dominion.[41] The Law
of Nature, or of reason, incorporated into and mediated through Roman law was
to have profound repercussions in subsequent political thought. Towards the
middle of the second century BC, soon after the Greeks had been subdued by the
Romans, Stoicism, in the modified form represented by Panaetius, found a home
in Roman thought.

The most significant Roman Stoics were the eclectic consul Cicero (106–43 BC)
and the Emperor Marcus Aurelius Antoninus (AD 121–180), the author of the

famous *Meditations*. Unlike their Greek counterparts, they did not concentrate their efforts upon the problems of logic and metaphysics, and for the most part they accepted on these matters the conclusions they had inherited, which allowed them to focus instead upon ethical and social problems.

Cicero

Cicero added little that was new to ethics and political philosophy, but he does exemplify the concerns of the later republic and the Greek influence upon Roman thought. He was an eclectic prepared to employ arguments appropriate to advancing his case. Like the Stoics, he believed in a universal fellowship of the human race, but he did not confine it to the wise, and in addition he allied it with the Roman idea of the Law of Nations.[42] It is a natural fellowship based upon the unifying principles of reason, speech, and natural equality (*On Duties*, I. 50, p. 21).[43] This universal society, encompassing the whole of humanity, found in Cicero no institutional expression. It is a fellowship established by the gods in which right reason, the 'royal power in the souls of men' (*Commonwealth*, I. xxxviii, p. 144) accords with nature. Reason in harmony with nature exhibits a law that is unchanging and universal. It restrains good men from wrongdoing, but cannot restrain the wicked, who have abandoned their better selves and who may evade human punishment but not the most severe of consequences deemed by god. It is a law that cannot be annulled, and no act of human legislatures can absolve us from the duty of obedience to it (*Commonwealth*, III. xxii, pp. 215–16). Cicero equates this Natural Law, or *jus naturale*, with the Law of Nations, *jus gentium*, in that it is ordained by nature and gives the substantive content of men's moral relations with each other, and the relations among the states in which they reside. *Jus civile*, or human positive law, is not wholly incorporated in *jus gentium*, but the whole of *jus ge..tium* should be incoporated in *jus civile* (*On Duties*, III. 69, p. 126). The meaning and content of these terms are not always consistent among Roman writers, as we will see.

How does this Natural Law, or the Law of Nations, translate into prohibitions or injunctions to act? Cicero does not go to any great lengths to articulate the duties of men to each other, preferring instead to emphasize the duties of citizens. His main prohibition, however, would be wide-ranging in its effects. There is nothing worse, and therefore nothing so much at variance with nature, than benefiting at the expense of another. To do so by theft or violence is total anathema to the common fellowship of mankind. In other words, respect for property is a basic human duty, the disregard of which 'is more contrary to nature than death or pain or anything else of the type' (*On Duties*, III. 24, p. 109) because it is destructive of human fellowship and community (*On Duties*, III. 22, p. 108, and III. 28, p. 110).

At this level of communal ties and obligations there does not appear to be any duty to make material sacrifices to benefit those peoples of other nations who are in need. We should simply desist from benefiting at their expense: 'each should attend to what benefits him himself, so far as may be done without injustice to another' (*On Duties*, III. 42, p. 115). Cicero explicitly says that we should not forgo personal benefits by surrendering them to others if we ourselves are in need of them (*On Duties*, III. 42, p. 115). In practical terms this would exclude ruthless exploitation, but not necessarily, as we will see, imperialism.

The world of human beings is a moral community united in reason and fellowship, but it is not our only sphere of obligation, and although our obligations under the Natural Law, or Law of Nations, cannot be renounced, Cicero does seem to suggest that our obligations to the state, our relatives, and our fellow citizens have a greater claim upon us in terms of the active discharge of moral responsibilities. The world may be one community, but it is a community composed of many communities, each of which has claims of loyalty and affection upon those individuals who are socially tied to it.

Whereas the early Stoics placed great emphasis upon the virtue of wisdom and the community of the wise, Cicero tilts the balance in favour of the virtue of justice, without which the natural sociability of man would be undermined, and the nobility of spirit consequent upon a love of learning would become little more than a form of savagery. He argues that human beings have a natural instinct to associate. They come together not out of fear, nor from the want of necessities, but because they are naturally gregarious (*Commonwealth*, I. xxv, p. 129). The social duties whose effect is to strengthen the social bond that unites us 'must be preferred to the duty that is limited to learning and knowledge' (*On Duties*, I. 157, p. 61).

There are different degrees of fellowship, ranging from the unlimited fellowship of the human species to the strictly limited fellowship of the family. The procreational instinct gives rise to the fellowship of marriage, children, and the household that is communally shared. Fellowship extends to other relations who cannot be contained within the one household, and intermarriage extends the bonds of fellowship to a .vider circle of relatives, and eventually to the establishment of political communities (*On Duties*, I. 54, p. 23). The Commonwealth, or 'the people's affair' (*Commonwealth*, I. xxvi, pp. 129–31), is a specific type of association in which individuals are 'united by a common agreement about law and rights and by the desire to participate in mutual advantages' (*Commonwealth*, I. xxv, pp. 129). Furthermore, there are bonds of language, tribe, and race that are held together by love and good will, strengthened by common ancestral memories and religious rites.

Of all these levels of fellowship Cicero makes it clear that 'none is more serious, and none dearer, than that of each of us with the republic' (*On Duties*, I. 57, p. 23; cf. III. 95, p. 137). No good man would shy away from sacrificing his life for the benefit of the state. To it we have a duty of public service because it is not a mere convenience for the better promotion of individual interests, a refuge in a storm, or a sanctum for private learning and undisturbed leisure. The state claims for itself the greater part of our physical and mental powers, and in return gives back for the benefit of private needs only that which is superfluous for its own

(*Commonwealth*, I. v, p. 110). The benefits that the state bestows upon us are so great that it is more venerable than a natural parent, and to it we owe a greater gratitude (*Commonwealth*, I. fragment 2, p. 152). This, of course, is similar to the case for political obligation put forward by the Laws in Plato's *Crito*.

The justification of the exercise of political power, for Cicero, must be on moral grounds which are consistent with Natural Law. In this respect he condoned the murder of Caesar. There could, in his view, be no fellowship between a people and a tyrant. Tyrants are unjust and arbitrary rulers unconstrained by standards of civilized conduct and common decency. They cannot even be afforded the title of human beings because of their wilful disregard of civilized conduct and beastly demeanour (*Commonwealth*, II. xxvi, pp. 178–9). Tyrants are cancerous growths upon humanity that should be cut out with the surgeon's knife (*On Duties*, III. 19, p. 107, and III. 32, p. 111).

The state, Cicero contended, should be organized in such a way that it will never become extinguished (*Commonwealth*, III. xxiii, p. 216). To this end one of the noblest preoccupations of the soul is the security of the state (*Commonwealth*, VI. xxvi, p. 267). War may sometimes be necessary to protect the state, but it can only be just if instituted to repel an invader or for the restitution of property for which a formal claim has been advanced. Furthermore, a war must be officially announced and declared (*Commonwealth*, III. xxiii, p. 217, and *On Duties*, I. 36, pp. 15–16). Those who have not been inhumane and cruel in the conduct of war, Cicero thought, should be spared when peace is restored. The state should show concern not only for those who have been overcome by force, but also for those who have laid down their arms and seek refuge. Here Cicero is referring to the well-established procedures of the religious fetial laws regulating the declaration and conduct of war.

Cicero argues that we are not born for ourselves. Our country and friends have claims upon us. Furthermore, we are born as humans to assist each other and have a duty to promote our common fellowship by exchanging goods, services and expertise. Injustice is caused not only by directly inflicting harm, but also by desisting from trying to prevent it being inflicted by others. He argues that 'the man who does not defend someone, or obstruct the injustice when he can, is at fault just as if he had abandoned his parents or his friends or his country' (*On Duties*, I. 23, p. 10). Cicero goes to some lengths to suggest that the wars by which Rome acquired its empire were just because they were in defence of its allies and undertaken only as a last resort in order to secure peace and eliminate injustices. He suggests that in this respect Rome in relation to its empire is best seen as a protectorate rather than a conqueror. Cicero was, of course, well aware that the allies Rome chose to protect were acquisitions.

In what remains of Cicero's *Commonwealth* we do not have his answer to Philus' question. He contends that Rome now has power over the whole world, enjoying immense benefits as a consequence. Philus rhetorically asks: 'Was it by justice or by prudence that our nation rose from the least among states [to be the greatest of all]?' (*Commonwealth*, III. xv, p. 211). In apparent disregard of his subscription to the principles of just war, and his view of Rome before Sulla as a protectorate, Cicero appears in one passage of *On Duties* to condone whatever means are necessary to increase the power, land, and revenues of Rome: 'Such are the deeds of men who are great; such deeds were achieved in our forefathers' day. Men who pursue these kinds of duties will win, along with the utmost benefit to the republic, both great gratitude and great glory for themselves' (*On Duties*, II. 85, pp. 98–9). He nevertheless abhorred ruthless imperialism, holding it responsible for the decline of the state, and certainly would not subscribe to anything like the doctrine of Reason of State.

Marcus Aurelius

The emperor Marcus Aurelius argued that everything in the cosmos is implicated and co-ordinated to constitute one ordered universe, pervaded by god, who has provided one substance, law, reason, and truth for all rational animals (*Meditations*, v, 16).[44] We know that god exists, not because we can have direct knowledge of the forms of his powers, but because we see his works all around us. We ourselves, although having bodies like the animals, are effluxes from the divinity because we have reason and intelligence like gods. He contended that everything is constituted for a purpose, towards which it is directed, being that which is advantageous or good for it. Man, the possessor of reason, is made for society and in it finds his good (*Meditations*, v, 16).[45] Rational animals are made to assist each other in society, and therefore injuries perpetrated against each other are acts of impiety against 'the highest divinity' (*Meditations*, IX, 1). Self-interested acts with no immediate or remote social purpose are in fact unnatural, that is, they go against reason (*Meditations*, IX, 23). Reason demands that we behave towards each other 'according to the natural law of fellowship with benevolence and justice' (*Meditations*, III, 11).

Marcus Aurelius sums up his philosophy in the following way:

If our intellectual part is common, the reason also in respect of which we are rational beings, is common: if this is so, common also is the reason which commands us what to do, and what not to do; if this is so, there is a common law also; if this is so, we are fellow-citizens; if this is so, we are members of some political community; if this is so, the world is in a manner a state. For of what other common political community will any one say that the whole human race are members? (*Meditations*, IV, 4)

He goes on to make his famous statement that, 'my nature is rational and social; and my city and country, so far as I am Antoninus, is Rome, but so far as I am a man, it is the world' (*Meditations*, VI, 43). The universal community in which every man is kin to every other man is united not by means of blood ties, but by something far more binding, intelligence or reason (*Meditations*, XII, 26).

The importance of the Roman Stoics is that they incorporated Greek philosophical ideas about a Universal Moral Order into the traditional legal ideas of Rome, providing a unifying principle for the empire in the community of reason and reasonableness. It was within the context of the Roman tradition that the concept of a just war arose. In its formative years it was closely attached to religious rites and institutions. As in Greece, the sanction of the gods in matters of war and peace was an extremely important public ritual, and during the period of the kings (735–508 BC) the laws of war and peace were integral to the *jus sacrum*. One of the duties of the college of priests was the administering of the *jus sacrum*. Whether Rome had been unjustly wronged or injured was a religious decision pronounced upon by the college of priests. During the republican period they would make the case for just cause before the Senate, and the Senate and the people of Rome decided whether to embark upon war. Such wars were at once just and pious. Gradually the role of the priests became less important, and the justness of a war became central to doctrine. Its justness became associated with the infringement of law, that is, Rome had to be deemed legally wronged before a war could be pronounced just. Thus war was subject to both a moral and a legal constraint. What Cicero added to this was to associate the justness of a war with the Stoic idea of a universal moral, or natural, law. In its mature form it acknowledged four just causes of war: first, if the frontiers of Rome were violated; second, if Roman ambassadors were insulted or their persons violated; third, if treaties made with Rome were broken; and, finally, if a friendly nation turned against Rome and gave support to an enemy.[46]

Rome instituted a formal procedure for pursuing its grievances against states which perpetrated wrongs against it. A leading statesman would head a delegation of ambassadors to demand reparations. After their return to Rome, thirty-three days would be allowed to lapse before sending the same delegation to the aggressor to threaten war. If no reparation was received the delegation would recommend war to the Senate, which might then decide to resort to force in pursuit of its claim. The same delegation would then return to the aggressor to declare war. Exceptions to this procedure were allowed in the case of civil war, or if the enemy had no recognizable state organization, or if an attack upon Rome was already under way.[47] Rome, as was illustrated in the work of Cicero, went to great lengths to deny that her expansion was motivated by greed, and protested that her wars were just. The safety of her allies was always paramount.[48] When it came to practical policy, however, Rome was not averse to allowing self-interest to overcome considerations of justice.[49]

A. P. d'Entrèves suggests that the establishment of a universally valid system of laws was the greatest achievement in the development of Natural Law. This system found expression in the law books of the Roman emperor Justinian, who claimed universal validity for it.[50] The purpose of Natural Law, as the Romans understood it, was to temper and make more acceptable their archaic and harsh civil law, *jus civile*. Roman expansion required a transformation in its laws to accommodate its newly acquired supranational empire, and Natural Law proved to be the appropriate agent. In order to minimize the association of law with force, Cicero was anxious to show the moral character of the *jus civile* and *jus gentium*. Justice on this reading did not result from law, but was prior to it.[51]

The Justinian code, which was a compilation of existing codes, embodied many inconsistencies. The Natural Law, *jus naturale*, for example, is sometimes different from the Law of Nations, *jus gentium*, and at other times identified with it. This reflects the equivocal meanings that they had from at least the time of Cicero. In practical terms the *jus gentium* was a body of customs and agreements constituted into a body of commercial law, applicable to both citizens and foreigners, and enforceable in the courts. As a legal ideal it was understood to be the universal element, as opposed to the parochial and particular elements, found in all legal codes. It is as a legal ideal that the *jus gentium* was often identified with Natural Law, or *jus naturale*, which according to Michael P. Zuckert is the law imposed on all creatures, 'that which nature has taught all animals'.[52] He suggests that much of the confusion about Roman jurists' conceptions of Natural Law arises out of confusing them with those of Stoicism, in which it is peculiar to humanity and discovered by right reason in conformity with nature, and with the later Christian conception, in which it stands above human law and acts as its judge. The *jus gentium* in the *Digest* is related to Natural Law, but is more strictly applicable to all of humanity, and in this respect it also can be deemed natural, but in a different sense from *jus naturale*.

Natural Law was not a written code, it is an ideal which imbues the spirit of the application of law in the courts and in this respect has some practical bearing upon it. In neither the Justinian *Institutes* nor the Ulpian *Digest* is Natural Law posited as superior to human positive law, or *jus civile*. It is not claimed that the former acts as a judge of the latter, nor that it should take precedence in cases of conflict.[53] Furthermore, it did not bestow upon human beings inalienable rights. Its importance was that it established the idea of the inherent value and worth of law, and of its equal applicability to everyone. It was a law based not on its power to compel, but instead upon its intrinsic worth.[54]

The relation of Rome to its neighbours was not one of master and slave, but one that depended upon circumstances. Romans were not as possessive of citizenship as the Greeks, and extenc..ed citizenship selectively first to Rome's Italian allies and then to the empire. Roman imperialism, as we have already seen, was not primarily conceived in territorial terms. Landed relations did play a part, but the fundamental conception was one of obedience to the commands of an *imperator*. In whatever relation Rome stood with an ally, it expected commands to be obeyed. Just as Greece was, for the Greeks, the heart of civilization, so was Rome for the Romans.[55]

The Christian World-View

Christians up to the time of Constantine's conversion (AD 312) mostly refused military service because of the deification of the emperor requiring idolatry, but also because of pacifist principles drawn from the New Testament. In the pre-Constantine empire persecuted Christians found a modified form of Stoicism, which preached equality before God and the hope of salvation, appropriate to their condition. The Natural Law in their hands became far more prescriptive and judgmental than it had been in the hands of the Roman jurists. Natural Law embodied natural justice, taught the intrinsic dignity and worth of every human soul, and was the moral criterion against which human laws should be tested. The ideal of the unity of the empire rapidly eroded with the transference of the imperial seat to Constantinople and the barbarian invasions. As the officially adopted religion of the empire, Christianity, with its emphasis upon equality and universality, did help to retard the process of disintegration.[56] Exploiting the ambiguity of the New Testament on the permitted use of war, the Church appropriated and refined the Roman tradition of justified war in order to permit, and even require, Christians to participate in the prosecution of just wars. St Ambrose and St Augustine (AD 354–430), for example, justify Christian involvement in war in order to secure the boundaries of the empire under Constantine against barbarian military threat. St Ambrose gives emphasis to the Platonic and Stoic virtues of prudence, justice, courage, and temperance, maintaining that living a life in accordance with them is a prerequisite of salvation. This entails the promotion of justice and, on occasion, its enforcement. St Ambrose followed Cicero in believing that desisting from preventing harm being done by another to a friend makes one as guilty as the perpetrator. Not only must there be a just cause for war, but its conduct must also be just, *jus in bello*. Even enemy soldiers must be treated as moral equals and dealt with in accordance with their good or bad conduct, and a distinction must be made between innocent and guilty parties on the enemy side when justice is applied to the vanquished. [57]

Augustine wrote at a time when Rome itself was sacked by the Visigoths in 411, and his own city of Hippo in North Africa, protected by the Roman army, was under constant threat of invasion, eventually falling to the Vandals in 431, the year after Augustine died. Augustine stated that the inhabitants of the City of God, which has existed since the beginning of time, and the Earthly City, which came into being after .ae Fall, share the same earth, constitute a world community which transcends state and ethnic limits, are the descendants of Adam, and are afflicted with original sin. As a consequence of the Fall man has corrupted everything that is good. The state, although corrupt, is necessary to maintain peace and accommodate man's social, but imperfect, nature. At the world level, Augustine argues, the multiplicity of languages divides men from one another, and when they are unable to communicate their thoughts to each other for want of a common language 'all the similarity of their common human nature is of no avail to unite them' (*City of God*, xix. 7, p. 861).[58]

To the end of pursuing peace a monarch may have to engage in wars, the justness of which depends upon whether they are perpetrated to avenge a wrong done by a nation in failing to return something unjustly acquired, that is, unjust aggression, or to punish its own citizens for wrongs against their own state. In addition, just war can only be waged by a legitimate authority, acting not out of revenge or malice. Central to Augustine's thinking is the view that war is both a consequence of and a remedy for sin. The end towards which wars must always aim is peace of some kind. Even in this earthly life, St Augustine tells us, there is nothing 'desired with greater longing' nor anything better to be enjoyed than peace (*City of God*, XIX. 11, p. 866). War was not evil in itself, but instead its usual accompaniments, of greed, the lust for power, and the love of cruelty, constitute the evils.[59] To punish a wicked ruler in order to prevent further wickedness being perpetrated, as long as the motive of revenge and the pleasure of inflicting suffering is absent, was for Augustine an act of love. Unjust wrongs had to be resisted for the sake of upholding Christian values, and he therefore exhorted Christians, for example, to protect the Roman Empire against marauding Saharan tribesmen.[60]

An additional just cause, not acknowledged by the Romans, was the kind of war which God Himself ordains.[61] Here we have the question of not only the justness of a war, but also its righteousness. As the agent of God, the ruler may make a subjective judgement which sanctifies any war he initiates in an attempt to rectify wrongs against the moral order, and wrongs may be perpetrated for the good of the vanquished in order to extirpate lust and vice from its community. Wicked rulers can therefore serve God's purpose by punishing other peoples who have sinned. Augustine's just war theory goes beyond Cicero's and the Romans'. Just war for reparation, or to protect a friendly ally, sought to re-establish the status quo, but Augustine's principles could be used to justify much more than this. War could be waged in order to inflict punishment for unlawful crimes, but also to avenge the moral degradation of sin. War was to uphold righteousness as well as legality.[62] Augustine argues that 'it is the injustice of the opposing side that lays on the wise man the duty of waging wars' (*City of God*, I. 26, p. 37).

Augustine pays homage to traditional Christian pacifism by denying the right of war to individuals who in harming others for a wrong received could not avoid being intent on revenge. Even private self-defence is prohibited because of the accompanying hatred and absence of love. Russell sums up Augustine's position when he argues that 'Private pacifism was thus joined to a justification of public warfare that underscored the later medieval emphasis on the legitimate authority necessary to wage just wars.'[63] In Augustine's theory the ruler or God decides upon the merits of, and authorizes, a just war. Only soldiers may legitimately act under such authority. Private citizens and the clergy are not sanctioned to kill (*City of God*, I. 26, p. 37).

Augustine, like Thucydides, recognized the pernicious consequences of civil war to be greater than those of foreign wars. The expansion of the empire, he believed, had increased the possibility and occasion of civil war, the consequences and miseries of which were far worse than foreign wars (*City of God*, XIX. 7, p. 861). Factious civil wars in Rome, Augustine argues, under the auspices of pagan gods, were far more brutal and devastating than anything ever known in foreign combat, and far worse than any calamity that befell Rome in the Christian era. The avenging of Marius' savagery by Sulla, for example, precipitated under the pretext of peace the slaughter of innocent and defenceless people whom the law of war would have spared because they bore no arms and offered no resistance. The murders, Augustine argues, were 'beyond all calculation' and did not stop 'until it was suggested to Sulla that some people should be allowed to live so that the conquerors should have some subjects to command' (*City of God*, iii. 28, p. 129).

The justness of foreign war in Augustine's theory, however, loses the objective criterion which the Romans and Stoics tried to supply. Augustine's theory licenses the holy war which was pursued with such righteous zeal during the crusades. Almost any war sanctioned by a ruler and believed to have the blessing of God could be deemed a holy war. Citizens do not have the right to resist the ruler's orders on grounds of conscience. They are absolved from culpable blame when acting in an official capacity even if they believe that the orders to kill an enemy are unjust. Augustine argues that 'one who owes a duty of obedience to the giver of the command does not himself "kill"—he is an instrument, a sword in its user's hand' (*City of God*, i. 21, p. 32).

In the face of imperial decline, the teachings of Christianity were imposed upon the rulers and subjects alike of a Christendom which, unlike the supra-continental Roman Empire, found its geographical limits gradually receding to the continent of Europe. By the fifth century what had previously belonged to Rome had become numerous small states, with a surviving relic centred on Constantinople. The political unity provided by Rome was gradually superseded, despite the existence of different types of Christianity, by a religious unity.

Notes

1. See e.g. Plato, *Protagoras*, trans. W. K. C. Guthrie (Harmondsworth, Penguin, 1987), 71.
2. Plato, *Laws*, trans. A. E. Taylor (London, Dent, 1934), §§889–90.
3. C. Phillipson, *The International Law and Custom of Ancient Greece and Rome* (London, Macmillan, 1911), 43.
4. Sophocles, *Oedipus the King*, in *Antigone, Oedipus the King, Electra*, trans. Robert Fagles (Harmondsworth, Penguin, 1994), 77 [864].
5. Sophocles, *Antigone*, in *Antigone, Oedipus the King, Electra*, trans. Robert Fagles (Harmondsworth, Penguin, 1994), 16 [450]. She says: 'Nor do I think that a decree of yours [Creon]— I A man—could override the laws of Heaven I Unwritten and unchanging. Not of today I Or yesterday is their authority; I They are eternal; no man saw their birth.'
6. *Aristotle on Rhetoric: A Theory of Civic Discourse*, trans. George A Kennedy (Oxford, Oxford University Press, 1991). Cf. his distinction between natural and conventional political justice: 'It is natural when it has the same validity everywhere and is unaffected by any view we may take about the justice of it. It is conventional when there is no original reason why it should take one form rather than another and the rule it imposes is reached by agreement, after which it holds good' (Aristotle, *Nicomachean Ethics*, trans. J. A. K. Thomson (Harmondsworth, Penguin, 1973), 157, v. 7).
7. Plato, *The Republic*, trans. Desmond Lee 2nd edn. (Harmondsworth, Penguin, 1987), 178. Cf. 'Thine own being also, fond man, is one such fragment, and so, for all its littleness, all its striving is ever directed towards the whole, but thou hast forgotten in the business that the purpose of all that happens is what we have said, to win bliss for

the life of the whole; it is not made for thee, but thou for it' (Plato, *Laws*, trans. A. E. Taylor (London, Dent, 1934), §903; also see §923).

8. Aristotle, *The Politics*, ed. Stephen Everson trans. based on Jonathan Barnes' revision of Jowett (Cambridge, Cambridge University Press, 1988).
9. Also see Jonathan Barnes, 'Partial Wholes', in Ellen Frankel Paul, Fred D. Miller, Jr., and Jeffrey Paul (eds.), *Ethics, Politics and Human Nature* (Oxford, Blackwell, 1991).
10. Plato, *Republic*, 258–9.
11. Plutarch, in Ernest Barker (ed. and trans.), *From Alexander to Constantine* (Oxford, Clarendon Press, 1956), 8.
12. Barker, *Alexander to Constantine*, 17.
13. Andrew Linklater, *Men and Citizens, in the Theory of International Relations*, 2nd edn. (London, Macmillan, 1990), pp. 21–2.
14. Alasdair MacIntyre, *A Short History of Ethics* (London, Routledge and Kegan Paul, 1967), 107.
15. Epicurus' letter to Menoeceus: Diogenes Laertius, in Brad Inwood and L. P. Gerson (trans.), *Hellenistic Philosophy* (Indianapolis, Hackett, 1988), 24 [10. 128].
16. Diogenes Laertius, in Inwood and Gerson, *Hellenistic Philosophy*, 27 [10, maxim xiv].
17. R. W. Sharples, *Stoics, Epicureans and Sceptics* (London, Routledge, 1996), 116–7.
18. Diogenes Laertius, in Inwood and Gerson, *Hellenistic Philosophy*, 28 [10, maxims xxxi–xxxv].
19. MacIntyre, *Short History of Ethics*, 108.
20. Diogenes Laertius, in Inwood and Gerson, *Hellenistic Philosophy*, 78–9 [7. 38–41].
21. Diogenes Laertius, in Inwood and Gerson, *Hellenistic Philosophy*, 96 [7. 134].
22. Constance Creede, 'Epictetus', in Ian P. McGreal (ed.), *Great Thinkers of the Western World* (New York, HarperCollins, 1992), 49.
23. See e.g. the section on Stoic fate in Inwood and Gerson, *Hellenistic Philosophy*, 127–35.
24. Cf. MacIntyre, *Short History of Ethics*, 105.
25. For this argument I have drawn upon the excellent discussion of fate and necessity in J. M. Rist, *Stoic Philosophy* (Cambridge, Cambridge University Press, 1977), 112–32. St Augustine interprets the Stoics in a similar way. He maintains that 'Among those things which they wished not to be subject to necessity they placed our wills, knowing that they would not be free if subjected to necessity' (*The Essential Augustine*, ed. Vernon J. Bourke (Indianapolis, Hackett, 1974), 184).
26. Diogenes Laertius, in Inwood and Gerson, *Hellenistic Philosophy*, 139–41 [7. 85–8 and 7. 108].
27. J. W. Gough, *The Social Contract* (Oxford, Clarendon Press, 1957), 15.
28. Diogenes Laertius, in Inwood and Gerson, *Hellenistic Philosophy*, 145 [7. 128].
29. R. N. Berki, *The History of Political Thought* (London, Dent, 1977), 57.
30. Diogenes Laertius, in Inwood and Gerson, *Hellenistic Philosophy*, 74–5 [7. 32].
31. Sharples, *Stoics, Epicureans and Sceptics*, 125.
32. Diogenes Laertius, in Inwood and Gerson, *Hellenistic Philosophy*, 160 [4. 62].
33. Sextus, in Inwood and Gerson, *Hellenic Philosophy*, 166 [M. 7. 159].
34. Carneades' view is expressed in Cicero, trans. G. H. Sabine and S. B. Smith *On the Commonwealth* (London, Collier Macmillan, 1986), 200–15.
35. Diogenes Laertius, in Inwood and Gerson, *Hellenistic Philosophy*, 137 [7. 89].
36. Diogenes Laertius, in Inwood and Gerson, *Hellenistic Philosophy*, 139 and 140 [7. 95 and 7. 108].

37. Ernest Barker, in Otto Gierke, *Natural Law and the Theory of Society 1500 to 1800*, trans. and introd. by Ernest Barker (Cambridge, Cambridge University Press, 1934), p. xxxv.
38. F. W. Walbank, *The Hellenistic World* (London, Fontana, 1992), 181.
39. E. Vernon Arnold, *Roman Stoicism* (Cambridge, Cambridge University Press, 1911), 100–3.
40. George Holland Sabine and Stanley Barney Smith, 'Introduction', in Cicero, *Commonwealth*, 32.
41. Charles Howard McIllwain, *The Growth of Political Thought in the West* (New York, Macmillan, 1932), 106.
42. Sharples, *Stoics, Epicureans, and Sceptics*, 127.
43. Cicero, *On Duties*, ed. and trans. M. T. Griffin and F. M. Atkins (Cambridge, Cambridge University Press, 1991).
44. *The Meditations of the Emperor Marcus Aurelius Antoninus*, trans. George Long (London, Collins, n. d.).
45. Cf. 'For we are made for co-operation, like feet, like hands, like eyelids, like the rows of the upper and lower teeth. To act against one another then is contrary to nature; and it is acting against one another to be vexed and turn away' (*Meditations*, II, 1).
46. See G. I. A. D. Draper, 'Grotius' Place in the Development of Legal Ideas about War', in Hedley Bull, Benedict Kingsbury, and Adam Roberts (eds.), *Hugo Grotius and International Relations* (Oxford, Clarendon Press, 1990), 179.
47. Paul Christopher, *The Ethics of War and Peace* (Englewood Cliffs, NJ, Prentice Hall, 1994), 13–14.
48. Michael Crawford, *The Roman Republic* (London, Fontana, 1992), 68.
49. Andrew Lintott, *Imperium Romanum* (London, Routledge, 1993), 34; Phillipson, *International Law and Custom*, 101.
50. A. P. d'Entrèves, *Natural Law*, rev. edn. (London, Hutchinson, 1972), 24–5.
51. F. Parkinson, *The Philosophy of International Relations: A Study in the History of Thought* (Beverly Hills, Calif., and London, Sage, 1977), 12–13.
52. Michael P. Zuckert, ' "Bringing Philosophy Down from the Heavens": Natural Right in the Roman Law', *Review of Politics*, 51 (1989), 76. Also see Phillipson, *International Law and Custom*, 83.
53. Barker, in Gierke, *Natural Law and the Theory of Society*, pp. xxxvi–xxxvii; Zuckert, ' "Bringing Philosophy Down from the Heavens" ', 76–7.
54. d'Entrèves, *Natural Law*, 35.
55. Denys Hay, *Europe: The Emergence of an Idea* (New York, Harper and Row, 1966), 4–5.
56. Parkinson, *The Philosophy of International Relations*, 14. Christianity was officially adopted in AD 383.
57. Christopher, *War and Peace*, 23–9.
58. St Augustine, *Concerning the City of God against the Pagans*, trans. Henry Bettenson, introd. by John O'Meara (Harmondsworth, Penguin, 1984).
59. F. H. Russell, *The Just War in the Middle Ages* (Cambridge, Cambridge University Press, 1975), 16.
60. Henry Chadwick, *Augustine* (Oxford, Oxford University Press, 1986), 104.
61. Christopher, *War and Peace*, 40.
62. Russell, *Just War in the Middle Ages*, 19.
63. Russell, *Just War in the Middle Ages*, 18.

9

CONSTRAINING THE CAUSES AND CONDUCT OF WAR: AQUINAS, VITORIA, GENTILI, AND GROTIUS

The Medieval Mind

The Earth, for the medieval Christian, stood at the centre of the universe. His view was geocentric rather than heliocentric. This did not mean that the Christian had an exalted opinion of his place in the universe. His Fall from Grace required humility not false pride. To be at the centre of the universe was at every point to be the furthest away from God in relation to the other planets. Furthermore, the Earth for the medieval Christian mind was made up of three continents: Europe, Asia, and Africa. Noah, after the Flood, had divided the world into continents and bestowed one upon each of his three sons. Shem was given Asia, from which the Jews originate. Japheth received Europe, from which Gentiles originate. And Ham received Africa, from which the different African peoples emerged. Such a view of geography had to be reconciled with a Christian cosmology. T ɔ Christian medieval mind inherited from the Greeks and Stoics the idea of an ordered cosmos in which everything had its place. God stood at the top of a hierarchy that reached down to the lowest forms of existence. This hierarchy encompassed the angels, people on other planets, human beings, animals, and inanimate objects. All these forms of existence were linked together in what Arthur Lovejoy has called 'The Great Chain of Being'. The chain was held together by three principles. The first was the principle of Plenitude, that is, the idea that God has created everything that it is possible to create, including those things that are good and evil. The second was Continuity. This principle derives from Aristotle's biological studies, in which he claimed that species so closely resemble each other in a classificatory scheme that they 'touch'. In other words, there is no conceivable gap between one species and another, that is, the chain is continuous between one form of existence and another. The third principle is that of Gradation. Each form of existence in this continuous chain is subordinate to that which comes after it. Human beings are superior to animals and inferior to spiritual beings on other planets.[1] It is only a short step from this cosmology to the placing of the three continents in a hierarchical relation. This was done by the Christian Fathers when they selectively invoked passages from Genesis in order to rank the different races. The reference to the enlargement of Japheth into the tents of Shem (Genesis, 9: 27) was a common citation. St Jerome, for example, used Genesis in support of his claim that Christians are destined to displace the earlier monopoly of the Jews in scholarship and scriptural knowledge. It was common among the Christian Fathers by the seventh century to view Jews as inferior to Christians because of their refusal to accept the New Testament. The reference to Ham's son Canaan becoming a servant of both Shem and Japheth was invoked to prove that Africans were clearly inferior to Gentiles and Jews. At the top of the hierarchy, then, stood the noble race of Gentiles, or Europeans, in the middle the churlish race of Jews, or Asians, and at the bottom the servile race of Africans.

Everything in the universe, for the medieval Christian mind, was regulated by law. Law is the single most important concept in medieval thought. The juristic character of all sorts of relationships, including that between the people and the ruler, and between lords and their vassals, as well as mercantile transactions cannot be overestimated. People believed in a hierarchy of law, with the laws of the state having a subordinate place. Human law, it was generally believed, should reflect the law that governed the universe. In this respect, the idea of making law was barely intelligible. The laws of the state were declaratory in that they reflected God's Natural Law.

Even though the idea of empire was never totally extinguished, with an emperor in Constantinople as the direct heir of the Roman Empire, and Charlemagne's revival of empire in the west in 800, the supranational unity with which people identified was primarily Christianity, and the world was divided into Christians and others. The territorial consciousness of Christendom was accelerated by the Muslim threat from the seventh to the tenth century, during which Christian territories, including Jerusalem, and parts of Europe, such as Spain and Sicily, were .ost to Islam. From the eleventh to the thirteenth century holy war in defence of the boundaries of Christendom constituted an almost permanent crusade. Pope Urban II, for example, sought in 1095 to prohibit knights fighting against fellow Christians, and exhorted them to wage wars against the infidel. Wars against the enemies of the faith were both authorized and sanctified by the papacy, completely destroying the vestiges of early Christian pacificism.[2] There were attempts by the Church nevertheless to regulate the conduct of war, by providing a rudimentary form of *jus in bellum* among Christians in order to constrain the activities of combatants by defining property and persons against which and whom it was unlawful to engage in hostilities, such as priests, innocent peasants, women, and children, as well as churches, agricultural animals, and fruit trees. There were also attempts to restrict warfare to certain seasons and days of the week, and to outlaw certain weapons such as the longbow and crossbow.[3] Such Church edicts had a negligible effect upon combatants, and it was the crusades themselves that served to reduce internecine disputes between Christians by providing a common enemy upon which to focus.

The political feasibility of a universal Christian empire had receded into the background by the time of St Thomas Aquinas, but it had not yet been replaced with the idea of the sovereign state. The most common political unit was the city-state with its own legislative authority. The universal element was the ideal of a rational Natural Law and the universal spiritual brotherhood of Christians in the Church.[4]

St Thomas Aquinas

The understanding of society from the time of Augustine to the time of Aquinas was transformed from one of voluntarism to rationalism. For Augustine people were bound together in society more by an agreement of will and common purpose than by a general conception of justice. The rationalist, however, gives greater emphasis to the discovery of justice by right reason in the Natural Law.[5] Aquinas exemplifies this move towards rationalism in his emphasis upon law and reason. At the same time he incorporates Aristotelianism into his theory with his emphasis upon the naturalness of political society, the priority of the common good over the individual, and the teleological nature of society.

For Aquinas the whole of the creation forms a linked hierarchy, with everything in it having a purpose. That purpose is to strive towards the perfection that each creature, or species, has been created to attain. Every form of being has a value and a place, with associated duties. Human beings are not isolated solitary creatures. Like Aristotle, Aquinas viewed humans as naturally social. Each is endowed with reason and can create with his own hands, but none is able to produce everything he needs. Society is necessary not only to sustain life, but also in order to live a full life, and the promotion of such is facilitated by political society, which also encourages the development of the spiritual life of the community (*Selected Political Writings*, 191).[6] The fact that humans possess language and can express their thoughts fully to each other is evidence for Aquinas that they are constituted to live in society.[7] Human beings together form an organism to which each individual is subordinate. This organism is the community, whose purpose is to promote the common good. The unity of the whole is conditional. The individuals who comprise it are also capable of acting independently of it. Similarly, society as a whole has a sphere of action different from that of any of its parts. The movement of a ship, by analogy, is the result of the combined rowing of the oarsmen, and no individual could achieve this on his own (*Selected Political Writings*, 193).

The purpose of human association is to enable individuals better to fulfil their purpose of being virtuous. In Aquinas's view, human society requires government in order to achieve this end. He distinguishes between two types of dominion: slavery, and voluntary subjection of free men for their common benefit. The latter, but not the former, *pace* Augustine, existed before the Fall and is therefore sanctioned by God in His original plan. Furthermore, the higher levels of personal virtue are associated with statesmanship, and therefore in order to attain them there must be a government (*Selected Political Writings*, 3–9).

Aquinas's view of human nature is optimistic in its potential, but pessimistic in its actual manifestations. In contrast to Augustine, he believes that the Fall from Grace damaged human virtue, leading to a loss of privilege, but did not irredeemably corrupt or destroy it.[8] All people, Aquinas contends, have the capacity for virtuous action, but this requires the exercise of self-discipline. Most of us, with the exception of the rare few, require mutual support to aid us in the development of our natural aptitude to be good. In most cases the exercise of the necessary discipline has to be imposed by means of force and fear in order to prevent harm being done to the rest of the community, and to instil the habit of doing voluntarily what was once compelled by fear.

The good of the individual and the good of the whole, or common good, are different. Individual interests differ, but it is the common good that unites a community. The individual apart from the community is unthinkable. An individual can only attain his or her potential through the community and political association. The pursuit of individual self-interest leads to fragmentation. Each community needs to be guided by a body promoting the common good, which constitutes the unifying principle of society (*On Law, Morality, and Politics*, 264).[9]

The government of the community formulates the laws that guide the individual towards perfection. The purpose of the civil law is to make the moral code explicit, thus enabling citizens to become more virtuous. The state, then, has an explicitly moral purpose in that it maintains justice and promotes the virtuous life: 'the true object of law is to induce those subject to it to seek their own virtue . . . [and] the proper effect of law is the welfare of those for whom it is promulgated' (*Selected Political Writings*, 117).

What is the source of human law? The whole universe is law-governed, and God is the orchestrator. Law is rational; it is the expression and embodiment of reason, with the exception of the law of sin. God instructs us by means of law, and through it he helps us ..chieve Grace. Aquinas distinguishes four types of rational law, each of which exhibits a different type of reason. The Eternal Law is the Divine Wisdom of God manifest in the whole of creation. It embodies all the purposes for which God's creatures were created and exemplifies God's reason in a rationally ordered universe (*Selected Political Writings*, 121). It is not open to humans to know this Law directly, nor to comprehend the mystery of the overall scheme of things. Humans can know it, however, in so far as Eternal Law is reflected in things and actions. Each person has some degree of knowledge of the truth, which is itself a reflection of the unchanging truth of the Eternal Law. In other words, Aquinas is suggesting, like Plato, that there is an immutable absolute transcendental rational law, whose appearances are manifest in the world.

What is the relationship between Eternal Law and other types of law? Aquinas's understanding of law is closely related to his view that human beings are naturally social and disposed to live in political communities. All law, including the Eternal, is likened to a kind of plan which directs things to an end. The overall plan is devised by a prime mover, and those who implement aspects of it by devising subordinate plans derive them from the first. Thus inferior magistrates derive their plans for governance from 'the king's command'. God's Eternal Law is the plan of government for the universe, and the 'plans of government' implemented by subordinate governors are therefore 'derived from the Eternal Law' (*Selected Political Writings*, 121).

The different types of law for Aquinas, then, stand in relation to the Eternal Law as derivations from it. This law provides the plan or model towards which all forms of law must look for guidance.

The second kind of law is the Natural Law. This law is the reflection of Divine reason in all the things which God has created. It refers to those things which make up our natures. Human beings, in Aquinas's view, have a natural inclination to be good. In common with other forms of existence, they seek to preserve themselves in accordance with their own nature. Self-preservation and an inclination to goodness are, then, Laws of Nature. There are natural inclinations that we have in common with animals. These are our instincts towards sexual relations and the rearing of children. Because of the rational nature of human beings there are certain instincts in the Natural Law that only apply to us. Those are our natural inclinations to strive to know God's truth, and to live with other human beings in a society. All actions related to these inclinations fall under the Natural Law: 'namely, that a man should avoid ignorance, that he must not give offence to others with whom he must associate and all actions of the like' (*Selected Political Writings*, 123).

In what way, then, do human beings participate in the Eternal Law through the possession of Natural Law or instincts? By being subject to law we may be said to participate in it: 'all things partake somewhat of the Eternal Law insofar as, from being imprinted on them, they derive their respective inclinations to their proper acts and ends' (*On Law, Morality, and Politics*, 20). Rational creatures participate in the Eternal Law in a more exalted way. In some manner both humans and angels have been endowed with reason, by means of which we come to learn what is good and evil. This knowledge of good and bad and the possession of a conscience in relation to it is nothing other than the Divine light shining in us. It is through the Natural Law that humans are said to participate in God's Eternal Law: it is because of this participation that we are able to distinguish good from evil, 'which pertains to the Natural Law' (*On Law, Morality, and Politics*, 20).

Is Natural Law universally valid? That is, is it the same for all men and women? The Law of Nature as far as general first principles are concerned is the standard of right conduct for us all. In relation to abstract or speculative reason the truth of the principles and the conclusion derived from them are the same for everyone. The truth that the three angles of a triangle add up to 180° is the same for everyone. Similarly in matters of practical reason the general principles of the Law of Nature remain the same; for example, that we must avoid doing harm unjustly to our fellow human beings, or that it is right to pay one's debts. In applying these principles to practical circumstances, however, exceptions may be admitted. There may be instances when the repayment of a debt precipitates great harm. For example, Aquinas contends that everyone agrees that it is a general principle of the Natural Law that we should act according to reason. From this principle, he suggests, we arrive at the immediate conclusion that we should repay our debts. This acts as a general rule, but may nevertheless admit of exceptions when applied to particular cases. In some circumstances it may be that the repayment of a debt could cause injury, and we would thus be acting irrationally rather than according to reason. It would be irrational, for instance, to repay money if that money were to be used to buy arms to wage war on your own country. In summary, then, the general principle is always right, that is, that we must act according to reason, but the conclusion we derive from the general principle in its practical application may not hold good in all practical circumstances.

The Natural Law may vary in another way. The general principles may hold good, but our ability to know the conclusions to be drawn from them may differ. In other words, reason, which is our capacity to know the conclusions to be drawn from the general principles, may be depraved by the passions or by some 'evil habit of nature'. For example, murder is against the Natural Law, but because of a corruption of reason in some societies it may be accepted as part of the way of life of those societies.

To sum up so far: human beings possess reason and know the difference between right and wrong. In this respect we participate in God's Eternal Law. We share with the animals a natural inclination to self-preservation and procreation. But as possessors of reason we are distinguished from animals by our natural inclinations to know God and to know his truths. Furthermore, we are naturally social and require to be governed by an authority motivated by a desire to promote the common good. Because we have different capacities to pursue good we need mutual assistance, and some need to be constrained by force and fear.

Human society, Aquinas contends, could not exist without human laws. Human laws are in effect the application and particularization of the principles of Natural Law to specific conditions. Just as individuals draw conclusions from the general principles of the Natural Law in making their own moral judgement, the state declares its laws to be derived from the same source. The laws of states in so far as they are conclusions drawn from the principles of Natural Law may differ from one state to another. For example, murder and theft are condemned by the principles of Natural Law, but the criteria and definitions of what constitute murder and theft, and the penalties for such crimes, may differ from state to state. They are no less legitimate because they vary in detail, as long as they are consistent with general principles of the Natural Law. Human laws require a great deal of ingenuity and skill in their formulation and offer a good deal of scope for change and improvement over time.[10]

Human law, for Aquinas, is distinguished into the Law of Nations and civil law. Aquinas differs from Cicero in that he does not identify the *jus gentium* and *jus naturale*, but instead approvingly cites Justinian's *Digest* in distinguishing them: 'the latter is common to all animals while the former is common to men only' (*On Law, Morality, and Politics*, 141). The Laws of Nations are the immediate conclusion from the Natural Law. By this Aquinas means that those things we share with animals, such as our natural propensity to procreate and nourish children, are absolute and universal. The Law or right of Nations is common to human beings only, and results from the application of Natural Law. Natural Law does not tell us in the abstract to whom a piece of land ought to belong, but in practical terms relating to its propensity for cultivation, reason may demonstrate that one man has a better claim than another to call it his property (*On Law, Morality, and Politics*, 140–1). Aquinas concurs with the definition of *jus gentium* offered by Gaius in the *Institutes*: 'Whatever natural reason decrees among all men is observed by all equally and is called right common among nations' (*On Law, Morality, and Politics*, 141).

Without the Laws of Nations no community could exist. From the principle of Natural Law 'do no harm to others', human law concludes that murder is unlawful. Other Laws of Nations refer to the practices of buying and selling and other such activities which regulate social relationships. Such laws are derived from the Natural Law because people are naturally social beings. The civil law is that body of law which applies the immediate conclusions from Natural Law, such as that murder is unlawful, to fit the particular circumstances.

There are limits, however, to what should be prescribed in human law. Law is not a perfect instrument for making people moral. It can regulate many of our visible actions, but it cannot make us do these actions for the right reasons. Human laws when they are passed have to take account of the condition of human beings. If they are impossible to comply with, then they serve no useful purpose. Only those vices which harm others and which detract from the public good should be made illegal. Thus murder and theft should be prohibited.

Because human reason is imperfect God feels it necessary to supplement human law with Divine Law. Divine Law is the fourth category of law that Aquinas identifies, and its main purpose is to regulate our outside bodily movements, but Divine Law ensures that the acts are carried out for the right reasons in order to allow human beings to participate in the Eternal Law in a manner in which they could not otherwise do. God's Divine Law is revealed in the Old and New Testaments. Such law is necessary in order to prepare human beings for their ultimate end beyond the powers of human reason, that is, eternal salvation. Human intelligence would be incapable of comprehending God's purpose without the aid of Grace and faith.

Aquinas assumes that the universal human community naturally coheres into smaller political units of varying degrees of autonomy. The moral code for him is universal, and, as well as regulating the conduct of individuals in their relations with each other, regulates relations among states. This does not mean that war is condemned outright. Within the Christian tradition the idea of just war, most notably articulated by Augustine, was widely accepted. The power of the papacy to initiate crusades against the infidel assumed the principle of a punitive just war.

Given that the end of government is to promote the common good, there may be occasion when the discharge of this obligation requires the repulsion of an external threat, or the need to seek reparations for a harm done to one's citizens by a hostile nation. A prince, or government—and those authorized in a public rather than a private capacity—in protecting society from harm, have the right to resort to the sword. Peace above all else is conducive to the well-being of the community, and it is this that the prince must preserve even if it means resorting to war (*Selected Political Writings*, 11). Aquinas argues that 'it is the king's duty to make sure that the community subject to him is made safe against its enemies. There is no point in guarding against internal dangers, when defence from the enemies without is impossible' (*Selected Political Writings*, 83). Killing is unlawful unless it is done in a public capacity and for the benefit of the common good, such as a soldier fighting the enemy. The intention to kill in self-defence in a private capacity is wrong. Should killing be the consequence of self-defence, on condition that a disproportionate degree of violence is not used in relation to the threat, then it is permissible because 'one is bound to take more care of one's own life than of another's' (*On Law, Morality, and Politics*, 226).

War cannot be legitimated by any old pretext. Its declaration must be subject to strict criteria. Aquinas's discussion of just war draws very heavily upon St Augustine. For Aquinas, a just war must satisfy three conditions. First, war must be declared by a proper authority, and not by private individuals, who were in a position to seek redress of grievances through the courts. Private individuals during the Middle Ages did claim a right to declare war, and many of the more powerful ones maintained armies and had diplomatic representation at the major courts. They entered into agreements and treaties independently of the sovereign ruler. Aquinas was here reflecting the emergence of more centralized political communities with the legitimate authority entrusted with both external and internal security. The legitimate authority, then, acts in accordance with the common good. We should not lose sight of the fact, however, that the legitimate authority was not always as clearly identifiable as it was later to become. Many rulers and princes stood in an ambiguous relation to the Roman Emperor, and many were in dispute with the papacy over legitimate jurisdiction. Many cities, as we saw in Chapter 6 on Machiavelli, were granted freedoms by the empire which made them relatively autonomous politically.

The second condition that Aquinas specifies for a just war is a just cause. In other words, the state against which war is waged must deserve to be attacked, or to defend oneself against. That state must have done something demonstrably wrong. Aquinas's conception of just war is far more limiting than that of Augustine. Imperialistic expansionism or the mere fear of a neighbouring state would not constitute just cause.

Thirdly, even though war is declared by a legitimate authority for a just cause, it may still be unjust if there is a wicked intention. Aquinas argues that 'it is necessary that the belligerents should have a rightful intention, so that they intend the advancement of good or the avoidance of evil' (*On Law, Morality, and Politics*, 221). In practical terms this can mean inflicting injury on an enemy in order to promote the good of justice, or in order to avoid greater harm. The punishment of evil-doers in order to restore moral harmony and concord has, in Aquinas's view, Divine authorization.[11] As long as the intention is honourable it is not an injustice in a just war to take the spoils of war as one's own. If the individual's intention for fighting in a just war is to profit by booty, rather than to promote justice, then the spoils of war are robbery, that is, the taking from someone something that is not one's due. Similarly in an unjust war those who profit from the spoils are commiting robbery and are bound to restore what they have taken (*On Law, Morality, and Politics*, 188).

To what extent are wars against the infidel, or unbelievers, justifiable? In other words, did Thomas Aquinas approve of, and justify, crusades instituted by the Church? The question of crusades was by the time Aquinas wrote less pressing than it had been, and the enthusiasm for upholding their ideals was on the wane. Aquinas does not give a systematic treatment to the issue of the Christian response to the infidel, but he does make some scattered remarks. Unbelief for Aquinas was one of the greatest sins, but he did not think that unbelievers could be forced to accept the Christian faith. This had to be a matter of will. Where there is a danger, however, of the blasphemous and evil practices of unbelievers 'hindering the faith of Christ' then war may be waged against unbelievers (*On Law, Morality, and Politics*, 250). Although he disapproved of the extension of infidel rule over believers and thought that the Church was justified in preventing it because of the effect that it would have upon the morale of the weaker members of the faith, the mere fact of being an infidel did not constitute justification for a holy crusade of conquest. On prudential grounds, in order to prevent greater harms ensuing, or on account of some positive good, it may be necessary for the occasional toleration of the rites of infidels, and although Aquinas is here talking of lands over which one has jurisdiction, this could also be extended to external relations, or wars. Lapsed believers, however, renege on an obligation to uphold the faith and may justifiably be persecuted.

Aquinas does address the question of whether a ruler is justified in taxing his subjects. The levying of tribute for private gain or aggrandizement is prohibited because 'rulers of countries are appointed by God, not that they may seek their own gain, but that they may prosper the common welfare' (*Selected Political Writings*, 91). It is just, however, that wealth, when required for maintaining the public good, be contribu..ed by citizens, in order to facilitate the ruler's discharge of his obligations (*Selected Political Writings*, 93). It would not be unjust in circumstances relating to 'safeguarding the common good' to exact levies by force (*On Law, Morality, and Politics*, 188). Aquinas simply assumes that military service is obligatory as part of our general obligation to pledge obedience to the legitimate ruler. He contends that 'even a good king, without being a tyrant, may take away the sons and make them tribunes and centurions and may take many things from his subjects in order to secure the common weal' (*On Law, Morality, and Politics*, 119).

Following Aquinas, Thomist theologians gave their imprimatur to the idea of a justified war waged for the benefit of the common good, while continuing to condemn those wars motivated by vice. The political practices of the newly emerging territorial units, along with military service and warfare, received conditional theological sanction. War was no longer merely a consequence of sinfulness, but a necessary concomitant of human communities consistent with human nature.[12]

European Expansionism: Vitoria and Gentili

The two principal sources of international allegiance in the later medieval period were the Holy Roman Empire and the Catholic Church, but it is generally believed that by then internationalism was on the wane. The attachment to one's country or town became increasingly important. The Church, however, remained strong, and its canon law was effectively truly international law. The political power of the Church was constrained by the Christian principle of rendering 'unto Caesar the things that are Caesar's', but, as we have already seen, endless disputes arose in practice, and were argued by jurists and theologians over the source and extent of secular and religious authority. The papacy, nevertheless, continued to call for crusades to protect the vulnerable eastern reaches of the Christian community against Islam.[13]

The medieval mode of warfare, centred upon orders of knights, provided ethical guidelines for gentlemanly conduct, the disregard of which was dishonourable. The code of chivalry prescribed a strict code of conduct in relation to how captured knights were to be treated, and the conditions of their ransom. Ordinary foot soldiers drawn from the lower levels of society were, however, dispensable, and when captured could be legitimately slain without compunction. The nature of warfare was, however, about to undergo considerable changes at the dawn of the modern era. The invention of firearms and gunpowder led to a reassessment of the use of cavalry and the importance of mounted knights in warfare. While the nobility still composed the officer class, there was a greater need for infantry in larger numbers to be integrated into new military formations, which included a new class of combatants, the artillery, capable of perpetrating vastly increased levels of destruction; these incurred mounting financial costs, which were serviced by new and ingenious forms of taxation. Such a transformation in warfare required a more centralized authority to co-ordinate and pay for the newly organized r...litary, and the imposition of a code of military discipline as a substitute for the chivalric code.[14] With the decline of the papacy and empire as focuses of unity, the idea of humanity was increasingly invoked as a restraint upon war. The Law of Nations constituted one such code that could be invoked to regulate not only the resort to war, but also its conduct.

Like Aquinas, Vitoria believes that the Natural Law can be known independently of revelation by the exercise of right reason. Natural Law is not innate, implanted in men's souls; it is natural because we have the capacity to judge what is right 'by natural inclination' (*Political Writings*, 169).[15] Something is contrary to the Natural Law 'when it is universally held by all [civilized people] to be unnatural' (*Political Writings*, 209). Vitoria implies that the Law of Nations and customary law are to be equated with human positive law, and not with the Natural Law. Their relation nevertheless is intimate. The Law of Nations, he contends, 'either is or derives from Natural Law' (*Political Writings*, 278). If Natural Law as a dictate of reason prohibits the killing of the innocent, the Law of Nations as a deduction from this determines who are to be regarded as innocent.[16] James

Turner Johnson suggests that for Vitoria the '*jus gentium* is a conscious, though culturally relative, expression of the Law of Nature'.[17]

There are some things in the Law of Nations, Vitoria suggests, which manifestly derive from the Law of Nature. There are others, however, whose title rests 'on the consent of the greater part of the world' (*Political Writings*, 281). Gentili is equally ambiguous about the relation between Natural Law and the Law of Nations. He does appear to equate the two (*Law of War*, I. i. 5),[18] but in fact wishes to separate them. The Law of Nature and of Nations does exist, he suggests, but it is extremely difficult to come to know. It is discernible, however, by recourse to a variety of sources. Light is shed upon it by recourse to authors and founders of laws who maintain that the Law of Nations is that law to which all nations commonly adhere, and which is the result of native reason. It is 'that which has successively seemed acceptable to all men' and is therefore regarded as the Law of Nature (*Law of War*, I. i. 10–11). From traders who have experience of many lands, knowledge of the commonly accepted laws and customs regulating commerce and trade indicate the content of the Law of Nations by which such matters are regulated. Furthermore, reason itself and the arguments and authority of philosophers, 'approved by the judgement of every age' (*Law of War*, I. i. 17), along with the Holy Scriptures, shed light upon the Law of Nature and Nations. In Gentili we have an emphasis upon the positive aspect of the Law of Nations, as that which is generally agreed or well established by custom, having its basis in natural reason and Natural Law. Gentili's position is further complicated by the fact that he thinks both the Law of Nature and the Law of Nations are expressions of the Divine Will. This to a large extent detracts from the view that he secularizes the Natural Law and the Law of Nations.[19]

Vitoria (*c.*1485–1546) and Gentili (1552–1608) follow both Augustine and Aquinas in maintaining that Christians have a right to wage war. Vitoria maintains that defensive and offensive war is permitted for Christians because it is allowed in Natural Law, Mosaic law, and the law of the Gospels, and by the example of saints and good men. But he does not rest the determination of just cause merely upon the subjective judgement of a prince. The prince has an obligation to consult wise men whose interest in a dispute is not clouded by anger or greed, and subjects of note have an obligation to weigh the justness of a war and to seek to prevent it if they are convinced of its injustice. Furthermore, a prince must be willing to negotiate in good faith with an opponent, and only in the last resort when all else has failed is war permitted on just grounds (*Political Writings*, 307–8). He argues that war is necessary for peace and security, and contributes to the good of humanity. Without war tyrants, thieves, and robbers would terrorize and oppress the innocent. The innocent have a right to teach the guilty a lesson (*Political Writings*, 297–8). For Gentili a just war by definition is one that is lawful (*Law of War*, I. ii. 20). Its purpose is the attainment of peace and the reign of reason, and because its aim is good, 'war itself is also good and just' (*Law of War*, I. v. 45). But it cannot be good and just unless it is necessary. In this respect, all reasonable channels of reaching a peaceful agreement should be exhausted, including a willingness to subject the dispute to independent arbitration (*Law of War*, I. iii. 20).

Unlike Augustine, who ruled out self-defence for the individual, and Aquinas, who permitted a limited right of self-defence on the principle of double effect but did not allow a private right of war because he thought the courts a more appropriate avenue of redress, Vitoria was much more forthright in allowing the private individual, and even the clergy, to wage war for the defence of property and of the person, as long as the injury responded to was unprovoked. The condition is that such a defence must be an immediate response to the injury. The response, however, does not have to be commensurate with the injury. A punch in the face may be responded to by resort to the sword in order to avoid a loss of honour by humiliation and disgrace. He does not allow a right of vengeance, nor a right to retrieve property by force to the individual after the event. He even seems to suggest that if the civil law permits killing in such circumstances, as it does, then it is permissible even if the Natural Law does not, because obedience to law is justification 'in the forum of conscience' (*Political Writings*, 300). Vitoria's understanding of war is rather widely conceived, and amounts effectively to the justifiable use of force for the protection of one's life or possessions. Gentili's jurist mind impels him to give a much more precise and technical definition which rules out the right of war for private individuals. States, and not individuals, are for him primarily the subjects of the Law of Nations. They are the public authorities to be regulated in their external relations by law. For Gentili, 'war is a just and public contest of arms', and 'not a broil, a fight, the hostility of individuals' (*Law of War*, I. ii. 18). The private individual has no right to incite the masses to take up arms against an enemy because he would be 'usurping the authority of the sovereign' (*Law of War*, I. iii. 32). Brigands and pirates do not wage war. They lack a just cause, but more importantly they do not have 'a state, a senate, a treasury, united and harmonious citizens, and some basis for a treaty of peace, should matters so shape themselves' (*Law of War*, I. iv. 40).

Vitoria and Gentili contend that any commonwealth has the legitimate authority to declare and enter into war. Gentili makes it a condition of war that for each party it 'must be publ.. and official and there must be sovereigns on both sides to direct the war' (*Law of War*, I. iii. 22). Vitoria contends that commonwealths, unlike private citizens, have the right to avenge wrongs and seize reparations on the authority of the prince if it is a perfect community, which means that it is self-sufficient and lacking nothing. Such commonwealths may be members of a larger empire, but they nevertheless retain the right of war. In the case of imperfect communities, the right of war is vested in a higher authority. Custom, however, Vitoria suggests, may override this. Communities subject to the same prince and holding the customary right of war had the authority to enter into hostilities. Suarez, like Grotius, endorsed the distinction to be made between the Law of Nations and the Natural Law, but challenged Vitoria's account of the customary right of some imperfect communities to wage war. Vitoria argued that wars waged by communities subject to the same prince were illegitimate, while those subject to different princes were not (*Political Writings*, 302–3 and n. 17).[20] Gentili contends that 'private individuals, subject peoples, and petty sovereigns' are never justified in waging war because necessity does not enter into their calculations. They are at liberty to settle disputes by resort to the justice of their superiors. Like Vitoria, however, he concedes that custom, compacts, or other special circumstances may extend the privilege of warfare to states or city-states which for one reason or another, including feudal ties, acknowledge a superior.

Like Augustine and Aquinas, Vitoria and Gentili believe that a just cause is necessary. Against this must be weighed the consideration of the possible harm incurred as a result of pursuing such a war. If the harm outweighs the good, war cannot be legitimate (*Political Writings*, 21). Justified war can only be for an injury committed, and the purpose of war must be to secure peace. Vitoria believes that this justifies all means necessary for bringing the war to a successful conclusion. Self-defence, he contends, is a self-evident ground for waging war, as is the pursuit of reparations from the enemy for harm done, or the forceful punishment of those princes who fail to bring wrongdoers to account or give restitution for the wrongs committed against a country.

Both Augustine and Aquinas recognized a just cause of war as vindictive justice, that is, the punishment of the moral guilt of the enemy. Vitoria extends the terms of reference of the condition of the right intention. He suggests that after the enemy has been defeated, reparations made, and peace restored, the commonwealth may teach the enemy a lesson. In other words he extends the right of vengeance against the injured party in order to deter future attacks and to punish those who have upset the tranquillity of peace: 'The simple rout of the enemy is not enough to cancel out the shame and dishonour incurred by the commonwealth; this must be done by the imposition of severe penalties and punishments' (*Political Writings*, 306). Vitoria justifies his contention by suggesting that the prince has authority not only in relation to his own subjects, but also in relation to foreigners in order to prevent the wicked from committing injustices against the innocent. This is the right of the prince by the terms of the Law of Nations, but more fundamentally it is grounded in Natural Law. Just as the Natural Law authorizes the use of execution and other penalties by the prince to restrain citizens within the commonwealth from inflicting harm on others, 'the whole world has the same powers against any harmful and evil men', and they are appropriately exercised by the princes of commonwealths (*Political Writings*, 305–6). Vitoria does, however, implore the prince to avoid provoking a potential enemy and giving any cause for war. A prince should love his fellow human beings as the Bible commands, and only in extreme cases of necessity should a prince allow himself to be 'dragged reluctantly but inevitably' into war (*Political Writings*, 327).

Is it possible that justice might reside on both sides in a just war? Vitoria gives an unequivocal negative answer to this question. If there is justice on both sides, he contends, then neither side can lawfully enter into conflict. There may be cases in which war is undoubtedly just for one side, but at the same time unjust for the other side, although it acts in good faith, mistakenly believing its cause is just. Such invincible error excuses sin, and renders the cause just on both sides, but objectively, of course, before the eyes of God, only one side has a truly just cause (*Political Writings*, 313). It must be presumed, unless there is evidence to the contrary, Vitoria suggests, that the soldiers on both sides fight in good faith, even if the justness of the war rests with one side. In such circumstances they are equally innocent of sin (*Political Writings*, 321). Gentili takes a more realistic view and suggests that war necessarily results in claims from both sides of the justness of their cause. The fact that one side has a juster cause does not mean that the other party has no justice on its side. If there is doubt about on which side justice lies, and both aim to achieve a just conclusion, then neither side can be considered unjust. In fact it is very rare that justice self-evidently resides on only one side in war, and it is much more often the case that each side has a just cause. The importance of this recognition is that Gentili is not merely looking at the constraints on the conduct of war from the point of view of the wronged party, but is emphasizing the applicability of the rule of law to both parties in the hostilities (*Law of War*, i. vi. 51–2).

Political communities and the government of those communities are for Vitoria natural and not conventional (*Political Writings*, 8–9). Together they comprise a family of communities, and the interests of one have in the end to be viewed against the interests of the whole. Any commonwealth, he contends, is part of the greater community of the world as a whole, and Christian countries together constitute a Christian commonwealth. If that which benefits one country results in a greater degree of harm being done to the world or Christendom, then in Vitoria's view it must be unjust: 'Thus if Spain declares war on France for reasons which are otherwise just, and even if the war is useful to the kingdom of Spain, if the waging of the war causes greater harm and loss to Christendom—for example, if the Turks are enabled in the mean time to occupy Christian countries—then hostilities should be suspended' (*Political Writings*, 22). For Gentili, the human race itself comprises a community. Human beings are social by nature and joined in common fellowship, and look upon the world as their home. There is a natural kinship or 'union of the human race' constituting a world-wide society which the actions of no sovereign can be allowed to destroy (*Law of War*, i. xvi. 119). It can therefore be considered as one universal commonwealth (*Law of War*, i. xv. 108, and iii. ii. 47.). On the grounds of this common fellowship Gentili wants to allow just grounds for intervention. It is commonly accepted, he suggests, that good and honest men will come to the aid of each other within civil society:

And if these things are true in the case of private individuals, how much truer they will be of sovereigns, who call one another kindred, cousins, brothers. They will be so much the more true of princes because, if one private citizen does not defend another, there is a magistrate who can avenge the wrongs of private individuals and make good their losses; but there is no one to mend the wrongs and losses of princes, unless it be the same prince, who would prefer to apply a remedy to an evil afterwards, rather than prevent the evil from being done in the beginning.   (*Law of Wars*, i. xv. 114)

Vitoria and Gentili go beyond the conditions of *jus ad bellum* to a consideration of *jus in bello*, that is, not only the just conditions for war, but also its just conduct. Gentili contends that not only must there be just cause, but that in addition 'all the acts of the war must be just' (*Law of War*, i. ii. 20). In seeking vengeance Vitoria suggests that it is permissible to slay the fleeing enemy in order to achieve the deterrent effect. He does, however, caution moderation and recommends not slaying all of the combatant enemy, because they cannot all be held responsible for the wrongdoing. He argues that such action would be against 'the public good, which is the purpose of war and peace' (*Political Writings*, 320). The infidel constitutes an exception because peace can never be genuinely expected with him, and therefore it is lawful to kill all those 'capable of bearing arms' (*Political Writings*, 321). The degree of injury and loss has to be balanced, and the extent of revenge moderated by considerations of cruelty and humanity; in other words, 'the punishment should fit the crime' (*Political Writings*, 321).

There will, he believes, be innocents, including children, who must be protected in war, and their innocence is generally discernible by their bearing or non-bearing of arms. It is not permissible under the Natural Law to slay such innocents by primary intent, even if they are Turks (*Political Writings*, 315). Vitoria therefore applies Aquinas's principle of double effect to the conduct of war. Just war is waged because of a wrong rendered, and by definition the innocent have not partaken in wrongdoing. To inflict harm intentionally upon the innocent in a just war is to give just cause to the innocent among the enemy to retaliate, resulting in justice on both sides (*Political Writings*, 315–16). There may be circumstances, however, when it is difficult to separate the innocent from the guilty, as for example during a justified attack on a fortress when a war could not be concluded without its destruction. In such cases, where there is no alternative, the innocent may be slain as long as the benefits considerably outweigh the harm done. There are also other special circumstances when innocents may be casualties of war. They may, for example, be justifiably enslaved if they are infidels and not Christians, a provision of the customary Law of Nations; their lands and property may be seized to prevent sustenance to the enemy; and they may be taken captive for purposes of ransom. In other words, the safeguards that Vitoria allows the innocent fare badly in cases of necessity, and those which protect their personal liberty hardly exist at all.

Furthermore, he suggests that if soldiers have been fighting licitly, and are genuinely defeated, con..ituting no further threat, then it is not permissible to slay them.[21] The aim of a just war should not be to destroy one's opponents, but through fighting to establish peace and security, and to attain justice for one's *patria* (*Political Writings*, 327). In a passage which considerably tempers his remarks on vengeance Vitoria maintains that a prince having attained victory must exercise Christian virtue and humility, viewing himself more as an impartial judge than as a prosecutor. He must ensure that justice is done in the eyes of the injured parties, while at the same time avoiding the complete ruin of the guilty commonwealth (*Political Writings*, 327).

The New World

By the sixteenth century, in addition to the emergence of a much stronger secular state, occasioned to some extent by the new military developments and a decline in the power of the papacy and the emperor, as well as transformations in ideas which overturned the orthodoxy, such as the rejection of the geocentric in favour of the heliocentric view of the universe, a new factor in the equation of international relations exercised men's minds. The discovery and exploration of the New World, resulting from new advances in shipbuilding and navigation, with the consequent colonization of the Americas, expansion of trade, and greater provision for sources of conflict, gave rise to a set of questions that had not previously been so prominent.

In Spain there had been centuries of fighting against the Moors of Africa. Spanish soldiers were crusaders in their own country, and when they took the last Moorish stronghold of Granada in 1492 the infidels were defeated. Spanish adventurers turned their attention in search of fortune to the newly discovered continent of America. The most famous of the Conquistadors were Cortés (1485) and Pizarro (*c.*1473). It was Cortés who defeated the Aztecs and conquered Mexico. Encountering the Aztecs was a disorienting experience for the Europeans. On the one hand their civilization was every bit as advanced as their own in architecture, dress, and design. The largest of their temples were as grand as the Egyptian pyramids, and their gardens as beautiful as those of Babylon. Yet they were heathens who practised the most barbaric human sacrifices and engaged in ritual cannibalism, as well as sodomy. Cortés succeeded in dominating the Aztecs through the acquiescence of their king, Montezuma. But in order to break their will Cortés decided to destroy their religion by desecrating their idols. After a long, heroic, and bitter struggle by the Aztecs against unfamiliar and superior weapons of war—cannons, armoured cavalry, muskets, and ships—they failed to expel Cortés and his men from Mexico. The Aztecs were enslaved, forced to convert to Christianity, subjected to the Inquisition, and their religion and the artefacts of their civilization destroyed.

The question of by whose authority Cortés conquered an area of the Americas larger than Spain was settled on 15 October 1522, when the Emperor Charles appointed him goverr._r and captain-general of New Spain. Pizarro extended the Spanish territories into Peru and Chile. By the time he was assassinated in 1541 the short period of discovery and conquest was coming to an end. The administration of the colonies was the responsibility of the Council of the Indies based in Seville. The Incas and Aztecs were less brutally treated under the new administration. The colonies were effectively sealed off from the outside world and from each other. Considerable restrictions were placed on their trading and manufacturing rights in order to protect Spanish interests. The vast development of trade and the importation of bullion were what maintained Spain's strong position in Europe throughout the sixteeenth century.The Spanish conquest of the Americas brought to the fore among theologians, lawyers, and theorists the question by what right a foreign power can hold dominion over a territory it discovers and occupies. To answer them, a fundamental theory of property needed to be provided in order to show how advanced countries could come to own the lands of primitive peoples, and even subject these people as slaves. The idea of property in Natural Law theory is fundamental to the concept of justice, and as we have already seen a significant element of the idea of just war relates to the violation of property rights and the restitution of the loss. Furthermore, with the growing importance of trade routes, the question of the extent to which the ocean could be considered the property of a nation became crucial.[22]

Vitoria's and Gentili's efforts to apply just war theory to the case of the American Indians constitute genuine attempts to make the precepts of the Natural Law truly universal. For all their protestations of universality, the medieval just war theorists were concerned with Christian belligerents and the justness of their causes, and not with the rights of non-Christian peoples.[23] Both Vitoria and Gentili contended that barbarians and infidels could have a just title to dominion and sovereignty and that the fact that they were unbelievers was not sufficient title for war. Gentili, for example, argues that the Spaniards were acting unlawfully in claiming natural enmity and 'the pretext of religion as the reason for their war with the Indians' (*Law of War*, I. xii. 89).

Vitoria had left Castile with a very slender title to the Americas when he dismissed many of the common justifications. He did not believe that the papacy had the secular jurisdiction to grant such possession, or that the emperor had a legitimate territorial right of expansion, nor did he believe that Natural Law gave anything but a tenuous claim. The Indians, he argued, were undoubtedly owners of public and private property; they were regulated by recognizable orders of authority and were not natural slaves in the Aristotelian sense, nor could they be deprived of their property on the grounds of madness and intellectual incapacity. They also had legitimate rulers. It could be argued that for want of better education they were the equivalent of children who had not yet reached the age of reason. A possible title might therefore be that of holding the Indians and their lands in trust, as a charitable act towards our barbarous neighbours until they came of age. This argument was used by many opponents of economic imperialism at the end of the nineteenth century to emphasize the duties of holding an empire and the responsibilities of preparing the populations for self-rule.[24]

The appearance of un..ersalism is undermined in practice by what amounts to an imposition of European Christian standards of conduct and rationality. Fundamentally Vitoria's arguments rest upon universal rights which take priority over those of specific communities, the contravention of which justifiably legitimates intervention by a foreign state to restore the rights and punish the perpetrators of the wrong. Vitoria assumed that not only Christians but also the American Indians could discover Natural Law by the exercise of right reason, and that just as the Spanish had to act in a manner appropriate to it, they had the right to expect the Indians to do likewise. The laudable intention to constrain heavily armed Spanish soldiers in their relations with native Indians by reference to the Natural Law broke down ultimately when the Indians, as Vitoria conceived it, acted in a manner at variance with that law.[25]

Vitoria and Gentili recognized a number of just claims to dominion which could provide strong pretexts for the justification of colonization. The Law of Nations accommodates both individuals and states in its provisions. In relation to individuals the Law of Nations allows unimpeded travel and communication on condition that harm is not perpetrated by the traveller. The traveller has a right to trade and enjoy those things that the indigenous peoples hold in common. This includes digging for gold or diving for pearls in the seas and rivers. Under the Law of Nations things that have not already been appropriated become the property of the 'first taker' (*Political Writings*, 280). Denial of these rights, or what Gentili called the privileges of nature, constitutes a just cause of war. A just cause, of course, gives the injured party claims to dominion that he would not previously have been able to press, and under the Law of Nations everything captured in war becomes the property of the victor (*Political Writings*, 231–92).

Furthermore, Vitoria grants a right to spread the gospel, but not forcibly to impose it, as a result of which converts secure rights of protection which if violated constitute just causes of war. He excuses them, however, of the charge of mortal sin for being non-believers in Christ because of their 'invincible ignorance', by which he means that they could not be expected to know of the faith without the word being spread, and could not reasonably be required to convert to it without sufficient demonstration of its efficacy (*Political Writings*, 269). The barbarians could not on rational grounds, given the untenability of their own beliefs, refuse to listen to the precepts of the Christian faith, and having heard it expounded in a reasonable and thorough manner, '*then the barbarians are obliged to accept the faith of Christ under pain of mortal sin*' (*Political Writings*, 271). In other words, the plea of invincible ignorance could no longer be accepted. Gentili agrees with Vitoria that religion cannot be the sole cause of war against the Indians. The laws relating to religion, he argues, are not a matter amongst men, but between men and God. Men cannot complain of an injustice because other men are faithful to a different religion (*Law of War*, I. ix. 64).

There might, however, be legitimate reasons for waging war on the American Indians which Gentili calls natural causes. Atheism, for example, was contrary to nature, and a war of vengeance was justified to 'avenge our common nature' (*Law of War*, I. xxv. 204). Like Vitoria, he believed that the Law of Nations prescribed rights of passage for travellers, and it was therefore unlawful to exclude people from harbours, obtaining provisions, engaging in commerce, or conducting trade (*Law of War*, I. xix. 138). The Spanish war with the Indians could be justified on the ground that the Indians refused to enter into commerce with the Spaniards. Gentili suggests, however, that the Spanish were not there to conduct commerce, but instead to exercise dominion in the belief that they had the right to appropriate lands that had recently been discovered, 'just as if to be known to none of us were the same thing as to be possessed by no one' (*Law of War*, I. xix. 144).[26] It was perfectly just, he argues, to oppose the Spaniards 'who are planning and plotting universal dominion' (*Law of War*, I. xiv. 103). Those who seek to extend their dominion are not short of pretexts for resorting to war.[27]

Gentili did, nevertheless, think that the Spaniards did have a just claim to wage war on the Indians. Vitoria and Gentili consider a just cause of war to be intervention on behalf of the innocent against certain categories of crime in breach of the Natural Law. Tyrannical oppression of the innocent, human sacrifice, euthanasia, and cannibalism, for Vitoria, provide just causes for intervention in 'defence of our neighbours' (*Political Writings*, 347 and 287–8). Gentili contends that he agrees with those who believed that the Spaniards had a just cause for war in punishing the Indians, 'who practised abominable lewdness even with beasts, and who ate human flesh, slaying men for that purpose' (*Law of War*, I. xxv. 198). Such practices violated the common sentiments of mankind and the law of nature.

Natural Rights and the Rule of Law: Grotius

Grotius is one of the few theorists of international relations whose approach designates the characterization of a whole tradition. Its roots go deep into classical and Christian thought, but he is thought, nevertheless, to epitomize the move from a religious to a secular conception of Natural Law, and indeed to dispense with the need for a Natural Law in a theory of human morality based upon Natural Rights. The purpose of the Law of Nations and of civil law is to protect and make possible the free use of these rights. What distinguishes the Grotian tradition is the conception that the whole of international relations, including the occasions for and conduct of war, become subject to the rule of law.

The first tentative steps towards establishing a Natural Rights theory were taken during the Reformation when the religious duty to resist tyrants became transformed into a right of resistance. After the massacre of St Bartholomew's Day (24 August 1572), Huguenots developed powerful theories which asserted the political rights of the subject against the sovereign. The importance of Huguenot theories of resistance was that they did not rest purely upon religious grounds. They formulated genuine political theories viewing civil society as the creation of a contract which in turn creates the moral right, and not just a religious duty, to resist rulers who did not fulfil their obligations to promote the common good.[28] Although Grotius is often accused of formulating a theory of absolutism in relation to internal politics, he is generally seen as the best early exemplification of the secularization of Natural Law and Natural Rights in the context of international relations. Tuck goes so far as to suggest that in Grotius the Natural Law is little more than an injunction to respect one another's rights.[29] Vincent quite rightly points out, however, that Grotius did not clearly distinguish a separate category of human rights separate from those of princes, states, and citizens.[30]

Justice and Injustice

By the time Grotius began to write, the vestiges of supranational power had almost disappeared, giving way both to a multiplicity of small political units and to the powerful nation-states of England, the Netherlands, Sweden, France, and Spain.[31] The rivalries between these countries, resulting in armed conflict and wholesale devastation, constituted a threat to civilization itself. Jonathan Scott contends that by 1625 'European warfare had become so endemic that it appeared to threaten moral knowledge as well as civilized life. The achievement of Grotius, at a time when war had almost conquered and destroyed politics, was to develop a language by which politics could reconquer and encompass war.'[32] War did not begin where law ended, but was itself subject to the Law of Nature and of Nations (*Prolegomena*, §§3 and 25).[33] The determination to articulate these constraints was occasioned, Grotius tells us, by his observation of a lack of restraint in relations among Christian nations 'such as even barbarous races should be ashamed of' (*Prolegomena*, §28). The desire to subject state relations to law would not have been a novelty to Grotius's readers. The practice of seventeenth-century states betrayed on the whole a great respect for law. Seldom was war declared without recourse to juridical claims based on feudal or dynastic titles. That Grotius did not choose to use contemporaneous examples, and instead relied upon classical illustrations, to some extent obscures the fact that he was theorizing the state practices of his time.[34]

Unlike the authors dealt with in Part I of this book, Grotius wants to argue that justice and injustice are not merely based on convention, but are instead objectively demonstrable. He wants to deny the claim made in Thucydides that nothing is unjust that is expedient (*Prolegomena*, §3). Grotius targets Carneades, who equated justice with expedience, as a representative of the moral scepticism he wished to discredit. He argues that human beings, unlike animals, are not wholly motivated by self-interest, and therefore morality cannot be reduced merely to expediency. Human beings distinguish themselves from animals by their natural peaceable, organized, and intelligent sociability. It cannot therefore be conceded that nature impels humans only to seek their own good or self-preservation (*Prolegomena*, §6). They are capable of conceiving and pursuing the general welfare motivated by general rather than self-interested principles. Human beings have the natural ability to discriminate what is beneficial and what is harmful to their sociable natures, declaring the former in accordance, and the latter at variance, with the Law of Nature (*Prolegomena*, §9). Because self-preservation is not the primary Law of Nature, Grotius is able to introduce into his theory a telling precept, that is, neither states nor individuals have an absolute right to self-defence. Wider considerations, based upon our natural sociableness and obligation not to put other people's lives at risk in order to save our own, act as a constraint.[35] Although justice is not based on expediency, expediency plays a part in its development. Because God has willed that we are weak and naturally social, society itself is both natural and expedient (*Prolegomena*, §16). It follows for Grotius that states and municipal laws are expedient, but have their foundation not in expediency, but in the Natural Law of human sociableness. In other words, justice is reinforced by, but not grounded in, expediency. Furthermore, because both states and individuals in Grotius's theory are the bearers of rights, he rejects the Realist contention that a different code of morality applies to states from that which is applicable to individuals. Individuals are principally the subjects of the Law of Nature and of Nations. The constraints they prescribe are not for the benefit of one or two nations, but for all. To ignore the Law of Nations for temporary advantage undermines the safeguards of peace and the possible long-term security of the state. The doctrine of *raison d'état* is therefore unjustifiable (*Prolegomena*, §§18 and 21).

Jus naturale and jus gentium

We saw in the case of Vitoria and Gentili that the relation between Natural Law and the Law of Nations was ambiguous. In the writings of Grotius, faithful to his determination not to conflate those things that should be distinguished, the distinction becomes much more pronounced.

Grotius was one of the most significant political thinkers of the seventeenth century and was extensively cited. His Natural Law theory differed from that of the discredited scholastics, and at the same time offered an alternative to the scepticism of Montaigne and Pierre Charron.[36] Grotius distinguishes law, or right, into natural and volitional types. Natural Law is a dictate of right reason, determining what is consistent with human nature to be by necessity morally right, and what is repugnant to it to be morally wrong (*Rights of War and Peace*, I. 1. x, and I. 2. i).[37] As the author of nature, God is the author of these logically deducible Natural Laws or Rights. Given our nature, such a law would be binding irrespective of its author. This has to be distinguished from volitional laws which are either human or divine. God's volitional Divine Law is that which it has pleased him to reveal, and which is binding either for a single people or universally (*Rights of War and Peace*, I. 1. xv). Human volitional laws are contingently related to the circumstances to which they are a response, and are either civil laws or the volitional Law of Nations, which must themselves be derived from, or at least must not subvert, the Natural Law. While acknowledging Gentili for saying much that was profitabl., Grotius criticizes him for inadequately distinguishing the Natural Law from the Law of Nations (*Prolegomena*, §38).

An indubitable and immutable human nature provides the basis for Natural Law. Starting from the basis of our natural sociableness, Grotius suggests that proofs of the Natural Law are almost as self-evident as the data we receive through the senses (*Prolegomena*, §39). Our moral reasoning, however, is not as certain as mathematical demonstrations because circumstantial factors often cloud the issues (*Rights of War and Peace*, II. 23. i). Nevertheless, Natural Law is so inextricably tied to human nature that even if God did not exist, and had no interest in the welfare of humanity, the law would remain valid (*Prolegomena*, §11).[38] This has often been taken to be Grotius's secularization of the Natural Law. Such a view is, however, ambiguous. Grotius clearly goes on to say that to think in this way is utterly wicked, because reason, tradition, and the proof of experience, including that of miracles, attest to God's existence and our obligation to render him unequivocal obedience. The source of Natural Law in Grotius is undoubtedly God. Its content, however, rests upon, and flows from, human nature and those natural traits implanted in us by

God—in other words, from the human condition. The logical necessity of the Law of Nature is what makes it scientifically deducible from God-given human nature. Grotius, then, clearly rejects the idea found in some versions of Roman Natural Law that it is common to all of God's creatures. It is instead that law which is common to all humankind, not on account of each person being a member of a community, but by the very fact of being human.

The idea of a right, or *jus*, in Roman law and Aquinas is that which is in conformity with law. It is the judgement of what is right or just in the making or conduct of war (*Rights of War and Peace*, I. 1. iii). Grotius, more clearly than Vitoria or Gentili, transforms this conception of right into something that we possess: it is a moral quality. In addition to being what is just, Grotius argues, a 'RIGHT is a moral quality annexed to the person, justly entitling him to possess some particular privilege, or to perform some particular act' (*Rights of War and Peace*, I. 1. iv). A right is something that we have. For Grotius there is a natural moral order in which the individual's rights are sustained by law. Law sustains rather than creates morality.[39] The Law of Nature becomes the assertion of the principle of having respect for one another's rights, that is, having rights implies a certain duty on the part of others to respect them.[40]

From our indubitable natural sociableness four fundamental rights of nature follow: first, to have people abstain from taking what is mine; second, to have that restored to me which is mine along with any profit; third, to honour promises; and fourth, to punish wrongdoing, which differs from the other rights in that it is not strictly speaking a moral power, and therefore has a somewhat ambiguous status (*Prolegomena*, §8).[41] Without such fundamental axioms human society could not exist, let alone flourish. In this respect the Natural Law stands as the foundation of all law.

There are two ways of coming to know its content. First, as a dictate of right reason it may be known a priori as compatible with our rational and social natures. Second, it may also be known with a high degree of probability by the more popular and less abstruse a posteriori method. That which is believed to be the case by all civilized nations must be deemed to have the same cause, which is nothing other than the 'common sense, as it is called, of mankind' (*Rights of War and Peace*, I. 1. 12). Stephen Buckle contends that in this respect Grotius's conception of Natural Law is both innate or rationalist, as well as historical.[42] It is important to note, however, that our coming to know it may have a historical dimension, but its timelessness is attested to by the fact that not even God can change it. In other words, its discovery and applicability are embedded in time, whereas its existence is not. The test of Natural Law must be that it logically derives from nature, or can 'be deducted from certain principles by a sure process of reasoning' (*Prolegomena*, §40). History is useful because it can confirm that certain judgements are universally held, and thus testify to the existence of the Law of Nature. The point is that the Law of Nature does not rest on the will of individuals. It has an objective existence as a criterion of human action. It is not its naturalistic quality, but its self-evidence as a rational precept of the human condition, that makes it a Law of Nature.

The Law of Nations, however, cannot be ascertained by any means other than the historical and empirical (*Prolegomena*, §46). In other words, it does not have an objective existence, and does not logically follow self-evidently from the indubitable data of human nature, but instead emanates from the will: 'whatever cannot be deducted from certain principles by a sure process of reasoning, and yet is clearly observed elsewhere, must have its origin in the free will of man' (*Prolegomena*, §40). In other words, it relates to what nations agree ought to be the case.

The Law of Nations is the product of human agreement and is in certain respects liable to change. Typically *jus gentium* refers to treaties establishing law between states.[43] It may also refer to the conventions which have grown up around the practices of states in their relations with each other. Just as the civil law is designed to benefit the state, by mutual consent the Law of Nations benefits 'the great society of states' (*Prolegomena*, §17). It is that law for the benefit of the society of humanity which is clearly observed by all nations, or the more civilized among them, but which cannot clearly be deduced from first principles. *Jus gentium* is that law which is consented to by nations and which supplements Natural Law, both of which together regulate international relations in their entirety.[44]

Community of the World

We are naturally related by blood, having the same distant ancestors in Adam and Eve (*Prolegomena*, §14). Haggenmacher contends that the international society of which Grotius speaks is ultimately Ciceronian in that its basic units are individuals rather than states.[45] Van Eikema Hommes, however, doubts whether it is accurate to interpret human society as a universal society of mankind whose will generates international law. The natural society of mankind is regulated by Natural Law, and the individual is the basic unit, whereas the international society of states, while constrained by the Natural Law, is regulated by *jus gentium*, or international positive law. Grotius did not, however, wish to restrict the Law of Nations exclusively to states in their various relations.

Jus gentium, then, is the product, not of the will of human society, but of the contractual will of states directed towards the common good.[46] Michael Donelan argues that this wider community is based upon the self-interestedness and not the altruism of the separate state.[47] Such a view fails to take account of Grotius's rejection of the ideas of Carneades and Grotius's insistence, as we have already seen, that humans distinguish themselves from animals by their very capacity to unite expediency with the broader conception of the common good. International law is directed to the advantage of the society of humankind, and not to the interest of particular states.

The idea of a universal society does not logically imply the idea of a need for a world government. Any advantage that might accrue would be offset by the practical disadvantages of managing such a huge territory and population (*Rights of*

War and Peace, ii. 22. xiii). Human corruption and ambition make it impossible to sustain social life and the free exercise of our Natural Rights without the intervention of civil authority. Such authority arises contingently by all manner of means, but the principle upon which it rests must be understood to be consent. The sovereign power exercised on behalf of civil society is charged with the protection of Natural Rights, although in cases of extreme necessity, such as the need to raise taxes in war, these seem to be able to be overridden. States and individuals in Grotius's theory are the possessors of rights, and both have obligations in an international context under the Natural Law and the Law of Nations.[48] Although he envisaged the possibility of international conferences to settle disputes, he can by no stretch of the imagination be seen as a precursor of the League of Nations or the United Nations. He did not think in terms of a supranational institution with executive functions.[49]

Grotius's analysis of just war is much more systematic and carefully defined than that of his predecessors. His aim was the prevention of war and, if this failed, the constraint of its conduct within acceptable bounds: the *jus ad bellum* and *jus in bello*. The former is a question primarily of political responsibility, while the latter is the responsibility of military command. Grotius more clearly distinguishes between just causes and the pretexts of war, that is, between war entered into because it is right and war motivated by expediency (*Rights of War and Peace*, ii. 1. i).[50] The just cause of a war was an entirely separate question from its just conduct.

Christian Gellinek suggests that the modern predilection for viewing peace as the opposite, or antithesis, of war should not delude us into thinking that Grotius saw them in the same relation. War could in fact be a legitimate way to arrive juridically at peace. The laws of war and peace are not in his mind separate categories.[51] All wars, Grotius argues, if they are to be legitimate, aim at peace and therefore must have just causes. Right reason does not proscribe force, and indeed prescribes it for the protection of society when rights are being violated. If authorized by a publi_ authority, wars may have the sanction of public opinion and right balanced in their favour, but they are none the less illegitimate or unlawful if they do not have a just cause. Grotius's first criterion draws upon the Christian tradition from St Augustine onwards, in identifying peace as the proper end of war, and a just cause as injury received or the prevention of injury. Unlike Augustine, who does not allow a private right of self defence, or Gentili, who does not extend the idea of war to private quarrels, Grotius allows private war. His definition of war, unlike Gentili's, embraces a much wider range of violent conflict. For Grotius war is a state of affairs between contending parties conducted by means of force (*Rights of War and Peace*, i. 1. ii). In private war only a plea of self-defence is permissible, but in public war 'sovereign powers have a right not only to avert, but to punish wrongs' (*Rights of War and Peace*, ii. 1. xvi).

The mere suspicion of hostile intent is insufficient to justify the declaration of war, but it does justify preparations for warfare and indirect hostilities (*Rights of War and Peace*, ii. 1. xvi). In other words, fear of an enemy, proposed by Thucydides, Machiavelli, and Hobbes to be a justifiable ground for war on the principle of expediency, is ruled out by Grotius. Grotius contends that 'it is not proper or reasonable that the fears of one party should destroy the rights of another' (*Rights of War and Peace*, I. 2. xiii).

Rulers are deemed by Grotius to be responsible not only for their own states and the conduct of their subjects in relation to other states, but also for the society of mankind as a whole.[52] He agrees with Vitoria and Gentili that intervention on behalf of the violated innocents is lawful. This constitutes his second criterion of just war. Grotius's third criterion of just war is an extension of this principle. States have a right to punish excessive violations of the Natural Law, whether the injuries are perpetrated against themselves or others with whom they have no direct involvement. Grotius contends that 'kings and those who are possessed of sovereign power have a right to exact punishments not only for injuries affecting immediately themselves or their own subjects, but for gross violations of the Law of Nature and of Nations, done to other states and subjects' (*Rights of War and Peace*, II. 22. xl). Punishment of a state for injustice is permissible, but less obviously deserved than in the cases of self-defence or the pursuit of reparations. Such wars will always be suspected of injustice unless 'there be manifest and enormous aggressions, with other conspiring causes, to vindicate nations for having recourse to arms' (*Rights of War and Peace*, II. 20. xliv). The fourth criterion of the justness of a war is the likelihood of success. Futile wars which defend liberty but put life in severe jeopardy are foolhardy. Resistance is not always just and praiseworthy in defence of liberty. Furthermore, war must be publicly declared by a legitimate authority in order that both sides may determine its justness, and, if necessary and willing, the sides must make amends before hostilities begin.

Like Gentili, Grotius contends that matters of religion are between man and his maker. It is a universal belief of mankind found in all true or false religions that there is a supreme being whose providence controls human affairs. Religion is the foundation of morality and provides the basis for political obligation and obedience to laws. All states therefore enact laws which prohibit and punish the violation of religion. But in the wider community, where civil laws do not prevail, violations of religion are judged by the sword by the standards of the Law of Nature and of Nations. The truth of Christianity, Grotius argues, rests upon evidence which goes beyond natural religion, such as the resurrection and the miracles performed by Christ and his Apostles. Christ would have no man embrace the new religion under the threat of punishment. Because of the historical element in Christianity, no one could be expected to embrace it on first hearing, or without some assistance from God. War could not then be justified by the mere fact that a nation did not uphold the Christian religion. The obstruction of those who seek to teach Christianity, which is not subversive to civil society, is however an entirely different matter (*Rights of War and Peace*, II. 20. xliv–xlix). Grotius is also convinced that war can be justly waged against those who persecute upholders of the Christian faith, or who deny the fundamental principles upon which society is based, namely the existence of a Divinity which has an active interest in human affairs (*Rights of War and Peace*, II. 20. xlvi and xlviii). The cannibals of the East Indies and the Americas (and not all were cannibals), who for Grotius were little better than beasts, could justifiably be punished by Europeans (*Rights of War and Peace*, II. 20. xl).

Acts performed in unjust war, whether or not the war be lawfully undertaken, are morally unjust, and those individuals who fight in them must repent before allowing to be admitted through the gates of heaven. A just war, if it disregards the rules of war, may be conducted unjustly and is therefore unlawful.

Even in the pursuit of just wars moderation should be practised. Grotius claims that his aim is to restrict the unrestrained licence of war to that which is permitted by nature, or to the choice of the better among the things permitted (*Rights of War and Peace*, III. 12. viii). Moderation must be exercised in relation to who and what constitute legitimate targets; the method and manner of attack; and the treatment of prisoners of war.

Grotius argues that you should exercise moderation in destroying those things which might lead the enemy to despair. Following Archidamus in Thucydides, he suggests that despair may make the enemy more difficult to defeat. Such moderation practised during times of war gives the appearance of confidence in victory, and may serve to conciliate the enemy and weaken their spirit. Grotius, in other words, is calling for compassion in the treatment of the enemy, but he is not denying the right to kill or seize those loyal to the enemy under the Law of Nations. The obverse side of this '*temperamenta Belli*' is that Grotius believes that the Law of Nations permits the killing of all people in enemy territory and the slaughter of captives and of those whose surrender is refused.[53] He says, for example, that 'whenever . . . war is declared against any power, it is at the same time declared against all the subjects of that power. And the Law of Nations authorizes us to attack an enemy in every place' (*Rights of War and Peace*, III. 4. viii). In this respect the Law of Nations may permit what the Law of Nature would condemn. Here either the Law of Nations has to be moderated by Natural Law, or the Law of Nations has to be altered to be brought in line with it.[54]

Grotius contends that there is a class of innocents whose rights must not be violated. It includes women who are not employed as soldiers, children, religious office holders, merchants, and farmers, as well as prisoners of war. Grotius subscribes to Aquinas's notion of double effect, with Vitoria's proviso of reasonable precautions, to allow the killing of innocents not by intention, but as a consequence of military action. In such cases the harm done must be outweighed by the good, and it is therefore always a delicate matter of judgement. 'Though there may be circumstances, in which absolute justice will not condemn the sacrifice of lives in war, yet humanity will require that the greatest precaution should be used against involving the innocent in danger, except in cases of extreme urgency and utility' (*Rights of War and Peace*, III. 11. vii). Thus the safety of innocents is not absolute and sacrosanct, but very strong reasons amounting to necessity are required to violate non-combatants.

On the question of the observance of treaties, Grotius contends that even if a pact is concluded as a result of extortion and fear and agreed upon by a country unjustly, the victim of aggression, the disadvantaged party, should still honour his obligation. If such pacts were invalidated by fear it would be almost impossible to moderate the severity of the conflicts, or bring wars conclusively to an end. The principle which underlines Grotius's view is the Natural Law that promises must be kept. Without good faith the institution of treaties would be severely undermined and the world society of nations would disintegrate.

To what extent treaties bind one's successors was a question of considerable concern to jurists and philosophers. Thucydides, Machiavelli, and Hobbes had no compunction about freeing a successor from the obligations of his predecessor and, indeed, believed that there was no compelling reason why the same ruler who made a treaty should keep faith if it became no longer to his, or her, advantage to do so. Grotius, on the other hand, argued that a treaty concluded with a monarch, who is later deposed, binds the parties to the agreement to fulfil their obligations to the signatory, and that those obligations are not therefore owed to the new monarch. We will see in the next chapter that Pufendorf sought to refine this position considerably by distinguishing between real and personal treaties.[55]

Theory of Property and the American Indians

In 1605 a Portuguese ship and its cargo were captured by a Dutch East India Company ship. The Portuguese sought to monopolize trade in the Indian Ocean. Grotius, who was employed to vindicate the Dutch,[56] defended Dutch attempts to defeat the Portuguese monopoly in the Indian Ocean. He drew upon Vitoria to argue that the American Indians had Natural Rights to public and private property, and could not be deprived of them on religious grounds, or on the pretext of converting them. They were subject to the same Natural Law as Christians and had to be treated accordingly. No title could be claimed on the grounds of their insanity or irrationality because they were extremely clever and wise people. Such arguments would deprive the Portuguese of the grounds for their claim to dominion in the Spice Islands.

Grotius's emphasis upon occupation in relation to his theory of property was also meant to deny the Portuguese a title to ownership of the seas on the ground that, unlike the land, it could not be occupied.[57] The sea, like the air, was held in common by mankind, and any attempt to occupy it for exclusive use was a violation of the use right of mankind, and could not be justified on the ground that it was necessary to the preservation of peace. The sea is so vast that everyone can share in its benefits, including sailing and fishing. Unlike ponds and rivers the sea is not naturally contained, and in fact constitutes more of the earth's surface than land (*Rights of War and Peace*, 1. 2. iii).[58] The idea of the freedom of the seas, like that of free movement and access to markets, benefits those who are capable of taking advantage of these rights. Those who are not may find themselves, as a result of these freedoms, the victims of exploitation.

The discovery of American Indians posed a difficult problem for those who subscribed to the Christian cosmology. If the world was one social community resting as it did for Grotius upon our common descent, then the American

Indians had to be descended from known peoples. A great deal of partly empirical but largely speculative literature devoted to the question was produced in the first half of the seventeenth century, to which Grotius himself contributed in the 1640s. The purpose of his intervention is not transparent. It may have been a personal attempt to discredit his rival De Laet, or the recognition of a real opportunity to seize the Americas in the context of the disarray caused by the Thirty Years War and revolts in Catalonia and Portugal.

He contended that, contrary to the view of some who believed them to be descended from the infidel Tartars and lost Jewish tribes, the American Indians had diverse origins: European Norse, Christian Ethiopian, and Chinese. This entitled them to better treatment than if they had been of mere barbarian ancestry.[59]

Grotius, like Vitoria, did allow some grounds for just war in the Americas and against those who sought to monopolize trade there: self-defence and the justifiable facilitation of free exchange on the ground of our natural fellowship and membership of a world society. Our natural sociableness dictates that it is a Law of Nature to honour our agreements, without which no sense of obligation could arise. Thus, property laws, for example, which develop out of the general use right allowed in nature, are not inconsistent with Natural Law but may be viewed as flowing from it. There are instances when using something is almost indistinguishable from owning it in so far as it becomes no longer available for anyone else's use. Thus eating something or making use of something may make it unavailable for someone else. As society becomes more complex, in order to avoid conflict, agreements are entered into, whether tacit or explicit, establishing individual ownership. From the simple use right appropriate to the primitive condition of humanity, Grotius allows title to private property on the ground that it diminishes conflicts and promotes the preservation of peace.

Grotius's theory of property generates title from a common use right, and possession was designed to defend Dutch commercial and colonial aspirations. Possession of mobile or movable property simply meant seizure, whereas fixed or immovable property like land required the marking of boundaries, or construction.[60] Vacant land used only by hunters and gatherers, that is, uncultivated land, remained common and available for appropriation.[61] In order to secure a permanent title on lands occupied but vacated, Grotius uses the popular example of a theatre seat which is held in common until occupied. The temporary vacation of the seat does not give another a right to take it. Great tracts of land in the Americas were occupied by European monarchs on behalf of the whole community and were a legitimate possession if there was an intention to divide the land into private sections for cultivation. This was a justification of both English and Dutch practice, and legitimated claims that should be respected by other European monarchs.[62] Occupancy is therefore an important criterion and discounts the possibility of claiming ownership on first sighting. Claims to property had to be public. Subjective thoughts generated no property rights because no one could guess at what someone intended to appropriate.

Hedley Bull argues that Grotius's conception of an international society, in which states are constrained by law and act to uphold the common good, became manifest in the Peace of Westphalia. The Peace did not mark the emergence of the modern international system of states, which began much earlier, nor the emergence of a system of nation-states, which came much later. Instead it constitutes the emergence of a society of states regulated by self-imposed and acknowledged rules and institutions. This is not to say that Grotius envisaged the principle of the balance of power that it incorporated, or the establishment of international conferences to settle European issues. Nor would the religious settlement have been altogether to his taste in allowing the confessional allegiance of states to their rulers, and therefore taking such issues out of the international arena.[63] Grotius's impetus towards the settlement should not, however, be exaggerated. He accepted in 1634 a sensitive diplomatic position as the Swedish ambassador in Paris under the administration of Chancellor Axel Oxenstierna, who continued the reckless imperial policies of Gustavus Adolphus in Germany under the guise of the leading Protestant bulwark against Catholicism, a policy which brought Sweden into conflict with France. Roelofsen argues that Grotius's role in Oxenstierna's war machine, although not a direct influence on policy, puts to rest the view of him as a dispassionate champion of the rule of law.[64] Whatever the details of Grotius's arguments and the likely unpalatable implications in modern society—owing to technological transformations and the democratization of both internal and international relations—of such doctrines as complete freedom of movement and access to markets, including the freedom of the seas, with its modern corollary of the exploitation of the ocean floor,[65] his lasting legacy, despite the fact that the doctrine of the Reason of State seems more evidently to have prevailed for three hundred years after his death, is the equation of morality with law, and the importance of regulating international relations with reference to it.

Notes

1. Arthur O. Lovejoy, *The Great Chain of Being* (Cambridge, Mass., Harvard University Press, 1974).
2. F. H. Russell, *The Just War in the Middle Ages* (Cambridge, Cambridge University Press, 1975), 35–6.
3. See Richard Shelly Hartigan, *The Forgotten Victim: A History of the Civilian* (Chicago, Precedent, 1982), 65–76.
4. Joan D. Tooke, *The Just War in Aquinas and Grotius* (London, SPCK, 1965), 139.
5. Paul Ramsey, 'The Just War According to St Augustine', in Jean Bethke Elshtain (ed.), *Just War Theory*, (Oxford, Blackwell, 1992), 19–20.
6. Aquinas, *Selected Political Writings*, ed. A. P. D'Entrèves (Oxford, Blackwell, 1974).
7. Antony Black, *Political Thought in Europe 1250–1450* (Cambridge, Cambridge University Press, 1992), 23.
8. Tooke, *The Just War in Aquinas and Grotius*, 96.

9. Aquinas, *On Law, Morality, and Politics*, ed. William P. Baumgarth and Richard J. Regan (Indianapolis, Hackett, 1988).

10. Black, *Political Thought in Europe*, 39.

11. Russell, *Just War in the Middle Ages*, 260–1.

12. Russell, *Just War in the Middle Ages*, 267.

13. Black, *Political Thought in Europe*, 87.

14. Torbjörn L. Knutsen, *A History of International Relations Theory* (Manchester, Manchester University Press, 1992), 44–6; and James Turner Johnson, *Just War Tradition and the Restraint of War* (Princeton, Princeton University Press, 1981), 179–87.

15. Francisco de Vitoria, *Political Writings*, ed. Anthony Pagden and Jeremy Lawrence (Cambridge, Cambridge University Press, 1991).

16. Richard Shelly Hartigan, 'Francisco Vitoria and Civilian Immunity', *Political Theory*, 1 (1973), 83.

17. Johnson, *Just War Tradition and the Restraint of War*, 97.

18. Gentili says: 'questions of war ought to be settled in accordance with the Law of Nations, which is the Law of Nature'. See Alberico Gentili, *The Three Books on the Law of War*, trans. John C. Rolfe, introd. by Coleman Phillipson (Oxford, Clarendon Press, 1933).

19. 'Let the Theologians keep silent about a matter which is outside of their province' (*Law of War*, I. xii. 92). He did think that jurists and theologians had different areas of competence, but this does not imply that he rejected the religious foundations of law and society.

20. Also see Quentin Skinner, *The Foundations of Modern Political Thought* (Cambridge, Cambridge University Press, 1978), vol. ii, 152–3.

21. Hartigan, 'Francisco Vitoria and Civilian Immunity', 83.

22. Thomas A. Horne, *Property Rights and Poverty* (Chapel Hill, NC, University of North Carolina Press, 1990), 9.

23. Johnson, *Just War Tradition and the Restraint of War*, 75.

24. See D. Boucher and A. Vincent, *A Radical Hegelian: The Political and Social Philosophy of Henry Jones* (Cardiff, University of Wales Press, 1993), chap. 7.

25. Johnson, *Just War Tradition and the Restraint of War*, 77.

26. Coleman Phillipson has misunderstood this passage in suggesting that Gentili thinks that the Spaniards justly waged war on the American Indians. See his introduction to Gentili, *Law of War*, 28a; and Coleman Phillipson, 'Albericus Gentili', in John MacDonell and Edward Manson (eds.), *Great Jurists of the World* (New York, Kelley, 1968; first pub. 1914), 123.

27. Furthermore Gentili suggests that the Spaniards have unjustly committed terrible acts of cruelty against the Indians (*Law of War*, III. viii. 529).

28. Skinner, *The Foundations of Modern Political Thought*, vol. ii, 334.

29. Richard Tuck, *Natural Rights Theories: Their Origin and Development* (Cambridge, Cambridge University Press, 1979), 67.

30. R. J. Vincent, 'Grotius, Human Rights, and Intervention', in Hedley Bull, Benedict Kingsbury, and Adam Roberts (eds.), *Hugo Grotius and International Relations* (Oxford, Clarendon Press, 1990), 242.

31. Tooke, *The Just War in Aquinas and Grotius*, 195.

32. Jonathan Scott, 'The Law of War: Grotius, Sidney, Locke and the Political Theory of Rebellion,' *History of Political Thought*, 13 (1992), 567.

33. Hugo Grotius, *Prolegomena*, repr. in M. G. Forsyth, H. M. A. Keens-Soper, and

P. Savigear (eds.), *The Theory of International Relations: Selected Texts from Gentili to Treitschke* (London, George Allen and Unwin, 1970).

34. C. G. Roelofsen, 'Grotius and the International Politics of the Seventeenth Century', in Hedley Bull, Benedict Kingsbury, and Adam Roberts (eds.), *Hugo Grotius and International Relations* (Oxford, Clarendon Press, 1990), 124.
35. Paul Christopher, *The Ethics of War and Peace* (Englewood Cliffs, NJ, Prentice Hall, 1994), 74.
36. Richard Tuck, 'Grotius and Seldon', in J. H. Burns and Mark Goldie (eds.), *The Cambridge History of Political Thought 1450–1700* (Cambridge, Cambridge University Press, 1988), 499.
37. Hugo Grotius, *The Rights of War and Peace*, trans. A. C. Campbell (Westport, Va., Hyperion, 1993; edn. first pub. 1901).
38. Also see Horne, *Property Rights and Poverty*, 10.
39. Knud Haakonssen, 'Hugo Grotius and the History of Political Thought', *Political Theory*, 13 (1985), 240.
40. R. J. Vincent, *Human Rights and International Relations* (Cambridge, Cambridge University Press, 1986), 25.
41. Haakonssen, 'Hugo Grotius', 242.
42. Stephen Buckle, *Natural Law and the Theory of Property: Grotius to Hume* (Oxford, Clarendon Press, 1991), 6.
43. Hendrik van Eikema Hommes, 'Grotius on Natural and International Law', *Netherlands International Law Review*, 30 (1983), 2.
44. Peter Pavel Remec, *The Position of the Individual in International Law According to Grotius and Vattel* (The Hague, Nijhoff, 1960), 28. Remec argues that 'The Law of Nations as such only supplements the Law of Nature in certain specific aspects, where the nations agree to such a regulation. Where no firm supplementary rule has been established by the consent of nations, one must find out what is permissible according to the Law of Nature and then direct his actions in consonance with these principles' (p. 81).
45. Peter Haggenmacher, 'Grotius and Gentili: A Reassessment of Thomas E. Holland's Inaugural Lecture', in Hedley Bull, Benedict Kingsbury, and Adam Roberts (eds.), *Hugo Grotius and International Relations* (Oxford, Clarendon Press, 1990), 172.
46. Van Eikema Hommes, 'Grotius on Natural and International Law', 64–5.
47. Michael Donelan, 'Grotius and the Image of War', *Millennium*, 12 (1983), 241.
48. A. Clare Cutler, 'The "Grotian Tradition" in International Relations', *Review of International Studies*, 17 (1991), 45.
49. Benedict Kingsbury and Adam Roberts, 'Introduction', in Hedley Bull, Benedict Kingsbury, and Adam Roberts (eds.), *Hugo Grotius and International Relations* (Oxford, Clarendon Press, 1990), 28–9.
50. Also see Haggenmacher, 'Grotius and Gentili', 164.
51. Christian Gellinek, *Hugo Grotius* (Boston, Mass., Twayne, 1983), 104.
52. Tooke, *The Just War in Aquinas and Grotius*, 226.
53. G. I. A. D. Draper, 'Grotius' Place in the Development of Legal Ideas about War', in Hedley Bull, Benedict Kingsbury, and Adam Roberts (eds.), *Hugo Grotius and International Relations* (Oxford, Clarendon Press, 1990), 198–9.
54. Remec, *Grotius and Vattel*, 108.
55. See J. L. Holzgrefe, 'The Origins of Modern International Relations Theory', *Review of International Studies*, 15 (1989), 19.
56. Horne, *Property Rights and Poverty*, 11.

57. Buckle, *Natural Law and the Theory of Property*, 14.
58. Also see W. E. Butler, 'Grotius and the Law of the Sea', in Hedley Bull, Benedict Kingsbury, and Adam Roberts (eds.), *Hugo Grotius and International Relations* (Oxford, Clarendon Press, 1990), 213–4.
59. See Joan-Pau Rubiés, 'Hugo Grotius's Dissertation on the Origin of the American Peoples and the Use of Comparative Methods', *Journal of the History of Ideas*, 52 (1991), 235.
60. Tuck, *Natural Rights Theories*, 61–2.
61. Hugo Grotius, *On the Law of War and Peace*, in M. G. Forsyth, H. M. A. Keens-Soper, and P. Savigear (eds.), *The Theory of International Relations: Selected Texts from Gentili to Treitschke* (London, George Allen and Unwin, 1970), II. ii. 4 and 17.
62. Barbara Arneil, 'John Locke, Natural Law and Colonialism', *History of Political Thought*, 13 (1992), 589 and 593.
63. Hedley Bull, 'The Importance of Grotius in the Study of International Relations', in Hedley Bull, Benedict Kingsbury, and Adam Roberts (eds.), *Hugo Grotius and International Relations* (Oxford, Clarendon Press, 1990), 75–7.
64. Roelofsen, 'Grotius and the International Politics of the Seventeenth Century', 129–30.
65. B. V. A. Röling, 'Are Grotius's Ideas Obsolete in an Expanded World?', in Hedley Bull, Benedict Kingsbury, and Adam Roberts (eds.), *Hugo Grotius and International Relations* (Oxford, Clarendon Press, 1990), 281–99.

10

PUFENDORF AND THE PERSON
OF THE STATE

Samuel, Freiherr von Pufendorf, although acknowledged in the early part of this century as one of the great international jurists with the publication of his three principal works on Natural Law by the Carnegie Endowment for International Peace, has commanded remarkably little attention among contemporary international relations theorists.[1] Nothing of his work has been reproduced in any of the recent anthologies of classic international theory.[2] Yet his importance as a thinker of some stature has been widely acknowledged by students of Natural Law and Natural Rights, social contract theories, and theories of property.[3] The scholarship of the last two decades has revealed the immense importance not only of Grotius but also of Pufendorf to the natural jurisprudence of the Scottish Enlightenment.[4]

Pufendorf was one of the most famous political philosophers of his day. Locke thought his *On the Law of Nature and Nations* better than Grotius's *On The Law of War and Peace*, and Vico described him as one of the 'three princes' of the Natural Law of Nations, taking his place alongside Grotius and Seldon.[5] It became a commonplace in accounts of the development of philosophy in writings up to the time of Kant to see Grotius breaking away from medieval scholasticism and Aristotelianism by providing a new foundation for Natural Law, and to see Seldon, Hobbes, and Pufendorf as his natural successors. Pufendorf saw himself in this line of descent, correcting the errors of his predecessors by giving a firmer foundation to the view he thought common to them all, that the Laws of Nature are in fact the laws of self-preservation and that from the nature of human beings the laws conducive to such an end can be deduced. These thinkers were at once departing from medieval scholasticism and providing answers to the moral scepticism of such modern thinkers as Montaigne (1533–92) who sought to cast doubt upon the natural capacities of humans to discover truth by means other than faith.[6] Pufendorf wanted to argue that the natural disposition of men was to be peaceable, and that the fundamental laws, or the absolute congenital obligations, relating to this disposition are not of men's making, and are therefore beyond their capacity to alter. Pufendorf, for all his concessions to the Reason of State, the importance of utility as an impetus to action, and the historically developing character of morality, unequivocally places himself in the tradition of a Universal Moral Order when he says:

Now by our assertion that the maintenance of peace toward all men as such is a natural state of man, we mean that it has been instituted and sanctioned by nature herself without any human intervention, and that it rests therefore, upon that obligation of Natural Law, by which all men are bound, in so far as they are endowed with reason, and which does not owe its original introduction to any convention of men. (*Law of Nature*, ii. ii. 11)

From these fundamental laws many others may arise as a consequence of human agreement, which may nevertheless be described as natural because they are consistent with our nature.

Why is Pufendorf an important thinker in the heritage of international relations theory? He was writing, of course, during the formative period of the modern states-based international system, and his writings were informed not only by a thorough grounding in philosophy, but also in his own professional studies of recent European history. He addressed the issues that arose as a consequence of the Thirty Years War and the Peace of Westphalia, which brought Europe's first continental war to an end. The war was more destructive than any known before, reflecting the modern innovations in military discipline and strategy.[7] The war was economically devastating and came to an end not because of military defeat, but because the participants had reached the limits of their endurance. In Germany alone it has variously been estimated that the population declined by one-third to two-thirds.[8] Pufendorf himself was a social casualty of the war. His economically devastated native Saxony held out few prospects for a young scholar, and he was compelled to accept employment as the tutor to the family of a Swedish diplomat in Denmark in 1658. In 1688 he became a professor of international law at Lund in Sweden. His readiness to accept such a position is indicative of the fact that the rise of the nation-state did not override the sense that scholars felt of belonging to a wider educated community.

The Thirty Years War was fought for a combination of reasons, principal among which were religious rivalries, reflected in the separate Catholic and Protestant peace conferences at Münster and Osnabrück respectively, and fear of the hegemonic designs of the Habsburg Holy Roman Emperor, Ferdinand II, and Philip IV of Spain. The Peace of Westphalia reflected the interests of its architects, France, Sweden, and Holland, in diminishing the universalist authority of the papacy and the Holy Roman and Spanish empires of the Habsburgs, which now became formally equal, at least juridically, with established and emergent states. The treaty essentially acknowledged the political and theoretical developments in the emergence of the modern state. The state had gradually come to claim a monopoly over declarations of war and peace, diplomatic representation, and the making of treaties with foreign powers.[9]

Conceptually the state was increasingly viewed as an abstract entity, distinct from the private person of the ruler and, more importantly, distinct from the power of the people whose absolute allegiance it demanded.[10] Westphalia thwarted the hegemonic aspirations of the emperor by conceding the right of over three hundred political entities to enter into making alliances and conduct their own foreign affairs without interference. It also conceded the right of France and Sweden to intervene if the emperor reneged on his renunciation of imperial ambitions.

Westphalia sanctioned the formal equality and legitimacy of an array of state actors, while at the same time postulating the principle of balance as the mechanism to prevent a preponderance of power.[11] It did not resolve dynastic disputes, but reduced them to a minimum. Although there were a number of wars of succession, the most significant of which was the Spanish, these were fought to prevent successions that might excessively favour a particular power, rather than to acquire new territory.[12] The Peace of Westphalia was largely successful in containing the hegemonic aspirations of the Habsburgs, but because it depended upon consolidating the strength of France and Sweden, it did not anticipate the ambitions of the Bourbon Louis XIV to dominate Europe. Far from preventing war, the Westphalian settlement provided criteria for when it may legitimately be resorted to. War transformed politics during the latter half of the seventeenth century and was the corollary of the process of state formation.

In the twenty-two wars fought during the period 1648–1713, religious disputes hardly figured at all.[13] Westphalia conceded the regulation of religious practices to individual states and emphasized the right of religious toleration and to educate children in the faith of the parents. Furthermore, Calvinism was acknowledged as a legitimate part of the Christian faith, and the Lutheran Church was formally established. The religious settlement was of course unsatisfactory to the papacy, and it did not prevent religious intolerance within states, but did alleviate religious friction between them.

Although the participants were not conscious of establishing a new system or state-centred international society, the Thirty Years War and the Peace of Westphalia brought to the fore conceptual issues that the political philosopher was compelled to address. In so far as Pufendorf presented an elaborate theory of the post-Westphalian state system, he was, as one of his most recent editors has commented, 'the first philosopher of modern politics'.[14] His main theoretical concern was not to re-establish order out of chaos, as Grotius's and Hobbes's had been, but to articulate and reconcile man's duties to humanity and, as a citizen, to a particular state. Westphalia raised to pre-eminence the problem of clearly demarcating the obligations of men and citizens. Pufendorf's summary of his own investigations and conclusions, *On the Duty of Man and Citizen* (1673) became a standard textbook in moral philosophy for nearly a century.[15]

A Science of Morals

Like many other seventeenth-century philosophers including Grotius, Pufendorf contested that certain knowledge could be achieved by first establishing fixed principles and then deducing a whole series of conclusions from them. His intention was to construct a demonstrative science of morals by appealing to indubitable data which, irrespective of the plurality of faiths sanctioned by Westphalia, no sane person could dispute. His aim was to refute the scholastics who followed Aristotle, and the Sceptics, who maintained that moral propositions were incapable of demonstration, by reasoning from axiomatic truths. Pufendorf emphatically contends: 'Now that knowledge, which considers what is upright and what base in human actions, the principal portion of which we have undertaken to present, rests entirely upon grounds so secure, that from it can be deduced genuine demonstrations which are capable of producing a solid science' (*Law of Nature*, I. ii. 4). By the word 'science' Pufendorf does not mean something quantitatively measurable and exact, but a systematic body of knowledge. It has to be said, however, that his early work *The Elements of Universal Jurisprudence* is more rigidly deductive and influenced by geometry than his later *On the Law of Nature and Nations*, by which time he had come to view Grotius's endeavours as too uncompromisingly formalistic and intellectualist.

Morality is not, for Pufendorf, a property of physical objects or motions, but an imposition of value by intelligence or reason upon them. This is Pufendorf's famous distinction between physical and moral entities. The very same physical acts performed by a dog without carrying any moral impropriety would, if performed by a man, provoke moral outrage. This, however, made morality none the less real, even though it had a historically evolving dimension, and none the less natural, even though, in part at least, it was the product of social construction. It was at once real and natural in that man's fundamental nature demanded it.

Moral action is, for Pufendorf, action according to rule, or law, and since morality is an imposition upon material existence it presupposes an imposer. There can, as far as Pufendorf is concerned, be no morality without reference to law and without its imposition by a supreme sovereign. Pufendorf, then, repudiates the idea, to which Aquinas and Grotius subscribe, that good exists independently of law, and sides with Duns Scotus in affirming that something is good because of its imposit...n by God. The autonomous existence that Grotius tentatively imputed to God and Natural Law is repudiated by Pufendorf.[16] For Pufendorf, the very idea of law entails the 'bidding of a superior' (*Law of Nature*, I. ii. 6) and its imposition by a power which can enforce it with sanctions. To set up an eternal rule as a standard of conduct, which is independent of God, and to which He Himself is obliged to conform, goes against what we generally believe about God. If God created us of His own free will, and chose to assign to us the natures which we possess, 'How, then, can an action of man be accorded any quality, if it takes its rise from an extrinsic and absolute necessity, without the imposition and pleasure of God?' (*Law of Nature*, I. ii. 6).

Natural Law is for Pufendorf law that is congruent with the very nature of man and is justifiably described as a 'dictate of right reason'. It is necessary to our very existence as human beings (*Duty*, I. 2. 16; *Elements*, def. XIII. 14; *Law of Nature*, II. iii. 13). The fact that it is a dictate of reason is not in itself a ground for obedience. Reason cannot judge the morality of any particular act without reference to law (*Law of Nature*, I. ii. 6). To have the force of law to which one is obligated presupposes its imposition by a superior. The Creator has destined for us a nature in accordance with which certain rules of conduct are consistent, and the following of these rules, or laws, is obligatory because God wills that we cultivate the nature He has given us (*Elements*, def. xii, 14; ob. iv. 3 and ob. iv. 10).[17]

Following from Pufendorf's contention that moral conduct is action according to rule or law, he makes an important distinction which places him clearly in the tradition of Universal Moral Order and distinctly at variance with Hobbes. He distinguishes between what he calls 'congenital' and 'adventitious' obligations or duties. The former are enjoined directly by Natural Law and refer to those obligations we owe to God as our creator, and to each other by the mere fact that we are human. The latter are obligations that we voluntarily assume, or which are imposed upon us by others, but which are nevertheless consistent with our nature (*Elements*, def. xii. I; *Duty*, i. 6. 1; *Law of Nature*, iii. iv. 3). The distinction between congenital and adventitious obligations, or duties, refers to their origin and should not be confused with the distinction between natural and civil obligations which refers to the force they have in community life. Pufendorf contends that a 'natural obligation is that which binds only by the force of Natural Law; a civil obligation is that which is reinforced by civil laws and authority' (*Law of Nature*, iii. iv. 6).

The point to be emphasized is that Pufendorf posits a moral order that is universal, in which men owe duties to each other by the mere fact of being human and subject to God's sovereignty. Even though, as we will see, these duties are sometimes severely qualified by our obligations as citizens, Pufendorf's theory constitutes an outright denial of the Realist contention that the moral order is confined to the internal relations of the state and that between states there can be no justice and injustice.

The State of Nature

Like Hobbes, only more explicitly, Pufendorf distinguishes between a hypothetical theoretical state of nature and the actual historical condition of human beings. Even though he is adamant that the former could never have existed, the fact that it was fictional did not detract from the theoretical contribution it could make to understanding the human predicament.[18] We have in Pufendorf's many accounts of the natural condition a pre-cultural phase in which sociality is hardly developed, and a pre-civil stage in which social relations are highly developed but political society is not yet instituted. Pufendorf does not subscribe to Hobbes's extreme individualism, nor is his state of nature characterized by a war of all against all. The principle of self-preservation does not absolve us from the obligations that the Natural Law impels us to perform towards other people (*Natural State of Men*, #9). On the other hand, while retaining Grotius's idea of natural sociality, he wants to show that it is subverted by human imperfections. The original condition of man is brutish, but soon he realizes that mutual aid, the sharing of a common humanity, and being subject to the Natural Law all impel him towards co-operation. Prior to the establishment of civil society it was 'established practice among humankind to transmit to others the discoveries made with the assistance of one's predecessors, to undertake joint projects, to engage in commerce, to dwell together, and to meet frequently with one another' (*Natural State of Men*, #6). Pufendorf maintains that his investigation takes man as he finds him here and now, 'tinged with depravity' (*Natural State of Men*, #3). It is of little use, he suggests, to posit an ideal condition of natural man to which civil law and practices must conform. An examination of the state of nature is supposed to impress upon the reader the need for civil society, even if this means enduring some of the imperfections of demanding and unreasonable rulers (*Natural State of Men*, #23).

Having indicated that Pufendorf aimed to produce a science of morals by means of demonstrative reasoning, and that his moral theory quite clearly places him in the tradition of a Universal Moral Order, what are the indubitable data to which he refers, and what rules or precepts can be deduced from them for the conduct of individuals in their relations with each other as members of humanity; in relation to each other as citizens of specific states; and in the relations among states? Pufendorf's experience of the disintegration of the Holy Roman Empire, a disunited Germany, and the devastation of the Thirty Years War led him, like many of his contemporaries, to postulate a state of nature. The method of reasoning he used was the same as that of Hobbes, the hypothetical resolutive compositive method in which all extraneous secondary qualities are stripped away, man is revealed in his true state, and an appropriate form of government is composed consistent with this nature.

It was Pufendorf's avowed aim to appeal to principles that would be accepted not only by Christians but by the whole of mankind (*Law of Nature*, preface, x). He wanted to ground Natural Law upon a foundation which avoided the disputes of rival doctrines over religious revelation. He thought that he could do this by making 'the basis of a.. Natural Law the social life of man' (*Law of Nature*, preface, ix). Religion was not to be severed from Natural Law. Instead a natural religion was to provide the basis, by which he meant a set of fundamental beliefs that every rational person could be brought to admit.[19] Among these would be included the belief that God created and controls the universe, and that He must have had some good purpose, the comprehension of which would indicate how He wished us to behave. In identifying the principal characteristics of humans we can discern which modes of behaviour are advantageous and which disadvantageous to existence. The former must be judged good, and the latter bad in relation to what we deduce to be God's purpose in creating us. Faced with these alternatives, individuals make rational calculations and free choices. The implication, for Pufendorf, is that in order to avoid those things disadvantageous to their nature human actions must be guided by the constraint of law.

For Pufendorf, in accordance with most Natural Law thinkers, political society is continuous with the state of nature, and not a radical departure from it.[20] In contrast with Hobbes, he denies that in the state of nature each person possesses a Natural Right to everything. We should not mistake the ability, or power, that we have to do something, or to acquire something, for a Natural Right to everything that it is in our power to obtain. Rights, properly so called, pertain to moral relationships with others of our kind.

Individuals, are not, he claims, the arbiters of what is right and wrong prior to the institution of a sovereign to pronounce upon such matters (*Law of Nature*, III. v. 2 and 3). Justice and injustice do not depend upon sovereigns, but are defined by Natural Law and bind the consciences of men. Civil law can attach the force of human sanction to that which is forbidden by the Natural Law, but it is, Pufendorf argues, 'no more possible for civil sovereignty to create goodness and justice by precept, than it is for it to command that poison lose its power to waste the human body' (*Law of Nature*, VIII. i. 5).

States, Pufendorf maintains, could never have been formed by compact had not some notion of justice and injustice existed prior to the institution of the state. What binding force could a pact have without the knowledge that it is just to keep it and unjust to break it? Indeed, if it is only the civil law that defines justice and injustice, what is to stop individuals renouncing their obligations and abolishing the distinction?

Self-love, with a consequent overriding determination for self-preservation, is common to both animals and humans. Like Grotius, Pufendorf saw the Laws of Nature as rules of preservation.[21] Self-love and self-interest are consistent with the Laws of Nature, and it is the principle of utility, in relation to the good of the individual and the common good, that determines which laws are to be assigned the force of civil law in a commonwealth (*Elements*, def. XIII. 18).

Human beings would be little different from animals, however, if it were not for the fact that they have an innate inclination to be social. Individuals are weak and fail to flourish without the assistance of others. Humans exhibit a capacity beyond that of animals for mutual assistance. From these fundamental features of human existence it can be deduced that God must have intended us to provide reciprocal assistance, and endowed us with a sociable nature in order to do so. God would not have endowed us with reason, Pufendorf argues, had his intention not been that the cultivation of society is proper to humans (*Elements*, ob. III. 1–6). By the term 'sociable' Pufendorf means 'an attitude of each man towards every other man, by which each is understood to be bound to the other by kindness, peace and love and therefore by a mutual obligation' (*Law of Nature*, II. iii. 15). From what we know of the human condition it follows that a fundamental Law of Nature must be to cultivate our sociableness, which in turn promotes peace to the advantage of humanity.

Self-preservation and the preservation of society, two principles that were later to constitute for Locke our duty to God, were for Pufendorf the fundamental Laws of Nature from which all others followed (*Elements*, ob. IV. 4).[22] It was, he contended, insufficient merely to desist from causing harm. Grotius, as we saw, tended to the view that our social duties are discharged by respecting others' rights, and particularly by not infringing their property rights. As opposed merely to desisting from causing harm to society, Pufendorf maintains, we have a duty actively to cultivate it. In *On the Duty of Man and Citizen* he emphasizes sociality over self-interest. He maintains that the fundamental law is 'every man ought to do as much as he can to cultivate and preserve sociality' (*Duty*, I. 3. 9). The obligation to do so is congenital rather than adventitious, and therefore, for Pufendorf, absolute (*Duty*, I. 6. 1).

He adumbrates three such duties pertaining to men as men which not only preserve but actively promote human society. The first is to desist from harming others, and it is the easiest to discharge since it does not require a positive action (*Duty*, I. 6. 2). The second requires every man to treat others as naturally his equal. This is because each individual not only has an intense interest in his own preservation, but also is acutely attuned to his own worth. A sense of dignity is evoked by the very sound of the name 'man' (*Duty*, I. 7. 1). And, finally, Pufendorf adds an injunction that requires the active promotion of society:

The third of the duties owed by every man to every man, to be performed for the sake of common sociality, is: everyone should be useful to others, so far as he conveniently can. For nature has established a kind of kinship among men. It is not enough not to have harmed, or not to have slighted others. We must also give, or at least share, such things as will encourage mutual goodwill.   (*Duty*, I. 8. 1)

Furthermore, sociality for Pufendorf, *pace* Grotius, is not merely a matter of respecting other people's property rights. Tully is simply wrong to suggest that 'Sociableness, for Pufendorf, as for Grotius, is characterised essentially by the negative duty of respecting what belongs to others'.[23] We see, then, a distinct departure from Hobbes's position. Self-preservation for Hobbes carried with it no moral duty to preserve others. Prudential considerations may dictate a policy of mutual co-operation, which does not rise out of, but is opposed to, our nature. For Hobbes (and Pufendorf certainly read him this way), the establishment of political society for the preservation of humanity is contrary to nature, and therefore entails renouncing those Natural Rights destructive of our fellow inhabitants of the state of nature.

Any adequate characterization of a state of nature must take into account the place of reason in guiding men in the direction of their long-term interests and away from the pernicious consequences of acting on the passions for short-term gain. Reason, Pufendorf contends, is not governed solely by its own advantage. Our natural sociableness inclines us towards peace and makes us averse to the war of all against all. Peace is our natural condition whether inside or outside a commonwealth, and 'to undertake a war without provocation, is both improper and unprofitable' (*Law of Nature*, II. ii. 9).[24]

It is not enough to say in criticism of this view, Pufendorf maintains, that in past times barbarity was prevalent and people delighted in living by brigandage, booty, and plunder. Among many of the ancients, Pufendorf says in defence, the reason of men was perverted by 'depraved habits and customs', but these could not themselves be deemed natural: 'For promiscuous thievery and robbery does not follow from a natural state, just as it is obviously not true of the relations of commonwealths, although they are natural' (*Law of Nature*, II. ii. 10).

Pufendorf specifically takes Hobbes to task for suggesting that robbery and pillage are not against the Laws of Nature. If the Law of Nature is violated we can justifiably retaliate, but we cannot presume to imitate such wicked behaviour in relation to others who are innocent. Furthermore, to restrain oneself from gratuitous and excessive violence in pillaging the possessions of others and to spare the tools of husbandry from the torch cannot, as Hobbes tried to persuade us, be to attain glory and avoid the charge of cowardice because of wanton cruelty, 'as if there were any glory in committing but half a crime upon recognizing the disadvantage of carrying it through to the end' (*Law of Nature*, II. ii. 10).

For Hobbes conflict arose in the state of nature because of natural equality and the absolute right of every person to all the fruits of the earth unconstrained by a moral law. We should not, Pufendorf argues, mistake the ability, or power, we have to do something or to acquire something for a natural right to everything that it is in our power to obtain. Rights pertain to moral relationships and for the most part entail correlative obligations. The right to property, for example, is not congenital, but adventitious. It arises in accordance with the needs of sociality, and may be called a Natural Right, even though it is socially constructed, because it is consistent with the nature that God has given to us.

The things that we may want have no obligation to present themselves to us, nor do we have a right to prevent all other persons, because of our natural equality, from enjoying those things that God has bestowed upon humanity in common. Nature itself does not prescribe what belongs to one man and what to another, and our right to things cannot arise without the consent of others. Similarly, we have no right over other people without their express, or tacit, consent which obligates them and gives us a right to compel them in the absence of compliance. We can only acquire a right over things if all other persons renounce their faculty or power to enjoy them, or use them, on equal terms with us. In this respect, and contrary to Hobbes, we gain a right that we did not previously have. Furthermore, Pufendorf is denying Grotius's claim that first possession confers a right, and the contentio.. that Locke was later to make, that mixing your labour with an entity creates a right to it, subject to the spoilage condition.[25]

Rights, for Pufendorf, although sanctioned by God, are inextricably related to our sociality, and have no validity outside a social context (*Law of Nature*, III. v. 3–6). It is wrong, however, to suggest, as Tuck does, that Pufendorf contended that all rights have correlative obligations and to associate him with the later and more radical doctrine of Bentham.[26] It is only when rights are narrowly conceived, as a right to have something, that Pufendorf says that there must be a correlative obligation in another. A right to do something does not automatically give rise to an obligation. A sovereign has the right to punish a lawbreaker, but the lawbreaker is not under an obligation to submit to it (*Law of Nature*, III. v. 1).[27]

In denying the existence of adventitious Natural Rights prior to agreement, Pufendorf does not want to undermine Natural Law, because the rights of which he speaks arise from our mutual consent and rely on moral obligations grounded in, and derived from, the fundamental Natural Law relating to our sociableness. In summary, Pufendorf agrees with Grotius that human beings are naturally social. It follows from this that the state of nature is itself a social condition in which right and wrong are prescribed by Natural Law and in which, in addition to our congenital obligations, we incur adventitious obligations by agreement, the discharge of which is morally compelled by the Natural Law.

Inconveniences of the State of Nature

Life without law, in Pufendorf's view, is contrary to human nature, and therefore it is part of the nature of things that positive law should be instituted. Law, however, even human positive law, has to be at the bidding of, or imposed by, an authority. It is therefore natural that human beings constitute governments for this purpose. Given that no one has adventitious rights over us, because of our natural equality, and that we are obliged to no other person without our consent, government must be based upon agreement. But why should we wish to establish an authority over ourselves, given that the state of nature is a social condition naturally inclined to peaceful relations?

Pufendorf argues that if in the state of nature someone fails to fulfil an obligation that has arisen from an agreement, then there is no authority to compel the performance, or put right an injury, although we may choose to empower an arbiter or rely on the interposition of common friends. Nevertheless, although nature wills that we live in common kinship and that it is wrong to injure others, this knowledge often exercises a feeble preventative force.

Co-operative ventures in pursuit of common ends without a superior to impose direction are hindered in the state of nature by two serious flaws in human nature. First is the diversity of opinion on the means to achieve the ends of joint enterprises, and the stubbornness of individuals in refusing to be swayed away from their original options; secondly, humans are indolent and disinclined to do what is required without being compelled to cease their procrastination and do their duty (*Duty*, II. 6. 4).

Pufendorf argues that the Law of Nature in itself is insufficient to restrain men who are not compelled to act lawfully by a superior. By far the greatest proportion of evils that befall humankind are inflicted upon man by man himself, and 'neither the fear of God nor the sting of conscience are found to have sufficient force to restrain the evil that is in men' (*Duty*, II. 5. 9). Even though the Natural Law is attended with God's vengeance, the delay in the punishment following the crime provides the wicked with opportunities to attribute the apparent ill fortune that befalls the impious to other causes. Pufendorf contends that

although conscience sufficiently indicates to each man what is to be done or left undone; nevertheless, few have such modesty of disposition that they are willing to follow this constantly where no present punishment, and one which strikes terror to the senses, has been set before the violator; especially where, through growing accustomed to them, the sweetness of vices has entered his heart, and, modesty being cast forth, the mind addicted to the passions has grown deaf to the admonitions of the reason.   (*Elements*, II. ob. v. 1)

Thus those with whom we share the state of nature are to be regarded as 'inconstant' friends. Perverse natures and the passion to dominate others or to possess more than we need may cause injury to others. But even those people who are of a more moderate disposition may arm themselves from fear of an anticipated injury. In this respect suspicion is prevalent, and even those of moderate disposition may attempt to undermine the strength of others because of distrust. It follows, for Pufendorf, that 'a cautious man who loves his own security will believe all men his friends but be liable at any time to become enemies; he will keep peace with all, knowing that it may soon be exchanged for war.' In other words, the state of nature is not one of perpetual war, because of a common humanity, mutual need, and interdependence, but at the same time it is not a harmonious condition, 'because of men's wickedness, their desires, and the passions which struggle vehemently against right reason'. This makes the condition an 'unstable and undependable peace' (*Natural State of Men*, #18). This is the reason why 'that country is considered happy which even in peace contemplates war' (*Duty*, II. 1. 11).

We have to distinguish, then, between society and political society in Pufendorf's theory, just as one has to do in relation to Locke. What is the impetus that compels us to take the step, or convert, from the one to the other, and by what means do we bring it about? It is not necessity, nor nature, nor sociability, but self-interest that motivates the institution of political society.[28] Here we see that in emphasizing our natural propensity to be social as Grotius, did, Pufendorf did not lose sight of Hobbes's emphasis upon self-interest.[29]

Pufendorf argues that without doubt human beings are filled with self-love and look out for their own interests to their full capacity. It must therefore be because of some personal utility that people seek political society. Certainly, the wants we have and the necessities with which we are faced could amply be accommodated in small communities, so it cannot be our sociability that directs us to political society. A community without an acknowledged superior would be prey to the depravities of human nature. It is in our own interests for security against members of our own communities, and against external threats, to found states in which we can more fully enjoy the benefits of association with fellow human beings and in which we can bequeath to our children habits of friendliness (*Elements*, II. ob. v. 14–15; *Law of Nature*, VII. i. 1–11; *Duty*, II. 5. 1–9).

What Pufendorf is attempting to do is to endorse a moral law that is absolute, or congenital, and universal, and at the same time to justify the existence of independent, autonomous states in terms of prudential considerations.[30] Since we cannot confer rights, or put ourselves under obligation without consent, and since political society entails giving up a degree of natural liberty and subjecting ourselves to a superior authority, or sovereign, the establishment of political society must be by means of contract. It is by constituting an authoritative civil sovereign that the moral obligations we find it difficult to enforce in a state of nature become laws with prescribed and enforceable penalties attached to them: 'Hence we are said to have an imperfect right [*jus imperfectum*] to the former, a perfect right [*jus perfectum*] to the latter, and similarly to be imperfectly obligated in the former case, perfectly obligated in the latter' (*Duty*, I. 9. 4). In other words, what was once compelled by conscience becomes enforceable by the force of positive law. Knud Haakonssen quite rightly points out that we should not lose sight of the fact that both imperfect and perfect rights and obligations 'have an equal moral foundation in Natural Law'.[31] The terms are not used consistently in the history of ethics, and it is well to point out that other writers talk of perfect obligations having counterpart rights, but of imperfect obligations having none. Taken in these senses, they have an unequal moral foundation and significant structural differences.[32]

Pufendorf read Hobbes's state of nature as a condition in which no sense of natural obligation prevailed, and was contemptuous of his derivation of moral obligation from a contract that had no moral foundation. Without a prior sense of obligation no contract can create it. Against Hobbes, Pufendorf argues that injustices can be committed independently of agreements, and that before an agreement is entered into its conformity with Natural Law should be ascertained (*Law of Nature*, I. vii. 12).[33] Human authorities cannot arise with the power to enforce obligation if the dictates of reason, that is the Natural Law, are not already morally obligatory. For Pufendorf, 'the obligation of Natural Law is of God, the creator and final governor of mankind, who by His authority has bound men, His creatures, to observe it' (*Law of Nature*, II. iii. 20; cf. *Duty*, II. 6. 14).

Establishing a political society with a civil sovereign who is the author and enforcer of positive law, converting our imperfect obligations into perfect obligations, entails the division of humankind into a plurality of political communities. The duties and obligations individuals have as human beings are at once supplemented and, as we will see, sometimes superseded or overridden by the obligations of citizenship.

Establishing States

Why is it necessary to subdivide the world into states in preference to establishing a cosmopolitan global authority? As we have seen, the condition of humankind is precarious because of the uncertainties of the observance and enforcement among a great multitude of people of the precepts of Natural Law. Self-preservation is best achieved by conformity to the Laws of Nature, the enforcement of which becomes effective when backed by the power of the state. Security is the principal motivation for converting social communities into political states.[34] States, although the creation of human artifice, are instituted by the command of God 'in so far as they serve as the means to the observance of Natural Law' (*Law of Nature*, VIII. iii. 2).

The security afforded by states is contingent upon prevailing circumstances. The size of a state and the degree of security required depend upon the strength and power of its neighbours. What was in antiquity a large and viable state may in modern times be too small in comparison with the vast empires that have arisen

(*Law of Nature*, vii. ii. 2). Like Hobbes, Pufendorf did not think a state should be so small as to be jeopardized by the addition of a few extra men to its enemy (*Duty*, ii. 6. 2: *Elements*, ii. ob. v. 1). Similarly, it should not be so big as to render the provision of security almost impossible. Pufendorf contends that society arose among the first individuals, but not to avoid the state of nature; on the contrary, the natural state arose as a consequence of the vast population increase that could not be encompassed by one society (*Law of Nature*, ii. ii. 7). Because of the 'huge dimensions' and diversity of mankind it is unrealistic to expect agreement on the details of a universal contract applicable to a multitude of different situations. Furthermore, the power of men is not so great that it could be exercised by one authority with equal force over all the world. The benefits gained from eliminating conflicts between states would be lost because of the outbreak of civil wars over the clash of group interests (*Law of Nature*, vii. iii. 2; *Elements*, ii. ob. v. 1).[35]

In summary, our natural inclination towards peace is disturbed by the vast growth in population and exacerbated by defects in human nature which lead many to disregard the Law of Nature and render the condition uncertain and precarious for all. It is impractical to unite the whole of such a vast multitude into one state, because the benefits gained by eliminating conflicts between nations would be lost by the diminution of the power of the state authority to contain internal disputes. A plurality of states, with contracts reflecting the diversity of mankind, is in Pufendorf's view the most effective form of security.

As Krieger has remarked, the procedure that Pufendorf prescribes for the establishment of a properly constituted state comprises one of the most elaborate systems of contract in the whole of the social contract tradition.[36] There are three stages in the process of establishing the state. First a pact, or contract, is made between those who desire to join together to improve their condition, expressing their intention and agreement to enter into a permanent society 'and to administer the means of their safety and security by common counsel and leadership; in a word, that they wish to become fellow-citizens' (*Duty*, ii. 6. 7). Such an agreement is conditional if an individual stipulates the form of government to which he would submit, and absolute if he is willing to abide by the majority decision. Secondly, on deciding the form of government a decree is made, followed, thirdly, by a further pact (*Law of Nature*, vii. ii. 7). This second pact is not an agreement exclusively among the people and, unlike Hobbes's version of the social contract, makes the ruler a party to the agreement. While appreciating Hobbes's desire to reduce the grounds for rebellion by excluding the sovereign from the promises made in the pact, Pufendorf cannot deny the reciprocal nature of an agreement:

When I subject myself to a prince, I promise him obedience, and stipulate for myself defence, while the prince in accepting me as a citizen promises me defence and stipulates from me obedience. Before that promise, neither of us was under an obligation, at least not a perfect one, I to obey him, or he to defend me. (*Law of Nature*, vii. ii. 9; cf. *Duty*, ii. 6. 9)

In other words, the social contract institutes a political society in which the rights and duties of citizens are supplemented with the rights and duties of the sovereign. They are not the same rights and duties, but 'peculiar rights' and 'possessions' conferred upon the 'highest authority' in whose hands the care of the state has been placed (*Law of Nature*, VII. ii. 8–12; *Duty*, II. 6. 6–14).

Personifying the State

In the later medieval and early modern periods the vocabulary in terms of which to conceptualize the state proved to be inadequate. The two principal contenders, *societas* and *universitas*, both had their shortcomings. A *societas* entailed a contractual relationship between individuals, implying no corporate identity, and this was the term used under private law to designate a partnership. It implied no identity beyond that of the individuals who comprised it. A *societas* was a partnership of individuals, each of whom was deemed capable of suing and of being sued independently of the whole, which was itself devoid of corporate personality. A *universitas*, or corporation, on the other hand, had conferred upon it a legal or fictitious personality. In this capacity it could possess proprietary rights, but was not deemed to have a will, intentions, or cognitive capacities. Furthermore a fictitious personality implied a higher legal authority to create it.[37] The difficulties of applying the terms *societas* and *universitas* to the state were to some extent evaded by understanding the state as a real moral person with a will and personality independent of those who comprised it. The apparent absurdity of a real person composed of numerous persons did not hinder the extent to which theorists were enticed by its powerful imagery. P. P. Remec tells us that it was Pufendorf who first applied the idea of the juristic moral person to the state and hence made it subject to the moral Law of Nature. His successors Wolff and Vattel extended the idea to designate states as the moral subjects of the Law of Nations.[38]

Hobbes, as we saw, understood the state as an artificial person, the embodiment of which was the persc.. of the sovereign exercising his will on behalf of the people. The sovereign essentially *represents* the people. He is the unity of the people.[39] Pufendorf thought this depiction of the state ingenious, but he goes much further than Hobbes in endowing the state with an individuality and personality distinct from the people who institute it and from the person of the ruler who exercises its authority. The three-stage procedure, comprising two contracts and one decree, institutes a new composite moral entity whose peculiar attribute is sovereignty. Moral entities are, for Pufendorf, individual persons or collections of persons united by a moral bond. The former he calls *simple* and the latter *composite* 'moral persons' (*Law of Nature*, I. i. 12). A composite moral person is ascribed one will, irrespective of the number of individuals who comprise it, and its actions are the actions of the whole body. Such entities may be endowed with rights and duties that none of the individuals comprising them could claim in their own right (*Elements*, I. def. IV. 3; *Law of Nature*, I. i. 13; *Duty*, II. 6. 10). The subjection and entwining of wills entailed in the social contract creates the state which is 'the most powerful of moral societies and persons' (*Law of Nature*, VII. ii. 5).[40]

Pufendorf is here talking not of a fictitious legal entity, but of a real autonomous moral person with the capacity to will, deliberate, and pursue purposes. The state has a personality and is the bearer of rights and duties. It would be anachronistic to read into Pufendorf's theory of the state the totalitarian and militaristic implications that were to become characteristic of the personification of the state in the theories of German Realists such as Bluntschli, Treitschke, and Bernhardi and the twentieth-century doctrines of Fascism and Nazism. The person of the state for Pufendorf had the limited objective of protecting its citizens, and had no justifiable expansionist designs. It was to be constrained by Natural Law and guided by the general rule: 'Let the safety of the people be the supreme law' (*Law of Nature*, vii. ix. 3).

Sovereignty is for Pufendorf the soul that animates the person of the state, but although instituted by human will, it is not the creation of it, nor dependent upon it. Sovereignty is consistent with nature in that it conforms with human sociality and right reason in better facilitating obedience to Natural Law. God sanctions sovereignty, but He does not confer it directly upon the rulers of states. He does so through the instrument of the human will. Pufendorf is undermining the doctrine of popular sovereignty without endorsing the divine right of kings (*Law of Nature*, vii. iii. 1–5).[41] Human beings acting in time perform God's will by instituting arrangements that are suggested by right reason and are consistent with the indubitable data of their nature. In so far as sovereignty is both human and divine, and in order to fulfil the purpose for which we associate and institute political society, it is in our interests to hold 'sacrosanct and inviolable' the civil sovereign. It is, Pufendorf argues, 'in the highest interest of mankind that the royal power be held sacred and free from the cavils of churlish men' (*Law of Nature*, vii. viii. 1 and vii. ii. 9 respectively). Does this mean that Pufendorf allows no right of resistance?

The sovereign, free from the interference of other persons and subject to no earthly superior, exercises natural liberty in guiding his conduct by what reason dictates. The sovereign, as a moral person, is subject to no human authority and occupies in that respect a place in the state of nature similar to that of the pre-civil individual (*Law of Nature*, ii. ii. 4). The people who instituted sovereignty, however, did so with a view to securing greater general compliance with the Laws of Nature, by securing for them the force of civil law. The people had a reasonable expectation that the sovereign would enact no civil law that was contrary to the Natural Law. Only a sovereign bent on the destruction of the state, Pufendorf maintains, would be insane enough to oppose the civil law to the Natural Law (*Law of Nature*, vii. i. 2). Pufendorf acknowledges that sovereigns can injure their subjects by violating their rights as both men and citizens, but he is willing only to allow the smallest concessions to citizens against the absoluteness of sovereignty. For the most part it is better to flee the country to escape the serious injuries that a sovereign is determined to inflict. When injuries are less serious it may be better to ignore them in deference to the dignity of the office, and for the sake of the stability of the state and well-being of fellow citizens (*Law of Nature*, vii. viii. 4 and v. viii. 5). The consequent injuries of the wrongdoing of sovereigns must by innocent citizens 'be classed among those evils to which man in his mortality is exposed, and which he must bear, like drought, floods and all other acts of nature' (*Law of Nature*, vii. ii. 14). In exceptional circumstances a citizen may justifiably resist 'the most open injuries of a superior' (*Law of Nature*, vii. viii. 5), but it is not permissible on that count for fellow citizens to disobey the sovereign and come to the aid of the injured citizen. The people as a whole is only justified in resisting when the actions of the sovereign threaten to destroy the state.[42]

Personification is the principal means by which the state can be identified as the natural actor in international relations. As an artificial or real moral person it is designated a deliberative agent. Having a will and personality of its own, it stands as a distinct and autonomous individuality in relation to other states. The personification of the state, like organic analogies, is designed to give substance to the cohesiveness of the group. Each individual is subordinate to, and part of, the larger living whole. Harm perpetrated against the state is harm done to one's own body. Resort to such theories is designed to impress upon the citizen the unconditional duties of political obligation. Internal political security is bought at the expense of generating a logic which restricts the conceptual vocabulary in terms of which to understand the external relations of states. In taking the state to be a person, whether natural or mechanical, the internal elements or constitution which stabilize its metabolism become the primary focus. The absence of the same features in the international sphere renders it inherently unstable.

The strong sense of agency ascribed to the state has the effect of relegating all relations of a non-governmental nature to relative insignificance. The state is the principal organ through which the will of the people is expressed. Its own will, which is more than the sum of its parts, is superordinate to and not co-ordinate with those of which it is composed. The vocabulary is one that has the inherent tendency of privileging the duties of citizenship over those of humanity, irrespective of whether the international sphere is conceived as a moral or amoral realm. It is a tendency that Pufendorf did not himself escape and, indeed, did much to reinforce.[43] The subject of international law, however rudimentary it may have been, became not peoples but states, whose conduct it was designed to regulate. States were the juristic persons of international law, in whatever terms that law was conceived.[44] Even the United Nations, despite its pronouncements on human rights, unequivocally endorses the inviolability of sovereignty and the integrity of the state. The Declaration on Principles of International Law expressly forbids intervention in the internal and external affairs of states. The 'personality of the state' is sacrosanct.[45]

States and the State of Nature

Like Hobbes, Pufendorf compares personified states in their relations with each other to individuals in a state of nature.[46] Individual sovereign states as composite moral persons exercise natural liberty. States, Pufendorf argues, are 'in a mutual state of nature' in that they have no common superior:

And so commonwealths and their officials may properly claim for themselves the distinction of being in a state of natural liberty, when they are girded with the powers which allow them its secure enjoyment, while it is a thing of little joy or use for those who enjoy individually a pure state of nature to have no superior, since the weakness of their own resources makes their safety hang by a thread. (*Law of Nature*, ii. ii. 4; cf. *Duty*, ii. 1. 6, and *Natural State of Men*, #7)

Here Pufendorf is suggesting that individuals do not have the strength to enjoy their natural liberty and must therefore form political societies. States, however, do on the whole have the strength to enjoy their natural liberty and need not, and indeed on practical grounds cannot, form a world government.[47]

Whereas Grotius believed that there could be law without a sanctioning authority, and that therefore international law, or the voluntary Law of Nations, had an independent integrity, Pufendorf compromised its integrity by denying that there could be any genuine international law in the absence of an authority to enforce it (*Law of Nature*, ii. iii. 23).[48] But this does not mean that he thought, as Thucydides, Machiavelli, and Hobbes did, that the sphere of international relations was devoid of ethics. Just as in the state of nature the Natural Law is the foundation of justice and injustice, the Natural Law also governs relations among sovereign states. The Law of Nature and the Law of Nations are one and the same thing (*Elements*, def. xiii. 24; *Law of Nature*, ii. iii. 23).

Pufendorf did, of course, acknowledge that customs and agreements regulate the conduct of states, but that they cannot have the force of law. Such customs may in fact contravene Natural Law. For example, the custom that ownership of property procured from an enemy 'in a formal war' becomes one's own may go 'beyond all bounds and reason, and far exceed the claim for which the war was begun' (*Law of Nature*, viii. vi. 20). A custom which is based on Natural Law has a greater moral worth than, and is qualitatively different from, those that are tacitly or explicitly the result of the 'simple agreement of nations' (*Law of Nature*, ii. iii. 23). Although a custom may appear obligatory because it is the result of something like a tacit agreement, a sovereign engaged in a legitimate war is under no moral compulsion to honour it if the Natural Law provides a course by which it can be ignored. Like Hobbes, Pufendorf acknowledges that honour and dishonour had no necessary connection with justice and injustice. Failure to observe a custom may be dishonourable but not necessarily unjust, and may occur at the risk of being accused of nothing more than 'ungentlemanliness' (*Law of Nature*, ii. iii. 23). Pufendorf, it must be emphasized, is not denying the regulatory capacity of Natural Law, custom, and conventional agreements; he is simply denying that they have the force of law in the required sense of being backed by a sovereign to demand compliance. In other words, the obligations of states under the Law of Nature, and those customs and agreements in accordance with it, are imperfect.

The Morality of War and Peace

Although he denies the reality of international law, and was not therefore concerned with questions of the legality of war, questions which were placed at the centre of international thought by the later writer Vattel, Pufendorf was nevertheless interested in questions of the morality of war. We have already seen that the idea of just war gives rise to three integrally related sets of issues: first, the justification of war itself as a mode of conduct, often taken for granted by just war theorists; second, the issues surrounding the conditions of the justifiable resort to war, which presuppose that war is a legitimate mode of conduct, questions of *jus ad bellum*; and third, issues relating to the conduct of war, questions of *jus in bello*. Grotius, as we saw, was predominantly concerned with specifying the conditions of just war; equally importantly he wanted to subject its prosecution to the rule of law. War was to be constrained within the bounds of humaneness.

Pufendorf was not unusual in giving short shrift to the question of the legitimacy of the use of war.[49] A serious enough violation of the fundamental Laws of Nature was in the last resort rectifiable by resort to war. Peace, for Pufendorf, as we saw, is the natural condition of mankind. States have the same right as individuals in a state of nature to exercise their natural liberties to 'defend themselves against unjust threats of violence' (*Law of Nature*, VIII. vi. 1). Such threats contravene the first Law of Nature, which forbids hurting people unjustly and compels us to act humanely towards fellow human beings. War is not, however, natural. It is not consistent with human nature and is permissible 'in defect of a more appropriate means' of securing one's rights (*Elements*, def. III. 6). Such appropriate means include a willing third party who is prepared to arbitrate, the pronouncement of whom, if favourable, adds credibility to one's cause, while 'at the same time, one is prevented from rushing into unjust and unnecessary wars because of greediness and lack of self-control' (*Natural State of Men*, #12).

War for Pufendor. is not, then, an instrument of policy as it was for Thucydides, Machiavelli, and Hobbes, but a last resort in protecting one's rights. Pufendorf contends that 'nature allows men war merely as a sort of extraordinary means of acting with one another' (*Elements*, I. def. XII. 22).

What, then, are the conditions of a just war? Nature permits war when it is waged for the purpose of securing peace, the natural condition of humanity (*Law of Nature*, VIII. vi. 2). In other words, Pufendorf, like his predecessors in the just war tradition, is emphasizing right intention as a just cause. Such wars may be just if they are motivated by the desire to protect ourselves and our property against unwarranted aggression, or to recover that which is owed to us. War may also be justly waged to secure reparation for injuries and damages sustained, and to force the offending party to guarantee that no repetition of the injury will occur. Wars are defensive when waged for protection and offensive for recovery and reparation.

Offensive wars are particularly difficult to justify, and the utmost caution should be exercised in establishing the facts of the matter, 'as nature does not allow one to plunge into war on the slightest provocation, even when one is fully convinced of the justice of his cause' (*Duty*, II. 1. 10). When it is apparent that an injustice has been done, recourse to means other than war should first be explored, such as a conference between the parties concerned; the use of arbitrators; or even the settlement of the dispute by lot (*Law of Nature*, VIII. vi. 4; cf. *Elements*, I. def. III. 5). The justice of one's cause does not, of course, guarantee success. To pursue such a course is tantamount tacitly to consenting to whatever outcome the vicissitudes of war may determine. War, then is likened to a game of chance, with the consequent risks of an unfavourable result and no legitimate cause for complaint about the outcome (*Elements*, I. def. XII. 59; *Duty*, II. 10. 2).

In agreement with such writers as Vitoria and Grotius, Pufendorf denies those grounds of war which Thucydides, Machiavelli, and Hobbes condone. A war is unjust, he claims, if it is waged because of a desire to acquire 'superfluous possession', or to exercise power over another, or for the sake of gaining fame by oppressing others. Whereas fear was a sufficient ground for Thucydides, Machiavelli, and Hobbes to enter into war with one's neighbour, Pufendorf makes it clear that 'fear alone does not suffice as a just cause for war' (*Law of Nature*, VIII. vi. 5). While fear may inspire us to improve our defences, it cannot justify being the first to resort to violence in order to secure a guarantee that there is no hostile intent.

Whereas writers like Aquinas allowed a wide degree of permissiveness to just causes, implying that significant differences in cultural practices may justify intervention, later writers became more restrictive. Vitoria and Suarez, for example, explicitly try to narrow the permissible grounds of war. Pufendorf was similarly restrictive. There can be no justification for attacking other peoples simply because we disapprove of their practices and ceremonies. Only when such behaviour inflicts palpable harm upon one of our own number is intervention justified.

On the second set of issues, those of *jus ad bellum*, he was as concerned as Grotius to establish the principles of just cause and right intention. Unlike Grotius, however, he did not add to the criteria of a properly just war that it be conducted humanely. Subject to the proviso that the end aimed for in war is peace, Pufendorf's view is that excesses in war are justifiable, a position that places him much closer to his predecessor Suarez and his successor William Paley than to Grotius, and one which Suarez and Paley nevertheless qualified severely. Paley, for example, while condoning excesses consistent with a justifiable cause and end of war, thought acts of barbarity, including 'the slaughter of captives', 'the violation of women', and the 'profanation of temples', to be 'prohibited not only by the practice of civilised nations, but by the Law of Nature itself, as having no proper tendency to accelerate the termination, or accomplish the object of the war'.[50]

A just cause, however, in the view of most just war theorists, can be undermined by unjust modes of behaviour in the conduct of war. In this respect the criteria for judging *jus in bello* are different from those applied to *jus ad bellum*. In the theory of Vitoria the two sets of criteria are inadequately distinguished. On the one hand he suggests that the justness of a war permits every course of action necessary to bring it to a successful conclusion. One may call this the principle of just necessity.[51] On the other hand he invokes moral criteria independently of judging the justness of a war in order to impose constraints on just necessity. On the important question of whether innocent civilians can be killed in war Vitoria suggests that 'it is never right to commit evil, even to avoid greater evils'.[52] The question for him is resolved into one of intention. If innocent civilians are killed as an unintended consequence of acts of war it is permissible on condition that 'it advances a just war which cannot be won in any other way', providing of course 'that the evil effects of the war do not outweigh the possible benefits sought by waging it'.[53] Grotius, as we saw, wanted to subject the conduct of war to the rule of law and was therefore opposed to the principle of just necessity. A war is just if the cause and the conduct are legitimate.

Pufendorf takes a more extreme view. Whoever violates the duties of peace against another demonstrates that he is an enemy and thus gives the victim a licence to use whatever degree of force is considered necessary to bring the war to an end. He says, for example, that 'a state of hostility of itself grants one the licence to do another injury without limit' (*Law of Nature*, VIII. vii. 2). Without this licence to go to extremes, Pufendorf argues, an end to the war would never be in sight. In this respect it is not unjust to return an injury that far outweighs the original injury inflicted by the enemy, because such acts are not to be likened to punishment. Here Pufendorf differs from Grotius, who believes that when the atrocity of crimes by other states is self-evident, then wars waged to inflict punishment are legitimate.[54] In Pufendorf's view, punishment requires a supreme sovereign, and is applicable therefore only within the state. The principle of retribution, that the punishment must fit the crime, is applicable only to civil tribunals where a superior authoritatively hands down the sentence, and the purpose of the punishment is primarily to reform the criminal. Grotius employs the principle of equivalence, intrinsic to the retributivist theory of punishment, as a constraint on nations: 'According to the Law of Nature, by a lawful war we acquire things which are either equal to that which, although it was owed to us, we could not otherwise obtain, or we inflict upon the guilty a loss that does not exceed an equitable m_asure of punishment.'[55] Pufendorf argues, however, that in war the force inflicted does not emanate from an authoritative superior in the international context, and the aim is not primarily to reform the offender, but to protect one's own security, property, and rights: 'To secure such ends it is permissible to use whatever means I think will best prevail against such a person, who, by the injury done me, has made it impossible for me to do him an injury, however I may treat him, until we have come to a new agreement to refrain from injuries for the future' (*Law of Nature*, VIII. vi. 7).

A sovereign in the conduct of a just war is not, then, obliged to conform to those customs which are commonly agreed among nations and which temper the excesses of war. An unjust war, however, may be partially mitigated by adherence to such customs, and the perpetrator may at least exhibit the saving grace of inflicting injuries with moderation (*Elements*, I. def. XIII. 2).

Certain constraints do, however, operate even in just wars. The Law of Nature of humanity restrains us against excessive violence and against unnecessary vindictiveness after a victory has been won. There is also a salutary prudential consideration. Fortunes change in war, and it is therefore sensible to moderate the licence to use any degree of force in case one's actions are taken as exemplars by the enemy when the tide turns.

Pufendorf and most Natural Law theorists would agree with Thucydides, Machiavelli, and Hobbes that craftiness and deceit are legitimate methods by which to conduct oneself in war. The Natural Law theorists, however, cannot condone the practice of fraud and deceit in the making of treaties, truces, or contracts. No peace could ever be stable, nor any sovereign trust another, if the means to peace were perverted by dishonesty. Pufendorf makes a distinction between those pacts which are designed to achieve a peace and in which keeping faith is imperative, and those pacts, or truces, which merely signal a temporary halt to hostilities. The latter are for Pufendorf rather curious in that the persons making them at once expect faith to be kept while at the same time signalling that they intend to remain an enemy. There can be, Pufendorf believes, no confidence in the faith of such agreements, and one must presume that the parties are laying traps for one another and hoping to find a way to cause injury by lulling one another into false security (*Law of Nature*, viii. vii. 2; cf. *Law of Nature*, viii. vi. 6, and *Duty*, ii. 16. 5).

The Sovereign's Right to Make Peace

Whereas everyone in the state of nature has a right to wage war and make peace with the enemy, only the moral entity of the person of the state exercises the rights of war in an international state of nature. Pufendorf quite clearly vests the right of war in the sovereign. Against Grotius he denies the claims of subordinate magistrates to exercise such power. The state is sacrosanct in retaining for itself special rights and duties that lesser moral persons do not have. The supreme sovereign entrusted with the safety of the people is ultimately responsible for all good and evil acts within the state (*Law of Nature*, vii. ix. 9).

The idea of the state having the monopoly of military power and being the sole arbiter in matters of war and peace is here being quite strongly asserted. This view can be contrasted with that of Vitoria, who over a hundred years earlier defended the private right to war, which he equated essentially with the use of force in self-defence. Commonwealths, in addition, have the right to avenge wrongs and seize reparations, on the authority of the prince if it is a perfect community, which means that it is self-sufficient and lacking nothing. Such commonwealths may be members of a larger empire but nevertheless retain the right of war. In the case of imperfect communities the right of war is vested in a higher authority. Custom, however, Vitoria suggests, may override this. Communities subject to the same prince and holding the customary right of war have the authority to enter into hostilities. Vitoria implies that the Law of Nations and customary law are to be equated with human positive law, and are not like the Natural Law dictates of reason. Suárez, like Grotius, endorsed the distinction to be made between the Law of Nations and the Natural Law, but challenged Vitoria's account of the customary right of some imperfect communities to wage war. Grotius argued that wars waged by communities subject to the same prince were illegitimate while those subject to different princes were not.[56] The decision to go to war is of such importance to the state, Pufendorf argues, that it cannot be held in the hands of anyone less than the sovereign. As Holzgrefe points out, in vesting the right of war in the sovereign, Pufendorf was reflecting the transition, completed by the end of the seventeenth century, during which feudal self-help ceased to be regarded as an act of warfare.[57] Pufendorf's denial of the right of war to subordinate magistrates also reflects his dissatisfaction with the outcome of the Peace of Westphalia for the German Empire. The right to negotiate and enter upon treaties granted to the different German territories licensed alliances with foreign powers and undermined the unity of the whole.

In the interests of the safety of the people Pufendorf argues that the sovereign has the right to raise such revenues as are necessary to that end, and 'since the relation in which states stand to one another is a peace none too stable, it is the part of supreme sovereigns to see to it that the valour and skill in arms of the citizens is fostered, and that everything required to repel invasion stands in readiness, such as forts, arms and troops' (*Law of Nature*, vii. ix. 13). Like Hobbes, Pufendorf believes that the sovereign has a duty to be forearmed and forewarned. The latter is to be achieved by permanent ambassadors, well-cultivated friendships, and 'prudent alliances' (*Law of Nature*, vii. ix. 13). The aim is to discern common interests with a view to the establishment of alliances guided by the principle of the welfare of the state (*Natural State of Men*, #22).

On the question of the limits of political obligation in time of peril, Pufendorf's is essentially a *de facto* theory, and despite apparent qualifications and conditions, practically his position is similar to that of Hobbes. A sovereign may temporarily lose the right to the allegiance of citizens if he is unable to protect them and they have insufficient strength to repel the enemy. This is simply the application of the Natural Law of self-preservation, motivated not by conscience, but by fear. When the sovereign is once again in a position to provide the protection required of him, citizens resume their obligations. Pufendorf does not, however, give any indication of how far we are obliged to go in assisting the former sovereign in regaining his position. However, he refers to the cessation of the obligation as a remission. What he is clear about is that no private citizen has the right to oppose the usurper for fear of the reprisals that experience shows are likely to follow (*Law of Nature*, vii. viii. 10).

We saw in the case of Hobbes how the principle of self-defence generated a good deal of equivocation over the extent to which a citizen is obligated to risk his life in war. Persons of a timorous nature, those able to substitute another, and those in imminent danger all qualified the obligation, and ultimately in the review and conclusion he adds to the Laws of Nature the injunction to do as much as is in one's power to protect in war that authority which provides protection in peacetime. Pufendorf is much more forthright in subjecting the individual to the state on questions of war. He argues that the life a person has would long ago have perished in a state of nature, and that the individual would of necessity have had to have risked it for self-protection. The individual owes not only his life but many other benefits to the state. It is therefore no injustice in cases of great necessity to compel citizens to risk their lives for the protection of the state, and even to be offered as hostages in guaranteeing the fidelity of pacts between states (*Law of Nature*, vii. ii. 4 and 6; *Natural State of Men*, #23; *Duty*, ii. 13. 2; cf. *Duty*, i. 5. 4 and i. 5. 18).[58]

Pufendorf is particularly concerned to withhold from the individual the right of conscience in the duty to fight for a sovereign. The right would be subject to such manifestly perverse motives as timidity and laziness in manufacturing pretexts for conscientious objection that the danger of sovereignty being severely undermined would be significant. Even in the case of an unjust war it would be dangerous to follow Grotius in releasing the individual from the obligation to fight. The best course is to leave the sovereign answerable to God for the justness of a war (*Law of Nature*, viii. i. 8).[59]

In summary, war, although regrettable and not a natural method of conduct, is nevertheless necessary, in the absence of any other course of action, to secure the rights of the sovereign state, all matters relating to which are vested in the sovereign. The state can legitimately expect the citizen to risk his life for its safety in recompense for past security and benefits. Conquest, as a matter of self-preservation, releases the subject temporarily from the obligations owed to an exiled sovereign on the ground that he can no longer provide protection.

Just as he wishes to reserve the right of war to the sovereign, Pufendorf also wishes to assert the sovereign's supremacy in matters of making peace. Pufendorf vests in the sovereign the right to decide with whom to make alliances and to render the service of the state to allies in just wars. Allies who lack circumspection, however, and enter upon unwise or unjust war, cannot expect the assistance promised. Pufendorf also makes it clear that promises of help to allies are conditional upon the capacity to discharge the obligation without undermining those obligations that the sove. .ign owes to his own citizens (*Law of Nature*, viii. v. 14).

On the question of the observance of treaties, Hugo Grotius contended that even if a pact is concluded as a result of extortion and fear and agreed upon by a country unjustly, the victim of aggression, the disadvantaged party, should still honour his obligation. If such pacts were invalidated by the plea of duress or fear it would be almost impossible to moderate the severity of conflicts or bring wars conclusively to an end. Pufendorf, on the other hand, contends that in all conscience the victim of unjust aggression forced to accept harsh peace terms may plead fear to exempt the state from the agreement and may justifiably seek to remedy the wrong when circumstances change and favour success. The preservation of the state is a prime obligation, and all treaties are to be assumed to contain the hidden clause 'insofar as it will not jeopardise the safety of our state' (*Natural State of Men*, #19).

To what extent treaties bind one's successors was a question of considerable concern to jurists and philosophers. Thucydides, Machiavelli, and Hobbes had no compunction about freeing a successor of the obligations of his predecessor and, indeed, believed that there were few compelling reasons why the same ruler who made a treaty should keep faith if it was no longer to his advantage. In Pufendorf's view the sovereign had a private and a public will, the person of the state being manifest in the latter. Following from this he distinguished between real and personal treaties. Real treaties are those concluded on behalf of the state, whether they are agreed to by a people or a monarch. Personal treaties are those agreements made by a monarch in his own personal capacity, and are not concluded in the name of the state; they are therefore not binding on his successors. A real treaty, on the other hand, does bind succeeding rulers or governments to its terms (*Law of Nature*, vii. ii. 4). Holzgrefe tells us that Pufendorf unequivocally expresses the modern view of the binding character of treaties upon successors.[60] This is not, however, entirely free of ambiguity. Pufendorf does make a qualification which considerably undermines the principle. He argues that it has now become the custom to renew even a 'real' treaty with a change of ruler, and that if no palpable advantage had been gained from it, and no transfers of benefits effected, exemption from the terms may be gained by pleading that the treaty was concluded on the faith of the original signatory and is not transferable to his successor:

Especially since treaties are made to promote the advantage of the state, and since a king can have a different feeling from his predecessor on that point, and can also by his right as king take another way in order to secure it, and so pay no attention to a treaty which he feels is now of no use to his kingdom.   (*Law of Nature*, viii. ix. 8)

In other words, the self-perceived interest of the state takes priority over commitments entered into by one's predecessors. It is certainly the case that in trying to accommodate self-interest with the universal standards of conduct expressed in the Natural Law, the ethical constraint often appears to be extremely weak, and even subordinate to the Reason of State.

In Pufendorf's historical writings the universal ethical content of the Natural Law is almost totally eclipsed by the principles of state necessity and state interest, so much so that Meinecke praises him as one of the great analysts of state interest and the Reason of State, dismissing his theoretical work as too abstract, divorced from history, and marred by a reliance upon Natural Law that obstructed the emergence of genuine insights about the special character of individual state formations.[61] Meinecke is wrong to distinguish so sharply between Pufendorf as a Natural Law philosopher and as a historical Realist. He criticizes Grotius for being grossly out of touch with the reality of state interest. 'International law and *raison d'état*', Meinecke argues, 'stand in natural opposition to one another.'[62] Pufendorf, in denying the existence of international law, provided the theoretical basis for the avoidance of imperfect obligations by states. Furthermore, Natural Law is itself a historically evolving body of rules consistent with the indubitable data of our existence, self-preservation, mutual dependence, and natural sociality. Pufendorf's philosophy is sensitive to the historical emergence of the state and the idea of sovereignty, trying to reconcile its duty to protect its citizens with the universal claims of humanity. Conceiving the state as a person inevitably generated its own logic of explanation and justification of international conduct. Like the individual in the state of nature, but in reality more self-sufficient, the state should regard others of its kind as friends who may presently become enemies. It should endeavour to live in peace, knowing that the Law of Nature is an inadequate constraint upon those determined to wreck it. The same may be said of the person of the state as is said of the individual: 'His vices render dealing with him risky and make great caution necessary to avoid evil from him instead of good' (*Duty*, i. 3. 4).

Rites of Passage

While there is a good deal of truth in the accusation that Pufendorf allowed the Hobbesian elements in his thought to submerge the Grotian,[63] we should not lose sight of the fact that he was a greater champion of the rights of non-Europeans than his predecessor Vitoria, his elder Grotius, or even his immediate contemporary Locke. In the name of humanity, dominion over the lands of the American Indians could be claimed on all sorts of pretexts. In asserting the rights of communities against universalist rights, Pufendorf represented a less partisan view of colonialism than Vitoria, Grotius, or Locke, who respectively represented the commercial and proprietorial interests of Spain, Holland, and England.

As we saw in Chapter 9, the Spanish conquest of the Americas brought to the fore among theologians, lawyers, and theorists the question by what right a foreign power could hold dominion over a territory it discovers and occupies. Vitoria recognizes a number of just claims to dominion which, even if not applicable in the Spanish case, can provide strong pretexts for the justification of colonization. The Law of Nations (*jus gentium*), which is, or is derived from, the Natural Law, allows unimpeded travel and communication on condition that harm is not perpetrated by the traveller. The traveller has a right to trade and enjoy those things that the indigenous peoples hold in common. Denial of these rights constitutes a just cause of war. Furthermore, Vitoria grants a right to spread the gospel, but not forcibly to impose it, as a result of which converts secure rights of protection which if violated constitute just causes of war. A just cause, of course, gives the injured party claims to dominion that he would not previously have been able to press.[64]

Both Vitoria and Grotius consider one such just cause to be intervention on behalf of the innocent against certain categories of crime in breach of the Natural Law. Tyrannical oppression of the innocent, human sacrifice, euthanasia, and cannibalism, for Vitoria, provide just causes for intervention in 'defence of our neighbours'.[65] Grotius's third criterion of just war is an extension of this principle. States have a right to punish excessive violations of the Natural Law, whether the injuries are perpetrated against themselves or against others with whom they have no direct involvement. The cannibals of the East Indies and the Americas, who for Grotius were little better than beasts, could justifiably be punished by Europeans.[66]

We have already seen how Grotius's theory of property generating title from a common use right and possession was designed to defend Dutch commercial and colonial aspirations. Possession of mobile or moveable property simply meant seizure, whereas fixed or immoveable property like land required the marking of boundaries, or construction.[67] Vacant land used only by hunters and gathers, that is, uncultivated land, remained common and available for appropriation.[68] To attain a permanent title to lands which were once occupied but now vacated Grotius, as we saw, used the example of a theatre seat which is held in common until occupied. When temporarily vacated it does not become vacant for another to take. Great tracts of land in the Americas were occupied by European monarchs on behalf of the whole community and were a legitimate possession if there was an intention to divide the land into private sections for cultivation. This was a justification of both English and Dutch practice, and legitimated claims that should be respected by other European monarchs.[69]

Pufendorf considerably restricts both the pretexts on which travellers may enter and enjoy the hospitality of foreign lands unimpeded and the just causes for which they may wage war against the inhabitants if the enjoyment of such rights under the Law of Nature is obstructed. The right of a stranger to expect hospitality is conditional upon the moral integrity of the stranger and the genuineness of his reasons for being away from home. Innocent but not over-curious travellers or guests and those forced to take refuge from storms on the high seas have a right to be treated humanely, and should they be attacked the state whose citizens have been harmed is justified in going to war, providing that the incidents are serious enough (*Law of Nature*, viii. vi. 5).

Pufendorf allows no automatic right to trade in goods that are not essential to life. He is very much a protectionist and not a free trader. Home industries may be protected against the competition of foreigners if profits are seriously affected or some other indirect harm is anticipated. Furthermore, one's own citizens may be favoured over foreigners by the imposition of tariffs, and valued items may be prevented from being exported if they are essential to the community. The grounds on which Vitoria allows Spanish subjugation of the Americans are all denied by Pufendorf. Fundamentally Vitoria's arguments rest upon universal rights which take priority over those of specific communities, the contravention of which justifiably legitimates intervention by a foreign state to restore the rights and punish the perpetrators of the wrong. Pufendorf, however, emphasizes the priority of the rights of the community, which as a moral person is capable of bearing such rights. No state that does not wish the same right of access and travel afforded to its own citizens is obligated by the Law of Nature to admit 'those who come to it unnecessarily and without good reason' (*Law of Nature*, iii. iii. 9). The state has a right to determine its own size and to consider the implications of an unrestricted influx of foreign settlers. Whereas it is humane to admit refugees forced from their homes,

The state should consider well beforehand, whether it is to its advantage for the number of its inhabitants to be greatly increased: whether its soil is fertile enough to support all of them well; whether we will not be too crowded if they are admitted; whether the band that seeks admittance is competent or incompetent; whether the arrivals can be so distributed and settled that no danger to the state will arise from them.   (*Law of Nature*, III. iii. 10; cf. *Elements*, I. def. v. 6)

The import of Pufendorf's arguments is that the American Indians are under no unconditional obligation to admit foreigners, and that to restrict access would not in itself constitute a just cause of war. In addition, the practices that Vitoria and Grotius found so abhorrent were not for Pufendorf grounds to subject their practitioners. Eating the flesh of members of their own religion is permissible. Eating that of strangers constitutes insufficient injury if 'those foreigners come to their shores as enemies and robbers'. Unjustifiable harm is inflicted only if 'those foreigners . . . come as innocent guests, or driven by storms' (*Law of Nature*, VIII. vi. 5).

Colonialism and Property Rights

Whereas Grotius's theory of property facilitated colonialism, Pufendorf's is far more restrictive. Both authors begin by suggesting that God gave the Earth to men in common. They did not own it collectively, but were granted a right to use it. This is what Pufendorf calls a negative community, as opposed to a positive community, in which property is communally owned (*Law of Nature*, IV. iv. 2).[70] It is the latter that Aristotle criticizes Plato for establishing among the Guardians. Because the things of the Earth are not infinite in supply, and use by one may prevent use by another, and because as the population increases competition for use increases, private property arises to prevent war (*Law of Nature*, IV. iv. 7).[71] It is for Pufendorf a moral quality which has no 'intrinsic effect upon things themselves, but only produces a moral effect in relation to other men' (*Law of Nature*, IV. iv. 1). Private property in so far as it is conducive to peace is consistent with nature, and although it is a human institution, it is nevertheless natural. Proprietorship develops historically in response to circumstances, and it is perfectly acceptable that elements of primitive community have been retained by 'backward peoples' (*Law of Nature*, IV. iv. 13).

For Grotius the use right gives users exclusive right over that which is used. No agreement as such is necessary, simply a sign of seizure or occupancy. Private property necessarily arises out of the original use right as communities become more complex. Agreements acknowledge what individuals have appropriated as their own.[72] Pufendorf, on the other hand, argues 'that dominion presupposes absolutely an act of man and an agreement, whether tacit or express' (*Law of Nature*, IV. iv. 4). In other words, use or occupancy does not in itself imply private ownership, nor is the fact that one has expended labour a title to property. As a moral quality, property requires agreement to create the moral effect of obligation. This agreement can be tacit or express. The original division of land among members of communities or nations required an express pact, alternatively,

Pufendorf suggests, agreements were made which allowed first occupancy of land not already designated to be a sign of ownership (*Law of Nature*, iv. iv. 9). In effect, then, tacit consent is deemed to acknowledge private ownership of those things which individuals take possession of, and which have not already been designated to someone in the original pact.

From the point of view of international relations, the important aspect of Pufendorf's theory of property, which serves considerably to restrict the grounds for colonial expansionism, is not private ownership, but his views on what he calls '*eminent domain*' and 'occupancy as a whole', or 'universal dominion' (*Law of Nature*, iv. vi. 4). The latter type of occupancy is quite different from the individual's title to property, in that it establishes the dominion of the whole group over all things in a particular territory. Whereas the ownership of the property of an individual may be transferred to a foreigner, 'universal dominion is preserved only in the state' (*Law of Nature*, iv. iv. 4). Here the state is clearly distinct from the person of the monarch, and those rights which are devolved to individuals within the universal domain are decided by the popular will (*Law of Nature*, iv. iv. 4), expressed presumably through the person of the state. The community, or state, as a whole has rights over property which no one outside it has, nor any individual distinct from his capacity as a member of that community. Eminent domain is the power that the whole community has over the property of its citizens, and constrains the use of private property within bounds consistent with the common good. Even the lands and other property of the Church fall within this domain and in cases of extreme necessity can be confiscated without compensation or restitution (*Elements*, i. def. v. 5).

Occupancy as a whole requires no signs of seizure or cultivation and, unlike Grotius, Pufendorf does not require that a clear intention to divide the land among individuals exist. Any land that appears to be unoccupied, and without a private owner 'should not at once be regarded as unoccupied and free to be taken by any man as his own, but it will be understood to belong to the whole people' (*Law of Nature*, iv. vi. 1). The community rights and eminent domain of which Pufendorf speaks are not restricted to states, but apply to societies as such. What this means is that even if one takes the American Indians to be living in a state of nature, as Grotius and Locke do, they must still be understood to exercise property rights of 'occupancy as a whole' and determine its use and distribution by title of eminent domain.

One of the fundamental problems of Pufendorf's theory legitimating community, private property, and the establishment of a plurality of states is his failure to explain how if property, or at least its initial distribution, requires agreement, anything less than the whole world community can authorize it. If all the world is given by God for the use of every individual in common, how and on what authority can small groups permanently appropriate portions, especially of immoveables like land, for common use? Only if this stage is legitimate can the further stage which serves to secure private property be justified, namely the creation of the state with universal dominion and eminent domain.

Notes

1. Samuel Pufendorf, *On the Duty of Man and Citizen According to the Natural Law* (1673), trans. W. A. Oldfather (Oxford, Clarendon Press, 1927); *The Elements of Universal Jurisprudence* (1658), trans. of the 1672 edn. by W. A. Oldfather (Oxford, Clarendon Press, 1931); *On the Law of Nature and Nations: Eight Books* (1672), trans. of the 1688 edn. by C. H. Oldfather and W. A. Oldfather (Oxford, Clarendon Press, 1934). *On the Duty of Man and Citizen*, a recent translation by James Tully, has been published by Cambridge University Press, 1991. *On the Natural State of Men*, first English translation (Michael Seidler), is published by Edwin Mellen Press, Lampeter, 1990. Both the recent translations are reviewed by F. Palladini, 'Translating Pufendorf', *History of Political Thought*, 16 (1995). *The Political Writings of Samuel Pufendorf* is edited by Craig L. Carr and translated by Michael J. Seidler and published by Oxford University Press, 1994. Of the secondary sources on classic international theory Andrew Linklater's *Men and Citizens in the Theory of International Relations*, 2nd edn. (London, Macmillan, 1990), is a notable exception in giving Pufendorf a prominent place. Charles Beitz devotes three pages to Pufendorf in his *Political Theory and International Relations* (Princeton, Princeton University Press, 1979).

2. See e.g. Howard P. Kainz (ed.), *Philosophical Perspectives on Peace* (London, Macmillan, 1987); John A. Vasquez (ed.), *Classics of International Relations*, 2nd edn. (Englewood Cliffs, NJ, Prentice Hall, 1990); Evan Luard (ed.), *Basic Texts in International Relations* (London, Macmillan, 1992); and Howard Williams, Moorhead Wright, and Tony Evans, eds., *A Reader in International Relations and Political Theory* (Buckingham, Open University Press, 1993).

3. See e.g. Michael Lessnoff (ed.), *Social Contract Theory* (Oxford, Blackwell, 1990); Stephen Buckle, *Natural Law and the Theory of Property: Grotius to Hume* (Oxford, Clarendon Press, 1991); Richard Tuck, *Natural Rights Theories: Their Origin and Development* (Cambridge, Cambridge University Press, 1979); and Robert Wokler, 'Rousseau's Pufendorf: Natural Law and the Foundations of Commercial Society', *History of Political Thought*, 15 (1994).

4. See e.g. Knud Haakonssen, 'Hugo Grotius and the History of Political Thought', *Political Theory*, 13 (1985); Knud Haakonssen, 'Natural Law and Moral Realism: The Scottish Synthesis', *Studies in the Philosophy of the Scottish Enlightenment* (Oxford, Clarendon Press, 1990); T. Mautner, 'Pufendorf and 18th Century Scottish Philosophy', in K. A. Modéer (ed.), *Samuel von Pufendorf 1632–1682* (Lund, Bloms Boktryckeri, 1986); and Peter Stein, 'From Pufendorf to Adam Smith: The Natural Law Tradition in Scotland', in *Europäisches Rechtsdenken in Geschichte und Gegenwart* (Munich, C. H. Beck, 1982).

5. John Locke, *Some Thoughts Concerning Education* (Cambridge, Cambridge University Press, 1902), 161; and Giambattista Vico, *The New Science*, 3rd edn., trans. Thomas Goddard Bergin and Max Harold Fisch (New York, Cornell University Press, 1968), §394, §493.

6. For Pufendorf's brief account of the importance of his predecessors see *Law of Nature*, preface, pp. v–vii. For a discussion of Pufendorf's much longer account in *Specimen controversiarum circa jus naturale ipsi nuper motarum* (1678), see Richard Tuck, 'The "Modern" Theory of Natural Law', in Anthony Pagden (ed.), *The Languages of Political Theory in Early-Modern Europe* (Cambridge, Cambridge University Press, 1987).

7. Gunther E. Rothenberg, 'Maurice of Nassau, Gustavus Adolphus, Raimondo

Montecuccoli and the "Military Revolution" of the Seventeenth Century', in Peter Paret (ed.), *Makers of Modern Strategy from Machiavelli to the Nuclear Age* (Princeton, Princeton University Press, 1986).

8. Kalevi J. Holsti, *Peace and War: Armed Conflicts and International Order 1648–1989* (Cambridge, Cambridge University Press, 1991), 28–9.

9. J. L. Holzgrefe, 'The Origins of Modern International Relations Theory', *Review of International Studies*, 15 (1989).

10. Quentin Skinner, 'The State', in T. Ball, J. Farr, and R. L. Hanson (eds.), *Political Innovation and Conceptual Change* (Cambridge, Cambridge University Press, 1989).

11. See Adam Watson, *The Evolution of International Society* (London, Routledge, 1992), 182–97.

12. Evan Luard, *International Society* (London, Macmillan, 1990), 96.

13. Holsti, *Peace and War*, 47.

14. James Tully, 'Introduction', in Samuel Pufendorf, *On the Duty of Man and Citizen*, trans. and ed. James Tully (Cambridge, Cambridge University Press, 1991), p. xx.

15. Stein, 'From Pufendorf to Adam Smith', 667.

16. See C. Phillipson, 'Samuel Pufendorf', in J. MacDonell and E. Manson (eds.), *Great Jurists of the World* (New York, Kelley, 1968; first pub. 1914), 317.

17. Cf. Buckle, *Natural Law and the Theory of Property*, 62–3.

18. Istvan Hont, 'The Language of Sociality and Commerce: Samuel Pufendorf and the Theoretical Foundations of the "Four-Stages Theory"', in Anthony Pagden (ed.), *The Languages of Political Theory in Early-Modern Europe* (Cambridge, Cambridge University Press, 1987), 256–7.

19. J. B. Schneewind, 'Pufendorf's Place in the History of Ethics', *Synthese*, 72 (1987), 134–5.

20. James Tully, *A Discourse on Property: John Locke and his Adversaries* (Cambridge, Cambridge University Press, 1980), 73.

21. Tuck, 'The "Modern" Theory of Natural Law', 105; Pufendorf, *Elements*, ob. III. i.

22. Pufendorf says 'That each should be zealous so to preserve himself, that society among men be not disturbed'. He was later to give a much more active role to the individual for promoting society.

23. Tully, *A Discourse on Property*, 86.

24. Also see Alfred Dutour, 'Pufendorf', in J. H. Burns and Mark Goldie (eds.), *The Cambridge History of Political Thought 1450–1700* (Cambridge, Cambridge University Press, 1988), 268.

25. Cf. Tully, *A Discourse on Property*, 86.

26. Tuck, *Natural Rights Theories*, 160–3.

27. For a convincing refutation of Tuck see Thomas Mautner, 'Pufendorf's Place in the History of Rights Concepts', in Timothy O'Hagan (ed.), *Revolution and Enlightenment in Europe* (Aberdeen, Aberdeen University Press, 1991), 13–22. Also see Buckle, *Natural Law and the Theory of Property*, 80.

28. For an interesting discussion of the foundation of political society in Pufendorf's theory see Leonard Krieger, *The Politics of Discretion* (London, University of Chicago Press, 1965), 117–32.

29. Krieger, *Politics of Discretion*, 105.

30. Cf. Linklater, *Men and Citizens*, 62–3.

31. Haakonssen, 'Hugo Grotius and the History of Political Thought', 256.

32. Onora O'Neill, *Towards Justice and Virtue: A Constructive Account of Practical Reasoning* (Cambridge, Cambridge University Press, 1996), 145.

33. Pufendorf argues that 'states could never have been formed, and when once formed could not have been preserved, had not some idea of justice or injustice existed before that time. For it is certain that pacts intervened in the establishment of states. Yet how could men have been able to persuade themselves that pacts were of any use at that time, had they not known beforehand that it was just to observe pacts and unjust to break them?' (*Law of Nature*, VIII. i. 5). Also see Michael Nutkiewicz, 'Samuel Pufendorf: Obligation as the Basis of the State', *Journal of the History of Philosophy*, 21 (1983), 15–29.
34. 'the real and principal reason why the fathers of families left their natural liberty and undertook to establish states, was in order that they could surround themselves with defences against the evils which threaten man from his fellow man' (*Law of Nature*, VII. i. 7).
35. Cf. Linklater, *Men and Citizens*, 66–8.
36. Krieger, *Politics of Discretion*, 120–1.
37. See Ernest Barker (ed.), *The Social Contract* (Oxford, Clarendon Press, 1961), introduction; Otto Gierke, *Natural Law and the Theory of Society 1500 to 1800*, trans. and introd. by Ernest Barker (Cambridge, Cambridge University Press, 1934); J. W. Gough, *The Social Contract* (Oxford, Clarendon Press, 1957), 43–8; and, Michael Oakeshott, *On Human Conduct* (Oxford, Clarendon Press, 1975), essay III.
38. Peter Pavel Remec, *The Position of the Individual in International Law According to Grotius and Vattel* (The Hague, Nijhoff, 1960).
39. Thomas Hobbes, *Leviathan, or the Matter, Forme, & Power of a COMMON-WEALTH*, ed. C. B. Macpherson (Harmondsworth, Penguin, 1981), 81 and 220.
40. To view the state as a moral person became a commonplace among writers on international relations. Thomas Reid, for example, combining elements of Grotius, Pufendorf, and Vattel in his theory of international relations, argues that 'A Nation incorporated and united into one Political Body becomes by this Union and Incorporation a Moral Person. It has a public Interest and good which it ought to pursue as every private man pursues his own private good. It has an Understanding and Will . . .' (Thomas Reid, *Practical Ethics: Being Lectures and Papers on Natural Religion, Self-Government, Natural Jurisprudence, and the Law of Nations*, ed. Knud Haakonssen (Princeton, Princeton University Press, 1990), 254). Haakonssen's commentary is excellent in providing useful cross-references, particularly with Vattel.
41. For an excellent discussion of Pufendorf's doctrine of sovereignty see Dufour, 'Pufendorf', 574–9.
42. See Krieger, *Politics of Discretion*, 143–4.
43. See David Boucher, 'Reconciling Ethics and Interests in the Person of the State: The International Dimension', in Paul Keal (ed.), *Ethics and Foreign Policy* (Sydney, Allen and Unwin, 1992), 44–65.
44. Robert L. Holmes, 'Can War be Morally Justified? Just War Theory', in Jean Bethke Elshtain (ed.), *Just War Theory* (Oxford, Blackwell, 1992), 202.
45. See C. A. J. Coady, 'The Problem of Intervention', in Paul Keal (ed.), *Ethics and Foreign Policy* (Sydney, Allen and Unwin, 1992), 72.
46. Pufendorf argues that 'An exact knowledge of the natural state can suggest to leaders of states many things concerning a state's external and internal affairs whose observance is extremely necessary' (*Natural State of Men*, #19).
47. See Mary Midgley, *Natural Law* (London, Elek, 1975), 173.
48. The author of the introduction to *The Elements*, Hans Wehberg, writes in relation to international law that Pufendorf's 'heart did not glow with enthusiasm for the greatness of the idea' (p. xxiii).

49. It was nevertheless an important question for Christians, and reference to the justifications of Augustine and Aquinas were often made. For example, Vitoria appeals, in addition, to Natural and Mosaic Law, to the 'example of saints and good men', and emphasizes the necessity for retaliating against tyrants and robbers (Francisco de Vitoria, *Political Writings*, ed. Anthony Pagden and Jeremy Lawrence (Cambridge, Cambridge University Press, 1991), 297–8).

50. William Paley, *Moral and Political Philosophy*, in *The Works of Dr Paley*, ii (London, George Cowie, 1837), 100–1.

51. The term is used by Holmes, 'Can War be Morally Justified?', 223.

52. Vitoria, *Political Writings*, 316.

53. Vitoria, *Political Writings*, 316–17

54. Hugo Grotius, *The Rights of War and Peace*, trans. A. C. Campbell (Westport, Va., Hyperion, 1993; edn. first pub. 1901), ii. 10, xliii.

55. Grotius, *Rights of War and Peace*, iii. 6, i.

56. Vitoria, *Political Writings*, 302–3 and n 17. Also see Skinner, *The Foundations of Modern Political Thought*, vol. ii. 152–3.

57. Holzgrefe, 'Origins of Modern International Relations Theory', 16.

58. Pufendorf argues that 'One who has never thought about the misery of that natural state bears the burdens which rulers impose on citizens with ill will, as if they were superfluous and contrived either to annoy the people or merely to nourish the ruler's ambition and extravagance. In contrast, someone who has correctly estimated the matter admits that it is no more suitable to complain about such burdens than about the price of clothes or shoes by which the body is protected against severe weather and injuries'. *Natural State of Men*, #23.

59. Pufendorf's position is also markedly contrary to Vitoria, who argues that 'if their conscience tells subjects that the war is unjust, *they must not* go to war even if their conscience is wrong, for "whatsoever is not of faith is sin" (Rom. 14: 23)' (Vitoria, *Political Writings*, 308).

60. Holzgrefe, 'Origins of Modern International Relations Theory', 19.

61. Friedrich Meinecke, *Machiavellism: The Doctrine of Raison d'État and its Place in Modern History* (London, Routledge, 1962; first pub. 1924), 230.

62. Meinecke, *Machiavellism*, 208.

63. Linklater, *Men and Citizens*, 73.

64. Vitoria, 'On the American Indians', in *Political Writings*, 231–92.

65. Vitoria, 'On the Evangelization of Unbelievers', in *Political Writings*, 347. Cf. 'On the American Indians', in *Political Writings*, 287–8.

66. Grotius, *Rights of War and Peace*, ii. 20. xl.

67. Tuck, *Natural Rights Theories*, 61–2.

68. Grotius, *Rights of War and Peace*, ii. 2. iv.

69. Barbara Arneil, 'John Locke, Natural Law, and Colonialism', *History of Political Thought*, 13 (1992), 589 and 593.

70. Arneil argues that Grotius postulates a positive community and thus common ownership of the Earth. My own reading accords with that of Stephen Buckle. See Arneil, 'John Locke, Natural Law and Colonialism', 597; Buckle, *Natural Law and the Theory of Property*, 36–7. It is significant that Pufendorf took Grotius to be describing a negative community.

71. See also Grotius, *Rights of War and Peace*, ii. 2. i.

72. See Tuck, *Natural Rights Theories*, 61; Arneil, 'John Locke, Natural Law, and Colonialism', 598; and Buckle, *Natural Law and the Theory of Property*, 42–3.

11

INTERNATIONAL AND COSMOPOLITAN
SOCIETIES: LOCKE, VATTEL, AND KANT

Property and Colonization: John Locke and Emer Vattel

It was Pufendorf's immediate contemporary John Locke—born in the same year (1632)—who offered a solution to the dilemma of how, if the whole world is given to mankind in common, individual property rights can arise without the consent of the whole. It was a solution that legitimated the appropriation of foreign lands that had not yet come under cultivation. His political theory also undermined the absolutist doctrines of sovereignty propounded by Grotius, Hobbes, and Pufendorf. Whereas Pufendorf acknowledged that states had imperfect rights and duties in relation to each other under the terms of Natural Law, he did not attempt systematically to elaborate upon them. Vattel, drawing inspiration from Christian von Wolff, wanted to show that the Law of Nations is in fact a modification of Natural Law, which took into account the different character of the moral person of the state from that of the individual. He distinguished the Law of Nations into the *necessary*, which binds the conscience of sovereigns, and the *voluntary* or positive which rests on the will of the sovereign and accommodates the practical and prudential considerations which have to be acknowledged in order to mitigate the effects of war.

Locke's theory incorporates the New World into his philosophical perspective, offering a justification for the appropriation of foreign lands based upon individual property rights. Locke follows Hobbes and Pufendorf, rather than Grotius, in identifying the Law of Nature with the Law of Nations (*Two Treatises*, ii. 276, §14).[1] Locke believed that the human condition was naturally social, and that God gave the Earth to men in common. Agreement, or consent, was not however necessary to create private property. If it were, Locke argues, private property would be contrary to God's intention. Private property existed in the state of nature from the outset in that every person had a property in himself over which no one, because of the principle of natural equality, could exercise dominion without consent. God wills that we sustain and protect this property in ourselves by cultivating and appropriating the things of nature. The use of the gifts of nature requires that we first take possession of those things. We do so by means of an instrument which inheres in the person, labour. It is labour, and not consent, which creates property in things: 'The *labour* that was mine, removing them out of that common state they were in, hath *fixed* my *Property* in them' (*Two Treatises*, II, 289, §28).

Locke does not allow unlimited accumulation of property in the state of nature. Individuals can appropriate without consent only so much as they can use. The principle of spoilage limits accumulation. It would be a sin to take goods out of the common sphere and allow them to perish (*Two Treatises*, II. 290, §31). The principle applies both to the produce of the Earth and to the accumulation of land. It is with the invention of money, by agreement to endow with exchange value that which is intrinsically valueless, that the unlimited accumulation of wealth is facilitated. In other words, whereas property does not rest upon consent, the 'disproportionate and unequal Possession of the Earth' does (*Two Treatises*, II. 302, §50).

The state of nature, although primitive, is populated by people who have a sense of justice and injustice. Each has executive power in enforcing the moral code of the Law of Nature. God has granted us life, a property in the person, and we have an obligation to preserve it, and as far as we can to preserve the life of others. Preservation of property in the person is enhanced by the efficient use of the resources of the Earth. We are also, therefore, under an obligation to God to make the land and all that lives and grows on it as productive as possible. The obligations to God are better discharged within a political society. The inconveniences of the state of nature, a law that is not written down, and wilful and innocent misinterpretation of the law with no common superior to arbitrate and no power to enforce it make it imperative by agreement to set up political society and government. Locke did not believe, however, that appropriated land should be allowed to lie waste (*Two Treatises*, II. 294 and 297, §§37 and 42). The accumulation of vast tracts of land if uncultivated was an offence against the Law of Nature. In this respect Locke shared the concern of many supporters and administrators of colonialism, who were concerned that the accumulation of land be limited to that which had suffici_.1t men to cultivate it.

It is not without significance that the American Indians are constantly invoked as examples of people currently living in a state of nature and subject to the principle of spoilage in the accumulation of property, slightly modified in some instances by a primitive form of money. England's war against the Dutch was becoming increasingly difficult to finance after the Great Plague of 1665 and the Fire of London of 1666. For some political commentators colonialism was seen to be the way out of financial difficulties, while for the majority it appeared to exacerbate them. Plantations in particular were seen to be a significant drain. Locke had a direct involvement with colonialism through his patron Lord Shaftesbury, and both were responsible for justifying the settlement of Carolina against the charge that such a policy would enfeeble England. Locke's knowledge of America was in fact extensive. He read books on its exploration and discovery, had investments there, and was practically involved with the administration of aspects of its affairs.[2] He believed that a properly managed colonial policy in America would be the key to England's economic success.[3]

The implication of Locke's discussions of the American Indians is that they fall short of adequately discharging their obligations to God. They still live in a state of nature and they fail to add to the common stock of mankind by improving the productivity of the land. In so doing they have no claim on vast territories in the Americas that '*lie waste*'. By this Locke means more than land which is simply left barren. Land that is not efficiently utilized, and whose produce is allowed to rot, regardless of its being enclosed, is 'still to be looked on as Waste, and might be the Possession of any other' (*Two Treatises*, ii. 295, §38). The lands of the more civilized peoples of the world are protected first by governments which are instituted for that purpose and which regulate use, and secondly by agreements among states that explicitly or tacitly renounce claims to the lands of the others. It is by mutual consent that states give up the common Natural Right which they originally had and establish territorial boundaries in the division of the Earth into 'distinct Parts and parcels'. Those primitive societies that have not taken their place among the civilized society of states are therefore not protected against peoples who settle, mix their labour, and make the land their own, because that land is still the common possession of mankind. Locke's intention to legitimate colonialism, while establishing the principle of European territorial integrity, is clear from the following passage:

there are still *great Tracts of Ground* to be found, which (the Inhabitants thereof not having joyned with the rest of Mankind, in the consent of the use of their common Money) *lie waste*, and are more than the People, who dwell on it, do, or can make use of, and so still lie in common. Tho' this can scarce happen amongst that part of Mankind, that have consented to the Use of Money. (*Two Treatises*, ii. 299, §45)

Locke, then, is a defender of colonial expansionism and justifies it with a theory of property that requires mixing one's labour, or that of one's employees, to create a title to specific tracts of land, or produce, that are otherwise considered vacant and open to all mankind in common. However, his theory does not legitimate colonialism if the inhabitants of occupied territories with a claim to the land are subdued by unjustifiable force. The use of force without right cannot legitimate conquest. Agreements reached under duress are void and incur no obligation. This position is very different from that of Hobbes, who might pronounce the unnecessary use of force dishonourable, but would have no grounds in international relations upon which to pronounce force unjust.

Both individuals and states are the subjects of the Law of Nations. Vattel (1714–67), writing almost a century later, reflects the extent to which the state had by the middle of the eighteenth century become the central actor in international relations. Vattel thought Natural Law the basis of the Law of Nations, but he did not identify the two (*Law of Nations*, 3a and 4).[4] Individuals were for him the subjects of Natural Law having rights and obligations in relation to each other. States, however, were different from individuals, and although related to each other in a condition analogous to the state of nature, the Laws of Nature had to be transformed into the Law of Nations. Like Pufendorf and Christian von Wolff (1679–1754), his own mentor, he contended that states were themselves corporate moral persons with rights and duties different from those of individual persons, and that as the creation of the individuals who comprise them they exercise on their behalf the duties that those individuals have to mankind as whole.[5] The state differs from an ordinary individual in that its decisions are not often the result of the whims of one man or of the rashness of the moment, but are based instead upon consultation and deliberation (*Law of Nations*, preface, 10a). Vattel contends that the state has 'an understanding and a will peculiar to itself' (*Law of Nations*, introduction, §2).

Because of the centrality of the sovereign state in Vattel's theory, his justification of the appropriation of the lands of North America is therefore subtly different from that of Locke. Vattel argues that God placed the Earth at the disposal of the human race for their habitation and subsistence. At first the population would have been so small as to permit tribes to live by hunting and gathering without the necessity of cultivation and the need for deviating from common ownership. As the population grew, nomadic tribes settled on territories in order by cultivation to increase the yield of the land and to avoid encroachments by others. The territories that these nations inhabited became by right their exclusive property. Scarcity and the need to increase the yield of the land by cultivation are therefore the origin of property. The right of a nation to such territory entails both ownership and sovereignty. Such rights, however, depend upon the efficient use of land, the cultivation of which is 'an obligation imposed upon man by nature' (*Law of Nations*, 37, §81), and those peoples who persist in refraining from cultivation do not have the same rights as those that do cultivate the land. Nations that do not encourage and promote the cultivation of the land are not fulfilling their obligations under the Law of Nations. In effect the lands of such people are still the common property of mankind, and all nations have an equal right to claim them by first possession. Nations have a right to occupy such territory 'so far as they can make use of it' (*Law of Nations*, 85, §209). In other words, first sighting or mere appropriation is not an adequate title. The peoples of North America, he argues, do not so much inhabit vast tracts of land as roam over them, and they have no grounds for complaint if the more industrious nations occupy part of their land and subject it to 'honest labour' (*Law of Nations*, 38, §81). To 'restrict the savages' within narrower boundaries is in fact in accordance with nature's intentions because their small numbers in North America make it impossible for them to populate and cultivate the whole country (*Law of Nations*, 85, §209).

Vattel does nevertheless think the seizing of territories from the civilized nations of Central and South America of dubious legality (*Law of Nations*, 37, §81) and praises the English Puritans of New England and Quakers of Pennsylvania for their moderation in purchasing lands from the American savages (*Law of Nations*, 85, §209). Vattel's justification of the appropriation of foreign unpossessed lands was based not on individual right, but upon the argument that it was contrary to nature to allow land to go uncultivated if it was needed to sustain the world's vastly increased population. Without agricultural communities the world could not sustain its population, and therefore agricultural communities had a right to occupy and work land that was not effectively being exploited by others.[6]

Just War: Locke and Vattel

Like Vitoria, Grotius, and Pufendorf, Vattel did not believe that conquest or the usurpations of property (*Law of Nations*, II. i, §5) or religious differences were a just cause of war. European nations which subjected the American Indians to avaricious rule on the pretext of teaching the true religion and civilizing them based their claim upon unjust and ridiculous grounds. Vattel thought, however, that allowing a right of intervention, as Vitoria, Grotius, and Pufendorf did to punish inhumane crimes against the Natural Law, provided too readily a pretext for zealots and brigands of all sorts to subject peoples of foreign lands. An individual in the state of nature or a nation has a right to punish only when the question of safety arises and when injury is done or threatened. In this respect, when no injury is received no right of punishment exists in matters that are not the concern of an outside state (*Law of Nations*, II. i. §7, and III. iii. §41). A nation has a humanitarian duty to provide assistance to those nations in need, but the prospective host nation has to be judge of the need and of whether it wishes to accept the assistance. In general a nation has no right to intervene in the affairs of another sovereign nation, because each is deemed an autonomous and independent moral person. When a nation is being torn apart by civil war, however, other considerations apply. Here Vattel allows the right of intervention to assist the party that has right on its side.[7] The intervention is not, however, motivated by justice, but by self-preservation.[8]

Unlike Hobbes, Locke falls squarely into the just war tradition with Grotius and Pufendorf, and he deviates from all three in the extent to which he denounces absolute government. Like Grotius, Hobbes, and Pufendorf, he employed the idea of a social contract, but he came to quite a different conclusion. Locke established the right to resistance by grounding it in a just war theory. His just war theory is the basis of justifying not only wars between states, but also the legitimate resistance of the use of arbitrary power within the state. The state of nature is a condition of natural equality regulated by the Law of Nature, with each individual possessing executive authority to call to account those who offend against it. It is the absence of a common authoritative judge which characterizes it as a state of nature. Unlike Hobbes, then, Locke takes the position of Grotius and Pufendorf in identifying the state of war as quite distinct from the state of nature. Whereas the latter has a propensity to generate the former, they are not equivalents. For Hobbes the state of nature and the state of war are identical because the latter is not characterized by physical force alone, but by a common disposition to use force. For Locke, '*Force without Right, upon a Man's Person, makes a state of War*, both where there is, and is not, a common Judge' (*Two Treatises*, II. 281, §19). Only where there is no common superior does the right of war reside in the individual. Even though the Law of Nature is not positive law, it gives rise to a juridical condition. Like Grotius, Locke describes the use of war as a punishment against offenders, to right either the wrong done against oneself or that against others. Reparations, however, are due only to the injured party (*Two Treatises*, II. 273, §11). Richard Cox suggests that here we have the doctrine of collective security in nascent form.[9]

Like Pufendorf, Locke reflects the greater centralization of military and political power during the seventeenth century by restricting the right of war to the sovereign authority within the state (*Two Treatises*, I. 238, §§131–2). How, then, can he justify resistance against the sovereign as the invocation of the right of war?

Although Locke does not go as far as Pufendorf, or his successors Wolff and Vattel, in suggesting that the state is a moral person with rights and duties peculiar to itself, he does, like Hobbes, resort to the analogy of the person of the state. We have already seen that Locke's theory of property was meant not only to legitimate individual appropriation but also to minimize the risk of war. It also legitimates the division of the world into territorial or state entities. A system of states is for Locke a natural consequence of his theory of property. Once an individual contracts to become part of political society, the state acts on his behalf in relation to all other individuals and states outside itself. In this respect the state, in addition to its political authority, has in relation to other states and individuals the natural power that everyone has in the state of nature (*Two Treatises*, II. 365, §§145–6). This renders the state of nature a permanent condition because as far as Locke is concerned states are the natural actors in the world and have no common superior to which to appeal. A use of force without right by one state upon another constitutes a state of war. Locke extends this argument to include the relationship between the sovereign authority and its own people.

Arbitrary government was the great fear of seventeenth-century England, and it seemed to Locke that both Charles II and James II were subverting the legal system by using it as a political weapon against the former opponents of the crown in the civil war.[10] Any magistrate acting *ultra vires* is effectively using force without right and ceases to retain the majesty of office. In other words, there is no common superior to which to appeal, and all parties revert to the state of nature in which the right of war can be invoked against the aggressor. The illegitimate use of force without right by a sovereign or a magistrate reintroduces the condition of natural equality that 'cancels all former relations of Reverence, Respect and Superiority' (*Two Treatises*, II. 422, §235). Vattel, like Locke, is a contract theorist. The contract establishes civil society, and the people choose by majority vote the type of government that suits their circumstances. He concurs with Locke in allowing to the people a right of resistance against those sovereign authorities which unlawfully abuse their powers.[11]

It has been suggested that Vattel's theory of international relations is merely a disguised form of utilitarianism, with elements of moralism which amount to nothing more than a 'precious sentimentalism'.[12] While the idea of self-preservation is central to his thesis, we must not lose sight of the additional element of self-perfection which mitigates against a crude utilitarian ethic because it entails a conception of the individual at odds with it. When Vattel suggests that the nation has a duty to place its own interests above those of other nations, and to do whatever it can to promote its own happiness and advancement, he does not mean it in any crude utilitarian way. He explains that 'I say whatever it *can* do, not meaning *physically* only, but *morally* also, what it can do lawfully, justly, and honestly' (*Law of Nations*, introduction, 6, §14; cf. I, §18). Even though Vattel considers prudence a virtue for sovereigns, he contends that it can never 'counsel the use of unlawful means in order to obtain a just and praise-worthy end'. Pufendorf explicitly denies the Realist claim that the welfare of the people must be the supreme law of the state. Vattel contends that 'we must hold as a sacred principle that the end does not justify the means' (*Law of Nations*, III. iii, §§43). The common good of one's own people and the good of the great society of nations depend upon the rejection of means that are unjust and dishonourable. As Andrew Linklater has suggested, Vattel is not a theorist who presses self-interest above all else. He does not suggest that a nation will not act without a view to some reciprocal benefit. What Vattel is more concerned with is the rigidity of an objective moral law being used to crush the liberty of conscience of each nation.[13]

The Equality of Nations

Pufendorf, Locke, Wolff, and Vattel in their different ways strengthen the inviolable nature of the state as an actor in international relations. Like Hobbes, they believe that individuals are free and equal in the state of nature, but unlike Hobbes they speak of a natural equality which is not physical or mental. It is a moral equality in so far as their obligations and rights are the same. States, being moral, and not artificial, persons related to each other as individuals, are in the state of nature similarly equal. Powerful nations do not have rights against small ones which small ones do not equally possess against them. Pufendorf, for example, contends that 'whatever right anyone asserts against another is appropriately enjoyed by the latter as well'.[14] For Vattel, just as a dwarf and giant are equally men, small and large republics are equally sovereign states (*Law of Nations*, introduction, §18). Might or force is not the basis of the right in the state of nature between either individuals or nations. Wolff argues, for example, that while a nation has a duty to develop its strength in order to fulfil its purpose of providing security for the persons who comprise it, it 'may not subject to its control by force of arms simply for the sake of increasing its own power'.[15] A wrong must be done or threatened before a just cause for war permits the subjection of another nation. In other words, right and might are not correlative. Wolff contends that 'Just as might is not the source of the Law of Nature, so that any one may do what he can to another, so neither is the might of nations the source of the Law of Nations, so that right is to be measured by might'.[16] While the principles of self-preservation and self-development may at times appear to postulate a utilitarian ethic, the moral foundations of their theories are in principle constraints which if deviated from impel the transgressor to give moral justifications for his actions.

Moral principles, like democratic constitutions, do not guarantee good practice; only when these principles are internalized and animate the actions of the state do they provide genuine constraints. In other words, a moral community is based upon mutual respect and a commitment to civilized behaviour which is as much internally generated as externally enforced; a sense of conscience is a prerequisite of discharging one's moral obligations to oneself and to others. As Vattel suggests, nations should not feel free to do whatever can be done with impunity, when it is contrary to the 'immutable laws of justice and the voice of conscience' (*Law of Nations*, preface, 10a).

A right, for Vattel, is the power to do what morality prescribes, that is, what is good in itself and in conformity with duty. Individuals in the state of nature are free and independent, and as with Locke, their consent is required if they are to be subjected to authority. Nations or states remain free and independent in the international state of nature unless they have voluntarily subjected themselves. As free and independent moral persons, nations are at liberty to make their own decisions about what their consciences demand in the fulfilment of their duties to other nations, without at the same time failing to discharge their duties to themselves. The obligations which individuals owe to humanity become the responsibility of the state of which they are citizens.

Following Leibniz and Wolff, Vattel makes a distinction between internal and external, and between perfect and imperfect rights and the corresponding obligations to which they give rise. An *internal* obligation is one which we are bound by conscience to honour and which has been deduced from rules regarding our duty. Obligations are *external* when viewed relative to other individuals who acquire rights as a result of our obligations. These external obligations and rights are either *perfect* or *imperfect*. Perfect rights are those whose corresponding obligations are perfect when they can be compelled or enforced, whereas imperfect obligations cannot. A right is imperfect when its corresponding obligation rests upon the conscience of the person obliged. Freedom entails the right to make judgements about what one's obligations are. Strictly speaking, then, there are no perfect external rights and obligations in the state of nature until agreements are made to create them, and in doing so that state is modified.[17] Nations, being free and equal, have a right to do what they wish as long as they are under internal obligations with no external perfect obligations entailed, and as long as they do not infringe the perfect rights of other states. Perfect rights and obligations among nations can only be created by agreement, and these, Vattel indicates, are limited in scope.

Vattel on Natural Law and the Law of Nations

Vattel is concerned to establish the point that the Law of Nations does not rest upon the consent of individual nations in order to impress upon sovereign states that the origin of their rights and duties is more fundamental and morally obliga-tory. In this respect Vattel wishes to dispel any confusion over those practices which are good and obligatory in themselves, and those which of necessity are merely tolerated (*Law of Nations*, preface, 11a). The Law of Nations, he argues, is in fact the application of the Law of Nature to the moral persons of states in their mutual relations (*Law of Nations*, preface, 3a). Like Wolff, Vattel distinguishes the Law of Nations into the *necessary* and *voluntary*. The necessary law, derived immediately from nature, binds the consciences of individuals and nations alike and must be observed in their personal conduct. It is necessary because its obli-gations are absolutely binding upon one's conscience. In this respect it is *internal* and consistent with the idea of a Universal Moral Order as I have characterized it. This law is not subject to change or alteration by human design, nor can individ-uals and states release themselves from its obligations (*Law of Nations*, preface, §§6–9).

Whereas one state may have a perfect right in conscience, the obligation to which it gives rise in another state is imperfect because that state has the right to judge for itself what its obligations are, and whether it can discharge them with-out detriment to itself. It is only by means of the consent of states that imperfect obligations can be transformed into perfect enforceable obligations.[18] The neces-sary law 'recommends the observance' of the voluntary Law of Nations in that the voluntary law's obligatory precepts are conducive to the common good and welfare of nations in their mutual relations (*Law of Nations*, preface, 11a). The voluntary Law of Nations does result from the will of sovereigns and is effectively positive international law. The source of both the necessary and the 268 voluntary Law of Nations is in the Law of Nature. Nations by will or consent may also give rise to the *arbitrary* Law of Nations. Agreements, treaties, and promises establish the *conventional* Law of Nations, which is binding upon the contracting parties, whereas the tacit consent implied in the subscription to common prac-tices establishes *custom* which must be observed by those nations which have accepted the principles t, 'long usage'. The obligatory nature of the arbitrary Law of Nations is nevertheless grounded in the binding force that the Law of Nature gives to the honouring of express and tacit promises. The necessary Law of Nations acts as a criterion in terms of which treaties and conventions may be judged lawful or unlawful, and customs just or unjust.

At the root of Vattel's necessary Law of Nations stands the crucial idea that nature has established a universal society among all mankind, and that the indi-vidual's limited attributes are convincing proof of nature's intention that we ren-der each other mutual assistance. Agreements to establish communities or nations are consistent with our natural interdependence, and therefore nature established the great society of nations, which similarly requires mutual assist-ance.[19] Like Pufendorf, Vattel denies that nations are as vulnerable as individuals; nations are therefore more self-sufficient. For this reason nations do not need to constitute themselves into a civil society.[20] Human society depends upon justice, without which the mutual assistance and respect afforded each other would become nothing more than 'a vast system of robbery' (*Law of Nations*, II. v, §63).

Because of the horrific consequences of war it is even more imperative that justice be observed among nations.

Vattel praises Cicero for acknowledging that the duties of the individual do not cease at state boundaries, and that the duties of nations are prescribed by the Law of Nature (*Law of Nations*, II. 1, §1). The human race, Vattel contends, constitutes a universal society whose interests and duties all men are bound to advance. Our common humanity obliges us to render mutual assistance to those in need. Our obligations are based upon a common human nature and therefore cannot be denied on grounds of religious differences. Vattel believes that we are naturally social because by nature we are not self-sufficient and depend upon others for protection and welfare. Agreements made among a limited number of individuals do not override these obligations to humanity, the difference being that they are now to be discharged by the state to which they have submitted their wills and given up their rights in order to advance the common good (*Law of Nations*, introduction, §11).

The state is obliged to discharge its duties to humanity provided that in doing so it does not neglect its duties to itself. It should, for example, come to the aid of a neighbouring state when it is being threatened by an enemy. Such action promotes the principle of mutual assistance and is at once an act of statecraft, as well as the fulfilment of one's duties and obligations. The state should not limit itself to the preservation of other states, but should also actively 'contribute to their advancement according to its ability and their need of help' (*Law of Nations*, II. i, §6). The Law of Nature when translated into the Law of Nations takes account of the fact that nations are more self-sufficient than individuals and less in need of frequent mutual assistance. Furthermore a good deal more circumspection is exercised by the state than by an individual in its assistance to other states because of the greater danger to its safety.

Vattel is not so naïve as to think that the ideals of humanity are not often ridiculed and departed from by statesmen, but to abandon the hope of impressing upon them their n..oral responsibilities 'would be to despair of human nature' (*Law of Nations*, II. i, §1). Ideally if humanity discharged its obligations we would all be citizens in a universal republic. Human nature is not, however, pure, and is corrupted by 'inordinate passions and mistaken self-interest' (*Law of Nations*, II. i, §16). Sad experience shows that the majority of nations have sought to strengthen themselves at the expense of other nations and have tried to dominate when the opportunity arose. Those who are good are under no obligation to make themselves the prey of the wicked. Thus the duty to assist the development of fellow nations may be mitigated by the duty towards oneself if a nation is perceived as an enemy or a potential threat. Nations are morally equal members of the great society of nations, and their obligations are imperfect. Each state has a perfect right to request of another that it fulfil its obligations under the Law of Nations, but that state judges for itself whether it is obliged and whether it is capable of fulfilling its obligations without detriment to itself (*Law of Nations*, II. i, §2). A denial of, or refusal to fulfil, the obligation has to be accepted by the requesting state because there is no independent authority to adjudicate the rival claims.

Vattel suggests that the great society of states depends upon the good faith of nations in their relations. Treaties are therefore sacred, and their breach is a violation of the Law of Nature (*Law of Nations*, II. xv, §§219–21). An injury occasioned by a treaty is not sufficient grounds to withdraw from it, because to allow such a vague plea to invalidate a treaty would jeopardize the whole system of treaties (*Law of Nations*, II. xii, §158). Nevertheless the requirement that a state protects and perfects itself led Vattel considerably to weaken his position. Simple injuries and inconveniences could not be used as a pretext to invalidate treaties, but pernicious effects could (*Law of Nations*, II. xii, §160).

The society of states of which Vattel speaks is a considerably weaker moral entity than the *civitas maxima* of his mentor Wolff. He did nevertheless recognize the efficacy of collective action in the interests of the whole. The collective will of nations could be imposed on a recalcitrant for the benefit of the whole. Because acts of oppression against neighbours have broader implications for the great society of states, individual nations may ally themselves to protect the threatened nation. Europe, he argued in conformity with widespread opinion, no longer constituted a disparate collections of nations, but had through constant interaction become a family or 'sort of Republic' of states, whose interests were interdependent. To attempt to equalize the power of states would, he believed, result in great injustices and unjustifiable acts of aggression. He did, however, endorse what he took to be the practice of European states, namely the attempt to balance preponderances of power with alliances to counter them. A vigilant eye must always be kept upon the probability of states taking advantage of alliances to subdue their partners. Vattel tells us that 'The safest plan, therefore, is either to weaken one who upsets the balance of power, as soon as a favourable opportunity can be found when we can do so with justice, or, by the use of all upright means, to prevent him from attaining so formidable a degree of power' (*Law of Nations*, III. iii, §49). The collective intervention of states was perfectly acceptable in order to ensure that the balance of power was maintained. Although Vattel does not think that it is the business of the state to set itself up as a judge of other nations, there are circumstances which warrant collective action for the preservation of the society of nations. If, for example, a nation were to make a virtue out of openly disregarding and trampling under foot the laws of justice in violation of the rights of others, the common safety of the society of nations would permit collective action to constrain and punish it. Vattel does not believe that a nation has a God-given right to exist. Warlike nations that enter conflicts for gain are nothing more than plunderers. Such action is a violation of and threat to the great society of mankind, and nations are justified in uniting to punish such brigand nations, even to the point of extermination (*Law of Nations*, III. iii, §34). Vattel argues that

if a nation, by its accepted principles and uniform policy, shows clearly that it is in that malicious state of mind in which no right is sacred to it, the safety of the human race requires that it be put down. To set up and maintain an unjust claim is an injury merely to the one who is affected by the claim; but to manifest a general contempt for justice is a wrong to all nations. (*Law of Nations*, II. v, §70)

The Right of War

Vattel, like Pufendorf and Locke, denies the right of private war to individuals except in the state of nature. Men have by nature been given the right of war in order to protect and preserve their rights (*Law of Nations*, ii. iv, §49). Once civil societies are established, war is declared and conducted in the name of the public authority, except in those instances when society can no longer protect its citizens. If men were always reasonable and motivated by the principles of justice and equity, disputes would be settled amicably. War is a regrettable and 'unfortunate expedient' when all else fails. Resort to war can only be because of an injury received, or to prevent a perceived injury from happening, and its motive must be 'the safety and common good of the citizens' (*Law of Nations*, iii. iii, §30). Each state has a perfect right to resist those that attempt to deprive it of its rights or property. In doing so the nation acts in accordance with its duty of self-preservation and self-development, from which its right derives (*Law of Nations*, ii. v, 65). The right to resist injustice, which is an injury, is a perfect right in that it entails a right to enforce compliance.

Before they embark upon such a drastic course of action it is reasonable to expect the disputants to discuss their differences and to attempt to arrive at a fair compromise. If one party refuses to comply with such a procedure then the other is justified in resorting to war. Vattel is quite clear, however, that might does not make right in such disputes:

> It is an error no less absurd than pernicious to say that war should decide controversies between those who, like Nations, acknowledge no superior judge. Victory is ordinarily on the side of strength and skill rather than on that of justice. It would be a bad rule of decision; but it is an efficacious means of constraining one who refuses a settlement according to justice, and it becomes just in the hands of the prince who employs it properly and in a lawful cause.   (*Law of Nations*, iii. iii, §38)

Vattel denies that justice can be on both sides in a dispute. It is impossible that two contrary claims are at the same time true. It is possible, however, that the two parties to a dispute both act in good faith, and when the details of a dispute are ambiguous it may be very difficult to determine on which side right stands. A nation that acts in good faith out of 'invincible ignorance or error' cannot, however, be accused of injustice (*Law of Nations*, iii. iii, §40).

On the question of whether a state is justified in waging war against another because of fear that its growing power eventually may lead to being subjected by it, Vattel attempts to combine justice and prudence. On the one hand a state that is growing in strength by lawful means is fulfilling its obligations under the Law of Nations to both itself and its citizens. On the other hand experience shows with alarming regularity that dominant powers almost invariably end up causing trouble for their neighbours, even to the extent of subjugating them when they can with impunity.

We have already seen that Vattel rejects the principles that the end justifies the means and that might is right. To employ unjust and dishonourable means to safeguard oneself without just cause is an affront to the great society of nations. The mere aggrandizement of a neighbouring state can never in itself provide a just cause for war. Power is not in itself evidence of the intention to perpetrate injuries. Vattel, as always, however, injects an element of realism at this point and implores us to take men as they are and not as they might be. It is a regrettable fact of the human condition, he argues, that wherever power has accrued followed by the capacity to use it with impunity, it is a reasonable assumption that the will to oppress accompanies it. A sovereign has a greater responsibility than an individual not to brush aside his suspicions, and must be vigilant at all times in protecting the interests of the nation. He must, however, have grounds for believing that another nation's intentions are dishonourable. The fact that power and the will to oppress so often go together does not mean that they invariably do so, but it does mean that the first signs of such a union may be acted upon without injustice (*Law of Nations*, III. iii, §44). It is not unreasonable to demand assurances from a state whose power is increasing, and in the absence of these, steps may justifiably be taken to restrain it.

In a great society of equal sovereigns it is unrealistic to think that both nations in a dispute, given their right to judge by their own consciences their moral obligations, would not claim justice on their side. Observance of the Necessary Law of Nations is a matter of conscience from which no nation can be released. Attempts by neutrals to enforce the necessary Law of Nations during the conduct of war, however, are only likely to exacerbate the situation. Something more palpable than the reliance upon individual conscience must nevertheless be invoked and be of more certain application. The Voluntary Law of Nations fulfils this function.

Whereas the Necessary Law of Nations should always guide a sovereign's own conscience, he should take account of the Voluntary Law of Nations, whose precepts are designed to secure the safety and welfare of the great society of nations, in formulating what he can demand of others. If any degree of law is to prevail and constrain the methods of such a violent instrument of redress as war, it must be presumed for practical reasons with regard to its effects that justice resides on both sides. In other words, we must separate questions about the effects of, and valid claims to, the acquisitions made in war, that is, their legality, from judgements about whether the cause is just. The Voluntary Law of Nations makes no pronouncements about the justice of the cause, and no side therefore can be accused of illegitimate methods on the ground of an unjust cause. Each side is permitted to do as the other does because of the presumption of equal justification, which is a practical expedient if war is to be regulated by law. The Voluntary Law of Nations permits no more in the conduct of war than the Law of Nature allows. Vattel denies, however, that the Voluntary Law of Nations makes what is wrong right, and that it confers true rights upon those who wage war unjustly. In conscience the acts are unjust, but through necessity and the determination to constrain the conduct of war the Voluntary Law of Nations makes them legal and lifts the threat of punishment (*Law of Nations*, III. xii, §192). We may take the example of acquisition during war as an example to illustrate what Vattel is driving at. According to the Necessary Law of Nations a just title can only accrue to a combatant if his cause is just. Unjust action cannot confer a right to conquered property. The Voluntary Law of Nations, however, in order to avoid endless disputes which exacerbate friction among nations, allows simple conquest as the basis of title without questioning the justice of the cause (*Law of Nations*, III. xiii, §§195–6).

Vattel's theory of international relations is a justification both of a states-based system and of universal moral obligations. He avoids the possible conflict between the duties of a citizen to the state and of a man to humanity by absolving the latter of his individual responsibility to discharge such obligations. Instead, the state is entrusted to act on his behalf. The citizen's moral obligations to humanity are therefore mediated by the state.

Kant's Cosmopolitanism

As we have already seen, the Spanish War of Succession has to be viewed in the broader context of dynastic politics and the attempt to circumvent Habsburg hegemony in Europe. The Utrecht Treaties (1713–14) gave the very clear indication that neither France nor England would allow the Austrian and Spanish Habsburgs to reunite. Furthermore the French Bourbons and Austrian Habsburgs were excluded from the Spanish succession, thus preventing the unification of the French and Spanish monarchies. It was not until 1718 that Austria reluctantly reconciled itself to the terms, and Spain, having done all it could to undermine them, was forced to accept the settlement in 1719–20. The Utrecht settlements were designed to defuse dynastic ambition and to prevent the establishment of universal monarchy by force. Providing a partial solution to the dynastic problem, the treaties reaffirmed the principle of balance of power rather than hierarchy. Like the Treaty of Westphalia, Utrecht addressed the specific problem of hegemony, but ـid nothing to tackle the problem of war that was endemic in the European states system. Although the participation of small states declined markedly after Utrecht, the major powers were frequent combatants.[21] Kant dismissed the principle of balance of power as a worthless mechanism, and sought instead to establish peace on a legalistic footing.

With the French Revolution, Burke, as we shall see, was not representative in his perception of its threat to the balance of Europe, and indeed the Partition of Poland was considered a much more serious issue by his contemporaries. A democracy, it was commonly thought, would be less inclined to go to war. Kant, although a citizen of Prussia, a country upon which, along with Austria, France declared war in 1792 because of the misperceived threat of counter-revolutionary intervention, was an admirer of the revolutionaries because of their emphasis upon the rights of man and individual self-determination. Kant's project for perpetual peace was formulated at a time when the French Revolution not only elevated the subject to the status of citizen, but also inaugurated a new era in the identity of the nation-state and nationalistic loyalty to it. Kant, without full knowledge of the legacy of the Revolution, nevertheless went some way to accommodate the new aspirations in his project. Republicanism, which entails citizen participation, and the guarantee of national integrity were incorporated into his cosmopolitanism in order to demonstrate that national self-determination and a universal moral law are not incompatible in the achievement of peace.

The editor of Kant's *Political Writings* argues that Kant deserves to be given a much more prominent place than he has hitherto held in the tradition of Western political thought. His intellectual peers are Aristotle, Plato, and Hobbes.[22] In the philosophy of international relations Kant has long been afforded this status. Chris Brown, for example, describes Kant as 'the greatest of all theorists of international relations'.[23] His primary concern in political philosophy was to emphasize the priority of establishing the rule of law among nations within the context of a properly organized confederation based upon agreement (*Idea for a Universal History, Political Writings*, 47). It is not agreement, however, that gives a rational foundation to cosmopolitanism. It is, as we will see, a demand of practical reason. Kant's theory of international relations was meant by him to be the culmination of his general moral theory.

He is dismissive of the unrealistic schemes of Grotius, Pufendorf, and Vattel, whom he calls 'miserable comforters'. It is they who have given credence to the idea of Right in international relations in which the depravity of human nature is to be seen at its most unconstrained. Their names are invoked in justification of war, whereas their diplomatic and philosophical codes are not even remotely legally binding. There is, Kant argues, 'no instance of a state ever having been moved to desist from its purpose by arguments supported by the testimonies of such notable men' (*Perpetual Peace, Political Writings*, 103). The Law of Nations for Kant is much more comprehensive than its formulation in the hands of Vattel. It encompasses the relations among nations as well as the relations among individuals who are members of different nations, including the position of the individual in relation to a foreign state. Kant argued that in order for a treaty of perpetual peace to be legally binding it must attain the formal consent of civilized nations. In other words, it cannot be effected in the absence of a legally constituted framework.

Like Hobbes and Grotius, Kant lends his name to one of Martin Wight's three famous traditions. The Kantian or revolutionary tradition is distinguished, according to Bull, by a rejection of the Machiavellian view that international politics is about interstate conflict, and of the Grotian view that it is characterized by conflict and co-operation. Only at a superficial level, Bull argues, did Kantians acknowledge that international politics was about state relations at all, and more fundamentally 'it was about relations among the human beings of which states were composed'.[24] Wight himself did not attribute this revolutionary cosmopolitanism to Kant. In fact no major thinker, Wight suggests, rejects the notion of a society of states and places in its stead the society of humankind, thus dissolving international relations.[25] Bull, however, calls Kant's views facile. It is a fallacy, Bull contends, to think that war will be abolished by abolishing sovereign states.[26] Similarly, Knutsen attributes to Kant the primary intention of redirecting the focus of international relations away from the 'fictitious Society of Nations' and towards the genuine international society of all men.[27]

It will become clear during the exposition of Kant's theory that his cosmopolitanism was not of a radical kind, and that he was quite happy to accommodate state sovereignty into his plan for perpetual peace, which incorporates three types of law: that among individuals within a state, civil or constitutional law; that between states, international right; and the law governing individuals in their relations with each other and with other states, cosmopolitan right. Cosmopolitan right is grounded in the idea of free commerce, and amounts for Kant to the right of hospitality, that is, the right not be treated as an enemy, or with hostility, by another individual or state. It affords no right of permanent residence in foreign lands. In other words, it amounts to little more than the rites of passage of which many traditional Natural Law theorists speak. The guarantee of rights in Kant's plan is much more firmly attached to sovereign states.

Natural Law, Natural Rights, and the Categorical Imperative

The Natural Law and Natural Rights theorists, ranging from the transcendent communitarianism of Aquinas to the individualistic and immanent approach of Pufendorf, in their various ways sought to take the indubitable data of nature, in principle knowable by all men, and present them as prescriptive universal laws to which all of humanity is subject.[28] Grotius, Pufendorf, and Vattel succeeded in liberating Natural Law and Natural Right from theology. Kant's critiques constituted a more radical departure from this tradition. In the preface to the second edition of the *Critique of Pure Reason* Kant discusses the relation between mind and external reality. He departs from traditional epistemology by suggesting that the assumption that the mind must conform to reality has proved abortive in our quest for knowledge o. external objects. Instead, Kant suggests, 'Let us then make the experiment whether we may not be more successful in metaphysics, if we assume that the objects must conform to our cognition.'[29] The things we know are mediated by thoughts or categories, and we cannot know things as they are in themselves. L. W. Beck calls this Kant's first Copernican revolution, in which understanding makes or constitutes nature rather than conforms to it. Kant's second Copernican revolution is the thought that reason, rather than apprehending or discovering the moral law, actually makes it.[30] In other words, the indubitable data of nature as a basis for universal ethical laws is jettisoned. Nature is for Kant the realm of causality and necessity, of phenomena and appearances. The order of nature is empirically determined, and in it the idea of 'ought' or morality has no meaning. In other words, we cannot deduce moral principles from experience or empirical data.[31]

It was futile to attempt to prove matters of morality by means of methods suited to the understanding of nature.[32] If morality is not to be derived from human nature, what is its source? Kant's theory is archetypally deontological,[33] which means that it is agent-centred and based on the idea of duty or right, which distinguishes it from theories which emphasize qualities of character needed to live the good life and from consequentialist theories such as utilitarianism which are based on the consequences of action.

The faculty of understanding has as its objects the phenomenal world. In contrast the faculty of reason has general ideas as its objects. Morality is quite different from our knowledge of the world of appearances, and is independent of the laws that govern them. Instead morality arises from subscription to universal laws which are internal to us and which presuppose human freedom. In other words, morality is not discovered or apprehended by reason, but is the product of it, and is only possible because reason is independent of the Laws of Nature. This is what Kant calls the transcendental sense of freedom.

Reason therefore plays quite a different function in Kant from the function proposed by traditional Natural Law theorists. Morality is not derived from nature or empirical principles; empirical principles derive from the senses and cannot be universal.[34] It is the realm of the intelligible or noumenal, and is characterized not by causal necessity but by freedom. Kant contends that the basis of morality is to be sought not in a knowledge of man's anthropology, 'but solely *a priori* in the concepts of pure reason'.[35] Moral philosophy gives man as a rational being a priori laws of morality, and in so far as they are rules for action, and not attempts to convey knowledge, they are the result of practical reason.[36] The moral laws also require sound judgement based on experience in order to discern instances when they might be applied, and in order to impress them upon the will and influence practice.

Kant assumes that reason functions in accordance with principles that the mind can come to know. Such rational principles are evident not only in thinking but also in morality. The principles are distinguishable from the activity in that they are indispensable for thinking rationally about, and acting in, the world. All things in nature are law-governed, but only a rational being has the capacity to act in accordance wit.. his or her conception of the law, that is, to act according to principles. To do so is to will. Actions cannot be derived from laws without reason, and the will therefore is practical reason. The conception of an objective principle necessarily binding on the will is a command of reason or an imperative.[37]

In the *Groundwork* Kant suggests that his intention is to establish the supreme principle of morality, namely the categorical imperative, which he expresses in five different ways. In the first he contends that 'I ought never to act except in such a way *that I can also will that my maxim should become a universal law*'.[38] He argues that it is not good enough merely to act in conformity with the moral law, but that we must act for the sake of that law itself. If what I do is the right thing for me to do, then it must also be the right thing for everyone else to do. In other words, the criterion of moral action is the test of whether what one proposes to do is also what others ought to do. Some principles of conduct will fail this test and will not therefore be moral. Moral categories are imperative, rather than hypothetical, because they are directives to act, and what is commanded is good in itself and not for some ulterior motive or benefit.[39] A hypothetical imperative for Kant is conditioned by the end willed. Its validity depends upon the willing of the end, and the act is a means to that end, and not as such an end in itself. In other words, it is not duty for duty's sake. The consequentialist reasoning of means and ends cannot as far as Kant is concerned provide a basis for a morality that is absolutely binding. A categorical imperative does not derive its validity from an end that is willed, but is instead an injunction to act in accordance with principles that are universally valid for all human beings, and do not depend upon the contingency of an end being willed.[40] Kedourie sums up Kant's position well when he says: 'Morality is independent of consequences and impervious to rewards.'[41]

Morality for Kant is the corollary of freedom and autonomy. The principle that human actions are necessarily free cannot be proved philosophically or empirically. In practical terms the idea of a rational agent presupposes freedom in both action and thought. This presupposition of freedom necessarily entails autonomy, and hence the categorical imperative. Morally free and autonomous individuals acting according to the moral law respect the autonomy of other individuals, treating them as ends in themselves rather than as means. This is what Kant calls the kingdom of ends, in which each person acts in the same manner as others, that is, according to law or impersonal principles with universal validity, fulfilling his own purposes and at the same time assisting the fulfilment of those of others. The equality of freedom posited in a kingdom of ends means that no one has the right to impose his will upon another for his own personal gain. The autonomous members of the kingdom of ends are not only subject to, but also the authors of, the law. What this means is that the rational person does not act according to a moral law that is imposed from outside.[42]

In summary, there are three fundamental principles of morality which Kant identifies as necessary and universal. The first is the principle of universality itself; the second, that of treating everyone as an end and never as a means; and third, the principle of autonomy in the context of a rational and universal kingdom of ends. Both domestic and international morality have the same basis, that is, what reason demands a priori.

Kant's attribution of Natural Rights to the individual prior to political society is an extension of this principle. Natural Rights are inextricably associated with the rational character of man, not in the traditional sense that they are apprehended by, or are the objects of, reason, but more fundamentally in that they are the products of reason.[43] The implications for Kant's Natural Law predecessors are quite profound. Grotius, Vattel, and Pufendorf, for example, go to great lengths to show that morality and self-interest are complementary principles in the moral order, and that self-interest provides an incentive to be moral. In other words, translated into Kant's vocabulary, morality is a means to an end, and therefore a hypothetical imperative because it is contingent and not universal. The fundamental moral law to which individuals are subject has an external source in nature as the indubitable data of rational deduction. For Kant the capacity of human beings to act according to reason means that they are able to deny the determination of inclinations and are free to choose morality for its own sake. The moral law does not have its source outside the individual in nature or external command, but instead each individual is its author in a community of ends.

Kant was born to parents who were devoutly religious and belonged to a fundamentalist sect known as the Pietists, whose teachings encouraged full participation of the congregation in all aspects of Church life, including reading and interpreting the Bible, from which God's divine revelation could be gleaned. Kant was profoundly affected by his religious upbringing, and although he later abjured fundamentalism his writings are infused with missionary zeal. The presupposition of the rational providence of God, or Nature, in a non-naturalistic sense, permeates the whole of his philosophy. It needs to be emphasized that Kant gave two different meanings to 'Nature', the first of which we have already encountered. It means the external world which is subject to mechanical causes and is the object of scientific explanation. The second sense of Nature to which he attributes purposes is the classical idea of something developing and reaching its *telos*.[44] Indeed, Kant's understanding of past events is teleological in that his account of human history asks us to assume, and indeed suggests that reason demands that we assume, that the human race is travelling upon a purposive journey.

The categorical imperative, Kant maintained, necessarily leads to the assertion of the existence of God. It imposes upon us the duty to seek the highest good, which is inconceivable without assuming its source as a perfect being. For Kant, in marked contrast to other thinkers I have associated with the tradition of a Universal Moral Order, God becomes the creature of men, created out of their need to assume him. The kingdom of ends and the idea of God are closely related. Practical reason finds the unity which it seeks in the highest good of the ideal or perfect community, the kingdom of ends, which has no empirical existence but which is nevertheless real as the object of the moral person's will.[45] The postulate of God is the ideal of perfection, with which our moral actions must strive to be in accord. As Waltz suggests, for Kant, 'If we are ever to fulfil the moral law, we must assume the existence of progress, an immortal soul, a God.'[46]

Kant's moral philosophy serves the same function as traditional Natural Law theories, in that irrespective of the contingencies of the application of a moral rule to different circumstances, the moral man is one who conducts himself on the supposition that there is an unconditional and absolute moral order to which all are subject in conformity with their rational character.[47] He differed from his predecessors in not accepting the traditional formulation of the distinction between perfect and imperfect duties. As we saw, such writers as Pufendorf and Vattel regarded duties as perfect if they could be enforced by external law, and imperfect if they could not. Perfect duties, then, were those which were owed to others and could be enforced. For Kant perfect duties allow of no exception on the ground of inclination, and include duties to oneself as well as to others.[48] Paton suggests that the exceptions which imperfect duties allow probably refer to the limitations that one maxim may place upon another. The distinction is also sharpened by Kant's view that a perfect duty is one which recommends a specific act, such as the paying of £1 to John Jones to acquit a debt. Imperfect duties recommend that we act in accordance with a maxim, for example, a maxim to act in accordance with the duty of benevolence. Over who should be the recipients and by how much, we exercise discretion.[49] Kant also differed from his predecessors in the way he went about establishing his conclusions, but like them he affirmed the existence of God, denounced sinners, and extolled the virtues of freedom and morality.

The formal principles of Kant's morality are criteria which all rational beings must apply to the justification of their conduct, but they do not give content to morality without being applied to the human condition. Although nature and morality are separate orders for Kant, he did nevertheless attempt to identify their points of interaction. A person presupposes his or her freedom as a part of the intelligible or noumenal world, and at the same time is determined by the Natural Laws of the phenomenal world to which he or she as a sentient being is subject. A person therefore may not take responsibility for his or her passions and desires, but does take responsibility for indulging them in contradistinction to morality.[50] The capacity of human beings to control their inclinations, because they are not completely determined by a pervasive natural order, means that they are capable of acting in accordance with their rational principles.[51]

Because a human being belongs to both the phenonemal world of inclinations and the noumenal world of reason, the moral law has to take account of these peculiar circumstances. Human beings do not have a holy will totally immersed in reason and free from the constraints of nature. A person has needs and wants that must be satisfied. Nor is a person wholly naturalistic, totally immersed in the satisfaction of inclinations and desires, free from rational constraints. In Kant's view the human condition embodies the essential end of perfectibility or of raising itself above the world of nature.

The political element in Kant reverberates with an optimism largely absent from the writers identified as belonging to the Empirical Realist tradition. Although in many respects he may agree with the view of human nature espoused by Thucydides, Machiavelli, and Hobbes, he does not share their pessimism about its potentiality. In answer to those who posited human nature as an insurmountable stumbling-block to permanent moral progress towards perpetual peace, Kant contends in his various writings that nature itself is the very vehicle by which such progress is attained.[52] Here 'nature' is being used in the second of the two senses outlined above.

It was beyond belief, in Kant's view, that the organic world of nature should be so perfectly regulated and that at the same time there could be no meaning and purpose to those things that happen in the realm of social existence.[53] If the philosopher cannot detect in the actions of human beings a rational collective design of its own, then such a design may be attributed to Nature (*Idea for a Universal History, Political Writings*, 42). There is something, even in the conflicts which occur because of the imperfections of human nature, which seems to pull us towards moral progress. This for Kant is the design of Nature. Conceived as a compelling mechanical process whose purpose is fulfilled regardless of our intentions, and whose laws are unknown to us, it is *fate*. Conceived as a purposive higher intelligent cause pointing the human race in the direction of an ultimate goal and predetermining the evolution of the world, it is *providence* (*Perpetual Peace, Political Writings*, 108). The operation of such causal agency is not to be observed empirically, nor is it to be inferred from circumstances. Kant contends that we must supply the idea mentally in order to conceive of such agency on the analogy of human artifice, but it would be presumptuous to suggest that we detect God's providence and wiser to attribute it to Nature.

Nature has in it a rational plan, Kant argues, which guides us and impels us to greater degrees of moral worth. This does not mean that Kant conceived of Nature as a deliberative intelligent agent. Instead, he contends that if we are to understand history we must assume that Nature has a plan. Given that his concern is with the development of freedom, Kant believes that Nature's plan is the education of the human race to its attainment. He concedes that such an idea seems implausible in theory, but it is one that in practice has 'dogmatic validity' (*Perpetual Peace, Political Writings*, 109).

Out of the conflict in the state of nature arises civil association, which in comparison with the higher forms yet to be developed is still relatively primitive. Over a long period of time and often helped by the experience of war, a federation of states will arise to establish perpetual peace. This is the highest political goal for which a politician can aim. For Kant, morality must always act as the guide to political action. Political expediency is no excuse for deviating from what is morally right. In his writings on international politics Kant brings to bear the conclusion of his whole philosophy.

Prior to the establishment of civil society, the dual nature of human beings is dominated by the sensual, or phenomenal, aspect. This state of nature is one of continuous violence and conflict in which experience, over a long period of time, develops the reasoning faculties. The conflicts and actions in which these savages engage seem senseless and purposeless, and even appear to inhibit the development of the natural capacities of the species (*Idea for a Universal History with a Cosmopolitan Purpose, Political Writings*, 48–9). The spectacle that human beings have presented in history is a sorry one. Their individual purposes conflict, and they have an eye only for the parts dissociated from the whole. The savages prefer 'incessant strife' and 'lawless freedom' to having to submit themselves to 'legal constraint' and the 'freedom of reason' (*Perpetual Peace, Political Writings*, 102–3).

Human beings are unsocial social beings. They are both attracted to social relations and averse to them. In a social setting we acquire and develop skills, yet on the other hand we seek privacy, and desire to cut ourselves off from society. We wish to direct everything according to our own ideas and expect others to resist because of a presumption of the same desire residing in them. Yet the irony is that this natural resistance to the will of others impels us to overcome our inclination to be lazy.[54] We wish not to be dominated, yet we wish to dominate. We wish to isolate ourselves from society, but at the same time seek honour and respect. The unsocial sociability of human beings facilitates their development. We may wish for a commodious life, but Nature wills that we live in discord.

In this condition where self-interest and conflict make life both unpleasant and precarious, we are forced through necessity to seek a constraining force which delivers human beings from their predicament. As Kant says: 'universal violence and the distress it produces must eventually make a people decide to submit to the coercion which reason itself prescribes (i.e. the coercion of public law), and to enter into a *civil* constitution' (*On the Common Saying: 'This May be True in Theory, but it does not Apply in Practice'*, *Political Writings*, 90). Nature or Providence guides us towards the achievement of higher moral goals. This does not mean that Kant believes that Nature imposes a duty upon us to achieve these goals, because only unconstrained free practical reason is able to do this. He means that we must assume that Nature has this purpose whether or not we are complicit in it. We progress teleologically towards an end, irrespective of whether we will many of the steps along the way. Even if the internal conflict does not compel us to accept the coercion of civil laws, war has the same effect. People find that other groups of people constitute a threat to them, and in order to stand up to this threat they are compelled to organize themselves internally into a state.

The solution to the problem of internal discord and external threat would not, Kant argues, be insoluble to a 'nation of devils' (*Perpetual Peace*, *Political Writings*, 112), because it does not require the moral improvement of human beings. All that is required is that intelligence is possessed and used to regulate the antagonistic relations which exist. People have to compel each other to submit to laws which apply to all. Only a civil society premised on the rule of law is consistent with the requirement of moral universalism and the autonomy of the individual. The individual's freedom of will must be reflected in society's institutions. Republican government is the precondition for such representation. Republicanism should not be confused with democracy. Monarchy, aristocracy, and democracy are forms of state each having a different focus of sovereignty. Republicanism and despotism are types of government. Republicanism entails the principle of separating the executive and legislative powers of government, and if it is to be in conformity with the idea of right it must have representative institutions. A monarch would eventually lose his influence over legislation and become the executive power while the representative institutions legislated.

States in their relations with each other, Kant contends, may be regarded as being like individual men who live in a state of nature and whose relations give rise to mutual conflict and injury: 'The depravity of human nature is displayed without disguise in the unrestricted relations which obtain between the various nations' (*Perpetual Peace*, *Political Writings*, 103). For Kant, the state of nature is by definition a condition of injustice because of the absence of legal constraints and the constant threat that violence will be resorted to in order to resolve disputes. Every state judges the merits of its own case, but to talk of an unjust enemy in the state of nature is something of a pleonasm because the condition is one of injustice (*The Metaphysics of Morals*, §60, *Political Writings*, 170). As civilized nations we look with disdain at savages who engage in continual conflict and who value their 'lawless liberty' more than the benefits of legal constraints. Given the aversion of civilized states to barbarism, it might reasonably be expected that states would wish to deliver themselves from the condition so resembling that of the savage in which they find themselves. On the contrary, however, every state prides itself on being free of external constraint, and its ruler, or head, is considered more or less glorious according to the number of men he has ready to sacrifice for a cause which they have had no part in bringing about, and for which the king or ruler does not himself place his life in danger (*Perpetual Peace, Political Writings*, 102–3). Kant maintains that all international right and the possession of external property by the state, whether 'acquired or preserved by war, are *provisional* until the state of nature has been abandoned' (*The Metaphysics of Morals*, §61, *Political Writings*, 171).

It is the same unsociableness that leads to the establishment of commonwealths, which Nature uses to bring about peace and harmony in the relations between states. War, through its destruction, has had and will continue to have positive benefits, in that out of internal devastation and exhaustion states may be forced through bitter experience to do what reason might well have taught them without such painful experiences (*Idea for a Universal History with a Cosmopolitan Purpose, Political Writings*, 47). As well as forcing states to enter into more peaceful relations with each other, Nature by means of war has caused people to be scattered all over the surface of the earth, and at the same time has made provision for sustenance in the most remote regions. War, Kant believes, 'seems to be ingrained in human nature, and even to be regarded as something noble to which man is inspired by his love of honour, without selfish motives' (*Perpetual Peace, Political Writings*, 111). In the current competitive condition of states in which ambition, avarice, and power-seeking dominate the motives of those who hold authority, war seems to be inevitable. Yet despite the thoughtlessness and unbridled passions of individuals, Nature works through war to bring about moral progress in the species. In the *Critique of Judgement* Kant suggests that war provides an impetus to the full development of those talents which are conducive to culture.[55] In fact he describes war as necessary for character-building: it is something sublime, in the absence of which a nation degenerates into the self-interestedness of commercialism and becomes cowardly and effeminate.[56]

No Right to Go to War

This does not mean that Kant believed that nations had a right to enter into war. International right, he argues, means nothing if it is taken to be a right to go to war. It would give states the right to judge what is lawful, not in conformity with the validity of universal laws, 'but by means of one-sided maxims backed up by physical force' (*Perpetual Peace, Political Writings*, 105; cf. *The Metaphysics of Morals, Political Writings*, 174). Matters of right cannot be resolved by force of arms. Victory may end a particular war, but it does not put to rest the 'warlike condition' in accordance with which all sorts of pretexts are invoked to perpetrate new wars (*Perpetual Peace, Political Writings*, 104).

Like Vattel, then, Kant thought it a sham to talk of just and unjust wars, or of punishing injustices by means of war. War cannot decide matters of morality, and victory does not make what is inherently wrong right. Unlike Vattel, however, who believed that states have a right to pursue by means of war what they regard as injuries in order to protect their interests, Kant repudiated the right of war. Whereas Grotius and Vattel, then, acknowledged the necessity of war and tried to submit its declaration and conduct to the rule of law, Kant denied its legitimacy and sought to institute a process to abolish it. This does not mean that he was a pacifist. He recognized the need for self-defence and national defence, as well as the need to repel the initial threat to any confederation of peace from outside hostile powers, whose hostility might take centuries to wane. In *The Metaphysics of Morals*, for example, he argued that international right permits the use of violence only to protect one's current property, and not to acquire more (§57, *Political Writings*, 168).

Unlike individuals in the state of nature instituting a commonwealth, states cannot successfully join together into one universal state. Nations, Kant claims, because of their views on the international rights of individual states, will not join together into one state of nations. The idea of a universal republic, although right in theory, would be rejected in fact (*Perpetual Peace, Political Writings*, 105). The extent of its territories and the immense difficulty of governing them and protecting the rights of citizens would make it impracticable and lead to internal strife (*The Metaphysics of Morals*, §61, *Political Writings*, 171). Furthermore, Kant argues that a world state is not feasible because of the diversity of language and religions among nations.[57] Only by means of what he variously calls a 'federal union', 'federative associate partnership or confederation', and 'permanent congress of states' can peace begin to be effectively kept between states.[58] A federation, Kant claims, is preferable to one where a state outgrows itself and absorbs all others into a 'Universal Monarchy'. In such a soulless despotism the range of government grows over a larger area and the laws become too general and lose their degree of definit..eness, undermining what is good and precipitating anarchy (*Perpetual Peace*, in *Political Writings*, 113). The evils of a universal despotism which war can precipitate impels states to seek deliverance not in a universal state under one ruler, but in 'a lawful *federation* under a commonly accepted *international right*' (*On the Common Saying, Political Writings*, 90).

Whereas the institution of commonwealths comes about by necessity and prudence, and could therefore be attained by a nation of devils forced by circumstances to unite, this is not the case in the international sphere. Here, even though wars and rivalry may modify and quell conflict, in the last analysis peace and justice can only be achieved by means of a choice consciously made by rulers to institute such a moral good. The moral end to institute perpetual peace between nations by conscious choice is not derived from the phenomenal world of appearances, but is a priori. Peace is an ethical duty because it is only in such a condition that men can fulfil their moral duty of treating others not as means but as ends in themselves. Kant contends that 'moral-practical reason within us pronounces the following irresistible veto: *There shall be no war*, either between individual human beings in the state of nature, or between separate states' (*The Metaphysics of Morals*, conclusion, *Political Writings*, 174). It is in the cosmopolitan federation of nations that Nature attains its highest purpose.

Every state desires to subject the whole world to its power, but Nature has so designed things as to act against this desire. Nature has deemed that nations be kept apart by ensuring, for example, that there are differences in languages and religion. Over time and as nations become more civilized, there is a greater degree of agreement between them on principles, and a better understanding of the need for peace notwithstanding the differences, facilitated by the demonstrable benefits of commerce which are dependent upon peace for the flourishing of trade. The gradual development of a pacific spirit is achieved not by reducing the power of each state, but instead by a balance which comes about as a result of their rivalry with each other.

Certain factors facilitate the development of peaceful relations. Kant believes that first, the economic and social cost of war, and its legacy in the national debt, will eventually make war prohibitive (*Idea for a Universal History*, *Political Writings*, 50–1; and *On the Common Saying*, *Political Writings*, 90). The immense cost of maintaining standing armies is a considerable drain on the resources of a nation, and serves to fuel ruinous competition as each tries to build bigger and better fighting forces. Kant's comments here reflect the experience of his own Prussia. In 1723, for example, there were less than 80,000 troops in the Prussian army. During Frederick the Great's long reign, 1740–86, the number increased to nearly 200,000 and took two-thirds of the state revenue to maintain.[59] Having such an army also contravenes one of Kant's basic principles because the state is using individuals not as ends in themselves but as means. Voluntary enlistment to protect the nation from external aggression does not constitute such a contravention (*Perpetual Peace*, *Political Writings*, 94–5). Second, a growing sense of morality among citizens, fostered by education and sustained by the competition among nations to exercise power and influence over each other, so that each attempts to emulate wha. the others have, has served to spread enlightenment to all nations, which itself promotes the cause of peace. The effectiveness of the rule of law in external relations, because it is not backed by force but instead rests upon voluntary agreement, is conditional upon the state achieving a certain degree of internal moral perfection. Third, the proliferation of economic relations and the necessity for laws governing them will, Kant contends, lead to the adoption of common rules world-wide to regulate business and trade. Healthy economic relations will engender more responsible and mature political relations.

Kant argues that we must continually strive to bring about the conditions conducive to perpetual peace on the presumption that it is a reality which can be attained. It is by doing so that we can bring about an end to war. The limitations of human knowledge render us incapable of proving that peace is not attainable, and therefore it would be presumptuous of us to adopt such a view. Even if the achievement of this goal is always to remain a pious wish, which is not a view to which Kant subscribes (*Perpetual Peace*, *Political Writings*, 130), there is still no reason to abandon the maxim of aiming to bring it about with relentless determination and perseverance. We have, Kant argues, a duty to pursue the goal of perpetual peace because we have to assume that the moral law within us is not deceptive and that it is the true guide to our actions. To think that the moral law deceives us is to subscribe to the repulsive view that reason is to be dispensed with. To do this is to see ourselves and our principles on the same level as the animals subject to phenomenal causal Laws of Nature (*The Metaphysics of Morals*, conclusion, *Political Writings*, 174).

In the context of what Kant perceives to be progress towards more harmonious relations among nations, he puts forward his own positive recommendations, which must receive the assent of the participating nations. These may at first be few in number, but by their positive example and the demonstrable benefits of a peaceable confederation, they will attract more, eventually encompassing the whole world. To rely upon the mechanism of the balance of power, which has built into it the use of war as an instrument of policy, in order to achieve a condition of permanent peace is, Kant suggests, 'a pure illusion' (*On the Common Saying, Political Writings*, 92).

Among the preliminary articles that must be agreed upon are the following. There must be no secret reservation to retain the material for prosecuting future wars. As a moral person the state's integrity must be respected as an autonomous free agent. States cannot be treated as a means, nor taken over or absorbed as if they were pieces of property. This is in conformity with the idea of an original contract in which each citizen must be deemed to have consented to the constitution. States must not use force to interfere in the government and constitution of other states. Standing armies should be abolished to avoid sending signals to other nations that one is equipped for war. National debts should not be incurred for the purpose of prosecuting wars. And, finally, nothing should be permitted in hostilities which would render confidence in a future peace impossible. This would include a prohibition on the use of assassins and poisoners; the violation of the terms of treaties of surrender; and the encouragement of treason.[60]

The principles relat..ng to prohibitions on secret articles, intervention, and the undermining of confidence would, he thought, need to be secured immediately, but those relating to the acquisition of states and the gradual abolition of standing armies and national debts to finance war could be more permissive and could be instituted gradually as long as their ultimate objective was never lost to view. Acceptance of the preliminary articles does not institute peace; they inaugurate the long and arduous process leading to it.[61]

The absence of war is not in Kant's view a state of peace. The cessation of hostilities is no guarantee of concord in the international state of nature. Without formally accepted and acknowledged legal constraints each state remains a permanent threat to others. A state of peace has to be formally instituted by the giving of guarantees in a legal context. In this respect Kant's precepts constitute a treaty for peace, that is, the placing of peaceful coexistence on a firm legal foundation. In this respect Kant is careful to attempt to accommodate the different obligations of men, citizens, and states. He suggests that any legal constitution has to conform to one of three types, and he goes on in his presentation of the definitive articles to relate one to each type. He enumerates three legal constitutions and three definitive articles. First he maintains that a constitution can be based on the '*civil right* of individuals within a nation (*ius civitatis*)' (*Perpetual Peace, Political Writings*, 98). The First Definitive Article maintains that the form of constitution in each state must be Republican because it comes the nearest to the moral ideal of individual freedom. Both are premised on the idea that obedience to external laws involves consenting to them. The constitution and laws to which rational human beings are subject and of which they are the authors must be deemed to be in principle capable of attaining their consent. The idea of rational consent in the context of a social contract acts as a principle or criterion by which to judge the justness of laws as those to which rational individuals would in principle consent. As Kant contends:

It is in fact merely an *idea* of reason, which nonetheless has undoubted practical reality; for it can oblige every legislator to frame his laws in such a way that they could have been produced by the united will of a whole nation, and to regard each subject, in so far as he can claim citizenship, as if he had consented within the general will. (*On the Common Saying, Political Writings*, 79)[62]

The universality of the law is not undermined by being subject to the principle of consent because it is a rational universal criterion inextricably associated with the freedom and autonomy of the individual in a kingdom of ends. Republicanism is the best form of constitution to bring about perpetual peace because the consent of the citizens of the state is required to determine the question of whether to go to war. Much more so than a ruler, the people who suffer the consequences of war are liable to be averse to entering into something that will bring misery and suffering upon themselves.

The second type of constitution is 'based on the *international right* of states in their relationships with one another (*ius gentium*)' (*Perpetual Peace, Political Writings*, 98). The Second Definitive Article is that 'The Right of Nations shall be based on a Federation of Free States' (*Perpetual Peace, Political Writings*, 102). This does not entail that each nation subjects itself to a higher power. If this were to happen they would transform themselves into one nation and one state. This, Kant argues, contradicts the principle underlying the reason why nations wish to bring about peace. The idea of a federation is to protect the rights of each separate nation in their mutual relations and to avoid fusion into one large state, while securing the liberty of each according to the international right of nations, which includes the right of self-determination but, as we have already seen, excludes the right of war.

The third type of constitution is 'based on *cosmopolitan right*, in so far as individuals and states, coexisting in an external relationship of mutual influences, may be regarded as citizens of a universal state of mankind (*ius cosmopoliticum*)' (*Perpetual Peace, Political Writings*, 98–9). The Third Definitive Article restricts cosmopolitan rights to those of universal hospitality. Foreigners entering a country, as long as they act peacefully and have no hostile intent, have a right not to be treated as enemies. This right is derived from the original right to 'communal possession of the earth's surface . . . which the human race shares in common' (*Perpetual Peace, Political Writings*, 106). Originally, each nation, Kant argues elsewhere, was a member of the community of land. It was not a legal community of possession, utilization, or ownership of the land. It was a community of 'reciprocal action' in which each had extensive relations with others, and could make overtures to engage in commerce without being treated as a foreign enemy. This right, in so far as it holds out the prospect of a unity of nations agreeing to universal laws to regulate their relations, is what Kant calls *cosmopolitan* right (*The Metaphysics of Morals*, §62, *Political Writings*, 172). In what amounts to a pointed criticism of the modern practice of colonialism, Kant argues that civilized nations have proved to be far more inhospitable that many less civilized nations. For many civilized nations which pride themselves on their piety, merely visiting foreign lands is tantamount to conquest. He argues that the original inhabitants of America, Africa, the Spice Islands, and the Cape of Good Hope are regarded as nothing, and their lands deemed to belong to no one. East India, or Hindustan, has been devastated by foreign troops under the pretext of setting up a trading post. Those countries that have engaged in such activities, Kant contends, far from gaining any economic benefits, have incurred huge losses. Unlike Locke and Vattel, he does not make out a case for the obligation of peoples to cultivate their lands to increase the fruits of the earth for the benefit of mankind, although he acknowledges that such a case could be made. A nation does not, Kant argues, have a right to seize the lands of another nation even if they lie uncultivated. The use of violence would be illegitimate to establish settlements, which should be done only in good faith by means of a treaty which avoids the exploitation of the ignorance of the savages (*The Metaphysics of Morals*, §62, *Political Writings*, 172–3). On a more optimistic note, however, Kant claims that social relations among peoples throughout the world have advanced to such an extent that they

have thus entered in var 'ng degrees into a universal community, and it has developed to the point where a violation of rights in *one* part of the world is felt *everywhere*. The idea of a cosmopolitan right is therefore not fantastic and overstrained; it is a necessary complement to the unwritten code of political and international right, transforming it into a universal right of humanity. Only under this condition can we flatter ourselves that we are continually advancing towards a perpetual peace. (*Perpetual Peace, Political Writings*, 108)

For the most part Kant's conception of world organization accommodates state sovereignty. The federalism of which he speaks is a society of nations, and not of individuals. Although he talks of the cosmopolitan right of hospitality, it is a right to be enjoyed in a state context. It gives no right to permanent residence in another state, only a right not to be treated as an enemy and with hostility. The preliminary and definitive articles, far from undermining state sovereignty, appear to reinforce it.[63]

In summary, Kant hoped that the pacific federation he proposed would serve as an example to other nations, who would come to see the benefits of arbitration rather than aggression. Conditions of mutual peaceful relations would prevail within the pacific federation, but by implication the federated states might have to engage in common defensive conflict against aggressive nations outside the federation. What Kant was aiming for was not a universal world state, nor a stateless world. Instead he hoped that the confederation which he envisaged would be able to secure the rights of individual human beings, as well as those of nations. In essence, it would amount to the peaceful settlement of disputes by nations, and the mutual acknowledgement of the rights to hospitality of each other's nationals the world over.

The plan itself cannot guarantee an end to conflict between states. It is optimistic to think that aggression will become increasingly futile as the benefits of peace become more obvious. The fear of relapse into senseless war and its consequences may, however, act as the assurance of the possibility of success. Kant suggests that nations faced with such a prospect will not, it is hoped, endanger the gains that have been made.

In Kant's view politics and morality are closely associated, and he is quite clear that the former is subordinate to the latter.[64] Every person has an intuitive understanding of what constitutes ethical conduct. Our ability and inclination to act morally are developed by practical reason. Politicians have in their care the well-being of society as a whole. In aiming to achieve that well-being they must have an idea of what it is, and this is a moral or ethical conception of the good of society. Politics, for Kant, is the carrying out of the theory of right.[65] The moral politician is one who facilitates the development of history towards the achievement of a morally educated people and a world in which relations between peoples are characterized by peace rather than by conflict. Kant is not denying that expediency and deceit may more often than not be characteristic of political activity, but, he believes, the constraints upon such conduct are becoming increasingly great. No men can escape the conception of right being applied to them in their private and public lives. Similarly, no man would openly renounce the idea of public right and overtly practise politics on the grounds of expediency, and this is especially true in the sphere of international right. Rather than reject moral principles in international politics, statesmen pay them all due honour, even if they are constantly devising in practice every conceivable means to avoid them (*Perpetual Peace, Political Writings*, 121). Kant argues that we must expose the expedient sophistry of politicians and show that when principles are subordinated to ends the business of bringing politics and morality into harmony is frustrated. The moral politician should act in accordance with the formal principle of practical reason, that is, in such a way as is consistent with the wish that your maxim become a universal law. Politics, Kant contends, 'must bend the knee before right' (*Perpetual Peace, Political Writings*, 125).

It is ironic that Kant's principle of moral self-determination should be taken over by his successors and made dependent upon national self-determination by such writers as Fichte. As we have seen, Kant was no nationalist, but his cosmopolitanism posits a confederacy of national self-determining units. His moral theory lent itself therefore to adaptation by more extreme nationalist theorists whose views on world unity were based upon domination rather than confederation.

Notes

1. John Locke, *Two Treatises of Government*, ed. Peter Laslett (Cambridge, Cambridge University Press, 1988).
2. Herman Lebovics, 'The Uses of America in Locke's *Second Treatise of Government*', *Journal of the History of Ideas*, 47 (1986), 575–6.
3. Barbara Arneil, 'Locke and Colonialism', *Journal of the History of Ideas*, 55 (1994), 593–7. Also see Barbara Arneil, 'John Locke, Natural Law, and Colonialism', *History of Political Thought*, 13 (1992).
4. Emer Vattel, *The Law of Nations or the Principles of Natural Law*, trans. C. G. Fenwick (Washington, DC, Carnegie Institution, 1916).
5. Christian Wolff, *The Law of Nations Treated According to a Scientific Method in which the Natural Law of Nations is Carefully Distinguished from that which is Voluntary, Stipulative and Customary*, trans. Francis J. Hemelt (Oxford, Clarendon Press, 1934), 'Prolegomena', §3.
6. Thomas Flanagan briefly discusses Vattel's position in 'The Agricultural Argument and Original Appropriation: Indian Lands and Political Philosophy', *Canadian Journal of Political Science*, 22 (1989).
7. F. G. Whelan, 'Vattel's Doctrine of the State', *History of Political Thought*, 9 (1988), 70.
8. Peter Pavel Remec, *The Position of the Individual in International Law According to Grotius and Vattel* (The Hague, Nijhoff, 1960), 150–1.
9. Richard H. Cox, *Locke on War and Peace* (Oxford, Clarendon Press, 1960), 150.
10. See Jonathan Scott, 'The Law of War: Grotius, Sidney, Locke and the Political Theory of Rebellion', *History of Political Thought*, 13 (1992), 565–86.
11. Whelan, 'Vattel's Doctrine of the State', 69.
12. Albert de Lapradelle, 'Emrich de Vattel', in John MacDonell and Edward Manson (eds.), *Great Jurists of the World* (New York, Kelley, 1968), 480–1. He describes that theory as a 'shrewd utilitarianism'.
13. Andrew Linklater, *Men and Citizens in the Theory of International Relations*, 2nd edn. (London, Macmillan, 1990), 88.
14. Samuel Pufendorf, *On the Natural State of Men*, trans. Michael Seidler (Lampeter, Edwin Mellen, 1990), #13.
15. Wolff, *The Law of Nations Treated According to a Scientific Method*, §72.
16. Wolff, *The Law of Nations Treated According to a Scientific Method*, 'Prolegomena', §18.
17. Remec, *The Position of the Individual in International Law*, 138.
18. Linklater, *Men and Citizens*, 85.
19. See Peter F. Butler, 'Legitimacy in a States-System: Vattel's *Law of Nations*', in *The Reason of States*, ed. Michael Donelan (London, Allen and Unwin, 1978), 50–1.
20. Linklater, *Men and Citizens*, 81.
21. Kalevi J. Holsti, *Peace and War: Armed Conflicts and International Order 1648–1989* (Cambridge, Cambridge University Press, 1991), 76.

22. Hans Reiss, in Immanuel Kant, *Political Writings*, ed. Hans Reiss (Cambridge, Cambridge University Press, 1991), 39–40.
23. Chris Brown, *International Relations Theory: New Normative Approaches* (London, Harvester Wheatsheaf, 1992), 14.
24. Hedley Bull, 'Martin Wight and the Theory of International Relations', *British Journal of International Studies*, 2 (1976), 105. Also see, Brian Porter, 'Patterns of Thought and Practice: Martin Wight's "International Theory" ', in Michael Donelan (ed.), *The Reason of States* (London, Allen and Unwin, 1978), 66–7; and Martin Wight, 'An Anatomy of International Thought', *Review of International Studies*, 13 (1987), 224–5.
25. Martin Wight, *International Theory: The Three Traditions*, ed. Gabriele Wight and Brian Porter (London and Leicester, University of Leicester Press, 1991), 45.
26. Hedley Bull, 'Society and Anarchy in International Relations', in H. Butterfield and M. Wight (eds.), *Diplomatic Investigations: Essays in the Theory of International Politics* (London, Allen and Unwin, 1966), 49.
27. Torbjörn L. Knutsen, *A History of International Relations Theory* (Manchester, Manchester University Press, 1992), 112.
28. Leonard Krieger, 'Kant and the Crisis of Natural Law', *Journal of the History of Ideas*, 26 (1965), 192–4.
29. Immanuel Kant, *Critique of Pure Reason*, trans. J. M. D. Meiklejohn (London, Dent, 1946), 12.
30. L. W. Beck, *A Commentary on Kant's Critique of Practical Reason* (Indianapolis, Library of Liberal Arts, 1960), 179 and 199–200. Also see Patrick Riley, *Kant's Political Philosophy* (Totowa, NJ, Rowman and Littlefield, 1960), 7. Riley argues against Rawls's and Beck's interpretation of Kant as a moral constructivist. He suggests that a good case can be made for believing that the moral law is not something constructed, but just 'there' (see pp. 56–7).
31. Roger Hancock, 'Kant and the Natural Right Theory', *Kant Studien*, 52 (1960–1), 440–1.
32. See Elie Kedourie, *Nationalism*, 4th edn. (Oxford, Blackwell, 1993; first edn. pub. Hutchinson, 1966), 13–14.
33. See Thomas Donaldson, 'Kant's Global Rationalism', in Terry Nardin and David R. Mapel (eds.), *Traditions of International Ethics* (Cambridge, Cambridge University Press, 1992), 137.
34. H. J. Paton, 'Analysis of the Argument', in H. J. Paton (ed.), *The Moral Law. Kant's Groundwork of the Metaphysics of Morals* (London, Routledge, 1991), 37.
35. Paton, *The Moral Law*, 55.
36. Krieger, 'Kant and the Crisis of Natural Law', 197.
37. Paton, *The Moral Law*, 76–7.
38. Paton, *The Moral Law*, 67.
39. James W. Ellington, 'Introduction', in Immanuel Kant, *Grounding for the Metaphysic of Morals*, ed. James W. Ellington (Indianapolis, Hackett, 1981), p. vii.
40. Paton, *The Moral Law*, 78.
41. Kedourie, *Nationalism*, 15.
42. Paton, *The Moral Law*, 100–1.
43. Hancock, 'Kant and the Natural Right Theory', 445–6.
44. G. A. Kelly, *Idealism, Politics and History: Sources of Hegelian Thought* (Cambridge, Cambridge University Press, 1969), 140.
45. See Howard Williams, *Kant's Political Philosophy* (Oxford, Basil Blackwell, 1983), 36–9.

46. Kenneth N. Waltz, 'Kant, Liberalism, and War', *American Political Science Review*, 56 (1962), 339.

47. Paton, translator's preface, *The Moral Law*, 7.

48. Paton, *The Moral Law*, 84–5.

49. See H. J. Paton, *The Categorical Imperative* (London, Hutchinson, n. d.), 148.

50. Paton, *The Moral Law*, 7.

51. Linklater, *Men and Citizens*, 101–2.

52. See W. B. Gallie, *Philosophers of Peace and War* (Cambridge, Cambridge University Press, 1979), 27–8.

53. Williams, *Kant's Political Philosophy*, 13.

54. Williams, *Kant's Political Philosophy*, 8.

55. Immanuel Kant, *The Critique of Judgement*, trans. James Creed Meredith (Oxford, Clarendon Press, 1991), II. 96 (433).

56. Kant, *The Critique of Judgement*, I. 112 (263).

57. Wolfgang Schwarz, 'Kant's Philosophy of Law and International Peace', *Philosophy and Phenomenological Research*, 23 (1962–3), 76.

58. See Gallie, *Philosophers of Peace and War*, 25.

59. J. H. Shennan, *International Relations in Europe 1689–1789* (London, Routledge, 1995), 63.

60. In *The Metaphysics of Morals* Kant contends that 'It must accordingly be prohibited for a state to use its own subjects as spies, and to use them, or indeed foreigners, as poisoners or assassins (to which class the so-called sharpshooters who wait in ambush on individual victims also belong), or even just to spread false reports' (*Political Writings*, 168).

61. See Gallie, *Philosophers of Peace and War*, 10. Gallie is generally dismissive of Kant's treatise on perpetual peace, considering it an incompetent attempt at popular polemics after years of serious philosophy.

62. Patrick Riley sums it up nicely when he says: 'the social contract is an "Idea of reason" which provides a standard for judging the adequacy of states and their laws, but which has nothing to do with actual agreement or with an actual promise to obey' ('On Kant as the Most Adequate of the Social Contract Theorists', *Political Theory*, 1 (1973), 450).

63. Riley, *Kant's Political Philosophy*, 116–18.

64. Riley, 'On Kant as the Most Adequate of the Social Contract Theorists', 452.

65. Williams, *Kant's Political Philosophy*, 40.

PART III

Historical Reason

12

REDEMPTION THROUGH INDEPENDENCE: ROUSSEAU'S THEORY OF INTERNATIONAL RELATIONS

The Emerging System of States

We have already seen how the Peace of Westphalia, which followed the Thirty Years War, provided the foundation for, and gave formal recognition to, the modern states system in Europe. It served to reduce the papacy and the Holy Roman Empire to the level of formal equality with the established states of Europe, and thus undermined their claims to universal authority.[1] By the mid-eighteenth century some states were recognizably nations, such as the five great powers, Britain, France, Austria, Prussia, and Russia. However, many smaller political units survived, some considerably diminished in status, such as Poland and Sweden and the former great colonial powers Spain, Portugal, and the United Provinces. These coexisted with the reduced supranational presence of the Holy Roman Empire and papacy and the almost decimated power of the Ottoman Empire. In addition the.: was a whole range of smaller political units, some of which existed within the territories of the larger. These included the ecclesiastical principalities in central Italy, and Avignon in France. There were also numerous secular principalities, of which there were about two hundred in Germany alone. Furthermore, and not without significance, were the city-states, which often little more than acknowledged notional allegiance to a distant ruler. All these entities maintained armies, engaged in diplomacy, and conducted themselves as independent agents in foreign affairs.[2]

Although the Peace of Westphalia failed to settle territorial disputes and placate rival claimant princes, and did little to diminish the outbreak of hostilities, it did mark the triumphant assertion of the modern state, which was in principle, if not always in fact, sovereign over its internal affairs and independent in its relations with other states.[3] Although no formal juridical equality of states could be assumed, the settlement circumscribed the territorial boundaries between them and unequivocally legitimized the principle of internal sovereignty. It was in this context, as we saw, that the concept of international law came into its own, ably assisted by such theorists, jurists, and diplomats as Grotius, Pufendorf, and Vattel. At the beginning of the eighteenth century the significant powers, with the exception of the Dutch Republic, were controlled by kings or princes. Dynastic disputes still played a significant role, but territorial, commercial, and security issues complicated the picture. Because most of the ruling houses were related, conflicts often took on the character of family disputes, but the principles of state relations were changing towards greater interdependence and collective security. Although the New World continued to be important, Europe was the main arena.[4]

The Peace of Westphalia (1648) sought to prevent any one power from becoming dominant, and was designed to undermine the hegemonic aspirations of the Habsburgs. Without being clearly articulated, and without a formal mechanism to effect it, the society of sovereign European states was to be regulated by a principle of equilibrium. It was ostensibly an anti-hegemonic system in which alliances and dynastic unions served to restrain the formation or emergence of unacceptable and threatening concentrations of power. The dynastic manœuvrings characteristic of the European system of states after the Peace of Westphalia were themselves a divisive force and gave rise to a series of wars of succession, the most significant of which was the Spanish, in which the Habsburgs and the Bourbons were the principal antagonists. The Utrecht settlement of 1714 partitioned the Spanish Empire and formalized the principles that had come to characterize international relations from the Peace of Westphalia; these became more explicit until the French Revolution, and the Vienna settlement of 1814–15 attempted to re-establish them. The fundamental concern of the territorial provisions of the Utrecht settlement was to establish and sustain an equilibrium. This is quite explicitly stated in the preamble of the treaty between England and Spain.[5] The idea of a balance of power, or an even distribution of power, maintained by an emerging conception of collective security was frequently invoked in international treaties down to the time of Bismarck, and was held by many jurists to be the primary prerequisite for the successful operation of international law.

France assumed the leadership of the anti-Habsburg coalition and under the auspices of Richelieu's statesmanship pursued a policy of internal consolidation, resulting in the creation of an absolute monarchy and the establishment of external anti-hegemonic alliances. When Louis XIV succeeded to the French throne he revived the aspirations that the Austrian and Spanish Habsburgs had been forced to abandon. During his reign, from 1661 to 1714, his grand design for a French-dominated Europe contravened the spirit of Westphalia and offended the general commitment of European states to the existence of a multitude of independent powers constantly realigning to maintain the delicate equilibrium.

The need to counter the threat of Louis XIV's France was acknowledged all over Europe. The Netherlands and Britain took the initiative in coalition-building, which was facilitated by the accession to the English throne by William of Orange. It was from this time onwards that the idea of a balance of power became widely discussed, and even some French writers like the theologian Fénelon, adviser to Louis XIV, acknowledged the desirability of maintaining the balance of power in Europe. He argued that the care to maintain a kind of equality and balance among neighbouring nations 'is that which secures the common repose; and in this respect such nations, being joined together by commerce, compose, as it were one great body and a kind of community'.[6] Reference to a community of European states became increasingly common throughout the eighteenth and nineteenth centuries, and as we shall see it is something both Burke and Hegel took for granted.

Rousseau's Ambiguity

Rousseau is notorious for the ambiguity that surrounds many of his most important doctrines. He did not attempt to be a systematic philosopher and largely reacted against the formalized rules of clear witty exposition practised by the Enlightenment *philosophes*.[7] Since Rousseau's death in 1778 interpreters of his thought have taken very different views on his intended meaning. His political philosophy has at once been condemned as proto-totalitarian and praised for its democratic sympathies. In his political theory of international relations he has mostly been misrepresented as an advocate of Abbé de Saint-Pierre's Project for Perpetual Peace,[8] misunderstood as an unremitting pessimist and an exponent of Realism who grasped the essential principles of power politics in opposition to Kantian Idealism,[9] or regarded as a structural or neo-Realist who portrayed war as endemic in the international system.[10]

Rousseau is more often than not characterized as the theorist who idealizes the noble savage in a state of nature free of interpersonal conflict, who when he begins to associate with others in society generates the inequalities and power relationships which engender conflict. It is suggested that the state of nature is an idyllic condition from which we have fallen and to which we can never return. Howard Williams, for example, portrays Rousseau's account of society as man's fall from Grace.[11] Society is the corrupter of humanity, and the state is the means of deliverance from this conflict, promising the possibility of domestic accord at the terrible price of the creation of a competitive anarchic state system in which war is inevitable, sometimes ameliorated, but impossible to eradicate.[12] Kenneth N. Waltz takes Rousseau to be the exemplar of the 'third image' in international relations. The first image attributes explanatory power to human nature, the second to the internal structure of the state, and the third to the structure of the international system itself. While all three are interrelated, the adoption of one as the primary focus often colours perceptions of the other two.[13] For Rousseau, Waltz tells us, the states system as it is provides a hostile environment in which the keeping of faith in a world which places very little value on it is bound to be to the detriment of one's state. Kings want only to increase their power over their subjects and to expand their territories. Peace furthers neither end. Would the situation be different if states reflected the General Will of their citizens rather than the particular wills of their monarchs? Waltz suggests that for Rousseau the absence of a sovereign at the international level necessarily implies that in relation to each other states do not share a General Will, and their policies inevitably reflect their particular wills. Conflict is inherent in the anarchic system of states in which the loosest of conventions and constraints exist and are constantly flouted because they are both unclear and unenforceable. Even states that are internally just in such a precarious and uncertain international system often embark upon unjust wars in order to enhance their security. Rousseau's solution to the problem, Waltz suggests, is the option of a federation of states.[14] While Rousseau did think that there is a solution to the problem, it is not in fact the one that Waltz attributes to him.

Such interpretations fail adequately to distinguish between Rousseau's explanation of what he takes to be the present corrupt and depraved condition of international relations, international relations as they would be in a world in which each state embodied the General Will of its citizens, and the international system as it would be if the conditions of freedom were met externally as well as within the state.

Looking at states as they are is necessarily 'realistic' in that it takes as its starting-point states and their relations as Rousseau saw them in his time: largely as a product of the Peace of Westphalia, which sanctioned the mechanism of force in preventing preponderances of power. He could detect nothing inherent in human nature which inevitably led to such a condition, and indeed believed that things could have been other than they were and might yet with extreme difficulty be different. Similarly, in the states system as currently constructed, with the personal interests and capricious whims of monarchs providing the motivating factors, consistent principles of state behaviour were impossible to identify. There could be no presumption that the interest of the state and its ruler coincided. Reform of the system without a fundamental transformation of the state would be futile. Where a state was transformed into one in which the General Will prevailed, the problem of international relations remained unresolved. Each state, even though it embodied the General Will of its citizens, was in relation to other states following its particular will. Reform of the international system would have had to reflect another important principle which made both men and states free. In order to be free a man must not be dependent upon another. Rousseau resolves this problem by making man dependent on the whole community, where he was not subjugated to the particular will of a master, but followed his own general will as expressed in the law. Internationally, relations of commerce in particular made states dependent and led to conflict among them. The solution was for states to become self-supporting and to withdraw from relations with other states. In other words, whereas the problem of corruption within society could not be solved by returning to the condition of the noble savage in a state of nature, Rousseau was advocating return to something like the condition of the noble savage for states.

State of Nature

Rousseau almost seemed to take a perverse pleasure in rejecting the conventional wisdom of the day and presenting ideas that were both novel and shocking. He rejects the view of Pufendorf that men are naturally social as well as Hobbes's contention that men are self-seeking and competitive by nature. Furthermore, he denies that history has brought progress in the condition of mankind.

Rousseau begins not with man in society, or as a moral being, or as God's creature, but with the isolated individual in a state of nature. Those who interpret Rousseau as a Realist philosopher of international relations tend to present his state of nature as if he believed that the golden idyllic age from which men have fallen and to which they can never return actually existed historically. Rousseau acknowledges that the idea of a state of nature is widely used, but he criticizes those who invoke it for projecting characteristics found in society upon men in their original condition. He argues that there never was a state of nature, nor a social contract established in the manner he suggests, and that therefore we should disregard recourse to the 'facts' when employing the concept of a state of nature in argument and rely instead upon 'right and reason' (*First Social Contract*, 114).[15] It is, then, a thought experiment. What purpose can such an idea have if it has no historical foundation? Rousseau argues that in positing basic postulates about human beings we are able to conjecture and reason conditionally, not on the true origin of the present state of things, but upon its contingency and how it may have been other than it is. The state of nature in Rousseau serves as a regulative idea against which the present condition of society and international relations may be judged.[16]

Criticisms of Hobbes

In a number of respects Rousseau begins his analysis by assuming many of the same things as Hobbes. His characterization of the state of nature, although different in detail from that of Hobbes, has much in common with that of his English predecessor. For Rousseau, unlike Pufendorf and Locke, the state of nature is not a social condition. Nor is it a moral condition. In the state of nature there is no justice and injustice. Men are portrayed as solitary and self-sufficient. It is a condition in which no one has the right to rule over another. Nature does not sanction legitimate authority or rule. Rousseau contends, however, that Hobbes is wrong to conclude that because man has no idea of goodness he is naturally evil, or will not help another individual to whom he has no obligation. Nor need we conclude from the idea that we have a right to those things we need that we have a right to everything. The savage man's concern for self-preservation only becomes prejudicial to the survival of others when one superimposes as Hobbes does the satisfaction of passions found only in society on the savage condition. While Rousseau thinks Hobbes a genius, he also thinks him perverse for imagining a race of people which thinks its welfare depends on the destruction of the entirety of its fellow human beings. He contends that Hobbes's motive for characterizing man in a perpetual state of war with his fellow men was his passionate desire to establish absolute rule and absolute obedience to it ('State of War', 45).

Hobbes's understanding of the state of nature would have been very different had he identified in man his one natural virtue.

Hobbes failed to identify the natural virtue of pity. It is pity, prior to all reflection, which mitigates the excesses of self-preservation. No man likes to see his fellow human beings suffer, and from pity all the rest of human virtues flow. Rousseau argues that 'Pity is what carries us without reflection to the aid of those we see suffering. Pity is what, in the state of nature, takes the place of laws, mores, and virtue, with the advantage that no one is tempted to disobey its sweet voice' ('Inequality', 55).[17] In his 'The State of War' Rousseau maintains that we have a natural revulsion to killing in cold blood. This, he says is a Natural Law written more indelibly in the heart than in reason ('State of War', 34). He seems to be suggesting that while there is no transcendental Natural Law of which we can have knowledge, there are natural sentiments which make us averse to certain kinds of action.

The state of nature for Rousseau is a condition in which human beings have little need of each other's company or support, and in which they have little or no need to associate beyond the drive to procreate. Savage man looks only to himself and desires peace and tranquillity. The state of nature is a condition of relative equality. While there are inequalities among men they are subject to natural limitations ('State of War', 37).

It is in origin of property that Rousseau identifies the source of inequality and most of the calamities that have befallen the human race. Power and reputation are the fruits of property. Labour, Rousseau argues, is the only conceivable source of a claim on property, and mixing your labour with land entitles you to the produce. The wheat in the field which results from my cultivating it is mine. My use of this field in successive years must have given rise to my claiming it as my own. On the other hand, the powerful see their strength and describe their need as 'a sort of right' to the property of others, which gives rise to a vicious conflict between 'the right of the strongest and the right of the first occupant'. Thus, Rousseau argues, 'Em..ging society gave way to the most horrible state of war . . . [and] brought itself to the brink of its ruin' ('Inequality', 68). In other words, what Rousseau is saying is that man's self-interestedness (*amour-propre*), or pride, is the wrong foundation for society and leads only to disputes. Egoistic individualism led to the breakdown of emerging society into a Hobbesian war of all against all. To resolve the conflict by basing the social contract on similar principles is a recipe for disaster.

Those accustomed to society are not content living within themselves and live only for the attention and recognition of others. It is in the judgement of others that man is aware of his own existence. The disputes which arose as a consequence of property led those advantaged by private ownership to propose the establishment of society in order to protect themselves and their property. In the state of nature there are of course natural inequalities of age, strength, ability, and health. People are unsuspectingly duped into consenting to those very institutions, based on egoistic individualism or self-love, that compound the artificial inequalities of honour, prestige, power, and privilege. The establishment of society immediately destroyed natural liberty and legitimated the acts of usurpation by which property had been acquired and inequality instituted, condemning the whole of the human race to 'labour, servitude and misery' ('Inequality', 70). What Rousseau wants to emphasize is that the passions that incline us to violence, aggression, and war are not pre-societal, but actually acquired in society itself. It is important to stress that Rousseau's *Social Contract* is an attempt to overcome the immorality and degradation consequent upon establishing a society based on a multiplicity of particular wills. A society based on the principle of the General Will, at the heart of which is the idea of the comon good, would eradicate the ills of modern society.

The state of war is for Hobbes a consequence of human nature. Without a Leviathan to keep states in awe they will always adopt the posture of war in relation to each other. States sustain a way of life and make life more commodious for their citizens, so that the posture of war against other states is never so unmitigated as it is in the state of nature. For Rousseau, war is the result of a corruption of human nature. It is a condition that prevails among states and not among individuals, and its consequences are far more destructive. Instead of alleviating violence, states accentuate it. Like Thucydides, Machiavelli, and Hobbes, Rousseau maintains that the weak consider themselves bound to the strong by informal agreements, alliances, and treaties. The strong, on the other hand, feel no similar obligation to the weak. Unlike the three Realists, however, Rousseau is not claiming that the strong have a right in nature to dominate the weak. He is simply stating a fact, and warns the Corsicans to steer clear of the great powers ('Corsica', 142).[18] He does not follow Machiavelli and Hobbes in propounding a doctrine of *raison d'état*. If states were motivated by their interests, their actions would be easier to predict. Instead it is the whims, momentary interests, and 'chance impulses' of ministers or their mistresses that determine policy. There can be no certainty or assurance in reading the behaviour of states because they act in accordance with no system of fixed principles: 'Nothing could be more frivolous than the political scienc_ of courts. Since it has no certain principles, no certain conclusions can be drawn from them; and all this fine theorising about the interest of princes is a child's game which makes sensible men laugh' (*Poland*, 192–3).[19] This amounts to a denial of Realism. The depravity into which monarchs have sunk prevents them from even rising above mere caprice in order to act in accordance with consistent principles of Reason of State.

Rousseau further distinguishes himself from exponents of Realism by denying the idea of Reason of State and the equation of might with right. He denies that right can be derived from might. Force is physical and from it no moral obligations can be generated. If force creates and sustains right, and without it men feel no obligation and cease to obey the ruling power, then right is superfluous: it adds nothing to force. Force does not create obligation, and one is obliged to obey only legitimate authority. No one has natural authority over his fellow men, and no amount of force can create that authority. It follows that authority must therefore arise out of convention. We must remember that Rousseau admired Machiavelli not as the teacher of *raison d'état* to princes, but as the teacher of republicans about the unscrupulous methods that princes were prepared to use in order to maintain their power (*Social Contract*, 183; 'Political Economy', 116).[20] To lay bare the principles of modern states and the modern international system would provide a similar service to those who value freedom and equality as opposed to subjection. In denying the principal contentions of Hobbes and refusing to equate might with right and to sanction the doctrine of *raison d'état*, Rousseau did not invoke the conventional idea of a transcendental Natural Law as the guide to states' conduct.

The Denial of Natural Law

Although Rousseau uses the vocabulary of the Natural Law school, and was thoroughly familiar with the writings of Grotius, Pufendorf, and Burlamaqui, the doctrine in his hands becomes transformed. Rousseau does not explicitly deny that the source of all justice is God. He even suggests that that which is good and conforms with order is so independently of conventions. He goes on to say, however, that our inability to receive justice from such an abstract source makes it necessary for us to establish governments (*Social Contract*, 160).[21] He relates Natural Law in the state of nature to natural sentiments which make us turn away from acts of cruelty. It is not a Law of Nature discoverable by, or consistent with, reason. Natural man has not yet developed rational capacities. This must await the institution of civil society. Robert Derathé, the foremost exponent of Rousseau as a Natural Law theorist, argues that it is in civil society that Rousseau re-establishes the connection between reason and the Law of Nature. He admits, however, that his interpretation holds only in relation to the moral theory and that he can find no way of reconciling the political theory of the General Will with the idea of a Law of Nature.[22]

In *The Social Contract* Rousseau mocks recourse to patriarchal grounds of authority by declining to talk of Adam's or Noah's generation of titles (*Social Contract*, 143). In the preface to the 'Discourse on the Origin of Inequality' he is critical of the doctrine of the modern Natural Law school. Modern exponents of Natural Law, Rousseau argues, restrict it to the moral relations among rational men, whose reason is the instrument through which it is known. Although their definitions of the Natural Law vary, they are all agreed that it is impossible to come to know its precepts and to obey them without being a 'great reasoner and profound metaphysician' ('Inequality', 35). Paradoxically, men must have required for the establishment of society only what a select few acquire within it, namely a highly developed rational faculty. Rousseau makes a similar point in *The Social Contract* when he talks of the substitution of justice for instinct. In order to make just laws, men should already be what they will become as a result of the laws (*Social Contract*, 164).

Throughout the chapters in this book on the idea of a Universal Moral Order, ranging from the Stoics to Pufendorf, we saw how a community of mankind lay at its heart. This community is typically seen to be subject to a moral law which in some way has to acknowledge and accommodate the institution of particularistic societies and states to which duties are owed.

Rousseau argues that it is a fallacy to think that there is a general society of mankind united under a universal moral law. There is no common feeling that makes humanity one, or any sense that in acting as an individual an end relative and general to the whole is being pursued. Rousseau denies that ideas of God and the Natural Law can be innate in men's hearts. If they were there would be no need to teach them, because we would be teaching what people already knew. Far from the moral community of humanity manifesting itself in society, that is, the universal giving rise to the particular, it is our experience of actually constituted society that has generated ideas of an imagined universal society. We must first become citizens in order to conceive of ourselves as men. What reason teaches the facts confirm. It is relatively late in human development that the laudable ideas of Natural Right and the brotherhood of man emerge; they do not become widely disseminated until the advent of Christianity, and even then they are intermittent and unsettled. Even under the laws of Justinian the humanity of the Romans extended only as far as the boundaries of the empire (*First Social Contract*, 104–9).

Men in the state of nature are still brutes and savages, whatever other qualities they may have possessed when looked at retrospectively. They knew nothing of human relationships and were not self-conscious of being free. Principles of Natural Law would simply be inapplicable within the state of nature because its inhabitants have no recognizable moral relations with, or obligations to, each other, and would lack the capacity to follow its precepts. Rousseau denies Pufendorf's and Locke's contention that men are naturally sociable, and strongly condemns the idea that there is a natural society of humanity. It is only with the development of self-consciousness, of oneself and of others in a society, that human potentialities develop. The inequalities found among men in society are not sanctioned by the moral Natural Law in a state of nature; they are in Rousseau's view most certainly the consequence of human law.

Exponents of Natural Law begin by identifying rules that it would be appropriate for men to agree upon as socially useful and give to them the name of Natural Law on no other grounds than the supposed good that would result from their universal observance. Such explanations of the nature of things are based on more or less arbitrary notions of what seems right. Rousseau's main contention against Natural Law jurists is that they assume what they seek to prove. They consistently fail to strip away those characteristics of man acquired in society. They take what men have socially acquired and project it back into a state of nature. In other words, Natural Law jurists fail to go back far enough or deep enough into the origins of man.

Rousseau and Historical Reason

Despite the fact that Rousseau used the fashionable vocabulary of Natural Rights, his ideas represented a considerable departure from what was conventionally associated with the doctrine. Primarily, he denied that humanity has an immutable moral nature, or that society is created to protect pre-existing and inalienable Natural Rights. His state of nature is not a moral condition, and its inhabitants are so deficient in reason that even if there were a moral law under which Natural Rights were subsumed they would not be capable of coming to know it. Human nature is not immutable. Rousseau maintains that the human race differs in character from age to age. The soul and passions of human beings, along with needs and pleasures, change. What was the ultimate happiness for the savage will reduce the civilized man to despair. Robert Wokler has pointed out that, more than any modern thinker, Rousseau believes that human nature is shaped by politics.[23] To use Hollis's term, man is plastic. His nature is malleable and susceptible of being moulded.[24] This is not to say that man is infinitely malleable. The historical process works on material that is limited in its potential. Natural man is impelled by the sentiments of self-love and pity, but he also possesses a free will and the capacity for perfectibility, or self-improvement. Rousseau was certainly of the opinion that man's plasticity was amenable to both exalted and depraved influences. A good society provides the environment for the development of virtuous citizens whose interests are in harmony with the common good. A corrupt society produces citizens motivated by their particular selfish wills.

The emergence from the state of nature is not for Rousseau the beginning of an inevitable decline: it is the point at which all that is greatest in humanity can be cultivated and flourish, or alternatively it has the potential for generating the utmost depravity. We as humans determine that course. The state of nature for Rousseau is not a moral condition. It is in fact barely a human condition. It is by entering into society that people acquire what is distinctly human. The individual becomes transformed 'from a stupid, limited animal into an intelligent being and a man' (*Social Contract*, 151). Justice is substituted for instinct, duty for physical impulse, and right for appetite. Only then can men's souls become elevated, their minds develop, their intellectual horizons broaden, and their feelings take on new depths. Rousseau's theory is constitutive in that the nature of man is related to the social relationships into which he is interwoven and which extend over long periods of time. Human nature and human community are inextricable, the latter being constitutive of the former.

The purpose of his 'Discourse on the Origin of Inequality' is to demonstrate not only the social and historical origins of human wickedness, but also the social origins of morality.[25] Humans would be the most exalted creatures if it were not for the abuse of their new condition, which often leads them to a condition lower than that which they left. In looking at the corruption and immorality around him Rousseau charts the path to degradation that men have trodden. Howard

Williams is wrong to claim that Rousseau objects to 'government and society in general'.[26] What he objects to is government which is premised on self-interest and whose principles have permeated the international society of states. The purpose of *The Social Contract* is the transformation of this condition.

Like Giambattista Vico, Rousseau sees the human world as a product of human intelligence. The evils that he sees around him—the power politics, insecurity, and immorality—are of human creation and, far from being structurally inherent and deterministic, can be overcome by human will. Thus, far from being the extreme pessimist that Realists portray him to be, Rousseau has faith in the human capacity for self-redemption, starting with the reconstitution of the state on ethical principles. The criterion of ethical conduct is to be not an abstract Natural Law divorced from the experience of human beings, nor principles based upon self-interest and capable of justifying any capricious act, but instead a criterion that is immanent in the real will of individuals, a criterion based upon the principle of a common good rather than self-interest, the idea of the General Will rather than a particular will. This is what he means at the beginning of *The Social Contract* when he says that 'I will always try in this inquiry to bring together what right permits with what interest prescribes, so that justice and utility do not find themselves at odds with one another' (*Social Contract*, 141). He goes on to say that the rights of a social order are the most sacred of all and are the foundation of all others. The rights are not natural, but instead 'founded upon conventions'. Unlike the human constitution, which is a work of nature, the constitution of the state is a work of art (*Social Contract*, 194).

The State as the Political Unit in International Relations

The existence of one society established on the principle of self-interest inevitably gives rise to a multiplici./ of societies for the purpose of self-protection against united forces. Natural compassion between individuals in a state of nature lost almost all its compunction in relations among societies. For Rousseau, then, the division of the world into separate societies is artificial, and the barriers that separate different nations are human artefacts.

The inconveniences that forced men in the state of nature to unite are compounded in the relations among nations. War, battles, and reprisals have given rise to perversions of reason which make it honourable and virtuous to kill one's fellow human beings.

In 'The State of War' Rousseau argues that there are natural limits on the inequalities among individuals, whereas the state, which is a human artifice, has no natural limits. Its size, strength, and security are relative to other states, with which it has to compare itself. Unlike a natural body, however, the members of a state do not cohere and act in unison. Often the individual wills acting disparately are more powerful than the public will, and the larger the state the more difficult it is to engender public spirit and act as a united entity. It is to the advantage of a state to destabilize others by methods designed to prevent the development of social cohesion and public-spiritedness, and thus to avoid its own relative position deteriorating in relation to its neighbours. The basic greed about which Rousseau talks in his essay on the origins of inequality is fuelled by the prospect of benefiting from the spoils of war. War then becomes transformed in men's minds from a contest between enemies and warriors into a free-for-all between brigands, thieves, and tyrants.

War, understood correctly, is the consequence of an overt mutual disposition among states to destroy or considerably weaken each other. This disposition constitutes a state of war, whilst its transformation into action constitutes a condition of war ('State of War', 40). War is not, however, a relation between individual human beings. It is a relationship between states in which private individuals are enemies only incidentally, not as citizens but as soldiers, defenders of their homelands. The state can have as its enemy only another state (*Social Contract*, 145–6). The public person of the state, or sovereign, is the only entity legitimately to enter into a relation of war. All other disputes are private conflicts.

Those who interpret Rousseau as a Realist take his commentary on Saint-Pierre's project for perpetual peace as an extremely pessimistic account of international relations. Once again, however, we should not lose sight of Rousseau's analysis of the current condition of relations among states, and what he thought might be possible in future. Rousseau is not suggesting that a world of multiple states inevitably leads to conflict. His analysis is much more subtle. He is saying that states as they are currently constituted, established as they are to further the particular interests of those who wish to consolidate and perpetuate inequalities, are bound to come into constant conflict. Saint-Pierre is therefore naïve to appeal to states as they are currently constituted to form a pacific confederation. It is not so much of Saint-Pierre's aspiration that Rousseau is critical as of the terribly naïve view that he had of the interests of rulers in contemporary Europe. They were, Rousseau argues, motivated not by a desire to achieve the common good, but by self-interest and the desire to dominate.

Saint-Pierre's constitution for a federation of Europe presupposes the co-operation of the ruling heads of state.[27] First, they should contract irrevocably to establish a permanent assembly in which disputes would be resolved by arbitration or judicial process. Second, the European sovereigns must agree upon the number of representatives, the procedures for rotating offices of responsibility, and the proportion of expenses to be levied from each country. Third, the federation should guarantee the *status quo* and renounce all prior claims to territory or possessions against each other, with the exception of future disputed successions or other claims that may arise. Such disputes would be resolved by arbitration, and resort to force should be absolutely prohibited. Fourth, terms should be agreed upon which any member may be proscribed for breaking the articles of the treaty, and provisions should be made for collective security in forcing recalcitrant states to capitulate to the terms of the treaty. And finally, the fifth article gives the assembly of the federation legislative powers. Initially it would be allowed to make provisional decisions on a simple majority vote, and after five years definitive decisions on a three-quarters majority vote, concerning matters for the common good of the commonwealth of Europe. None of the five articles should be altered without the unanimous consent of all parties.

In justification of the plan Saint-Pierre suggests that it must be demonstrated that such a scheme would bring about lasting peace, and that it is in the interest of sovereigns to establish a federation of Europe. On the first issue, he contends that once a federation of Europe is established no state, or small alliance of states, would transgress the agreed articles at the risk of being brought back into line by the united forces of the whole. Such a federation need fear no rebellion from its members. The motives for which states enter into war—conquest, self-defence, to weaken a powerful neighbour, to maintain a state's rights, to settle a dispute where negotiation has failed, or to fulfil the terms of a treaty obligation—would all become redundant with the establishment of the federation. Aspirations of conquests would have to be abandoned because of the impossibility of making them, but likewise all fear of being conquered would be eliminated, and there would no longer be any need to attempt to weaken one's neighbours because of a fear of their growing power. States would no longer need to go to war to maintain their rights. Past rights would be acknowledged under the terms of article three of the treaty, and disputes that might arise over rights in future would be settled by arbitration. Finally, having no potential enemy to fear, a state would have no need of protective alliances and would not therefore be called upon to fulfil treaty obligations of the sort currently in existence.

The question of whether a federation of Europe is in the interests of each state is again answered in the affirmative. States, Saint-Pierre suggests, labour under the illusion that there are gains to be made from wars. More often than not the victorious side is left enfeebled, and is consoled only by the thought that the vanquished is left more enfeebled than itself. This purported advantage is itself a mere appearance because in relation to non-disputants the victorious state has become less powerful. The longer-term costs of the depletion of resources in war are also rarely calculated. The higher tax burden, disruption of trade, depopulation through casualties, and also the decrease in the birth rate all weaken the state, which would be much stronger with a smaller territory to protect and a population not exhausted by the ravages of war, but sustained by good laws. Furthermore, a state subjecting itself to the benefits of federation rather than to the fortunes of war eliminates much of the uncertainty that currently prevails. Previous disputes are renounced, established successions according to the conventions of the land are affirmed, trade facilitated, agriculture developed as a consequence of improved security, extraordinary taxes for military adventures eliminated, and the possibility created for the better flourishing of the arts and sciences.

Rousseau concludes his comments on Saint-Pierre's project by emphasizing that its author assumes men not as they ought to be but as they are in reality: 'unjust, grasping and setting their own interest above all things' ('Saint-Pierre's Project', 87). Such men should, however, be assumed to have enough reason to know their own interests and enough courage to act upon them for the sake of their happiness. 'If, in spite of all this, the project remains unrealised, that is not because it is utopian; it is because men are crazy, and because to be sane in a world of madmen is in itself a kind of madness' ('Saint-Pierre's Project', 88).[28]

In his judgement on the project Rousseau sounds a note of cynicism. The Abbé Saint-Pierre, he argues, reasons soundly on how the federation would work after it was instituted, but exhibits the judgement of a child on how it was to be set up ('Saint-Pierre's Project', 94). The rulers of European states as they are currently constituted have only two objects in mind: externally to expand their rule into new territories, and internally to make their rule more absolute. The establishment of a federation of Europe would circumvent both designs. It would freeze not only the boundaries of the state, but also its constitution. To secure a prince against rebellion at the same time is to secure a people against tyranny. No prince, Rousseau argues, is likely to accept being forced to be just not only to foreigners but also to his own subjects. What Saint-Pierre fails to realize is that foreign adventurism and the entrenchment of internal despostism go hand in hand; they are mutually supportive. Foreign adventures provide the prince with the pretext for raising taxes to support a standing army, which he uses to suppress the people further. The prince's ministers similarly have no interest in peace because it is to their advantage to perpetuate war and plunge him into difficulties in order to make him more reliant upon them. They use war in order to manipulate the prince, undermine their rivals in his eyes, and scheme towards consolidating their own power and wealth. With peace the prince is able to become independent of them and diminish their influence. Rousseau contends that it is not so much that the scheme for perpetual peace is impractical, but that it will never be adopted by men like these. Such men oppose schemes for lasting peace by ridicule, and demean the proposals in the eyes of the prince. It is ridiculous to envisage such a project succeeding 'under the present circumstances' ('Saint-Pierre's Project', 100). Self-interested rulers will not agree to federation.

Rousseau acknowledges that Henry IV's and Sully's abortive but well-planned attempt to establish a Christian commonwealth by means of conquest was laudable in intent. It would now, however, be an anachronism. The Westphalian settlement legitimated the principle of the balance of power, and any ruler who tried to realize Henry IV's project by means of force would be defeated by an alliance of the other European states. Unification by means of force was certainly no longer feasible, and any attempt to institute it might well result in doing 'more harm in a moment than it would guard against for ages' ('Saint-Pierre's Project', 100). Both a federation by agreement and a federation by force are not in Rousseau's view feasible solutions to European conflict among states.

The Solution

Although Rousseau paints an extremely pessimistic picture of the condition of states in their relations with each other, he is not always despairing about the prospects of a transformation. He says in the 'Geneva Manuscript' that 'far from thinking that there is neither virtue nor happiness for us and that heaven has abandoned us without resources to the depravation of the species, let us attempt to draw from the ill itself the remedy that should cure it. Let us use new associations to correct, if possible, the defect of the general association' (*First Social Contract*, 110). The solution for the internal ills of the state does not in itself solve the problem of conflict in international relations. The reason for this is that

the will of the state, however general it may be in relation to its members, is no longer so in relation to other states and to their members, but becomes for them a private and individual will which has its rule of justice in the Law of Nature, which enters equally into the principle established. For then the great city of the world becomes the political body whose Law of Nature is always the General Will, and whose states and diverse peoples are merely private individuals. ('Political Economy', 114)

Rousseau's preoccupation with freedom and independence finds political expression in numerous tracts, including 'Constitutional Project for Corsica', the 'Discourse on Political Economy', and *The Social Contract*. Independence is action unconstrained by external social or moral laws, and freedom is acting in conformity with the moral law, free of other constraints. Both independence and freedom meet two negative criteria. Both require the absence of subjection to another person and to one's own lower nature. Man in the state of nature is capable of being independent because he is solitary and the qualitative distinction between higher and lower nature does not apply. His freedom in the civil condition is more difficult to attain. To avoid personal servitude Rousseau proposes to make individuals dependent not on other individuals or institutions but upon the whole community, which protects the goods and person of every citizen with the united force of all. He is liberated from subjection to his lower nature in uniting with others, and in so doing the individual obeys only himself as the author of the laws to which he subscribes. Freedom is equated with obedience to law, and law is equated with the expression of the General Will of the whole community. Inequalities are in fact forms of dominance and dependence, and as we have seen they are artificially instituted to the detriment of the whole society. Rousseau is not suggesting that there should be no inequalities, only that there should be none based on birth. He argues that 'the state should grant no distinctions save for merit, virtue, and patriotic service; and these distinctions should be no more hereditary than are the qualities on which they are based' ('Corsica', 148). In order to avoid dependency of one region upon another within the state Rousseau would as far as possible reduce to a minimum the gross inequalities which currently exist.

The virtuous person is the person whose will is in conformity with the General Will. Patriotism, or love of one's country, is what most effectively promotes this identity, because when we love a people we more readily want what they want. The sympathy, sentiment, and obligations we feel towards our fellow citizens are all the more powerful in being circumscribed by community. The moral rights we acquire as citizens arise out of conventions. Conceptions of a Universal Moral Order of humanity arise out of our circumscribed communities, and do not exist prior to them. Like Pericles, Rousseau extols the virtue of a passionate love of one's country which is 'a hundred times more ardent and delightful than that of a mistress' ('Political Economy', 121; cf. *Poland*, 168). The community of the whole world dilutes the sentiment of humanity and provides little or no foundation for obligations to each other as fellow human beings rather than citizens. The most virtuous acts, Rousseau contends, arise out of the sentiment of patriotism ('Political Economy', 121). Each people has, or ought to have, a national character. If it did not it would have to be given one. It is national traditions and institutions that shape the character of a people and give rise to its genius. Education 'must give souls a national formation' by instilling in the young the whole cultural heritage of its people. A people whose love of liberty and country has been brought to the 'highest pitch' will not easily be conquered (*Poland*, 190). A free nation, in Rousseau's view, is not dependent upon any other nation for anything. Contrary to Kant's belief that progress in international relations will develop out of greater interdependence, Rousseau believes that interdependence creates the conditions for international conflict.

In characterizing the international relations of his time, and in identifying the corrupt motivating principles of modern European states, he warns even peaceful states to keep a watchful eye on their neighbours. But this does not mean that he thinks the states system as currently constituted is permanent and structurally determining. Rousseau himself contends that 'arguing from the actual to the possible seems like good logic to me' (*Social Contract*, 195). To transcend such a situation is to set free not only the oppressed but also the oppressor, for 'he who believes himself the master of others does not escape being more of a slave than they' (*Social Contract*, 141). Rousseau in fact deplores relationships of dependence. The state that appears to be in the dominant position invariably ends up becoming dependent upon the weaker. Freedom for Rousseau, both at a personal level and for states, becomes compromised when one party wants to deprive another of its freedom and mostly ends up losing its own. He warns the Poles, for example, that a people that wants to retain its freedom ought to abjure aspirations of conquest.[29] This is because he believes that there is an optimum size for each state, beyond which the social bond begins to weaken. He maintains that in general a smaller state is proportionately stronger than a larger state (*First Social Contract*, 122). He warns that the needs of states grow in the same way as those of individuals, not by necessity but by an increase in unnecessary desires. Extra expenditure is incurred in order to provide a pretext to increase income. Conquest which satisfies this desire is often driven by a different motive from the one proclaimed. Far from wanting to increase the wealth and territory of the nation, its leaders wish to increase their authority at home by war, expanding the number of troops and diverting the minds of the people with foreign wars. Nothing is more miserable, Rousseau argues, than a conquering people, because the increase in the size of its territory leads to increased expenditure on administration. Not only does a territory within the state have to maintain its own administration, but it also has to contribute to the upkeep of the central administration ('Political Economy', 131). Conquest is a form of servitude which makes the conqueror dependent upon the conquered. Even the great nations have overextended themselves in this respect and fallen into decay. Rousseau's advice is that a state should strive to be self-sufficient in order to avoid dependence on another. His advice to the Corsicans, for example, is to 'depend on yourselves only', and not to allow foreign masters to exploit internal dissension in order to make them dependent ('Corsica', 142–3).

If a state maintains its independence it will neither need to conquer nor be vulnerable to conquest. He advises both the Corsicans and the Poles that if they wish to be self-sustaining, happy, free, and peaceful nations they must revive the laudable and wholesome aspects of their customs. Money should be replaced if possible by stronger and more patriotic motives for performing 'great deeds' (*Poland*, 177; cf. 'Corsica', 143).They should foster a healthy and courageous warrior spirit without allying it with ambition. This can be accomplished by the establishment of a citizens' militia, requiring the whole nation to undergo military training. Traditional trades should be encouraged and agriculture developed. In the 'Project for Corsica' Rousseau argues that the development of agriculture is the only sound means of making a state independent in external affairs. No amount of wealth is a substitute for self-sufficiency in the production of food. To be dependent upon another state for imports of food is to be at its mercy. Commerce, while it produces wealth, leads at the same time to dependency. Rousseau equates agriculture, however, with freedom ('Corsica', 145). He is also aware that the temptations of the city draw young men away from agricultural life. His remedy is to make land the basis of the rights and status of citizens, and to strengthen family ties by making paternity conditional upon land ('Corsica', 155). Furthermore, he would not leave the depletion of resources to the discretion of the individual. He advocates the intelligent, planned, and sustainable exploitation of such resources as the forest.

In Rousseau's view Christianity, with its emphasis upon otherworldliness, has both undermined the internal unity of the state and accentuated the possibility of conflict in relations amo..g nations because of its aspirations to become a universal religion. It can clearly be inferred from Rousseau's discussion of the civil religion in *The Social Contract* that a return to a more nationally based religion modelled on paganism would contribute considerably towards reducing international conflict, particularly wars of religion. His discussion here can plausibly be viewed as an extension of his concern with national independence. All states in ancient times, he argues, placed at their head a god associated with a particular cult. Their separate and particular religions were undifferentiated from their governments. The sphere of the gods was circumscribed by national boundaries. The gods of pagan nations had no claims over people from different nations. They were not jealous gods. To serve the state was also to serve its god. The state was a theocracy in which the pontiff was the prince and the priest the magistrate. The only way to convert a people was to conquer it and expel its gods. Rousseau does not, however, want explicitly to say that paganism is superior to Christianity. Pagan religions, he contends, are false because they cultivate credulity and encourage superstition. They replace the true worship of divinity with empty ritual. At their worst they destabilize the state when they become exclusive and tyrannical, intolerant of all who do not worship their god. Rousseau follows Hobbes in wanting to reunite religion with the sovereign. He acknowledges that a national religion is never likely to be established again, by which he means that no people will universally accept the same dogmas. Rousseau rejects both paganism and Christianity in favour of a 'purely civil profession of faith, the articles of which it belongs to the sovereign to establish, not exactly as dogmas of religion, but as sentiments of sociability, without which it is impossible to be a good citizen or a faithful subject' (*Social Contract*, 226).

Rousseau's emphasis upon small self-sustaining communities to which citizens are intimately and passionately related, and in which the General Will is the expression of their real wills, has typically engendered the criticism that his project of redemption is impractical given the emergence of today's advanced, progressive, and interdependent state. It is suggested that his theory is a curiosity, and an idle one at that.[30] Such critics fail to see the irony in their strictures. They are simply reasserting what Rousseau was rejecting. Advancement in the arts and sciences, including widespread trade and interdependence, based as they are upon particular and selfish interests, is the cause of the problem. Whatever proposals may be put forward to reform the modern states system, any which rely upon the co-operation of the prevailing establishment would merely perpetuate the delusion under which Saint-Pierre laboured. Such critics would in Rousseau's view exemplify the corrupt rationality of modern man and his inability to recognize his real or true interest.

Notes

1. F. Parkinson, *The Philosophy of International Relations: A Study in the History of Thought* (Beverly Hills, Calif., and London, Sage, 1977), 44.
2. Franklin L. Ford, *Europe 1780–1830*, 2nd edn. (London, Longmans, 1989), 51–61.
3. Adam Watson, *The Evolution of International Society* (London, Routledge, 1992), 186.
4. J. H. Shennan, *International Relations in Europe 1689–1789* (London, Routledge, 1995), 1.
5. See Watson, *Evolution of International Society*, 199.
6. François Fénelon, 'The Balance of Power as a Source of Stability' trans. William Gaunt, in Evan Luard (ed. and introd.), *Basic Texts in International Relations* (London, Macmillan, 1992), 385.
7. Maurice Cranston, 'Remembering Rousseau', *Encounter*, 51 (1978), 38.
8. Kenneth N. Waltz, *Man, the State and War: A Theoretical Analysis* (New York, Columbia University Press, 1959), 6–7 and 165–86; F. Melian Stawell, *The Growth of International Thought* (London, Thornton Butterworth, 1929), 140–68; and Howard P. Kainz (ed.), *Philosophical Perspectives on Peace* (London, Macmillan, 1987), 39. Also see the introduction by G. Lowes Dickinson to Rousseau's *A Project for Perpetual Peace*, trans. E. M. Nuttall (London, F. Warne, 1927), p. xxii.
9. Stanley Hoffman, *The State of War: Essays on the Theory and Practice of International Politics* (New York, Praeger, 1965), 54–87.

10. Waltz, *Man, the State and War*, 6–7 and 165–86.
11. Howard Williams, *International Relations in Political Theory* (Buckingham, Open University Press, 1992), 70.
12. Ian Clark, *Reform and Resistance in the International Order* (Cambridge, Cambridge University Press, 1981), 62.
13. Waltz, *Man, the State and War*, 160.
14. Waltz, *Man, the State and War*, 185.
15. Jean Jacques Rousseau, *The First Version of the Social Contract* trans. Judith R. Masters (The Geneva Manuscript) in *Rousseau on International Relations*, ed. Stanley Hoffmann and David P. Fidler (Oxford, Clarendon Press, 1991). Elsewhere Rousseau contends that '. . . it is here less a question of history and facts than of right and justice, and that I wish to examine things according to their nature rather than according to our prejudices' (Rousseau, 'The State of War', in *International Relations*, 36).
16. Michael C. Williams, 'Rousseau, Realism and *Realpolitik*', *Millennium*, 18 (1989), 190.
17. Jean-Jacques Rousseau, 'Discourse on the Origin of Inequality', in *The Basic Political Writings*, trans. Donald A. Cress (Indianapolis, Hackett, 1987).
18. Rousseau, 'Constitutional Project for Corsica' trans. Frederick Watkins, in *International Relations*, 139–61.
19. Rousseau, *Considerations on the Government of Poland* trans. Frederick Watkins, in *International Relations*.
20. Rousseau, 'Discourse on Political Economy', in *The Basic Political Writings*.
21. Rousseau, *On the Social Contract*, in *The Basic Political Writings*.
22. Robert Derathé, *Jean-Jacques Rousseau et la science politique de son temps* (Paris, University of Paris Press, 1950). For an excellent account and criticism of Derathé's interpretation see David Cameron, *The Social Thought of Rousseau and Burke: A Comparative Study* (London, Weidenfeld and Nicolson for the London School of Economics, 1973), 69–76.
23. Robert Wokler, 'Rousseau's Pufendorf: Natural Law and the Foundations of Commercial Society', *History of Political Thought*, 15 (1994), 373.
24. Martin Hollis, *Models of Man* (Cambridge, Cambridge University Press, 1977).
25. Arthur M. Melzer, 'Rousseau's Moral Realism: Replacing Natural Law with the General Will', *American Political Science Review*, 77 (1983), 640.
26. Williams, *International Relations in Political Theory*, 70.
27. In 1754 Rousseau agreed to edit and abridge Saint Pierre's *Project for Making Peace Perpetual in Europe* (1713).
28. Rousseau, 'Abstract and Judgement of Saint-Pierre's Project for Perpetual Peace', in *International Relations*.
29. See M. Levin, 'Rousseau on Independence', *Political Studies*, 18 (1970), 497.
30. See Chris Brown, *International Relations Theory: New Normative Approaches* (London, Harvester Wheatsheaf, 1992), 58.

13

EDMUND BURKE AND HISTORICAL REASON IN INTERNATIONAL RELATIONS

During the eighteenth century Britain, conscious of its geographical detachment from continental Europe, saw itself as holding the balance of power. This self-proclaimed role was expressed in almost every annual Mutiny Act from 1727 to 1867. These acts charged the British army with the task of preserving 'the balance of power in Europe'.[1] It would be an overstatement to say that during the eighteenth century Europe constituted a system of states regulated by the principle of the balance of power for the common good. It was often self-interest rather than consciously acting in conformity with the mechanism of a system which motivated states to construct alliances to constrain the power of rival states. The fact that the principle of the balance of power was deliberately pursued did, however, promote the idea of a good that was greater than the self-interest of one state.[2] The community of states regulated their relations by means of four integral institutions: international law, which was often a codification of well-established customary practices; recognition or legitimacy acknowledging internal sovereignty and subscribing to the principle of non-interference; a constant diplomatic presence and continuing dialogue; and finally, the resort to limited war as a means of adjusting imbalances.[3] It was not, then, a system that prevented war—indeed, war was intrinsic to its aim of restoring or maintaining the balance of power—but it was nevertheless limited war aimed at diminishing rather than wholly destroying the power of a state. When Burke argues that war 'is the sole means of justice among nations' ('Letters on a Regicide Peace, I', *Works*, vi. 156) and contends that the 'annihilation of France' is not desirable for Great Britain, nor for 'Europe as a whole' ('A Letter to a Member of the National Assembly', *Works*, iv. 292–3),[4] he is consciously invoking the principles of the practice of international relations as he saw them in his own time. Commentators have tended to highlight Burke's critique of rationalism and radicalism in the *Reflections* in relation to his fears for the internal stability of both France and England. They emphasize his fear that basic English values are in danger of being destroyed.[5] In addition, however, and very prominent among his concerns in his vehement condemnation of the French

Revolution and its aftermath, was the expression of outrage at the flagrant attack upon the traditionally accepted idea of a European balance, and a call upon Great Britain to fulfil its self-appointed function of restoring the balance. This is not to deny that he was probably more alarmed at the implications of the application of the principles of the rights of man to the English constitution by radicals inspired by the French Revolutionaries. Indeed, to destroy the institutions and constitution of the state was itself a threat to the balance of Europe. The balance of power became such an established concept during the eighteenth century that Burke merely reflected its general acceptance as the acknowledged code of international relations when he called it the 'common law of Europe' ('Letters on a Regicide Peace, IV', *Works*, vi. 259).

Colonialism

Although Burke is infamous for his vehement attack on the French Revolution, he made an important and lasting contribution to articulating a conception of imperial relations which emphasized the responsibilities of empire. He lived during a period when the American, Irish, and Indian questions were at the forefront in British politics. The prevailing conception of colonial relations was one of a God-given right of the mother country to extract raw materials and to compel the colonized country to accept manufactured products in exchange.[6] The economies of colonies were subordinate to the British economy, and foreign trade was restricted to transportation by British ships. Ireland, for example, was the principal market for English export trade and was compelled to sell wool to no other country but England, and was prohibited from processing it into manufactured commodities. Even though Ireland was dependent upon America for potash to bleach its linen, Irish ships were prohibited from trading with the colonies.[7] Similarly the Navigatic.. Acts and ordinances restricting manufacture were designed to subordinate the American economy to Britain.[8] Burke wished to see a much greater degree of economic and political autonomy and a more equitable enjoyment of civil liberties and the privileges of citizenship within an imperial context. He never questioned the existence of the empire as such, but rather envisaged it as a loose federation of states with co-ordinated parliaments, all relatively autonomous, but nevertheless subordinate to, but not dominated by, the British Parliament, which would retrieve and perform the functions of colonial governments only when they proved incapable of performing them for themselves.

The American War of Independence, which Burke had unsuccessfully campaigned to avert, was itself, for Burke, not only a threat to liberty in the empire, but also a threat to the balance of Europe. The 1778 American treaty with France augured the prospect that an American defeat would seriously weaken France in Europe and inordinately strengthen the position of George III, with the further possible erosion of civil liberties by his court style of government. If Britain were to be vanquished then France would become the pre-eminent power in Europe, constituting a threat to British security and almost certainly leading to a revival of the aborted French invasion of 1778.[9]

The loss of America heralded a change of attitude towards colonial relations, reflecting a growing sense of a country saturated with religion and the spirit of reform which occupied the high moral ground. Empire, justified in terms of economic and strategic national interest unadorned with the sense of a moral purpose or mission, was simply incompatible with Britain's own self-image as the very embodiment of the highest standards of civilized conduct. Burke was at the forefront of developing this new moral conception of imperial responsibilities. It became increasingly unacceptable to consider colonies as children who must obey their parents. They were to be regarded as children who grew and matured, and who one day would become independent of the parent, having inherited the best of what the parent had to offer.

Nowhere was the changing attitude to empire more clearly articulated than in the debates surrounding the question of Britain's role in India. By the middle of the eighteenth century the East India Company had become transformed from a trading organization, whose employees respected the laws and customs of their host, adopted Indian habits and manners of dress, and often married native women, into a political force, entirely corrupt and contemptuous of traditional structures of government. The directors of the East India Company wielded immense patronage, and employment in the service of the company offered the opportunity for a young man to make his fortune in a short space of time.[10] The successes of Clive in India made the rewards of trading look relatively insignificant in relation to the prizes to be gained by military and political intrigue. Under Warren Hastings the East India Company pursued a policy of imperial expansion which necessitated the resort to war for its prosecution. To use Burke's famous description: 'The constitution of the Company began in commerce, and ended in empire. . . In fact the East-India Company in Asia is a state in the disguise of a merchant' (*Warren H...tings*, i. 23).[11]

The supporters of Warren Hastings did not deny that he acted like a despot; on the contrary it was the only appropriate way to act when dealing with people of oriental character.[12] It is well known that Burke embellished the facts and exaggerated the charges against Hastings in a vendetta designed not to gain a conviction, but to raise the whole problem of the moral basis of imperial relations. Burke argued that no government had the right to exercise arbitrary power, irrespective of its geographical location. The government of India, he contended, had to be conducted in conformity with that country's traditions and for the benefit of its people.

We find in Burke's theory of international relations elements from all three of the traditions identified in this book. At different times and in response to different circumstances any one of the traditions may appear to dominate his thought, but on other occasions he is equally likely to dismiss them. We cannot be sure, when Burke is invoking a manner of argument, whether he does so because of a sincerely held belief in the principles which lay at its foundation, or because he wants to achieve the maximum rhetorical and dramatic effect.[13] He does, however, make conscious attempts to formulate a criterion for the conduct of states, at the centre of which stands a conception of Historical Reason which on the whole tends to dominate.

Burke's Realism

I was at pains in Chapter 2 to emphasize that the tradition of Historical Reason tried to combine the positive elements of Empirical Realism and Universal Moral Order. It attempted to show that the conduct of states reflected their interests without being wholly immersed in them. It tried to show that the policy of states was not wholly capricious. Regulatory principles provided the manifold, not so abstract that they were divorced from the temporal world and its interests, and yet not so finite that they could not be distinguished from immediate pragmatic self-interest. It is because Burke consciously wished to preserve the insights of Empirical Realism and Universal Moral Order in his formulation of the criterion of Historical Reason that commentators have been so easily led to interpret him as a pragmatic utilitarian Realist, and alternatively as a Natural Law political philosopher.

There are endless examples in Burke, if taken in isolation, which can be used to sustain an Empirical Realist interpretation of his position. He never for a moment questioned the division of the world into states, a word he used to encompass everything enclosed within the territorial boundaries of a country, including the government and the nation. Patriotism was for him more natural than humanitarianism. He says, for example, that 'Next to the love of parents for their children, the strongest instinct both natural and moral that exists in man is the love of his country' (*Warren Hastings*, i. 141). It was, in his view, the first duty of states 'to take care of themsel. :s'.[14] This was a matter of expedience and prudence.[15] Prudence was for Burke the highest of the virtues, and was 'the director, the regulator, the standard of them all' ('Appeal from the New to the Old Whigs', *Works*, v. 20). Rules of prudence are usually imprecise and can never be universal ('Regicide Peace I', *Works*, vi. 92). The course of action a state takes must be dictated by its interests in the circumstances in which it finds itself. That interest, however, need not be short term nor merely parochial ('Thoughts on French Affairs, 1791', *Works*, iv. 326–92). Nothing in morality or politics can be asserted as universal. There are always exceptions which call for their modification, not by the application of logic, 'but by the rules of prudence' ('Appeal from New to Old Whigs', *Works*, v. 20). In his support of the American colonists and Irish toleration, for example, he goes to great pains to reject the relevance of abstract principles to the course of action the British government ought to take. Irrespective of whether the British Parliament had the right to tax the American colonies,[16] it was not expedient for it to do so. Britain's interests were simply not being served by refusing to repeal the tea tax. Commercial and practical considerations should influence governmental decisions, leaving abstract theorizing to the metaphysicians and philosophers ('Speech on American Taxation 1774', *Works*, ii. 147). It was, he argued the following year, in Britain's interest to forget about abstract principles and to make the American colonists happy by conciliating.[17]

In condemning Irish persecution and pleading for toleration and the extension of civil liberties to Catholics, Burke bases his argument on civic, not universal, justice, and political utility. Persecution was unjust not because it was contrary to Natural Right, but because no good reason could be given in justification of a policy which penalized loyal citizens. Furthermore it was in the interests of the state to cultivate the support of its citizens and reward the Irish Catholics, as a matter of expediency, for their loyalty during the American rebellion.[18] Ireland was a strategically important part of the empire, and therefore as much as possible should be done to allay political instability. Ireland's voluntary co-operation would provide much greater stability in the empire than continued oppression. As O'Gorman suggests, 'it was not so much the case that the persecution was wrong; it was futile'.[19] The American Revolution had such a dramatic effect on British affairs that it now became 'prudent to be just' ('Speech at Bristol previous to the Election in that City, 1780', *Works*, iii. 33).[20] For Burke, institutions adapt to circumstances as a result of 'necessities and expediencies'. The modifications are rarely the result of the application of a theory. Indeed, theories are themselves derived from experience (*Reflections*, *Works*, iv. 190).

If Burke is to be placed in the Empirical Realist tradition he needs to have more in common with its exponents than the exhibition of elements of utilitarian pragmatism. Does he, for example, subscribe to the doctrine of *raison d'état*? Is his attitude towards religion purely instrumental? And does he deny the existence of universal moral rules? To all of these questions it is not possible to give an unequivocal answer.

Burke admits that the principle of *raison d'état* is entirely legitimate in the vast majority of circumstances if it is to justify concealing the true motive or ground for a public action. '..1 that case silence is manly and it is wise' ('Letters on Regicide Peace I', *Works*, vi. 171). In other words, reason itself may dictate the suspension of public disclosure. Furthermore, while he cannot condone deceit and delusion, he believes that it is politic to be sparing with the truth. Being economical with the truth was something he was not averse to practising himself for political advantage.[21] The 'great interests of a state' must occasionally take precedence over all considerations ('Regicide Peace I', *Works*, vi. 108). Thus truth, because it frequently lacks certainty, may often be a casualty in the avoidance of unwelcome political consequences, including war ('Speech on the Acts of Uniformity', *Works*, iii. 299).

Burke was not, however, an admirer of Machiavelli's Realism, and he criticized him opaquely in the satire on Bolingbroke's opinions, *A Vindication of Natural Society*, and explicitly in the 'Speech on Mr Fox's East India Bill'. In the former he refers to Machiavelli as 'this great political Doctor' for suggesting that a prince consider times of peace as breathing spaces in which to prepare for the next war (*Vindication*, *Works*, i. 12). Burke expresses sympathy for Machiavelli in having to 'bear the iniquities of those whose maxims and rules of government he published' (*Vindication, Works*, i. 23). We may assume that his approval of Machiavelli in this satire signals real disapproval. Bolingbroke was, of course, an admirer of Machiavelli, and Burke is sending up Bolingbroke at this point. In his 'Speech on Mr Fox's East India Bill (1783)', Burke explicitly criticizes Machiavelli for corrupting the minds of readers by not expressing disapproval of the 'horrible and detestable proceedings' he describes (*Works*, iii. 81). In the *Reflections* Burke is even more explicit in his condemnation of Machiavelli: 'where men follow their natural impulses, they would not bear the odious maxims of a Machiavelian policy, whether applied to the attainment of monarchical or democratic tyranny' (*Reflections, Works*, iv. 89).

As in all matters, Burke could not admit of a rigid principle being universally applicable. He was therefore prepared to acknowledge that in the avoidance of a greater evil things may have to be done of which one would not normally approve. Such necessities cannot, however, justify following the same course of action in all cases: 'Because we have done one humiliating act, we ought with infinite caution to admit more acts of the same nature' ('Regicide Peace I', *Works*, vi. 168). It is in his attacks upon Warren Hastings, whom Macaulay described as a fertile mind 'so little restrained by conscientious scruples', that Burke makes his most vehement denunciations of the principle of *raison d'état*.[22]

Hastings was accused of vicious, unprincipled, and criminal conduct in exceeding the authority vested in him by the British government and the East India Company; in wilfully subverting the traditional laws of India which Britain held in trust when it entered into a virtual act of union with the Indian people; and, finally, of conduct at variance with the fundamental principles of humanity (*Warren Hastings*, i. 14, 15, 40, 44, 60, 61, 92, 93, 231, 486; ii. 2–3). In his defence Hastings argued that the whole history of India was his precedent for the exercise of arbitrary rule, and that he had inherited that style of governance from the Moguls (Mughals). It was wrong, he maintained, to apply European standards of morality to a country to which they were alien (*Warren Hastings*, i. 94, 97, 99, 104, 107, 485). His conduct, although despotic, was intended not for personal gain, but to safeguard the interest and financial security of the government. In other words, Hastings justified his methods by appeal to the principle of *raison d'état*, 'in the Time of the most pressing Necessity'.[23]

Burke's case against Hastings can be reduced to one simple proposition: it can never be justifiable to subvert the principle of the rule of law, because 'it is the security of the people of England, it is the security of the people of India, it is the security of every person that is governed, and of every person that governs' (*Warren Hastings*, i. 504). To exercise arbitrary power is to substitute will for law; it is government by force rather than by justice and authority (*Warren Hastings*, i. 103, 486). All power, Burke contends, 'is limited by law, and ought to be guided by discretion and not by arbitrary will' (*Warren Hastings*, ii. 2). Hastings had no right to make 'his own will the sole rule of his government' (*Warren Hastings*, ii. 4). In Burke's view, no legal code or constitution can rationally sanction the exercise of arbitrary power in place of the rule of law (*Warren Hastings*, i. 105 and

ii. 4). He challenges Hastings to state to what code of law he claims to be subject and by what law, if any, he can justify his conduct (*Warren Hastings*, i. 107).

Although the doctrine of *raison d'état* could justify concealing the true grounds of a policy, it could, then, never justify the subversion of the rule of law by the exercise of arbitrary will. Burke is certainly presenting us with a severely qualified account of the legitimacy of *raison d'état*. He deviates from its classic formulations in refusing to identify the will of the sovereign with law and in not wishing to condone the central tenet of the doctrine, namely that the end justifies the means.

Burke argued that Hastings's resort to arbitrary rule could not be justified on any possible grounds. What, however, were the grounds of Burke's objections? Hastings's claim to have been delegated or to have inherited arbitrary power could not rest upon prescription. The British constitution was, for Burke, prescriptive. By this Burke meant 'it is a constitution whose sole authority is, that it has existed time out of mind' ('Speech on the State of Representation 1782', *Works*, iii. 354). Arbitrary power was never any part of this constitution, and therefore could not have been delegated to Hastings.[24] Furthermore, it was never any part of the Muhammadan constitution, sanctioned by law and the Qu'rān, nor of the Institutes of Genghis Khan or Tamerlane (*Warren Hastings*, i. 104–14 and ii. 4). In other words, Hastings could derive no prescriptive right from the constitutions of Asia to rule by arbitrary will.

Burke as a Universal Moralist

What is interesting is that Burke is not satisfied to rest his case on prescription. It is unlikely that he thought that he could win a legal victory against Hastings, but he was determined to take the moral prize. In enunciating the principle of trusteeship for the governance of India, Burke frequently appeals to God's universal and immutable laws of morality as a standard against which Hastings should be judged. Is there a case, then, for suggesting that Burke rightly belongs to the tradition of a Universal Moral Order when he articulates a criterion of state conduct? It is certainly the case that he wished to refute Hastings's appeal to moral relativism in justification of his conduct. In defiance of the principle of 'geographical morality' Burke contends that

the laws of morality are the same everywhere; and that there is no action, which would pass for an act of extortion, of peculation, of bribery, and of oppression in England, that is not an act of extortion, of peculation, of bribery, and of oppression in Europe, Asia, Africa, and all the world over.   (*Warren Hastings*, i. 94)[25]

He maintains that God is the source of all authority, and that those in whom it is invested are subject to 'the eternal laws of Him that gave it, with which no human authority can dispense' (*Warren Hastings*, i. 99). The Eternal Laws of justice, humanity, and equity are primeval, and the human positive laws which share their character are declaratory of them (*Warren Hastings*, i. 14, 99, 101, 231, and 504; ii. 410 and 439). These laws of justice are our birthright, placed in our breasts as guides to conduct. They are immutable and independent of human design, pre-exist society, and are destined to survive its destruction (*Warren Hastings*, i. 14, 99; ii. 410).

It is appeals such as these which have enabled commentators to enlist Burke in the service of a common humanity against the totalitarian excesses of Hitler and Stalin,[26] and which prompted Cobban to dissociate Burke altogether 'from the immoralism of the school . . . whose principle, whether derived from theoretical Machiavellianism or from practical expediency, was *raison d'état*'.[27] In Burke the separation between morality and politics, effected by Machiavelli, and the equation of morality with expediency, effected by Hobbes, were, the Natural Law interpreters tell us, firmly rejected in subordinating politics to 'the universal law of reason and justice ordained by God'.[28]

Burke's resort to Natural Law is, however, somewhat perplexing. In fact, his attitude to religion in general, although there is no cause to doubt a genuine belief, is in one crucial respect very like that of Thucydides, Machiavelli, and Hobbes.[29] Burke tended when talking about religion to praise it in terms of its social and political utility, rather than its truth or theological virtues. Religion stands at the foundation of society and is a source of energy in the people ('Speech on Conciliation with the Colonies', *Works*, ii. 187; 'Regicide Peace IV', *Works*, vi. 404; *Reflections*, *Works*, iv. 98). It is, he tells us, 'our boast and comfort, and one great source of civilization amongst us, and among many other nations' (*Reflections*, *Works*, iv. 99–100). Religion is a source of happiness and consolation. It is an opiate in that it pacifies the victims of injustice with the promise of salvation. The importance of religion to the stability of society requires freedom of conscience and thus religious toleration.[30] We have received our natures from God, who for the virtuous perfection of His people has willed the existence of the state (*Reflections*, *Works*, iv. 107). The state and religion are therefore inseparable. Toleration is a matter ۍ political expedience, whereas atheism must be suppressed with the full weight of the law because it strikes at the very foundation of the state (*Reflections*, *Works*, iv. 99).[31] This is not to say that Burke was unaware of the dangers of religious fanaticism, both dissenting and established, to the political stability of the state.

In essence, Burke's view of Christianity is instrumental; it serves a politically and socially useful purpose, and this he was at pains to demonstrate, irrespective of what he thought of its theological truth. Similarly Burke uses Natural Law for political ends. He frequently invokes it for rhetorical impact in order to sustain principles which in different cicumstances he would back with prescriptive authority. As we have already seen, he is quite prepared to let the authority of the British constitution rest on prescription when advocating extreme caution in parliamentary reform, but the same ground could with difficulty be extended to India and the conduct of Warren Hastings. In this instance prescription is reinforced with the rhetorical weight of Natural Law. There is no doubt that for Burke God is the prime mover in human affairs who has set us out on a journey, but our destination is of our own choosing. Man is, then, 'in a great degree a creature of his own making' (*Reflections, Works*, iv. 101). God, in Burke's writings, is shrouded in mystery. He is the 'Governor of the Universe', 'the mysterious Governor' and 'Great Disposer' whom he often invokes, in the same way that Machiavelli invokes Fortuna, to explain the inexplicable (*Warren Hastings*, i. 94; 'Regicide Peace I', *Works*, vi. 87 and 182). God's interventions and dispensations may mysteriously rescue a nation from ruin, for example, but it would be utter folly to put one's trust 'in an unknown order of dispensations, in defiance of the rules of prudence' ('Regicide Peace I', *Works*, vi. 182).

We saw in discussing the writers who exemplify the tradition of a Universal Moral Order that the power of individual reason to apprehend the abstract principles of Natural Law, or the moral Natural Rights of man, was a central tenet in postulating a transcendental and transhistorical code of conduct. The Enlightenment belief that right reason can discover the true principles upon which to base our laws and institutions without the slightest regard for historical precedent or traditional practices was merely an extension of the rationalism of the Natural Law theorists.[32] Burke, however, was contemptuous of such reliance upon individual reason, and unceremoniously rejected the applicability of abstract principles like the so-called rights of man to concrete political situations. He contends that 'The individual is foolish. The multitude, for the moment, is foolish when they act without deliberation; but the species is wise, and when time is given to it, as a species, it almost always acts right' ('Speech on the State of Representation', *Works*, iii. 355).

Burke relentlessly maintains that it is potentially dangerous, and always foolish, to deduce from abstract principles practical policies for the conduct of affairs. Metaphysicians and abstract speculative philosophers, with whom he is little impressed, derive their theories from experience, and it is therefore fallacious to think that experience conforms to the principles deduced and to criticize governments for not corresponding to them ('Speech on the State Representation, ii. 357). No rational person, he contends, would presume to direct his or her affairs by 'abstractions and universals' ('Speech on the Second Reading of a Bill for the Relief of Protestant Dissenters, 1773', *Works*, iii. 316). Their 'abstract perfection' is in fact 'their practical defect' (*Reflections, Works*, iv. 65). Politics is an eminently practical activity requiring an enormous amount of experience, more than one man can acquire in a lifetime, and it is therefore extremely reckless to dismantle an established constitution or replace it on the basis of the metaphysical rights of man. These 'pretended rights', Burke tells us, 'are all extremes: and in proportion as they are metaphysically true, they are morally and politically false' (*Reflections, Works*, iv. 67).

It is well to note at this point that right reason was not the only way in which the Natural Law could be discovered. We saw, for example, that Grotius contended that there are two ways of coming to know Natural Law, the first by means of the exercise of right reason a priori, and the second by the a posteriori method, that is, that which is believed by all civilized nations to be the case must be assumed to be derived from the same source, namely God. Burke's occasional appeals to Natural Law are clearly of this second order, and the fact that he rejected abstract reasoning cannot therefore be taken as unequivocal evidence that he rejected a Universal Moral Order. What differentiates Burke in this respect from Grotius is that Burke does not contend that the confirmation of Natural Law is its deduction from indubitable principles through logically certain reasoning.

It would seem from what I have contended that Burke, in formulating a criterion of moral conduct, wished to depart from the traditions of Empirical Realism and Universal Moral Order, while retaining elements of both. I want to suggest that Burke self-consciously departed from these traditions and tried to overcome their deficiencies by developing a criterion whose foundation is Historical Reason.[33] He was aware that the multiplicity of discrete actions required a manifold of principle, for otherwise there 'would be only a confused jumble of particular facts and details, without the means of drawing out any sort of theoretical or practical conclusions' (Religious Opinions, *Works*, iii, 317).[34] On the other hand it is madness to be guided solely by principles. Abstractly speaking liberty is good, but abstract liberty is nowhere to be found ('Speech on Conciliation with the Colonies', *Works*, ii. 185).

Historical Reason

'The circumstances', Burke tells us, 'are what render every civil and political scheme beneficial or noxious to mankind' (*Reflections, Works*, iv. 7–8). These circumstances give rise to infinite variations, and nothing can be settled among them by the application of 'any abstract rule' (*Reflections, Works*, iv. 65).

What is needed is a combination of the two extremes. This is surely what Burke is suggesting when he says that 'A statesman, never losing sight of principles, is to be guided by circumstances' ('Religious Opinions', *Works*, iii. 317), and when he contends that the rights of man are to be found not in a pre-societal state of nature or in the abstract speculations of metaphysicians, but 'in a sort of *middle*, incapable of definition, but not impossible to be discerned' (*Reflections, Works*, iv. 67).[35] What this means is that the principles and rules which guide conduct are to be discerned in the historical process itself, that is, the process from which they emanated and in which our individual and national characters are formed.

Hindson and Gray are misleading us when they suggest that Burke believed human nature to be transhistorical and permanently fixed.[36] Only in relation to its most basic characteristic is this the case. Because of his emphasis upon history and circumstance Burke sees human nature, that is, our socially produced second natures, as at once historically and geographically variable. Burke does have a conception of a universal human nature, particularly in relation to experience of the sublime and the beautiful, but his political insights are almost exclusively directed at the accommodation of our second natures.[37]

The 'civil social man' (*Reflections, Works*, iv. 64) about whom Burke speaks is the product of both our own making and circumstance. Human beings are interdependent within the context of specific societies, and their actions invariably have a bearing upon the lives of others. In other words, the social relationships into which we enter have implicated in them certain degrees of responsibility for one's conduct. The conventions and constraints which modify our behaviour arise out of our social relations. Burke argues that 'the *situations* in which men relatively stand produce the rules and principles of that responsibility, and afford directions to prudence in exacting it' ('Regicide Peace I', *Works*, vi. 158). This is why Burke prefers to talk not of the rights of man, but of the rights of Englishmen who enjoy them as an inheritance from their forefathers to which they are entitled 'without any reference whatever to any other more general or prior right' (*Reflections,Works*, iv. 35). If the civil social man differs according to circumstance, then the type of government appropriate to his character will not be the same everywhere and anywhere. There can be no ideal form of government to which all states should conform; 'the circumstances and habits of every country, which it is always perilous and productive of the greatest calamities to force, are to decide upon the form of its government' ('Appeal from New to Old Whigs', *Works*, v. 44).

Similarly, it is the character of states, their common heritage, perceived affinities, and resemblances which lead them to associate, and which in turn give rise to the constraints which they feel obliged to acknowledge. Common sympathies rather than formal legal requirements determine the nature of the historic relationships among states. We should not, Burke contends, rely too heavily in our international relations upon the abstractions embedded in formal treaties and agreements. It is also unwise to rely upon the interests of states as guarantees of their formal commitments. Interests and passions are just as likely to render useless those formal undertakings: 'Entirely to trust to either, is to disregard our own safety, or not to know mankind' ('Regicide Peace I', *Works*, vi. 155). In other words, Burke is resorting to what I have called the criterion of Historical Reason in postulating a standard of state conduct:

Men are not tied to one another by papers and seals. They are led to associate by resemblances, by conformities, by sympathies. It is with nations as with individuals. Nothing is so strong a tie of amity between nation and nation as correspondence in laws, customs, manners, and habits of life. They have more than the force of treaties in themselves. They are obligations written in the heart. They approximate men to men, without their knowledge, and sometimes against their intentions. The secret, unseen, but irrefragable bond of habitual intercourse holds them together, even when their perverse and litigious nature sets them to equivocate, scuffle, and fight, about the terms of their written obligations. ('Regicide Peace I', *Works*, vi. 155–6)

The title to authority is not power, or divine sanction, but prescription. Its ground, or the reason why we obey the authority, is presumption. We prefer the certainty of a time-honoured and settled form of government, or set of arrangements, to the uncertainty of untried projects. The constitutions of countries or the relations in which nations stand with each other are not the result of the choice of one day, or one generation of people, but are 'made by the peculiar circumstances, occasions, tempers, dispositions, and moral, civil, and social habitudes of the people, which disclose themselves only in a long space of time' ('Speech on the State of Representation 1782', *Works*, iii. 355). Prescription, and not abstract philosophizing, establishes our rights, the authority of government, and our political obligations.

The European Balance

As civil social entities we are shaped by, belong to, and create the states which guide our nations. Each nation is a unique individuality with its own special features developed over countless ages. There is no question in Burke's mind that the international system is state-based. States are the units within which individuals acquire and develop their characters. In Burke's mind there are prescriptions, prejudices, and customs that are peculiar to nations, but he does not think that there is any set pattern of development through which they must necessarily go ('Regicide Peace I', *Works*, vi. 86). Each nation has a spirit which constitutes its vitality. A nation is not merely a geographical entity, or 'momentary aggregation, but it is an idea of continuity which extends in time as well as in numbers and space' ('Speech on the State of Representation 1782', *Works*, iii. 355). It is, for Burke, 'a moral essence' ('Regicide Peace I', *Works*, vi. 86 and 163), enduring throughout the ages and binding together the dead, living and yet to be born. Change is intrinsic to the historical process as society adapts to varying circumstances (*Reflections*, *Works*, iv. 23), but sudden and unprecedented change without reverence for the antiquity of institutions and the sediment of reason that saturates them is anathema to a stable nation, and the utmost care must be taken 'not to inoculate any scion alien to the nature of the original plant' (*Reflections*, *Works*, iv. 34; cf. pp. 94–5). A nation and its constitution are delicate things which must be cared for and cherished, and their defects must be attended to 'as to the wounds of a father, with pious awe, and trembling solicitude' (*Reflections*, *Works*, iv, 105). The characterization of beauty which Burke gives is equally applicable to a nation and its constitution. One of the principal properties of beautiful objects is

that the line of their parts is continually varying its direction; but it varies it by a very insensible deviation; it never varies it so quickly as to surprise, or by the sharpness of its angle to cause any twitching or convulsion of the optic nerve. Nothing long continued in the same manner, nothing very suddenly varied, can be beautiful; because both are opposite to that agreeable relaxation which is the characteristic effect of beauty. (*A Philosophical Inquiry into the Origin of our Ideas of the Sublime and Beautiful*, *Works*, i. 200)

To a people proud of their heritage there can be no more terrible a revolution than 'a change in the national spirit' ('Regicide Peace I', *Works*, vi. 85).

There is a natural aristocracy in any nation whose refined sensibilities, breadth of reading, powerful intellects, commanding conversation, wider vision, and lack of exposure to the vile and sordid qualify it to take the lead in society and governance. The natural aristocracy is the soul of a nation, in the absence of which the nation would cease to exist ('Appeal from New to Old Whigs', *Works*, v. 100–2). It serves to constrain the potential excesses of both the monarchy and the populace in politics. The natural aristocracy is the very embodiment of the manners of a gentleman. The spirit of a gentleman and of religion are the twin pillars upon which European manners rest, and which foster arts and learning and the development of commerce.

Burke shared the widespread belief that Europe constituted something like one large state or society of nations. Although the states were formally separate and sovereign, they were ethically and culturally united in a wider community. Their law, Christian religion, and manners, as well as their politics and economics, were all fundamentally the same, with some local variations, and all derived from the same sources in the customs of the Germanic peoples and Goths, from the feudal institutions that grew out of them, and from the Roman law that integrated them all into a system. The similarity of association, ways of life, university education, and personal relations, with their satisfying variations, ensured that 'no citizen of Europe could be altogether an exile in any part of it' ('Regicide Peace I', *Works*, vi. 157).

The spirit of a gentleman pervaded Europe, and although its associated manners and sentiments exhibited circumstantial variation, its source was ancient chivalry. It was this system of civilized manners and common sympathy which distinguished what Burke variously called 'the community of Europe', 'the great commonwealth of Christendom', 'the brotherhood of Christendom', and 'the system of Europe'[38] from the countries of Asia, and from even the most glorious periods in ancient history (*Reflections*, *Works*, iv. 83–4). In Burke's view, the importance of manners is greater than that of laws. With laws we are only occasionally in contact, but the manners upon which they depend are pervasive. It is manners that mould us, which agitate or calm, civilize or barbarize, refine or debase in a persistent insensible process ('Regicide Peace I', *Works*, vi. 149–50).

For Burke, Europe was a system whose principal actors were states. Their common sympathies, laws, manners, customs, and habitual associations, and the situations in which they stood relative to each other, generated the rules and responsibilities of their relations. These ties and obligations, written not on paper but in the hearts of citizens of Europe, were more binding than any formal treaty could be in itself. While these invisible ties were not able to eliminate European conflict, nor totally to allay mutual suspicions, the common sympathies and shared sentiments served to temper the rancour of disagreements between nations. War was therefore less barbarous, and peace more tranquil among nations in the European community of states ('Regicide Peace I', *Works*, vi. 155–6).

What then were the principal features of this commonwealth of states that served to regulate their relations? In addition to the shared manners and common sympathies, the principles of the balance of power and the duty of vicinity were widely acknowledged, justifying both war as a regulatory mechanism operating within the system, and armed intervention in the internal governance of states that constituted palpable threats to the common civilization which the system of

European states presupposed. These, for Burke, were elements in the common law of Europe.

David Hume believed that maintaining a balance of power among states was based upon self-evident reasoning and common sense. Even though the term 'balance of power' itself was of recent origin, the practice was apparent throughout history. Among the many examples he invokes is Thucydides' representation of the Spartan league, which was formed out of fear of the growing powers of Athens and her allies. Burke, without enquiring into the antiquity of the principle, believed that the balance of power was accepted by all countries. The question which exercised the minds of their rulers was not whether there should be a balance, but in which direction it was inclined. In other words, it had become a prescriptive principle reinforced by presumption and prejudice. It was 'the known common law of Europe'.[39]

The balance of power, then, was a law of politics, but unlike Natural Laws it was not independent of human will. It was not a given which automatically responded to stimuli, but an achievement, a policy to be pursued. The balance of power in Europe was in Burke's view at once delicate and multiple. It was a constellation of balances with five centres. Great Britain, France, and Spain comprised the 'Great Middle Balance'. Northern Europe constituted a distinct balance, as did Germany externally and internally and Italy. In all of these systems, Burke contended, England was entrusted with the balance ('Letters on a Regicide Peace III', *Works*, vi. 259).

Burke was acutely aware that the very idea of balance could not accommodate a preponderance of power. He was as concerned about the potential of Great Britain to become over-powerful in Europe as he was about France's. It was always in the interest of Britain to ensure that the power of France was kept within moderate bounds. It would be detrimental to its interest to see the power of France destroyed. Great Britain should be cautious, in fearing France, not to destroy the balance of power. It should not, for example, seize the whole West Indies, leaving the remaining feeble Spa..ish possessions 'at our mercy, without any power to balance us in the smallest degree' ('Remarks on the Policy of the Allies with Respect to France 1793', *Works*, v. 270). In 1792–3 Burke was adamant that Spain, which had to rely upon France or England, in the central, or middle, balance, should be given no reason to suspect that Great Britain sought to take advantage of the confusion that reigned in France. To destroy the balance would cause Spain to harbour the same fears about an uncontrolled preponderance of power as Great Britain harboured towards France ('Remarks on the Policy of the Allies with Respect to France 1793', *Works*, v. 270; 'Heads for Consideration on the Present State of Affairs 1792', *Works*, v. 215–32). Burke warned that the balance of Europe was intricate and complex, and that France was not as awesome to all states as she was to Great Britain. In warning against being carried away by ambition he sounded a chilling note of caution: 'I dread our being too much dreaded . . . It is impossible but that, sooner or later, this state of things must produce a combination against us which may end in our ruin' ('Remarks on the Policy of the Allies', *Works*, v. 278–9).

Burke was not so naïve as to think that the policy of balance of power reduced the likelihood of war in Europe; it was indeed the mechanism for maintaining the balance. Nor was he blind to the fact that self-interest, rather than the common interest of Europe, often prevailed in the national policies of states. France, although not the inventor of the policy of balance, was the architect of the Peace of Westphalia. During the period between the Peace of Westphalia and the Peace of Utrecht France did develop hegemonic designs under the absolute monarchy of Louis XIV, aspirations which Charles II and James II also entertained. It was nevertheless the case, in Burke's view, that France, *'acting upon the common old principles of state policy'*, had traditionally acted as the trustee of the balance and independence of Germany. With the Revolution, however, Westphalia had become 'an antiquated fable' ('Thoughts on French Affairs, 1791', *Works*, iv. 339).[40]

Any attempt to upset the balance of power and to dominate the system of Europe, or to constitute a sufficient threat of domination, was for Burke a just cause of war. Because of the absence of a properly constituted and sovereign authority to adjudicate disputes between nations, war, although the source of much evil and violence, 'is the sole means of justice amongst nations. Nothing can banish it from the world' ('Regicide Peace I', *Works*, vi. 156). Burke is far from suggesting that the international sphere is a moral vacuum devoid of principles of justice, nor is he attributing war and conquest to human nature as Thucydides, Machiavelli, and Hobbes did. What he is suggesting is that the situations in which European nations stand have produced the rules and conventions which govern their conduct. Given that there is no ultimate authority to enforce these prescriptive rules, justice in accordance with them can only be secured by resort to war. The Spanish War of Succession, for example, was for Burke a just war in that it prevented the union of two crowns and succeeded in preserving the balance of power. Furthermore, the regicide Jacobin government of France, in its acts and general demeanour, was a justification for the combination of European powers to restrain the French ('Regicide Peace I', *Works*, vi. 144–5 and 169–70).

France had deliberately abandoned a policy of balance of power and no longer accepted 'the public law of Europe, the ancient conventions of its several states, or the ancient opinions which assign to them superiority or pre-eminence of any sort' ('Regicide Peace III', *Works*, vi. 260). In other words, France could no longer be deemed to accept the same principles or speak the same language as other European states in their mutual relations. Burke maintains that 'The rights and liberties she was bound to maintain are now a system of wrong and tyranny which she is bound to destroy' ('French Affairs', *Works*, iv. 339).

The external policies of France were in themselves sufficient grounds for just war, but even more insidious and pernicious was the revolutionary change in its internal affairs, which constituted for Burke such a complete breach with the manners and sympathies of the community of Europe as to present a serious and palpable threat to the internal politics of France's neighbours. It was a government of a new species born of a revolution in ideology, a 'college of armed fanatics' espousing principles totally anathema to the traditional social and political values of Europe ('Letter to a Member of the National Assembly', *Works*, iv. 290). The French government was regicide by establishment, proclaiming all monarchy as the usurpation of authority. It was a government of state-established Jacobinism destructive of existing laws and institutions and contemptuous of existing titles to property. Furthermore, its established church was atheism, which destroyed the clergy and everything holy. In place of the immemorial system of manners sacred to all European states, the French government 'settled a system of manners, the most licentious, prostitute, and abandoned, that ever has been known, and at the same time the most coarse, rude, savage, and ferocious' ('Regicide Peace I', *Works*, vi. 150).

Such a radical departure from the customary foundations of European society in itself constituted a threat, not only to the internal governments of neighbouring states undermined by the spread of seditious ideas,[41] but also to the balance if successive states went the way of France. Burke feared a domino effect ('Remarks on the Policy of the Allies', *Works*, v. 270), and maintained that in such circumstances there was not only a right, but a duty to intervene in the internal affairs of France; what is more he denied the sovereign integrity of states by suggesting that such a duty was part of the common law of Europe. On what, then, did he base this contention?

In order to establish the credibility of his contention, Burke argued on the basis of a variety of principles. First, he invoked precedent to justify his method. Legal jurists frequently extend to the international sphere laws that were firmly established in civil communities. Secondly, he was aware that such a method would give rise to the criticism that argument by legal analogy could have no force. A law applicable within one legal system could not claim universal legitimacy. In anticipation of such a criticism Burke contended that some laws are not merely positive but the result of legal reasoning rather than of a statutory process. These laws 'belong to universal equity, and are universally applicable' ('Regicide Peace I', *Works*, vi. 159). In other words, he invoked the authority of reason, as the French Revolutionaries and his English critics did in asserting the rights of man. Burke was not, however, invoking the abstract reasoning of which he vehemently disapprc . ed. His argument was based firmly on, and never lost sight of, the empirical conditions from which he established the principle of the duty to intervene.

Burke argues that ownership of property entails correlative responsibilities. No one has a right to do whatever he likes with his property. Any addition or improvement must not constitute a nuisance or impinge upon the rights of neighbours. No new use can be made of one's property that is detrimental to one's neighbours. A neighbour who suffers harm in this way, or anticipates harm as a consequence of proposed innovations, can present the case before a judge. The law of neighbourhood, with the consequent right of vicinage, constrains the enjoyment of property, and any proposed innovations may be prohibited pending adjudication to prevent irreparable damage. The right of the vicinage to denunciate an innovation does not hold, however inconvenient it may be, if it complies with the established use of the property.

The same law of neighbourhood holds among nations and bestows 'on the grand vicinage of Europe a duty to know, and a right to prevent, any capital innovation which may amount to the erection of a dangerous nuisance' ('Regicide Peace I', *Works*, vi. 160). The whole of French society had been destroyed and decomposed. In its place a republic of robbers and wrongdoers stood. To do nothing would be to be an accomplice in its crimes. The new French political arrangements could plead no prescription. The French example, if left to its own devices, would have the most pernicious influence on its neighbours. The vicinage of Europe had a duty to denounce this nuisance before the consequences of the construction of 'so infamous a brothel' became extensive ('Regicide Peace I', *Works*, vi. 161). In the absence of a properly constituted judiciary the vicinage itself is the judge: 'It is, preventively, the assertor of its own rights, or remedially, their avenger ('Regicide Peace I', *Works*, vi. 160). The counterpart of legal action in civil society was therefore war in international relations. It was the duty of the vicinage to know, and its right to act, if any untoward occurrences posed a serious danger to the whole.

The 'principle of interference', along with the principle of the balance of power, comprised 'the basis of the public law of Europe' ('Regicide Peace I', *Works*, vi. 161).[42] Burke is certainly not justifying intervention on the merest of pretexts. One incident in itself is insufficient to incur denunciation by the vicinage. The mischief had to be cumulative and exhibit malicious design and deliberation. The country deemed to be a threat must possess credible power and the will or energy of mind to constitute a danger ('Regicide Peace I', *Works*, vi. 161).

The public law of Europe was unable to constrain Napoleon, who amassed a preponderance of power and vast territorial gains. The German translator of Burke's *Reflections*, Friedrich von Gentz, who was himself a theorist of balance of power and who developed Burke's ideas, became an adviser to Metternich and worked closely with him in restoring the pre-Napoleonic system of Europe. The Concert of Europe, which was the result of the Vienna settlement, benefited from a temporary convergence of interests. Britain and Russia wished to re-establish Austria and Prussia as strong powers, as well as to rehabilitate France under the restored Bourbon monarchy. The five countries together claimed a collective right of intervention, and succeeded, at least partially, for three decades or so, despite a growing divergence of interests, in controlling the lesser European states which were outside the Concert.[43]

Something has already been indicated of Burke's conception of the relations of Britain to the rest of the world outside Europe, but a few pertinent elements may be added at this point. As long as any part of North or South America remained in the possession of an imperial power it had, for Burke, to be considered part of the European system of states ('Regicide Peace III', *Works*, vi. 224). Such territories were necessarily included in calculating the balance of power in Europe. He did not, however, believe that a uniform system of government was appropriate to all of the colonies. No abstract ideal of imperial relations could be applicable to all of the contingently different circumstances. Government was a practical device instituted for the benefit of mankind, and not for the gratification of speculative philosophers and visionary politicians. 'I never was', says Burke, 'wild enough to conceive, that one method would service for the whole; that the natives of Hindustan and those of Virginia could be ordered in the same manner; or that the Cutchery court and the grand jury of Salem could be regulated on a similar plan' ('Letter to the Sheriffs of Bristol', *Works*, ii. 272).

In relation to America, for example, whatever Britain may desire, government had to accommodate the nature of the people and their particular circumstances ('Speech on Conciliation with the Colonies', *Works*, ii. 176). The Americans, Burke contended, were characterized by 'a fierce spirit of liberty' which disposed them to be hostile to any form of government that was not free ('Speech on Conciliation with the Colonies 1775', *Works*, ii. 191; and 'Letter to the Sheriffs of Bristol', *Works*, ii. 273). American liberties and religion were descended from those of Englishmen, and not from abstract principles. To use force against the Americans would at once harm them and Britain itself. To resort to force to sub- due the spirit of the Americans would deviate from the principles of both the British and Americans. Force could never be more than a temporary measure, and could not obviate the need for repetition. Government by perpetual conquest is no government at all, and in fact damages the very thing that force is used to pre- serve. Furthermore, Burke contended, force has not in the British experience been the instrument by which to rule the colonies. Colonial government had developed over time and in response to circumstances; there was no prescription that favours force ('Speech on Conciliation with the Colonies', *Works*, ii. 184).

An empire is not like a single state. It is an aggregate of states owing allegiance to a common head, but it would be foolish to demand a blind allegiance. The sub- ordinate states will have developed privileges and immunities appropriate to their conditions, and to respond to every claim of privilege against the imperial authority with the charge of treason is imprudent and provocative in the extreme. It will engender a belief that obedience to the imperial government is tantamount to slavery ('Speech on Conciliation with the Colonies', *Works*, 199).

Imperial governments cannot rebel against nature. It is a natural fact that blood flows less vigorously at the extremities of the body than at its centre. Distance adds difficultie. to ruling effectively, and to exercise oppressive govern- ment at the periphery leads to a weakening of the centre. The centre gains strength only if the periphery is vigorous, which requires not an iron hand, but a circumspect loosening of the rein of government in the extremities. In other words, good imperial government requires a degree of relative autonomy, which judiciously combines liberty and subordination ('Conciliation with the Colonies', *Works*, ii. 190; 'Speech on American Taxation 1774', *Works*, ii. 150). The *imperial character* of Britain entails superintending and guiding the subordinate legislatures without extinguishing any. The imperial legislatures are co-ordinate with each other, but subordinate to the head. Britain has necessarily 'to restrain the violent, and to aid the weak and deficient, by the overruling plenitude of her power. She is never to intrude into the place of others, whilst they are equal to the common ends of their institution' (*Warren Hastings*, i. 103; cf. i, 108–14, 118).[44]

Burke believed that the spirit of a nation, its liberties, privileges, and, national dignity must be accommodated in imperial relations, but it never occurred to him to question whether national pride and liberty were compatible with colonialism. As long as a degree of autonomy was granted commensurate to the perceived capacities of the colonized for self-determination, he thought that imperial relations could be mutually beneficial. The very fact that he spent a considerable part of his career defending the privileges of the Americans, Irish, and Indians against the encroaching despotism of imperialism indicates that the idea of empire fell far short of the practice, as it did throughout the nineteenth century.

In his writings on international relations Burke appealed to three sets of principles in prescribing a nation's conduct: your own country's historically evolved principles, those of the nations with which you have relations, and universal principles. In the case of two countries like Great Britain and America, whose principles and liberties coincide because the latter nation derived its from the former, it is on the whole unnecessary and probably unsafe to make any, or appeal to, universal generalizations. The authority of the principles is derived from prescription, presumption, and prejudice. When two dissimilar nations enter into relations, as was the case with Great Britain and India, a coincidence in fundamental principles, it appears, as long as they were to be found adhered to in other nations as well, was for Burke an indication of their universality and divine origin. For example, the principle of the rule of law, and its commensurate rejection of arbitrary power, was common both to the British constitution and to all the legal codes by which India had been governed. The Institutes of the Mughal Empire, the Qu'rān, the Institutes of Tamerlane, the common law and statute law of Great Britain, and every 'good constitution' have provisions which are 'security against that worst of evils, the government of will and force instead of wisdom and justice'. It seems a reasonable inference to make from Burke's manner of argument that just as we look to history for the collective reason of the ages which confers prescriptive authority upon current practices, we look to comparative history for the underlying and universal principles applicable to all nations. In other words, although he appeals to universal moral laws, irrespective of his often rhetorical intent, they are not to be discovered by a priori or abstract philosophizing. Here he subscribes to Grotius's second method, the a posteriori, of coming to know with a high degree of probability what the Natural Law is. However equivocal and unsatisfactory the result, Burke was consciously trying to formulate a criterion of individual and state conduct that incorporated the positive elements of the traditions of Empirical Realism and Universal Moral Order.

Notes

1. Martin Wight, *Power Politics*, ed. Hedley Bull and Carsten Holbraad, 2nd edn. (Harmondsworth, Penguin, 1986), 172; also see p. 174.
2. Evan Luard (ed.), *Basic Texts in International Relations* (London, Macmillan, 1992), 380.
3. Adam Watson, *The Evolution of International Society* (London, Routledge, 1992), 202–6.

4. Edmund Burke, *Works*, (World's Classics; London, Henry Frowde for Oxford University Press, 1907), 6 vols.

5. Stephen K. White, *Edmund Burke: Modernity, Politics, and Aesthetics* (Thousand Oaks, Calif., Sage, 1994), 1.

6. J. H. Plumb, *England in the Eighteenth Century* (Harmondsworth, Penguin, 1971), 124.

7. Plumb, *England in the Eighteenth Century*, 124.

8. F. Melian Stawell, *The Growth of International Thought* (London, Thornton Butterworth, 1929), 182.

9. Frank O'Gorman, *Edmund Burke: His Political Philosophy* (London, Allen and Unwin, 1973), 74.

10. Burke contends that 'Young men (boys almost) govern there, without society, and without sympathy with the natives. They have no more social habits with the people than if they still resided in England; nor, indeed, any species of intercourse but that which is necessary to make a sudden fortune, with a view to a remote settlement' (Burke, 'Speech on Mr Fox's East India Bill (1783)', *Works*, iii. 79).

11. Edmund Burke, *Speeches on the Impeachment of Warren Hastings* (Delhi, Discovery Publishing House, 1987), 2 vols.

12. White, *Edmund Burke*, 49.

13. For a reading of Burke as a dramatist of moral and political society see Paul Hindson and Tim Gray, *Burke's Dramatic Theory of Politics* (Aldershot, Avebury, 1988). For a discussion of the crucial and integral importance of rhetoric to Burke's method of argument see I. W. Hampsher-Monk, 'Rhetoric and Opinion in the Politics of Edmund Burke', *History of Political Thought*, 9 (1988). Hampsher-Monk's distinction between philosophy and rhetoric is instructive: 'The crucial aspect of rhetoric which distinguishes it from philosophy is that it is not concerned with rational proof, but with persuasion; and to achieve this it must start from the beliefs of the body of people to be persuaded, whether those beliefs be true or not' (p. 462).

14. Cited in F. Parkinson, *The Philosophy of International Relations: A Study in the History of Thought* (Beverly Hills, Calif., and London, Sage, 1977), 163.

15. In a parody of Bolingbroke designed to allude to the absurdity of his view that natural was superior to artificial religion, Burke argued a case against artificial society, holding up the elements of the doctrine of the Reason of State as contrary to nature, and the most telling indictment of artificial society. See Burke, 'A Vindication of Natural Society: Or a View of the Miseries and Evils Arising to Mankind from Every Species of Artificial Society', *Works*, i. 23–4. It is reasonable to assume that he was at least giving a partial endorsement to the doctrine of the Reason of State. Although, as we will see, he believed that necessity often dictated Reason of State, he simply could not condone arbitrary government in the name of the Reason of State. This fear of arbitrary power reflected a widespread eighteenth-century obsession with tyranny. Its expression in literature and political drama is explored in J. T. Boulton, 'Arbitrary Power: An Eighteenth Century Obsession', *Studies in Burke and his Time*, 9 (1967–8).

16. Burke did not for a moment question this right; it was a mere metaphysical abstraction not worthy of consideration in relation to pressing practical matters. He was prepared to accept the policy if it could be shown to be reasonable, a matter of common sense, or 'the means of attaining some useful end' ('Speech on American Taxation 1774', *Works*, ii. 102).

17. Burke, 'Speech on Moving the Resolutions for Conciliation with the Colonies', 1775, *Works*, ii. 202. He contends that 'My idea, therefore, without considering whether we

yield as matter of right, or grant as matter of favour, is *to admit the people of our colonies into an interest in the constitution'* (p. 203).

18. See R. R. Fennessy, *Burke, Paine and the Rights of Man* (The Hague, Nijhoff, 1963), 58–9.

19. O'Gorman, *Edmund Burke*, 90; also see p. 82.

20. For the view that Burke was a utilitarian pragmatist, in different degrees, see J. Morley, *Burke* (London, Macmillan, 1879); Alfred Cobban, *Edmund Burke and the Revolt against the Eighteenth Century* (London, Allen and Unwin, 1960); and O'Gorman, *Edmund Burke*. On the utilitarian view see David Cameron, *The Social Thought of Rousseau and Burke: A Comparative Study* (London, Weidenfeld and Nicolson for the London School of Economics, 1973), 67–9; C. B. Macpherson, *Burke* (Oxford, Oxford University Press, 1980), 4, 13–14, and 36; and Hindson and Gray, *Burke's Dramatic Theory of Politics*, 1–2. Jeremy Waldron seems anxious to label Burke a utilitarian, but recognizes that he is not a 'mainstream utilitarian' (*Nonsense upon Stilts: Bentham, Burke and Marx on the Rights of Man* (London, Methuen, 1990), 94).

21. The most famous example is his dramatic description of the murder of Marie-Antoinette's sentinel to give force to contention that on 6 Oct. 1789 the lives of the king and queen were under threat. See Burke, *Reflections on the Revolution in France, Works*, iv. 77–8: 'Instantly he [the sentinel] was cut down. A band of cruel ruffians and assassins, reeking with his blood, rushed into the chamber of the queen, and pierced with a hundred strokes of bayonets and poniards the bed, from whence this persecuted woman had but just time to fly almost naked'. Despite the fact that Burke's son met the sentinel in Cologne some years later, Burke never took the opportunity to revise his account. In this instance, and in many more, it might be more accurate to say that he stretched the truth, rather than practised its economy.

22. T. B. Macaulay, *Essays and Lays of Ancient Rome* (London, Longman's Green, 1899), 614. He says of Burke's pursuit of Hastings: 'His imagination and his passions, once excited, hurried him beyond the bounds of justice and good sense' (p. 652).

23. Cited by W. H. Greenleaf, 'Burke and State Necessity: The Case of Warren Hastings', in R. Schnur (ed.), *Staatsrason* (Berlin, Duncker and Humblot, 1975), 358.

24. '*He* have arbitrary power! My lords, the East-India Company have not arbitrary power to give him; the king has no arbitrary power to give him; your lordships have not; nor the Commons; nor the whole legislature' (Burke, *Warren Hastings*, i. 99).

25. Burke wrote that he thought a conviction impracticable, but that his reputation was at stake and required acquitting before posterity. See the editor's introduction to *The Writings and Speeches of Edmund Burke, vi, 1786–1788*, ed. P. J. Marshall (Oxford, Clarendon Press, 1991), 1–2.

26. See P. J. Stanlis, *Edmund Burke and the Natural Law* (Ann Arbor, University of Michigan Press, 1958); and Russell Kirk, *Edmund Burke: A Genius Reconsidered* (New Rochelle, NY, 1967). Cf. J. G. A. Pocock, 'Introduction' to *Reflections on the Revolution in France* (Indianapolis, Hackett, 1987), p. xlviii; and Conor Cruise O'Brien, 'Introduction', in Edmund Burke, *Reflections on the Revolution in France* (Harmondsworth, Penguin, 1968), 56–62.

27. Cobban, *Edmund Burke and the Revolt*, 48.

28. Ross Haffman and Paul Levack, 'Introduction', in *Burke's Politics* (New York 1949), p. xv.

29. Conor Cruise O'Brien suggests that Burke's association with the Church of England was an attachment of convenience for which he showed no theological enthusiasm. His family background made him more well disposed to Catholicism than it was politic to admit in the late eighteenth century ('Introduction', in *Reflections*, 29–30).

30. See Michael Freeman, *Edmund Burke and the Critique of Political Radicalism* (Oxford, Blackwell, 1980), 142.
31. 'atheism is against, not only our reason, but our instincts' (Freeman, *Edmund Burke*, 142; and Fennessy, *Burke, Paine and the Rights of Man*, 59).
32. David Cameron suggests that the essence of the Enlightenment's conception of Natural Law is 'its belief in the individual's rational capacity to discern the rights of nature' (*Social Thought of Rousseau and Burke*, 58–9).
33. See my 'The Character of the History of the Philosophy of International Relations and the Case of Edmund Burke', *Review of International Studies*, 17 (1991), 140–1.
34. Cf. 'By this unprincipled facility of changing the state as often, and as much, and in as many ways, as there are floating fancies or fashion, the whole chain and continuity of the commonwealth would be broken. No one generation could link with the other. Men would become little better than the flies of a summer' (*Reflections, Works*, iv. 104).
35. Harold Laski conveys something of what Burke was trying to do when he says of the Irishman: 'Admitting while he did that politics must rest upon expediency, he never failed to find good reason why expediency should be identified with what he saw as right' (*Political Thought in England from Locke to Bentham* (Oxford, Oxford University Press, 1942), 173–4).
36. Hindson and Gray, *Burke's Dramatic Theory of Politics*, 177.
37. White, *Edmund Burke*, 35.
38. See e.g. Burke, *Works*, ii. 31; vi. 94, 144, 156, 158, and 191.
39. David Hume, 'Of the Balance of Power', in *Essays Moral, Political and Literary* (Oxford, Oxford University Press, 1963), 339–48.
40. Cf. Burke, 'Regicide Peace II', *Works*, vi. 191–2.
41. Burke's *Reflections* begins with an attempt to counter Dr Richard Price's radical arguments. Price and Burke are at odds in their interpretations of the 1688 Glorious and Bloodless Revolution. Price maintains that the British monarch was one of the few legitimate monarchs in the world owing his exercise of authority to the choice of the people. See Richard Price, *Political Writings* (Cambridge, Cambridge University Press, 1991), 186. Thomas Paine's *The Rights of Man*, the most famous of many replies to Burke, was so popular that it served to generate support of organizations campaigning for political reform. See Gregory Claeys, 'The French Revolution Debate and British Political Thought', *History of Political Thought*, 11 (1990), 67.
42. Also see Burke, *Warren Hastings*, ii. 480.
43. Franklin L. Ford, *Europe 1780–1830*, 2nd edn. (London, Longman, 1989), 271–300; and Watson, *Evolution of International Society*, 242–4.
44. Cf. Boucher, 'Character of the History of the Philosophy of International Relations', 147–8.

14

HEGEL'S THEORY OF INTERNATIONAL
RELATIONS

Hegel is probably second only to Marx in the extent to which he has been held responsible for some of the most contemptible developments in modern European history. In popular opinion after the turn of this century, as well as among the ranks of distinguished philosophers, Hegel was persistently vilified. His philosophy was taken to have justified the subordination of the interests of the individual to those of the state, whose authority was based upon sheer brute force, and whose relations with other states were conducted in a moral vacuum and regulated by the principle that might is right. He has been accused of being the philosopher of Prussian militarism and German egotism, the consequences of which became manifest in the First and Second World Wars and in the rise of Nazi and Fascist totalitarianism in Europe. Because of Marx's professed early admiration for him, Hegel could also be held responsible for Communist totalitarianism.

Some of the most distinguished intellectuals of this century, including George Santayana, John Dewey, L. T. Hobhouse, and Karl Popper, held variants of these views, and attributed ͟ Hegel a strong degree of culpability. Hobhouse's famous attack on the metaphysical theory of the state continued to be reissued during the inter-war years and after, while Santayana and Dewey updated the critiques they had written during the First World War to make them pertinent to the Second. It was the events surrounding the Second World War that were the occasion for Popper's infamous invective against Plato, Hegel, and Marx.[1] Even some followers of Hegel's philosophical outlook, like J. S. Mackenzie, Ernest Barker, and R. G. Collingwood, did not feel able totally to absolve him of blame.[2]

Hegel, even when most heavily beleaguered by critics, was never without defenders in Great Britain. They strongly denied that any relation could be sustained between Hegel's philosophy and the cults of materialism and militarism that had captured the modern German mind. Such defenders denied that Hegel equated the legitimacy of the state with force, and contended that it was for him the will of the people and their disposition towards order that constituted the cohesive binding elements in the state. It was maintained that Hegel's emphasis was upon the spiritual and not the carnal might of the state. It is not the idealism of Kant, Fichte, Goethe and Hegel but the reaction against it after 1831 that can be blamed for 'the fetish of Force and Fraud and Frightfulness'.[3]

T. M. Knox's exchange with E. F. Carritt conducted in the pages of *Philosophy* at the beginning of the Second World War was a brave and significant step in the rehabilitation of Hegel, in that the approach Knox took in dispelling the claim that Hegel 'was an exponent of "Prussianism" and "frightfulness" '[4] attained a high level of scholarship, of which the detractors fell far short, and which subsequent defenders emulated and surpassed. This altogether more scholarly approach has led to the elimination of the more outlandish claims, and instead of a state absolutist, totalitarian, and fascist, he is now portrayed as a liberal or conservative in varying degrees. Instead of a megalomaniac preacher of state expansionism and world domination, he is portrayed as a sober and temperate thinker refusing to condemn war outright. He at once suggested that war has certain positive benefits and acknowledged its obvious evils. Instead of an insensitive and evil purveyor of the doctrine that might is right, and a disdainful ridiculer of international law, Hegel is portrayed as regretful that such formal constraints are no more than an ought-to-be. He looks instead to custom and various forms of recognition based upon the family, community, civil society, the state, and states in their mutual relations as constraining influences.[5]

The Actual is the Rational

Whatever view one ultimately takes of Hegel's political philosophy and his theory of international relations, it can be said with confidence at the outset that for him, contrary to what some of his critics took him to believe, philosophical enquiry was non-predictive and non-prescriptive. Only in nature, in which there is a constant cyclical process and continuous repetition, can the logic of the past be projected into the future. The rationality or reason discernible in history, or the realm of Spirit, exhibits a capacity for real novelty, and therefore its future course cannot be predicted. This is because events in nature are determined by external necessity, whereas historical developments occur out of the 'drive toward *perfectibility*'.[6] It is the business of philosophy not to construct ideals, which exist only in the philosopher's opinions and are subject to any flight of fancy which takes his imagination, but to understand what is actual. Each philosopher comprehends his own times in thought and comes on the scene too late to offer injunctions about what ought to be (*Philosophy of Right*, 20–3).

It is a mistake, however, to attribute to Hegel, as Andrew Vincent does, the view that 'the philosopher's function is to describe passively'. In this respect what Hegel says about the conduct of states and the activity of war is not a mere description of 'the actual state of affairs of his time'.[7] The philosopher does not accept actuality as he finds it, but assumes that it is rational and intelligible (*Philosophy of Right*, 11).[8] He attempts to discern and exhibit the underlying rationality or reason which has informed the development of history, or the progress of Spirit. The intelligibility which the philosopher discovers in the rational development of history is different from, and a transformation of, the ordinary understanding of the participants in the events. The philosopher cannot be satisfied with the empirical finiteness of the given, but must bring to the comprehension of the subject a conception of the unity and overall coherence exhibited in it. Only in relation to the whole can the phenomenal aspect of the subject reveal the reason immanent in it.[9] Thought thinking about thought must reveal itself as rational. The philosopher brings with him to history the conviction 'that Reason rules the world, and that world history has therefore been rational in its course'.[10] Hegel argues:

Even the ordinary, average historian, who believes and says that he is merely receptive to his data, is not passive in his thinking; he brings his categories along with him, and sees his data through them. In every treatise that is to be scientific, Reason must not slumber, and reflection must be actively applied. To him who looks at the world rationally, the world looks rational in return.[11]

In the preface to *Elements of the Philosophy of Right* Hegel's conviction is expressed in the famous aphorism: 'What is rational is actual; and what is actual is rational' (*Philosophy of Right*, 20).[12] What this means, of course, is that war as a persistent element in human history has to be rationally accounted for. This is one of the reasons why, in Hegel's view, 'war should not be regarded as an absolute evil' (*Philosophy of Right*, §324). This is not to say, however, that everything that exists must necessarily be rational. Actuality, for Hegel, is a technical term that is not coextensive with existence. Those things that are transitory and contingent and which have no necessary existence, cannot claim to be actual.[13] Actuality excludes 'contingent', and 'worthless' existence. Actuality is, for Hegel, the unity of the universal and particular, that is, the resolution of the former into the latter. Particularity, although having the appearance of self-sufficiency, is maintained by the whole. What is truly actual has an existence that is necessary and not contingent. Without the unity of universal and particular, 'nothing can be *actual*, even if it may be assumed to have *existence*' (*Philosophy of Right*, §270A).[14] If philosophy seeks to discover the rational plan unfolding in history, the progressive revelation of freedom in the world, then those things that are out of step with it or are not 'fulfilled according to that plan' do not deserve to be called actual.[15] It is only in the state, for example, that freedom, the essence of humanity, is fully realized. A state that does not manifest this realization, and is contingently and fortuitously a denial of it, is not actual: it is a 'bad state . . . which merely exists' (*Philosophy of Right*, §270A).

The criteria of what constitutes actuality are by no means unambiguous. The conclusions they generate when applied are not at all self-evident. Slavery, for example, seems manifestly to contravene the principle of freedom, and therefore even though it exists, it would appear that it lacks actuality and is contingent and inessential. This, however, is not entirely the case. Slavery is indeed an 'untrue appearance' in that it is opposed to the concept of the person as free, and thus ought to be condemned. The wrong of slavery, Hegel maintains, is the responsibility not only of the will of the enslaver, but also of the enslaved.

Slavery in fact occupies a necessary position in the transition of the human from a natural existence to a truly ethical one. In other words, slavery occurs at a time when 'a wrong is still right', and in which 'the wrong *is valid*' (*Philosophy of Right*, §57A).

In essence, then, Hegel thinks that reality is intelligible and knowable and that its development is the rational and progressive revelation of freedom in the world. That which is not in accordance with this rational development, and which is therefore not necessary, may well have existence, but it is not actual.

The Philosophical Project

We cannot fully understand Hegel's theory of international relations without an acquaintance with his broader philosophical project. He was concerned to overcome all dualisms that hampered the achievement of genuine knowledge. Much more self-consciously than Burke, Hegel systematically undermined traditional epistemology and subjected the premises of empiricism and universalism to dissolving critical scrutiny.

Traditional epistemology was concerned to establish a criterion of knowledge, that is, a standard by which to judge what was and what was not genuine knowledge itself. Epistemology was at once the foundation of the various sciences and the prerequisite of philosophical enquiry. This foundationalism is what Rorty calls 'systematic', as opposed to 'edifying' philosophy. The latter is sceptical about the very idea of a search for 'universal commensuration'.[16]

The philosophy of Descartes and Locke made it possible to pose as the central problem of philosophy the explanation of the transition from our conscious states to the reality of which we are conscious, that is, the project of making our ideas conform to reality. It was the failure of this project which led Kant to pose the problem differently. . .e rejected the demand that thought must correspond to its objects because it denied the possibility of knowing anything about them a priori. Instead he proposed to effect a Copernican revolution by assuming that objects must conform to our thought.[17] Knowledge can be achieved, Kant contended, only if we organize experience in conformity with our a priori categories and the forms of space and time. It is only by means of such an imposition that we can have knowledge of things, not in themselves, but as they are mediated by our forms and categories. Kant, like his predecessors, against whom he was reacting, continued the attempt to reconcile opposites, but was ultimately unable to resolve the dualism between thought and things. Things as they are in themselves cannot reveal their authentic character in thought because of the mediation of the instrument of knowledge through which they are known.

Hegel, in identifying what Richard Norman calls the 'Dilemma of Epistemology',[18] was able to complete the Copernican revolution which Kant had begun. He acknowledged that before undertaking a philosophical enquiry it is natural to think that one should investigate the instrument or medium for attaining such knowledge.[19] This, however, presupposes what one sets out to prove, that is, a criterion of true knowledge prior to the investigation which is supposed to establish it.[20] As Hegel puts it: 'to want to have cognition *before* we have any is as absurd as the wise resolve of Scholasticus to learn to *swim before he ventured in to the water*'.[21]

Instead of assuming dualities and proceeding to reconcile their differences as Kant and his predecessors had done, Hegel first assumed the unity of the universe, without denying its diversity. From this starting-point he did not have to reconcile differences, or overcome dualisms, but instead account for the differentiation of the unity. It is not therefore with minds independent of their objects, or with thoughts severed from the thinker, that Hegel concerns himself, but with the process of thinking itself, that is, the logic of the operation of mind. Knowledge, Hegel suggests, appears as a phenomenon, but the criterion of its truth cannot be external to it. It is only through a critical description of the phenomena of knowledge that their validity can be revealed. In other words, an account of knowledge is not to be given in terms of its conformity to a pre-existing formula, but instead as it actually emerges and develops. The purpose of this is to dispense with Kant's mistaken dichotomy between things as they are for us and as they are in themselves. The criterion of validity which Hegel employs is internal to the forms of consciousness themselves. By remaining within a form of consciousness he is able at once to describe and to criticize it. This is possible, as Norman suggests, 'because the internal description involves both a description of the object and a description of the knowledge, and the one can be tested against the other'.[22]

Spirit, for Hegel, is the principle of the unity of the universe. The essence of Spirit is freedom, which means that it is self-sufficient and self-determining, requiring nothing outside itself. Spirit knows itself as freedom, and at the same time is active in realizing its own potentiality in the world. It is completely rational self-consciousness which expresses itself in and knows itself through the actions of individuals.

The principle of Spirit remains abstract and general in that its potential is implicit or a mere possibility without human activity or will to make it actual. The activity which actualizes the principle of the Spirit must arise from the needs, volitions, and passions of humans. To bring something into being, or to fulfil a purpose, must in some way satisfy my own interests and embody something of my own purpose: 'This is the infinite right of the subjective individual to satisfy himself in his activity and work.'[23] The interests, or passions, are the energy or driving force which constitutes the uniqueness of an individual's character. The universal Idea of Freedom and the particular passions, or character, of individuals are unified and made concrete in the 'ethical Freedom' of the state.

Spirit, then, can accomplish nothing without the passions of individuals, and those individuals who accomplish most are what Hegel calls world-historical individuals. They are the instruments of Spirit, transcending all obstacles and heralding new epochs. Hegel variously characterizes them as completely ignorant of their historical mission; as having flickering awareness of their world-historical significance; and as being fully conscious of their role.[24] In his major writings, however, he describes world-historical individuals as having no consciousness of being the embodiment of the will, and the instrument, of World Spirit.[25] World-historical individuals of the calibre of Alexander, Caesar, and Napoleon are just as much the product of their times as their times are the product of their heroic actions.[26] These heroes break free of the constraints that bind lesser mortals and make actual that which is nascent or potential in their times (*Philosophy of Right*, §348).[27] Such men are not to be judged by their motives and intentions, or by the psychological factors which drive them to exhaustion. They are to be judged by the results of their work, even though they themselves may be unaware of what they are.

In Hegel's view, 'a state is well constituted and internally strong if the private interest of the citizens is united with the universal goal of the state, so that each finds its fulfilment and realisation in the other'.[28] The state is, for Hegel, the realization of Spirit and the ethical totality in which freedom is possessed and enjoyed by the individual. It is with the state that world history must concern itself. We will see in due course why the state, for Hegel, is the natural actor in international relations.

Spirit realizes itself, then, in the phenomena of history, and it is to history we must look if we are to know the rational progress of freedom in the world. The philosopher does not study this history in order to learn lessons and make recommendations about what courses of action to take in international relations. What history teaches us, Hegel contends, is that nations and governments never learn anything from history, and do not act upon lessons that they have derived from it. The particular historical circumstances of an era are peculiar to itself, and decisions about what has to be done have to be made within that context itself. Unlike the Realists Thucydides and Machiavelli, Hegel is not suggesting that we study history for the practical lessons we can learn from it. For Hegel, as we have seen, the purpose of philosophy is to comprehend and reveal as rational that which is actual. Within t..e Hegelian system anything partial and one-sided has to be accounted for and its deficiencies overcome by integrating it into a more adequate picture of the whole.

Realism and Universal Moralism

The philosophical bases of the Realist and Universal Moral Order traditions were subjected to criticism in many different contexts by Hegel throughout his career. His examination of Natural Law theory, for example, divides the subject into empirical, or naturalistic, and formal, or universalistic, methods of enquiry. The former type, of which Hobbes would be an instance, derives rights from natural instincts, passions, and desires. Nature, or man in a pre-political condition, is taken to be the basis of rights. These rights are not strictly speaking moral, but prudential imperatives. Formalistic methods of enquiry, like that of Kant, derive rights from abstract principles that are in fact incapable of generating a moral content. Both methods have severe limitations and deficiencies.

The empirical, or naturalistic, method lacks a criterion for distinguishing the accidental from the necessary features of existence. Fundamental principles are arbitrarily abstracted from the multiplicity of elements comprising a complex social situation, and read back into the chaos of an original condition or position, stripped of its social complexity, and designated the true causes of human conduct. The guiding principle must be the retention of just so much as is necessary for the characterization of what is found in reality. In other words, what we want to justify in a current institution simply requires the imposition of an appropriate quality or capacity into the original condition which at once generates and justifies what we set out to demonstrate. We are left, however, without any unifying principle. Any number of the multiplicity of elements which coexist, and which by comparison with the arbitrarily designated fundamental principles are posited as unreal, can present themselves as equally as viable alternatives to the supposedly crucial or essential elements (*Natural Law*, 58–65).[29]

The empirical method of selecting and elevating to the status of fundamental those aspects of experience or human nature which account for or explain and justify an existing condition is, of course, the method of Thucydides, Machiavelli, and Hobbes, who were discussed in Part I of this book. Although Hegel is critical of the method, he is not totally dismissive. Empiricism has a great deal that is positive in its emphasis upon experience. It, like philosophy proper, concerns itself with what is, and not with what ought to be and which is therefore not actual. Within empiricism is to be found the crucial principle of freedom: 'namely, that what ought to count in our human knowing, we ought to see *for ourselves*, and to know *ourselves* as *present* in it.'[30] One of the great merits of Hobbes was that he 'tried to trace the social union, the nature of state power, back to principles which lie in ourselves, which we recognise as our own'.[31] Like Burke, Hegel appreciated the value of a method which obstinately opposed any 'artificial framework of principles' (*Natural L...v*, 69). Empiricism could justifiably reproach abstract philosophizing for corrupting and perverting a content which the former has given.

Where empiricism falls down and contradicts itself is in its attempts to become more than a negative force against philosophy and present a philosophy of its own. Empiricism rarely remains pure:

And what is alleged to be an empirical method is only weaker in abstraction and has been less self-sufficient in distinguishing and fixing its restricted concepts which it has not itself selected; on the contrary, it is entangled in such concepts as have become fixed in the culture of the day as 'healthy common sense' and so seem to have been drawn directly from experience. (*Natural Law*, 69–70)

In other words, empiricism itself is theory-laden, but much less self-consciously so than abstract philosophy.

It is clear, then, that Hegel could not endorse the view of Thucydides, Machiavelli, and Hobbes that the principles of international relations can be derived from human nature. Now that it has been shown that Hegel found the

method of empiricism generally wanting, the question arises whether he subscribed to some of the important conclusions associated with the Realist tradition. Did he, for example, understand the state as power, and international
relations as the exercise of such power in the external sphere?

Hegel, it is true, did admire Machiavelli, but he praised him for different
reasons from, for instance, the arch-Realist Heinrich von Treitschke. It is a gross
misrepresentation to suggest that Hegel had aspirations to become a second
Machiavelli.[32] His interpretation of Machiavelli was strictly historicist. He saw
Machiavelli's exhortation to expel the barbarians from Italy as a political response
appropriate to the contemporaneous circumstances. Hegel was quite clear about
the fact that Machiavelli's imperatives could not be elevated to the status of general principles applicable to any and every comparable situation. They were valid
in relation to the unique conditions which prevailed in Italy, and could be understood and appreciated only with reference to the history of the times.[33] Hegel
went on to castigate Frederick the Great for casting empty moral aspersions upon
Machiavelli. In a disapproving tone, he cited an example of the shallowness of
Frederick's moral censures. Having taken Machiavelli out of context and repri-
manded him for recommending that treaties between states should be taken
lightly, Frederick himself, in his conduct and literary works, denied that treaties
were binding when they no longer suited the interest of the state.[34] Treitschke, on
the other hand, apologetically explained why Frederick the Great had a distorted
view of Machiavelli, whose doctrines had been perverted by the eighteenth-
century purveyors of 'visions of universal brotherhood'.[35] Instead of accusing
Frederick of duplicity, as Hegel had done, Treitschke described him as 'one of
Machiavelli's greatest practical disciples'.[36] He praised Machiavelli himself, not for
the appropriateness of his political precepts for sixteenth-century Italy, but
because he 'was the first to declare distinctly that the State is Power'.[37] While
admitting with Machiavelli that 'the state is absolute physical power', Treitschke
did, nevertheless, wish to suggest that it must be restrained by conscience and
reason.[38] Despite the in..usion of an ill-grafted moralism upon the principle of
raison d'état, Treitschke's view of the state was purely utilitarian: its essence is
power, and its highest moral duty is the maintenance of that power.[39]

Hegel, on the contrary, is quite explicit in his rejection of equating the state
with power, and in condemning the principle that might is right. He is often criticized for the statement attributed to him by one of his students, K. G. von
Griesheim, that (in Knox's translation) 'The march of God in the world, that is
what the state is'.[40] The military allusion is perhaps unfortunate, but it is clear that
he does not wish to associate the state with the brute force of nature, as Realists
typically do. For him, the basis of the state 'is the power of reason actualising itself
as will' (*Philosophy of Right*, §258A). The principle of the 'right of might' rests
upon egotism and is, for Hegel, no 'proof of rational freedom and civic honour,
but rather a proof of barbarism'.[41] In other words, it is with the power of Spirit,
whose essence is freedom, that Hegel wishes to associate the state, and not with
the physical force of nature. This distinction is in fact the basis of his criticism
of Carl Ludwig von Haller, who was a Swiss by origin but was nevertheless

influential among the Prussian nobility. Four volumes of Haller's six-volume work, *Restauration der Staatswissenschaft* (Restoration of the Science of the State), appeared between 1816 and 1820. Haller was critical of the political theories that had become dominant in European thought from the beginning of the seventeenth century. He was critical of social contract theories because of their fictitious accounts of natural equality and because of their mistaken belief that mere mortals can ever deliver themselves from the state of nature. The state of nature is a divine creation and is coexistent with our social life; in fact it is a mixture of social and non-social elements, at the root of which stands a natural inequality which generates relationships of dominance and dependence. Haller argued that 'where strength and need meet, a relationship develops in which the former acquires domination and the latter dependence. It is therefore the Eternal Law of God that the more powerful dominates, must dominate, and will always dominate'.[42] In this respect the state is nothing more than a composite of private relationships which has no purpose of its own, nor is it the expression of a General Will. In fact, it is nothing more than a household on a larger scale.

Hegel contemptuously dismisses Haller by contending that 'what is meant by power in this context . . . is not the power of justice and ethics, but the contingent power of nature' (*Philosophy of Right*, §258 n). The state for Hegel is a higher form of association than civil society, and unlike it the state is not dominated by the particular interests of individuals, nor can it rightly be conceived as the promoter or protector of those interests. Should such interests dominate the state, whether they are those of a monarch or of the people, government is arbitrary and despotic (*Philosophy of Right*, §278; cf. §279). The basis of the state is will and not force, and its social cohesiveness rests not upon fear but upon 'the basic sense of order which everyone possesses' (*Philosophy of Right*, §268A). Force and violence are necessary in establishing states, but we should not confuse their origin with their basis. The basis of right is not force but 'the spirit of the people, custom, and law'.[43]

The vehicle of significant change through which Spirit reveals itself as rational is often world-historical individuals, carriers of the will of the World Spirit. Like Machiavelli's men of *virtù* and Rousseau's legislators, at first they appear morally ambivalent. Hegel contends that

A world-historical individual is not so circumspect as to want this, that, and the other, and to take account of everything; rather, he commits himself unreservedly to one purpose alone. So it happens that such individuals treat other interests, even sacred ones, in a casual way—a mode of conduct certainly open to moral censure. But so great a figure must necessarily trample on many an innocent flower, crushing much that gets in his way.[44]

This, however, in no way absolves world-historical individuals of moral responsibility. All individuals aware of their freedom 'are responsible for any ethical and religious deterioration, and for the weakening of ethics and religion'.[45] World-historical individuals are to be praised only for accomplishing great things which are judged 'right and necessary'.[46]

The essence of the state is freedom and therefore the acknowledgement and recognition of its universal interest and one's pursuit of it as an ultimate end must be self-conscious and voluntary (*Philosophy of Right*, §260). What is important is that the ends of the individual and those of the state coincide, each recognizing itself in the other. If the individual does not recognize his purposes in those of the state, the foundation of the state must rest insecure (*Philosophy of Right*, §265).

At this stage we can provisionally conclude that any resemblance between the conclusions of Hegel and those of the Realists will be to some extent coincidental, but not entirely accidental. Even though he rejects the philosophical foundations of Realism, that is, the use of nature as a criterion of conduct, he is nevertheless committed to a theory which incorporates and unifies subjective and universal interests.

Hegel's rejection of a one-sided universalism and of the claims of all higher laws doctrines can be dealt with more briefly. He was, for example, unrelentingly critical of the formalism of Kant's moral criterion of universalizability. Kant's theory is formal in that it is strictly universalist,[47] and secondly because it does not purport to derive from, but instead imposes itself upon, experience.[48] Hegel does not wish to deny that rational activity must be universalizable, but it must not be formal, abstract, and hypothetical. The universality of which Hegel speaks must be actual in the laws and customs of the state. It is therefore inadequate to posit as moral criteria the principles of universalizability and non-contradiction. They are merely formal criteria with no content. In Hegel's view the absence of self-contradiction as a formal principle turns out to be self-annihilating. For example, if the injunction to help the poor was elevated to a universal maxim the poor would disappear and cancel the maxim. If we retain poverty in order to fulfil our duty we in fact prevent the duty being fulfilled (*Natural Law*, 80).[49] The point that Hegel wants to make is this: contradiction has to contradict something, and it is that something which has to be presupposed. If the principle of theft is universalized it is not contradictory in itself. Only if property is presupposed to be of value and of importance to society can the universal principle of theft be convicted of contradiction. In other words, the content of Kant's moral principles is in fact derived from an existing social condition and is not the product of his formalism. As Hegel pertinently says: 'It is not, therefore, because I find something is not self-contradictory that it is right; on the contrary, it is right because it is what is right.'[50]

The fact that formalism frees itself from a stultifying finite empiricism is testimony to its 'loftiness of outlook' (*Philosophy of Right*, §133A). It presents, however, a universalism divorced from experience and a criterion of conduct so abstract that it cannot be reconciled with the will and interest of the individual. Kant's idea of perpetual peace, for example, is divorced from experience in that it fails to take account of the individuality of states[51] and presupposes agreement between the states, which, dependent as it is upon the 'particular sovereign wills', irrespective of the grounds of agreement, 'would therefore continue to be tainted with contingency' (*Philosophy of Right*, §333; cf. §324).[52] This is not a dispute about whether war brings beneficial or negative results. In this respect it is not a consequentialist argument. Constraints in war and the requirements of international law arise between two or more autonomous states because of mutual recognition and respect, and not because there is a cosmopolitan morality impelling them. As Janna Thompson correctly observes, Hegel's theory is a radical rejection of universal morality and an assertion of the 'moral primacy of the community'.[53]

Historical Reason

What Hegel wants to do is to retain what is good in both empiricism and formalism, without succumbing to the deficiencies of either. This moral criterion of conduct constitutes what I have called in this book the tradition of Historical Reason. Moral duty and moral standards, apart from the historical circumstances of social and political life in relation to which they developed, are mere abstractions. Practical principles arise in connection with the activities of individuals in their social and political relations.[54] It is only within an ethical order, or ethical actuality, that individuals can exercise their right to follow their subjective consciences (*Philosophy of Right*, §153). Within such an order or community the determination of one's moral duty is relatively easy. The person 'must simply do what is prescribed, expressly stated, and known to him within his situation' (*Philosophy of Right*, §150). Understanding practical and rational principles is not a matter of explaining their origin. The historical origin of something, as we have seen, may be very different from its philosophical significance. The reason why an institution or practice originally arose may be very different from its philosophical significance (*Philosophy of Right*, §3).[55] In other words, we want to know not the origin, but the process by which our institutions and principles come to be what they are. It is a process of emanation. The beginning cannot explain the end, but the end of the process does explain the beginning.

Like Burke, then, Hegel denies the possibility of constructing a politically stable state on abstract a priori principles. In this respect there can be no ideal constitution or political institutions that is universally applicable irrespective of time and circumstance. This is why it is misleading to refer to Hegel, as G. K. Browning does, as an ethical absolutist.[56] A constitution, for example, will reflect the character and development of the self-consciousness of a particular nation, and must therefore be 'more than a product of thought. Each nation accordingly has the constitution appropriate and proper to it' (*Philosophy of Right*, §274). The same is also true of a nation's penal code, which Hegel takes to be a 'product of its time and of the current condition of civil society' (*Philosophy of Right*, §218). It follows, for Hegel, that 'harsh punishments are not unjust in and for themselves, but are proportionate to the conditions of their time; a criminal code cannot be valid for every age, and crimes are semblances of existence which can meet with greater or lesser degrees of repudiation' (*Philosophy of Right*, §218).

Relations among states have developed over a long period of time and reflect the level of consciousness attained at any particular epoch. World history is the history of nation-states, and these states are characterized in each epoch by a different self-conception which manifests itself as a national principle evident in the social structure, and particularly in the constitution, of designated world-historical peoples. We tend to think of Hegel as the philosopher of the state, but what he is actually talking about is not particular nation-states as such embodying the World Spirit but typically systems of states, including those of the oriental world, particularly the Persian Empire, the Greek system of states, and the Roman Empire, but in his own day of course the state system of the Germanic, or northern European, peoples. Take, for example, the Persian Empire as an illustration. Hegel argues that it was an empire in the modern sense because it consisted in a number of states, which despite being dependent had their own individualities, customs, and laws. Hegel argues that 'the Persian Empire extends over a multitude of nations, and leaves to each one its particular character. Some have even kings of their own; each one its distinct language, arms, way of life and customs.'[57]

Individuality of States

We have seen that for Hegel the individual can fulfil himself as a moral person only within the state. Freedom is manifest in the state, and through the state individuals know themselves as free.[58] Furthermore, however, it is only in the state that the person attains complete recognition and the full realization of his individuality. This necessarily entails that the state itself, as a state among other states, is fully recognized by them. It is Hegel's theory of individuality, which for him is a technical term, that enables us to elucidate why he believed the international community was necessarily one in which states were the principal actors, and why war had an integral role to play in relations among states, in the ethical development of the individual, and in the inner strength of the state. This aspect of Hegel is what Mervyn Frost and Chris Brown call his constitutive theory of the self. In brief, Hegel's constitutive theory traces the development of the self-consciousness of the individual through the family, civil society, and the state. The ethical family provides the loving community within which personality can first emerge. Based as it is on unconditional love, it can only provide the starting-point for individuality. In civil society the individual takes responsibility for setting and achieving his own goals in the sphere of private property and the market economy sustained by political institutions. In this sphere individuals are contestants in competition with each other and experience the law not as something of their own making or a reflection of their own will, but instead as external constraints. The state is for Hegel the realization of Spirit and the ethical totality in which freedom is enjoyed by the individual. The individual's freedom is not fully realized, however, until the state itself is recognized by other states. Colonial status denies this recognition, and the people are subject to an external power and thus fail to achieve full freedom. It is, for Hegel, with the state that world history must concern itself.

Personality for Hegel entails self-consciousness, and self-consciousness of one's individuality requires recognition. It is not enough, however, to attain mere recognition. It must be reciprocal. In other words, unless one recognizes the other as an independent self-consciousness, one's own self-esteem can hardly be raised by the judgement of someone whom one regards as worthless.[59] In the *Phenomenology of Spirit* Hegel traces the tortuous process by which this full recognition of self-consciousness and freedom is attained. Self-consciousness requires consciousness of an other in whom one sees oneself. The other at the same time is conscious of himself in oneself, or of the I in the Thou; each wants recognition, but neither is prepared to give it at the cost of undermining his own self-certainty. This equality of individuals whose identity resides in each other, and over which neither has control, results in the struggle for recognition. The purpose of this struggle, by each risking his life to kill the other, is to raise one's self-certainty to the level of truth, that is, to prove one's independence and autonomy. Hegel maintains that 'the individual who has not risked his life may well be recognised as a *person*, but he has not attained to the truth of this recognition as an independent self-consciousness'.[60] What Hegel is saying is that unless you have faced the possibility of your own death and come to the realization that the world will continue without you, you cannot attain full self-consciousness of being an independent individual.

Should either succeed in killing the other, the whole purpose of the struggle, namely recognition, cannot be achieved. Death renders one of the parties incapable of conferring recognition, and because it requires a reciprocal act, both parties are left in their different ways incapacitated. It is the realization of the necessity of life to self-consciousness that gives rise to the attempt not to kill the other, but to force his submission to one's will. This is the master–slave relation, which results in the exact opposite of what one would expect. The master does not achieve recognition, because the slave is a dependant and not an autonomous self-conscious will. The consciousness of the slave is forced to retreat back into itself only to become transformed. The slave achieves self-consciousness through work for the master. The objects the slave creates are the enduring expressions of his identity. The fear he experiences for his life in service to a master impresses upon him the consciousness of his own existence.

Is Hegel suggesting, then, as the *Phenomenology* clearly implies, that the attainment of universal self-consciousness through mutual recognition and respect requires risking one's life and subjecting oneself to service? In the *Philosophy of Mind* Hegel suggests that these extreme forms of achieving recognition and self-consciousness of one's own individuality have a historical as well as a logical dimension. In order to avoid any misunderstanding, Hegel suggests in the *Zusatz* to §432 that the process that he describes occurs in its extreme only in a natural condition. Within civil society and the state the recognition for which consciousness fought is already given. Universal self-consciousness, the condition in which each regards the other as a free rational being, occurs in the sphere of ethical life, or *Sittlichkeit*.

Individuals realize themselves in obedience to the laws and customs of society. These laws and customs are embodied in the actions of the individual and constitute the person's individuality, and they are therefore regarded not as external, but instead as the reflection of his own being. It is in the state, Hegel argues, that

the citizen derives his honour from the post he fills, from the trade he follows, and from any other kind of working activity. His honour thereby has a content that is substantial, universal, objective, and no longer dependent on an empty subjectivity; honour of this kind is still lacking in the natural state where individuals, whatever they may be and whatever they may do, want to compel others to recognise them.[61]

The recognition afforded the individual within the state does not, however, absolve him of risking his life, but as we shall see, the citizen has a duty to do so for the sake of his own moral development and for the higher individuality of the state.

The state is itself an individual that demands recognition and achieves it by struggle, and that undergoes a process of moral development towards full self-consciousness of itself as free and autonomous. Like the individual person, the sovereignty of the state must possess self-certainty and exists 'only as subjectivity'. The truth of subjectivity and of personality can be realized only as a subject and person. The individuality of the state is manifest in the individual person of the constitutional monarch (*Philosophy of Right*, §279; cf. §321). In an allusion to Kant, Hegel contends that princes and their cabinets are less likely to be swayed by enthusiasms and passions than the people. In other words, Hegel is intimating that to place one's hope in a republican form of government to eliminate war and establish perpetual peace must be forlorn (*Philosophy of Right*, §329A).[62] The sovereign as the manifestation of the individuality of the state retains sole responsibility for its relations with other states, each of which is *a being-for-itself* independent of the others. This being-for-itself consists in the independence of the state and 'is the primary freedom and supreme dignity of the nation' (*Philosophy of Right*, §322 and §329). In other words recognition and hence full self-consciousness depe..ds upon the existence of other states. Each state 'has a primary and absolute entitlement to be a sovereign and independent power *in the eyes of others*, i.e. *to be recognised* by them' (*Philosophy of Right*, §331). This formal entitlement is in itself abstract. Formal recognition depends upon the internal constitution of the state, and upon external perception of it. Recognition, as for the individual person, entails struggle. To wage war against a state implies that recognition is being denied it, but in fact the very opposite is the case. By waging war the existence of a state is being acknowledged, and full recognition is conferred when peace is finally agreed.[63]

A state too must undergo a process whereby it attains its rational self-consciousness of being-for-itself. Hegel contends that in order to become free and self-determining all nations must experience the harsh discipline of subservience. The examples he gives are those of Athens and Rome, which had to go through periods of subjection before progressing to their own self-consciousness of individuality. He does not suggest, then, that each individual person must experience slavery or a tyranny of harsh discipline. The moral progress of a nation, however, does entail in the course of its history such experiences. In this respect, 'Slavery and tyranny are, therefore, in the history of nations a necessary stage and hence *relatively* justified.'[64]

The criteria of conduct which states observe in their relations with other states are, like the internal constitution of a state, historically developing. Of all those peoples in antiquity the Greeks and the Jews loved freedom most, but even they did not look upon other peoples as equally worthy of existence. The Greeks viewed other peoples as barbarians, while the Jews simply looked upon non-Jews as other, or gentiles. Because a consciousness of national individuality was not widespread and the reciprocal acknowledgement of each people's right to an essential existence was lacking, Rome had no sense of the equality of the right to exist. After the destruction of Carthage, Rome's relations with other nations, which had originally been respectful, were characterized by pure force.

What, then, is required if states are to afford each other mutual recognition and acknowledge their equal right to exist? Hegel's answer is that there must be a family of states like that which had come into being in modern Europe. This system of states, although politically fragmented, constituted one people. Within this system a balance of power was maintained to protect any one of them from 'the violence of the powerful', and a diplomacy emerged 'in which all the members of the great European system, however distant, felt an interest in that which happened to any one of them'.[65] European states constrain each other not only in the declaration of war, but also in its conduct once war has been declared. Like Burke, Hegel has a great deal of faith in the regulatory capacity of custom in international relations. It is not a cosmopolitan ideal or principle that impresses itself upon the individual European states to act humanely in their relations with each other, but primarily their own national customs universalized. It is these, and not international law as such, that constitute 'the universal aspect of behaviour which is preserved under all circumstances' (*Philosophy of Right*, §339). Hegel suggests, in fact, that generally speaking, 'international law rests on social usage'.[66]

International Obligations

Does this mean, then, that an international ethical community exists as the basis of international law and cosmopolitan obligation? Is there a shared *Sittlichkeit* that makes the emergence of a General Will possible? Vincent suggests that these are logical possibilities and that Hegel does not actually preclude them.[67] It is true to say, however, that whatever transpires, and Hegel made no predictions in this respect, a state-based system of international relations is the necessary precipitate of his philosophy. He says unequivocally that 'the state is an individual, and negation is an essential component of individuality. Thus, even if a number of states join together as a family, this league, in its individuality, must generate opposition and create an enemy' (*Philosophy of Right*, §324A). For states to renounce their individuality and self-awareness in order to create a new totality is for Hegel almost unthinkable (*Philosophy of Right*, §322). The state, as we have seen, is the manifestation, or the actuality, of Spirit. In this respect it is 'the absolute power on *earth*' (*Philosophy of Right* §331; cf. §322).

Although states are individuals, they are not like private persons. Each state is sovereign and completely independent. Private individuals are interdependent in innumerable ways, while the state is largely a self-sustaining whole whose needs can be satisfied internally. In their relations with each other every state is a particular will. The rights of the state are not actualized as a universal will, as those of private persons are in the constitutional powers exercised over them. The rights of a state are actualized in its particular will. The state as a concrete whole has for the content of its particular will its own interest and welfare, which cannot be superseded as those of the individual person can by consciousness of belonging to a greater whole. Its own welfare 'is the supreme law for a state in its relations with others' (*Philosophy of Right*, §336). This means that in making treaties or in justifying wars the principles that govern the state are not abstract and universal, but actual conditions which affect or threaten its welfare. The justification of the welfare of the state is different from that of the individual person whose existence is abstract in the absence of the ethical life of the state. Hegel argues that

The immediate existence [*Dasein*] of the state as the ethical substance, i.e. its right, is directly embodied not in abstract but in concrete existence [*Existenz*], and only this concrete existence, rather than any of those many universal thoughts which are held to be moral commandments, can be the principle of its action and behaviour. (*Philosophy of Right*, §337)

Because a state is the determinant of its own interest and welfare, no abstract principles can dictate which among its extensive relations it will be most sensitive about and most easily take to be injured or in breach of agreement. The stronger its individuality the more likely a state is to take offence at any affront to what it determines as its honour. Where each state views itself as right, there is in international relations a clash of rights because no universal principle can be applied to adjudicate its actual claims. The appointment of arbitrators or mediators is contingent and rests upon the acquiescence or agreement of the particular wills in dispute. In the absence of agreement between sovereign states whose individual wills conflict, war is the means by which disputes are settled (*Philosophy of Right*, §333–4).

Hegel did, however, believe that international law was obligatory even though it did not have the characteristics of positive state law. It is clear that international law does not have the ethical status of civil law. Civil law expresses the General Will of the community, whereas international law expresses the agreement of particular wills on their immediate common welfare. Whereas Hegel was contemptuous of any political theory that based the state upon contract, international law for him did in fact 'possess the formal nature of *contracts* in general' (*Philosophy of Right*, §322). International law does not, however, possess the legal status of civil contracts, or of civil law. The absence of a legitimately constituted sovereign body to guarantee the rights and obligations established under civil contract means that in the international sphere the rights that states derive from their agreements fall 'short of true actuality'.[68] Civil contracts are directly related to 'the individuality and dependence' of citizens and do not constitute the model by which 'absolutely independent and free nations' are to be regulated (*Natural Law*, §124). Hegel's opinion of the ethical and legal status of interstate agreements is betrayed in his reference to them as 'so-called *international* law'.[69] In other words, international law is not properly law. It is the expression of several particular wills, and not the result of a General Will.

In so far as international contracts fall short of actuality, to what extent are they obligatory? James Leslie Brierly suggests that 'Hegel left nothing but contract as a possible explanation of the relations of states to one another, and even for that he provided no foundation'.[70] We are left with the problem that Hobbes failed to solve. In the transition of pre-social men from the state of nature into society, why should they be obliged by their promises in the absence of the moral framework which gives them legitimacy? Much has been made of Hegel's statement that international agreements ought to be honoured, and that relations between states *ought* to be governed by right (*Philosophy of Right*, §330 and §333).[71] Is Hegel here stating his own moral preference or saying something which *is* obviously the case? If international law is to be effective, obviously it *ought* to be obeyed. The whole point, however, is that the principle of international right upon which this ought is based is not a valid one: universal right is not actual and cannot be the ground of obligation. As sovereign entities, states at once create international law by agreement and stand above it. International relations are therefore not regulated by the principle of the rule of law, and treaties are observed or suspended according to the sense of welfare which each particular will has.

If international right is not the ground of obligation, what is? Here, I think, we may pronounce Brierly wrong in suggesting that Hegel provided no foundation for international contracts. Power may be lacking to enforce international obligations, but this does not mean that there are no obligations. It means that they are unenforceable should a state decide to renege on them. The obligation remains irrespective of the power to enforce its discharge.[72]

The foundation of this obligation has two sources. First, national customs—a nation's sense of propriety and decency—will be universalized and held up by it as humanitarian principles (*Philosophy of Right*, §338). They are not, of course, mere customs because they constitute the relations in which mutual recognition is afforded. Mutual recognition entails mutual respect. Agreements are of little use *per se* unless the will exists to keep them. Bernard Bosanquet articulates better what Hegel's theory implies. The state is responsible for organizing the moral organism in which the conditions for the good life of its citizens are sustained. Our very conceptions of humanitarianism and universal principles, in the absence of an international General Will, are learned and imparted within the social, cultural and ethical fabric of the advanced civilized nations. It is the nation from which the ideals emanate, and which constitutes the principal instrument through which to contribute to humanity. Patriotism and humanitarianism are therefore not opposed.[73]

The second source of international obligation is the code of customary conduct which will have emerged as a result of the historical relationships into which states have entered, and of the co-operative endeavours that are integral to them, the terms of which may sometimes find formal expression in international law. The fact that there is no determinate system of justice in the international sphere does not necessarily mean that there is no morality. It should be remembered that for the most part the morality of citizens is not enforced by law, and that the constraints upon conduct are voluntarily subscribed to at the risk of nothing more than being rebuked, frowned upon, or sent to Coventry, should one transgress. The conduct of citizens in relation to each other is informed by common sympathies and practices that give rise to moral constraints. Although states, unlike citizens, do not belong to an organized whole, they do share common experiences and sympathies that constitute the common *Sittlichkeit* in which obligations arise, and which, in the words of Viscount Haldane, 'it is "bad form" or "not the thing" to disregard'.[74]

The Justification of War

Hegel never saw active service in a war, but during most of his life European states were at war with each other. On the principle that the actual is the rational, war, like everything else, has to be accounted for. Unlike Rousseau, who objected to the Abbé de Saint-Pierre's Project for Perpetual Peace on the grounds that it was desirable but impracticable, Hegel objects to Kant's *On Perpetual Peace* because it was both undesirable and impracticable. War, for Hegel, is by no means the 'normal' condition of relations between states. Should a clash of rights precipitate armed conflict between states, their shared sense of decency and humane conduct serves to regulate the prosecution of war. War is taken by all parties to be something which ought, once it has started, to come to an end, and therefore all avenues that may facilitate this end should be exempt from attack. Hegel in fact wants to maintain a clear distinction between civil and military relations. In war the domestic institutions of the state, family life, and private individuals ought to be allowed to go about their business unimpeded by a foreign enemy. In this respect Hegel somewhat naïvely suggests that 'Modern wars are accordingly waged in a humane manner, and persons do not confront each other in hatred' (*Philosophy of Right*, §338A).[75]

It is important to bear in mind that nothing Hegel says is a justification of any particular war. Each war has its own mundane causes arising from each state's conception of its welfare. Hegel is offering a philosophical explanation and justification of war which, as we have seen, postulates the necessity for struggle in achieving state recognition and individuality, or rational self-consciousness. Furthermore, in sustaining its individuality the state may be required to prosecute its own case by means of warfare when its rights clash with those of another state. This is only one side of Hegel's explanation of war.

The other side is concerned with identifying the importance of war in cementing the relationship between the individual person and the state, and in developing and sustaining the moral integrity of its institutions. It is to this second side that we must now turn, that is, to the internal health of the state as a factor in its relations with other states. The risking of one's life for the state in war serves a number of crucial ethical purposes. First, it impels the individual citizen to recognize and acknowledge that his interests and desires as a member of civil society are only transitory. His own family and civil or economic life depends upon the existence and maintenance of the state. The call upon citizens to make the ultimate sacrifice does not have as its end the protection of the life and property of the citizen. This would be to conceive of the state, as Hobbes does, as a civil society. It is absurd to understand war as the sacrifice of that which war is supposed to safeguard.

The individual person who realizes himself only as the citizen of a state is subordinate to the ethical whole, and must dedicate himself to it. The state is a higher individuality in relation to which the rights and interests of individual persons are only transitory. In consequence, the individual has a duty to lay down his life for the state 'to preserve this substantial individuality' (*Philosophy of Right*, §324 and §70A). It is the realization of belonging to a greater whole whose preservation is paramount, and which incorporates and transcends the particular wills of its members, that constitutes the ethical moment of war.

During long periods of peace, Hegel believes in contrast with Kant, citizens of a state begin to delude themselves into thinking that the material values of civil society are paramount. This is because during times of peace the state makes few calls upon its citizens, and their private activities can be pursued in relative seclusion. Perpetual peace would lead to the pursuit of individual interest at the expense of the common good.

The second ethical function of war, following directly from the first, is to reinforce the idea that the unity has greater significance than the parts. War, then, as well as impelling the .ndividual person's acknowledgement of belonging to a wider whole, provides the impetus for greater social cohesion: 'in war the power of the association of all with the whole is in evidence; this association has adjusted the amount which it can demand from individuals, as well as the worth of what they may do for it of their own impulse and their own heart'.[76] Risking one's life for the state is of far greater significance than merely fearing death. Courage in the service of the state is the true valour of a nation in which the individual 'counts as one among many' (*Philosophy of Right*, §327). Valour, then, is 'not so much the deed of a *particular* person as that of a *member* of a whole' (*Philosophy of Right*, §328).

In addition, the propensity for self-interest to become translated into corruption during prolonged periods of peace is mitigated by war. As a result of war internal dissension may evaporate and the nation emerge strengthened (*Philosophy of Right*, §324).[77]

War does not merely exist: it is actual, that is, it has a place in the rational development of individual self-consciousness, as Hegel describes it in the

Phenomenology of Spirit, and in the development of the state, as espoused in the *Philosophy of Right.* Whereas empirically the occasion and justification of war may be fortuitous and contingent, or accidental, philosophically war has a rationale consistent with the development of World Spirit.

Notes

1. John Dewey, *German Philosophy and Politics*, 2nd edn. (1915; repr. New York, Books for Libraries, 1970); George Santayana, *Egotism in German Philosophy*, 2nd edn. (London, Dent, 1940; 1st edn. 1916); L. T. Hobhouse, *The Metaphysical Theory of the State* (London, Allen and Unwin, 1951; first pub. 1918); and Karl Popper, *The Open Society and its Enemies* (London, Routledge and Kegan Paul, 1977; first pub. 1945).

2. J. S. Mackenzie, 'Might and Right', in Louise Creighton et. al., *The International Crisis: The Theory of the State* (London, Oxford University Press, 1916), 111; Ernest Barker, 'Nietzsche and Treitschke: The Worship of Power in Modern Germany' (Oxford Pamphlets; London, Oxford University Press, 1914), 4; and R. G. Collingwood, 'The Prussian Philosophy', in David Boucher (ed.), *Essays in Political Philosophy* (Oxford, Clarendon Press, 1989), 202–3.

3. John Watson, 'German Philosophy and the War', *Queen's Quarterly*, 23 (1916), 375. For similar arguments see John Watson, 'German Philosophy and Politics, *Queen's Quarterly*, 22 (1915); J. H. Muirhead, *German Philosophy in Relation to the War* (London, Murray, 1917); Hilda D. Oakeley, 'The Idea of a General Will', in Creighton et al., *The International Crisis: The Theory of the State* (London, Oxford University Press, 1916); Henry Jones, 'Why We are Fighting', *Hibbert Journal*, 13 (1914–15); and Henry Jones, speech, North Wales Heroes Memorial (Bangor, Caxton Press, 1917).

4. T. M. Knox, 'Hegel and Prussianism', in Walter Kaufmann (ed.), *Hegel's Political Philosophy* (New York, Doubleday, 1970), 14. The whole exchange between Knox and Carritt is reprinted in this volume, as well as subsequent debates on whether Hegel was a liberal or conservative, and a Prussian patriot or German nationalist.

5. For representative discussions of the issues see Z. A. Pelczynski (ed.), *Hegel's Political Philosophy: Problems and Perspectives* (Cambridge, Cambridge University Press, 1971); Shlomo Avineri, *Hegel's Theory of the Modern State* (Cambridge, Cambridge University Press, 1972); Raymond Plant, *Hegel* (London, Allen and Unwin, 1973); Charles Taylor, *Hegel and Modern Society* (Cambridge, Cambridge University Press, 1979); D. P. Verene (ed.), *Hegel's Social and Political Thought: The Philosophy of Objective Spirit* (New Jersey, Humanities Press, 1976); Judith N. Shklar, *Freedom and Independence: A Study of the Political Ideas of Hegel's Phenomenology of Mind* (Cambridge, Cambridge University Press, 1976); Steven B. Smith, *Hegel's Critique of Liberalism: Rights in Context* (Chicago and London, University of Chicago Press, 1989); and Allen W. Wood, *Hegel's Ethical Thought* (Cambridge, Cambridge University Press, 1990).

6. G. W. F. Hegel, *Introduction to the Philosophy of History*, trans. Leo Rauch (Indianapolis, Hackett, 1988), 57; cf. p. 20. Also see G. W. F. Hegel, *Lectures on the History of Philosophy*, trans. E. S. Haldane (London, Kegan Paul, Trench, Trübner, 1892), i. 29 and 31–2; G. W. F. Hegel, *Elements of the Philosophy of Right*, trans. H. B. Nisbet and ed. Allen W. Wood (Cambridge, Cambridge University Press, 1991),

12–13; and G. O'Brien, *Hegel on Reason and History* (Chicago and London, The University of Chicago Press, 1975), 47–53. Wood's edition of *Elements of the Philosophy of Right* is cited in the text as *Philosophy of Right*.

7. Andrew Vincent, 'The Hegelian State and International Politics', *Review of International Studies*, 9 (1983), 195; also see pp. 196, 197, 200, and 202.

8. Cf. G. W. F. Hegel, *Philosophy of Mind*, trans. William Wallace and A. V. Miller (Oxford, Clarendon Press, 1971), *Zusatz* to §435.

9. Hegel, *Lectures on the History of Philosophy*, 29 and 31.

10. Hegel, *Philosophy of History*, 12.

11. Hegel, *Philosophy of History*, 14.

12. Cf. 'The insight to which philosophy ought to lead, therefore (in contrast to what happens to those ideals), is that the real world is as it ought to be' (Hegel, *Philosophy of History*, 39).

13. G. W. F. Hegel, *The Encyclopaedia Logic*, trans. T. F. Geraets, W. A. Suchting, and H. S. Harris (Indianapolis, Hackett, 1991), §6A.

14. Emil L. Fackenheim sums up Hegel's position quite pertinently: 'For Hegel the actuality of the rational is a *specific historical condition*; and only if and when that condition exists is the recognition of the rational in the Actual a philosophical possibility' ('On the Actuality of the Rational and the Rationality of the Actual', *Review of Metaphysics*, 23 (1970), 693).

15. Hegel, *Philosophy of History*, 39. Cf. Muirhead's characterization of Hegel's position: 'Not everything that is actual is its own justification, but what is justified in it is that which is of a piece with the order of the world' (*German Philosophy in Relation to the War*, 29).

16. Richard Rorty, *Philosophy and the Mirror of Nature* (Oxford, Basil Blackwell, 1980), 367–8.

17. Immanuel Kant, *Critique of Pure Reason*, trans. J. M. D. Meiklejohn (London, Dent, 1943), 12.

18. Richard Norman, *Hegel's Phenomenology: A Philosophical Introduction* (London, Chatto and Windus for University of Sussex Press, 1976), 12.

19. G. W. F. Hegel, *Phenomenology of Spirit*, trans. A. V. Miller, with analysis of the text and foreword by J. N. Findlay (Oxford, Oxford University Press, 1977), §73.

20. Hegel, *Phenomenology of Spirit*, §81.

21. Hegel, *Encyclopaedia Logic*, §10.

22. Norman, *Hegel's Phenomenology*, 20.

23. Hegel, *Philosophy of History*, 25.

24. Avineri, *Hegel's Theory of the Modern State*, 233.

25. Hegel, *Introduction to the Philosophy of History*, 33; Hegel, *Philosophy of Right*, §348.

26. Hegel, *Philosophy of Mind*, *Zusatz* to §381.

27. See also Hegel, *Introduction to the Philosophy of History*, 33–4.

28. Hegel, *Phenomenology of Spirit*, 27. It is in *The Philosophy of Right* that this unity is most fully articulated and elaborated.

29. G. W. F. Hegel, *Natural Law: The Scientific Ways of Testing Natural Law, its Place in Moral Philosophy, and its Relation to the Positive Sciences of Law*, trans. T. M. Knox, introd. by H. B. Acton (Pennsylvania, University of Pennsylvania Press, 1975). Also see Smith, *Hegel's Critique of Liberalism*, 65–70; and J.-F. Suter, 'Burke, Hegel, and the French Revolution', in Z. A. Pelzcynski (ed.), *Hegel's Political Philosophy: Problems and Perspectives* (Cambridge, Cambridge University Press, 1971), 59–60.

30. Hegel, *Encyclopaedia Logic*, §38.

31. Cited by Manfred Riedal, *Between Tradition and Revolution: The Hegelian Transformation of Political Philosophy* (Cambridge, Cambridge University Press, 1971), 98.
32. Ernst Cassirer, *The Myth of the State* (New Haven, Yale University Press, 1946), 122.
33. G. W. F. Hegel, *Political Writings*, trans. T. M. Knox and introd. by Z. A. Pelczynski (Oxford, Clarendon Press, 1964), 220–1.
34. Hegel, *Political Writings*, 223.
35. Heinrich von Treitschke, *Politics*, trans. Blanche Dugdale and Torben de Bille, 2 vols. (London, Constable, 1916), i. 87.
36. Treitschke, *Politics*, i. 87.
37. Treitschke, *Politics*, ii. 587. H. W. Davis cites an apposite letter in which Treitschke praises Machiavelli: 'He is indeed a practical statesman, more fitted than any other to destroy the illusion that one can reform the world with cannon loaded only with ideas of Right and truth. But even the political science of this much descried champion of brute force seems to me moral by comparison with the Prussia of today. Machiavelli sacrifices Right and Virtue to a great idea, the might and unity of his people; this one cannot say of the party which now rules in Prussia. This underlying thought of the book, its glowing patriotism, and the conviction that the most oppressive despotism must be welcome if it ensures might and unity for his mother-country—these are the ideas which have reconciled men to the numerous reprehensible and lawless theories of the great Florentine' (*The Political Thought of Heinrich von Treitschke* (London, Constable, 1914), 5).
38. Treitschke, *Politics*, ii. 587.
39. Treitschke, *Politics*, i. 94. Cf. R. G. Collingwood, *The New Leviathan* rev. edn., ed. David Boucher (Oxford, Clarendon Press, 1992), 223.
40. *Hegel's Philosophy of Right*, trans. T. M. Knox (Oxford, Oxford University Press, 1967), 279. Kaufmann accuses Knox of mistranslating the passage and suggests that it should read: 'It is the way of god with [literally: in] the world that there should be [literally: is] the state' (W. Kaufmann (ed.), *Hegel's Political Philosophy* (New York, Doubleday, 1970), 4). Nisbet's translation reads: 'The state consists in the march of God in the world' (*Philosophy of Right*, § 258A).
41. Hegel, *Philosophy of Mind*, *Zusatz* to §432. Hegel is here talking about the practice of duelling.
42. Cited by Robert M. Berdahl, *The Politics of the Prussian Nobility: The Development of a Conservative Ideology* (Princeton, Princeton University Press, 1988), 236.
43. Hegel, *Philosophy of Mind*, *Zusatz* to §432; cf. §433.
44. Hegel, *Introduction to the Philosophy of History*, 35.
45. Hegel, *Introduction to the Philosophy of History*, 36.
46. Hegel, *Introduction to the Philosophy of History*, 34.
47. Smith, *Hegel's Critique of Liberalism*, 70.
48. Norman, *Hegel's Phenomenology*, 69.
49. Hegel uses Kant's own example of a person enriching himself by denying that a deposit has been entrusted to him after the death of the owner. To test this by means of the universalizability criterion, in Hegel's view, entails no contradiction. If I keep the deposit I no longer regard it as someone else's property. As Hegel says: 'Alteration of the *point of view* is not contradiction' (*Phenomenology of Spirit*, §437; cf. *Natural Law*, 77 and *Philosophy of Right*, §135).
50. Hegel, *Phenomenology of Spirit*, §437.
51. 'Individuality' is a technical term in Hegel's philosophy to which we will return later in this chapter.

52. Cf. also Hegel, *Political Writings*, 208.

53. Janna Thompson, *Justice and World Order: A Philosophical Inquiry* (London, Routledge, 1992), 112.

54. Montesquieu is particularly important in this respect. Although he failed to attain the highest philosophical insight, Montesquieu recognized that the laws of the nation were not the result of abstract reason, nor could they be abstracted from experience and raised to the level of universals. Each had to be understood in relation to the whole as systems composing the living individuality of the nation. Hegel says, for example that 'it was above all Montequieu who, in his celebrated work *L'Esprit des lois*, focused on and attempted to expand in detail both the thought that laws, including those of civil law in particular, are dependent on the specific character of the state, and the philosophical view that the part should be considered only with reference to the whole' (*Philosophy of Right*, §261; cf. §3A and *Natural Law*, 128–9).

55. Cf. Hegel, *Encyclopaedia Logic*, §143.

56. G. K. Browning, 'The Night in which all Cows are Black: Ethical Absolutism in Plato and Hegel', *History of Political Thought*, 12 (1991), 391–404.

57. G. W. F. Hegel, *The Philosophy of History*, trans. J. Sibree (New York, Dover, 1956), 187–8.

58. Hegel, *Philosophy of History*, 41–2: 'For we must understand that the state is the realisation of freedom, i.e. of the absolute end-goal, and that it exists for its own sake. We must understand, further, that all the value that human beings possess, all of their spiritual reality, they have through the state alone.' Andrew Vincent sums up Hegel's view in the following terms: 'We are not just social creatures but state creatures' (*Theories of the State* (Oxford, Blackwell, 1987), 119).

59. This point is well made in Wood, *Hegel's Ethical Thought*, 89.

60. Hegel, *Phenomenology of Spirit*, §187; cf. *Philosophy of Right*, §57.

61. Hegel, *Philosophy of Mind*, *Zusatz* to §432. The right of property is particularly important for recognition. Property facilitates moral development and self-realization through entering into contractual arrangements: 'Contract presupposes that the contracting parties *recognise* each other as persons and owners of property; and since it is a relationship of objective spirit, the moment of recognition is already contained and presupposed within it' (*Philosophy of Right*, §71; also see §274).

62. For a discussion of Hegel's views on hereditary monarchy see M. Tunick, 'Hegel's Justification of Hereditary Monarchy', *History of Political Thought*, 12 (1991).

63. Hegel, *Political Writings*, 201.

64. Hegel, *Philosophy of Mind*, *Zuzatz* to §435. Cf. Hegel, *Introduction to the Philosophy of History*, 27.

65. *Philosophy of History*, 430–2.

66. Hegel, *Philosophy of Mind*, §547.

67. Vincent, 'The Hegelian State and International Politics', 197 and 200. In his *Theories of the State*, 134, Vincent accepts that the states-based system is for Hegel 'logically necessary'.

68. Hegel, *Philosophy of Mind*, §547.

69. Hegel, *Philosophy of Mind*, §547.

70. James Leslie Brierly, *The Basis of Obligation in International Law* (Oxford, Clarendon Press, 1958), 36.

71. See e.g. Michael H. Mitias, 'Hegel on International Law', *Clio*, 9 (1980), 274–80.

72. Hegel, *Philosophy of Right*, §330: 'the relation must always remain one of obligation'; §333: 'international law remains only an obligation'.

73. Bernard Bosanquet, *Social and International Ideals* (London, Macmillan, 1917), 134 and 16 respectively.
74. Viscount Haldane, *Selected Addresses and Essays* (London, Murray, 1928), 68.
75. Hegel's contention that civilian interests and institutions should be excluded from legitimate targets in war should be compared with his views on the extension of the arbitrary powers of the police during times of war (*Philosophy of Right*, §234).
76. Hegel, *Political Writings*, 144.
77. Also see Hegel, *Phenomenology of Spirit*, §§474–6; Hegel, *Philosophy of Mind*, §§545–7; and Hegel, *Natural Law*, 93–4.

15

MARX AND THE CAPITALIST WORLD SYSTEM

The Changing International Scene

Hegel during the course of his life was witness to a grand European expansionism which by the turn of the nineteenth century, although pervasive in the Americas and extensive in Asia, had not yet created a Eurocentric world system dominated by the great powers. He saw the rise and demise of the Napoleonic Empire. By the terms of the Treaty of Vienna (1815) the European states system was rebuilt upon legal foundations and the delicate balance of power was reaffirmed with little or no regard for suppressed and emergent nationalist aspirations which were later to dominate and change the face of European politics. As well as those features that continued or were restored, there were some that were new. Primarily, prior to 1798 Russia, Austria, Prussia, France, and England had come to be the main players in international relations, but the polite etiquette and formal diplomatic language of the *ancien régime* extended sovereign equality to a whole array of lesser polities. The traumas of the struggle for Europe between 1792 and 1815 highlighted the realities o. power and destroyed the polite fiction of equality. There were now fewer polities on the map of Europe, with many having consolidated themselves into larger entities. Furthermore, the conception of the state changed with the elevation of the subject to the status of citizen.

Between 1818, when France took its place alongside Russia, Britain, Austria, and Prussia in the Concert of Europe, and the time of Hegel's death in 1831, the great powers orchestrated the maintenance of the system by means of agreeing to, or acquiescing in, collective intervention in the domestic issues outside their formal jurisdiction. The interventionism which the French Revolution sanctioned, and which Burke used against France itself, provided a convenient practical principle for repressing revolutionary activities against existing states. Hegel also witnessed the birth of the Industrial Revolution, and was an astute observer of the adverse effects of the market on some sections of civil society, the accentuated social and economic problems generated by German capitalism, and its intensified and aggressive world expansionism.

In the Americas colonies were rebelling against empire. In 1823 the United

States promulgated the Monroe Doctrine, which declared that in future the countries of the American continent were not to be viewed as potential colonies for European powers. Furthermore, any attempt to win back the newly established South American republics would be viewed by the United States as a threat to its peace and security. In the decade after 1815 Argentina, Colombia, and Mexico rebelled against Spain and were recognized by Britain as independent republics in 1825, the same year as it recognized Brazil.

The collapse of the Concert of Europe under the strain of resurgent nationalism found expression in the 1848 revolutions and was epitomized by the unification of Germany and Italy; accelerated industrial growth with its consequent economic and social problems; and the creation of a world capitalist system of states out of colonialism, encouraged by strident nationalism. These were all developments about which Marx wrote in his capacity as a political activist, journalist, and philosopher, considerably influenced by Hegel and often in collaboration with Engels.

Marx and Hegel

As early as 1837, the year in which Marx transferred from the University of Bonn to Berlin, he had extensively read Hegel and the works of some of his followers and was an active member of the Doctors' Club, which was important within the Young Hegelian movement.[1] From 1843 Marx came to believe that Hegel's idealism was fundamentally defective. He nevertheless continued to believe that conceiving historical change as a dialectical development generated by contradictions was of considerable importance. While using Feuerbach's materialism to develop his own critique of Hegel's idealism, Marx used Hegel to go beyond Feuerbach to formulate what has come to be called historical materialism, or the materialist conception of history.[2]

Modern international relations theory has recently taken a normative turn and begun seriously to explore the place of ethics in the relations among states. Such theorists at once reject what was the dominant aspiration in various guises in the discipline, namely the search for objective explanation, and deny the Realist contention that talk of morality and ethical principles disguises the underlying motivations, namely power and security. If ethical principles are to play a role in international relations, they must have some basis of justification. As I suggested in Chapter 1, a number of theorists have sought to identify the source of the principles of international ethics in either cosmopolitanism or communitarianism, while maintaining at the same time that these two categories adequately conceptualize normative thinking in international relations since the time of Kant. There are, of course, different types of cosmopolitanism, and Marx's is typically identified as one of its main variants along with utilitarianism and Kantianism. Similarly, communitarianism comes in different guises, but Hegel is exemplified as its principal exponent. In order to dissociate the broader implications of modern communitarianism from the specifically Hegelian and idealist versions, such international relations theorists as Mervyn Frost and Chris Brown prefer to use the term 'constitutive theory'.[3] Both authors jettison Hegelian metaphysics and present their own ideas in a secular Hegelianism.

When looked at in terms of the categories of communitarianism and cosmopolitanism, the theories of Hegel and Marx appear starkly antithetical. Marx is seen as a cosmopolitan thinker who sees capitalism as a world-wide phenomenon diminishing the importance of national boundaries and emphasizing the world character of the two main protagonists, the proletariat and the bourgeoisie. If Marx is a cosmopolitan thinker, there must be some firmer basis for a world community than class cohesiveness. After all, the community towards which he looks forward is classless. What sort of cosmopolitanism is Marx advocating? Broadly speaking, cosmopolitanism can be distinguished into two types: institutional cosmopolitanism and moral cosmopolitanism. Communitarian critics of cosmopolitanism usually launch their attacks on the institutional kind, arguing for the necessity of the concepts of national community and national identity.[4] Although the implications of a classless and stateless world seem to be the unity of the human race in a moral rather than institutional cosmopolitanism, it is by no means inevitable in the works of Marx and Engels that nations and communities will disappear. When we use the categories of cosmopolitanism and communitarianism to explore the theories of international relations of Hegel and Marx we find that the states-based international system of Hegel, with its emphasis upon individuality, recognition and international right, stands in marked contrast to Marx's emphasis upon a stateless international community in which alienation, exploitation, and estrangement are overcome in a universal moral community.

On the other hand, when we shift the emphasis to particularism and universalism we are able to bring the thoughts of Hegel and Marx much closer together on the question of international ethics. In both theorists ethical constraints in international relations are constituted by the historical process.

In Hegel's communitarianism and Marx's cosmopolitanism we find elements of both particularism and universalism. O'Neill suggests, for example, that 'Hegel embeds the stages of particularity in the history of more inclusive universal reason.'[5] Marx, on the other hand, while holding some notion of a universal human essence, traces its manifestations in the particularities of distinct historical epochs. They both see history as the gradual unfolding of freedom in the world. They are both historicists but not relativists. Both have an ideal of human nature in that humans are deemed by both to have a capacity to attain freedom, and both believe that the historical process in which the stages of attainment are manifest reveal not one universal nature but changing natures constituted by the historical conditions. Each of the stages is an inadequate attainment of freedom. Because each stage has the idea of human freedom as his guiding principle, each is able to make judgements about the merits of one epoch over another.

For Marx, Hegel's dialectic was detached from reality. It simply could not reconcile the world of ideas with the material conditions of life. Marx contended that

Hegel's idealist abstractions could be avoided by taking the material conditions of life as the starting-point of any philosophical enquiry. In other words, for Marx, Hegel's 'dialectic stands on its head. You must turn it the right way up again if you want to discover the rational kernel that is hidden away within the wrappings of mystification.'[6]

From Nationalism to Materialism

Taking the material conditions of life, the modes by which they were produced, and the social relations to which they gave rise, Marx and Engels concluded that all history has been the history of class struggle. The composition of the classes, the nature of the struggle, and the modes of production to which they were related had dialectically evolved, resulting in the polarization of the proletariat and the bourgeoisie, who were engaged in nothing less than veiled civil war, under the auspices of capitalism.

Capitalism was the first truly international mode of production, and broke down national barriers to the exploitation of a world market. The impetus for such expansion is the competition among capitalists for resources, cheap labour, and investment opportunities. Conflict between capitalists is inherent in the system. Marx often refers to this competition as war. In order to survive the cyclical patterns of boom and recession, capitalists have desperately to search for ways to cut costs and open up new markets. Capitalist international expansionism at the same time gave rise to an international working class. The war among capitalists is mitigated by their united or common class interest, conflict against the proletariat.[7] Marx and Engels were not concerned with globalization developed by relations among states, although they were aware of the importance of such relations in the past and of conquest in creating larger political entities. Globalization under capitalism, howev_r, was of much greater significance.[8]

With Marx materialism rather than nationalism provided the basis for understanding societies, and class became the essential form of group cohesion for analysis. Conflict between classes, rather than between states, constituted the central focus for Marx's conception of history. As Williams succinctly puts it: 'Marx sees politics not from the perspective of one national state but from the perspective of a progressive view of history with the international working class as its agent.'[9] After the 1848 revolutions and the unrelenting upsurge of nationalist aspirations Marx and Engels could not completely ignore nationalism. They acknowledged that as well as class oppression, national oppression was a factor that had to be accommodated in their analyses of capitalism. They identified the Irish and Poles as victims of national oppression and argued that liberation from national domination was a requisite step prior to taking their place in the international struggle of the proletariat.

Given the denial of state centrality in world politics, his denunciation of inequality and injustice, and the implicit rejection of the established world order in preference for radical change or revolution, Marx has to a large extent, until relatively recent times, been relegated to the margin of the modern international relations community. His main contribution to international relations theory has been in contemporary analyses of imperialism with their emphasis upon the capitalist world structure, structural power, and the structural instruments of oppression exercised in the context of the centre–periphery relationship.[10] The main difference between Marx's conception of colonialism and the theories of imperialism of modern neo-Marxists is that on the whole Marx, although contemptuous of the particular acts of capitalist colonialists in exploiting the Orient, believed that in the long term capitalist intervention had the effect of raising barbarous societies to the level of history and facilitating progress towards socialism and communism.

On the other hand, neo-Marxists like Galtung and Gunder Frank contend that capitalist intervention in the Third World is detrimental to the economic growth of those countries and actually precipitates underdevelopment.[11] The discovery of critical theory by a number of contemporary international relations theorists, among them Andrew Linklater, has successfully intruded an important post-Marxian perspective into the discipline.[12] This, however, is a heterogeneous tendency encompassing and surpassing the critical theory developed from the Frankfurt School. Such writers as Robert Cox and Justin Rosenberg have deployed historical materialism in their attempts to challenge the dominant assumption of Realist international relations that 'the geopolitical core of the discipline's subject matter is ontologically distinct from the wider structures of social production'.[13]

The Three Traditions

With Marx's emphasis upon the material conditions of life and upon a universalist humanitarianism we find elements from both the Realist and Universal Moral Order traditions being employed. In addition, however, the dominant tendency in Marx is to understand human nature as a developing phenomenon in conjunction with the modes of production and the division of labour associated with them. Similarly, international relations take on different characteristics as the division of labour and the mode of production change. Where one places Marx on the three-dimensional map presented in this book is a matter of interpretation. Any interpretation, however, needs to be sustained with the presentation of cogent reasons.

A strong case can be made for including Marx in the Empirical Realist tradition, and it is only fair to present it as forcefully as possible. First, in various places Marx denied the existence of transcendental laws. It is the material conditions of our existence, and in particular the economic conditions, that shape and determine our lives. It is human beings who create the material conditions in accordance with their needs and desires, and not in accordance with abstract laws laid down by God, or dictated by Natural Right. We saw in the case of Machiavelli that human beings were not in perfect control of their environment. Fortuna could always intervene to frustrate the most carefully prepared plans. In Marx this lack of control over circumstances and of our environment became more pronounced. It was human beings who created the modes of production, but the modes became so complex that we lost control of them. These impersonal economic forces shaped our existence. We were trapped within the structures of the system. It was the modes of production themselves that embodied contradictions that weakened the system and led to its collapse. In this respect Marx developed Mandeville's theory of unintended consequences and applied it to the operation of the economic system, and arrived at conclusions very different from those of Mandeville.

Secondly, the Realist or empirical tradition, with its emphasis upon temporal and material existence, embodied a tendency to emphasize that social existence can be understood scientifically. Machiavelli, for instance, believed that by collecting examples from history, or by studying different terrain, useful precepts could be formulated and used as guides to action. Hobbes too, more explicitly than Machiavelli, believed that he had founded a science of politics. It was, however, Euclid's geometry rather than the experimental science of his day that inspired him. Marx himself claimed to be providing a scientific basis for explaining the human condition. In providing such a basis he relied heavily upon the work of classical political economy. He learned much, for example, from Ricardo's theory of rent. It is from this theory that Marx derived his idea of surplus value, which was central to his theory of the dynamics and decay of capitalism. He developed Bentham's theory of sinister interests at work in society, and formulated a theory which portrays capitalists as alien powers persuading the working class that the economic system works to the benefit of all, while really it operates purely in the interests of the bourgeoisie.

Why, then, are the material conditions of life important in Marx's philosophy? Marx contends that his predecessors in philosophy were too preoccupied with the realm of ideas to the neglect of the material world. Their premises were at variance with reality. He maintained that, unlike those of his predecessors, his own premises were not arbitrary because he took as his starting-point 'real individuals, their actions and their material conditions of life, those which they find existing as well as those which they produce through their actions'.[14] In whatever way we might try to distinguish human beings from animals, in terms of rationality or consciousness, this does not get to the real heart of the matter because human beings themselves began to distinguish themselves from animals the moment that they *produced* the means of their own subsistence: 'By producing food man indirectly produces his own material life itself'.[15]

In the 'Lordship and Bondage' section of Hegel's *Phenomenology* one of the most important points to arise was that individuality for the slave was attained through work. Individuality was given an enduring and objective form by means of working upon the world. The self-conscious individual was self-realizing. Hegel's significant achievement, in Marx's view, was to comprehend man's development as a process. Marx says of Hegel 'that he thus grasps the nature of *work* and comprehends objective man, authentic because actual, as the result of his *own work*.'[16] Because individuality entailed a struggle for recognition at the level of consciousness, Hegel failed to identify the foundation of self-consciousness in the material conditions of life. In other words, he failed to identify self-consciousness with the prevailing modes of production and the relations to which they gave rise.[17] For Marx, then, it was only by means of the historical process that man became a human being. At the outset he was merely a generic being who belonged to a tribe or herd.

For Marx the way in which production is organized is of crucial importance because it expresses the life of human beings. The *mode of life*, as Marx calls it, is what people are. People are what they do; in the ways in which they express themselves, they are themselves. This is a crucial and pivotal aspect of Marx's thought because here we have the reason why economics is important to the understanding of social existence. He sums up his position in the following terms: 'As individuals express their life, so they are. What they are, therefore, coincides with what they produce, with *what* they produce and *how* they produce. The nature of individuals thus depends on the material conditions which determine their production.'[18] This, then, is the fundamental reason why much of Marx's thought is concerned with analysing the different modes of production, and capitalism in particular. It was from this analysis that he developed his philosophy of history.

Marx sometimes referred to his method as dialectic, but he certainly never saw it as an abstract formula that could be applied to circumstances as a blueprint for understanding. A general philosophy of history with a structure of set principles could only result in transhistorical theories unrelated to fact and possessing no genuine explanatory power. To move from the transhistorical claim that all production takes place in a context of social relations to the contention that a prerequisite of capitalist production is the existence of a propertyless class of wage labourers is not achievable by the application of a set formula, but requires detailed historical stuc /.

We saw that in the tradition of Empirical Realism a low view of human nature was assumed, with actions motivated by the basic instincts of seeking pleasure and avoiding pain. In the second tradition, Universal Moral Order, human nature was viewed as embodying the capacity, and having the potential, for real moral progress. This tradition held out great faith in the reasoning capacities of human beings to apprehend an absolute standard of conduct to guide human action. It is true that some of Marx's characterizations of human action and motivation under capitalism comply with the picture of human nature assumed by Realists. When he discusses these characteristics they are clearly specific to capitalism, and therefore historically confined. Marx suggests that capitalism 'has left remaining no other nexus between man and man than naked self-interest, than callous "cash payment"' (*Communist Manifesto*, 70).[19]

Marx does have a notion of what he calls 'species being', which at first glance appears to conform with the optimistic view of human nature portrayed in the second tradition. Species being is the essence of life and finds expression when a person is in harmony with nature. It is this that has to provide the basis of Marx's cosmopolitanism. The person expresses this species being in the things that he or she makes, whether they are artistic creations or products for consumption. When the capitalist takes away the object of labour and gives wages in return, the labourer becomes alienated from his or her species being. This process, Marx suggests, undermines the labourer's superiority over animals and transforms it into an inferior relationship. People are deprived of nature, the very thing to which they stand in an intimate relation. Nature is, for Marx, the 'inorganic body' of the person; it is that which is formed and transformed as an expression of his, or her, species being. As Marx suggests: 'A direct consequence of man's alienation from the product of his work, from his life's activity, and from his species-existence, is the *alienation* of *man* from *man*'.[20]

Marx's notion of 'species being' or 'species-existence' implies that there is an ideal of humanity from which man has become alienated. He seems to have a universal and transcendental idea of what man should be in opposition to what man had become at that time. In the *Communist Manifesto*, however, Marx appears to deny any suggestion of an eternal human essence. He says, 'Communism abolishes eternal truths, it abolishes all religions and all morality, instead of constituting them on a new basis; it therefore acts in contradiction to all past historical experience' (*Communist Manifesto*, 85–6). He is in fact suggesting that everything is the product of prevailing circumstances, and ultimately of the prevailing mode of production.

Bertell Ollman, Norman Geras, and Lawrence Wilde have all argued that Marx does have a conception of human essence which is not incompatible with what he says in the *Communist Manifesto*, and in relation to which the concept of alienation has to be understood.[21] For Wilde this essence consists in that which differentiates human beings from animals, that is, their capacity for creative production that can be distinguished and identified only in its manifestations in history. This essence is one which changes with history in that the capacity for creativity finds new expression as circumstances change. The human essence, for example, can become manifest in political activity, but the origin and genesis of the manifestation will be more deeply rooted in civil society, and in particular in the organization of production. Alienation on this interpretation is the alienation of the human essence of creative activity that occurs within the process of commodity production.[22] The existence of a cosmopolitan community based on this idea of human essence is impeded not only by alienation, which is a consequence of being at the mercy of impersonal structures and forces of human creation, but also by exploitation of one group by another through the control of the labour power of another for profit, and estrangement of communities or nations from each other because of suspicion and hostility.

Although we have a universalist humanitarianism in Marx with an emphasis upon human essence, this essence is really little more than a capacity which in terms of content and realization wholly depends upon the historical process, that is, the social relations of production. In criticism of Bentham, Marx distinguishes between 'human nature in general, and . . . human nature as modified in each specific historical epoch'.[23] He says in the *Theses on Feuerbach* that 'the human essence is no abstraction inherent in each single individual. In its reality it is the ensemble of the social relations'.[24] Marx is in fact, along with Hegel, best understood as an exponent of a historically developing international ethics. For him human nature is not something given, but develops over time: not in accordance with any absolute standards of morality, but in accordance with the type of society in which people live. He does, in fact, explicitly deny that there is a universal human nature. He argues that 'every century has its peculiar nature, it also produces its peculiar natural men'.[25] History constitutes a continuous transformation of human nature and undermines any claim that a universal morality can reside in an absolute human essence.[26]

It needs to be emphasized, then, that morality is not an absolute standard, but is integrally related to the mode of production and its associated society. Injustice and justice only have meaning and sense relative to the historical epoch and mode of production with which they are associated. Thus slavery is just within the ancient mode of production because it is integral to that system of life. To criticize the ancient world for being based on slavery is futile.[27] Transactions between people are just when they are the natural consequences of the system of relations of a particular mode of production. Thus because capitalism presupposes the idea of voluntary action in the making of contract, 'slavery, on the basis of the capitalist mode of production, is unjust; so is fraud in the quality of commodities'.[28] The material conditions of life are the foundation of all other relations, including moral relations.

When this is translated into the international sphere, as well as defining the relations between individuals, the mode of production defines relations in the international sphere. The types of relations which states enjoy are nothing other 'than the expression of a particular division of labour. And must not these change when the division of labour changes?'[29]

Capitalism and the World

Marx and Engels did not address themselves directly to formulating a fully developed theory of international relations. They did, however, write a great deal about the propensity for capitalism to develop world-wide markets; on specific incidents and events involving colonies and their colonizers; and on the ideas of a nation and class; in addition, Engels was fascinated with military history. It is from these sources that we are able to construct the theory that is only intimated in their work.

In the *Grundrisse* Marx implicitly subscribed to Hegel's view that history was nothing other than the development of consciousness in the world. History, then, was the progressive revelation of freedom. Its progress was to be distinguished into three phases. The first primitive stage was characterized by relations of dependency, whether within the family, within the tribe, or under feudalism by dependency upon a lord. The early forms of social relations were characterized by a herd instinct, or common consciousness. Individuals were barely distinguishable from nature, which appeared to them as an irresistible and mighty force. Progress in freeing themselves from nature and thus developing the capacities that distinguished humans from animals had hardly begun. At this level of consciousness, societies were estranged from each other, and each was the source of the others' difficulties. These primitive communities entered into disputes over land occupation and displaced each other from their territories of settlement. War, for these primitive settlements, was a unifying force. Communal labour, which was necessary for occupying the land in order to sustain life, was also necessary to defend that occupation against those who threatened to displace your own community.[30]

Any notion of belonging to a common species, or of conceiving larger and inclusive moral orders, was beyond the capacity of these primitive humans. Universal moral ties were inconceivable. The primitive communities were superseded by higher forms of association effected by conquest, in which estrangement between communities was replaced by a hierarchical and more inclusive social structure, and this gave rise to estrangement between classes. The conquerors dominated the conquered and established new conditions of production, and gave rise to larger inclusive communities.

The second form of human association was distinguished by relations of mutual independence. The development of exchange relations, which at first arose between communities, was in addition to war the mechanism by which the internal structure of primitive communities became transformed. The money economy transformed the relations of personal dependence into those of an apparent greater independence characterized under capitalism, for example, by freely contracting individuals exchanging labour power and capital. Under conditions of mutual independence, productive capacities were enhanced, and the human was liberated from nature and learned to dominate it and harness its productive potential. This individual freedom was in fact illusory, and one form of domination was succeeded by another. It was the capitalist structure itself that now dominated individuals with impersonal forces, and what appeared to be personal independence simply generated a total dependence of individuals upon a world-wide market. In addition, what appeared to be a universal community of a common species was merely related by money, and not by universal moral ties.

The formal freedom and equality that capitalism posited, and effectively negated by class domination, an oppressive division of labour, and the tyranny of the market, were nevertheless of crucial importance in the development of socialism and communism. The third phase of social development realized the freedom and equality that was only potential in the second mode of association. It was a phase in which national and social barriers were surmounted and a truly international and universal moral society established, namely a classless and stateless international society devoid of the forms of alienation to which capitalism gave rise.[31]

In the preface to *A Contribution to the Critique of Political Economy* Marx contends that

In the social production of their existence, men inevitably enter into definite relations, which are independent of their will, namely relations of production appropriate to a given stage in the development of their material forces of production. The totality of these relations of production constitutes the economic structure of society, the real foundation, on which arises a legal and political superstructure and to which correspond definite forms of social consciousness.[32]

Each successive mode of production marks a stage in the 'economic development of society'. He distinguished four such stages before socialism: the Asiatic, ancient slave economies, feudal serf economies, and the capitalist bourgeois mode of production. There was no suggestion that every society had to follow this line of development, nor that stages could not be skipped. Similarly, remnants of previous stages could coexist with later stages in any one society, and between societies the whole range could be coexistent. Countries in the contemporary world exhibited the Asiatic mode of production at the same time as Europe exhibited fully developed capitalism.

Of all the modes of production to emerge prior to socialism, only capitalism had the potential and capacity to encompass the whole world in its system of productive relations. In the *Communist Manifesto* Marx and Engels argued that under capitalism a world market had been established which had given considerable impetus to the development of communications, commerce, and navigation (*Communist Manifesto*, 69). Because of the exploitation of the world market, production and consumption in each country had taken on a cosmopolitan character. As Marx said 'In place of the old wants, satisfied by the productions of the country, we find new wants, requiring for their satisfaction the products of distant lands and climes' (*Communist Manifesto*, 71). Capitalist values became universalized over the whole world and effectively broke down national barriers. The continuous improvements in the instruments of production, along with the enhanced means of communication, gave capitalism an irresistible impetus which dragged even barbarous nations into the sphere of civilization. Marx argued that

While on the one hand capital must thus seek to pull down every local barrier to commerce, i.e. to exchange, in order to capture the whole world as its market, on the other hand it strives to destroy space by means of time, i.e. to restrict to a minimum the time required for movement from one place to another. The more developed capital is, and thus the more extensive the market through which it circulates and which constitutes the spatial route of its circulation, the more it will aspire to greater extension in space for its market, and thus to greater destruction of space by time.[33]

Capitalism compelled all nations to comply with bourgeois methods of production and to adopt bourgeois values: 'In one word, it creates a world after its own image' (*Communist Manifesto*, 71). National self-sufficiency and local parochialism were replaced by international interdependence. This universalization of capitalist values was achieved at both the material and intellectual levels. Local literature, he maintained, gave way to an international literature.

Just as the mode of production to which the bourgeoisie was related was universal in its scope, the class which it brought into being, and which would ultimately destroy it, was itself truly universal. The state itself, which was so central in the international system for most of the theorists discussed in this book, was described by Marx and Engels as an instrument of the ruling class employed to regulate competition among themselves and to oppress the proletariat (*Communist Manifesto*, 69). This does not mean that they believed that it was consciously employed in this manner, merely that it is an expression of class interest, no doubt mistakenly believed by the bourgeoisie to represent the interests of all.

At other times the state was described by Marx and Engels as constituting a bureaucracy with its own interests, attempting to alleviate and mediate class conflict in order to sustain its own power.[34] Either way, the state was something to which the proletariat owed nothing more than a strategic allegiance. The primary loyalty of the proletarian was to his class, rather than to the nation or the state. The sufferings of the proletariat were universal, and its emancipation must also be universal.[35] The conditions of subjection were the same everywhere under capitalism, and in consequence the worker had been stripped of every vestige of national character (*Communist Manifesto*, 77–8). In their struggles against the bourgeoisie, the proletarians of all countries had a common interest independent of national ties (*Communist Manifesto*, 79).[36]

Even though the aim was to rid the world of class conflict, the level at which the struggle took place between the proletariat and the bourgeoisie was at first the national level: 'The proletariat of each country must, of course, first of all settle matters with its own bourgeoisie' (*Communist Manifesto*, 78). Modern nationalism was for Marx and Engels bourgeois. It was the territorial consolidation by the bourgeoisie of their economic social and political power under the auspices of the sovereign nation-state.[37] Along with the consolidation of capitalist power, the modern nation-state and a national proletariat were necessary, but nevertheless transitory, phases in the development of history. Although the emphasis and the force of the argument changed after the nationalist revolutions of 1848, Marx was consistent in maintaining the universal character of capitalism, which could not be constrained by national boundaries, and the universal interest of the proletariat. Only under capitalism was this universality possible.

As nationalist aspirations became stronger as a force which simply had to be reckoned with, both Marx and Engels acknowledged that national self-determination was indispensable to the development of socialism. Their view was consequentialist in the sense that if a certain development, including nationalism, contributes to the development of history and not to its regression, that is, if the overall consequences are favourable, then it is to be valued and encouraged.[38] Initially Marx and Engels were on the whole hostile to nationalist movements because they were potentially retrogressive and retarded the development and demise of capitalism. Initially, for example, Marx believed that Irish nationalism would inhibit the growth of capitalism in both England and Ireland. He urged Irish workers to join the Chartist cause, which he thought would perpetuate a workers' revolution and simultaneously liberate Ireland.[39] With the increasing number of Irish emigrants forced by famine to seek their fortune in English cities, an antagonism arose between English and Irish workers. Ireland was firmly placed on the British political agenda in 1867 with the resurgence of Fenianism. More importantly, the stance taken by Marx and Engels no longer appeared progressive. They came to believe that Irish nationalism could be used to undermine British aristocratic landed interests in both Ireland and Britain by breaking down the last remnants of feudalism.[40] Nationalist movements, then, could be commensurate with the development of socialism. If nationalist movements were progressive, that is, if they promoted the development of socialism, they could be accepted. If they were regressive, that is, likely to inhibit the growth of socialism, they had to be condemned. The nation provided a suitable context for generating capitalist growth, and that is why both Marx and Engels supported German and Italian unification. As Petrus contends, Marx and Engels 'supported national self-determination under particular conditions but never as a binding principle'.[41]

Oppressed nations had first to achieve national liberation before the proletariat could liberate themselves from the bourgeoisie. The accommodation of nationalism became much more pronounced in Engels's writings than it had been in those of Marx. Gallie shows how Engels came to believe that the socialist parties of Europe, particularly those at the centre of impending social changes, among them the German Social Democrats and French Workers' Party, should cultivate appropriate images and portray themselves as responsible and patriotic, capable of being trusted with the nation's defence. Each party should portray itself as the authoritative voice of the proletariat conscripts, and the only party capable of averting European war. Peace was possible because each of the socialist parties had close affinities with the others. They were similar in their economic aims, and harboured no mutual suspicions and reciprocal rivalries that might precipitate conflict.[42]

Colonialism

The inexorable evidence of the omnipotence of capitalism lay in the conquest, subjection, and destruction of non-European societies in the wake of capitalist expansionism. In the *Communist Manifesto* Marx and Engels identified the ancient and feudal modes of production preceding capitalism. All modes have within them the seeds of both their own development and destruction. As the contradictions inherent in each mode became more intense, the economic system broke down and was superseded by a higher form of production. Each mode was necessary to the emergence and development of the one that followed. In *A Contribution to the Critique of Political Economy* Marx argued that each mode had to exhaust its potentialities before the higher relations of production could appear out of the mode that was superseded.[43] He did, however, modify his views by suggesting that the course of European history could not be transposed into a universal philosophy of history applicable to all societies.[44]

It is clear from the works of Marx and Engels that each of the modes was dialectically related to the rest. Through a series of contradictions which were eventually overcome, higher levels of production were eventually achieved until socialism emerged and prepared the way for communism. Each of the modes was dynamic and embodied within itself its developmental propensities and tensions, which led to its eventual degeneration. There is, however, as I have already suggested, a further mode that Marx and Engels add to account for those economic formations which do not correspond to any of those earlier identified. This mode is called the Asiatic and is a form of primitive communism.[45] There is nothing peculiarly oriental about it, other than its inordinate durability in Asia. Its communal ownership of land centred upon village communities was, as far as Marx and Engels were concerned, characteristic of primitive stages in societies all over the world from India to Ireland.[46] From the time of the revolt of the Indian Army in 1857, both Marx and Engels tended to use the term 'Asiatic' as a synonym for 'primitive'.[47] As a mode of production it did not share the characteristics of ancient, feudal, or capitalist modes. It was not dialectically related to them, did not have an inner dynamism for development, and did not appear to have inherent within it the seeds of its own degeneration and collapse.

As a contemporary phenomenon the Asiatic mode of production was non-European, and Marx was insistent that its development need not follow the pattern typical of European economic progress.[48] He was in fact of the view that capitalism forced those barbarous countries subjected by the Asiatic mode of production to become part of the capitalist system. The Asiatic mode of production, on Marx's own account, could be transformed into capitalism by the direct intervention of bourgeois expansionism. Both Marx and Engels, especially in their earlier writings, looked favourably upon colonization because of this capacity to transform primitive economic formations.

In order to understand their attitude to colonization we need to know what the Asiatic mode was; why it did not contain the seeds of its own decay; and why Marx and Engels believed that it was necessary for it to be transformed by capitalist intervention.

Marx and Engels do not discuss the Asiatic mode of production at any great length, nor do they ever attempt systematically to relate it to the course of European economic development. However, both writers had a good deal to say about colonial matters. Engels, for example, was particularly interested in Ireland, while Marx, who was the reluctant London correspondent of the *New York Daily Tribune*, had become well enough versed in Indian, Chinese, and Middle Eastern affairs to be able to write authoritatively about them.

The principal difference between the Asiatic mode of production and those that succeeded it in Europe is that the former is not based upon private property relations in land. The existence of a state usually entailed a class society, and its function, whether it represented its own interests, or was simply the instrument of the ruling class, was to ensure social cohesion. In Asia, however, the oriental despot was synonymous with the state, and was the effective landlord who co-ordinated economic activity.[49] With the state as the landlord, private ownership of land, the prerequisite of a feudal economy, was nothing more than nominal.[50] In effect, the Asiatic mode of production was not a class system,[51] and therefore technically fell outside history as Marx and Engels conceived it in the *Communist Manifesto*, where they contended that 'The history of all hitherto existing society is the history of class struggles' (*Communist Manifesto*, 67).[52]

The particularly harsh geographic and climatic conditions, according to Marx, made it necessary to have public works schemes in order to irrigate areas which would otherwise be unproductive. The level of civilization was so low that even the need for meticulous care in the use of water did not generate the creation of voluntary associations of individuals to solve their common problems. It was therefore necessary for the state to interfere by providing public works programmes. The extent of the programmes fluctuated from one oriental despot to another. Marx did, however, exaggerate the extent of public works and the extent to which equality prevailed among individuals within communities. The communities themselves, nevertheless, did provide a useful foundation upon which to build an autocratic despotism.[53]

Because public works were controlled by central government, and because agriculture and commerce were dispersed all over the country, farming and commercial activities became interlinked within the confines of small communities which were self-sustaining in 'productive capacity and surplus production'.[54] The village system of production had remained the same from time immemorial. Officials had strictly demarcated functions concerned with the preservation of peace, the distribution of water, the protection of crops, and the preservation of village boundaries.

It was a system, however, that stultified the imagination, inhibited development, and allowed oriental despotism to flourish. It was a system in which the individual failed to achieve independence from the community.[55] The human mind was constrained by its limited environment and was susceptible to superstition and subjection to traditional rules and customs. The Asiatic mode of production subjected hu..ian beings to the forces of nature, rather than elevating them above them. The self-developing propensities of social life were transformed into the acceptance of the whims of unchanging destiny. Nature, far from being subjected by man, had become sovereign. Human degradation before the feet of nature was testified to by the worship of the monkey and the cow. Asiatic modes of production could not be transformed by their own internal dynamics because the human condition was so much subjected to nature. Instead of their using nature to liberate themselves, nature had been used to enslave them.[56]

In Marx's view, these societies were so primitive that they had not yet reached a level where history began. Marx's attitude to the transformation of these Asiatic modes of production was quite clear. Even though on a personal level he was appalled by the misery and suffering caused by the colonizing process, he believed that the Asiatic countries performed a necessary function in bringing about the final demise of European feudalism, and enabled capitalism to develop to the stage where it could no longer contain its contradictions. In the *Communist Manifesto* Marx and Engels argued that the opening-up of the world through discovery and colonization gave considerable impetus to commerce, navigation, and industry which facilitated the rapid decline of the decaying feudal society (*Communist Manifesto*, 68). In *Das Kapital*, volume ii, this view was reiterated. The expansion of the world market; increased circulation of commodities; the fierce competition between European countries for the riches of Asia and America; and the colonial system itself had 'all contributed materially towards destroying the feudal fetters on production'.[57] In Marx's view Britain was the only country to have brought about a social revolution in India, and in so doing it was fulfilling a dual mission: the destruction of Asiatic society and the laying of foundations for the generation of Western society in Asia. The first condition of the regeneration of India was political unity, and this Britain had accomplished by means of the sword.

Whatever the motivation for bringing about the social revolution in India, Britain acted as the unconscious instrument of the destiny of mankind.[58] The fruits of British colonialism, however, could not be enjoyed by the Indians until the British bourgeoisie had been superseded by the industrial proletariat or, alternatively, the Hindus themselves were sufficiently well organized to throw off British imperialism.[59] The irony was that such unity was not possible until the social transformations brought about by British colonization itself.

The fact that colonization would transform the Asiatic mode of production to a capitalist mode presented a practical problem. Marx pointed out in 1858 that once the revolution had succeeded in Europe it would have to face the possibility of being crushed by the bourgeois societies outside Europe.[60] In 1882 Engels suggested how European socialist societies might respond to the threat from the semi-civilized societies of Asia and the Middle East. He prophesied that in countries where a European population was in occupation, like Canada, the Cape, and Australia, they would become independent. In countries inhabited by the native population and subjected to colonial power, like India, Algeria, and the possessions of Holland, Portugal, and Spain, they would need to be taken over by the proletariat and shown the way to independence as quickly as possible. However, the European proletariat in the process of self-emancipation could not conduct colonial wars and would have to allow the colonies to run their own course. It was likely, Engels believed, that the 'semi-civilized' colonized countries of the world would follow in due course the example of North America and Europe. It was simply idle speculation, in his view, to conjecture on the course which the semi-civilized countries would have to take before arriving at socialism. Engels contended that 'One thing alone is certain: the victorious proletariat can force no blessings of any kind upon any foreign nation without undermining its own victory by so doing. Which of course by no means excludes defensive wars of various kinds.'[61]

During the period when the proletariat of each nation was liberating itself and setting up a dictatorship of the proletariat to assist the transition from capitalism through socialism to communism, different countries would be at different stages of class struggle. In these circumstances a defensive war against external aggressors was justifiable. In so far as the world was organized into nations and states,

Marx and Engels saw war as a function of prevailing economic conditions. There were indications in their writings, however, that war was not necessarily and inextricably related to economic factors.

Gallie and Kubálková and Cruickshank, for example, argue that war for both Marx and Engels is an independent variable. It was used to further economic ends, but could not itself be explained by those ends. In *Anti-Dühring*, for instance, Engels suggested that war was as old as the existence of communities that existed side by side, and in *The Origin of the Family* he argued that prior to wars waged for pillage, war was waged to avenge attacks or expand territory which was insufficient in size.[62] While both Marx and Engels wished to emphasize the economic motivation of war, they both admitted that prior to the differentiation of society into the vertical division of classes, in primitive societies wars were waged as a matter of course.

The question that now arises is that if wars occur independently of and prior to class societies, when classes disappear in post-capitalist society, what will happen to the division of the world into nations or communities? If they persist, will war remain a feature of international or inter-community relations? Although the implications of a classless and stateless world seem to be the unity of the human race, it is by no means inevitable that nations and communities will disappear. In a letter to Bebel, for example, Engels wrote that 'as soon as it becomes possible to speak of freedom the state as such ceases to exist. We would therefore propose to replace *state* everywhere by "community".'[63] Kubálková and Cruickshank also find it difficult to accept that after the revolution there would be no division of the world into communities. They point out that Marx in *Das Kapital*, volume iii, acknowledged the possibility of there being variations in the way in which the common mode of production exhibited itself in surface manifestations. Similarly, they contend that Engels even allowed for minimum inequalities to surface in the conditions of life from one community to another.[64]

The presumption of international class solidarity was seriously undermined by the wars of the early twentieth century, when not only did capitalist countries wage war upon each other, but workers were prepared to fight fellow workers on behalf of the state and in the name of patriotism. Marx's theory needed to be extended to accommodate these developments. Polemicists such as Hobson, Lenin, and Bukharin developed theories of imperialism which sought to explain the durability of capitalism and the phenomenon of national patriotism and its relation to class solidarity. In general they believed that imperialism and war are closely associated with the temporary, but higher, form of monopolistic capitalism.

In conclusion I want to reiterate the point that Marx is best seen as an exemplar of the tradition of Historical Reason. Human beings are constituted by the social relations of production and international ethics, and the international system itself is a function of the mode of production. Marx's version of cosmopolitanism is one in which the universal moral community has little or no place until the end of a process considerably enhanced and facilitated by the particularistic circumstances of capitalism.

Notes

1. Karl Marx, letter to his father dated 10 Nov. 1837, printed in *The Marx–Engels Reader*, 2nd edn., ed. Robert C. Tucker (New York, Norton, 1978), 8.
2. See Lawrence Wilde, *Marx and Contradiction* (Aldershot, Gower, 1989), 19.
3. Chris Brown, 'The Ethics of Political Restructuring in Europe—The Perspective of Constitutive Theory', in Chris Brown (ed.), *Political Restructuring in Europe: Ethical Perspectives* (London, Routledge, 1994); and Mervyn Frost, *Ethics in International Relations: A Constitutive Theory* (Cambridge, Cambridge University Press, 1996). For discussions of the cosmopolitan/communitarian distinction see Janna Thompson, *Justice and World Order: A Philosophical Inquiry* (London, Routledge, 1992); and Chris Brown, *International Relations Theory: New Normative Approaches* (London, Harvester Wheatsheaf, 1992).
4. For discussions of this distinction see the chapters by Onora O'Neill and Charles Beitz in Brown (ed.), *Political Restructuring in Europe*.
5. Onora O'Neill, *Towards Justice and Virtue: A Constructive Account of Practical Reasoning* (Cambridge, Cambridge University Press, 1996), 29.
6. Karl Marx, preface to the second German edition of *Capital* (London, Dent, 1934), 3 vols. ii. 873.
7. Thompson, *Justice and World Order*, 63.
8. Andrew Linklater, 'Marxism', in Scott Burchill and Andrew Linklater with Richard Devetak, Matthew Paterson, and Jacqui True, *Theories of International Relations* (London, Macmillan, 1996), 123.
9. Howard Williams, *International Relations in Political Theory* (Buckingham, Open University Press, 1992), 120.
10. K. J. Holsti maintains that Marxist philosophy fails to address the central questions in international relations and therefore has little to offer the discipline (*The Dividing Discipline: Hegemony and Diversity in International Theory* (London, Allen and Unwin, 1987), 61–81). On the other hand John Maclean has argued that we can separate Marx's method from his particular analysis of capitalism, and apply it with profit (metaphorically speaking) to the study of international relations. John Maclean, 'Marxism and International Relations: A Strange Case of Mutual Neglect', *Millennium*, 17 (1988), 295–320.
11. See André Gunder Frank, 'The Development of Underdevelopment', in Michael Smith, Richard Little, and Michael Shackleton (eds.), *Perspectives on World Politics* (London, Croom Helm, 1981); and Johan Galtung, *The European Community: A Superpower in the Making* (London, Allen and Unwin, 1981).
12. See e.g. R. B. J. Walker, 'Realism, Change, and International Political Theory', *International Studies Quarterly*, 31 (1987); Mark Hoffman, 'Critical Theory and the Inter-Paradigm Debate', *Millennium*, 16 (1987), and 'Going Critical? A Response to Hoffman', *Millennium*, 17 (1988); Yosef Lapid, K. J. Holsti, Thomas J. Biersteker, and Jim George, 'Exchange on the "Third Debate"', *International Studies Quarterly*, 33 (1989); and Andrew Linklater, *Beyond Realism and Marxism: Critical Theory and International Relations* (London, Macmillan, 1990).
13. Justin Rosenberg, *The Empire of Civil Society: A Critique of the Realist Theory of International Relations* (London, Verso, 1994), 6.
14. Karl Marx, *The German Ideology*, in *Writings of the Young Marx on Philosophy and Society*, ed. Loyd D. Easton and Kurt H. Guddat (New York, Doubleday, 1967), 409.

15. Marx, *The German Ideology*, in *Writings of the Young Marx*, 409.

16. Marx, 'Critique of Hegelian Dialectic and Philosophy in General' from the 1844 Manuscripts in *Writings of the Young Marx*, 315.

17. See Richard Norman, *Hegel's Phenomenology: A Philosophical Introduction* (London, Chatto and Windus for University of Sussex Press, 1976), 52–3. Also see *Karl Marx: Pre-Capitalist Economic Formations*, ed. E. J. Hobsbawm (London, Lawrence and Wishart, 1964), 36, 68, and 96.

18. Marx, *The German Ideology*, in *Writings of the Young Marx* , 409. Cf. Karl Marx, *Contribution to the Critique of Political Economy* in *Writings of the Young Marx*, 20.

19. *Manifesto of the Communist Party*, in *The Political Writings, i: The Revolutions of 1848* (Harmondsworth, Penguin, 1973).

20. Karl Marx, *Economic and Philosophical Manuscripts*, in *Writings of the Young Marx on Philosophy and Society*, ed. Loyd D. Easton and Kurt H. Guddat (New York, Doubleday, 1967) 295.

21. Bertell Ollman, *Alienation: Marx's Concept of Man in Capitalist Society* (Cambridge, Cambridge University Press, 1971); Norman Geras, *Marx and Human Nature* (London, Verso, 1983); Lawrence Wilde, 'Marx's Concept of Human Essence and its Radical Critics', *Studies in Marxism*, 1 (1994).

22. Wilde, 'Marx's Concept of Human Essence and its Radical Critics', 23–7; and Wilde, *Marx and Contradiction*, 105.

23. Karl Marx, *Capital* (London, Everyman, 1974), i. 671 n. 2.

24. *Marx–Engels Reader*, thesis vi, p. 145.

25. Karl Marx, *The Philosophical Manifesto of the Historical School of Law*, in *Writings of the Young Marx*, 97.

26. See Eugene Kamenka, *The Ethical Foundations of Marxism* (London, Routledge 1972), 123; and Linklater, *Beyond Realism and Marxism*, 36.

27. Friedrich Engels, *Anti-Dühring* (Moscow, Progress, 1977), 223.

28. Cited in Allen W. Wood, 'The Marxian Critique of Justice', *Philosophy and Public Affairs*, 1 (1971–2), 255; and Norman Geras, 'The Controversy about Marx and Justice', in Alex Callinicos (ed.), *Marxist Theory* (Oxford, Oxford University Press, 1989), 211–67.

29. Marx, letter to P. V. Annenkov dated 28 Dec. 1846 in *Marx–Engels Reader*, 139. Cf. *The German Ideology*, in *Writings of the Young Marx*, 410.

30. Marx, *Pre-Capitalist Economic Formations*, 89 and 92.

31. For illuminating accounts of these three stages in the development of freedom see Andrew Linklater, *Men and Citizens in the Theory of International Relations*, 2nd edn. (London, Macmillan, 1990), 150–61, and *Beyond Realism and Marxism*, 34–45.

32. Marx, *Contribution to the Critique of Political Economy*, 20–1.

33. David McLellan, *Marx's Grundrisse* (London, Paladin, 1973), 141.

34. Karl Marx, *Critique of Hegel's Philosophy of Right*, trans. and ed. Joseph J. O'Malley (Cambridge, Cambridge University Press, 1970) (written in 1843). Also see Karl Marx, *The Class Struggles in France* and *The Eighteenth Brumaire of Louis Bonaparte*, in *The Political Writings, ii: Surveys from Exile* (Harmondsworth, Penguin, 1973).

35. Karl Marx, *Contribution to the Critique of Hegel's Philosophy of Right: Introduction*, in *Marx–Engels Reader*, 64.

36. Also see Alan Gilbert, 'Marx on Internationalism and War', *Philosophy and Public Affairs*, 7 (1978), 348.

37. Joseph A. Petrus, 'Marx and Engels on the National Question', *Journal of Politics*, 33 (1971), 806 and 810.

38. Chris Brown, 'Marxism and International Ethics', in Terry Nardin and David R. Mapel (eds.), *Traditions of International Ethics* (Cambridge, Cambridge University Press, 1992), 230.

39. Horace B. Davis, 'Nations, Colonies and Social Classes: The Position of Marx and Engels', *Science and Society*, 29 (1965), 27.

40. Karl Marx and Friedrich Engels, *Ireland and the Irish Question*, ed. R. Dixon (New York, Doubleday 1972).

41. Petrus, 'Marx and Engels on the National Question', 816; and V. G. Kiernan, *Marxism and Imperialism* (London, Arnold, 1974), 216.

42. W. B. Gallie, *Philosophers of Peace and War* (Cambridge, Cambridge University Press, 1979), 85–91.

43. Marx, *Contribution to the Critique of Political Economy*, 21.

44. This point is well made by M. Evans, referring to a letter written by Marx to Mikhailovsky (M. Evans, *Karl Marx* (London, Allen and Unwin, 1975), 74).

45. Engels distinguished between the Asiatic mode and primitive communism. The former is a type of state communalism, and the latter is a society without a state. I owe this point to Lawrence Wilde.

46. Engels, n. 13 to the 1888 edition of the *Communist Manifesto*, 67. In a letter to Engels dated 14 Mar. 1868, Marx says: 'the Asian or Indian forms of property constitute the initial ones everywhere in Europe, (repr. in Marx, *Pre-Capitalist Economic Formations*, 139). Also see W. H. Shaw, *Marx's Theory of History* (London, Hutchinson, 1974), 169.

47. Kiernan, *Marxism and Imperialism*, 169.

48. Shlomo Avineri, *Karl Marx on Colonialism and Modernisation* (New York, Doubleday, 1968), 5.

49. Karl Marx, 'India', in *On Colonialism* (Moscow, Progress, 1976), 79.

50. George Lichtheim, 'Marx and the "Asiatic Mode of Production"', in Shlomo Avineri (ed.), *Marx's Socialism* (New York, Liber-Atherton, 1973), 190–1; and, Marx, *Pre-Capitalist Economic Formations*, 79.

51. See Hobsbawm, introduction to Marx, *Pre-Capitalist Economic Formations*, 34.

52. Daniel Thorner has identified a number of striking similarities between Marx's 1853 article on India and Hegel's account of India in the *Philosophy of History*. Thorner argues that Marx and Hegel agree in believing that 'India was stationary and was still outside World history; Indian village arrangements were fixed and immutable; the common Hindu was indifferent to politics and political revolution; India was predestined to be conquered and subjugated; in India the most arbitrary despotism had enjoyed full swing' (Daniel Thorner, 'Marx on India and the Asiatic Mode of Production', *Contributions to Indian Sociology*, old series (1966), 44).

53. Victor Kiernan, 'History', in David McLellan (ed.), *Marx: The First 100 Years* (London, Fontana, 1983), 70–1.

54. Marx, *Pre-Capitalist Economic Formations*, 70 and 91.

55. Marx, *Pre-Capitalist Economic Formations*, 83.

56. Marx, 'The Future Results of the British Rule in India', in *On Colonialism*, 41.

57. Repr. in Marx and Engels, *On Colonialism*, 304.

58. Marx, 'The Future Results of the British Rule in India', in *On Colonialism*, 41.

59. Marx, 'The Future Results of the British Rule in India', in *On Colonialism*, 85.

60. Marx, letter to Engels, 8 Oct. 1858, in *On Colonialism*, 320.

61. Engels, letter to Karl Kautsky, 12 Sept. 1882, in *On Colonialism*, 342.

62. Gallie, *Philosophers of Peace and War*, 76; and V. Kubálková and A. A. Cruickshank,

Marxism-Leninism and the Theory of International Relations (London, Routledge and Kegan Paul, 1980), 49.

63. R. N. Berki, 'On Marxian Thought and the Problem of International Relations', *World Politics*, 24 (1971), 85.

64. Kubálková and Cruickshank, *Marxism-Leninism and the Theory of International Relations*, 57.

16

IDENTITY, HUMAN RIGHTS, AND THE EXTENSION OF THE MORAL COMMUNITY: THE POLITICAL THEORY OF INTERNATIONAL RELATIONS IN THE TWENTIETH CENTURY

In Chapter 1 of this book I introduced a number of contemporary characterizations of the history of the political theory of international relations, ranging from Carr's Idealism and Realism, through Wight's and Bull's Hobbesian, Grotian, and Kantian traditions, to the cosmopolitan/communitarian dualism of Brown and Thompson and finally O'Neill's universalism versus particularism. I suggested that all of these characterizations were deficient in one way or another, and I went on in Chapter 2 to offer an alternative triadic conception. Each tradition, it was suggested, offered a criterion of state conduct: the first two are antithethical, representing the subjective and objective springs of state action, and the third, that of Historical Reason, offers an immanent criterion. It was further suggested that for the most part, elem ts of each tradition of thought are to be found in the writings of any one thinker. A Realist, for example, may find the logical implications of his or her moral theory unpalatable, or unacceptable, and seek to modify them in some way with reference to a universal constraint, or with reference to humane considerations which have emerged in the course of the practice of relations among states.

In this final chapter I want to look at some of the substantive issues that modern political theorists of international relations have addressed. It will become apparent that elements from these three traditions still pervade the discussions about human rights and self-identity, the moral status of the nation and state, and the question of extending the moral community beyond state borders. Historicism has become the orthodoxy of late-twentieth-century intellectual debate, and within the political theory of international relations postmodernism is thought to exemplify the tendency of the suspension of universal and foundationalist criteria of moral criticism. Postmodernism in international relations is associated with the names of, among others, Richard K. Ashley, R. B. J. Walker, and James Der Derian, who challenged most of the standard assumptions in international relations, especially those associated with Realism, and in particular power, the state with its inside/outside perspective, and the idea of sovereignty and non-intervention. With their emphasis upon knowledge and knowledge creation, postmodernist theorists have mounted a challenge to what they call the dominant discourse. They question the separation in modern thought of power and knowledge. Far from knowledge being independent of power, power is capable of producing knowledge. The complex power relationships which permeate all aspects of life generate their own forms of knowledge, which serve to regulate the behaviour and thought of individuals. There is no knowledge which is not at the same time a set of power relations. The emphasis, often, is upon the role of power, ideology, and ideas in the construction of reality. The idea of sovereignty itself is one such construction of knowledge and power defining who is to be excluded and who included within its terms of reference. The power knowledge relations are historically contingent, and therefore postmodernism seeks to expose the deep structure of these relationships by means of a form of historical enquiry, which Foucault calls the archaeology of knowledge, or genealogy, following Nietszche. Postmodernism does not claim to unmask the various power relations from an independent vantage point. Knowledge, the theorists claim, is never unconditioned. There are only different perspectives and what Foucault calls regimes of truth, each of which prevails by subjugating others.[1]

What is being questioned is the status of the present and how it came to have authority, and what has been left out, or forgotten, in the history of legitimizing it. The postmodernist wants to know what procedures have been adopted for selecting some aspects of history and passing over others in the legitimation of the power structures of the present. The purpose is normative in that postmodernism seeks to show that current constraints are contingent and conditional, and might therefore be other than they are. They identify layers of practices replacing each other over time. The aim is to liberate the individual from current power constraints and open up future possibilities. In international relations they identify the dominant discourse as Realism and show how it structures and constitutes reality, ordering the world to the advantage of some and to the disadvantage of others. Because no knowledge is unconditional and free from power relations, the implication is that we liberate ourselves from the current structures only to enter new relations of power. This is why Mervyn Frost thinks that postmodernism does not really offer us a normative theory. History is in permanent flux; human nature is extensively malleable. Postmodernism cannot claim a privileged position for its discourse, and like all others sets up new power relations. This, of course, gives it little normative purchase in giving answers to difficult questions in international relations. The irony is that, like the Realists of whom they are critical, postmodernists take the central category of analysis to be power and power relations. This is why Frost calls them super-Realists.[2]

I want to suggest in this chapter that while elements of the traditions of Empirical Realism and Universal Moral Order are pervasive it is nevertheless the elements of the tradition of Historical Reason that have come to dominate, not only through postmodernism, but through most aspects of the modern political theory of international relations.

Human Rights, Man's Wrongs, and the Feminist Voice

For over three hundred years rights talk, especially in the universalist mode, has dominated ethical discourse. As we saw, it was never without its forceful and influential detractors. Rousseau, Burke, Hegel, and Marx all gave credence to the historically developing character of rights and, by implication, the non-universal or particularist nature of rights. None of them, however, was a relativist. Rousseau's belief in natural equality and innate revulsion, Burke's emphasis upon tradition in the context of appeals on behalf of the Indians to universal humanitarian considerations, Hegel's historicist account of the stages of consciousness and forms of life unfolded in the context of universal reason, and Marx's emphasis upon the impact of the modes of production upon human nature, tempered by the universalist notion of a species being, all in their different ways exhibit a tension between particularism and universalism. None wanted to deny that some ways of life are better than others, and all offered criteria by which we could make such judgements.

In contemporary 'domestic' and international politics the appeal to universal rights has achieved unprecedented prominence. Governments are frequently brought to task for their human rights abuses. The United Nations and a great many non-governmental organizations monitor human rights throughout the world, and cases are brought against governments in the various international courts by individuals who claim their human rights are being violated. The claim made by philosophers that human rights are moral rights in the sense that they are said to exist prior to and independently of institutional legal and non-legal rules, and are usually co...rasted with positive law, is not in their view compromised by their institutionalization in the constitutional law of many states, or to a lesser extent in international law. It is claimed that the fact that they have come to have legal sanction does not mean that they depend for their existence on that legal sanction.

Increasingly in an age of globalization, the internationalization of production, finance, and culture, along with the heightened recognition of a common ecological plight, there has been widespread concern about the excessively individualist and potentially divisive character of appeals to universal rights. Many feminists, for example, associate appeals to rights with male-dominated political discourse and culture, and would replace the ethic of rights with that of care. Similarly communitarian philosophers have sought firmly to embed moral practices within the traditions and cultures of specific societies. This assertion of particularism against universalism gives credence to the idea of special rights appropriate to certain persons and spheres of life within which they have social meaning and valid claims to be recognized and sustained, not only by the particular groups involved but also within the wider community constituted by this social pluralism.

Questions of universalism and particularism necessarily have an international dimension and have given rise in various guises to the question of international and cosmopolitan morality. There has been something of a renaissance in international relations political theory. The fundamental question that links political theory and international relations theory is simply 'who are you?' or self-referentially 'who am I?' In other words, it is the question of identity. This is not just a question of boundaries under a different guise at which authority and legitimacy begin and end. Identities are not necessarily territorially bound, although they may in some instances, such as national identity, seek to be so, and when they are they may become integral to the identity of competing national groups as, for example, in Palestine and the former Yugoslavia.[3]

The question of identity is not perennial and transhistorical. The question is relational, not relative, in that it is asked in a context of conventions which endows it with a point. If one gets the point of the question, then, in J. L. Austin's terms, one gains uptake. We live our lives, as Mervyn Frost suggests, in the context of social institutions which are constitutive of our identity. Who we are is bound up with what we do and who we do it with. 'Identity', it has recently been suggested, 'determines how you are treated, what is expected of you, what you expect of yourself, what jobs are available to you . . .'[4]

Religious identification may transcend sectarianism and become genuinely universalist. Here my identity as a Sunni or Shiite Muslim, with one of the two different views about the succession to the Prophet, for example, will unite me with other believers of Islam outside my polity, and may on many issues be my primary mode of attachment and motivation. The teaching of God as revealed to his messenger Muhammad and expressed in the Qur'ān, the reported sayings of the Prophet, or Sunna, and the will of God, which can only be enacted through the *umma*, the communal society which is not territorially based, takes priority over my identity as a c..izen of this or that particular polity. The power of religion in shaping domestic and international politics has tended to be ignored by political and international theorists in the secularized West, but this form of identification clearly has to be integrated into understanding developments not only in the Middle East, but also in Eastern Europe.[5] Islamic revivalism has had a profound effect on such Islamic countries as Nigeria, Pakistan, Afghanistan, and Iran, with significant consequences not only for domestic politics but also because of the destabilizing effects it has on regional and world politics.[6] In the Somali Democratic Republic, for example, it is impossible to understand the return of relative order in North Mogadishu, in comparison to South Mogadishu, without reference to Islam and the introduction of Muslim fundamentalist law which punishes theft with the severing of hands and feet. Similarly, any attempt to theorize or to explain post-1989 events in Eastern Europe would be greatly impoverished without taking into account the relative degrees of importance that religion, and religious identity, took on in the different countries.

Chris Brown argues that global and particularistic loyalties clash precisely because the question of identity is so crucial to the constitution of the person. The competing normative claims upon individuals arise out of different sources which may barely be compatible. Culturally transmitted identities in which strict hierarchies are observed and respected by the participants may well be distasteful to the cosmopolitan liberal, but for the person whose culture has so thoroughly permeated him or her the perception of being unjustly exploited or subordinated may not even arise.[7]

The question of attachments and self-identity is complicated by factors which go beyond self-perception. Self-identification is of little value without recognition, recognition by those with whom one wishes to be associated, and externally by those whose acknowledgement of one's identity is deemed important. Recognition comes in all sorts of ways, and the lack of it may have all sorts of consequences. In order to qualify as a state, for example, to take Northedge's criteria, it is not enough that its leaders deem it to be so because it has a physical identity and possesses internal sovereignty.[8] It must also have external sovereignty, that is, recognition by the community of states. It must be welcomed into the club of the United Nations. Such issues are related, of course, to the politics of inclusion and exclusion in which all societies engage, and which critics opposed to the notion of cosmopolitanism invoke as evidence of a deep-seated need for individuals to 'belong' in and be anchored to historically identifiable communities. Walzer contends that it is always a matter of priority that societies establish rules that define membership.[9] States themselves are the classic expression of these patterns with their systems of inclusion and exclusion relating to ideas on sovereignty, citizenship, and territoriality.[10] Both R. B. J. Walker and Andrew Linklater remark that the patterns of inclusion and exclusion that are currently taken for granted are historically contingent, a point of course that cuts little ice with those empirical theorists of international relations who are not interested in the origins or causes of current patterns but are more concerned with their consequences.[11]

There are other forms of identity, however, which call out for recognition and whose voices are not heard, or simply not understood, in either international relations theory or the practice of international relations itself. The self-perception of Africans during the nineteenth century as proud and dignified tribesmen was negated by Europeans in considering them 'inferior peoples' who from the point of view of the ruthless could be legitimately exploited, and who from the point of view of the more humane should be ruled over until such time as they became capable of self-government. Either way Africans were to have no say in the matter.

In the modern wave of feminism the identity of 'women', for example, was first forged in relation to men. The identities and differences were explored between the sexes, often attributing what were traditionally regarded as biological differences to cultural or sociological gender differences. The causes of women's oppression were sought in gender relations, and the exclusion of women from the public sphere by means of the public/private dichotomy. By excluding the personal from politics, women's voices had been silenced. Some feminists quickly realized that the focus upon comparison had led to a homogenization of the category of women. What feminist theory needed to establish was not only the respects in which women are different from and the same as men, but also the ways in which they are different from each other, and that these differences should be celebrated rather than ignored. While feminists were slow to demand a voice and a place in international relations issues the focus upon difference gave impetus to a much more internationally oriented outlook.

Feminist writers in international political theory have been particularly concerned to press home the point that the sub-discipline must take the politics of identity seriously.[12] International relations are portrayed as indifferent to gender. What goes on at the international level is deemed to have no bearing on the role of women or their status relative to men in society. The identities that are more often than not taken as significant in international relations, such as the state, the nation, ethnic groupings, the military, international organizations, international law, and multinational corporations, give rise to perceptions of the configuration of alignments and forces. Civic virtue and military preparedness have been inextricably related from ancient times to the present. For Machiavelli, the archetype for modern Realism, a well-organized and dedicated citizen militia, embodying the virtues of Republican Rome, is synonymous with civic responsibility and pride. The military, however, is predominantly a male preserve, and to focus upon it as a category excludes women not only from the discourse, but also from the idea of good citizenship itself. Such is the power of the discourse, however, that instead of challenging the centrality of the military to the idea of good citizenship some feminists have sought to dismantle the social and legal barriers in order to make the concept of the military gender-inclusive. In the process the critical cutting edge of feminism, instead of transforming, reinforces and legitimates the view that the military is central to the social order and that only by gaining access to it can women fulfil their civic aspirations.[13] Elshtain contends that entering into the discourse of war, which so thoroughly imbues all types of literature, reminds us of the pov..r of received narratives effectively to shape and constrain what we take reality to be. To challenge this received discourse is a recognition of how received doctrines 'may lull our critical faculties to sleep, blinding us to possibilities that lie within our reach'.[14] Women were, of course, afforded formal equality with men in article 1 of the Universal Declaration of Human Rights (1948), which was reaffirmed in subsequent conventions on economic and political rights, racial discrimination, and apartheid. Women's rights have been specifically affirmed in the UN Declaration on the Elimination of Discrimination against Women (1967) and conventions on the political rights of women (1952), marriage (1962), and the nationality of married women (1957). Such formal recognition of women as rights holders at the international level was given impetus by the establishment in 1947 of the Commission on the Status of Women, and by the United Nations' Decade for Women (1976–85) following International Women's Year (1975) with its conference in Mexico City, which internationalized women's issues and created a powerful transnational pressure group, with regular world meetings. Following the World Conference of 1980 in Copenhagen a new convention on the elimination of discrimination against women was issued by the UN (1981), and it has subsequently been adopted by over ninety countries.[15]

Recognition (or the declaration) of women's fundamental rights internationally at a formal level is something quite different from recognition in practice or as a key factor in explaining and theorizing international relations. Human rights conventions are difficult to ground and largely lack teeth, requiring the agreement of states for their enforcement.[16] Many states simply do not agree to accept those aspects of the conventions they do not like. The onward and upward view of progress in the universal acceptance of human rights has been severely shaken. The newly acquired freedoms consequent upon the collapse of communism have led to some of the grossest mass violations of human rights in parts of Eastern Europe. Furthermore, some governments have declared themselves opposed to the ideology of human rights. At the United Nations Conference in Vienna in 1993 delegates were presented with the Bangkok Declaration, subscribed to by the unlikely combination of China, Cuba, Indonesia, and Iran, which challenged the assumption that freedom and fundamental human rights are worthy ideals to pursue. It was contended that they are ideas which have never been universal and which have little legitimacy in the traditions of most countries. The emphasis, it was contended, should be much more upon the idea of economic development as intrinsic to a conception of freedom and basic rights.[17]

John Vincent argues that humanitarian intervention may be said to correlate with the right that everyone has not to be treated outrageously. This may be derived from a basic right to life, in terms of both security against violence and a right to subsistence. When these rights are violated, at most we have an obligation to render aid up to a point where something of equal moral importance is not sacrificed, and at least we have an obligation not to be accomplices in the deprivation of human rights by providing economic or military aid to the offending regime. The obligations fall upon us all as individuals, but this does not prevent us from discharging them most successfully through our governments. Failure of governments to uphold the basic rights of their citizens may be grounds for pronouncing them illegitimate. In the case of failure to sustain subsistence rights, the implications may be quite far-reaching because it may be that the international economic system, and not the domestic government, is at fault. This gives rise to the question of economic justice and the redistribution of resources.[18] John Rawls's *A Theory of Justice* distinguishes strongly between the internal and external relations of states. A social structure that gives rise to inequalities is unjust unless it can be rationally justified. In the international sphere, however, inequalities of wealth do not need such justifications. The reason for this is that Rawls believes society to be a co-operative venture productive of a social surplus for mutual advantage, which is in excess of the aggregate of individual goods. Principles of justice have to ensure the fair distribution of these goods. The so-called world society is a collection of coexistent states and not a co-operative venture in the same sense as a state-based society, and is therefore not in need of principles for the redistribution of wealth. The rules of justice needed for a world society and arrived at by means of a second contract to which states are parties, with the customary veil of ignorance, are rules of coexistence, such as respect for state autonomy and self-determination, sovereignty, and non-interference, and conventions of war. Charles Beitz, Brian Barry, and Janna Thompson, on the other hand, do not accept that internal justice is a special case. Global inequalities are also in need of justification. Beitz contends that in an interdependent world economic inequalities amount to a taxation on the poor countries in order for others to benefit from living in just societies.[19]

Rex Martin's theory of human rights diverges considerably from the Natural Rights theories associated with the tradition of Universal Moral Order. His theory recognizes the contingency of their recognition and promotion. In this respect he articulates a theory which is in keeping with the tradition of Historical Reason. While he relates human rights to civil rights, he would not want to deny valid moral claims which are independent of human rights and of any legal system to enforce them. Martin has put forward a vigorous challenge to the view that we possess human rights prior to and independently of legal systems. In other words, he is denying the principal contention of the Natural Rights-based theories of the tradition of Universal Moral Order. Martin argues that it is essential to take into account the practices of recognition, promotion, and maintenance of such rights. Human rights, he argues, depend upon being more than valid moral claims. Valid moral claims have two distinct elements: each is a justifiable claim *to* something, and in so far as it is attached to specifiable people it is a claim *against* someone. What in addition to being a morally valid claim do human rights require in order to qualify as rights? Martin argues that justificatory arguments for human rights must connect up with the actual moral beliefs and practices of a community. This is not to suggest that people only have duties they believe themselves to have, but that any duties assignable to them have in some way to fit into or be derivable from the critical moral principles attached to the overall system of moral beliefs in existence in a society. People cannot have duties of which they could not become reflectively aware. In other words, a human right cannot be a human right unless in addition to being a valid moral claim it is reflectively available, that is, unless it is also recognized as such. Such recognition without the will to promote and protect it is merely a nominal right and provides no normative direction for persons. A nominal right may have a paper existence, but it does not function as a right. A right is fully fledged not merely because it is a valid moral claim, but also because embodied in the very notion of right are the procedures and practices of recognition and maintenance. It must be stressed, however, that human rights do have the appropriate moral backing, but they have something else in addition: 'A human right is defective, not as a morally valid claim but as a right, in the absence of appropriate practices of recognition and maintenance. The absolute difference between morally valid claims and human rights, then, is that rights do, and claims do not, include such practices within their concept.'[20]

There are other factors which are not merely historically related to human rights but which are in fact revealed by philosophical analysis to be constitutive of them. The great human rights documents are addressed not primarily to individuals, although individuals are the beneficiaries, but principally to governments of states. In so far as this is the case any account of human rights cannot ignore governmental practices of recognition and maintenance in characterizing them. Even rights *to* freedom from torture and injury claimed *against* individuals are also at once addressed to governments which are expected to protect and maintain these rights. Human rights on Martin's view both are morally valid claims recognized by governments and are given the backing of law. In other words, they are equated with civil rights (legal rights), but it is not suggested that all civil rights are also human rights. Some civil rights may lack the necessary moral backing.

Human rights are universal in that they are claims to something, but are they universal in being claims against everyone? Martin thinks not. His contention is that to press a claim involves directing a request or demand at specific persons or agencies. Human rights talk assumes that individuals live in organized societies, and that the goods to which they refer as claims to something are conceived and enjoyed in such social contexts. Claims are not primarily addressed to individuals as such, that is, to all of humanity, but are typically made against representatives or agents of organized societies, and principally this means governments. Even the claimants live in some organized society and are for the most part making their claim against representatives or officials of that society to have their human rights protected and maintained. Martin concludes that 'These important points, though little noted, set a powerful constraint on the sense in which human rights can be regarded as universalism.'[21]

Such a view which claims philosophically to disclose what is historically embedded in the notion of a human right has, however, to face up to some difficulties. We are presented with the ideal characterization of an organized society capable of converting morally valid claims into human rights by recognizing and maintaining them with the backing of law. But it is precisely in circumstances where there is a systematic refusal to acknowledge valid moral claims, or a breakdown of the capacity to do so, that we are most likely to want to talk about violations of human rights. I.. cases where civil society has broken down into a form of barbarism, and respect for human life or bodily integrity is not equally afforded to all, we may in Martin's terms talk of the denial of valid moral claims, providing that the perpetrators could in principle become reflectively aware of their obligations, but we could not justifiably use the much stronger condemnatory language of human rights violations. It may well be the case that the only validity that human rights is capable of having is through recognition and maintenance, but it is an entirely different claim to suggest that this is part of what we mean by a human right. The appeal to human rights becomes most shrill when the will or capacity to sustain them does not exist, or has ceased to exist. When rape and genocide are systematically perpetrated in the context of a civil war, and where there are no agencies representative of the whole society willing to or capable of maintaining the rule of law and protecting people's rights, we would have to say that these people no longer have human rights, but it is precisely in such circumstances that they are most frequently invoked. Let me illustrate. In the Bosnian situation ethnicity has been the predominant category in terms of which to characterize the conflict, yet victims of the conflict may not always, or primarily, see their identities as Muslims, Serbs, or Croats above that of, say, their identity as women. As MacKinnon points out, women's human rights are more systematically violated in ways that men's rarely are. To see Serbian aggression as an ethnic conflict, or civil war, among equal aggressors masks the extent to which rape and misogyny are integral to the strategy of genocide in this conflict. Most human rights conventions empower states to act against states, not individuals to act on their own behalf or on behalf of others. Typically, states and not individuals are identified as the violators. MacKinnon argues that no state effectively protects women's human rights within their borders, and that none is prepared to set standards internationally for bringing to account the violators of women's human rights. Any account of human rights must be able to account for and accommodate human rights language in contexts such as these, because it is in these contexts that they are thought to be most in need of asserting.[22] This is a similar criticism to that which is directed at Gauthier for formulating a theory of social or distributive justice in which the sick, weak, infirm, and mentally defective do not have valid claims to the co-operative surplus which results from constrained maximization.

Richard Rorty's defence of human rights, or the human rights culture, is more radically historicist than that of Martin. Rorty is an American postmodernist who is an anti-foundationalist thinker. He explicitly denies the basis upon which the tradition of Universal Moral Order rests. He argues that there are no universal or fundamental moral principles upon which to ground modern ideas of morality or politics. He also denies that there is any universal human nature upon which we could ground the Realist view of international relations. Our ideas and beliefs about such matters are simply contingent and ungroundable. He describes himself as a bourgeois liberal ironist. A liberal is someone who believes that 'cruelty is the worst thing we can do'.[23] The ironist, being sufficiently historicist and nominalist, is aware of the contingency of his or her own fundamental beliefs. Liberal ironists would count among these ungroundable fundamental beliefs their desire that human suffering be reduced and that humiliation perpetrated by human beings upon one another cease. In other words, they do not ground their beliefs on such a foundation as a universal human nature. As Rorty says, 'There is no *neutral*, noncircular way to defend the liberal's claim that cruelty is the worst thing ... We cannot look back behind the processes of socialization which convinced us twentieth-century liberals of the validity of this claim and appeal to something which is more "real" or less ephemeral than the historical contingencies which brought those processes into existence.'[24]

In demonstrating the contingency of things and beliefs Rorty shows how the search for foundations is an impossible enterprise. In his book *Philosophy and the Mirror of Nature* he calls those who search for unifying universal theories systematic philosophers, and those who are critical of our current vocabularies and deny that philosophy is the search for truth he calls edifying philosophers. In *Contingency, Irony and Solidarity* Rorty argues that these are the sort of philosophers who attempt to dissolve rather than solve inherited problems. Truth is not a property of the world, but is instead a property of language, which is a human creation. Furthermore, truth is not a matter of correspondence to an independent reality but instead what comes to be believed as a result of 'free and open encounters'.[25] Rorty relies upon Wittgenstein and Donald Davidson to show that language itself has no foundations but is a product of time and chance. In other words, it is contingent.

Liberal societies, Rorty argues, are not held together by philosophical beliefs. They hold together because they have common vocabularies and common hopes. The vocabulary plays on the hopes by telling stories about desired futures to be generated by the sacrifices of the present.[26] In the ideal liberal society intellectuals would be ironists. The non-intellectuals would, however, accept their liberal vocabulary along with its stories and dreams, but nevertheless still be commonsensically nominalist and historicist. In other words, they would acknowledge their own contingency without having any serious doubts about the particular contingency they have happened to become. The fundamental premise of Rorty's theory is that belief without philosophical foundations is capable of guiding action. Furthermore, he contends that belief may still be worth dying for even when its adherents are aware that it is nothing more than the result of historical contingencies.[27] Rorty maintains that the existence of a human rights culture appears to owe nothing to increased moral knowledge, nor to any notion of an ahistorical human nature. The redundancy of such ideas, he suggests, arises because they fail the classic pragmatist tests. If, as Dewey argued, all enquiry is directed at practical problem-solving, or if we invoke Peirce's criterion that every belief is action-guiding, then foundationalist philosophy has not solved any of our moral problems, nor does it seem to have provided practical guides to action.[28]

Rorty's denial of anything like human essences, or human nature, or foundations of any kind makes it impossible to invoke any notion of transhistorical principles at times when human institutions and traditional notions of decency and behaviour are collapsing, as in the case of Auschwitz and more recently the conflict between Serbs and Muslims in Bosnia. At such times we want to appeal to some notion of human solidarity and declare that because these people, the Muslims and Jews, are like us it is inhuman to be committing such crimes against them. Rorty wants to argue in the final chapter of *Contingency, Irony and Solidarity* that the notion of we or us is crucial in understanding the idea of moral obligation. The ideas of a fellow comrade, a co-national, a fellow Catholic, all invoke strong senses of being one of us. Rorty says quite emphatically: 'I want to deny that "one of us human beings" (as opposed to animals, vegetables, and machines) can have the same sort of force as the previous examples. I claim that the force of "us" is, typically, contrastive in the sense that it contrasts with "they" which is also made up of human beings—the wrong sort of human beings.'[29] To say one rescued Jews from the horrors of Auschwitz because they were fellow human beings would be, Rorty contends, a poor explanation of a generous action. Those Danes and Italians who rescued Jews at the risk of their own lives would surely, if questioned, have said that they did so because they were their neighbours, or fellow Milanese, fellow Jutlanders, or members of the same profession, rather than fellow human beings.

Rorty's claim that few rescuers would have cited a common humanity as the motive for acting righteously is, of course, testable. There are in fact many accounts by rescuers of why they harboured or saved Jews. Many do appeal to a common humanity, and in research into the motivations of rescuers it has been suggested that predominantly some universal principle of humanity was being appealed to.[30] Many of the rescuers felt somewhat alienated from their own communities, and may because of this have sought a reference point outside. It may also be that they were moved by more immediate considerations and rationalized their actions in terms of universal principles.

In his Amnesty lecture Rorty argues that inhuman treatment or the refusal to treat people equally is justified by the perpetrators in treating the victims as non-human or pseudo-human. Firstly, the victim can be portrayed as an animal as opposed to a human. This is how the Nazis portrayed Jews. In fact they portrayed them as vermin. Secondly, humans can be portrayed as children as opposed to adults and therefore as not having a claim to equal treatment. A Black, for instance, may be referred to as 'boy'. A third form of exclusion is to use 'man' as the generic term for men and women. Rorty suggests that in Catherine MacKinnon's view, for most men, being a woman is not synonymous with being human.

Philosophers have tried to find some essential ingredient that defines human nature in order to avoid arbitrary exclusions, but, Rorty argues, 'We have come to see that the only lesson of either history or anthropology is our extraordinary malleability. We are coming to think of ourselves as the flexible, protean, self-shaping, animal rather than as the rational animal or the cruel animal.'[31] Our human rights culture is one such recent shape that human nature has taken. Here, as with the other arguments I have touched upon, it is clearly the case that the type of universalism posited by exponents of the tradition of a Universal Moral Order is being rejected without reverting to a wholehearted subjectivism. What is presented is a conception of the self and the rights associated with it as historically constituted.

National Identity

The fact that our selves are multifaceted and that a whole array of social institutions are constitutive of our identities means that the calls upon our loyalty and commitment, the factors that shape us and the demands we make upon others, come from a diversity of directions, often in the form of legal obligations or strictly defined organizational norms, but also often in the form of conventional or moral claims arising in the context of our participation in a practice. This is what Walzer calls the divided self, divisible into interests and roles, identities, and the subject and object of self-criticism.[32] We stand, as Dilthey suggested, at the centre of a system of interactions. The priorities of sets of claims over others have to be ranked, by ourselves or by others, informally or formally. Some have an informal ranking, in that the obligation one feels to a friend to spend one's leisure time with him or her in comparison with spending time with one's children may be lower or higher on the scale depending upon what sort of person one is. On the other hand obligations may be formal, or even legally defined. Responsibilities to care for one's children are much more strictly delimited than those we have for taking care of friends. These are our social and legal responsibilities. The relationships in which we stand to each other and the complex of expectations and responsibilities to which they give rise require to be maintained and sustained. The state has traditionally in the modern period been the sustainer of this constellation of values. The basic structural security to which all our social institutions look for support has to be sustained. The modern state is, of course, historically contingent, and much modern international relations theory is critical of its centrality and the privileged position it has, especially in Realist theories which still dominate the discipline. The fact remains, however, that as the sustainer of all our cultural, social, and political institutions and practices it is the predominant agent through which citizens are collective actors on the world scene. There have undoubtedly been great transformations in the agenda of international relations, issues of power and security, economic forces with the undoubted growing influence of non-governmental transnational organizations, and marked erosions of sovereignty in identifiable spheres of state activity, such as its freedom of action in managing a national economy in an economically interdependent world in which multinational corporations wield considerable influence especially in resource-rich but economically poor developing countries. The globalization of communications, the internationalization of culture, the growing prominence of the issue of human rights, and the capacity of what Rorty calls sad and sentimental stories[33] to extend our empathy to others and thus broaden the sentimental community in which we move have all served to bring into prominence the question of our relationship with and obligations to individuals as individuals, irrespective of nationality or citizenship.

Whatever the trend may be towards alternative ways of responding to the major crises of our age, nuclear proliferation, the extreme hunger and poverty of 20 per cent of the world's population, the imbalance in the ecosystem, and increasingly repressive regimes and the systematic violation of human rights,[34] we continue to look in times of crises to the acknowledged and legitimate authority of the state to act as a deliberative agent in setting goals and devising plans to attain them. But what is the source of identity that is able to act through the state?

National identity is a historically contingent fact of social life, and one can envisage other focuses of social cohesiveness such as religion, gender, colour, or class being just as strong or stronger on certain issues. One's identity as a Christian, a woman, black, or working class makes a strong claim to transcend nationality as the source of one's primary loyalty and identity. National identity has, however, predominated. Even Marx's and Engel's internationalism eventually had to accommodate the nation-state by suggesting that the revolution first entailed the working class having to come to terms with their own national bourgeoisie. If we take ethnicity as a factor in international relations, for example, the state is taken out of focus and relegated to the background, while ethnic unity and identity come into focus in the foreground. The Kurds, who are Sunni Muslims and who were nomadic pastoral people, inhabit an area which they call Kurdistan, comprising neighbouring territories in Iraq, Iran, and Turkey. Their identity is transposed over the nation-states they inhabit, but understanding their predicament, their persecution, and their urbanization necessarily entails coming to terms with national identity. The establishment of national boundaries after the First World War severely restricted Kurdish freedom of movement and their traditional seasonal migration, leading to the urbanization of many of their number. Their aspiration for self-determination, and its denial, cannot be divorced from the question of national identity. This is not to ignore the internal divisions among rival groups of Kurds such as the Kurdish Democratic Party (KDP), which has invoked the aid of the Iraqi state against the Patriotic Union of Kurdistan (PUK).

Much of the contemporary literature on national identity gives emphasis to the historically constituted self. The idea of changing individual identity, not a fixed and final nature, figures prominently. The nation is seen to be a legitimate source of moral obligation. National identity has to be responsive to change and renew itself with each successive generation. In this respect Renan was right to see it as a daily plebiscite, and some forms of national identity may be incapable of meeting the challenge. As Liah Greenfield suggests, a national identity is at base a matter of dignity, providing reasons to be proud.[35] How effectively it does this and what criteria it highlights as crucial to the identity are again historically and geographically contingent. It should be noted at this point that communitarianism, or constitutive theory, does not give a blanket endorsement to nations and nation-states.[36]

By whatever means national identity comes into existence, it is too large and abstract an entity to generate the sort of unconditional loyalty that at times of emergency it demand.. The idea of nationality has to be sustained by more concrete and immediate attachments. National consciousness, Janna Thompson argues, rests on the foundation of the overlapping social relations which sustain the groups and communities that individuals value.[37] What was referred to above as the individual standing at the centre of a system of interactions is the key to the way in which our particularistic community attachments, however numerous they may be, are interwoven in ways that attach us to broader and broader overlapping communities, which in some way the nation has come to represent. Conflicts of interest may frequently occur between the obligations of the various identities one shares, but the question of which are primary at any particular time depends not only upon the contingencies of the circumstances, but also upon the kind of person one happens to be. Principles are always mediated by persons, and when translated into the special circumstances of each, what one regards as a duty may for another person be outweighed by other obligations.

It is when the source of dignity and pride is threatened that national identity takes on the more pernicious aspects of nationalism. Fichte, for example, deplored the French influence upon German life and defined the spirit of the latter in opposition to the former. The identification of an oppressor, real or imagined, a scientific and, or, historical explanation of the cause and effects of that oppression, and finally by a prescription for emancipation and the retrieval of dignity are the elements which when taken to extremes have transformed national identity into one of the most pernicious ideological forces in modern times.[38] The unacceptable face of nationalism has tended to be that presented as its typical manifestation,[39] and Hobsbawm had some justification for suggesting that the age of nationalism, understood in such pejorative terms, was over,[40] only to be immediately proved wrong with a vengeance. The resurgence of nationalism in Eastern Europe, and especially its identification with ethnicity and ethnic cleansing, the modern euphemism for genocide, has demonstrated the continuing destructive force of harnessing the strong emotional ties of national identity to the ideals of political liberation.

Elshtain has argued that nationalism is intrinsically neither good nor bad. It is possible for it to be both.[41] It has recently been suggested that both political theory and international theory have become impoverished because of a failure adequately to theorize about nationalism.[42] In relation to matters of international justice, in particular, 'it is above all important to determine whether nationalist ideas have any validity from a moral point of view: whether it is true that people ought to identify with their nation and defend it, and if so, what this means as far as international relations are concerned'.[43] It is nevertheless the case that much normative political theory of international relations conceptualizes the last two hundred years in terms of the rights and obligations of the citizen and their relation to the rights and obligations of humanity, characterized in terms of men versus citizens, communitarianism versus cosmopolitanism, nationality versus universality, or cultural relativism versus human rights. The attempts to ground our rights and duties come from two categorically distinct standpoints. What is at issue between the contending contemporary approaches is what has always been at issue in the poli..cal theory of international relations, that is, the source of our moral claims and obligations.

On the one hand the community, often assumed to be synonymous with the self-determining nation, is identified as the context within which rules and conventions emerge; these give rise to our special moral rights and duties towards our fellow citizens and have priority over any we might have to humanity as a whole. Indeed, those duties towards humanity to which the community subscribes, by being party to conventions on human rights, are mediated by the political apparatus of the community or nation, namely the state. As Miller and Walzer remind us, we must not fall into the trap of using 'nation' as a synonym for 'state'. A nation is a community of people with an aspiration to be politically self-determining, and the state is the set of political institutions that they aspire to achieve.[44] This community-generated morality is maintained and sustained, both formally, by being codified in law, and informally, by being embedded in social practices. Vincent sees this as a form of cultural relativism, not invented by post-imperialist nationalist movements but certainly popularized by them.[45] Such views, broadly speaking, are related to the tradition of Historical Reason, but as we have seen there is nothing necessarily relativistic about the theories that it tolerates.

Alternatively, the source of our rights and duties is identified outside the national community, in a higher law, or as a dictate of reason. In order to avoid cultural imperialism, which is the imposition of a dominant state's standards upon less powerful states, or cultural relativism, which is the denial that there can be any transcultural standards for judging the moral basis of the actions of states, it is argued, it must be assumed that there is a community of humankind. This is what Michael Donelan calls the 'primordial community of mankind'.[46] What is being presupposed is that moral discourse cannot proceed without there being some basic shared values. The problem here, as Vincent suggests, is to reconcile the idea that there are human rights that everyone should enjoy by virtue of being human, and at the same time to acknowledge that their content and importance are subject to contention.[47] Natural Law theorists, of course, acknowledge this problem. They are aware that the basic abstract principles governing the primordial community, when translated into human positive laws governing specific communities, vary in their application and interpretation. They argue, however, that there are self-evident goods which all communities hold in common, and which are presupposed in our relations with each other. In John Finnis's view these goods are life, sociability, being practically reasonable, delight in art and literature (aesthetic experience), a desire for knowledge, and some form of religious experience. These goods are pursued in different ways.[48] The way that we seek knowledge, and indeed what is regarded as knowledge, have changed considerably over time, but the fact that people pursue knowledge by different processes of reasoning—even the sceptic is making a claim to knowledge in denying that there can be certainty in these matters—demonstrates a commitment to the value of knowledge.

The historicist, of course, would argue that when the pursuit of what is claimed to be the same value c . er space and time is contextualized, it strains credulity to think of it as in any fundamental sense the same value. And even if there is a coincidence of values at a very abstract level, in what way can this be said to constitute a moral community which has claims on us as individuals? A resemblance of attributes, whether moral or physical, may be sufficient for the purposes of classification, identifying us as human beings or certain types of human being, but something more is required to designate something a society or community—a collection of people with which we feel a certain solidarity. Rorty, for example, argues that our sense of solidarity, our sense of someone being one of us, with its associated beliefs, is historically specific and does not transcend time and institutions. Such beliefs, even when those who hold them are conscious of their contingency, are capable of regulating action and even of inspiring people to die for them. He denies that a sense of identity centred on humanity as the relevant focus can have the same power to move an individual as solidarity with co-religionists, co-nationals, revolutionary comrades, and so on. He argues that 'our sense of solidarity is strongest when those with whom solidarity is expressed are thought of as "one of us", where "us" means something smaller and more local than the human race. That is why "because she is a human being" is a weak, unconvincing explanation of a generous action.'[49] Michael Sandel expresses this difference well when he contends that communities are constitutive of the shared identities and self-understandings of those who participate in them. Our membership of a community shapes what we are and what we take to be morally significant, and what is significant finds expression in the institutional arrangements of that community. We are simply not autonomous individuals capable of constructing or choosing a morality for ourselves.[50]

What is presupposed in the general liberal account of the individual is that human nature is universal. Constitutive theory, on the other hand, thinks human nature circumstantial. Human nature is a product of the different social formations in which people find themselves. The role of politics in this formative process is much more pronounced in constitutive theory than in liberalism. A political structure is part of the social fabric that shapes individuals. Thus republicanism as a political structure provides the conditions constitutive of republicans. In order to avoid the charge of conservatism, constitutive theory needs to show how development and change can be incorporated into the theory without presupposing an ahistorical pre-social individual as the reference point.

Brown, like Frost, relies on Hegel for his account of the development of individuality. He quite explicitly rejects Hegelian metaphysics and presents us with what he calls a 'demythologised' account of his ideas.[51] Through the family the individual develops a personality and sense of belonging in the world based on unconditional love. Taking responsibility for one's projects in the context of civil society, and participating in the world of private property, the market, and the institutions which sustain them, constitute a further stage in the development of consciousness. The problem, however, is that

Civil society leaves individuals in a state of contestation, striving against one another and experiencing the law as an external force; this is not satisfactory. The fully rounded human individual should not have to experience constraint as external, or other individuals as opponents. Laws must be internalised and others experienced as fellow citizens. The role of the rational ethical, state—based on the rule of law and the separation of powers—is to perform this task.[52]

All three institutions have to be present in order to constitute the fully rational person. It is only in relatively recent times that such conditions have developed. Previous societies have to be seen as slowly developing these institutions and, in comparison with the present, inadequately constituting the freedom of their individuals.

Brown wants to suggest in relation to the question of restructuring in Europe that for Hegel it is the family, civil society, and the state that play their roles in constituting the individuality of the person, but the nation, although it may be useful in this process, has no necessary connection with it. In fact, to extend the point, Hegel is not nationalistic. He has wrongly been interpreted as advocating a German God state, whereas his concern is always with the Germanic peoples, northern Europeans, who together comprise the modern states system. The ethical state in Hegel's theory could not condone the oppression or persecution of one nation by another within its domain. As Brown suggests: 'It is the ethical quality of the state rather than its national characteristics which makes it worthy of support'.[53]

It is hardly ever noticed that Hegel's philosophy of the state is also in fact a philosophy of history in which one states-based system replaces another. Under these different states systems different types of freedom are achieved. In the Greek world we have a system of *poleis*. In the Roman world we have a system of states within an empire, and in the Germanic world we have a system of constitutional states. Brown gives emphasis to the fact that in the Greek *polis* an unreflective freedom is attained, but only for some, namely the citizens sustained by a system of slavery. The ideas relating to the different practices that prevail under different systems restrict the conception of freedom available to them. It is when the ideas can no longer be sustained and the practices become intolerable that the system comes under strain and forces change.

In Brown's view, Hegel's philosophy and constitutive theory in general have a number of advantages. First, it offers an alternative, but as rich an account of freedom as any liberal individualism can provide, with the advantage that the individual and the state are not viewed in opposition with each other. It gives reasons why a particular kind of state has ethical significance, but unlike some other forms of communitarianism, it does not base the ethical community or state on nationality. States may be based on nations, but they need not always be so. Second, the state is the central ethical institution, and its claims upon the individual are immense, yet they are constitutional and regulated by the rule of law. And, third, Hegel offers us a historicist account of rationality and freedom without lapsing into relativism. Historicism essentially relates ideas and practices to the prevailing circumstances, while relativism contends that we have no transhistorical or transcultural criteria by which to judge one against another. Hegel is able to do this, however, only because of his metaphysics, which Brown explicitly rejects. Hegel unfolds the particularist manifestations of freedom in the context of universal reason, or the *Geist* or Spirit unfolding itself in the world. This is why one stage of freedom can be for Hegel better than another. Fourth, Brown contends that constitutive theorists can share with many cosmopolitans a commitment to human rights. These human rights, they claim, have to be realized in a state. It needs to be emphasized that the source of these rights is seen to be the various communities which give them expression. In other words, the individual does not possess them independently of the community. Fifth, the theory emphasizes that human beings are individuals only as a result of being in relationships with others, and the type of person each becomes depends to a large extent on the type of society each lives in.

In applying these notions to the current situation in Europe, Brown argues that the ideological battle between East and West seems to have resulted in a victory for liberalism. The paradox is, however, that at a time when liberal individualism in the West is seen to point in the direction of cosmopolitanism and underplay the claims of the nation-state, in the East the claims of the nation are resurgent. With the collapse of communism and the reintroduction, and in some cases the introduction, of market forces and private property, social cohesiveness needs to find new expression, especially if these newly emergent nations are to face the restructuring problems of the present and build a foundation for the future. Such a project, Brown argues, requires a strong sense of solidarity, or to put it in Bosanquet's words, there must be a sense of a General Will as opposed to the liberal conception of being part of a joint enterprise for mutual benefit. In other words, there must be a strong sense of belonging to a community. Brown argues that only when looked at from the point of view of liberal cosmopolitanism do the claims of nationality and national self-determination appear to be backward and against the trend of integration. When looked at from the perspective of communitarian or constitutive theory, as he prefers to call it following Frost, the claims of the nation may be taken more seriously. The advantage of this theory, as opposed to liberal cosmopolitanism, is that it demonstrates the role of the community in constituting the individual. It denies the priority of the individual over the community.

This position of Brown's does not necessarily exclude the development of a world community of some sort, but the development of greater contact between individuals across state boundaries and the emergence of global interdependence does not in itself constitute a community. Such developments may be necessary but not sufficient conditions for the emergence of a world community. As Brown rightly contends, 'such contact need not generate the essentially moral consciousness of common identity that is required'.[54] There can be no doubt that through the work of numerous aid agencies and the increase in mass communication a concern for the human rights of those who live beyond our borders continues to grow. A widening sense of identity with others has accompanied greater world interdependence. But if there is to be a sense of world community, what sort of community is it? Cosmopolitans like Beitz and Singer often talk of a world community of humanity having the greater claim on us and having priority over the more particularistic obligations to one's family, friends, and co-nationals. But this need not be the only view. Degrees of obligation can be acknowledged which require not that we give priority to all fellow human beings, but that we should not be indifferent to them. Brown argues that even this degree of community may be difficult to achieve at the global level.

For example, he argues that global and particularistic loyalties clash precisely because the question of identity is so crucial to the constitution of the person. The competing normative claims upon the individuals arise out of different sources which may barely be compatible. Culturally transmitted identities in which strict hierarchies are observed and respected by the participants may well be distasteful to the cosmopolitan liberal, but for the person whose culture has so thoroughly permeated him or her the perception of being unjustly exploited or subordinated may not even arise.[55] The irony of the position is, of course, that often such a clash can be seen as between universalism and particularism only from one side. In a clash of ideas between Islam and liberal universalism, for example, each would see the other as particularist because both claim to be universal doctrines applicable for everyone.

The idea of national identity and of the nation as a source of moral obligation, and even as the foundation of obligation to one's co-nationals, is not incompatible with the idea of universal human rights and of duties to humanity. But the idea of compatibility can be expressed in different ways. The real issue revolves around the relative moral standing of the nation, state, and global society, and which set of obligations is decreed to have priority over the others.

First, we have the view that human rights percolate upwards from the community, to the self-determining nation, and through it find expression in the international community. This is the point that Walzer is making when he argues that maximal morality, the type embedded in our societies and social practices, precedes universal minimal morality, which is in fact abstracted from the former.[56] Eleanor Roosevelt was well aware of the role of the community in upholding and sustaining human rights when she asked: 'Where, after all, do universal human rights begin? In small places, close to home . . .'[57] A sense of national identity embraces universal concepts such as natural rights and the right to self-determination.[58] The United Nations Covenants on Civil and Political Rights and on Economic, Social, and Cultural Rights maintain self-determination as a fundamental right of all peoples. This was asserted as a human right in 1960 by a Declaration adopted by the General Assembly on the Granting of Independence to Colonial Countries and Peoples (Resolution 1514, XV). Effectively this is an assertion of the rights of individuals within national groups, and an acknowledgement that national self-determination is the condition for enjoying other human rights. Freedom of the nation precedes freedom of the individual.

Bernard Bosanquet argued nearly eighty years ago that patriotism was perfectly compatible with humanitarianism, and indeed the source and sustainer of all that has been elevated to the status of universal principles. In this he was following T. H. Green's example in believing that human progress has consisted in a consciousness of a good which the person holds in common with others.[59] It is the idea that my well-being is not transitory. It is held in common with a group of people whose well-being is taken to be the same as my own, and in which I am interested by the very fact that I am interested in myself. In other words, my well-being and that of the group are almost inextricable. Any duties that I have to humanity arise because of a gradual extension or widening conception of those people I regard as included in the common good. It is the recognition of more and more people as our neighbours and their inclusion in the moral community that gives rise to our obligations towards them. Green argues that it is who we are prepared to regard as our neighbour, and not the 'sense of duty to a neighbour' that has changed.[60]

Where the state is seen as the basic unit in international relations, this does not preclude the idea of an international morality. Such views are expressed in terms of an international society of states which in their relations with each other have both moral rights and responsibilities. Sovereign states are the subjects of international law, and individuals are its objects. To uphold a principle of intervention would open the way for interference by foreign states in the domestic affairs of others on the most tenuous of moral pretexts. One may call this the legal sceptical consequentialist or prudential justification of an international system based on states. Alternatively, the acknowledgement of sovereignty may entail mutual respect for each other's natural rights as 'moral individuals', and a subscription to the principle of non-intervention is an expression of respect for these rights. The ground of the moral obligation is typically Natural Law in such classic thinkers as Pufendorf, Wolff, and Vattel. But one may take the system of states itself, and not the universal moral community of humanity, as the society of shared values from which moral argument can proceed.

Extending the Moral Community: Justice beyond Borders

I want in this section to show briefly that, whether from a so-called cosmopolitan or communitarian starting-point, the same substantive end is desired by many political theorists of international relations, an extension of the moral community which posits a certain degree of universalism, while at the same time seeking to preserve difference and respect for diverse identities. It is the means or mechanism by which the extension takes place that remains at issue: whether, for example, it is to take place by means of Linklater's critical theory perspective on overcoming estrangement, Walzer's attempt to show how thin universalism develops out of thick particularism, Mervyn Frost's constitutive theory of shared norms, Janna Thompson's overlapping communities, Rorty's extension of sentimental empathy, or O'Neill's constructivist universalism uniting justice with virtue. It is, then, a project which brings up to date the Idealist aspiration of extending the moral community to become more and more inclusive of people we are willing to acknowledge as our neighbours. The Idealist aspiration, however, had its dangers. The Idealists tended to be what Walzer calls covering-law universalists. Taking the ideas of freedom and individual choice as central to human development, from the vantage point of the present, and viewing any impediments to self-realization as regressive historical tendencies, they were able, despite being communitarians, to eschew relativism. But in doing so they were affirming a way of life as right and desirable for world moral progress. Many of the British Idealists justified imperialism on the grounds that the more civilized nations had a duty to raise the lower nations to the level of being capable of self-government.

Contemporary theorists who acknowledge that particularistic communities and the nation (but not necessarily the state) have to be accommodated in any theory of cosmopolitanism seek to avoid the implications of the Idealist path. Linklater suggests that what is needed is a balance between the need to identify transnational values and respect for cultural differences.[61] The task of a critical theory of international relations, he tells us, is to go beyond Marxism and develop a more adequate theory in which to anchor the state than the Marxist tradition

has provided. Following from this, critical theory 'must regard the practical project of extending community beyond the nation-state as its most important problem—and not just as a backdrop to the allegedly more basic struggle between
antagonistic social classes'.[62]

Linklater offers us a philosophical history that has at its core the idea of the
development of human freedom. It is an ideal development in which the individual's feelings of estrangement and powerlessness are overcome in more and more
adequate social and international arrangements. This philosophical history,
inspired by Kant, Hegel, Marx, and Collingwood, comprises a scale of forms the
essence of which is the Kantian idea of the contribution made by various human
associations to the achievement of world citizenship. Human freedom progresses
by first overcoming the estrangement felt by individuals who as members of tribes
have rights but have none in their relations with other tribes. Individuals are
wholly immersed in the particularism of their own tribe, and are dominated by
nature and the fear of ostracism, that is, being cut off from the only source of their
identity; they have no sense of making their own history or of having obligations
to others outside their community. Awareness of their ability to create history and
to enter into relations other than those of antagonism with outside communities
is a precondition of emancipation from this condition. The establishment of
political society is a move beyond tribalism to a common acceptance of a legal
system in which all citizens are equal and the possessors of rights. Law now takes
priority over custom in the integration of members of different cultural communities into one political unit. The estrangement between states is overcome in the
creation of a universalistic political community in which individuals hold rights
as humans. The process is one which includes the recognition of the equality of
other states by states, the development of rules which regulate their conduct in
their mutual relations, and finally the extension of these rules to the states system.
This presumes the evolution of a common rational nature and the cultivation of
an obligation which extends beyond the bounds of the obligations of citizenship
to a more advanced ..10ral consciousness which acknowledges obligations to
humanity as a whole. The result is the transformation of state sovereignty into a
global political order, 'in which all men have inalienable rights, including the
right of access to material resources subject to their control; a type of international community in which they have rights simply as human beings and solely
for the purpose of promoting their individual development'.[63] The current condition of international relations as defined by Realists is in Linklater's view at a
point where states are inadequately conscious of their ability to overcome the
structural systemic forces in the international system which they deem to be out
of their control. The task of critical theory is to provide an account of ways of acting in the international environment which would enable people to circumvent
international systemic constraints and take control of their history.[64]

Linklater's philosophical history entails the acknowledgement that social and
inter-societal relations are historical creations which reveal man's capacity to create forms of life capable of breaking down inter-societal estrangements, which are
barriers to personal development. The account he gives does not depend upon

historical verification, because it is an ideal characterization of the development of human freedom. The ideality of it does, however, depend upon the acceptance of the initial premises. As with Marx, there is the assumption that there is a human essence, or species being, from which individuals are alienated in the smaller restrictive associations in which they are trapped. The human formations identified as tribes and states do constitute types of estrangement which lead to a sense of powerlessness, and the larger associations, including the universal community, contribute to greater individual freedom. Progress is defined as growth in the recognition of a private sphere in which the autonomy of the individual becomes manifest in personal relations not only within society but also externally without hindrance. It is an individualistic conception of human freedom as one which entails the growing realization that the constraints upon the individual's actions are the product of human will and can be modified. It assumes that historical development, albeit ideal, converges on a common conception of rationality and a heightened moral consciousness. Implicit in the whole account is the idea that forms of attachment and obligation which arise from particularistic associations, such as the family, tribe, or nation, are primitive, imperfect, and even irrational in comparison with the ideal end of a global community in which obligations are owed to each other as individuals and not as members of lesser associations. Progress is defined by Linklater as the process of ascending to the level of ethical universalism. It is by no means clear, however, to what extent cultural diversity would be valued at this level, at which a Western liberal conception of freedom predominates. It posits an emotional and ethical attachment to the human community as such, giving little consideration to the extent to which identity is constituted in the process of recognition by and participation in a variety of particularistic communities which often prescribe obligations for us, not at the expense of others but in establishing priorities. Brian Barry's version of universal justice as impartiality is constructed with this very problem in mind. He acknowledges in opposition to Godwin that we must be able to distinguish the degree of our obligations to family, friends, and colleagues from those to humanity as a whole and recognize that the agents for discharging certain of our obligations may have to be the institutions of the state.[65] Linklater has himself more recently recognized the untenability of dismissing these attachments and acknowledged the universal prevalence of the politics of inclusion and exclusion.

Walzer's path to justice in the international sphere has given rise to some confusion. In his *Spheres of Justice* Walzer is radically pluralist, denying the existence of any universal laws of justice. He refuses to ground our ordinary notions of justice in such fundamental principles as equal treatment, desert, or inalienable rights. We should, he contends, see justice as the product of particular political communities at identifiable times, and our accounts of justice should be constructed within the terms of reference dictated by these communities. Within any society, particularly liberal societies, there will be a variety of social goods whose distribution is governed by different criteria in their respective spheres of activity.[66]

Elsewhere Walzer has suggested that there is a minimal code of universal morality constituting cross-cultural requirements of justice, such as the expectation not to be deceived, treated with gross cruelty, or murdered.[67] Walzer in fact posits the idea of an international society which he grounds not on natural or a hypothetical contract in a Rawlsian original position, but on ideals and principles that have become commonly accepted by leaders of states and their citizens. This is because he wants to endorse difference while subscribing to a 'thin' universalism. As I suggested earlier, the universalism in Walzer is not prior to but instead a distillation of the 'thick' morality associated with communities. This is not what he calls covering-law universalism, which gives priority to a way of life as uniquely right, and which can be used as the basis for imperialist arguments. Instead, his universalism is reiterative, acknowledging that subject to minimal universal constraints there are many different and valuable ways of life that have equal rights to flourish in their respective locations and deserve equal respect to our own.[68]

Mervyn Frost is committed to the state as the basic unit in international relations. These units together constitute a society of states. He takes the international system as given, and tries to identify the settled norms associated with it and largely accepted by its members. He then seeks to establish a background theory which can be used to justify the settled norms and give some guidance in the difficult ethical cases in international relations. Frost maintains that the absence of the kind of foundations for ethical theory of which philosophers once dreamed does not mean that moral argument cannot take place and that moral conclusions cannot be reached by reasoning from the premises that we hold in common. Like the Natural Law theorists he believes that a community of shared values must be presupposed in order for moral argument to take place. He differs, however, in believing that far from the community of values being independent of the modernizing states system, it is this system itself which provides 'the idiom within which normative argument takes place'.[69] Whatever proposals are made for a modification of the international system will have to be made in the modern idiom of the state, the discourse that already provides the vocabulary for discussion. Among the settled norms that he identifies is the belief that the states system in which each state is sovereign is a good worth preserving. From this certain other norms follow: that it is bad for states to extend their sovereignty by the subjugation of other states, and that the preservation of the system by means of a balance of power is a good. Patriotism for one's country is deemed a good, and it is a settled norm that states first and foremost protect the interests of their citizens. Both self-determination and non-intervention are deemed to be goods. There are also goods relating to international law, and to peace, in so far as war needs special justification. Norms are accepted regarding the justifications for and conduct of war, economic sanctions, collective security, and institutional diplomacy. Modernization within states and economic co-operation between states are settled norms. Furthermore, it is a norm that democratic institutions and respect for human rights are good things.[70] Frost wants to provide a background theory justifying the maintenance of the sovereign state system which is compatible with respect for individual rights. The relationship in which individual rights and institutions stand is one of mutual inclusion: neither is prior to and each is dependent upon the other. What needs to be explained is not why putative contractees in a state of nature accept constraints on their actions in return for the protection of their rights, but instead how the claim to have a right necessarily entails such constraints within the context of state-related and rights-related norms. As individuals we are constituted by the relations in which we stand to others. We have value and worth as individuals by being recognized as members of the communities in which we participate, the family, occupation, civic society, legal framework, and ultimately the state. The constituted self is composed of multiple forms of recognition, and what is not provided in one institution may be remedied in another. Hegel, for example, shows how individuality is achieved by the different forms of recognition that are afforded in the family, civil society, and the state, and how what is deficient in the one is remedied but not replaced by another. In his explicit subscription to Hegel's theory, Frost argues that the state should not be seen, as contract theorists see it, as a voluntary association for protecting property and individuals' rights, but instead as the whole which grounds their individuality: not as something that is experienced as alien to them, but as something whose laws are seen as the reflection and manifestation of their own wills. It is in the consciousness that my interests are contained and preserved in the unity of the state that I attain full individuality and freedom. Within the state individuals are constituted as free, but that freedom as a citizen only fully flourishes when the state is recognized as autonomous by other states. The international system of states provides an additional constitutive level of recognition.[71] In summary, the contradiction between sovereignty and individual rights that was such a prominent feature of contract theory no longer arises. In contract theory, individuality, the condition for exercising rights, pre-exists the state, and protecting those rights often comes into conflict with state sovereignty. On Frost's theory, rights arise as individuality is constituted, not pre-socially, but through the family, civil society, and the state. Individuals' rights and state sovereignty are complementary rather ...an contradictory. In Frost's theory, states themselves constitute a society in which individual freedom achieves ultimate realization. States that are not recognized as states by other states, and which perhaps have the status of colonies, are not free and self-determining, and therefore their people are not fully free.

From the point of view of international justice Janna Thompson sees her idea of overlapping consensus among overlapping or interlocking communities, the consciousness of which is the basis of the ethical life of the nation, extending beyond state boundaries. She shares with the theorists of cosmopolitan democracy the idea that there is nothing inviolable about nation-states.[72] States themselves often comprise more than one nation, and nations could in principle form the basis of cosmopolitan schemes. Indeed, many interlocking and overlapping communities, such as religions, social movements, learned societies, and so on, are already transnational. The conditions of justice in an ever-increasing association of interlocking communities will be freedom of association and the openness of communities.[73]

This differs from the Natural Law foundation to the community of humankind in positing a historical identity to the moral obligations incurred, first to the family, then in turn to the tribe, the nation, the state, and finally to humanity. The broadening of the community within which the common good prevails brings with it an extension of the obligations owed to a larger number of people and eventually to humanity as a whole. Curiously, this is a position that Rorty advocates from his postmodern bourgeois liberal point of view. He urges that we should extend our sense of 'we' to those whom we have previously regarded as 'they': 'The right way to take the slogan "We have obligations to human beings simply as such" is as a means of reminding ourselves to keep trying to expand our sense of "us" as far as we can.'[74] What Rorty wants to argue is that 'nothing relevant to moral choice separates human beings from animals except historically contingent facts of the world, cultural facts'.[75] These are the realizations that we shape our own future, and that we can transform ourselves into whatever we are courageous enough to imagine. This substitutes for Kant's question 'what is man?' the quite different question of what sort of world can we make in the future. In other words, we are dispensing with the search for foundations in ethics and epistemology.

In rejecting the search for foundations we can move away from an emphasis upon rational argument and acknowledge that what makes us different from the animals is not the fact that they feel and we know, but instead the fact that we feel for each other to a much greater extent than they do. It is the education and manipulation of sentiments rather than rational argument that will overcome the tendency for people to regard other people as less than human. The aim of focusing on sentiment in this way is to extend our concept of those whom we are prepared to regard as one of us. Rational argument did not persuade the Serbs that the Muslims deserve equal respect as humans, nor many men that intelligent women do so, nor the Nazis that intelligent Jews deserve equal status as humans. Rorty favourably cites Annette Baier, who contends that Hume's notion of corrected sympathy is preferable to Kant's idea of a law discerning reason. In this respect trust replaces obligation as the fundamental moral notion. The extension of the moral or human rights community then becomes a question not of a progressive widening of the moral law, but instead a progress in sentiments. The question then becomes not that of the rational egotist, who asks 'Why should I be moral?' but instead 'Why should I care about a stranger, a person who is no kin to me, a person whose habits I find disgusting?' The traditional answer is that the only morally relevant factor is recognition of each other as members of humanity. This, however, begs the question of whether such species membership constitutes a strong enough tie to generate trust, the sort of trust that is associated with more concrete relationships like family and kinship. Rorty argues that the better answer is one that relies on 'sad and sentimental stories'. He states quite clearly in *Contingency, Irony and Solidarity* 'that detailed descriptions of particular varieties of pain and humiliation (in e.g. novels or ethnographies), rather than philosophical or religious treatises, were the modern intellectual's principal contributions to moral progress'.[76] Feelings of solidarity with others arise, and in this context similarities and dissimilarities strike us as important at any historical time. Which are important is a matter of contingency. He claims that his position is not incompatible with extending as far as possible the terms of reference of 'we' to those whom we have historically regarded as 'they'.

Onora O'Neill's constructivism in ethics, that is, the determination to reason from available starting-points and methods in order to 'reach *attainable* and *sustainable* conclusions for relevant audiences',[77] leads her to reject arbitrary particularist accounts of justice and virtue. Even accounts of ethical action based upon the idea of appropriate recognition, in her view, do not resolve the problem of identifying which characteristics of the person have to be appropriately recognized and why. They address at once the scope and content of ethics in attempting to give an account of who ought to be recognized, and what such recognition would entail.[78] There is still a need to back up the account with a metaphysics of the person, or some recourse to a perfectionist idea of the good which particularist accounts tend to avoid.

O'Neill has argued that modern writers on ethics have tended to sever the traditional connection between justice and virtue. She associates cosmopolitans, or universalists, with arguing the case for justice and communitarians with propounding a constitutive and embedded view of the virtues. What is crucial for her is the distinction between perfect and imperfect obligations. Her use of these terms differs from that of Pufendorf, who thought that perfect obligations were imperfect obligations with the force of law added. O'Neill's distinction rests upon the idea that perfect obligations are those which have determinate correlative rights and rights-holders, whereas imperfect obligations differ in structure in that they have no correlative rights attached to them. In her view this makes them no less obligatory. She acknowledges that it is necessary to have institutions which establish rights and responsibilities in order to protect the vulnerable from systematic and gratuitous injury. To show that social virtues, such as charitableness, compassion, pity, and generosity of spirit, cannot in themselves adequately protect the vulnerable and cannot therefore take the place of social justice does not make them redundant. There may still be a whole range of required and necessary action that is not itself a matter of justice or claimable as a right.[79]

Universal imperfect obligations are owed by all, but not to all. They do not have correlative rights and therefore cannot be claimed against specific persons. They typically find embodiment not in relationships but in character. They serve in many different situations and are therefore portable in nature. Generosity and charitableness of character are virtues that can be expressed in numerous situations. This need not mean that they are psychologically based. The virtues that are deemed important may be fostered by institutions and traditions. In this way the individual and institutional embodiments of virtue become mutually supportive. Special imperfect obligations are those that the historicist or communitarian tends to focus upon as embedded in traditions and institutions.[80]

This is not to suggest that virtues are inextricably tied to contexts. Indeed, possession of the virtues of character may often enable one to transcend the constraints of a context and provide a degree of independence which insures against the vicissitudes of the moment. In any situation rights and virtues are not mutually exclusive. Virtues often accompany the discharge of perfect obligations.

O'Neill argues that an agent must adhere to some inclusive principles of action in order to give unity and coherence to the diversity of ethical spheres in which he or she operates. These principles will inevitably be abstract, too abstract in fact to include the 'thick' ethical concepts that have currency within the more narrowly restricted areas of ethical life. In judging what to do, or what is appropriate, in any situation, agents have to supplement their inclusive abstract principles with the more descriptive and less abstract specific thick principles forged for more restricted areas of ethical activity. These thicker principles, specifying for example legal requirements or the terms of specific relationships and the rights arising out of them, 'cannot be fixed without relying on a framework of more inclusive and indeterminate principles'.[81]

Any substantive account of justice, then, must as a preliminary establish some abstract, as opposed to idealized, inclusive principles of justice. Here O'Neill is alluding to Walzer's idea of different spheres of justice within which different goods are valued and different criteria of distribution employed. Different societies will very likely establish their own sets of priorities for goods and attribute to them different social meanings. O'Neill's point is that without certain inclusive abstract principles of both justice and virtue, such spheres remain discrete and disjunctive. Walzer's thin universalism, which posits highly abstract principles of justice generated by the different spheres, is meant in some way to accommodate such a criticism. Where O'Neill and Walzer differ, however, is in their respective starting-points. For O'Neill, abstract inclusive universal principles can be 'constructed' with reference to establishing certain criteria of action which cannot be universalized. Put succinctly, justice from this Kantian perspective is about refusing to base actions, ways of life, or institutions on principles that are not universally acceptable. It is not a question of requiring uniform action.[82] The principles are not directly translatable into prescriptive action. In this respect they are under-determined and allow for considerable variety in the concrete details of just action consistent with them.

If a principle is to be universalizable it must satisfy a dual condition. A person must be able to accept it as a principle for all within a certain ethical sphere. If a principle disables some from adopting it, then it cannot be universalizable. Such principles can be acted upon only on condition that at least some others do not or cannot adopt them. To subscribe to an inclusive principle of injury, for example, cannot be universalizable, because the injuring of some will disable them from injuring others. It is an exclusive and not an universalizable principle. On this account, the core of injustice would be the subscription to principles that if enacted would lead to foreseeable injury to some people. An inclusive principle rejecting injury is not the same as a commitment to non-injury. The latter would require, for example, pacifism and non-retaliation. It would also require acquiescing to injuries which rational persuasion failed to avert. A rejection of injury as an inclusive principle is less demanding. It requires only that we do not place the principle of injury at the core of our life, institutions, or practices.[83] What this means is not that all injury can be avoided, but that avoidable *systematic* and *gratuitous* injury should be rejected. Furthermore, indirect injuries may be perpetrated by damage to the social environment where, for example, an erosion of trust destroys social relationships. A commitment to the principle of deception, like injury, cannot be universalized, because fraud, cheating, lying, and deception require a social background which rejects these modes of acting. A commitment to the destruction of the natural and built environment is similarly a form of committing injury because such systematic and gratuitous destruction generates vulnerabilities and precipitates direct injury to individuals. In addition, it is an inclusive principle that cannot be universalized as a way of life, because the irreversible destruction of resources relies upon the fact that at least some are committed to preserving parts of the natural world which will enable those committed to destruction to continue their activities. From these basic principles of the rejection of injury and deception, the thick fundamental requirements of justice in specific situations are not capable of being deduced. The basic principles are a manifold in relation to which actions, institutions, and practices are developed in order to circumvent avoidable gratuitous and systematic injury.

The complexities of embedding the principles of the rejection of injury, deception, and destruction of the environment are applicable to both international and domestic issues of justice. Avoidable injurious activities and practices perpetrated by states or institutions in the international system must be rejected, but the form that institutional eradication of such injustices is to take is by no means self-evident. The cosmopolitan, on the other hand, who takes the individual as the subject of a universal moral law, what Beitz calls moral or ethical cosmopolitanism, is not thereby committed to an institutional cosmopolitanism.[84] The key idea here, as Pogge suggests, 'is that every human being has a global stature as an ultimate unit of moral concern'.[85] The idea of a global moral community of humanity does not logically preclude the division of the world into smaller administratively manageable units in whatever political form may be deemed most appropriate: states, federations, empires. Typically in the modern era, that unit has been the sovereign state, often coinciding with a desire on the part of a community for national self-determination. The point that the Natural Law theorist would want to make is that the division is not absolute and that states are merely more convenient administrative apparatuses to sustain the common good of the communities they serve. Together these states in co-operation with each other serve the common good of humanity. In such a view there is an overlaying of responsibilities, laws, rights, and obligations, and at some point a conflict of duties may arise between one's obligations as a citizen and as a person. Kant's cosmopolitanism, for instance, is fully cognizant of the existence of a primordial community of humankind and of the impracticality of a world state. The best that can be hoped for is a peaceful federation of states. The world order rests on three types of right: constitutional right, that is, ideally a republican form of government in each state; international right, the rights of states; and cosmopolitan right, the rights of individuals in relation to each other. His criterion of morality, however, is universal. The modern Kantian ethical cosmopolitan Onora O'Neill fully acknowledges that nationality and other forms of community have an importance, and that securing a national state may be instrumental in achieving justice for some, as for example looks to be the case with the Kurds. On the other hand the achievement of a national state may be just as likely to be the instrument of injustice to others, as the nationality problem in the former Soviet Union testifies.[86]

Institutional design and reform at both the domestic and international levels of ethical concern have to be judged on the basis of their potential to lessen avoidable direct and indirect injury to the person, social fabric, and built and natural environments by redistributing goods to the vulnerable in order to enhance their capabilities, irrespective of whether they fall within the same borders. What is particularly interesting about O'Neill's argument is that she readily acknowledges that the development of institutions to eliminate as far as possible avoidable systematic and gratuitous injury can very rarely come about *de novo*. Conceptions of reform and the will to make changes more often than not build upon current institutions and traditions. It is a matter of modifying what is to hand, redesigning parts rather than the whole, and re-establishing relations that have become disengaged. The purpose is to shape institutions in such a way that they better embody abstract principles of justice.[87]

Justice is, as we saw, a matter of perfect obligation. Its requirements fall upon everyone and are matched by correlative rights. Virtues, on the other hand, are a matter of imperfect obligation. Their requirements fall upon everyone but specify no one as their recipients. Can principles of virtue, like principles of justice, also be inclusive, or are they always embedded in situations? As with justice, there must be certain principles of virtue which connect, or act as a manifold for, the different spheres of activity in which an agent moves in the world: 'The spheres of action must be linked not only by public institutions that co-ordinate or subordinate them, but by continuities of character which support continuities of activity, including feeling, relationships and community.'[88] Without some consistency of character in differe..t situations, life would be erratic and unpredictable, and the basis for trust and sustainable relationships would be eroded. O'Neill's point is that virtues are inextricably related to justice and must be embodied not only in individuals but also in institutions, traditions, and the common culture of social groups. Institutions established on principles of justice cannot be sustained for long if they operate in a culture of corruption. The virtues of justice such as fairness, reciprocal respect, truthfulness, probity, and fidelity are essential to the maintenance of just institutions.

In addition, there are what O'Neill call the social virtues, which supplement and support the principles and practice of justice. These virtues are fundamentally related to the inclusive universal principle that we must reject '*directly expressed indifference* to others'. She maintains that it is a false idealization of human capacities to assume that provided that people are treated justly, that is to say that no systematic or gratuitous injury is perpetrated against them, they will exhibit a high degree of rationality, self-sufficiency, and autonomy in sustaining their capabilities and capacities for action. 'On the contrary', O'Neill maintains, 'capacities and capabilities for action are always fragile; even the seemingly autonomous may be so only because they are secure in others' care and concern. Hence systematic indifference to others cannot be a principle for all, and rejection of systematic indifference is correspondingly required of all.'[89]

In this overview of the modern political theory of international relations it will have been apparent that there is a growing tendency to emphasize the desirability of extending the moral community to include all of humanity, without at the same time advocating institutional cosmopolitanism. The arguments for the extension of this community, while positing varying degrees of a 'thin' universalism, whatever its source, do not want to deny the value and importance of the historicity of the thick morality of particularistic societies. Indeed, there is widespread acknowledgement that this thick morality is to differing degrees, at least partially, constitutive of the individual. Even liberal individualism and Marxian cosmopolitanism make concessions to the historically constituted self. What I am suggesting, then, is that the ideas associated with the tradition of Historical Reason have thoroughly permeated all strands of the political theory of international relations. This is not to deny that these ideas coexist and are still in competition with ideas associated with the traditions of Empirical Realism and Universal Moral Order.

Notes

1. See Richard Devetak, 'Postmodernism', in Scott Burchill and Andrew Linklater with Richard Devetak, Matthew Paterson, and Jacqui True, *Theories of International Relations* (London, Macmillan, 1996).
2. Mervyn Frost, *Ethics in International Relations: A Constitutive Theory* (Cambridge, Cambridge University Press, 1996), 68.
3. Onora O'Neill, 'Justice and Boundaries', in Chris Brown (ed.), *Political Restructuring in Europe: Ethical Perspectives* (London, Routledge, 1994), 77.
4. Marysia Zalewski and Cynthia Enloe, 'Questions of Identity in International Relations', in Ken Booth and Steve Smith (eds.), *International Relations Theory Today* (Cambridge, Polity, 1995), 282.
5. Jean Bethke Elshtain makes a similar point in 'International Politics and Political Theory', in Ken Booth and Steve Smith (eds.), *International Relations Theory Today* (Cambridge, Polity, 1995), 269.
6. Barbara Allen Robeson, 'The Islamic Belief System', in Richard Little and Steve Smith (eds.), *Belief Systems and International Relations* (Oxford, Blackwell, 1988), 105. James Piscatori suggests that while Islam is a more powerful and enduring force than Arabism in the contemporary world, 'the "Islamic challenge" to world order has not been as great as has been feared' ('Islam and World Politics', in *Dilemmas of World Politics: International Issues in a Changing World* (Oxford, Oxford University Press, 1992), 331).
7. Chris Brown, 'International Political Theory and the Idea of World Community', in Booth and Smith (eds.), *International Relations Theory Today*, 97.

8. F. S. Northedge, *The International Political System* (London, Faber and Faber, 1976), 141–5.

9. M. Walzer, *Spheres of Justice: A Defence of Pluralism and Equality* (Oxford, Basil Blackwell, 1985).

10. Andrew Linklater, 'The Question of the Next Stage in International Relations Theory: A Critical-Theoretical Point of View', *Millennium*, 21 (1992), 82; R. B. J. Walker, *Inside/Outside: International Relations as Political Theory* (Cambridge, Cambridge University Press, 1993), 179.

11. James Mayall, 'Nationalism in the Study of International Relations', in A. J. R. Groom and Margot Light (eds.), *Contemporary International Relations: A Guide to Theory* (London, Pinter, 1994), 183.

12. See e.g. V. Moghadam, *Identity Politics: Cultural Reassertion and Feminism in International Perspectives* (Boulder, Colo., Westview, 1993).

13. Cynthia Enloe, *Does Khaki Become You? The Militarisation of Women's Lives* (London, Pluto, 1983), 16–17.

14. Jean Bethke Elshtain, 'Reflections on War and Political Discourse: Realism, Just War, and Feminism in a Nuclear Age', in *Just War Theory* (Oxford, Blackwell, 1992), 276.

15. Marianne Haslegrave, 'Women's Rights: The Road to the Millennium', in Peter Davies (ed.), *Human Rights* (London, Routledge, 1988). Also see Margot Light and Fred Halliday, 'Gender and International Relations', in A. J. R. Groom and Margot Light (eds.), *Contemporary International Relations: A Guide to Theory* (London, Pinter, 1994), 46.

16. R. J. Vincent, *Human Rights and International Relations* (Cambridge, Cambridge University Press, 1986), chap. 2.

17. Orlando Patterson, 'Freedom, Slavery and the Modern Construction of Rights', in Olwen Hufton (ed.), *Historical Change and Human Rights* (New York, Basic Books, 1995), 132–3.

18. Vincent, *Human Rights and International Relations*, 127.

19. Charles R. Beitz, *Political Theory and International Relations* (Princeton, Princeton University Press, 1979), 150.

20. Rex Martin, *A System of Rights* (Oxford, Clarendon Press, 1993), 85.

21. Martin, *A System of Rights*, 91.

22. Catherine A. MacKinnon, 'Crimes of War, Crimes of Peace', in Stephen Shute and Susan Hurley (eds.), *On Human Rights* (New York, HarperCollins, 1993).

23. Richard Rorty, *Contingency, Irony and Solidarity* (Cambridge, Cambridge University Press, 1989), p. xv.

24. Rorty, *Contingency, Irony and Solidarity*, 197–8.

25. Rorty, *Contingency, Irony and Solidarity*, 68.

26. Rorty, *Contingency, Irony and Solidarity*, 86.

27. Rorty, *Contingency, Irony and Solidarity*, 189.

28. Richard Rorty, 'Human Rights, Rationality, and Sentimentality', in Stephen Shute and Susan Hurley (eds.), *On Human Rights* (New York, HarperCollins, 1993), 119.

29. Rorty, *Contingency, Irony and Solidarity*, 190.

30. See Norman Geras, *Solidarity and the Conversation of Humankind* (London, Verso, 1995).

31. Rorty, 'Human Rights, Rationality, and Sentimentality', 115.

32. Michael Walzer, *Thick and Thin: Moral Arguments at Home and Abroad* (Notre Dame, Ind., University of Notre Dame Press, 1994), 85–6.

33. Richard Rorty, ' Human Rights, Rationality, and Sentimentality'. Continuing his

assault on the 'Enlightenment Project', Rorty argues that the 'last two centuries are most easily understood not as a period of deepening understanding of the nature of rationality or of morality, but rather as one in which there occurred an astonishingly rapid progress of sentiments, in which it has become much easier for us to be moved to action by sad and sentimental stories' (p. 134).

34. Paul Ekins, *A New World Order: Grassroots Movements for Global Change* (London, Routledge, 1992).

35. Liah Greenfeld, *Nationalism: Five Roads to Modernity* (Cambridge, Mass., Harvard University Press, 1992), 487–8.

36. Chris Brown, 'The Ethics of Political Restructuring in Europe—The Perspective of Constitutive Theory', in Chris Brown (ed.), *Political Restructuring in Europe: Ethical Perspectives* (London, Routledge, 1994), 174; and Ryszard Legutko, 'Cosmopolitans and Communitarians: A Commentary', in Brown (ed.), *Political Restructuring in Europe*, 231.

37. Janna Thompson, *Justice and World Order: A Philosophical Inquiry* (London, Routledge, 1992), 175.

38. These are the criteria of ideological politics that Kenneth Minogue puts forward in his *Alien Powers: The Pure Theory of Ideology* (London, Weidenfeld and Nicolson, 1985).

39. See Elie Kedourie, *Nationalism* 4th edn. (Oxford, Blackwell, 1993; 1st edn. pub. Hutchinson, 1966); and Kenneth Minogue, *Nationalism* (London, Batsford, 1967)

40. E. J. Hobsbawm, *Nations and Nationalism since 1780* (Cambridge, Cambridge University Press, 1990).

41. Elshtain, 'International Politics and Political Theory', 271.

42. Sanjay Seth, 'Political Theory in the Age of Nationalism', *Ethics and International Affairs*, 7 (1993), 76.

43. Thompson, *Justice and World Order*, 127.

44. David Miller, *On Nationality* (Oxford, Clarendon Press, 1995), 18–19; Michael Walzer, 'Nation and Universe', *The Tanner Lectures on Human Values*, 11, ed. G. B. Peterson (Salt Lake City, University of Utah Press, 1990), 554–5.

45. Vincent, *Human Rights and International Relations*, 37.

46. Michael Donelan, 'The Political Theorists and International Theory', in M. Donelan (ed.), *The Reason of States* (London, Allen and Unwin, 1978), 90.

47. Vincent, *Human Rights and International Relations*, 56.

48. See John Finnis, *Natural Law and Natural Rights* (Oxford, Oxford University Press, 1980).

49. Rorty, *Contingency, Irony and Solidarity*, 191.

50. M. J. Sandel, *Liberalism and the Limits of Justice* (Cambridge, Cambridge University Press, 1982), 173 and 179.

51. Brown, 'Ethics of Political Restructuring', 173.

52. Brown, 'Ethics of Political Restructuring', 171.

53. Brown, 'Ethics of Political Restructuring', 175.

54. Brown, 'Idea of World Community', 94

55. Brown, 'Idea of World Community', 97.

56. Walzer, *Thick and Thin*, 13.

57. Quoted by MacKinnon, 'Crimes of War, Crimes of Peace', 83.

58. Elshtain, 'International Politics and Political Theory', 271.

59. Of recent international political theory writers Michael Walzer and Andrew Linklater explicitly acknowledge his influence. See Walzer, *Just and Unjust Wars: A Moral Argument with Historical Illustrations* (New York, Basic Books, 1977), 28 n. 28;

Andrew Linklater, *Men and Citizens in the Theory of International Relations*, 2nd edn. (London, Macmillan, 1990), 25–7 and 30–2; Andrew Linklater, 'Men and Citizens in International Relations', in Howard Williams, Moorhead Wright, and Tony Evans (eds.), *A Reader in International Relations and Political Theory* (Buckingham, Open University Press, 1993), 320–1

60. T. H. Green, *Prolegomena to Ethics*, 4th edn. (Oxford, Clarendon Press, 1899), 247.
61. Linklater, 'The Question of the Next Stage in International Relations Theory', 84.
62. Andrew Linklater, *Beyond Realism and Marxism: Critical Theory and International Relations* (London, Macmillan, 1990), 171. Cf. Linklater, 'The Question of the Next Stage in International Relations Theory', 93.
63. Linklater, *Men and Citizens*, 201.
64. Linklater, *Beyond Realism and Marxism*, 14.
65. Brian Barry, *Justice as Impartiality* (Oxford, Clarendon Press, 1995).
66. Michael Walzer, *Spheres of Justice*. For a succinct and lucid account of the argument of this book see David Miller, 'Introduction', in David Miller and Michael Walzer (eds.), *Pluralism, Justice and Equality* (Oxford, Oxford University Press, 1995).
67. Michael Walzer, 'Interpretation and Social Criticism', *The Tanner Lectures on Human Values*, 7, ed. S. M. McMurrin (Salt Lake City, University of Utah Press, 1988), 22.
68. Walzer, 'Nation and Universe'.
69. Frost, *Ethics in International Relations*, 85.
70. Frost, *Ethics in International Relations*, 106–12.
71. Frost, *Ethics in International Relations*, 137–59.
72. See Danielle Archibugi and David Held (eds.), *Cosmopolitan Democracy: An Agenda for a New World Order* (Cambridge, Polity Press, 1995); and David Held, *Democracy and the Global Order: From the Modern State to Cosmopolitan Governance* (Cambridge, Polity Press, 1995).
73. Thompson, *Justice and World Order*, chap. 9.
74. Rorty, *Contingency, Irony and Solidarity*, 192 and 196.
75. Rorty, 'Human Rights, Rationality and Sentimentality', 116.
76. Rorty, *Contingency, Irony and Solidarity*, 192.
77. Onora O'Neill, *Towards Justice and Virtue: A Constructive Account of Practical Reasoning* (Cambridge, Cambridge University Press, 1996), 63.
78. O'Neill, *Towards Justice and Virtue*, 92.
79. O'Neill, *Towards Justice and Virtue*, 190.
80. O'Neill, *Towards Justice and Virtue*, 149.
81. O'Neill, *Towards Justice and Virtue*, 157.
82. Onora O'Neill, 'Transnational Justice', in David Held (ed.), *Political Theory Today* (Cambridge, Polity Press, 1991), 297.
83. O'Neill, *Towards Justice and Virtue*, 161–6.
84. Charles R. Beitz, 'Cosmopolitan Liberalism and the States System', in Chris Brown (ed.), *Political Restructuring in Europe*, 124–5.
85. Thomas Pogge, 'Cosmopolitanism and Sovereignty', in Chris Brown (ed.), *Political Restructuring in Europe: Ethical Perspectives* (London, Routledge, 1994), 90.
86. O'Neill, 'Justice and Boundaries', 78–9.
87. O'Neill, *Towards Justice and Virtue*, 182–3.
88. O'Neill, *Towards Justice and Virtue*, 185.
89. O'Neill, *Towards Justice and Virtue*, 200–1.

BIBLIOGRAPHY

ADKINS, A. W. H., 'The *Arete* of Nicias: Thucydides 7.86', *Greek, Roman and Byzantine Studies*, 16 (1975), 379–92.

AIRAKSINEN, TIMO, and BERTMAN, MARTIN A. (eds.), *Hobbes: War among Nations* (Aldershot, Avebury, 1989).

ALKER, Jr., HAYWARD, R., 'The Dialectical Logic of Thucydides' Melian Dialogue', *American Political Science Review*, 82 (1988).

ALLEN, J. W., 'Marsilio of Padua and Medieval Secularism', in F. J. C. Hearnshaw (ed.), *The Social and Political Ideas of Some Great Medieval Thinkers* (New York, Barnes and Noble, 1923).

ANDREWES, ANTONY, *Greek Society* (Harmondsworth, Penguin, 1991).

ANGLO, SYDNEY, *Machiavelli* (London, Paladin, 1971).

ANTIPHON, 'On Human Nature', repr. in Ernest Barker, *Greek Political Theory* (London, Methuen, 1918).

AQUINAS, ST THOMAS, *On Law, Morality, and Politics*, ed. William P. Baumgarth and Richard J. Regan (Indianapolis, Hackett, 1988).

—— *Selected Political Writings*, ed. A. P. d'Entrèves (Oxford, Blackwell, 1974).

ARCHIBUGI, DANIELLE, and HELD, DAVID, eds., *Cosmopolitan Democracy: An Agenda for a New World Order* (Cambridge, Polity Press, 1995).

ARISTOPHANES, *Lysistrata*, in *Lysistrata, The Acharnians, The Clouds*, trans. Alan H. Sommerstein (Harmondsworth, Penguin, 1973).

ARISTOTLE, *Aristotle on Rhetoric: A Theory of Civic Discourse*, trans. George A. Kennedy (Oxford, Oxford University Press, 1991).

—— *Nicomachean Ethics*, trans. J. A. K. Thomson (Harmondsworth, Penguin, 1973).

—— *The Politics*, ed. Stephen Everson trans. based on Jonathan Barnes' revision of Jowett (Cambridge, Cambridge University Press, 1988).

ARNEIL, BARBARA, 'John Locke, Natural Law, and Colonialism', *History of Political Thought*, 13 (1992).

—— 'Locke and Colonialism', *Journal of the History of Ideas*, 55 (1994).

ARNOLD, E. VERNON, *Roman Stoicism* (Cambridge, Cambridge University Press, 1911).

ARON, RAYMOND, 'What is a Theory of International Relations?', *Journal of International Affairs*, 21 (1967).

AUGUSTINE, St, *Concerning the City of God against the Pagans*, trans. Henry Bettenson, introd. by John O'Meara (Harmondsworth, Penguin, 1984).

—— *The Essential Augustine*, ed. Vernon J. Bourke (Indianapolis, Hackett, 1974).

AVINERI, SHLOMO, *Hegel's Theory of the Modern State* (Cambridge, Cambridge University Press, 1972).

—— *Karl Marx on Colonialism and Modernisation* (New York, Doubleday, 1968).

—— 'The Problem of War in Hegel's Thought', *Journal of the History of Ideas*, 22 (1961).

BALL, TERENCE, 'Hobbes' Linguistic Turn', *Polity*, 17 (1985).

BANKS, MICHAEL, 'The Evolution of International Relations Theory', in Michael Banks (ed.), *Conflict in World Society* (London, Wheatsheaf, 1984).

BARKER, ERNEST, *Greek Political Theory* (London, Methuen, 1977).

—— 'Nietzsche and Treitschke: The Worship of Power in Modern Germany' (Oxford Pamphlets; London, Oxford University Press, 1914).

—— (ed.), *The Social Contract* (Oxford, Clarendon Press, 1961).

—— (ed. and trans.), *From Alexander to Constantine* (Oxford, Clarendon Press, 1956).

BARNES, JONATHAN, *Early Greek Philosophy* (Harmondsworth, Penguin, 1987).

—— 'Partial Wholes', in Ellen Frankel Paul, Fred D. Miller, Jr., and Jeffrey Paul (eds.), *Ethics, Politics and Human Nature* (Oxford, Blackwell, 1991).

—— *The Presocratic Philosophers* (London, Routledge, 1992).

BARRACLOUGH, GEOFFREY, *History in a Changing World* (Oxford, Blackwell, 1957).

BARRY, BRIAN, *Justice as Impartiality* (Oxford, Clarendon Press, 1995).

BAUMGOLD, DEBORAH, *Hobbes's Political Theory* (Cambridge, Cambridge University Press, 1988).

BECK, L. W., *A Commentary on Kant's Critique of Practical Reason* (Indianapolis, Library of Liberal Arts, 1960).

BEITZ, CHARLES R., 'Cosmopolitan Liberalism and the States System', in Chris Brown (ed.), *Political Restructuring in Europe: Ethical Perspectives* (London, Routledge, 1994).

—— *Political Theory and International Relations* (Princeton, Princeton University Press, 1979).

BEJCZY, ISTVÁN, 'The State as a Work of Art: Petrarch and his *Speculum principis* (xiv, I)', *History of Political Thought*, 15 (1994).

BENTHAM, JEREMY, 'A Plan for an Universal and Perpetual Peace', in Howard P. Kainz (ed.), *Philosophical Perspectives on Peace* (London, Macmillan, 1987).

BERDAHL, ROBERT M., *The Politics of the Prussian Nobility: The Development of a Conservative Ideology* (Princeton, Princeton University Press, 1988).

BERKI, R. N., *The History of Political Thought* (London, Dent, 1977).

—— 'On Marxian Thought and the Problem of International Relations', *World Politics*, 24 (1971).

BLACK, ANTONY, *Political Thought in Europe 1250–1450* (Cambridge, Cambridge University Press, 1992).

BONDANELLA, PETER E., *Machiavelli and the Art of Renaissance History* (Detroit, Wayne State University, 1973).

BOOTH, KEN and SMITH, STEVE (eds.), *International Relations Theory Today* (Cambridge, Polity Press, 1995).

BOSANQUET, BERNARD, *Social and International Ideals* (London, Macmillan, 1917).

BOUCHER, DAVID, 'British Idealism, the State, and International Relations', *Journal of the History of Ideas*, 55 (1994).

—— 'The Character of the History of the Philosophy of International Relations and the Case of Edmund Burke', *Review of International Studies*, 17 (1991).

—— 'The Duplicitous Machiavelli', *Machiavelli Studies*, 3 (1990).

—— 'Reconciling Ethics and Interests in the Person of the State: The International Dimension', in Paul Keale (ed.), *Ethics and Foreign Policy* (Sydney, Allen and Unwin, 1992).

—— *Texts in Context: Revisionist Methods for Studying the History of Ideas* (Dordrecht, Martinus Nijhoff, 1985).

—— ed., *The British Idealists* (Cambridge, Cambridge University Press, 1997).

—— and KELLY, PAUL, 'The Social Contract and its Critics', in David Boucher and Paul Kelly (eds.), *The Social Contract from Hobbes to Rawls* (London, Routledge, 1994).

—— and VINCENT, ANDREW, *A Radical Hegelian: The Political and Social Philosophy of Henry Jones* (Cardiff, University of Wales Press, 1993).

BOULTON, J. T., 'Arbitrary Power: An Eighteenth Century Obsession', *Studies in Burke and his Time*, 9 (1967–8).

BRADLEY, F. H., *Ethical Studies*, 2nd edn. (Oxford, Clarendon Press, 1927).

BRIERLY, JAMES LESLIE, *The Basis of Obligation in International Law* (Oxford, Clarendon Press, 1958).

BROWN, C. W., 'Thucydides, Hobbes, and the Derivation of Anarchy', *History of Political Thought*, 8 (1987).

—— 'Thucydides, Hobbes, and the Linear Causal Perspective', *History of Political Thought*, 10 (1989).

BROWN, CHRIS, 'The Ethics of Political Restructuring in Europe—The Perspective of Constitutive Theory', in Chris Brown (ed.), *Political Restructuring in Europe: Ethical Perspectives* (London, Routledge, 1994).

—— 'International Political Theory and the Idea of World Community', in Ken Booth and Steve Smith (eds.), *International Relations Theory Today* (Cambridge, Polity Press, 1995).

—— *International Relations Theory: New Normative Approaches* (London, Harvester Wheatsheaf, 1992).

—— 'Marxism and International Ethics', in Terry Nardin and David R. Mapel (eds.), *Traditions of International Ethics* (Cambridge, Cambridge University Press, 1992).

BROWNING, G. K., 'The Night in which all Cows are Black: Ethical Absolutism in Plato and Hegel', *History of Political Thought*, 12 (1991).

BRUEL, CHRISTOPHER, 'Thucydides' View of Athenian Imperialism', *American Political Science Review*, 68 (1974).

BRUNT, P. A., 'The Hellenic League against Persia', in *Studies in Greek History and Thought* (Oxford, Clarendon Press, 1993).

—— 'Thucydides and Alcibiades', in *Studies in Greek History and Thought* (Oxford, Clarendon Press, 1993).

BUCKLE, STEPHEN, *Natural Law and the Theory of Property: Grotius to Hume* (Oxford, Clarendon Press, 1991).

BULL, HEDLEY, *The Anarchical Society: A Study of Order in World Politics* (London, Macmillan, 1984).

—— 'The Grotian Conception of International Society', in Herbert Butterfield and Martin Wight (eds.), *Diplomatic Investigations: Essays in the Theory of International Politics* (London, Allen and Unwin, 1966).

—— 'Hobbes and the International Anarchy', *Social Research*, 48 (1981).

—— 'The Importance of Grotius in the Study of International Relations', in Hedley Bull, Benedict Kingsbury, and Adam Roberts (eds.), *Hugo Grotius and International Relations* (Oxford, Clarendon Press, 1990).

—— 'Martin Wight and the Theory of International Relations,' *British Journal of International Studies*, 2 (1976).

—— 'Martin Wight and the Theory of International Relations', in Martin Wight, *International Theory: The Three Traditions*, ed. Gabriele Wight and Brian Porter (London and Leicester, Leicester University Press, 1991).

—— 'Society and Anarchy in International Relations', in Herbert Butterfield and Martin Wight (eds.), *Diplomatic Investigations: Essays in the Theory of International Politics* (London, Allen and Unwin, 1966).

—— KINGSBURY, BENEDICT, and ROBERTS, ADAM, (eds.), *Hugo Grotius and International Relations* (Oxford, Clarendon Press, 1990).

BURCHILL, SCOTT, LINKLATER, ANDREW, DEVETAK, RICHARD, PATERSON, MATTHEW, and TRUE, JACQUI, *Theories of International Relations* (London, Macmillan, 1996)

BURCKHARDT, JACOB, *The Civilisation of the Renaissance* (London, Phaidon, 1944; first pub. 1860).

BURKE, EDMUND, *The Writings and Speeches of Edmund Burke, VI, 1786–1788*, ed. P. J. Marshall (Oxford, Clarendon Press, 1991).

—— *Works* (World's Classics; London, Henry Frowde for Oxford University Press, 1907), 6 vols.

—— 'An Appeal from the New to the Old Whigs', *Works*, v. *A Philosophical Inquiry into the Origin of our Ideas of the Sublime and Beautiful* (1756), *Works*, i.

—— 'Heads for Consideration on the Present State of Affairs 1792', *Works*, v.

—— 'Letters on a Regicide Peace, I, II, III, IV', *Works*, vi.

—— 'On a Motion for leave to bring in a Bill to repeal and alter certain Acts respecting Religious Opinions: May 11, 1792', *Works*, iii.

—— *Reflections on the Revolution in France, Works*, iv.

—— 'Speech at Bristol previous to the Election in that City, 1780', *Works*, iii.

—— *Speeches on the Impeachment of Warren Hastings* (Delhi, Discovery Publishing House, 1987), 2 vols.

—— 'Speech on American Taxation 1774', *Works*, ii.

—— 'Speech on a Motion made in the House of Commons, May 7, 1782, for a Committee to inquire into the State of the Representation of the Commons in Parliament', *Works*, iii.

—— 'Speech on Moving the Resolutions for Conciliation with the Colonies', 1775, *Works*, ii.

—— 'Speech on Mr Fox's East India Bill 1783', *Works*, iii.

—— 'Thoughts on French Affairs, 1791', *Works*, iv.

BURN, A. R., *The Penguin History of Greece*, (Harmondsworth, Penguin, 1990).

—— *Pericles and Athens* (London, English Universities Press, 1956).

BURNHAM, JAMES, *The Machiavellians: Defenders of Freedom* (London, Putman, 1943).

BUTLER, PETER F., 'Legitimacy in a States-System: Vattel's *Law of Nations*', in Michael Donelan (ed.), *The Reason of States* (London, Allen and Unwin, 1978).

BUTLER, W. E., 'Grotius and the Law of the Sea', in Hedley Bull, Benedict Kingsbury, and Adam Roberts (eds.), *Hugo Grotius and International Relations* (Oxford, Clarendon Press, 1990).

BUTTERFIELD, HERBERT, *The Statecraft of Machiavelli* (New York, Collier Macmillan, 1967).

CAMERON, AVERIL, *The Later Roman Empire AD 284–430* (London, Fontana, 1993).

CAMERON, DAVID, *The Social Thought of Rousseau and Burke: A Comparative Study* (London, Weidenfeld and Nicolson for the London School of Economics, 1973).

CARLYLE, R. W., and CARLYLE, A. J., *A History of Medieval Theory in the West* (Edinburgh, Blackwood, 1970) 6 vols.

CARR, E. H., *The Twenty Years' Crisis 1919–1939* (London, Macmillan, 1939; 2nd edn. 1946).

CARRITT, E. F., 'Hegel and Prussianism', *Journal of Philosophy*, 15 (1940).

—— *Morals and Politics* (Oxford, Oxford University Press, 1935).

CASSIRER, ERNST, *The Myth of the State* (New Haven, Yale University Press, 1946).

CHABOD, F., *Machiavelli and the Renaissance* (New York, Harper Torchbooks, 1958).

CHADWICK, HENRY, *Augustine* (Oxford, Oxford University Press, 1986).

CHRISTOPHER, PAUL, *The Ethics of War and Peace* (Englewood Cliffs, NJ, Prentice Hall, 1994).

CICERO, *On Duties*, ed. and trans. M. T. Griffin and F. M. Atkins (Cambridge, Cambridge University Press, 1991).

—— *On the Commonwealth* trans. G. H. Sabine and S. B. Smith (London, Collier Macmillan, 1986).

CLAEYS, GREGORY, 'The French Revolution Debate and British Political Thought', *History of Political Thought*, 11 (1990).

CLARK, IAN, *Reform and Resistance in the International Order* (Cambridge, Cambridge University Press, 1981).

CLOUGH, CECIL H., *Machiavelli Researches* (Pubblicazioni della Sezione romanza dell'Istituto Universitario orientale, Napoli Studi, V. 3, 1967).

COADY, C. A. J., 'The Problem of Intervention', in Paul Keale (ed.), *Ethics and Foreign Policy* (Sydney, Allen and Unwin, 1992).

COBBAN, ALFRED, *Edmund Burke and the Revolt against the Eighteenth Century* (London, Allen and Unwin, 1960).

COGAN, MARC, 'Mytilene, Plataea, and Corcyra: Ideology and Policy in Thucydides, Book Three', *Phoenix*, 35 (1981).

COLLINGWOOD, R. G., 'Lectures on Moral Philosophy for M-T 1921', MS, Collingwood Papers, DEP 4, Bodleian Library, Oxford.

—— *The New Leviathan*, rev. edn., ed. David Boucher (Oxford, Clarendon Press, 1992).

—— 'The Prussian Philosophy', in David Boucher (ed.), *Essays in Political Philosophy* (Oxford, Clarendon Press, 1989).

—— *Roman Britain* (London, Oxford University Press, 1924).

CONNOR, W. R., 'A Post Modernist Thucydides?', *Classical Journal*, 72 (1977).

CONWAY, STEPHEN, 'Bentham on Peace and War', *Utilitas*, 1 (1989).

CORNFORD, F. M., *Thucydides Mythistoricus* (London, Arnold, 1907).

COULTON, G. G., *Studies in Medieval Thought* (London, Nelson, 1940).

COX, RICHARD H., *Locke on War and Peace* (Oxford, Clarendon Press, 1960).

CRANSTON, MAURICE, 'Remembering Rousseau', *Encounter*, 51 (1978).

CRAWFORD, MICHAEL, *The Roman Republic* (London, Fontana, 1992).

CREEDF, CONSTANCE, 'Epictetus', in Ian P. McGreal (ed.), *Great Thinkers of the Western World* (New York, HarperCollins, 1992).

CROCE, B., *Politics and Morals* (London, Allen and Unwin, 1945).

CUTLER, A. CLARE, 'The "Grotian Tradition" in International Relations', *Review of International Studies*, 17 (1991).

DAVIES, J. K., *Democracy and Classical Greece*, 2nd edn. (London, Fontana, 1993).

DAVIS, HORACE B., 'Nations, Colonies and Social Classes: The Position of Marx and Engels', *Science and Society*, 29 (1965).

DAVIS, H. W. *The Political Thought of Heinrich von Treitschke* (London, Constable, 1914).

—— *The Medieval Contribution to Political Thought* (Oxford, Clarendon Press, 1939).

DERATHÉ, ROBERT, *Jean-Jacques Rousseau et la science politique de son temps* (Paris, University of Paris Press, 1950).

DEVETAK, RICHARD, 'Postmodernism', in Scott Burchill and Andrew Linklater with Richard Devetak, Matthew Paterson, and Jacqui True, *Theories of International Relations* (London, Macmillan, 1996).

DEWEY, JOHN, *German Philosophy and Politics*, 2nd edn. (1915; repr. New York, Books for Libraries, 1970).

DICKINSON, G. LOWES, 'Introduction', in Rousseau, *Project for Perpetual Peace*, trans. E. M. Nuttall (London, 1927).

DIETZ, MARY C., 'Trapping the Prince: Machiavelli and the Politics of Deception', *American Political Science Review*, 80 (1986).

DILTHEY, W., *Selected Writings*, ed. and trans. H. P. Rickman (Cambridge, Cambridge University Press, 1976).

DONALDSON, THOMAS, 'Kant's Global Rationalism', in Terry Nardin and David R. Mapel (eds.), *Traditions of International Ethics* (Cambridge, Cambridge University Press, 1992).

DONELAN, MICHAEL, *Elements of International Political Theory* (Oxford, Clarendon Press, 1990).

—— 'Grotius and the Image of War', *Millennium*, 12 (1983).

—— 'The Political Theorists and International Theory', in M. Donelan (ed.), *The Reason of States* (London, Allen and Unwin, 1978).

DOYLE, MICHAEL W., 'Liberalism and World Politics', *American Political Science Review*, 80 (1986).

DRAPER, G. I. A. D., 'Grotius' Place in the Development of Legal Ideas about War', in Hedley Bull, Benedict Kingsbury, and Adam Roberts (eds.), *Hugo Grotius and International Relations* (Oxford, Clarendon Press, 1990).

DUFOUR, ALFRED, 'Pufendorf', in J. H. Burns and Mark Goldie (eds.), *The Cambridge History of Political Thought 1450–1700* (Cambridge, Cambridge University Press, 1988).

EDMUNDS, LOWELL, *Chance and Intelligence in Thucydides* (Cambridge, Mass., Harvard University Press, 1975).

EDWARDS, PAUL (ed.), *The Encyclopedia of Philosophy* (New York, Collier Macmillan, 1967).

EHRENBERG, VICTOR, *The Greek State* (Oxford, Blackwell, 1960).

EKINS, PAUL, *A New World Order: Grassroots Movements for Global Change* (London, Routledge, 1992).

ELIAS, NORBERT, *The Court Society* (Oxford, Blackwell, 1983).

ELLINGTON, JAMES W., 'Introduction', in Immanuel Kant, *Grounding for the Metaphysic of Morals*, ed. James W. Ellington (Indianapolis, Hackett, 1981).

ELSHTAIN, JEAN BETHKE, 'International Politics and Political Theory', in Ken Booth and Steve Smith (eds.), *International Relations Theory Today* (Cambridge, Polity, 1995).

—— 'Reflections on War and Political Discourse: Realism, Just War, and Feminism in a Nuclear Age', in *Just War Theory* (Oxford, Blackwell, 1992).

ENGELS, F., *Anti-Dühring* (Moscow, Progress, 1977).

ENLOE, CYNTHIA, *Does Khaki Become You? The Militarisation of Women's Lives* (London, Pluto, 1983).

d'ENTRÈVES, A. P., *Natural Law*, rev. edn. (London, Hutchinson, 1972).

EPICURUS, letter to Menoeceus: Diogenes Laertius, in Brad Inwood and L. P. Gerson (trans.), *Hellenistic Philosophy* (Indianapolis, Hackett, 1988).

ERMATH, MICHAEL, *Wilhelm Dilthey: The Critique of Historical Reason* (Chicago, University of Chicago Press, 1978).

EVANS, GRAHAM, 'Some Problems with a History of Thought in International Relations', *International Relations*, 4 (1974).

EVANS, M., *Karl Marx* (London, Allen and Unwin, 1975).

FACKENHEIM, EMIL L., 'On the Actuality of the Rational and the Rationality of the Actual', *Review of Metaphysics*, 23 (1970).

FARRAR, CYNTHIA, *The Origins of Democratic Thinking: The Invention of Politics in Classical Athens* (Cambridge, Cambridge University Press, 1988).

FÉNELON, FRANÇOIS, 'The Balance of Power as a Source of Stability', trans. William Gaunt, in Evan Luard (ed. and introd.), *Basic Texts in International Relations* (London, Macmillan, 1992).

FENNESSY, R. R., *Burke, Paine and the Rights of Man* (The Hague, Nijhoff, 1963).

FILMER, Sir ROBERT, *Observations Concerning the Originall of Government, Upon Mr. HOBS Leviathan*, repr. in *Patriarcha and other Political Works of Sir Robert Filmer*, ed. Peter Laslett (Oxford, Basil Blackwell, 1949).

FINLEY, M. I., *The Ancient Greeks*, rev. edn. (Harmondsworth, Penguin, 1971).

—— *Aspects of Antiquity: Discoveries and Controversies*, 2nd edn. (Harmondsworth, Penguin, 1977).

—— *Politics in the Ancient World* (Cambridge, Cambridge University Press, 1991).

FINNIS, JOHN, *Natural Law and Natural Rights* (Oxford, Oxford University Press, 1980).

FLANAGAN, THOMAS, 'The Agricultural Argument and Original Appropriation: Indian Lands and Political Philosophy', *Canadian Journal of Political Science*, 22 (1989).

FORD, FRANKLIN L., *Europe 1780–1830*, 2nd edn. (London, Longmans, 1989).

FORDE, STEVEN, 'Classical Realism', in Terry Nardin and David R. Mapel (eds.), *Traditions of International Ethics* (Cambridge, Cambridge University Press, 1992).

—— 'Thucydides on the Causes of Athenian Imperialism', *American Political Science Review*, 80 (1986).

FORSYTH, MURRAY, 'Thomas Hobbes and the External Relations of States', *British Journal of International Studies*, 5 (1979).

FORSYTH, M. G., KEENS-SOPER, H. M. A., and SAVIGEAR, P. (eds.), *The Theory of International Relations: Selected Texts from Gentili to Treitschke* (London, George Allen and Unwin, 1970).

FRANK, ANDRÉ GUNDER, 'The Development of Underdevelopment', in Michael Smith, Richard Little, and Michael Shackleton (eds.), *Perspectives on World Politics* (London, Croom Helm, 1981).

FRANKEL, JOSEPH, *National Interest* (London, Macmillan, 1970).

FREEMAN, KATHLEEN, *The Pre-Socratic Philosophers* (Oxford, Blackwell, 1946).

FREEMAN, MICHAEL, *Edmund Burke and the Critique of Political Radicalism* (Oxford, Blackwell, 1980).

FROST, MERVYN, *Ethics in International Relations: A Constitutive Theory* (Cambridge, Cambridge University Press, 1996).

FUKUYAMA, FRANCIS, *The End of History and the Last Man* (Harmondsworth, Penguin, 1992).

GAGARIN, MICHAEL, and WOODRUFF, PAUL, 'Introduction', *Early Greek Political Thought from Homer to the Sophists* (Cambridge, Cambridge University Press, 1995).

GALLIE, W. B., *Philosophers of Peace and War* (Cambridge, Cambridge University Press, 1979).

—— *Understanding War* (London, Routledge, 1991).

GALTUNG, JOHAN, *The European Community: A Superpower in the Making* (London, Allen and Unwin, 1981).

GARDNER, J. F., 'Introduction', in *Caesar: The Conquest of Gaul*, trans. S. A. Handford and ed. J. F. Gardner (Harmondsworth, Penguin, 1982).

GARLAN, YVON, *War in the Ancient World* (New York, Norton, 1975).

GARST, DANIEL, 'Thucydides and Neorealism', *International Studies Quarterly*, 33 (1989).

GAT, AZAR, 'Machiavelli and the Decline of the Classical Notion of the Lessons of History in the Study of War', *Military Affairs*, 52 (1988).

GAUTHIER, DAVID P., *The Logic of Leviathan* (Oxford, Clarendon Press, 1969).

GEERKEN, J. H., 'Machiavelli: Magus, Theologian or Trickster?', *Machiavelli Studies*, 3 (1990).

GELLINEK, CHRISTIAN, *Hugo Grotius* (Boston, Mass., Twayne, 1983).

GENTILI, ALBERICO, *The Three Books on the Law of War*, trans. John C. Rolfe, introd. by Coleman Phillipson (Oxford, Clarendon Press, 1933).

GEORGE, JIM, *Discourses of Global Politics: A Critical (Re)Introduction to International Relations* (Boulder, Colo., Rienner, 1994).

GERAS, NORMAN, 'The Controversy about Marx and Justice', in Alex Callinicos (ed.), *Marxist Theory* (Oxford, Oxford University Press, 1989).

—— *Marx and Human Nature* (London, Verso, 1983).

GERAS, NORMAN, *Solidarity and the Conversation of Humankind* (London, Verso, 1995).

GERMINO, DANTE, 'Second Thoughts on Leo Strauss's Machiavelli', *Journal of Politics*, 28 (1966).

GERWITH, ALAN, *Marsilius of Padua and Medieval Political Philosophy* (New York, Columbia University Press, 1951).

GIERKE, OTTO, *Natural Law and the Theory of Society 1500 to 1800*, trans. and introd. by Ernest Barker (Cambridge, Cambridge University Press, 1934).

GILBERT, A. H., *Machiavelli's Prince and its Forerunners* (Durham, NC, Duke University Press, 1938).

GILBERT, ALAN, 'Marx on Internationalism and War', *Philosophy and Public Affairs*, 7 (1978).

GILBERT, FELIX, 'Machiavelli: The Renaissance of the Art of War', in Peter Paret (ed.), *Makers of Modern Strategy from Machiavelli to the Nuclear Age* (Princeton, Princeton University Press, 1984).

GILPIN, R. G., 'The Richness of the Tradition of Political Realism', *International Organisation*, 38 (1984).

GLOVER, T. R., *The Ancient World* (Harmondsworth, Penguin, 1972).

GOODMAN, M. D., and HOLLADAY, A. J., 'Religious Scruples in Ancient Warfare', *Classical Quarterly*, 36 (1986).

GOODWIN, G. L., *World Institutions and World Order* (London, Bell and Sons, 1964).

GOUGH, J. W., *The Social Contract* (Oxford, Clarendon Press, 1957).

GRAZIA, SEBASTIAN DE, *Machiavelli in Hell* (Princeton, Princeton University Press, 1989).

GREEN, T. H., *Prolegomena to Ethics*, 4th edn. (Oxford, Clarendon Press, 1899).

GREENFIELD, LIAH, *Nationalism: Five Roads to Modernity* (Cambridge, Mass., Harvard University Press, 1992).

GREENLEAF, W. H., 'Burke and State Necessity: The Case of Warren Hastings', in R. Schnur (ed.), *Staatsrason* (Berlin, Duncker and Humblot, 1975).

—— 'Hobbes: The Problem of Interpretation', in Maurice Cranston and Richard Peters (eds.), *Hobbes and Rousseau* (New York, Doubleday Anchor, 1972).

—— *Order, Empiricism and Politics* (Oxford, Oxford University Press for the University of Hull, 1964).

GRIFFITHS, MARTIN, *Realism, Idealism and International Politics* (London, Routledge, 1992).

GROOM, A. J. R., and LIGHT, MARGOT (eds.), *Contemporary International Relations: A Guide to Theory* (London, Pinter, 1994).

GROTIUS, HUGO, *Prolegomena*, repr. in M. G. Forsyth, H. M. A. Keens-Soper, and P. Savigear (eds.), *The Theory of International Relations: Selected Texts from Gentili to Treitschke* (London, George Allen and Unwin, 1970).

—— *The Rights of War and Peace*, trans. A. C. Campbell (Westport, Va., Hyperion, 1993: edn. first pub. 1901).

GUICCIARDINI, FRANCESCO, 'The Balance of Power among the Italian States', in Evan Luard (ed.), *Basic Texts in International Relations* (London, Macmillan, 1992).

—— *Dialogue on the Government of Florence*, ed. Alison Brown (Cambridge, Cambridge University Press, 1994).

GUTHRIE, W. K. C., *The Greek Philosophers from Thales to Aristotle* (London, Routledge, 1991).

—— *The Sophists* (Cambridge, Cambridge University Press, 1971).

HAAKONSSEN, KNUD, 'Hugo Grotius and the History of Political Thought', *Political Theory*, 13 (1985).

—— 'Natural Law and Moral Realism: The Scottish Synthesis', in *Studies in the Philosophy of the Scottish Enlightenment* (Oxford, Clarendon Press, 1990).

HAFFMAN, ROSS, and LEVACK, PAUL, 'Introduction', in *Burke's Politics* (New York, 1949).

HAGGENMACHER, PETER, 'Grotius and Gentili: A Reassessment of Thomas E. Holland's Inaugural Lecture', in Hedley Bull, Benedict Kingsbury, and Adam Roberts (eds.), *Hugo Grotius and International Relations* (Oxford, Clarendon Press, 1990).

HALDANE, Viscount, *Selected Addresses and Essays* (London, Murray, 1928).

HALE, J. R., *Machiavelli and Renaissance Italy* (Harmondsworth, Penguin, 1961).

HALL, EDITH, 'Asia Unmanned: Images of Victory in Classical Athens', in John Rich and Graham Shipley (eds.), *War and Society in the Greek World* (London, Routledge, 1993).

HAMPSHER-MONK, I. W., 'Rhetoric and Opinion in the Politics of Edmund Burke', *History of Political Thought*, 9 (1988).

HANCOCK, ROGER, 'Kant and the Natural Right Theory', *Kant Studien*, 52 (1960–1).

HANSON, A. H., 'Political Philosophy or Political Science', an inaugural lecture (Cambridge, Leeds University Press, 1956).

HANSON, DONALD W., 'Thomas Hobbes's "Highway to Peace"', *International Organization*, 38 (1984).

HARTIGAN, RICHARD SHELLY, *The Forgotten Victim: A History of the Civilian* (Chicago, Precedent, 1982).

—— 'Francisco Vitoria and Civilian Immunity', *Political Theory*, 1 (1973).

HASLEGRAVE, MARIANNE, 'Women's Rights: The Road to the Millennium', in Peter Davies (ed.), *Human Rights* (London, Routledge, 1988).

HAY, DENYS, *Europe in the Fourteenth and Fifteenth Centuries* (London, Longman, 1970).

—— *Europe: The Emergence of an Idea* (New York, Harper and Row, 1966).

HEATER, DEREK, *Citizenship* (London, Longman, 1990).

HEGEL, G. W. F., *Elements of the Philosophy of Right*, trans. H. B. Nisbet and ed. Allen W. Wood (Cambridge, Cambridge University Press, 1991).

—— *The Encyclopaedia of Logic*, trans. T. F. Geraets, W. A. Suchting, and H. S. Harris (Indianapolis, Hackett, 1991).

—— *Hegel's Philosophy of Right*, trans. T. M. Knox (Oxford, Oxford University Press, 1967).

—— *Introduction to the Philosophy of History*, trans. Leo Rauch (Indianapolis, Hackett, 1988).

—— *Lectures on the History of Philosophy*, trans. E. S. Haldane (London, Kegan Paul, Trench, Trübner, 1892), 3 vols.

—— *Natural Law: The Scientific Ways of Testing Natural Law, its Place in Moral Philosophy, and its Relation to the Positive Sciences of Law*, trans. T. M. Knox and introd. by H. B. Acton (Pennsylvania, University of Pennsylvania Press, 1975).

—— *Phenomenology of Spirit*, trans. A. V. Miller, with analysis of the text and foreword by J. N. Findlay (Oxford, Oxford University Press, 1977).

—— *The Philosophy of History*, trans. J. Sibree (New York, Dover, 1956).

HEGEL, G. W. F., *Philosophy of Mind*, trans. William Wallace and A. V. Miller (Oxford, Clarendon Press, 1971).

—— *The Philosophy of Right* (Chicago, Benton, 1952).

—— *Political Writings*, trans. T. M. Knox and introd. by Z. A. Pelczynski (Oxford, Clarendon Press, 1964).

—— *Reason in History*, trans. Robert S. Hartman (Indianapolis, Bobbs-Merril, 1953).

HELD, DAVID, *Democracy and the Global Order: From the Modern State to Cosmopolitan Governance* (Cambridge, Polity Press, 1995).

HELLER, MARK A., 'The Use and Abuse of Hobbes: The State of Nature in International Relations', *Polity*, 13 (1980).

HERODOTUS, *The Histories*, trans. Aubrey de Sélincourt, rev. edn. (Harmondsworth, Penguin, 1972).

HERZ, JOHN H., *Political Realism and Political Idealism: A Study in Theories and Realities* (Chicago and London, The University of Chicago Press, 1951).

HINDSON, PAUL, and GRAY, TIM, *Burke's Dramatic Theory of Politics* (Aldershot, Avebury, 1988).

HOBBES, THOMAS, *A Dialogue between a Philosopher and a Student of the Common Laws of England*, ed. Joseph Cropsey (Chicago and London, The University of Chicago Press, 1971).

—— *The Elements of Law Natural and Politic*, 2nd edn., ed. M. M. Goldsmith (New York, Barnes and Noble, 1969).

—— *The English Works of Thomas Hobbes of Malmesbury*, ed. Sir William Molesworth (London, John Bohn, 1841).

—— *Leviathan, or The Matter, Forme, & Power of a COMMON-WEALTH, Ecclesiasticall and Civill*, ed. C. B. Macpherson (Harmondsworth, Penguin, 1981).

—— 'The Life of Mr Thomas Hobbes of Malmesbury' (Exeter, The Rota, 1979), 4.

—— *Man and Citizen*, ed. Bernard Gert (London, Harvester, 1978).

—— 'Of the Life and History of Thucydides', in *The English Works of Thomas Hobbes of Malmesbury*, ed. Sir William Molesworth (London, John Bohn, 1841), viii.

HOBHOUSE, L. T., *The Metaphysical Theory of the State* (London, Allen and Unwin, 1951; first pub. 1918)

HOBSBAWM, E. J., *Nations and Nationalism since 1780* (Cambridge, Cambridge University Press, 1990).

HOFFMAN, MARK, 'Critical Theory and the Inter-Paradigm Debate', *Millennium*, 16 (1987).

HOFFMAN, STANLEY, *Duties beyond Borders: On the Limits and Possibilities of Ethical International Politics* (New York, Syracuse University Press, 1981).

—— *The State of War: Essays on the Theory and Practice of International Politics* (New York, Praeger, 1965).

HOLLIS, MARTIN, *Models of Man* (Cambridge, Cambridge University Press, 1977).

HOLMES, ROBERT L., 'Can War be Morally Justified? Just War Theory', in Jean Bethke Elshtain (ed.), *Just War Theory* (Oxford, Blackwell, 1992).

HOLSTI, KALEVI J., *The Dividing Discipline: Hegemony and Diversity in International Theory* (London, Allen and Unwin, 1987).

—— *Peace and War: Armed Conflicts and International Order 1648–1989* (Cambridge, Cambridge University Press, 1991).

HOLZGREFE, J. L., 'The Origins of Modern International Relations Theory', *Review of International Studies*, 15 (1989).

HOMMES, HENDRIK VAN EIKEMA, 'Grotius on Natural and International Law', *Netherlands International Law Review*, 30 (1983).

HONT, ISTVAN, 'The Language of Sociality and Commerce: Samuel Pufendorf and the Theoretical Foundations of the "Four-Stages Theory"', in Anthony Pagden (ed.), *The Languages of Political Theory in Early-Modern Europe* (Cambridge, Cambridge University Press, 1987).

HORNBLOWER, SIMON, *A Commentary on Thucydides* (Oxford, Clarendon Press, 1991).

—— *Thucydides* (London, Duckworth, 1987).

HORNE, THOMAS A., *Property Rights and Poverty* (Chapel Hill, NC, University of North Carolina Press, 1990).

HUIZINGA, J., *The Waning of the Middle Ages* (Harmondsworth, Penguin, 1976).

HUME, DAVID, 'Of the Balance of Power', in *Essays Moral, Political and Literary* (Oxford, Oxford University Press, 1963).

INWOOD, BRAD, and GERSON, L. P. (trans.), *Hellenistic Philosophy* (Indianapolis, Hackett, 1988).

JOCELYN, H. D., 'The Roman Nobility and the Religion of the Republican State', *Journal of Religious History*, 4 (1966–7).

JOHNSON, JAMES TURNER, *Just War Tradition and the Restraint of War* (Princeton, Princeton University Press, 1981).

JONES, HENRY, *The Principles of Citizenship* (London, Macmillan, 1919).

—— 'Why We are Fighting', *Hibbert Journal*, 13 (1914–15).

—— speech, North Wales Heroes Memorial (Bangor, Caxton Press, 1917).

JUDD, PETER H., 'Thucydides and the Study of War', *Columbia Essays in International Affairs*, 11 (1966).

KAINZ, HOWARD P., (ed.)., *Philosophical Perspectives on Peace* (London, Macmillan, 1987).

KAMENKA, EUGENE, *The Ethical Foundations of Marxism* (London, Routledge, 1972).

KANT, IMMANUEL, *The Critique of Judgement*, trans. James Creed Meredith (Oxford, Clarendon Press, 1991).

—— *Critique of Pure Reason*, trans. J. M. D. Meiklejohn (London, Dent, 1943).

—— *Groundwork of the Metaphysics of Morals*. See entry for Paton, H. J. (ed.), *The Moral Law*.

—— *Political Writings*, ed. Hans Reiss (Cambridge, Cambridge University Press, 1991)

KAUFMANN, WALTER (ed.), *Hegel's Political Philosophy* (New York, Doubleday, 1970).

KEALE, PAUL (ed.), *Ethics and Foreign Policy* (Sydney, Allen and Unwin, 1992).

KEDOURIE, ELIE, *Nationalism*, 4th edn. (Oxford, Blackwell, 1993; 1st edn. pub. Hutchinson, 1966).

KEEGAN, JOHN, *A History of Warfare* (London, Hutchinson, 1993).

KELLY, G. A., *Idealism, Politics and History: Sources of Hegelian Thought* (Cambridge, Cambridge University Press, 1969).

KEOHANE, R. O., 'Theory of World Politics: Structural Realism and Beyond', in A. Finifter (ed.), *Political Science: The State of the Discipline* (Washington, DC, American Political Science Association, 1983).

KERFORD, G. B., 'Anaxagoras of Clazomenae', in Paul Edwards (ed.), *The Encyclopedia of Philosophy* (New York, Collier Macmillan, 1967).

KIERNAN, V. G., *Marxism and Imperialism* (London, Arnold, 1974), 216.

KIERNAN, VICTOR, 'History', in David McLellan (ed.), *Marx: The First 100 Years* (London, Fontana, 1983).

KIRK, RUSSELL, *Edmund Burke: A Genius Reconsidered* (New Rochelle, NY, 1967).

KITTO, H. D. F., *The Greeks*, rev. edn. (Harmondsworth, Penguin, 1971).

KLOSKO, G., and RICE, D., 'Thucydides and Hobbes's State of Nature', *History of Political Thought*, 6 (1985).

KNOTOS, ALKIS, 'Success and Knowledge in Machiavelli', in Anthony Parel (ed.), *The Political Calculus* (Toronto, Toronto University Press, 1972).

KNOX, T. M., 'Hegel and Prussianism', *Journal of Philosophy*, 15 (1940).

—— 'Hegel and Prussianism', in Walter Kaufmann (ed.), *Hegel's Political Philosophy* (New York, Doubleday, 1970).

KNUTSEN, TORBJÖRN L., *A History of International Relations Theory* (Manchester, Manchester University Press, 1992).

KOEBNER, RICHARD, *Empire* (Cambridge, Cambridge University Press, 1961).

KRIEGER, LEONARD, 'Kant and the Crisis of Natural Law', *Journal of the History of Ideas*, 26 (1965).

—— *The Politics of Discretion* (London, University of Chicago Press, 1965).

KUBÁLKOVÁ, V., and CRUICKSHANK, A. A., *Marxism-Leninism and the Theory of International Relations* (London, Routledge and Kegan Paul, 1980).

KYMLICKA, WILL, *Contemporary Political Philosophy: An Introduction* (Oxford, Oxford University Press, 1990).

LAPID, YOSEF, HOLSTI, K. J., BIERSTEKER, THOMAS J., and GEORGE, JIM, 'Exchange on the "Third Debate"', *International Studies Quarterly*, 33 (1989).

LAPRADELLE, ALBERT DE, 'Emrich de Vattel', in John MacDonell and Edward Manson (eds.), *Great Jurists of the World* (New York, Kelley, 1968).

LASKI, HAROLD, *Political Thought in England from Locke to Bentham* (Oxford, Oxford University Press, 1942).

LAUTERPACHT, H., 'The Grotian Tradition in International Law', *British Yearbook of International Law*, 27 (1946).

LEBOVICS, HERMAN, 'The Uses of America in Locke's *Second Treatise of Government*', *Journal of the History of Ideas*, 47 (1986).

LEGUTKO, RYSZARD, 'Cosmopolitans and Communitarians: A Commentary' in Chris Brown (ed.), *Political Restructuring in Europe: Ethical Perspectives* (London, Routledge, 1994).

LESSNOFF, MICHAEL (ed.), *Social Contract Theory* (Oxford, Blackwell, 1990).

LEVIN, M., 'Rousseau on Independence', *Political Studies*, 18 (1970).

LICHTHEIM, GEORGE, 'Marx and the "Asiatic Mode of Production"', in Shlomo Avineri (ed.), *Marx's Socialism* (New York, Liber-Atherton, 1973).

LIGHT, MARGOT, and HALLIDAY, FRED, 'Gender and International Relations', in A. J. R. Groom and Margot Light (eds.), *Contemporary International Relations: A Guide to Theory* (London, Pinter, 1994).

LINKLATER, ANDREW, *Beyond Realism and Marxism: Critical Theory and International Relations* (London, Macmillan, 1990).

—— 'Marxism', in Scott Burchill and Andrew Linklater with Richard Devetak, Matthew Paterson, and Jacqui True, *Theories of International Relations* (London, Macmillan, 1996).

—— 'Men and Citizens in International Relations', in Howard Williams, Moorhead Wright, and Tony Evans (eds.), *A Reader in International Relations and Political Theory* (Buckingham, Open University Press, 1993).

—— *Men and Citizens in the Theory of International Relations*, 2nd edn. (London, Macmillan, 1990).

—— 'The Question of the Next Stage in International Relations Theory: A Critical-Theoretical Point of View', *Millennium*, 21 (1992).

LINTOTT, ANDREW, *Imperium Romanum* (London, Routledge, 1993).

LITTLE, RICHARD, and SMITH, MICHAEL, *Perspectives on World Politics*, 2nd edn. (London, Routledge, 1991).

—— and SMITH, STEVE (eds.), *Belief Systems and International Relations* (Oxford, Basil Blackwell, 1988).

LOCKE, JOHN, *Some Thoughts Concerning Education* (Cambridge, Cambridge University Press, 1902).

—— *Two Treatises of Government*, ed. Peter Laslett (Cambridge, Cambridge University Press, 1988).

LOVEJOY, ARTHUR O., *The Great Chain of Being* (Cambridge, Mass., Harvard University Press, 1974).

LUARD, EVAN, *International Society* (London, Macmillan, 1990).

—— (ed.) *Basic Texts in International Relations* (London, Macmillan, 1992).

LUNENFELD, MARVIN, 'The Art of War in Renaissance Florence: Leonardo, Machiavelli and Soderini', *Machiavelli Studies*, 3 (1990).

MACAULAY, T. B., *Essays and Lays of Ancient Rome* (London, Longman's Green, 1899).

MACHIAVELLI, NICCOLÒ, *Machiavelli: The Chief Works and Others*, ed. Allan Gilbert (Durham, NC, Duke University Press, 1989), 3 vols.

—— *The Art of War* in *Chief Works*, 561–726.

—— *First Decennale*, in *Chief Works*.

—— 'A Description of the Method Used by Duke Valentino in Killing Vittellozzo Vitelli' in *Chief Works*, 163–9.

—— *The Discourses*, ed. Bernard Crick, trans. Leslie J. Walker, rev. Brian Richardson (Harmondsworth, Penguin, 1970).

—— *The Florentine History*, trans. W. K. Marriot (London, Dent, 1976).

—— 'The [Golden] Ass', in *Chief Works*, 750–72.

—— *The History of Florence*, in *Chief Works*, 1025–435.

—— *The Legations*, in *Chief Works*, 120–60.

—— *The Prince*, trans. George Bull (Harmondsworth, Penguin, 1974).

—— *The Prince*, trans. Harvey C. Mansfield Jr. (Chicago, Chicago University Press, 1985).

—— 'Tercets on Ambition', in *Chief Works*, 735–9.

MCILWAIN, CHARLES HOWARD, *The Growth of Political Thought in the West* (New York, Macmillan, 1932).

MACINTYRE, ALASDAIR, *A Short History of Ethics* (London, Routledge and Kegan Paul, 1967).

MACKENZIE, J. S., 'Might and Right', in Louise Creighton et al., *The International Crisis: The Theory of the State* (London, Oxford University Press, 1916).

MACKINNON, CATHERINE A., 'Crimes of War, Crimes of Peace', in Stephen Shute and Susan Hurley (eds.), *On Human Rights* (New York, HarperCollins, 1993).

MACKINNON, D. M., 'Natural Law', in H. Butterfield and M. Wight (eds.), *Diplomatic Investigations: Essays in the Theory of International Politics* (London, Allen and Unwin, 1966).

MACLEAN, JOHN, 'Marxism and International Relations: A Strange Case of Mutual Neglect', *Millennium*, 17 (1988).

MCLELLAN, DAVID, *Marx's Grundrisse* (London, Paladin, 1973).

MACPHERSON, C. B., *Burke* (Oxford, Oxford University Press, 1980).

MALLET, MICHAEL, 'The Theory and Practice of Warfare in Machiavelli's Republic', in Gisela Bock, Quentin Skinner, and Maurizio Viroli (eds.), *Machiavelli and Republicanism* (Cambridge, Cambridge University Press, 1990).

MANICAS, PETER T., 'War, Stasis, and Greek Political Thought', *Comparative Studies in Society and History*, 24 (1982).

MARCUS, AURELIUS, *The Meditations of the Emperor Marcus Aurelius Antoninus*, trans. George Long (London, Collins, n.d.).

MARSHALL, P. J., 'Introduction', in *The Writings and Speeches of Edmund Burke, VI, 1786– 1788*, ed. P. J. Marshall (Oxford, Clarendon Press, 1991).

MARSILIUS OF PADUA, *Defensor minor and De translatione imperii*, trans. Fiona Watson and Cary J. Nederman (Cambridge, Cambridge University Press, 1993).

—— *Defensor pacis*, trans. Alan Gerwith (Toronto, Toronto University Press, 1986).

MARTIN, REX, *A System of Rights* (Oxford, Clarendon Press, 1993).

MARX, KARL, *Capital* (London, Dent, 1934), 3 vols.

—— *The Class Struggles in France*, in ed. David Fernbach, *The Political Writings*, ii: *Surveys from Exile* (Harmondsworth, Penguin, 1973).

—— *Capital* (London, Everyman, 1974) 2 vols.

—— *Contribution to the Critique of Hegel's Philosophy of Right: Introduction*, in *The Marx–Engels Reader*, 2nd edn., ed. Robert C. Tucker (New York, Norton, 1978).

—— 'Critique of Hegelian Dialectic and Philosophy in General' from the 1844 Manuscripts, in *Writings of the Young Marx on Philosophy and Society*, ed. Loyd D. Easton and Kurt H. Guddat (New York, Doubleday, 1967).

—— *Critique of Hegel's Philosophy of Right*, trans. and ed. Joseph J. O'Malley (Cambridge, Cambridge University Press, 1970).

—— *The Eighteenth Brumaire of Louis Bonaparte*, in *The Political Writings*, ii: *Surveys From Exile* (Harmondsworth, Penguin, 1973).

—— 'The Future Results of the British Rule in India', in *On Colonialism* (Moscow, Progress, 1976).

—— *The German Ideology*, in *Writings of the Young Marx on Philosophy and Society*, ed. Loyd D. Easton and Kurt H. Guddat (New York, Doubleday, 1967).

—— 'India', in *On Colonialism* (Moscow, Progress, 1976).

—— *Karl Marx: Pre-Capitalist Economic Formations*, ed. E. J. Hobsbawm (London, Lawrence and Wishart, 1964).

—— *Writings of the Young Marx on Philosophy and Society*, ed. Loyd D. Easton and Kurt H. Guddat (New York, Doubleday, 1967).

—— and ENGELS, FRIEDRICH, *Ireland and the Irish Question*, ed. R. Dixon (New York, Doubleday, 1972).

—— and —— *Manifesto of the Communist Party*, in *The Political Writings*, i: *The Revolutions of 1848* (Harmondsworth, Penguin, 1973).

—— *The Marx–Engels Reader*, 2nd edn., ed. Robert C. Tucker (New York, Norton, 1978).

MATTINGLY, GARRETT, 'Machiavelli's *Prince*: Political Science or Political Satire?', *American Scholar*, 27 (1958).

—— *Renaissance Diplomacy* (London, Cape, 1955).

MAUTNER, THOMAS, 'Pufendorf and 18th Century Scottish Philosophy', in K. A. Modéer (ed.), *Samuel von Pufendorf 1632–1682* (Lund, Bloms Boktryckeri, 1986).

—— 'Pufendorf's Place in the History of Rights Concepts', in Timothy O'Hagan (ed.), *Revolution and Enlightenment in Europe* (Aberdeen, Aberdeen University Press, 1991).

MAYALL, JAMES, 'Nationalism in the Study of International Relations', in A. J. R. Groom and Margot Light (eds.), *Contemporary International Relations: A Guide to Theory* (London, Pinter, 1994).

MEINECKE, FRIEDRICH, *Machiavellism: The Doctrine of Raison d'État and its Place in Modern History* (London, Routledge and Kegan Paul, 1962; first pub. 1924).

MELZER, ARTHUR M., 'Rousseau's Moral Realism: Replacing Natural Law with the General Will', *American Political Science Review*, 77 (1983).

MIDGLEY, MARY, *Natural Law* (London, Elek, 1975).

MILLER, DAVID, 'Introduction', in David Miller and Michael Walzer (eds.), *Pluralism, Justice and Equality* (Oxford, Oxford University Press, 1995).

—— *On Nationality* (Oxford, Clarendon Press, 1995).

MINOGUE, KENNETH, *Alien Powers: The Pure Theory of Ideology* (London, Weidenfeld and Nicolson, 1985).

—— *Nationalism* (London, Batsford, 1967).

MINOGUE, K. R., 'Theatricality and Politics: Machiavelli's Concept of Fantasia', in B. Parekh and R. N. Berki (eds.), *The Morality of Politics* (London, Allen and Unwin, 1972).

MITIAS, MICHAEL H., 'Hegel on International Law', *Clio*, 9 (1980).

MOGHADAM, V., *Identity Politics: Cultural Reassertion and Feminism in International Perspectives* (Boulder, Colo., Westview, 1993).

MOMIGLIANO, ARNALDO, 'Some Observations on Causes of War in Ancient Historiography', *Studies in Historiography* (London, Weidenfeld and Nicolson, 1966).

MORGANTHAU, H. J., *Politics among Nations*, 5th edn. (New York, Knopf, 1978).

MORLEY, J., *Burke* (London, Macmillan, 1879).

MORROW, JOHN, 'British Idealism, "German Philosophy" and the First World War', *Australian Journal of Philosophy and History*, 28 (1982).

MUIRHEAD, J. H., *German Philosophy in Relation to the War* (London, Murray, 1917).

MURRAY, GILBERT, *Euripides and his Age* (London, Oxford University Press, 1965).

NARDIN, TERRY, *Law, Morality and the Relations of States* (Princeton, Princeton University Press, 1983).

NEDERMAN, CARY J., *Community and Consent: The Secular Political Theory of Marsiglio of Padua* (Lanham, Rowman and Littlefield, 1994).

—— 'Introduction', in *Defensor minor and De translatione imperii* (Cambridge, Cambridge University Press, 1993).

—— 'The Problem of Empire in Marsiglio of Padua', *History of Political Thought*, 16 1995).

—— and FORHAN, KATE LANDON, 'Introduction', in Cary J. Nederman and Kate Landon Forhan (eds.), *Medieval Political Theory—A Reader* (London, Routledge, 1993)

NICHOLSON, PETER P., 'Philosophical Idealism and International Politics: A Reply to Dr Savigear', *British Journal of International Studies*, 2 (1976).

NORMAN, RICHARD, *Hegel's Phenomenology: A Philosophical Introduction* (London, Chatto and Windus for University of Sussex Press, 1976).

NORTHEDGE, F. S., *The International Political System* (London, Faber and Faber, 1976).

NUTKIEWICZ, MICHAEL, 'Samuel Pufendorf: Obligation as the Basis of the State', *Journal of the History of Philosophy*, 21 (1983).

OAKELEY, HILDA D., 'The Idea of a General Will', in Louise Creighton et al., *The International Crisis: The Theory of the State* (London, Oxford University Press, 1916).

OAKESHOTT, MICHAEL, *Experience and its Modes* (Cambridge, Cambridge University Press, 1933)

—— *Hobbes on Civil Association* (Oxford, Blackwell, 1975).

—— *On Human Conduct* (Oxford, Clarendon Press, 1975).

—— *Rationalism in Politics and Other Essays*, new and expanded edn., ed. T. Fuller (Indianapolis, Liberty, 1991).

O'BRIEN, CONOR CRUISE, 'Introduction', in Edmund Burke *Reflections on the Revolution in France*, ed. Conor Cruise O'Brien (Harmondsworth, Penguin, 1968).

O'BRIEN, G., *Hegel on Reason and History* (Chicago and London, The University of Chicago Press, 1975).

OCKHAM, WILLIAM OF, *A Short Discourse on Tyrannical Government*, ed. A. S. McGrade (Cambridge, Cambridge University Press, 1992).

O'GORMAN, FRANK, *Edmund Burke: His Political Philosophy* (London, Allen and Unwin, 1973).

OLLMAN, BERTELL, *Alienation. Marx's Concept of Man in Capitalist Society* (Cambridge, Cambridge University Press, 1971).

OLSEN, WILLIAM C., and GROOM, A. J. R., *International Relations Then and Now: Origins and Trends in Interpretation* (London, Routledge, 1991).

OLSHKI, LEONARDO, *Machiavelli the Scientist* (Berkeley, Gillick, 1945).

O'NEILL, ONORA, 'Justice and Boundaries', in Chris Brown (ed.), *Political Restructuring in Europe: Ethical Perspectives* (London, Routledge, 1994).

—— *Towards Justice and Virtue: A Constructive Account of Practical Reasoning* (Cambridge, Cambridge University Press, 1996).

—— 'Transnational Justice', in David Held (ed.), *Political Theory Today* (Cambridge, Polity Press, 1991).

ORR, ROBERT, 'The Time Motif in Machiavelli', *Political Studies*, 17 (1969).

ORWIN, CLIFFORD, 'The Just and the Advantageous in Thucydides: The Case of the Mytilenian Debate', *American Political Science Review*, 78 (1984).

ORWIN, CLIFFORD, '*Stasis* and Plague: Thucydides on the Dissolution of Society', *Journal of Politics*, 50 (1988).

PALEY, WILLIAM, *Moral and Political Philosophy*, in *The Works of Dr Paley*, ii (London, George Cowie, 1837).

PALLADINI, F., 'Translating Pufendorf', *History of Political Thought*, 16 (1995).

PALMER, MICHAEL, 'Alcibiades and the Question of Tyranny in Thucydides', *Canadian Journal of Political Science*, 15 (1982).

—— 'Machiavellian *virtù* and Thucydidean *areté*: Traditional Virtue and Political Wisdom in Thucydides', *Review of Politics*, 51 (1989).

PAREL, ANTHONY, 'Introduction: Machiavelli's Method and his Interpreters', in Anthony Parel (ed.), *The Political Calculus* (Toronto, University of Toronto Press, 1972).

—— 'Machiavelli *Minore*', in Anthony Parel (ed.), *The Political Calculus* (Toronto, University of Toronto Press, 1972).

PARIS, JOHN OF, *On Royal and Papal Power*, in Cary J. Nederman and Kate Landon Forhan (eds.), *Medieval Political Theory—A Reader* (London, Routledge, 1993).

PARKER, ROBERT, 'Greek States and Greek Oracles', *History of Political Thought*, 6 (1985).

PARKINSON, F., *The Philosophy of International Relations: A Study in the History of Thought* (Beverly Hills, Calif., and London, Sage, 1977).

PATON, H. J., 'Analysis of the Argument', in H. J. Paton (ed.), *The Moral Law. Kant's Groundwork of the Metaphysics of Morals* (London, Routledge, 1991).

—— *The Categorical Imperative* (London, Hutchinson, n.d.).

—— (ed.), *The Moral Law, Kant's Groundwork of the Metaphysic of Morals* (London, Routledge, 1991).

PATTERSON, ORLANDO, 'Freedom, Slavery and the Modern Construction of Rights', in Olwen Hufton (ed.), *Historical Change and Human Rights* (New York, Basic Books, 1995).

PELCZYNSKI, Z. A. (ed.), *Hegel's Political Philosophy: Problems and Perspectives* (Cambridge, Cambridge University Press, 1971)

PETERMAN, LARRY I., 'Machiavelli's Dante and the Sources of Machiavellianism', *Polity*, 28 (1987).

PETRUS, JOSEPH A., 'Marx and Engels on the National Question', *Journal of Politics*, 33 (1971).

PHILLIPSON, COLEMAN, *The International Law and Custom of Ancient Greece and Rome* (London, Macmillan, 1911).

—— 'Samuel Pufendorf' and 'Albercus Gentili', in J. MacDonell and E. Manson (eds.), *Great Jurists of the World* (New York, Kelley, 1968; first pub. 1914).

PISCATORI, JAMES, *Dilemmas of World Politics: International Issues in a Changing World* (Oxford, Oxford University Press, 1992).

PITKIN, HANNA FENICHEL, *Fortune is a Woman* (Berkeley, University of California Press, 1984).

PLANT, RAYMOND, *Hegel* (London, Allen and Unwin, 1973).

PLATO, *Gorgias*, trans. Walter Hamilton (Harmondsworth, Penguin, 1971).

—— *Laws*, trans. A. E. Taylor (London, Dent, 1934).

—— *Protagoras*, trans. W. K. C. Guthrie (Harmondsworth, Penguin, 1987).

—— *The Republic*, trans. Desmond Lee 2nd edn. (Harmondsworth, Penguin, 1987).

—— *Theaetetus*, trans. F. M. Cornford (Indianapolis, Bobbs-Merrill, 1957).

PLUMB, J. H., *England in the Eighteenth Century* (Harmondsworth, Penguin, 1971).

PLUTARCH, *The Rise and Fall of Athens: Nine Greek Lives*, trans. Ian Scott-Kilvert (Harmondsworth, Penguin, 1960).

POCOCK, J. G. A., 'Introduction', in Edmund Burke, *Reflections on the Revolution in France* (Indianapolis, Hackett, 1987).

—— *The Machiavellian Moment* (Princeton, Princeton University Press, 1975).

POGGE, THOMAS, 'Cosmopolitanism and Sovereignty', in Chris Brown (ed.), *Political Restructuring in Europe: Ethical Perspectives* (London, Routledge, 1994).

POLYBIUS, *The Histories of Polybius*, trans. Evelyn S. Shackburgh (Bloomington, Ind., Indiana University Press, 1962).

POOLE, J. C. F., and HOLLADAY, A. J., 'Thucydides and the Plague of Athens', *Classical Quarterly*, n.s. 29 (1979).

POPPER, KARL, *The Open Society and its Enemies* (London, Routledge and Kegan Paul, 1977; first pub., 1945).

PORTER, BRIAN, 'Patterns of Thought and Practice: Martin Wight's "International Theory"', in Michael Donelan (ed.), *The Reason of States* (London, Allen and Unwin, 1978).

POST, GAINES, *Studies in Medieval Legal Thought* (Princeton, Princeton University Press, 1964).

POUNCEY, PETER R., *The Necessities of War: A Study of Thucydides' Pessimism* (New York, Columbia University Press, 1980).

PREZZOLINI, GIUSEPPE, *Machiavelli* (London, Hale, 1968).

PRICE, RICHARD, *Political Writings* (Cambridge, Cambridge University Press, 1991).

PRICE, RUSSELL, '*Ambizione* in Machiavelli's Thought', *History of Political Thought*, 3 (1982).

PROCTOR, DENIS, *The Experience of Thucydides* (Warminster, Aris and Phillips, 1980).

PUFENDORF, SAMUEL, *The Elements of Universal Jurisprudence* (1658), trans. of the 1672 edn. by W. A. Oldfather (Oxford, Clarendon Press, 1931).

—— *On the Duty of Man and Citizen According to the Natural Law* (1673), trans. W. A. Oldfather (Oxford, Clarendon Press, 1927).

—— *On the Duty of Man and Citizen*, trans. and ed. James Tully (Cambridge, Cambridge University Press, 1991).

—— *On the Law of Nature and Nations: Eight Books* (1672), trans. of the 1688 edn. by C. H. Oldfather and W. A. Oldfather (Oxford, Clarendon Press, 1934).

—— *On the Natural State of Men*, trans. Michael Seidler (Lampeter, Edwin Mellen, 1990).

PUFENDORF, SAMUEL, *The Political Writings of Samuel Pufendorf*, ed. Craig L. Carr, trans. Michael J. Seidler (Oxford, Oxford University Press, 1994).

RAMSEY, PAUL, 'The Just War According to St Augustine', in Jean Bethke Elshtain (ed.), *Just War Theory* (Oxford, Blackwell, 1992), 19–20.

RAWLS, JOHN, *A Theory of Justice* (Oxford, Oxford University Press, 1992).

REBHORN, WAYNE A., *Foxes and Lions: Machiavelli's Confidence Men* (Ithaca, NY, Cornell University Press, 1988).

REID, THOMAS, *Practical Ethics: Being Lectures and Papers on Natural Religion, Self-Government, Natural Jurisprudence, and the Law of Nations*, ed. Knud Haakonssen (Princeton, Princeton University Press, 1990).

REMEC, PETER PAVEL, *The Position of the Individual in International Law According to Grotius and Vattel* (The Hague, Martinus Nijhoff, 1960).

RIEDAL, MANFRED, *Between Tradition and Revolution: The Hegelian Transformation of Political Philosophy* (Cambridge, Cambridge University Press, 1971).

RILEY, PATRICK, *Kant's Political Philosophy* (Totowa, NJ, Rowman and Littlefield, 1960).

—— 'On Kant as the Most Adequate of the Social Contract Theorists', *Political Theory*, 1 (1973).

RIST, J. M., *Stoic Philosophy* (Cambridge, Cambridge University Press, 1977).

ROBERTSON, BARBARA ALLEN, 'The Islamic Belief System', in Richard Little and Steve Smith (eds.), *Belief Systems and International Relations* (Oxford, Blackwell, 1988).

ROBINSON, JOHN MANSLEY, *An Introduction to Early Greek Philosophy* (Boston, Houghton Mifflin, 1968).

ROELOFSEN, C. G., 'Grotius and the International Politics of the Seventeenth Century', in Hedley Bull, Benedict Kingsbury, and Adam Roberts (eds.), *Hugo Grotius and International Relations* (Oxford, Clarendon Press, 1990).

RÖLING, B. V. A., 'Are Grotius's Ideas Obsolete in an Expanded World?', in Hedley Bull, Benedict Kingsbury, and Adam Roberts (eds.), *Hugo Grotius and International Relations* (Oxford, Clarendon Press, 1990).

ROMILLY, JACQUELINE DE, *The Great Sophists in Periclean Athens* (Oxford, Clarendon Press, 1992).

—— *Thucydides and Athenian Imperialism* (Oxford, Blackwell, 1963).

RORTY, RICHARD, *Contingency, Irony and Solidarity* (Cambridge, Cambridge University Press, 1989).

—— 'Human Rights, Rationality, and Sentimentality', in Stephen Shute and Susan Hurley (eds.), *On Human Rights* (New York, HarperCollins, 1993).

—— *Philosophy and the Mirror of Nature* (Oxford, Basil Blackwell, 1980).

ROSENBERG, JUSTIN, *The Empire of Civil Society: A Critique of the Realist Theory of International Relations* (London, Verso, 1994).

ROTHENBERG, GUNTHER E., 'Maurice of Nassau, Gustavus Adolphus, Raimondo Montecuccoli and the "Military Revolution" of the Seventeenth Century', in Peter Paret (ed.), *Makers of Modern Strategy from Machiavelli to the Nuclear Age* (Princeton, Princeton University Press, 1986).

ROUSSEAU, JEAN-JACQUES, 'Abstract and Judgement of Saint-Pierre's Project for Perpetual Peace' in *Rousseau on International Relations*, ed., Stanley Hoffmann and David P. Fidler (Oxford, Clarendon Press, 1991).

—— *Considerations on the Government of Poland*, trans. Frederick Watkins, in *Rousseau on International Relations*, ed. Stanley Hoffmann and David P. Fidler (Oxford, Clarendon Press, 1991), 162–96.

—— 'Constitutional Project for Corsica', trans. Frederick Watkins in *Rousseau on*

International Relations, ed. Stanley Hoffman and David P. Fidler (Oxford, Clarendon Press, 1991), 139–61.

—— 'Discourse on Political Economy', in *The Basic Political Writings*, trans. Donald A. Cress (Indianapolis, Hackett, 1987), 111–40.

—— 'Discourse on the Origin of Inequality', in *The Basic Political Writings*, trans. Donald A. Cress (Indianapolis, Hackett, 1987), 25–82.

—— *First Version of the Social Contract* trans. Judith R. Masters (The Geneva Manuscript), in *Rousseau on International Relations*, ed. Stanley Hoffmann and David P. Fidler (Oxford, Clarendon Press, 1991), 101–38.

—— *On the Social Contact*, in *The Basic Political Writings*, trans. Donald A. Cress (Indianapolis, Hackett, 1987).

—— 'The State of War', in *Rousseau on International Relations*, ed. Stanley Hoffman and David P. Fidler (Oxford, Clarendon Press, 1991).

ROUTH, D. A., 'The Philosophy of International Relations: T. H. Green versus Hegel', *Politica*, 3 (1938).

RUBIÉS, JOAN-PAU, 'Hugo Grotius's Dissertation on the Origin of the American Peoples and the Use of Comparative Methods', *Journal of the History of Ideas*, 52 (1991).

RUNCIMAN, W. G., 'Doomed to Extinction: The *Polis* as an Evolutionary Dead-End', in Oswyn Murray and Simon Price (eds.), *The Greek City from Homer to Alexander* (Oxford, Clarendon Press, 1990).

RUSSELL, F. H., *The Just War in the Middle Ages* (Cambridge, Cambridge University Press, 1975).

SALISBURY, JOHN OF, *Policraticus*, ed. and trans. Cary J. Nederman (Cambridge, Cambridge University Press, 1990).

SANDEL, MICHAEL, *Liberalism and the Limits of Justice* (Cambridge, Cambridge University Press, 1982).

SANTAYANA, GEORGE, *Egotism in German Philosophy*, 2nd edn. (London, Dent, 1940; 1st edn. 1916).

SCHLATTER, R., 'Thomas Hobbes and Thucydides', *Journal of the History of Ideas*, 6 (1945).

SCHMITT-PANTEL, PAULINE, 'Collective Activities and the Political in the Greek City', in Oswyn Murray and Simon Price (eds.), *The Greek City from Homer to Alexander* (Oxford, Clarendon Press, 1990).

SCHNEEWIND, J. B., 'Pufendorf's Place in the History of Ethics', *Synthese*, 72 (1987).

SCHWARZ, WOLFGANG, 'Kant's Philosophy of Law and International Peace', *Philosophy and Phenomenological Research*, 23 (1962–3).

SCOTT, JONATHAN, 'The Law of War: Grotius, Sidney, Locke and the Political Theory of Rebellion', *History of Political Thought*, 13 (1992).

SETH, SANJAY, 'Political Theory in the Age of Nationalism', *Ethics and International Affairs*, 7 (1993).

SEXTUS, EMPIRICUS, *Selections from the Major Writings on Scepticism, Man and God* (Indianapolis, Hackett, 1985).

SHARPLES, R. W., *Stoics, Epicureans and Sceptics* (London, Routledge, 1996).

SHAW, W. H., *Marx's Theory of History* (London, Hutchinson, 1974).

SHENNAN, J. H., *International Relations in Europe 1689–1789* (London, Routledge, 1995).

SHIPLEY, GRAHAM, 'Introduction: The Limits of War', in John Rich and Graham Shipley (eds.), *War and Society in the Greek World* (London, Routledge, 1993).

SHKLAR, JUDITH N., *Freedom and Independence: A Study of the Political Ideas of Hegel's Phenomenology of Mind* (Cambridge, Cambridge University Press, 1976).

SHOTTER, DAVID, *Augustus Caesar* (London, Routledge, 1991).

SKINNER, QUENTIN, 'Hobbes's *Leviathan*', *Historical Journal*, 7 (1964).

—— *The Foundations of Modern Political Thought* (Cambridge, Cambridge University Press, 1978), 2 vols.

—— *Machiavelli* (Oxford, Oxford University Press, 1981).

—— 'The State', in T. Ball, J. Farr, and R. L. Hanson (eds.), *Political Innovation and Conceptual Change* (Cambridge, Cambridge University Press, 1989).

SLOMP, G., 'Hobbes, Thucydides and the Three Greatest Things', *History of Political Thought*, 11 (1990).

SMITH, MICHAEL JOSEPH, *Realist Thought from Weber to Kissinger* (Baton Rouge, La., Louisiana State University Press, 1986).

SMITH, STEVE, 'The Forty Years' Detour: The Resurgence of Normative Theory in International Relations', *Millennium*, 21 (1992).

SMITH, STEVEN B., *Hegel's Critique of Liberalism: Rights in Context* (Chicago and London, University of Chicago Press, 1989).

—— 'Hegel's Views on War, the State, and International Relations', *American Political Science Review*, 77 (1983).

SOPHOCLES, *Antigone, Oedipus the King, Electra*, trans. Robert Fagles (Harmondsworth, Penguin, 1994).

SOURVINOU-INWOOD, CHRISTINE, 'What is *Polis* Religion?', in Oswyn Murray and Simon Price (eds.), *The Greek City from Homer to Alexander* (Oxford, Clarendon Press, 1990).

STANLIS, P. J., *Edmund Burke and the Natural Law* (Ann Arbor, University of Michigan Press, 1958).

STAWELL, F. MELIAN, *The Growth of International Thought* (London, Thornton Butterworth, 1929).

STEIN, PETER, 'From Pufendorf to Adam Smith: The Natural Law Tradition in Scotland', in *Europäisches Rechtsolenken in Geschichte und Gegenwart* (Munich, C. H. Beck, 1982).

STERLING, RICHARD W., *Ethics in a World of Power* (London, Oxford University Press, 1958).

STRAUSS, LEO, *The City and Man* (Chicago, University of Chicago Press, 1978).

—— *The Political Philosophy of Hobbes: Its Basis and its Genesis* (Oxford, Clarendon Press, 1936).

—— *Thoughts on Machiavelli* (Seattle and London, University of Washington Press, 1969).

SULLIVAN, EILEEN P., 'Liberalism and Imperialism: J. S. Mill's Defence of the British Empire', *Journal of the History of Ideas*, 44 (1983).

SULLIVAN, ROBERT R., 'Machiavelli's Balance of Power Theory', *Social Science Quarterly*, 54 (1973).

SUTER, J.-F., 'Burke, Hegel, and the French Revolution', in Z. A. Pelzcynski (ed.), *Hegel's Political Philosophy: Problems and Perspectives* (Cambridge, Cambridge University Press, 1971).

TAYLOR, CHARLES, *Hegel and Modern Society* (Cambridge, Cambridge University Press, 1979).

TELLEGEN-COUPERUS, OLGA, *A Short History of Roman Law* (London, Routledge, 1993).

THOMPSON, JANNA, *Justice and World Order: A Philosophical Inquiry* (London, Routledge, 1992).

THOMPSON, K. W., 'Idealism and Realism: Beyond the Great Debate', *British Journal of International Studies*, 3 (1977).

THORNER, DANIEL, 'Marx on India and the Asiatic Mode of Production', *Contributions to Indian Sociology*, old series (1966).

THUCYDIDES, *History of the Peloponnesian War,* trans. Rex Warner rev. edn. (Harmondsworth, Penguin, 1972).

TOOKE, JOAN D., *The Just War in Aquinas and Grotius* (London, SPCK, 1965).

TREITSCHKE, HEINRICH VON, *Politics,* trans. Blanche Dugdale and Torben de Bille (London, Constable, 1916), 2 vols.

TUCK, RICHARD, 'Grotius and Seldon', in J. H. Burns and Mark Goldie (eds.), *The Cambridge History of Political Thought 1450–1700* (Cambridge, Cambridge University Press, 1988).

—— 'The "Modern" Theory of Natural Law', in Anthony Pagden (ed.), *The Languages of Political Theory in Early-Modern Europe* (Cambridge, Cambridge University Press, 1987).

—— *Natural Rights Theories: Their Origin and Development* (Cambridge, Cambridge University Press, 1979).

TULLY, JAMES, *A Discourse on Property: John Locke and his Adversaries* (Cambridge, Cambridge University Press, 1980).

—— 'Introduction' to Samuel Pufendorf, *On the Duty of Man and Citizen,* ed. James Tully (Cambridge, Cambridge University Press, 1991).

TUNICK, M., 'Hegel's Justification of Hereditary Monarchy', *History of Political Thought,* 12 (1991).

UNDERSTEINER, MARIO, *The Sophists,* trans. Kathleen Freeman (Oxford, Blackwell, 1954).

VASQUEZ, JOHN A. (ed.), *Classics of International Relations,* 2nd edn. (Englewood Cliffs, NJ, Prentice Hall, 1990).

VATTEL, EMER, *The Law of Nations or the Principles of Natural Law,* trans C. G. Fenwick (Washington, DC, Carnegie Institution, 1916).

VERENE, D. P. (ed.), *Hegel's Social and Political Thought: The Philosophy of Objective Spirit* (New Jersey, Humanities Press, 1976).

VICO, GIAMBATTISTA, *The New Science,* trans. Thomas Goddard Bergin and Max Harold Fisch, 3rd edn. (New York, Cornell University Press, 1968).

VILLARI, PASQUALE, *The Life and Times of Niccolò Machiavelli,* trans. Linda Villari (London, Benn, 1929).

VINCENT, ANDREW, 'The Hegelian State and International Politics', *Review of International Studies,* 9 (1983).

—— *Theories of the State* (Oxford, Blackwell, 1987).

VINCENT, R. J. 'Edmund Burke and the Theory of International Relations', *Review of International Studies,* 10 (1984).

—— 'Grotius, Human Rights, and Intervention', in Hedley Bull, Benedict Kingsbury, and Adam Roberts (eds.), *Hugo Grotius and International Relations* (Oxford, Clarendon Press, 1990).

—— 'Hedley Bull and Order in International Politics', *Millennium,* 17 (1988).

—— *Human Rights and International Relations* (Cambridge, Cambridge University Press, 1986).

—— 'Western Conceptions of a Universal Moral Order', *British Journal of International Studies,* 4 (1978).

VITORIA, FRANCISCO DE, *Political Writings,* ed. Anthony Pagden and Jeremy Lawrence (Cambridge, Cambridge University Press, 1991).

WALBANK, F. W., *The Hellenistic World* (London, Fontana, 1992).

WALDRON, JEREMY, *Nonsense upon Stilts: Bentham, Burke and Marx on the Rights of Man* (London, Methuen, 1990).

WALKER, R. B. J., *Inside/Outside: International Relations as Political Theory* (Cambridge, Cambridge University Press, 1993).

WALKER, R. B. J., 'Realism, Change, and International Political Theory', *International Studies Quarterly*, 31 (1987).

WALTZ, KENNETH N., 'Kant, Liberalism, and War', *American Political Science Review*, 56 (1962).

—— *Man, the State and War: A Theoretical Analysis* (New York, Columbia University Press, 1959).

—— *Theory of International Politics* (New York, McGraw-Hill, 1979).

WALZER, MICHAEL, 'Interpretation and Social Criticism', *The Tanner Lectures on Human Values*, 7, ed. S. M. McMurrin (Salt Lake City, University of Utah Press, 1988).

—— *Just and Unjust Wars: A Moral Argument with Historical Illustrations* (New York, Basic Books, 1977).

—— 'Nation and Universe', *The Tanner Lectures on Human Values*, 11, ed. G. B. Peterson (Salt Lake City, University of Utah Press, 1990).

—— *Spheres of Justice: A Defence of Pluralism and Equality* (Oxford, Basil Blackwell, 1985).

—— *Thick and Thin: Moral Arguments at Home and Abroad* (Notre Dame, Ind., University of Notre Dame Press, 1994).

WARRENDER, HOWARD, *The Political Philosophy of Hobbes* (Oxford, Clarendon Press, 1966).

WATSON, ADAM, *Diplomacy* (London, Routledge, 1982).

—— *The Evolution of International Society* (London, Routledge, 1992).

WATSON, JOHN, 'German Philosophy and Politics', *Queen's Quarterly*, 22 (1915).

—— 'German Philosophy and the War', *Queen's Quarterly*, 23 (1916).

WESTLAKE, H. D., 'The Influence of Alcibiades on Thucydides, Book 8', in *Studies in Thucydides and Greek History* (Bristol, Bristol Classical Press, 1989).

WHEELER, NICHOLAS J., and BOOTH, KEN, 'The Security Dilemma', in John Baylis and N. J. Rengger (eds.), *Dilemmas of World Politics* (Oxford, Clarendon Press, 1992).

WHELAN, F. G., 'Vattel's Doctrine of the State', *History of Political Thought*, 9 (1988).

WHITE, HAYDEN V., *The Greco-Roman Tradition* (New York, Harper and Row, 1973).

WHITE, JAMES BOYD, *When Words Lose their Meanings* (Chicago, University of Chicago Press, 1984).

WHITE, STEPHEN K., *Edmund Burke: Modernity, Politics, and Aesthetics* (Thousand Oaks, Calif., Sage, 1994).

WIGHT, MARTIN, 'An Anatomy of International Thought', *Review of International Studies*, 13 (1987).

—— *International Theory: The Three Traditions*, ed. Gabriele Wight and Brian Porter (London and Leicester, University of Leicester Press, 1991).

—— *Power Politics*, ed. Hedley Bull and Carsten Holbraad, 2nd edn. (Harmondsworth, Penguin, 1986).

—— 'Why is There No International Theory?', in H. Butterfield and M. Wight (eds.), *Diplomatic Investigations: Essays in the Theory of International Politics* (London, Allen and Unwin, 1966).

WILDE, LAWRENCE, *Marx and Contradiction* (Aldershot, Gower, 1989).

—— 'Marx's Concept of Human Essence and its Radical Critics', *Studies in Marxism*, 1 (1994).

WILEY, BASIL, *The Eighteenth Century Background* (London, Penguin, 1965).

WILLIAMS, HOWARD, *International Relations in Political Theory* (Buckingham, Open University Press, 1992).

—— *Kant's Political Philosophy* (Oxford, Basil Blackwell, 1983).

—— WRIGHT, MOORHEAD, and EVANS, TONY (eds.), *A Reader in International Relations and Political Theory* (Buckingham, Open University Press, 1993).

WILLIAMS, MICHAEL C., 'Rousseau, Realism and *Realpolitik*', *Millennium*, 18 (1989).

WILSON, JOHN, ' "The Customary Meanings of Words were Changed" —Or were they? A Note on Thucydides 3,82.4', *Classical Quarterly*, 32 (1982).

WOKLER, ROBERT, 'Rousseau's Pufendorf: Natural Law and the Foundations of Commercial Society', *History of Political Thought*, 15 (1994).

WOLFF, CHRISTIAN, *The Law of Nations Treated According to a Scientific Method in which the Natural Law of Nations is Carefully Distinguished from that which is Voluntary, Stipulative and Customary*, trans. Francis J. Hemelt (Oxford, Clarendon Press, 1934).

WOLIN, SHELDON, *Politics and Vision* (Boston, Little, Brown, 1960).

WOOD, ALLEN W., *Hegel's Ethical Thought* (Cambridge, Cambridge University Press, 1990).

—— 'The Marxian Critique of Justice', *Philosophy and Public Affairs*, 1 (1971–2).

WOODRUFF, PAUL, 'Introduction' in *Thucydides on Justice, Power and Human Nature* (Indianapolis, Hacket, 1993).

ZALEWSKI, MARYSIA, and ENLOE, CYNTHIA, 'Questions of Identity in International Relations', in Ken Booth and Steve Smith (eds.), *International Relations Theory Today* (Cambridge, Polity, 1995).

ZUCKERT, MICHAEL P., ' "Bringing Philosophy Down from the Heavens": Natural Right in the Roman Law', *Review of Politics*, 51 (1989).

INDEX